THE
AMERICAN
CINEMA

ANDREW SARRIS is film critic for the
Village Voice and professor of cinema
at Columbia University. He is a member
of the National Society of Film Critics
and the New York Film Critics Circle. Mr. Sarris was editor-in-chief of
Cahiers du Cinema in English from 1965
to 1967, and an associate editor of *Film
Culture* from 1955 to 1965. He is the
author of *The Films of Josef von Sternberg, Interviews with Film Directors,
The Film, Confessions of a Cultist, The
Primal Screen, The John Ford Movie
Mystery,* and *Politics and Cinema.*

THE AMERICAN CINEMA

DIRECTORS
AND
DIRECTIONS
1929–1968

by Andrew Sarris
With a New Afterword
by the Author

THE UNIVERSITY OF
CHICAGO PRESS

The University of Chicago Press, Chicago 60637

94 93 92 91 90 89 88 87 86 85   5 4 3 2 1

Published by arrangement with E. P. Dutton

Library of Congress Cataloging-in-Publication Data

Sarris, Andrew.
  The American cinema.

  Reprint. Originally published: 1st ed.   New York :
Dutton, 1968. With new afterword.
  Includes index.
  1. Moving-picture producers and directors—United
States—Dictionaries.   I. Title.
PN1998.A2S24   1985   791.43'0233'0922   85–24494
ISBN 0–226–73500–1 (paper)

To Molly

ACKNOWLEDGMENTS | I am deeply indebted to Stephen Gottlieb, Michael McKegney, Eugene Archer, and Patrick Bauchau for their stimulating comments on the manuscript. I am grateful also to Jonas Mekas for his kindness in providing a haven for my critical opinions in the pages of *Film Culture* and *The Village Voice*.

CONTENTS

PREFACE

The need for an updated film history is self-evident. Time keeps marching on, with new movies arriving and old movies acquiring new perspectives. Lewis Jacobs's *The Rise of the American Film* stopped at 1939. The forties, the fifties, the sixties have had to shift for themselves, a few thousand features a decade spreading memories and associations so widely, indiscriminately, and unpredictably that no conceivable chronicle could ever serve as a final judgment on the subject. Far from rendering final judgments, this book is intended to reappraise the American sound film from the transitory vantage point of 1968. The sociologically oriented film historians — Jacobs, Grierson, Kracauer, Rotha, Griffith, Leyda, Sadoul, *et al.*—looked on the Hollywood canvas less as an art form than as a mass medium. Hollywood directors were regarded as artisans rather than as artists, and individual movies were less often aesthetically evaluated than topically synopsized. Inevitably, something was left out, and that something is the very personal art of the talkies, an art that has flourished through nearly forty years of obtrusive obscurity. The evidence was on the screen all the time, but no one bothered to look very hard.

Still, if my distinguished predecessors tended to focus on the forest at the expense of the trees, they did endow film scholarship with a commendable seriousness of purpose. A serious approach to old movies is particularly indispensable at a time when the very existence of old movies is jeopardized by the shocking negligence of the so-called film industry, and at a time also when the appreciation of old movies is hindered by the pernicious frivolities of pop, camp, and trivia. The enemies of cinema have found their new battle cry in the condescending cackle one hears in so-called art houses. This book is intended for those perennial cinephiles, the solitary moviegoers.

For practical purposes, the term "American" should be

more precisely defined. Since the criteria of selection for this historical survey are aesthetic rather than social or industrial, "American" will embrace many undubbed English-language films produced abroad. As much as this encroachment on British and international cinema may smack of imperialistic presumption, the doctrine of directorial continuity within the cultural marketplace of the English language takes precedence here over ethnographic considerations. This point of view is perhaps more representative of New York, a distribution center, than of Hollywood, a production center. The distinction is not worth an extended debate, but it might be noted that we do not intend to overemphasize "Americana" in American films. It is this exaggerated concern with what is "distinctively" American that has led to the unfortunate denigration of Ophuls, Sternberg, and Lubitsch for their alleged exoticism. *That* is carrying social consciousness too far.

As for what constitutes a movie by our temporary definition, the necessary evil of specialization must be invoked. Quite simply, a movie is a movie is a movie. It is what most people are thinking of when they propose "going to the movies." It is generally encumbered by a plot, actors who portray characters, and a running time of one hour or more. This hardly represents the totality of cinema, especially in these feverish times. The vast realms of documentary, animated and experimental film-making are pointedly excluded. Flaherty is mentioned arbitrarily for the sake of an aesthetic principle; otherwise, the survey is limited to what has been variously described as the narrative, fictional, theatrical, commercial, conventional, hybrid, and impure motion picture. Even such popular fare as comedy two-reelers, serials and television films are ignored here because of the problems of historical classification. The feature film that emerged full-grown from the head of Cinema's Zeus, D. W. Griffith, happens to be the subject under scrutiny. Let us say for the moment that this is just one kind of cinema, but the one that most people would identify, rightly or wrongly, as *the* Cinema.

The framework of this book appeared originally in the Spring 1963 *Film Culture* (No. 28), and aroused considerable controversy. Many critics objected to my placing directors in categories, particularly categories with whimsical titles. After some thought, I have decided to retain the categories and even expand them. There is no such thing as an objective film history. Each historian weights his presentation by the arrangement of chapters, the length of paragraphs, the tone of sentences, the choice of words. The historian's categories are usually implicit in his text, but he usually strives to preserve the spurious façade of "objectivity" by not seeming to have strong opinions. I choose to make my categories explicit for the convenience of my readers. Also, I feel that marginal distinctions are the most important distinctions a critic can make. They indicate a critical sensibility at work over the entire expanse of the cinema, not just in the currently fashionable sectors. To put it bluntly, many alleged authorities on film disguise their ignorance of the American cinema as a form of intellectual superiority. I have no quarrel with such snobbery, but there is no point in compromising with it. There are now enough dedicated moviegoers in the reading public to make the most adventurous speculations seem more reasonable than they did in 1963.

The film titles that are in italics in the individual filmographies represent the highlights of a director's career. The implied valuation is relative in that the worst film of a great director may be more interesting though less successful than the best film of a fair to middling director. Hence, by arranging the directors in categories we maintain some perspective on careers as coherent identities whereas the italics make the distinction between those movies that made it and those that did not. All in all, the italics both in the filmographies and in the directorial chronology from 1915 to 1967 near the end of the book are intended as guides for the film enthusiast who lacks the lifetime in the darkness to check out every possibility of personal expression in the cinema.

TOWARD A THEORY OF FILM HISTORY

I. The Forest and the Trees

The cinema by any definition is still very young, but it is already old enough to claim not only its own history but its own archaeology as well. The earliest artifacts have been traced back to the 1880's and 1890's in the United States, France, or England, depending on the nationality of the archaeologist. Conflicting proofs and patents of invention have been submitted for Thomas A. Edison, William Kennedy Laurie Dickson, William Friese-Greene, Louis Aimé Augustin Le Prince, Louis and Auguste Lumière, and many other shadowy figures out of the nineteenth-century camera obscura of art, science, and capitalism.

To the extent that the cinema is a creature of the scientific spirit, it has inherited expectations of infinite development and improvement. It is as if this machine art were designed to transcend the vagaries of human inspiration. A Shakespeare may appear once in a millennium, but the express train of twentieth-century history cannot wait a century or even a decade for the world to be remade from the moonbeams of a movie projector. Too much was expected of the medium, and too little was demanded of its scholars. The extravagant rhetoric of disillusionment obscured the incredibly perfunctory attention given to thousands upon thousands of movies. Therefore the first task of a theory of film history is to establish the existence of these thousands of movies as a meaningful condition of the medium.

Even though most movies are only marginally concerned with the art of the cinema, the notion of quality is difficult to grasp apart from the context of quantity. Comprehension becomes a function of comprehensiveness. As more movies are seen, more cross-references are assembled. Fractional responsibilities are more precisely defined; personal signatures are more clearly discerned.

It follows that comprehensive film scholarship from primary sources depends for its motivation upon a pleasurable response to the very act of moviegoing. Conversely, the compleat film historian must be recruited from the ranks of the authentic moviegoers rather than the slummers from the other arts. Not that an uncritical enthusiasm for movies is desirable in our chronicler. Film history devoid of value judgments would degenerate into a hobby like bridge or stamp collecting, respectable in its esoteric way, but not too revelatory. Or, as has been more the fashion, the collectivity of movies could be clustered around an idea, usually a sociological idea befitting the mindlessness of a mass medium.

The trouble up to now has been not seeing the trees for the forest. But why should anyone look at thousands of trees if the forest itself be deemed aesthetically objectionable? Of course, the forest to which I refer is called Hollywood, a pejorative catchword for vulgar illusionism. Hollywood is a foresty word rather than a treesy word. It connotes conformity rather than diversity, repetition rather than variation. The condescending forest critic confirms his preconceptions by identifying those elements that Hollywood movies have in common. Thus he also justifies his random sampling of Hollywood's output. If you've seen one, you've seen 'em all. And if you've seen a few, you certainly don't need to see them all. Hence the incessant carping on Hollywood "clichés:" Boy Meets Girl. The Happy Ending. The Noble Sacrifice. The Sanctity of Marriage. The Gangster Gets His Just Deserts. The Cowboy Outdraws the Villain. Girl and Boy Feel a Song Coming On. Presumably if you've laughed at one such convention, you've laughed at them all.

There is no denying that Hollywood movies emerge through a maze of conventions. Pressures from the studio, the censor, and the public have left their mark on film history. There is no artistic justification for the handcuffing of Burgess Meredith's George after he has mercifully shot the Lennie of Lon Chaney, Jr., in *Of Mice and Men*. Nor for the arrest of Gale Sondergaard at the end of *The Letter*. Nor for the mysterious going-away tears shed by Carole Lombard's Amy in *They Knew What They Wanted*. The citations of censor-dictated punishments of crime and sin could take up volumes and volumes. Hollywood movies have been hobbled also by front-office interference and a Scribean script policy that decreed the simplest, singlest, and most vulgar motivations for characters.

But the forest critic is not concerned with particulars. It is the system that he despises. It is the system that he blames for betraying the cinema. This curious feeling of betrayal dominates most forest histories to the point of paranoia. Somewhere on the western shores of the United States, a group of men have gathered to rob the cinema of its birthright. If the forest critic be politically oriented, he will describe these coastal conspirators as capitalists. If aesthetically oriented, he will describe them as philistines. Either way, an entity called the cinema has been betrayed by another entity called Hollywood. It is hard to find a parallel to this stern attitude in any of the other arts. A bad novel is not reviewed as if the author and publisher had betrayed literature. A bad painting is not castigated for disgracing the medium that produced Poussin and Delacroix. Perhaps the closest parallel can be found in certain critical attitudes toward the type of play performed on Broadway, London's West End, and the Parisian boulevards. The factor shared by theatre and cinema in this regard is the possession of buildings in which the public gathers to watch plays or films as the particular edifice complex dictates. The forest critic cannot help wondering what would happen if these buildings were consecrated to what he considers to be genuine art. What he seeks is the union of crowd spectacle with coterie taste. His generally liberal leanings convince him that the masses can indeed be saved from their own vulgarities.

The forest critic is not entirely lacking in historical proofs of betrayal. An unimpeachable witness such as George Stevens has testified: "When the movie industry was young, the film-maker was its core and the man who handled the business details his partner. . . . When he finally looked around, he found his partner's name on the door. Thus the film-maker became the employee, and the man who had the time to attend to the business details became the head of the studio." The so-called system can be blamed for the blighted careers of D. W. Griffith, Josef von Sternberg, Orson Welles, Erich von Stroheim, and Buster Keaton, and for the creative frustrations of innumerable other directors. The problem with these examples is that in most instances the forest critics repudiated the afflicted directors long before the industry curtailed their careers. Forest critics have never championed individuality for its own sake. A Griffith has been denounced for not keeping up with the times. A Sternberg has been condemned for his preoccupation with eroticism. A Welles has been flayed for his flamboyant egotism. The principle of the forest has been upheld at the expense of the topmost trees, and this is indeed the supreme irony of forest criticism. Far from welcoming diversity, the forest critic seeks a new uniformity. He would have Hollywood march off en masse like Birnam Wood to whatever Dunsinane the forest critic desires. Instead of one version of *The Grapes of Wrath,* there would be three hundred. Instead of one biography of Émile Zola, there would be a thousand critiques of anti-Semitism throughout the ages. Every movie would deal Realistically with a Problem in Adult Terms, or employ the Materials of the Medium in a Creative Manner. Thus the goals of forest criticism are ultimately impersonal. If John Ford decides to make a thirties adventure movie like *Seven Women* in the sixties, he is hopelessly out of step with cinemah. Similarly Charles Chaplin's *Countess from Hong Kong,* Orson Welles's *Falstaff,* and Howard Hawks's *El Dorado* are not synchronized with the express train of history. The medium marches on at its own pace. It is impervious to the melancholy twilight periods of its greatest artists.

The forest critic has had recourse to other snobberies over the years, and brief rebuttals to the battle cries of foreign "art" films, documentary, and the avant-garde might be in order at this point. In fact, the same careless arguments are heard today. The same rebuttals obviously apply.

THE FOREIGN FILM IS BETTER: The first serious cults of the foreign film sprang up in the twenties around the German and Russian cinemas, notable respectively for expressive camera mobility and revolutionary theories of montage. The giants of this era were Murnau, Lang, and Pabst in Germany, and Eisenstein, Pudovkin, and Dovjenko in Russia. The French cinema of Renoir, Vigo, Becker, Cocteau, Pagnol, Duvivier, Carné, Feyder, and Autant-Lara attracted some cultists in the thirties and early forties. The Italian neorealism of Rossellini, Visconti, and De Sica dominated the late forties and early fifties. The current line of the xenophiles among American critics is less localized. Hollywood's alleged betters may be found in Sweden (Ingmar Bergman), Denmark (Carl Dreyer), Japan (Mizoguchi,

Kurosawa, Ozu), India (Satyajit Ray), Poland (Has, Polanski, Skolimowski, Wajda), not to mention the familiar hunting grounds of France, Italy, and England. Film for film, Hollywood can hold its own with the rest of the world. If there have been more individualized works from abroad, there have also been fewer competent ones. If Hollywood yields a bit at the very summit, it completely dominates the middle ranges, particularly in the realm of "good-bad" movies and genres. Invidious comparisons are inevitable to some extent because of the arithmetic of distribution. Since a lower percentage of foreign films are available in America, indiscriminate viewing of Hollywood movies leads to an unscientific sampling of merit. Language barriers and the sheer exoticism of the unknown contribute to critical distortions. By the same token, American movies are often overrated abroad.

DOCUMENTARY FILMS ARE MORE REALISTIC THAN FICTIONAL MOVIES, HENCE MORALLY AND AESTHETICALLY SUPERIOR: One might just as well say that books of nonfiction are more truthful than novels. A great deal of semantic confusion is caused here by the duality of the cinema as a recording medium like the printing press, phonography, radio, lithography, and television, and as an art form.

AVANT-GARDE FILMS POINT THE WAY FOR COMMERCIAL MOVIES: It is difficult to think of any technical or stylistic innovations contributed by the avant-garde. Avant-garde critics and film-makers have had to be dragged screaming into the eras of sound, color, and wide-screen. Avant-garde impulses seem to be channeled toward the shattering of content taboos, political, religious, and sexual. Luis Buñuel and René Clair have come out of the avant-garde, and some think that Cocteau never left it, but few avant-garde mannerisms stand for long the withering gaze of the camera.

Though the forest critic may still point to foreign "art" films, the documentary, and the avant-garde, he knows full well that the masses he wants to save are enthralled more by ordinary movies than by lofty cinema. He himself is fascinated by the vulgar spectacles he deplores in his scholarly treatises, and in his fascination is the secret of his yearning. If the stupidities on the screen can stir even his own refined sensibilities, what ecstasies would he not experience if the dream mechanism were controlled by tastes comparable to his own? Greta Garbo edited by the *Partisan Review,* and all that. The forest critic cannot admit even to himself that he is beguiled by the same vulgarity his mother enjoys in the Bronx. He conceals his shame with such cultural defense mechanisms as pop, camp, and trivia, but he continues to sneak into movie houses like a man of substance visiting a painted woman. If he understood all the consequences involved, he would not want movies liberated from their vulgar mission. He appreciates the fact that always and everywhere there were temples of temptation dedicated to the kind of furtive pleasure that was mercifully free from the stink of culture. Nonetheless his intellectual guilt compels him to deny serious purpose and individual artistry to the mass spectacles he has been educated to despise.

The forest critic makes the mistake of crediting the power of the medium for making a "bad" movie seem entertaining. He overlooks the collectivity of creation in which "good" and "bad" can co-exist. Greta Garbo is genuinely "good" in *Camille* and Robert Taylor is genuinely "bad." George Cukor's direction of Garbo is extraordinary, but his direction of Laura Hope Crews is much too broad. In that same year (1937) Ernst Lubitsch obtained a restrained performance from Miss Crews in *Angel.* Thus our notions of "good" and "bad" are cast adrift in a sea of relativity. The collectivity that makes the cinema the least personal of all the arts also redeems most movies from complete worthlessness. But collectivity is not necessarily impersonality. Collectivity may just as easily be a collection of distinctive individualities. Ideally the strongest personality should be the director, and it is when the director dominates the film that the cinema comes closest to reflecting the personality of a single artist. A film history could reasonably limit itself to a history of film directors. It would certainly be a good start toward a comprehensive film history, but it would hardly explain everything to be found in thousands of movies. Nor is there any theory that would explain everything for all time. The performances of Humphrey Bogart, for example, seem more meaningful today than they did in their own time. By contrast, the image of Greer Garson has faded badly.

Film history is both films *in* history and the history of films.

The forest critic tends to emphasize the first approach at the expense of the second. He treats the movies of the thirties as responses to the Great Depression. By this criterion, few movies met their responsibilities to the oppressed and the underprivileged. For every *I Was a Fugitive from a Chain Gang* and *Our Daily Bread,* there were a score of "Thou Swell" romances in which money was no object. Yet the escapism of the thirties was as much a reflection of the Great Depression as any topical film on unemployment. The most interesting films of the forties were completely unrelated to the War and the Peace that followed. Throughout the sound era, the forest critic has been singling out the timely films and letting the timeless ones fall by the wayside. Unfortunately, nothing dates faster than timeliness. Hence the need for perpetual revaluation.

The theory of film history toward which this book is directed aims at nothing more than taking the moviegoer out of the forest and into the trees. The thousands of sound films in the English language exist for their own sake and under their own conditions. They constitute their own history, be it sublime or ridiculous or, as is more likely, a mixture of both. This particular study will start at the top with the bundles of movies credited to the most important directors, and work downward, director by director, movie by movie, year by year, toward a survey of what was best in American sound movies between 1929 and 1966. This survey is obviously a labor of love beyond the boundaries of art. The movies have been their own justification. Piece by piece, scene by scene, moment by moment, they have paralleled my own life. I was born in the midst of the convulsions over sound. I grew up with the talkies. Film history constitutes a very significant portion of my emotional autobiography. Fortunately, the resources of archives, television, museums, and revival houses make it possible to reappraise nostalgic memories in the clear, cold light of retrospection. Old movies come out of their historical contexts, but they must be judged ultimately in the realm of now.

II. The Auteur Theory

I first employed the term "auteur theory" in an article entitled "Notes on the Auteur Theory in 1962" (*Film Culture* No. 27, Winter 1962–63). The article was written in what I thought was a modest, tentative, experimental manner. It was certainly not intended as the last word on the subject. Indeed, it invited debate in a dialectical spirit of pooled scholarship, though without much hope of attracting attention in a publication with a readership of less than ten thousand. I had been writing articles in *Film Culture* for seven years without fueling any fires of controversy, but on this occasion a spark was ignited in far-off San Francisco by a lady critic with a lively sense of outrage. As often happens, the attack on the theory received more publicity than the theory itself. Unfortunately, the American attacks on the auteur theory only confirmed the backward provincialism of American film criticism. Not that the auteur theory is beyond criticism. Far from it. What is beyond criticism is the historical curiosity required to discuss any critical theory on film. A character in Bernardo Bertolucci's *Before the Revolution* observes that you can argue only with those with whom you are in fundamental agreement. "Let us polemicize," a Polish critic once wrote me. The affectionate aggressiveness of this attitude demands a modicum of mutual respect and a tradition of scholarly community sadly lacking in American film criticism.

First of all, the auteur theory, at least as I understand it and now intend to reaffirm it, claims neither the gift of prophecy nor the option of extracinematic perception. Directors, writers, actors (even critics) do not always run true to form, and the critic can never assume that a bad director will always make a bad film. No, not always, but almost always, and that is the point. What is a bad director but a director who has made many bad films? Hence, the auteur theory is a theory of film history rather than film prophecy. Of the directors listed in this book's Pantheon, Flaherty, Griffith, Keaton, Lubitsch, Murnau, and Ophuls are dead. Lang, Renoir, and Sternberg are involuntarily inactive, Chaplin, Ford, and Welles involuntarily intermittent. Only Hawks and Hitchcock of this group still enjoy reasonable commercial viability as they pass into their seventies, but it is difficult to imagine that their ultimate critical standing will be at stake in the next few seasons. Auteur criticism has been accused of sentimentality toward old directors. In Hollywood, particularly, you're only as good as your last picture, and no one in that power-oriented micropolis wants to waste time on has-beens. Since auteur criticism is based on an awareness of the past, it finds the work of old directors rich in associations. Not the work of all old directors, however. William Wellman, Henry King, and Frank Lloyd are not without their defenders, but the sum totals of their careers reveal more debits than credits. The ranking of directors is based on total rather than occasional achievement.

But why rank directors at all? Why all the categories and lists and assorted drudgeries? One reason is to establish a system of priorities for the film student. Another is the absence of the most elementary academic tradition in cinema. The drudgeries in the other, older, arts are performed by professional drudges. Film scholarship remains largely an amateur undertaking. In America especially, a film historian must double as a drudge. The rankings, categories, and lists establish first of all the existence of my subject and then my attitude toward it. "Taste," Paul Valéry remarked, "is made of a thousand distastes." François Truffaut's *Politique des auteurs,* first promulgated in the *Cahiers du Cinéma* No. 31 of January 1954, can be credited (or blamed) for the polemical stance of the term "auteur."

Politique des auteurs referred originally to the policy at *Cahiers* to be for some directors and against others. For Truffaut, the best film of Delannoy was less interesting than the worst film of Renoir. This was an extreme example of the *politique* in action. It served as a shock statement for the criticism of cruelty. The term "auteur" is more perplexing, as I should be the first to recognize after all the controversies the term has caused me. Strictly speaking, "auteur" means "author," and should be so translated when the reference is to literary personalities. When Truffaut writes of Gide or Giraudoux, and refers to them incidentally as "auteurs," there is no special point being made, and "author" is both an adequate and accurate translation. It is another matter entirely when Truffaut describes Hitchcock and Hawks as "auteurs." "Author" is neither adequate nor accurate as a translation into English mainly because of the inherent literary bias of the Anglo-American cultural Establishment. In terms of this bias, Ingmar Bergman did not become an author until his screenplays were published in cold print. The notion that a non-literary director can be the author of his films is difficult to grasp in America. Since most American film critics are either literary or journalistic types with no aspirations or even fantasies of becoming film directors, the so-called auteur theory has had rough sledding indeed. Truffaut's greatest heresy, however, was not in his ennobling direction as a form of creation, but in his ascribing authorship to Hollywood directors hitherto tagged with the deadly epithets of commercialism. This was Truffaut's major contribution to the anti-Establishment ferment in England and America.

However, Truffaut cannot be considered a systematic historian of the American cinema. Nor a comrade in arms for Anglo-American auteurists and New Critics. Truffaut, Godard, Chabrol, Rohmer, Rivette, and other *Cahiers* critics may have stimulated the Anglo-American New Criticism into being, but they did not long sustain its heresies. Of course, even *Cahiers* criticism was never so monolithic as its more vulgar American antagonists supposed. Nor were (or are) all French critics and periodicals camped under the *Cahiers* standard. Nor does the *nouvelle vague* constitute a continuing advertisement for auteur criticism. The critics of each country must fight their own battles within their own cultures, and no self-respecting American film historian should ever accept Paris as the final authority on the American cinema.

If Truffaut's "Politique des auteurs" signaled a break with anything, it was with a certain segment of the French cinema that was dominated (in Truffaut's view) by a handful of scriptwriters. The target was the well-upholstered, well-acted, carefully motivated "Tradition of Quality" represented by Claude Autant-Lara, Marcel Carné, René Clair, René Clément, Henri Clouzot, André Cayatte, Jean Delannoy, Marcel Pagliero, and a host of even lesser figures. This "Old Guard" was responsible for films like *Devil in the Flesh, The Red and the Black, Forbidden Games, Gervaise, Wages of Fear, Diabolique, Justice Is Done,* and *Symphonie Pastorale,* in short, what American reviewers considered the class of French film-making into the late fifties. Against these alleged creatures of fashion, Truffaut counterposed Jean Renoir, Max Ophuls, Robert Bresson, Jacques Becker, Jean Cocteau, and Jacques Tati as authentic auteurs.

Truffaut was involved in nothing less than changing the course of the French cinema. His bitterest quarrels were with film-makers, whereas the bitterest quarrels of the New Critics in England and America were with other critics. Truffaut's critical antagonists in Paris were generally not guilty of condescending to the American cinema. The editors of *Positif* may have preferred Huston to Hitchcock, and the MacMahonists may have preferred Losey to Hawks, but no faction had to apologize for its serious analyses of American movies. Even the French Marxists denounced the more capitalistic output from Hollywood in intellectually respectful terms. Long before the giddy rationalizations of pop, camp, and trivia, French critics were capable of discussing such lowbrow genres as Westerns and *policiers* with a straight face. The fact that many French critics had small English and less American actually aided them in discerning the visual components of a director's style.

Nevertheless a certain perversity in Truffaut's position still haunts the auteur theory and the New Criticism. Truffaut used American movies as a club against certain snobbish tendencies in the French cinema. This suggests the classic highbrow gambit of elevating lowbrow art at the expense of middle-brow art. Auteur critics are particularly vulnerable to the charge of preferring trash to art because they seek out movies in the limbo of cultural disrepute. An anti-auteur critic can score points simply by citing the titles of alleged auteur masterpieces. Without having seen the films, is anyone likely to believe that *Kiss Me Deadly* is more profound than *Marty,* that *Seven Men from Now* is more artistically expressive than *Moby Dick,* that *Baby Face Nelson* is more emotionally effective than *The Bridge on the River Kwai,* that *Bitter Victory* is more psychologically incisive than *The Defiant Ones,* that *Rio Bravo* is more morally committed than *The Nun's Story,* that *Gun Crazy* will outlive *The Heiress* or that *Psycho* will be admired long after *A Man for All Seasons* has been forgotten? Again, these propositions cannot be seriously debated. One kind of critic refuses to cope with a world in which a movie called *Baby Face Nelson* could possibly be superior to *The Bridge on the River Kwai.* The other kind of critic refuses to believe that a movie called *Baby Face Nelson* could possibly be less interesting than *The Bridge on the River Kwai.* One of the fundamental correlations in auteur criticism is that between neglected directors and neglected genres. To resurrect Ford and Hawks, it is necessary also to resurrect the Western. To take Minnelli seriously, it is necessary to take musicals seriously. However, auteur criticism is quite distinct from genre criticism. Genre criticism of the Western, for example, presupposes an ideal form for the genre. Directors may deviate from this form, but only at their own peril. The late Robert Warshow's celebrated essay on the Western described how a variety of directors failed to achieve Warshow's idealized archetype of the genre. By contrast, auteur criticism of the Western treats the genre as one more condition of creation.

Ultimately, the auteur theory is not so much a theory as an attitude, a table of values that converts film history into directorial autobiography. The auteur critic is obsessed with the wholeness of art and the artist. He looks at a film as a whole, a director as a whole. The parts, however entertaining individually, must cohere meaningfully. This meaningful coherence is more likely when the director dominates the proceedings with skill and purpose. How often has this directorial domination been permitted in Hollywood? By the most exalted European standards, not nearly enough. Studio domination in the thirties and forties was the rule rather than the exception, and few directors had the right of final cut. Educated Americans were brought up on the jaundiced Hollywood chronicles of F. Scott Fitzgerald, Nathanael West, John Dos Passos, Ring Lardner, and John O'Hara. The vulgar but vital producer-entrepreneur was the sun king in these sagas, and sensitive literary types were left out in the shade. In retrospect, however, the studio system victimized the screenwriter more than the director. It was not merely a question of too many scribes spoiling the script, although most studios deliberately assigned more than one writer to a film to eliminate personal idiosyncrasies, whereas the director almost invariably received sole credit for direction regardless of the studio influences behind the scenes. This symbol of authority was not entirely lacking in substance even in Hollywood, or perhaps especially in Hollywood where the intangibles of prestige loom large. There were (and are) weak and strong directors as there were weak and strong kings, but film history, like royal history, con-

cerns those who merely reign as well as those who actually rule.
Indeed, the strength of a John Ford is a function of the weakness
of a Robert Z. Leonard just as the strength of a Louis XIV is a
function of the weakness of a Louis XVI. The strong director
imposes his own personality on a film; the weak director allows
the personalities of others to run rampant. But a movie is a
movie, and if by chance Robert Z. Leonard should reign over a
respectable production like *Pride and Prejudice,* its merits are
found elsewhere than in the director's personality, let us say in
Jane Austen, Aldous Huxley, Laurence Olivier, Greer Garson,
and a certain tradition of gentility at Metro-Goldwyn-Mayer.
Obviously, the auteur theory cannot possibly cover every vagrant
charm of the cinema. Nonetheless, the listing of films by directors remains the most reliable index of quality available to us
short of the microscopic evaluation of every film ever made.

Even the vaunted vulgarity of the movie moguls worked in
favor of the director at the expense of the writer. A producer was
more likely to tamper with a story line than with a visual style.
Producers, like most people, understood plots in literary rather
than cinematic terms. The so-called "big" pictures were particularly vulnerable to front-office interference, and that is why the
relatively conventional genres offer such a high percentage of
sleepers. The culturally ambitious producer usually disdained
genre films, and the fancy dude writers from the East were seldom wasted on such enterprises. The auteur theory values the
personality of a director precisely because of the barriers to its
expression. It is as if a few brave spirits had managed to overcome the gravitational pull of the mass of movies. The fascination of Hollywood movies lies in their performance under pressure. Actually, no artist is ever completely free, and art does not
necessarily thrive as it becomes less constrained. Freedom is desirable for its own sake, but it is hardly an aesthetic prescription.

However, the auteur critic does not look to the cinema for
completely original artistic experiences. The cinema is both a
window and a mirror. The window looks out on the real world
both directly (documentation) and vicariously (adaptation). The
mirror reflects what the director (or other dominant artist) feels
about the spectacle. Modern cinema tends to fog up the window
in order to brighten the reflection. It would seem that a theory

that honored the personality of a director would endorse a cinema in which a director's personality was unquestionably supreme. Paradoxically, however, the personalities of modern directors are often more obscure than those of classical directors who were encumbered with all sorts of narrative and dramatic machinery. The classical cinema was more functional than the modern cinema. It knew its audience and their expectations, but it often provided something extra. This something extra is the concern of the auteur theory.

The auteur theory derives its rationale from the fact that the cinema could not be a completely personal art under even the best of conditions. The purity of personal expression is a myth of the textbooks. The camera is so efficient a manufacturer of "poetic" images that even a well-trained chimpanzee can pass as a "film poet." For all its viciousness and vulgarity, the Hollywood system imposed a useful discipline on its directors. The limited talents of a Gregory La Cava could be focused on an exquisite department-store-window whimsy involving Claudette Colbert and a family of mannequins. The genre expectations of *She Married Her Boss* took care of the rest of the movie, but in those few moments in the department-store window, the La Cava touch was immortalized as a figure of style.

Nonetheless the auteur theory should not be defended too strenuously in terms of the predilections of this or that auteur critic. Unfortunately, some critics have embraced the auteur theory as a shortcut to film scholarship. With a "you-see-it-or-you-don't" attitude toward the reader, the particularly lazy auteur critic can save himself the drudgery of communication and explanation. Indeed, at their worst, auteur critiques are less meaningful than the straightforward plot reviews that pass for criticism in America. Without the necessary research and analysis, the auteur theory can degenerate into the kind of snobbish racket that is associated with the merchandizing of paintings. The burden of proof remains with the critic, auteur-oriented or otherwise, and no instant recipes of aesthetic wisdom will suffice. Welles is not superior to Zinnemann "of course," but only after an intensive analysis of all their respective films. Where the auteur critic parts company with the anti-auteur critic is in treating every Welles film as well as every Zinnemann film as part of a career whole. The auteur critic thus risks the resentment of the reader by constantly judging the present in terms of the past. The auteur critic must overcome this resentment by relating the past to the present in the most meaningful way possible. Fortunately, readers are becoming more rather than less knowledgeable about the past with each passing year.

Ian Cameron's article "Films, Directors and Critics" in *Movie* of September 1962 raises an interesting objection to the auteur theory: "The assumption which underlies all the writing in *Movie* is that the director is the author of a film, the person who gives it any distinctive quality. There are quite large exceptions, with which I shall deal later. On the whole we accept the cinema of directors, although without going to the farthest-out extremes of the *la politique des auteurs* which makes it difficult to think of a bad director making a good film and almost impossible to think of a good director making a bad one."

Cameron was writing particularly of the policy at *Cahiers du Cinéma* in which the films of favored directors were invariably assigned to the specialists in those directors. The result was that no favored director was ever panned. Ironically, Cameron and his colleagues found themselves in the same bind in *Movie* when David Lean's *Lawrence of Arabia* came up for consideration. Since none of the *Movie* critics liked Lean or the film enough to search for meanings in the mise-en-scène, *Lawrence* was left in the lurch without any review at all. Cameron defended the exclusion on the grounds that the best review of any film will be written by the critic who best understands the film, usually because he is the most sympathetic to it. Cameron, like the editors of *Cahiers,* thus upheld the criticism of enthusiasm as a criterion for his publication. Why does this sound so heretical in the United States? Simply because most movie reviewers fancy themselves as magistrates of merit and paid taste consultants for the public. The "best" movie reviewer is the "toughest" movie reviewer, and a reputation is made and measured by the percentage of movies the reviewer pans. The more movies panned, the more honest the reviewer. Everyone knows how assiduously the movie companies seek to corrupt the press. Hence, what better proof of critical integrity than a bad notice? Besides, the journalistic beat of the movie reviewer takes in all movies, not just the ones he likes. The highbrow critic can pick and choose; the lowbrow reviewer must sit and suffer. Walter Kerr has defined the difference between reviewing and criticism as the difference between assuming that your reader has not seen the work in question and assuming that he has. Reviewing is thus a consumer report for the uninitiated; criticism a conversation with one's equals. It is the economic structure of the cinema that gives the reviewer more power than the critic, but whereas in the other arts the critic makes up in academic prestige what he lacks in the market power of the reviewer, the film scholar has until very recently lacked both power and prestige. That is why film scholars can be slandered as "cultists" by philistinish movie reviewers.

However, the more fastidious film publications neglect their obligations to the medium by restricting their critiques to the films and directors they like. The film scholar should see as much as possible and write about as much as possible. To avoid passing judgment on a film because of lack of sympathy is an act of intellectual arrogance. Nothing should be beneath criticism or contempt. I take a transcendental view of the role of a critic. He must aspire to totality even though he knows that he will never attain it. This transcendental view disposes of the either/or tone of many opponents of the auteur theory. This tone suggests that the critic must make an irrevocable choice between a cinema of directors and a cinema of actors, or between a cinema of directors and a cinema of genres, or between a cinema of directors and a cinema of social themes, and so on. The transcendental view of the auteur theory considers itself the first step rather than the last stop in a total history of the cinema. Eventually we must talk of everything if there is enough time and space and printer's ink. The auteur theory is merely a system of tentative priorities, a pattern theory in constant flux. The auteur critic must take the long view of cinema as if every film would survive in some vault forever. Auteur criticism implies a faith in film history as a continuing cultural activity. The last thing an auteur critic desires is to keep a reader from seeing a movie. Debate is encouraged, but the auteur critic is committed to the aesthetic values he has derived from the artists who have inspired him. The auteur critic seeks to communicate the excitement he has felt to his readers, but he does not substitute his own sensibility for that of the artist under analysis. The ideal auteur critic should sacrifice his own personality to some extent for the sake of illuminating the personality of the director. In practice, however, no critic can entirely escape the responsibility of his own values. Elucidation must yield at some point to evaluation. All that is meaningful is not necessarily successful. John Ford's sentimentality in *The Informer* is consistent with the personality he expresses throughout his career, but the film suffers from the sentimentality just the same. Alfred Hitchcock's *Marnie* makes a meaningful statement about sexual relationships, but the script and acting leave much to be desired. *Red Line—7000* is no less personal a project for Howard Hawks than *El Dorado,* but there is all the difference in the world between the self-parody of *Red Line* and the self-expression of *El Dorado.* Orson Welles manifests his vision of the world with more lucidity and grace in *The Magnificent Ambersons* than in *Macbeth,* and Sternberg is more poetic, if less personal, in *Morocco* than in *Anatahan.* Even the greatest directors have their ups and downs. No one has ever suggested the contrary. At a certain level of achievement, however, even the failures of a director can be fascinating. Actually, a careful analysis of a director's career often turns up neglected masterpieces that replace the "official" masterpieces. Ford, for example, is seldom cited for *Steamboat 'Round the Bend* and *The Searchers,* but these films look more interesting today than *The Informer* and *The Grapes of Wrath.*

The best directors generally make the best films, but the directors must be discovered through their films. "That was a good movie," the critic observes. "Who directed it?" When the same answer is given over and over again, a pattern of performance emerges. The critic can talk about meaning and style in the work of a director. But how does a critic determine whether a movie is good or bad? This is a more difficult question. At first, there was only the vaguest idea of what a movie should be like to qualify as a work of art. Then as more and more movies were made, it was possible to impose relative standards. D. W. Griffith was the first great film-maker simply because his films were so much more accomplished than anyone else's.

After Griffith, film criticism became richer in associations. If Aristotle had been alive to write a *Poetics* on film, he would have

begun with D. W. Griffith's *Birth of a Nation* as the first definition of a feature film as a work of bits and pieces unified by a
central idea. Griffith is thus one of the definitions of cinema.
Subsequent definitions include Murnau, Lang, Lubitsch, Flaherty, Eisenstein, Dreyer, Hitchcock, Renoir, Ford, *et al.* In
every instance, the film preceded the film-maker in the critic's
consciousness. The films have continued to accumulate more
than fifty years after *Birth of a Nation.* The bits and pieces have
multiplied beyond measure. The auteur theory is one of several
methods employed to unify these bits and pieces into central
ideas.

To look at a film as the expression of a director's vision is not
to credit the director with total creativity. All directors, and not
just in Hollywood, are imprisoned by the conditions of their craft
and their culture. The reason foreign directors are almost invariably given more credit for creativity is that the local critic is
never aware of all the influences operating in a foreign environment. The late Robert Warshow treated Carl Dreyer as a solitary
artist and Leo McCarey as a social agent, but we know now that
there were cultural influences in Denmark operating on Dreyer.
Day of Wrath is superior by any standard to *My Son John,* but
Dreyer is not that much freer an artist than McCarey. Dreyer's
chains are merely less visible from our vantage point across the
Atlantic.

The art of the cinema is the art of an attitude, the style of a
gesture. It is not so much *what* as *how.* The *what* is some aspect
of reality rendered mechanically by the camera. The *how* is what
the French critics designate somewhat mystically as mise-en-
scène. Auteur criticism is a reaction against sociological criticism that enthroned the *what* against the *how.* However, it would
be equally fallacious to enthrone the *how* against the *what.* The
whole point of a meaningful style is that it unifies the *what* and
the *how* into a personal statement. Even the pacing of a movie
can be emotionally expressive when it is understood as a figure of
style. Of course, the best directors are usually fortunate enough
to exercise control over their films so that there need be no glar-
ing disparity between *what* and *how.* It is only on the intermediate and lower levels of film-making that we find talent wasted
on inappropriate projects.

Not all directors are auteurs. Indeed, most directors are virtually anonymous. Nor are all auteurs necessarily directors. There is much more of Paddy Chayefsky than of Arthur Hiller in *The Americanization of Emily,* which is another way of saying that *Emily* is written but not really directed. Players, particularly comic players, are their own auteurs to varying degrees. It can be argued that Leo McCarey directed the funniest picture of the Marx Brothers in *Duck Soup,* but he can hardly be credited with molding their anarchic personalities. The trouble with the Marx Brothers, in comparison with Chaplin, Keaton, and Lloyd in the silent era, was that they never controlled their own films either as directors or producers. W. C. Fields did his most memorable turns as unrelated bits of vaudeville in the muck of third-rate scenarios. We remember fragments more than we remember films. Even Garbo was of only fragmentary interest in Robert Z. Leonard's *Susan Lennox—Her Fall and Rise.* Would Garbo's image be as lustrous today without her performances in *Camille* (George Cukor), *Ninotchka* (Ernst Lubitsch), and *Queen Christina* (Rouben Mamoulian)? Good sequences in bad movies can be cited *ad infinitum, ad gloriam.* How about good performances by bad actors? Or good novels by bad novelists? Good and bad seem to become less frivolous matters with acting and writing than with direction. Most cultivated people know what they like and what is art in acting and writing, but direction is a relatively mysterious, not to say mystical, concept of creation. Indeed, it is not creation at all, but rather a very strenuous form of contemplation. The director is both the least necessary and most important component of film-making. He is the most modern and most decadent of all artists in his relative passivity toward everything that passes before him. He would not be worth bothering with if he were not capable now and then of a sublimity of expression almost miraculously extracted from his money-oriented environment.

I.
PANTHEON
DIRECTORS

These are the directors who have transcended their technical problems with a personal vision of the world. To speak any of their names is to evoke a self-contained world with its own laws and landscapes. They were also fortunate enough to find the proper conditions and collaborators for the full expression of their talent. Works of special interest in each director's filmography are indicated by italics.

CHARLES CHAPLIN (1889–   )

FILMS: 1914—Making a Living, Kid Auto Races at Venice, Mabel's Strange Predicament, Between Showers, A Film Johnnie, Tango Tangles, His Favorite Pastime; Cruel, Cruel Love; The Star Boarder, Mabel at the Wheel, Twenty Minutes of Love; Caught in a Cabaret, Caught in the Rain, A Busy Day, The Fatal Mallet, Her Friend the Bandit, The Knockout, Mabel's Busy Day, Mabel's Married Life, Laughing Gas, The Property Man, The Face on the Barroom Floor, Recreation, The Masquerader, His New Profession, The Rounders, The New Janitors, Those Love Pangs, Dough and Dynamite, Gentlemen of Nerve, His Musical Career, His Trysting Place, Tillie's Punctured Romance, Getting Acquainted, His Prehistoric Past. 1915—His New Job, A Night Out, The Champion, In the Park, The Jitney Elopement, The Tramp, By the Sea, Work, A Woman, The Bank, Shanghaied, A Night in the Show. 1916—Carmen, Police, The Floorwalker, The Fireman, The Vagabond, *One* A.M., The Count, *The Pawnshop,* Behind the Screen, *The Rink.* 1917 —*Easy Street, The Cure, The Immigrant, The Adventurer.* 1918— Triple Trouble, *A Dog's Life,* The Bond, *Shoulder Arms.* 1919— *Sunnyside,* A Day's Pleasure. 1920—*The Kid.* 1921—The Idle Class. 1922—Pay Day. 1923—*The Pilgrim, A Woman of Paris.* 1925—*The Gold Rush.* 1928—*The Circus.* 1931—*City Lights.* 1936—*Modern Times.* 1940—*The Great Dictator.* 1947—*Monsieur Verdoux.* 1952—*Limelight.* 1957—A King in New York (unreleased in New York). 1967—The Countess from Hong Kong.

Chaplin's "primitive" Sennett films are listed above because the evolution of the actor preceded the evolution of the director. The apparent simplicity of Chaplin's art should never be confused with lack of technique. For Chaplin, his other self on the screen has always been the supreme object of contemplation, and the style that logically followed from this assumption represents the antithesis to Eisenstein's early formulations on montage. The late André Bazin brilliantly analyzed this fundamental opposition between montage and the one-scene sequence thus: "If burlesque triumphed before Griffith and montage, it is because most of the gags came out of a comedy of space, of the relation of man to objects and to the exterior world. Chaplin, in *The Circus,* is actually in the lion's cage and both are enclosed in a single frame on the screen." However, Chaplin, unlike Keaton, eventually subordinated his physical ties to the exterior world to the interior, almost schizophrenic relationship between director and actor. The physical objects that remained mechanical props in Keaton's cinema became universal symbols in Chaplin's. The breathtaking ballet with a global balloon in *The Great Dictator* derives its effect, not from the physical properties of balloons, but from a symbolic extension of megalomania. The circle Chaplin traces on the ground in *The Circus* is less an image in space than an image of time and life. The loss of plasticity and specificity in Chaplin's films coincided with a loss of humor and a gain of meaning. Ultimately Chaplin lost most of his audience, and in *Limelight* he celebrated the occasion by imagining his own death, a conception of sublime egoism unparalleled in the world cinema. To imagine one's own death, one must imagine the death of the world, that world which has always dangled so helplessly from the tips of Chaplin's eloquent fingertips.

Chaplin dabbled in Marxian (*Modern Times*) and Brechtian (*Monsieur Verdoux*) analysis, but the solipsism of his conceptions negated the social implications of his ideas. The idea of the actor has always contradicted the idea of the masses, just as the close-up has always distorted the long view of history. Chaplin's sensitivity to the eternal perverseness of woman further clouded his vision of the world. What, after all, is the final close-up of *City Lights* but the definitive image of a man who feels tragically unworthy of his beloved?

Chaplin has been criticized for abandoning the Tramp, a creature who had engulfed his creator in the public's mind. Chaplin might be criticized with equal justice for having grown old and reflective. The bitter melancholy of *Limelight* carries over into *A King in New York,* a film widely misunderstood as an anti-American tract. For Chaplin, however, America is like Dawn Addams, a fantasy and a delusion, a marvelous world that he may yet revisit but that he will never reconquer. Viewed as a whole, Chaplin's career is a cinematic biography on the highest level of artistic expression.

Chaplin the director was denied Chaplin the actor on only two occasions: *A Woman of Paris* (1923) and *The Countess from Hong Kong* (1967). Even in these two relatively objective enterprises, Chaplin makes cameo appearances. Curiously, *A Woman of Paris* was considered ahead of its time, and *The Countess from Hong Kong* behind its time, but both movies reveal Chaplin's roots in the theatre. Without Chaplin's physical grace at the center of the action, all the stage machinery becomes more visible. Yet Chaplin communicates his own personality to such disparate players as Adolphe Menjou, Edna Purviance, Marlon Brando, and Sophia Loren. The continuity of his career is maintained even in the absence of his acting persona, which proves that in the cinema feelings are expressed *through* actors, not *by* actors.

ROBERT FLAHERTY (1884–1951)

FILMS: 1922—*Nanook of the North.* 1926—Moana. 1927 —White Shadows of the South Seas (with W. S. Van Dyke). 1931— *Tabu* (with F. W. Murnau). 1934—*Man of Aran.* 1937—Elephant Boy (with Zoltan Korda). 1948—*Louisiana Story.* Shorts: 1925—The Pottery Maker. 1927—The Twenty-Four Island. 1931 —Industrial Britain. 1942—The Land.

Robert Flaherty was not merely the "father" of the documentary but also one of its few justifications. Actually, his films slip so easily into the stream of fictional cinema that they hardly seem like documentaries at all. From the beginning, Flaherty intuitively sensed the limitations of the impersonal camera and the restrictions of the formal frame. By involving himself in his material, he established a cinematic principle that parallels Werner Heisenberg's Uncertainty Principle in physics, namely, that the mere observation of nuclear (and cinematic) particles alters the properties of these particles. One of the most beautiful moments in the history of the cinema was recorded when Nanook smilingly acknowledged the presence of Flaherty's camera in his igloo. The director was not spying on Nanook or attempting to capture Nanook's life in the raw. He was collaborating with Nanook on a representation rather than a simulation of existence. What Flaherty understood so well was the potential degeneration of the documentary into voyeurism when the images of the camera were not reprocessed in the mind of the artist.

Tabu remains an interesting footnote to Flaherty's career, and his clash with Murnau acquires a fateful inevitability in retrospect. Where Flaherty expressed man's adaptability to nature, Murnau pondered on man's place in the universe. Where Flaherty was concerned with the rhythm of living, Murnau was obsessed with the meaning of life.

Flaherty was written off by some schools of documentary in the thirties for his presumed exoticism. The charge made more sense in the days when people believed that documentaries could reform the world. Today Flaherty seems touchingly romantic in his desire to find people who have escaped the corruption of civilization. Flaherty's cinema is one of the last testaments of the "cult of nature," and, as such, is infinitely precious.

JOHN FORD (1895–   )

FILMS: 1917—The Tornado, The Trail of Hate, The Scrapper, The Soul Herder, Cheyenne's Pal, Straight Shooting, The Secret Man, A Marked Man, Bucking Broadway. 1918—Phantom Riders, Wild Women, Thieves' Gold, The Scarlet Drop, Hell Bent, Delirium, A Woman's Fool, Three Mounted Men. 1919—Roped, A Fight for Love, The Fighting Brothers, Bare Fists, The Gun Packers, Riders of Vengeance, The Last Outlaw, The Outcasts of Poker Flat, Ace of the Saddle, Rider of the Law, A Gun Fightin' Gentleman, Marked Men. 1920—The Prince of Avenue A, The Girl in Number 29, Hitchin' Posts, Just Pals. 1921—The Big Punch, The Freeze-Out, The Wallop, Desperate Trails, Action, Sure Fire, Jackie. 1922—Little Miss Smiles, Silver Wings, The Village Blacksmith. 1923—The Face on the Bar-Room Floor, Three Jumps Ahead, Cameo Kirby. 1924— Hoodman Blind, North of Hudson Bay, The Iron Horse, Hearts of Oak. 1925—Lightnin', Kentucky Pride, The Fighting Heart, Thank You. 1926—The Blue Eagle, The Shamrock Handicap, Three Bad Men. 1927—Upstream. 1928—Four Sons, Mother Machree, Napoleon's Barber, Riley the Cop. 1929—Strong Boy, Black Watch, Salute. 1930—*Men Without Women,* Born Reckless, *Up the*

River, The Seas Beneath. 1931—The Brat, *Arrowsmith*. 1932—
Air Mail, Flesh. 1933—Pilgrimage, *Doctor Bull*. 1934—*The Lost
Patrol*, The World Moves On, *Judge Priest*. 1935—*The Whole
Town's Talking, The Informer, Steamboat 'Round the Bend*. 1936—
The Prisoner of Shark Island, Mary of Scotland, The Plough and the
Stars. 1937—Wee Willie Winkie, *The Hurricane*. 1938—Four
Men and a Prayer, Submarine Patrol. 1939—*Stagecoach, Young
Mr. Lincoln*, Drums Along the Mohawk. 1940—*The Grapes of
Wrath, The Long Voyage Home*. 1941—*Tobacco Road*, Sex Hy-
giene (Army documentary), *How Green Was My Valley*. 1942—
The Battle of Midway (Navy documentary). 1943—December 7th,
We Sail at Midnight (Navy documentaries). 1945—*They Were Ex-
pendable*. 1946—*My Darling Clementine*. 1947—The Fugitive.
1948—*Fort Apache*, Three Godfathers. 1949—*She Wore a Yel-
low Ribbon*. 1950—When Willie Comes Marching Home, *Wagon-
master, Rio Grande*. 1951—This Is Korea (Navy documentary).
1952—What Price Glory, *The Quiet Man*. 1953—*Mogambo*.
1954—*The Sun Shines Bright*. 1955—*The Long Gray Line*,
Mister Roberts. 1956—*The Searchers*. 1957—*The Wings of
Eagles, The Rising of the Moon*. 1958—The Last Hurrah. 1959—
Gideon of Scotland Yard, Korea (documentary), *The Horse Soldiers*.
1960—Sergeant Rutledge. 1961—*Two Rode Together*. 1962—
The Man Who Shot Liberty Valance. 1963—How the West Was
Won (with Henry Hathaway and George Marshall), *Donovan's Reef*.
1964—Cheyenne Autumn. 1965—Young Cassidy (finished and
signed by Jack Cardiff), 1966—*Seven Women*.

If John Ford had died or retired at the end of 1929, he would
have deserved at most a footnote in film history. *The Iron Horse*
and *Four Sons* attracted some attention in their time, and seem to
be the only Ford silents in the American museum repertory. *The
Iron Horse* is clearly influenced by Griffith, and *Four Sons* by
Murnau. Neither work is a revelation in itself, though there are
privileged moments in these films that belong to Ford alone.
Above all, there is a nostalgia for lost innocence on the family
level of history. Ford's technical competence has been established even at this early stage in his career, but up to 1929 he
cannot be considered one of the major artists of the medium. His
personal vision has not been developed to the level of a Lubitsch
or a Lang at this stage of film history.

If Ford had died or retired at the end of 1939, he would have deserved at least a paragraph for *The Informer* and *Stagecoach,* the former allegedly the first creative American sound film, and the latter representing the renaissance of the Western. He would now be a faded, dated establishment figure like Marcel Carné, a vulnerable target for all the New Critics after Bazin. Dated also would be the calculated expressionism and maudlin sentimentality of *The Informer.* Ford's style still lingered in the shadow of Murnau's in 1935, but no one had seemed to notice *Steamboat 'Round the Bend* and *The Whole Town's Talking* that same year. Ford has never been sufficiently appreciated for the verve and snap of his visual storytelling. Critics of the thirties always joked about the fact that the Hollywood system compelled Ford to make three *Wee Willie Winkie*s for every *Informer.* The joke, then as now, was on the critics. Despite the monstrous mythology of Shirley Temple, *Wee Willie Winkie* contains extraordinary camera prose passages from the wide-eyed point of view of a child. What the critical establishment of the thirties admired in Ford was his ability to avoid so-called woman's pictures despite studio pressures. Nor was Ford too much interested in the fancier forms of sexual intrigue. Being Irish and Catholic and action-oriented to boot, he tended to gravitate to public places where men spoke their minds openly. The Left has always been puritanical, but never more so than in the thirties when Hollywood's boy-girl theology threatened to paralyze the class struggle. In such an epoch, even an Irish-Catholic conservative like Ford could be mistaken for a progressive force.

Ford's critical reputation reached its peak and then began its decline during the forties. *The Grapes of Wrath, The Long Voyage Home* and *How Green Was My Valley* firmly established Ford as *the* Hollywood director despite the extraordinary challenges of Orson Welles and Preston Sturges. The New Dealish propaganda of *The Grapes of Wrath* has dated badly, as has John Steinbeck's literary reputation. Ford's personal style was particularly inimical to Steinbeck's biological conception of his characters. Where Steinbeck depicted oppression by dehumanizing his characters into creatures of abject necessity, Ford evoked nostalgia by humanizing Steinbeck's economic insects into heroic champions of an agrarian order of family and community. By the time of *How Green Was My Valley,* Ford had mastered his narrative style to the point that he could embroider it with those pauses and contemplations that expressed his feelings. Even in *Tobacco Road,* Charlie Grapewin's Jeeter Lester was transformed from a greedy barnyard animal to a seedy but serious mainstay of tradition. Ford had more in common with Welles than anyone realized at the time. Ford was forty-six when he made *How Green Was My Valley,* and Welles was only twenty-five when he made *Citizen Kane,* but both films are the works of old men, the beginnings of a cinema of memory.

Ford's *The Battle of Midway* is ostensibly a documentary, but it is as personal a statement as any of his fiction films. He focuses here on the ordinary scale by which the most gallant heroes are measured. It is not the battle itself that intrigues Ford, but the weary faces of rescued fliers plucked out of the Pacific after days of privation. World War II was the last war to be endorsed by the intellectual establishment as a valid artistic subject. Ford proceeded into the fifties to photograph the Korean war, an act symptomatic of his downfall with the taste-makers.

Only the Lindsay Anderson–Gavin Lambert generation of *Sequence* and *Sight and Sound* kept Ford's reputation alive in the period beginning with *They Were Expendable* in 1945 and ending with *The Sun Shines Bright* in 1954. The British critics could appreciate Ford for the flowering of his personal style at a time when the rest of the world (this critic included) were overrating Carol Reed and David Lean for the efficient, impersonal technicians that they were. Finally, the New Critics in London and Paris rediscovered Ford after he had been abandoned even by the *Sequence–Sight and Sound* generation. The last champions of John Ford have now gathered around *Seven Women* as a beacon of personal cinema.

The late André Bazin damaged Ford's reputation with New Critics by describing Ford's technique as a hangover from the scenario-dominated thirties. Bazin overrated the use of deep-focus in *The Little Foxes* as the antithesis to Ford's "invisible editing" in *Stagecoach.* What Ford had been evolving all through his career was a style flexible enough to establish priorities of expression. He could dispose of a plot quickly and efficiently when he had to, but he could always spare a shot or two for a mood that belonged to him and not to the plot. A Ford film, par-

ticularly a late Ford film, is more than its story and characterizations; it is also the director's attitude toward his milieu and its
codes of conduct. There is a fantastic sequence in *The Searchers*
involving a brash frontier character played by Ward Bond. Bond
is drinking some coffee in a standing-up position before going
out to hunt some Comanches. He glances toward one of the bed-
rooms, and notices the woman of the house tenderly caressing
the Army uniform of her husband's brother. Ford cuts back to a
full-faced shot of Bond drinking his coffee, his eyes tactfully
averted from the intimate scene he has witnessed. Nothing on
earth would ever force this man to reveal what he had seen.
There is a deep, subtle chivalry at work here, and in most of
Ford's films, but it is never obtrusive enough to interfere with the
flow of the narrative. The delicacy of emotion expressed here in
three quick shots, perfectly cut, framed, and distanced, would
completely escape the dulled perception of our more literary-
minded film critics even if they deigned to consider a despised
genre like the Western. The economy of expression that Ford has
achieved in fifty years of film-making constitutes the beauty of
his style. If it had taken him any longer than three shots and a
few seconds to establish this insight into the Bond character, the
point would not be worth making. Ford would be false to the
manners of a time and a place bounded by the rigorous necessity
of survival.

Ford's major works can be traced in a rising parabola from
Steamboat 'Round the Bend to *Seven Women,* but even when
Ford is in less than top form there are marginal compensations.
His sentimentality extends to his casting not only of leads but
also of the most minute bit roles. As Jean Mitry once observed,
there is a John Ford world with a distinctive look to it. *How
Green Was My Valley* established Maureen O'Hara as the definitive Ford heroine just as *Stagecoach* established John Wayne as
the definitive John Ford hero. The extraordinary rapport of the
Wayne-O'Hara team through *Rio Grande, The Quiet Man,* and
Wings of Eagles adds a sexual dimension to Ford's invocation of
tradition in human experience. *How Green Was My Valley* is
also notable for introducing Ford's visual treatment of the past
as a luminous memory more real than the present, and presumably more than the heroic future. Ford and Hawks, the directors

closest to the Griffith tradition, project different aspects of Griffith's personality: Ford the historical perspective and unified vision of the world, and Hawks the psychological complexity and innate nobility of characterization.

Ford can never become fashionable again for the rigidly ideological critics of the Left. Too many of his characters wear uniforms without any tortuous reasoning why. Even the originally pacifistic *What Price Glory* is transformed by Ford into a nostalgic celebration of military camaraderie with the once-raucous Charmaine emerging from the dim shadows as an idealization of the Chivalric Code. As a director, Ford developed his craft in the twenties, achieved dramatic force in the thirties, epic sweep in the forties, and symbolic evocation in the fifties. His style has evolved almost miraculously into a double vision of an event in all its vital immediacy and yet also in its ultimate memory image on the horizon of history.

Ford's failures tend to be objective rather than subjective in that he tends to be faithful to his own feelings at the expense of his material. *Mary of Scotland* is patently biased in favor of Mary against Elizabeth even in Maxwell Anderson's blank-minded verse version. Ford completes the travesty of historical objectivity by treating Katharine Hepburn's Mary as a soft-focused, unfairly slandered Madonna of the Scottish moors. (Curiously, it is not until *Seven Women* that Ford can bear to look at women with a degree of sexual ambiguity.) *When Willie Comes Marching Home* seemed to be a Preston Sturges project that Ford directed with undue seriousness, and *The Last Hurrah* lost much of its satiric sparkle in the transition from novel into film. *The Fugitive,* like *The Informer,* runs counter to Ford's sense of order. Graham Greene's renegade priest and Liam O'Flaherty's renegade informer are clearly beyond Ford's comprehension, and in both instances Ford's casual Catholicism cannot grapple with the causal Catholicism in the two novels. Nor with the Left-wing politics of the two novelists. *Cheyenne Autumn* is a failure simply because Ford cannot get inside the Indians he is trying to ennoble.

Ultimately, Ford's cinema must be considered a continent full of mountain peaks and desert valleys. *The Horse Soldiers* is weakest when the characters are talking abstractly about war, but the march of the little boy soldiers lingers in the mind long after all the dialogues have been forgotten. Tyrone Power may have played very broadly in *The Long Gray Line,* but who can forget the first materialization of his family at the kitchen table or Maureen O'Hara's standing in the doorway and watching a son-substitute go off to war. Ford is more than the sum of his great moments, however. A storyteller and poet of images, he made his movies both move and be moving.

D. W. GRIFFITH (1875–1948)

FILMS (partial list 1908–1914): 1908—The Adventures of Dollie, For the Love of Gold, After Many Years, The Taming of the Shrew, The Song of the Shirt. 1909—Edgar Allan Poe, The Curtain Pole, The Politician's Love Story, The Voice of the Violin, The Medicine Bottle, The Drunkard's Reformation, The Suicide Club, Resurrection, The Cricket on the Hearth, What Drink Did, The Violin Maker of Cremona, The Lonely Villa, Her First Biscuits, A Convict's Sacrifice, The Mended Lute, The Sealed Room; 1776: or, The Hessian Renegades; In Old Kentucky, Leather Stockings, Pippa Passes, A Change of Heart, In the Watches of the Night, Through the Breakers, Lines of White on a Sullen Sea, Nursing a Viper, The Restoration, The Light That Came, The Red Man's View, A Corner in Wheat. 1910—In Old California, As It Is in Life, The Unchanging Sea, Ramona, In the Season of Buds, A Child of the Ghetto, The Face at the Window, Muggsy's First Sweetheart, The House with Closed Shutters, The Usurer, Rose o' Salem Town, The Iconoclast, That Chink at Golden Gulch, The Message of the Violin, Waiter No. 5, The Lesson. 1911—The Two Paths, The Italian Barber, His Trust, His Trust Fulfilled, The Manicure Lady, What Shall We Do with Our Old, Fisher Folk, The Lily of the Tenements, The Heart of a Savage, A Decree of Destiny, The Lonedale Operator, The Spanish Gypsy, Paradise Lost, How She Triumphed, Enoch Arden, The Primal Call, Fighting Blood, The Last Drop of Water, The Squaw's Love, The Revenue Man and the Girl, Her Awakening, The Battle, Through Darkened Vales, The Miser's Heart, The Failure, A Terrible Discovery. 1912—For His Son, A Mender of Nets, The Goddess of Sagebrush Gulch, A Girl and Her Trust, The Female of the Species, The Lesser Evil, The Old Actor, A Temporary Truce, Lena and the Geese, Man's Lust for Gold, Man's Genesis, The Sands of Dee, A

Change of Spirit, A Pueblo Legend, An Unseen Enemy, A Feud in the Kentucky Hills, The Musketeers of Pig Alley, My Baby, Friends, The Massacre, The New York Hat, The God Within, Greed, The One She Loved. 1913—Broken Ways, The Sheriff's Baby, The Mothering Heart, The Battle at Elderbush Gulch, Judith of Bethulia, The Battle of the Sexes. 1914—The Escape, Home Sweet Home, The Avenging Conscience, The Mother and the Law. 1915—*The Birth of a Nation.* 1916—*Intolerance.* 1918—*Hearts of the World,* The Great Love, The Greatest Thing in Life. 1919—A Romance of Happy Valley, The Girl Who Stayed at Home, *Broken Blossoms, True Heart Susie,* The Fall of Babylon, The Mother and the Law, Scarlet Days, The Greatest Question. 1920—The Idol Dancer, The Love Flower, *Way Down East.* 1921—*Dream Street.* 1922— *Orphans of the Storm,* One Exciting Night. 1923—*The White Rose.* 1924—America, *Isn't Life Wonderful?* 1925—Sally of the Sawdust, That Royle Girl. 1926—Sorrows of Satan. 1928—Drums of Love, The Battle of the Sexes. 1929—Lady of the Pavements. 1930 —*Abraham Lincoln.* 1931—*The Struggle.* 1940—One Million, B.C. (signed by Hal Roach, but reputedly directed by Griffith).

It is about time that D. W. Griffith was rescued from the false pedestal of an outmoded pioneer. The cinema of Griffith is no more outmoded, after all, than the drama of Aeschylus. When one observes in the bird-in-a-cage telephone-booth image in Hitchcock's *The Birds* a derivation of a similarly objective viewpoint in Griffith's *Broken Blossoms,* the alleged antiquity of Griffith becomes more dubious than ever. Only in film history is half a century treated as a millennium. This is particularly true of the liberal, technological, or Marxist historians who have embraced a theory of Progress in contradistinction to all other arts. By their standards, the cinema does not rise or fall, as do all other arts, in relation to the artists involved. Instead, the cinema is subject to a certain mystical process of evolution by which Griffith's Babylonian crane shots are on the bottom rung of a ladder that mounts to Eisenstein's Odessa Steps. Conversely, the fallacious assumption that the cinema rose progressively from Griffith to Murnau to Eisenstein in the period from 1915 through 1928 implies that the cinema was betrayed from 1929 onward. The fact remains that Griffith, Murnau, and Eisenstein had differing visions of the world, and their technical "contributions" can never be divorced from their personalities. The recent rediscovery of Griffith in New York and Paris centered not on the relatively familiar landmarks, *The Birth of a Nation* and *Intolerance,* but on such underrated masterpieces as *Broken Blossoms, True Heart Susie, Way Down East, Dream Street,* and *Orphans of the Storm.*

We might observe that Griffith's silent films, like Sternberg's and Stroheim's, are often carelessly evaluated in terms of their absurd titles. When Griffith is mistakenly called naïve, the titles of his films are usually responsible even when the images belie them. However, in recent years, both Jean Renoir and Josef von Sternberg have explicitly repudiated the titles connecting their films. Griffith was certainly not a writer in any serious literary sense, but a film-maker of extraordinary complexity and depth. When Richard Barthelmess first confronts Lillian Gish in *Broken Blossoms,* the subtle exchange of emotions between the two players would defy the art of the greatest novelist, but the scene is almost invariably measured by the dime-magazine title that "explains" it. The same critics and historians who denounced the intrusion of dialogue into the silent film were guilty of reducing the glorious images of the silent cinema to the feeble conventions of the explanatory title. Very early in his career, Griffith mastered most of the technical vocabulary of the cinema, and then proceeded to simplify his vocabulary for the sake of greater psychological penetration of the dramatic issues that concerned him. Like all great artists, his art had become so deceptively simple by the time of *Abraham Lincoln* that most critics assumed that he was in decline. Yet today the stark simplicity of *Lincoln* looks infinitely greater than the once-fashionable razzle-dazzle of Mamoulian's *Applause.*

The debt that all film-makers owe to D. W. Griffith defies calculation. Even before *The Birth of a Nation,* he had managed to synthesize the dramatic and documentary elements of the modern feature film. He traced the paths of his players across natural landscapes without the slightest trace of incongruity. Indeed, the rural countryside of *True Heart Susie* and *The White Rose* is in complete harmony with the careless rapture of Lillian Gish and Mae Marsh. For Griffith, a tree was more than a tree. Its strength and vulnerability expressed metaphorically the emotional life of his heroines. Modern audiences have lost this sense of psychological harmony with nature to the extent that the trees in, say, Antonioni's compositions serve as metaphors of cosmic indifference. The harmonies of Griffith have become the dissonances of Antonioni. The moral order to which Griffith's scenarios refer no longer exists. What remains to delight the modern connoisseur are torrents and torrents of classical acting, forceful, direct and full-bodied, cleanly and inventively directed with full psychological accountability. Literary pundits may see great profundities in Monica Vitti's inscrutable smile, but it is much harder for an actress to express feelings like joy and fear than to let her director express them for her with literary metaphors of vision. Lillian Gish is an infinitely greater actress than Monica Vitti because Griffith's cinema demands a rediscovery of behavioral reality, whereas Antonioni's divests characters of their personalities for the sake of a literary statement on alienation and boredom.

Griffith devised a grammar of emotions through his expressive editing. The focal length of his lens became a function of feeling. Close-ups not only intensified an emotion; they shifted characters from the republic of prose to the kingdom of poetry. Griffith's privileged moments are still among the most beautiful in all cinema. They belong to him alone, since they are beyond mere technique. Griffith invented this "mere" technique, but he also transcended it.

HOWARD HAWKS (1896–   )

FILMS: 1926—The Road to Glory, Fig Leaves. 1927—The Cradle Snatchers, Paid to Love. 1928—*A Girl in Every Port*, Fazil, The Air Circus. 1929—Trent's Last Case. 1930—*The Dawn Patrol*. 1931—The Criminal Code. 1932—The Crowd Roars, *Scarface*, Tiger Shark. 1933—Today We Live. 1934—*Twentieth Century*, Viva Villa! (completed and signed by Jack Conway). 1935—Barbary Coast. 1936—*Ceiling Zero, The Road to Glory*, Come and Get It (with William Wyler). 1938—*Bringing Up Baby*. 1939—*Only Angels Have Wings*. 1940—*His Girl Friday*. 1941—Sergeant York, Ball of Fire. 1943—*Air Force*. 1944—*To Have and Have Not*. 1946—*The Big Sleep*. 1948—*Red River*, A Song Is Born.

1949—I Was a Male War Bride. 1952—*The Big Sky, Monkey Business,* O'Henry's Full House (The Ransom of Red Chief episode). 1953—*Gentlemen Prefer Blondes.* 1955—The Land of the Pharaohs. 1959—*Rio Bravo.* 1962—*Hatari!* 1964—*Man's Favorite Sport.* 1965—Red Line—7000. 1967—*El Dorado.*

Howard Hawks was until recently the least known and least appreciated Hollywood director of any stature. His name is not mentioned in the indices of Kracauer's *Theory of Film, Grierson on Documentary* (which discusses many Hollywood directors), Lewis Jacobs's *The Rise of the American Film,* and Roger Manvell's *Penguin Film* series. Paul Rotha's *The Film Till Now* makes one brief reference to Hawks: "A very good all-rounder" [who] "stays in the mind with *The Crowd Roars, Scarface, Ball of Fire,* and *The Big Sleep.*" By contrast, Hawks had been greatly admired in France since *Scarface* in 1932. But then it was easier to see *Scarface* in Paris than in New York through the thirties and forties. Many revival houses featured a double bill of *The Public Enemy* and *Little Caesar,* but *Scarface* was always withheld from circulation by the Howard Hughes interests. (It would be interesting to know where and when the late Robert Warshow saw *Scarface,* to which he refers briefly in his famous essay on *The Gangster as Tragic Hero.*) Once Hawks was discovered, however, he revealed a consistent personal style and view of the world. If anything, *Man's Favorite Sport, Red Line —7000,* and *El Dorado* are quintessentially and self-consciously Hawksian. The same lines and basic situations pop up in film after film with surprisingly little variation. Call it classicism or cliché, the fact remains that for a director whose credentials are so obscure to English-speaking critics, Hawks has retained a surprising degree of control over his assignments, choosing the ones he wanted to do, and working on the scripts of all his films. The Hawksian hero acts with remarkable consistency in a predominantly male universe.

If Ford's heroes are sustained by tradition, the Hawksian hero is upheld by an instinctive professionalism. Even during the Depression, Hawksian characters were always gainfully employed. The idea that a man is measured by his work rather than by his ability to communicate with women is the key to Hawksian masculinity, as the converse is the key to Antonioni's femininity. Whereas Ford's attitude to his women can be defined in terms of chivalry, the Hawksian woman is a manifestation of the director's gallantry.

Like his heroes, Howard Hawks has lived a tightrope existence, keeping his footing in a treacherous industry for more than forty years without surrendering his personal identity. It is impossible to single out any one of his films as a definitive summation of his career, and it is unlikely that he will ever discard the mask of the commercial film-maker, although he comes very close in *El Dorado* when one of his characters recites Poe's "Eldorado" almost as a tribute to perceptive French criticism of both Poe and Hawks.

Throughout his career Hawks has adjusted to technological changes without blazing a trail for others to follow. He came late to the talking film after Vidor, Lubitsch, von Sternberg, and Mamoulian had explored its potentialities, extremely late to the color film, and, despite an honorable effort in *Land of the Pharaohs,* he does not seem to have been enchanted by the world of the wide screen. His technique is a function of his personality and the material with which he has chosen to work. His scenarios, which invariably emphasize action within a short time span, do not lend themselves to decorative mannerisms. When he has been confronted with epic subjects in *Red River* and *Land of the Pharaohs,* he has split his story into two short segments of time a decade or so apart. He has never used a flashback, and even in the thirties he seldom resorted to the degenerative montage of time lapses. His tracking, cutting, and framing have never attracted much attention in themselves, and this is not so much a virtue as it may seem. Critics who argue that technique should not call attention to itself are usually critics who do not wish to call attention to technique. If Hawks does not choose to use technique as reflective commentary on action, it is because his personality expresses a pragmatic intelligence rather than a philosophical wisdom.

Hawks has an uncanny technical flair for establishing the mood of the film at the outset and sustaining this mood to the end. The atmosphere established in the opening fog-enshrouded shots of *Barbary Coast, Road to Glory* and *Only Angels Have*

Wings casts a spell that is uniquely Hawksian. The opening, wordless sequences in *Rio Bravo* present all the moral issues of the film. The low-angle shot of Wayne looking down at Martin with sorrowful disdain tells the audience all it has to know about the two men, and Hawks even tilts his camera to isolate the relationship from its background and to intensify the reciprocal feelings of shame and disappointment. However, Hawks never tilts his camera again in the film, and the intensity of the opening tapers off into comic understatement. This is typical of the director's tendency to veer away from dramatization and verbalization of feelings that are implicit in the action.

Hawks consciously shoots most of his scenes at the eye level of a standing onlooker. Consequently, even his spectacles are endowed with a human intimacy which the director will not disturb with pretentious crane shots. Hawks will work within a frame as much as possible, cutting only when a long take or an elaborate track might distract his audience from the issues in the foreground of the action. This is good, clean, direct, functional cinema, perhaps the most distinctively American cinema of all. It is certainly not the last word on the art of film-making, but its qualities are more unusual than most critics have imagined. However, even at the time of their release, the Hawks films were generally liked for their solid professionalism. The director has worked with the most distinguished cameramen in Hollywood: Gregg Toland, Lee Garmes, James Wong Howe, Tony Gaudio, Ernest Haller, Russell Harlan, and Sid Hickox. Hawks himself has never been less than a professional, but he has been more as well. His technique has served ultimately to express his personal credo that man is the measurer of all things.

Aside from a few gibes at red-baiting in *His Girl Friday,* Hawks has never indicated any specific political orientation. The religious lunatic in *Twentieth Century,* the revivalism in *Sergeant York,* and the mordant piety after the brutal fact in *Red River* constitute what little there is of religion in the world of Howard Hawks. Except for *Sergeant York,* Hawks has never dealt with the very poor as a class, and except for *Bringing Up Baby,* he has never dealt with the very rich as a class. To the best of my memory there has never been a divorce or a gratuitous suicide in any of the director's films. Hawks rejected *Fourteen*

Hours as a directorial assignment because he explicitly disapproved of the theme of suicide as a form of neurotic escape. (Henry Hathaway later accepted this assignment.) Curiously, however, *Dawn Patrol, Today We Live, Ceiling Zero,* and *Road to Glory* have quasi-suicidal climaxes in which characters accept fatal missions, but the moral arithmetic balances out because in each instance the martyr is a replacement in an obligatory situation. However, it may be significant that all these sacrificial episodes occurred in films of the thirties, an era in which the Hawksian virtues were most appropriate. A director of parts as well as a unified whole, Hawks has stamped his distinctively bitter view of life on adventure, gangster and private-eye melodramas, Westerns, musicals, and screwball comedies, the kind of thing Americans do best and appreciate least. Now that his work has been thoroughly revived and revaluated throughout the English-speaking world, there is little point in belaboring the point for the few remaining stragglers who maintain that his art is not really Art with a serving of espresso in the lobby. That one can discern the same directorial signature over a wide variety of genres is proof of artistry. That one can still enjoy the genres for their own sake is proof of the artist's professional urge to entertain.

ALFRED HITCHCOCK (1899–   )

FILMS: 1925—The Pleasure Garden. 1926—The Mountain Eagle, The Lodger. 1927—Downhill, Easy Virtue, The Ring. 1928 —*The Farmer's Wife,* Champagne, The Manxman. 1929—*Blackmail.* 1930—Juno and the Paycock, *Murder.* 1931—The Skin Game. 1932—East of Shanghai, Number Seventeen. 1935—*The Man Who Knew Too Much, The 39 Steps,* Strauss' Great Waltz. 1936—*Secret Agent.* 1937—*Sabotage.* 1938—*The Lady Vanishes, A Girl Was Young.* 1939—Jamaica Inn. 1940—*Rebecca, Foreign Correspondent.* 1941—Mr. and Mrs. Smith, *Suspicion.* 1942—*Saboteur.* 1943—*Shadow of a Doubt.* 1944—Lifeboat. 1945—Spellbound. 1946—*Notorious.* 1947—The Paradine Case. 1948—Rope. 1949—*Under Capricorn.* 1950—*Stage Fright.* 1951—*Strangers on a Train.* 1953—*I Confess.* 1954— *Dial M for Murder, Rear Window.* 1955—*To Catch a Thief, The*

Trouble with Harry. 1956—*The Man Who Knew Too Much, The Wrong Man.* 1958—*Vertigo.* 1959—*North by Northwest.* 1960 —*Psycho.* 1963—*The Birds.* 1964—Marnie. 1966—*Torn Curtain.* 1969—Topaz, Frenzy.

Alfred Hitchcock is the supreme technician of the American cinema. Even his many enemies cannot begrudge him that distinction. Like Ford, Hitchcock cuts in his mind, and not in the cutting room with five different setups for every scene. His is the only contemporary style that unites the divergent classical traditions of Murnau (camera movement) and Eisenstein (montage). (Welles, for example, owes more to Murnau, whereas Resnais is closer to Eisenstein.) Unfortunately, Hitchcock seldom receives the visual analysis he deserves in the learned Anglo-American periodicals devoted ostensibly to the art of the cinema. Pages and pages will be expended on Resnais's synchronized tracks in *Last Year at Marienbad,* but the subtler diminuendo of Hitchcock's cross-tracking in the American remake of *The Man Who Knew Too Much* will pass by unnoticed. Truffaut, Chabrol, and Resnais can pay homage to Hitchcock, but the Anglo-American admirers of Truffaut, Chabrol, and Resnais will continue to pass off Hitchcock as a Continental aberration. "The Master of Suspense" is thus virtually without honor in his own countries.

Hitchcock's art is full of paradoxes. *The Birds,* for example, reveals a rigorous morality coupled with a dark humor, but the theme of complacency that runs through all his work is now so explicit that it is generally misunderstood. Hitchcock requires a situation of normality, however dull it may seem on the surface, to emphasize the evil abnormality that lurks beneath the surface. Hitchcock understands, as his detractors do not, the crucial function of counterpoint in the cinema. You cannot commit a murder in a haunted house or dark alley, and make a meaningful statement to the audience. The spectators simply withdraw from these bizarre settings, and let the décor dictate the action. It is not Us up there on the screen, but some play actors trying to be sinister. However, when murder is committed in a gleamingly sanitary motel bathroom during a cleansing shower, the incursion of evil into our well-laundered existence becomes intolerable. We may laugh nervously or snort disgustedly, but we shall never be quite so complacent again. Hitchcock's repeated invasions of everyday life with the most outrageous melodramatic devices have shaken the foundations of the facile humanism that insists that people are good, and only systems evil, as if the systems themselves were not functions of human experience. Much of the sick, perverse, antihumanistic humor sweeping through America today is an inevitable reaction to the sickening sentimentality of totalitarianism masquerading as all-encompassing humanism. Hitchcock has never been accepted as part of this fashionable sickness, and his unfashionableness is all to his credit. He insists, almost intolerantly, upon a moral reckoning for his characters and for his audience. We can violate the Commandments at our own psychic peril, but we must pay the price in guilt at the end. Hitchcock can be devious, but he is never dishonest.

Hitchcock's reputation has suffered from the fact that he has given audiences more pleasure than is permissible for serious cinema. No one who is so entertaining could possibly seem profound to the intellectual puritans. Furthermore, did not Santayana once observe that complete understanding extinguishes pleasure? No matter. Hitchcock's art will always delight the specialist because so much of it is rendered with an air of casualness. The iron is encased in velvet, the irony in simplicity—simplicity, however, on so many levels that the total effect is vertiginously complex. Beneath the surface melodrama of every Hitchcock film is a lively comedy of manners. In this regard, *The Farmer's Wife* of 1928 displays Hitchcock's flair for satiric pantomime much as Dreyer's *Master of the House* reveals the Great Dane apart from the shadow of eternity. Hitchcock's style is alive to the expressive potentialities of the slightest encounter. His cutting is the means by which he contradicts what people say by what they do. In the beginning of his career, he was attracted to montage as a mental language. In *Murder* (1930) a sleuth-type character thinks of the hot meal he is missing at home in order to stay at a dingy hotel, and Hitchcock cuts to a spatially abstract shot of roast duckling purely as a mental expression of a gourmet's grief. Hitchcock quickly abandoned this experiment in favor of the intricate editing of objects and glances within a scene. His films abound with objects as visual correlatives—the missing finger in *The 39 Steps*, the crashing cymbals (not symbols) in both versions (1935 and 1956) of *The Man Who Knew Too Much*, the milk chocolates on the assembly line in *Secret Agent*, the knife and time bomb in *Sabotage*, the doctored drink in *The Lady Vanishes*, the twitching eye in *A Girl Was Young*, the monogrammed pillowcase in *Rebecca*, the reverse-sailing windmills in *Foreign Correspondent*, the conjugally crossed skis in *Mr. and Mrs. Smith*, the sinister glasses of milk in *Suspicion* and *Spellbound*, the magisterial Statue of Liberty in *Saboteur*, the incriminating ring in *Shadow of a Doubt*, the concealed compass in *Lifeboat*, the key to the winecellar in *Notorious*, the hypnotic portrait in *The Paradine Case*, the omnipresent trunk in *Rope*, the shrunken head in *Under Capricorn*, the bloodstained doll in *Stage Fright*, the incriminating cigarette lighter in *Strangers on a Train*, the falling bicycle in *I Confess*, the latchkeys in *Dial M for Murder*, the wedding ring in *Rear Window*, the cat in *To Catch a Thief*, the bothersome corpse in *The Trouble with Harry*, the hallucinatory coiffure in *Vertigo*, the crop duster in *North by Northwest*, the motel shower in *Psycho*, the besieged telephone booth in *The Birds*, the papier-mâché flames in *Torn Curtain*. Hitchcock's objects are never mere props of a basically theatrical mise-en-scène, but rather the very substance of his cinema. These objects embody the feelings and fears of characters as object and character interact with each other in dramas within dramas.

The late James Agee perceived the novelistic nuances of Hitchcock's visual storytelling in *Notorious*, but most American reviewers have failed to appreciate the Hitchcockian virtues of vividness and speed as artistic merits. Hitchcock's economy of expression can be compared favorably to that of any of his colleagues or imitators. There is, for example, a Hitchcockian touch in John Huston's direction of *Reflections in a Golden Eye*. Marlon Brando's Captain Penderton is following a private with whom he is obsessed. There is a sound of a car crash behind Brando. The private and his buddies all turn to look at the crash. Brando keeps staring at the private. The Hitchcockian equivalent of this sequence occurs in *Strangers on a Train* at a tennis match involving a troubled participant played by Farley Granger. The visual coup of the sequence is the familiar joke of spectators at a tennis match swiveling their heads back and forth to follow the action. All heads swivel but one—that of a psychopathic murderer played by Robert Walker. The difference of camera placement and editing between the Hitchcock sequence and the Huston sequence is the difference between visual directness and visual obliqueness. Hitchcock gives the audience the point immediately with a device designed for maximum vividness. Huston's effect is slower in making its point. Paradoxically, however, Hitchcock is more oblique psychologically than Huston. Hitchcock's characters are ostensibly obsessed by the issues of a contrived melodrama. The Walker character has proposed to the Granger character an exchange of murders so that the police would be left without a plausible motive for either murder. The Granger character has never taken the proposition seriously enough to reject it flatly, and he is horrified to discover that he is an accomplice to one murder and expected to keep his end of the bargain by committing another. Walker stalks Granger everywhere, most memorably at the tennis match. It is only under the surface of the melodrama that the darker humor of homosexual obsessiveness comes into play as an added layer of meaning. Huston's treatment of homosexuality is much closer to the surface. Indeed, the Brando characterization of Captain Penderton is less subtle and repressed than the Carson McCullers original out of her Gothic novel. Hitchcock is ultimately more cinematic; Huston more literary. Hitchcock operates on many levels, Huston only on one. The beauty of Hitchcock's style is a function of its speed and efficiency in operating a time mechanism. Huston's personality is not expressed so much through the medium itself as in a sour reaction to its emotional facility.

Hitchcock has worked with big stars from Nita Naldi to Julie Andrews and from Ivor Novello to Paul Newman, but he has generally managed to impart Hitchcockian humor to the most distinctive personalities. The ultra-Hitchcockian performances are those of James Stewart in *Rope, Rear Window, The Man Who Knew Too Much,* and *Vertigo* and Cary Grant in *Suspicion, Notorious, To Catch a Thief,* and *North by Northwest.* Stewart and Grant gave Hitchcock the means he could not have got from any other actors. In return, Hitchcock gave Stewart and Grant meanings they could not have got from any other director. Nonetheless Hitchcock has seldom been the favorite director of his players. Thespians traditionally prefer weaker wills and more adaptable visions of life.

BUSTER KEATON (1895–1966)

FILMS: Roscoe ("Fatty") Arbuckle two-reelers, directed by and starring Arbuckle: 1917—The Butcher Boy, Rough House, His Wedding Night, Fatty at Coney Island, Oh, Doctor!; Out West. 1918 —The Bell Boy, Goodnight Nurse, Moonshine, The Cook. 1919— A Desert Hero, Backstage, A Country Hero, The Garage. 1920— The Saphead (feature film directed by Winchell Smith and starring Keaton). Two- and three-reelers produced by and starring Keaton: 1920—The High Sign (written and directed by Keaton and Eddie Cline), One Week, Convict 13, The Scarecrow, Neighbors. 1921— The Haunted House, Hard Luck, The Goat (written and directed by Keaton and Malcolm St. Clair), The Playhouse (directed by Keaton and Cline), *The Boat*, The Paleface. 1922—*Cops,* My Wife's Relations, The Blacksmith, *The Frozen North, The Electric House, Daydreams.* 1923—*Balloonatics,* The Love Nest (directed by Keaton). Features produced by and starring Keaton: 1923—The Three Ages (directed by Keaton and Cline), *Our Hospitality* (directed by Keaton and Jack Blystone). 1924—*Sherlock Jr.* (directed by Keaton), *The Navigator* (directed by Keaton and Donald Crisp). 1925—Seven Chances (directed by Keaton), Go West (directed by Keaton). 1926 —*Battling Butler* (directed by Keaton), *The General* (directed by Keaton and Clyde Bruckman). 1927—*College* (directed by James Horne), *Steamboat Bill Jr.* (directed by Charles "Chuck" Reisner). 1928—The Cameraman (directed by Edward Sedgwick, Jr.). 1929 —Spite Marriage (directed by Sedgwick). 1930—Free and Easy (directed by Sedgwick). Doughboys (directed by Sedgwick). 1931— Speak Easily (directed by Sedgwick). 1932—Parlor, Bedroom and Bath (directed by Sedgwick), The Passionate Plumber (directed by Sedgwick). 1933—Sidewalks of New York (directed by Jules White and Zion Myers), What, No Beer? (directed by Sedgwick).

Keaton appeared in close to sixty films after 1933, most memorably in *San Diego I Love You, Sunset Boulevard, Limelight,* and

A Funny Thing Happened on the Way to the Forum, but only in *Limelight* with Chaplin was there a spark of the creative fire behind the deadpan mask. Even Samuel Beckett contributed to the desecration of the Keaton mask by involving the actor of absurdity before its time in a dreary exercise called *Film,* the most pretentious title in all cinema.

That Buster Keaton had regained a certain critical eminence before his death is due largely to the tireless efforts of the film cultists in the little magazines. What the late James Agee described as the "Golden Age of Comedy" (and Silence) has been distilled into the precious essence of Chaplin and Keaton or Keaton and Chaplin. (By contrast, the intermittent inspiration of Lloyd, Langdon, Arbuckle, Sennett, Laurel and Hardy, et al., seems relatively one-dimensional.) The difference between Keaton and Chaplin is the difference between poise and poetry, between the aristocrat and the tramp, between adaptability and dislocation, between the function of things and the meaning of things, between eccentricity and mysticism, between man as machine and man as angel, between the girl as a convention and the girl as an ideal, between the centripetal and the centrifugal tendencies of slapstick. Keaton is now generally acknowledged as the superior director and inventor of visual forms. There are those who would go further and claim Keaton as pure cinema as opposed to Chaplin's essentially theatrical cinema. Keaton's cerebral tradition of comedy was continued by Clair and Tati, but Keaton the actor, like Chaplin the actor, has proved to be inimitable. Ultimately, Keaton and Chaplin complement each other all the way down the line to that memorably ghostly moment in *Limelight* when they share the same tawdry dressing room as they prepare to face their lost audience.

Keaton's most striking visual coups involve the collision between an irresistible farce and an immovable persona. Immovable and imperturbable. At least on the surface. Time has transformed the surface calm of Keaton's countenance into a subtle beauty. There is a moment in *The General* when Keaton, exasperated by the stupidity of his Southern Belle sweetheart, makes a mock gesture to choke her, but then kisses her instead. This kiss constitutes one of the most glorious celebrations of heterosexual love in the history of the cinema. Unlike Chaplin, Keaton does not idealize women as projections of his own romantic fantasies. Keaton is more like Chabrol in *Les Bonnes Femmes* in perceiving the beauty of women through all their idiocies and irritations. Their beauty and their indispensability. Keaton accepts woman as his equal with clear-eyed candor, whereas Chaplin's misty-eyed mysticism is the façade of a misogynist.

A complete revival of Keaton's career is promised for 1968. Until that fateful moment of reappraisal, the evidence of *Cops, Sherlock Jr., The Navigator,* and *The General* is sufficient to stamp Keaton as the most enduringly modern of classical directors. A stylistic footnote is in order here. When Jean-Luc Godard frames Jean-Paul Belmondo in an iris improvised out of Jean Seberg's rolled-up magazine spyglass, the knowledgeable film aesthete identifies this mannerism in *Breathless* as a tribute to Samuel Fuller's iris frame in *Forty Guns.* Fuller's viewpoint represented that of a real spyglass. *Breathless* was released in Paris in 1960 and in New York in 1961. *Forty Guns* came out in New York in 1957. Back in 1926, Keaton devised the same iris frame (in *The General*) out of a tablecloth burned through by a careless cigar. Keaton's Confederate fugitive, hiding under a Union table, sees his sweetheart through the hole in the tablecloth as in a locket tintype. It is a measure of Keaton's classicism that he conceals this poetic effect within a contrived plot. By contrast, Fuller and Godard flaunt the effect in a manner that can be described as self-consciously decadent.

FRITZ LANG (1890–   )

FILMS: 1919—Halb-Blut, Der Herr der Liebe, Die Spinnen (Part One): Der Goldene See, Hara Kiri, Die Spinnen (Part Two): Das Brillanten Schiff. 1920—Das Wandernde Bild. 1921—Vier um die Frau, Der Müde Tod. 1922—*Dr. Mabuse, Der Spieler.* 1924 —*Die Niebelungen.* 1926—*Metropolis.* 1928—*Spione,* Frau im Mond. 1932—*M;* Das Testament von Dr. Mabuse. 1933—Liliom. American period: 1936—*Fury.* 1937—*You Only Live Once.* 1938 —You and Me. 1940—The Return of Frank James. 1941— Western Union, *Manhunt.* 1943—*Hangmen Also Die.* 1945— *Ministry of Fear, The Woman in the Window, Scarlet Street.* 1946—

Cloak and Dagger. 1948—Secret Beyond the Door. 1950—House by the River, American Guerilla in the Philippines. 1952—*Rancho Notorious,* Clash by Night. 1953—The Blue Gardenia, *The Big Heat.* 1954—Human Desire. 1955—*Moonfleet.* 1956—While the City Sleeps, Beyond a Reasonable Doubt. 1960—Journey to the Lost City (English-German languages). 1961—*The Thousand Eyes of Dr. Mabuse.*

Fritz Lang's cinema is the cinema of the nightmare, the fable, and the philosophical dissertation. Lang's apparent weaknesses are the consequences of his virtues. He has always lacked the arid sophistication lesser directors display to such advantage. Lang's plots generally go inexplicably sour or sentimental at the very end. His characters never develop with any psychological precision, and his world lacks the details of verisimilitude that are so important to realistic critics. However, Lang's vision of the world is profoundly expressed by his visual forms. Where Renoir's *The Human Beast* is the tragedy of a doomed man caught up in the flow of life, Lang's remake, *Human Desire,* is the nightmare of an innocent man enmeshed in the tangled strands of fate. What we remember in Renoir are the faces of Gabin, Simon, and Ledoux. What we remember in Lang are the geometrical patterns of trains, tracks, and fateful camera angles. If Renoir is humanism, Lang is determinism. If Renoir is concerned with the plight of his characters, Lang is obsessed with the structure of the trap. It must be stressed that Lang's cinema has not declined over the years. The same objections can be directed at both *Metropolis* and *Moonfleet,* and yet both films share the same bleak view of the universe where man grapples with his personal destiny, and inevitably loses. The last sea image of *Moonfleet* is Lang's chilling reconstruction of the legend of the Flying Dutchman. There is something of the voyeur in Lang; vide the flashlight sequence in *Metropolis* and the false mirror in the last *Mabuse.* His films take place in a closed world, but their formal brilliance and intellectual conceptions are incontestable. Lang is the cerebral tragedian of the cinema, and his lapses into absurdity are the evidence of a remote sagacity, an intellect that transforms images into ideas.

A curious pattern of paranoia runs through Lang's films from the first *Mabuse* in 1922 to the last in 1961. The pattern persists in his best Hollywood films—*Fury, You Only Live Once, Manhunt, Hangmen Also Die, Ministry of Fear, The Woman in the Window, Scarlet Street, Rancho Notorious,* and *The Big Heat.* As the servant of an allegedly optimistic film industry, Lang is singularly successful in undercutting audience expectations of a moral balance regained. Lang's prevailing image is that of a world ravaged and in flames. The hero is nearly burned to death in *Fury* and actually shot to death with his wife in *You Only Live Once.* The hero's wife is raped and murdered in *Rancho Notorious,* as is her child in a direct evocation of the bouncing-ball murder of the innocents in Lang's *M.* The hero's wife in *The Big Heat* is blown up when she presses the starter of the car, and her husband must then not only revenge her death but also assuage his guilt at being the intended victim of the bomb-planter. The most memorable violence in *The Big Heat* involves, not explosives, however, but scaldingly hot coffee flung in Gloria Grahame's face by Lee Marvin, and later, in a revenge worthy of Kriemhild, in Marvin's face by Grahame. In view of these outrages, Lang's violent mise-en-scène implies, the world must be destroyed before it can be purified.

Nonetheless Lang makes sentimental exceptions to this paranoia in the pure, trustworthy love of beautiful girls, a love capable of destroying the most intricately insidious conspiracies ever devised by evil minds. Romantic love with its intimations of Christian self-sacrifice flows through both the German and American periods of Lang's career, as strongly in *Spione* as in *The Ministry of Fear.* Sentimental exceptions aside, Lang might argue that in a century that has spawned Hitler and Hiroshima, no artist can be called paranoiac; he *is* being persecuted.

ERNST LUBITSCH (1892–1947)

FILMS: 1915–1918—twelve comedy shorts. 1918—Die Augen der Mumie Ma (The Eyes of the Mummy), The Ballet Girl, Carmen. 1919—Meyer from Berlin; My Wife, the Movie Star; The Schwab Maiden, The Oyster Princess, Rausch (Intoxication), *Mad-*

ame Dubarry (Passion), *Die Puppe* (The Doll). 1920—Kohlhiesel's Daughters, Romeo and Juliet in the Snow, Sumurun (One Arabian Night), Anne Boleyn (Deception). 1921—The Wildcat. 1922— The Loves of Pharaoh. 1923—Die Flamme (Montmartre). American period: 1923—Rosita. 1924—*The Marriage Circle,* Three Women, Forbidden Paradise. 1925—Kiss Me Again, *Lady Windermere's Fan.* 1926—*So This Is Paris.* 1927—The Student Prince. 1928—The Patriot, Eternal Love. 1929—*The Love Parade.* 1930 —Paramount on Parade (with Edmund Goulding, Victor Schertzinger, Rowland V. Lee, Edward Sutherland, Lother Mendes, Frank Tuttle, Dorothy Arzner, Edwin H. Knopf, Victor Heerman, Otto Brower), *Monte Carlo.* 1931—*The Smiling Lieutenant.* 1932— The Man I Killed, *One Hour With You* (Cukor directed from Lubitsch plan, signed by Lubitsch), *Trouble in Paradise,* If I Had a Million (with King Vidor, James Cruze, Norman Z. McLeod, Stephen S. Roberts, William A. Seiter, Norman Taurog, Bruce Humberstone). 1933—*Design for Living.* 1934—*The Merry Widow.* 1937— *Angel.* 1938—Bluebeard's Eighth Wife. 1939—*Ninotchka.* 1940 —*The Shop Around the Corner.* 1941—That Uncertain Feeling. 1942—*To Be or Not to Be.* 1943—*Heaven Can Wait.* 1946— *Cluny Brown.* 1948—That Lady in Ermine (completed by Otto Preminger after Lubitsch's death, signed by Lubitsch).

In the well-mannered, good-natured world of Ernst Lubitsch, grace transcends purpose. *To Be or Not to Be,* widely criticized as an inappropriately farcical treatment of Nazi terror, bridges the abyss between laughter and horror. For Lubitsch, it was sufficient to say that Hitler had bad manners, and no evil was then inconceivable. What are manners, after all, but the limits to man's presumption, a recognition that we all eventually lose the game of life but that we should still play the game according to the rules. A poignant sadness infiltrates the director's gayest moments, and it is this counterpoint between sadness and gaiety that represents the Lubitsch touch, and not the leering humor of closed doors. Describing Lubitsch as the continental sophisticate is as inadequate as describing Hitchcock as the master of suspense. Garbo's pixilated speech in *Ninotchka* is pitched delicately between the comic and the cosmic, and in one breathtaking moment, Garbo and Lubitsch sway on the tightrope between grace and purpose.

Lubitsch was always the least Germanic of German directors, as Lang was the most Germanic. The critics were always so obsessed with what Lubitsch naughtily left off the screen that they never fully evaluated what was left on. It seems incredible that Lubitsch's silent *Lady Windermere's Fan* was an improvement on Wilde's original. Everyone remembers Wilde's epigrams, which were largely irrelevant to the plot, but Lubitsch redeemed Wilde's silly melodramatics through the sardonic wit of his images and players. There were many Lubitsch imitators in the thirties, but none could penetrate beyond the master's most superficial mannerisms.

Lubitsch's German period ran between 1915 and 1923, the American period from 1923 to the director's death in 1947, or three times as long. Consequently, Lubitsch, unlike Lang and Murnau, is more an American director than a German director, and must be evaluated accordingly, particularly after 1933 for such neglected masterpieces as *Design for Living, The Merry Widow, Angel, The Shop Around the Corner, To Be or Not to Be, Heaven Can Wait,* and *Cluny Brown,* all in all, a dazzling display of stylistic unity transcending varied source materials. The conventional critics of the time decided that Gary Cooper and Fredric March were miscast for *Design for Living,* Chevalier was too old for *The Merry Widow,* Marlene Dietrich too stiff for *Angel,* James Stewart and Margaret Sullavan too cute for *The Shop Around the Corner,* Carole Lombard and Jack Benny too disparate for *To Be or Not to Be,* Gene Tierney and Don Ameche too guileless for *Heaven Can Wait,* and Jennifer Jones and Charles Boyer too strained for *Cluny Brown.* And that was that. However, Lubitsch has had the last laugh in that the magical qualities of his films have survived the topical distractions of his detractors. If *Angel* evokes Pirandello as *The Shop Around the Corner* evokes Molnar, it is because Lubitsch taught the American cinema the importance of appearances for appearance's sake (Pirandello) and the indispensability of good manners (Molnar). Lubitsch was the last of the genuine continentals let loose on the American continent, and we shall never see his like again because the world he celebrated had died—even before he did—everywhere except in his own memory.

F. W. MURNAU (1889–1931)

FILMS: 1919—Der Knabe in Blau. 1920—Satanas, Sehnsucht, Der Buckelige und die Tänzerin, Der Januskopf, Abend . . . Nacht . . . Morgen, Der Gang in die Nacht. 1921—Marizza, Gennant die Schmugglermadonna; Schloss Vogeloed. 1922—*Nosferatu,* Der Brennende Acker, Phantom. 1923—Die Austreibung. 1924—Die Finanzen des Grossherzogs, *The Last Laugh.* 1926—Tartuffe, *Faust.* 1927—*Sunrise.* 1928—Four Devils. 1930—Our Daily Bread (City Girl). 1931—*Tabu* (with Robert Flaherty).

The tradition Murnau represents is that of the director who decides how much of the world will be revealed to his audience. The aesthetic of camera movement over montage implies the continuousness of a visual field outside the frame of a film. What we see on the screen is what the director has chosen to show us. He could have shown us more or less or something else, but he chose to show us what he has shown us for a specific purpose. In *Faust,* the screen is momentarily dark. Suddenly it is illuminated by a candle, and we see a man carrying the candle down some stairs. The man, the candle, the stairs have materialized out of the darkness. The world has been manifested by the director. Spottiswoode or Arnheim would demystify this luminous moment by explaining the technical processes involved, but they could never fully express the magical effect of these processes upon an audience. This is the difference between viewing the cinema as the sum of its machinery and regarding it as the creation of its artists. Any director can track if he has the facilities at his disposal. Any director can illuminate a dark screen. But only Murnau could have given the meanings and moods to tracking and lighting that he did.

The limiting factor in Murnau's cinema is his conception of characters in terms of universals. His Everyman in *Faust, The Last Laugh, Sunrise,* and *Tabu* is no man in particular, and paradoxically, no man in general. Murnau's characters, like Lang's, are creatures of their private destinies. The director's fateful camera angles, again like Lang's, constitute the signature of a modern tragedian. Murnau's enclosed cosmos even in *Tabu* is the logical consequence of studio cinema, and the ultimate presumption of his mise-en-scène. It might be supposed that after the extraordinary artistry of *Sunrise* and *Tabu,* Murnau's future in the American cinema seemed limitless. His tragic death in a car accident shortly after he had signed a Paramount contract removed for all time the staggering possibilities of a Murnau-Sternberg-Lubitsch triumvirate at one studio. On the other hand, the acute pessimism of *Tabu* seems today a fitting testament for a suicidally inclined artist.

Murnau's influence on the cinema has proved to be more lasting than Eisenstein's. Murnau's moving camera seems a more suitable style for exploring the world than does Eisenstein's dialectical montage, and the trend in modern movies has been toward escaping studio sets so as to discover the real world. Also, the modern cinema tends to be less manipulative and more expressionistic, less concerned with how the audience feels than with how the artist feels. The trolley ride from the country to the city in *Sunrise* is one of the most lyrical passages in the world cinema. It is also a prophetic passage in that it heralds the cinema of the future as the art of the traveler. Back in the silent era Murnau saw cinema as an international language to the extent of printing signs in Esperanto in *The Last Laugh.* Murnau never really made the transition to the sound film, but it is difficult to see how his style could have been adversely affected by the elimination of titles as breaks in the continuousness of his visual field. Indeed, there is a sequence in *Sunrise* in which music and pantomime are directly substituted for speech, as if the cinema were not silent at all, but merely straining to be heard through a technological barrier.

MAX OPHULS (1902–1957)

FILMS: 1930—Dann Schon Lieber Lebertran. 1931—Die Lachende Erben, Die Verliebte Firma. 1932—*Die Verkaufte Braut, Liebelei.* 1933—Une Histoire d'Amour, On a Vole un Homme. 1934—*La Signora di Tutti.* 1935—*Divine.* 1936—Komödie um

Geld, Ave Maria of Schubert (short), La Valse Brilliante (short) *La Tendre Ennemie.* 1937—Yoshiwara. 1938—Werther. 1939—Sans Lendemain. 1940—De Mayerling à Sarajevo. 1947—*The Exile.* 1948—*Letter from an Unknown Woman.* 1949—*Caught, The Reckless Moment.* 1950—*La Ronde.* 1951—*Le Plaisir.* 1953 —*Madame de . . .* 1955—*Lola Montès* (released in mutilated English-language version, Sins of Lola Montes, in New York, 1959).

The cinema of Max Ophuls translates tracking into walking. His fluid camera follows his characters without controlling them, and it is this stylistic expression of free will that finally sets Ophuls apart from Murnau and Hitchcock. However, the track is such a conspicuous element of film technique that Ophuls has never been sufficiently appreciated for his other merits. Even when he is most bitter, he never descends to caricature. His humor is never malicious, his irony never destructive. Like Renoir, he was one of the first genuinely international directors, the kind of artist who did not slur over national differences in the name of a spurious universality, but who defined national differences as functions of a larger unity. Consequently, Ophuls's American films, particularly *Caught* and *The Reckless Moment,* express a perceptive vision of America's glamorous fantasies (*Caught*) and the obsessive absorption with family at the expense of society (*The Reckless Moment*). Conversely, his treatment of European subjects in *The Exile* and *Letter from an Unknown Woman* lent grace and sensibility to the American cinema at a time when it was reeling from its false realism.

We claim Max as our own only to the extent that he happened to pass in our midst during his long voyage to sublimity. His influence was not so decisive as Murnau's or so pervasive as Renoir's. In the final analysis, Ophuls is, like all great directors, inimitable, and if all the dollies and cranes in the world snap to attention when his name is mentioned, it is because he gave camera movement its finest hours in the history of the cinema. When Joan Fontaine mounts the staircase to her lover's apartment for the last time, Ophuls's camera slowly turns from its vantage point on a higher landing to record the definitive memory-image of love. For a moment we enter the privileged sanctuary of remembrance, and *Letter from an Unknown*

Woman reverberates forever after with this intimation of mortality. Love, the memory of love, the mortality of love comprise the Ophulsian heritage. If Ophuls seemed inordinately devoted to baroque opulence, his devotion was nevertheless strong-minded enough to contemplate an underlying human vanity tinged with sadness at its impending doom. The sensuous fabrics and surfaces of the Ophulsian world never completely obscure the grinning skeletons in the closets, and luxury never muffles tragedy.

The main point is that Ophuls is much more than the sum of all his camera movements. What elementary aestheticians overlook in Ophuls is the preciseness of his sensibility. His women may dominate subjectively, but his men are never degraded objectively. James Mason in *Caught* does not know what Barbara Bel Geddes is feeling when he proposes to her, but Ophuls conveys through the acting sensibility of Mason that a man need not understand what a woman feels to be capable of providing love. The Bergman-Antonioni problem of communication between the sexes does not arise in Ophuls simply because the director recognizes the two separate spheres of men and women. The Ophulsian view is never feminist, like Mizoguchi's, or feminine like Bergman's and Antonioni's. No Ophulsian male, for example, is ever caught with his pants down like Gunnar Bjornstrand in *Smiles of a Summer Night* or Gabriele Ferzetti in *L'Avventura,* and no Ophulsian female ever displays the smug complacency toward her own moral superiority evidenced in the superior expressions of Eva Dahlbeck and Monica Vitti. We have instead the desperate effort of Wolfgang Liebeneiner in *Liebelei* to recapture his lost innocence with Magda Schneider on a sleigh ride that is mystically reprised by the camera after they both have died. It is not merely the moving camera that expresses the tragedy of lost illusions, but the preciseness of the playing. There is a direct link between Liebeneiner and Gérard Philipe's jaded count in *La Ronde* looking deep into Simone Signoret's eyes to find something he has forgotten forever. There is the same delicacy of regret nearly twenty years apart.

Some critics, particularly in England, have objected to the softening of Schnitzler's cynicism in the Ophuls versions of *Liebelei* and *La Ronde,* not to mention the Ophulsian rendering of De Maupassant in *Le Plaisir.* Ophuls himself once observed that

Schnitzler wrote *Liebelei* after *Reigen,* and not before. The implication is clear. It is cynicism, and not idealism, that is generally the mark of youthful immaturity, or rather it is the cynic who is generally the most foolish romantic. A cynic delights in the trivial deceptions lovers practice on each other, and his attitude is particularly fashionable in a culture dedicated to the happy ending. There is a time in every film critic's life when he thinks that Billy Wilder is more profound than John Ford, and that nastiness is more profound than nobility. However, the acquiring of moral wisdom comes with mortal awareness, and vice begins paying back all its youthful debts to virtue. At such a moment, Ophuls becomes more profound than Schnitzler and De Maupassant, and *Madame de* becomes infinitely more tragic than *The Bicycle Thief.* By showing man in his direst material straits, De Sica and Zavattini imply a solution to his problems. Ophuls offers no such comforting consolation. His elegant characters lack nothing and lose everything. There is no escape from the trap of time. Not even the deepest and sincerest love can deter the now from its rendezvous with the then, and no amount of self-sacrifice can prevent desire from becoming embalmed in memory. *"Quelle heure est-il?"* ask the characters in *La Ronde,* but it is always too late, and the moment has always passed.

This is the ultimate meaning of Ophulsian camera movement: time has no stop. Montage tends to suspend time in the limbo of abstract images, but the moving camera records inexorably the passage of time, moment by moment. As we follow the Ophulsian characters, step by step, up and down stairs, up and down streets, and round and round the ballroom, we realize their imprisonment in time. We know that they can never escape, but we know also that they will never lose their poise and grace for the sake of futile desperation. They will dance beautifully, they will walk purposively, they will love deeply, and they will die gallantly, and they will never whine or whimper or even discard their vanity. It will all end in a circus with Lola Montès selling her presence to the multitudes, redeeming all men both as a woman and as an artistic creation, expressing in one long receding shot, the cumulative explosion of the romantic ego for the past two centuries.

JEAN RENOIR (1894–   )

FILMS: 1924—La Fille de l'Eau. 1926—*Nana.* 1927—Charleston, Marquitta. 1928—La Petite Marchande d'Allumettes. 1929—*Tire au Flanc,* Le Tournoi, Le Petit Chaperon Rouge, La P'tite Lili, Le Bled. 1931—On Purge Bébé, *La Chienne.* 1932—La Nuit du Carrefour, *Boudu Sauve des Eaux.* 1933—Chotard et Compagnie. 1934—*Toni, Madame Bovary.* 1935—*Le Crime de Monsieur Lange.* 1936—La Vie Est à Nous, *Une Partie de Campagne,* Les Bas Fonds. 1937—*La Bête Humaine.* 1939—*La Regle du Jeu.* 1940—La Tosca (with C. Koch and Luchino Visconti). 1941—*Swamp Water.* 1943—This Land Is Mine. 1944—Salute to France (allegorical documentary). 1945—*The Southerner.* 1946—*Diary of a Chambermaid.* 1947—*The Woman on the Beach.* 1951—*The River.* 1954—*The Golden Coach.* 1956—*French Can Can.* 1957—*Paris Does Strange Things.* 1960—*Le Dejeuner sur l'Herbe.* 1961—Dr. Cordelier. 1963—*The Elusive Corporal* (Renoir wrote and produced Une Vie sans Joie in 1924, and Albert Dieudonne directed.)

Renoir's career is a river of personal expression. The waters may vary here and there in turbulence and depth, but the flow of personality is consistently directed to its final outlet in the sea of life. If the much-abused term "humanism," could be applied to Renoir's art and to no one else's, it might still provide an accurate definition for his work as a whole. In Renoir's films, man's natural surroundings are almost always prominently featured, and it is this emphasis on man in his environment photographed by an unblinking camera that is the true precursor of neorealism. As Murnau represents the formal antithesis to Eisenstein's montage principles, Renoir represents the thematic alternative to Eisenstein's dialectic. However, the fact that Renoir is a warm director and Eisenstein a cold one cannot be explained entirely through forms and themes. Directorial personality is, as always, the crucial determinant of a film's temperature. Murnau, after all, is cold, and Ophuls is warm, and both move their cameras. Chaplin is warm, and Keaton is cold, and both have evolved from the Sennett tradition. Lubitsch is warm, and Preminger is cold, and both are descended from the Viennese school. However, Renoir's preoccupation with his actors implies a concern with the unifying principles of humanity. *The Diary of a Chambermaid* is Renoir's definitive Resistance film. Never before had his characterizations been so Manichean. On one side were the fascists, the reactionaries, and the opportunists, and on the other, the enlightened aristocrats and the people, and the issue between the two groups could be resolved only by violence. Yet, before and after his committed periods, whether Marxist or patriotic, Renoir developed the themes of brotherly accommodation. Consequently, Renoir's career is not merely biography but also history. He has never looked back to an imaginary Golden Age, and he has never exploited past successes. The easy paths of cynicism and sentimentality have never appealed to him, and his unyielding sincerity is one of the glories of the cinema. If Renoir had not come to America in 1940, his work might have developed into an elaboration of the class structure as seen from the multiple viewpoint of *The Rules of the Game*. Renoir's American experience undoubtedly contributed to his transition from objectivity to subjectivity. In the American cinema, one must ultimately root for one side or another. The exceptions to this rule, most notably Hitchcock and Preminger, only confirm the rule. However, Renoir's conversion was only surface deep, and the multiple viewpoint was never really abandoned even in *The Diary of a Chambermaid*. The problem with most conventional critiques of Renoir's films is that humanism is invariably associated with crudity of expression, but there is nothing crude about Renoir's technique once its purposes have been fully understood. Only when style is confused with meaningless flourishes does Renoir's economy of expression seem inadequate for textbook critics.

JOSEF VON STERNBERG (1894–)

FILMS: 1925—*The Salvation Hunters.* 1926—The Sea Gull, The Exquisite Sinner. 1927—*Underworld.* 1928—*Last Command, The Dragnet, Docks of New York.* 1929—The Case of Lena Smith,

Thunderbolt. 1930—*The Blue Angel, Morocco.* 1931—*Dis-
honored, An American Tragedy.* 1932—*Shanghai Express,* Blonde
Venus. 1934—*The Scarlet Empress.* 1935—*The Devil is a
Woman,* Crime and Punishment. 1936—The King Steps Out. 1937
—*Claudius* (unfinished). 1939—Sergeant Madden. 1941—*The
Shanghai Gesture.* 1944—The Town. 1952—Macao. 1954—
Anatahan. 1957—Jet Pilot.

Although Josef von Sternberg's directorial career spans almost
thirty years, he was a meaningful force in the cinema primarily
between 1927 and 1935, an interval we might ironically designate as his Paramount Period. Until very recently, even his work
of this period had not been seriously evaluated since the mid-
thirties, when movies were supposed to crackle crisply to the pro-
letarian point. Sternberg was then considered slow, decadent,
and self-indulgent, while gloriously ambiguous Marlene Dietrich was judged too rich for the people's blood—it was a time
for bread, not cake. Paradoxically, Sternberg and Dietrich look
deeper and more dazzling than ever, while most of the cinema of
the bread lines looks excessively mannered.

Even today, however, the art of Josef von Sternberg is too
often subordinated to the mystique of Marlene Dietrich, with
whom the director was associated in seven of his more familiar
movies. Unfortunately, the Svengali-Trilby publicity that en-
shrouded *The Blue Angel, Morocco, Dishonored, Shanghai Express, Blonde Venus, The Scarlet Empress,* and *The Devil Is a
Woman* obscured the more meaningful merits not only of these
particular works but of Sternberg's career as a whole. In fact, the
director's filtered feminine mystique neither originated nor disappeared with Marlene Dietrich, but ecstatically embraced such
other photogenic features as those of Georgia Hale, Evelyn
Brent, Betty Compson, Olga Baclanova, Esther Ralston, Fay
Wray, Sylvia Sidney, Frances Dee, Laraine Day, Gene Tierney,
and Janet Leigh. It is also part of the record that he made films
before *The Blue Angel* and after *The Devil Is a Woman.* At all
times, Sternberg's cinema of illusion and delusion has transcended the personality of even his most glittering star the better
to reflect his own vision.

In a sense, Sternberg entered the cinema through the camera
rather than the cutting room, and thus became a lyricist of light

and shadow rather than a master of montage. The control he achieved over his studio surroundings encouraged him to concentrate on the spatial integrity of his images rather than on their metaphorical juxtaposition. Sternberg's cinema, for better or worse, represents a distinctively Germanic camera movement — from Murnau and Lang — in contrast to Eisenstein's fashionably Marxist montage.

Even today, however, critics and audiences may be reluctant to endorse Sternberg's story sense. Apart from "classical" assignments like *An American Tragedy* and *Crime and Punishment,* his plots seem farfetched, his backgrounds bizarre, and his character motivations obscure, at least by conventional standards of storytelling. As in a dream, he has wandered through studio sets representing Imperial Russia (*The Last Command, The Scarlet Empress*), China (*Shanghai Express, The Shanghai Gesture*), North Africa (*Morocco*), Spain (*The Devil Is a Woman*), Austria (*The Case of Lena Smith, Dishonored*), France (*The Exquisite Sinner*), and Germany (*The Blue Angel*). Even his American locales focus primarily on the dregs or fringes of society from the festive criminality of *Underworld, The Dragnet* and *Thunderbolt* to the bawdy, brawling backwaters and back streets of *The Salvation Hunters, Docks of New York,* and *Blonde Venus.* Everyday life, as such, seldom appears in Sternberg's cinema. His characters generally make their entrance at a moment in their lives when there is no tomorrow. Knowingly or unknowingly, they have reached the end or the bottom, but they will struggle a short time longer, about ninety minutes of screen time, to discover the truth about themselves and those they love. Although there is much violence and death in Sternberg's world, there is relatively little action. The various murders, duels, executions, suicides, and assaults serve merely as poetic punctuation for lives drifting to their destination in reflective repose. Death in this context is less a conclusion than a termination. The paradox of violence without action is supplemented by the paradox of virtue without morality. There are no codes or systems in these dream worlds; the characters retain their civilized graces despite the most desperate struggles for psychic survival, and it is their poise under pressure, their style under stress, that grants them a measure of heroic stature and stoic calm.

Sternberg's films are poetic without being symbolic. We need not search for slumbering allegories of Man and God and Life, but rather for a continuous stream of emotional autobiography. Sternberg's exoticism is, then, less a pretense than a pretext for objectifying personal fantasies. His equivalent literary genre is not the novel or the short story or the theatrical spectacle, but the closet drama unplayable but for the meaningful grace of gesture and movement. There persists an erroneous impression that the art of a *Morocco* or a *Shanghai Express* consists of the magnifying of trivialities. Yet there is nothing trivial about the size of Sternberg's emotions, and nothing disproportionate in the means employed to express them, critics from John Grierson to Susan Sontag notwithstanding. Also there is conscious humor in the director's awareness of his own absurdity, though some spectators still imagine they are laughing *at* Sternberg when they are merely laughing *with* him. The colorful costumes, the dazzling décors, the marble-pillared palaces merely underscore by ironic contrast the painfully acquired wisdom of the all too human prisoners of grandiose illusions. The limitations of this aesthetic are self-evident. An insufficient grasp of one's time and place is hardly a positive virtue even for the most lyrical poet. It is only when we look around at the allegedly significant cinema of Sternberg's contemporaries that we recognize the relative stature of a director who chose to write with a camera in the first person long before Alexandre Astruc's *caméra-stylo* made such impious subjectivity fashionable and such personal poetry comprehensible.

ORSON WELLES (1915–   )

FILMS: 1941—*Citizen Kane.* 1942—*The Magnificent Ambersons,* Journey into Fear (signed by Norman Foster). 1946—The Stranger. 1948—*Lady from Shanghai.* 1950—Macbeth. 1955—*Othello.* 1958—*Touch of Evil.* 1962—*Mr. Arkadin.* 1963—The Trial. 1967—*Falstaff.* 1968—*The Immortal Story.*

That Welles, the aging *enfant terrible* of the American Cinema, is still the youngest indisputably great American director is an ominous symptom of decadence in the industry as a whole. It can even be argued that Welles's films are now less American than European in outlook and that in ten years or less there may be no American cinema of great artistic significance. It is more likely, however, that we are too dazzled by the phantasms of the sixties to perceive their ultimate aesthetic contours.

With *Mr. Arkadin* and *The Trial,* Welles's career took a curious turn. This Man from Mars who projected radio dynamics to that RKO-Radio classic *Citizen Kane* went surprisingly sour on the sound track. The ear of the expatriate had lost contact with the nuances of American speech. It may be no accident that Welles has gradually turned away from the psychological density of the fictionalized biography (*Citizen Kane*) and the filmed novel (*The Magnificent Ambersons*) to the psychological abstractions of fantasy (*Lady from Shanghai*), allegory (*Touch of Evil*), fable (*Mr. Arkadin*), hallucination (*The Trial*), and reverie (*Falstaff*).

Welles seemed to have been rehearsing all his life for *Falstaff,* and it is not surprising that he should be carted away in a coffin like one of Murnau's vampires in *Nosferatu.* Indeed, Welles has been the foremost German expressionist in the Anglo-Saxon world ever since *Citizen Kane* infected the American cinema with the virus of artistic ambition. The conventional American diagnosis of his career is decline, pure and simple, but decline is never pure and never simple. Welles began his career on such a high plateau that the most precipitous decline would not affect his place in the Pantheon. *Citizen Kane* is still the work that influenced the cinema more profoundly than any American film since *Birth of a Nation.* If the thirties belong to Lubitsch's subtle grace and unobtrusive cutting, the forties belong to the Wellesian resurrection of Murnau's portentous camera angles. The decade of plots gave way to a decade of themes, and the American cinema had lost its innocence and charm forever. From the beginning, Welles imposed a European temperament on the American cinema. Even today, Arthur Penn acknowledges the influence of Welles. Certainly the cinema is no poorer for having inspired a young man from Wisconsin to act out his Faustian fantasies on the screen until they consumed him.

The Wellesian persona looms large in Wellesian cinema.

Apart from *The Magnificent Ambersons,* in which his presence was exclusively vocal narration, every Welles film is designed around the massive presence of the artist as autobiographer. Call him Hearst or Falstaff, Macbeth or Othello, Quinlan or Arkadin, he is always at least partly himself, ironic, bombastic, pathetic, and, above all, presumptuous. The Wellesian cinema is the cinema of magic and marvels, and everything, and especially its prime protagonist, is larger than life. The dramatic conflict in a Welles film often arises from the dialectical collision between morality and megalomania, and Welles more often than not plays the megalomaniacal villain without stilling the calls of conscience. Curiously, Welles is far from being his own best actor. Actually, no actor-director in history has been as generous to his colleagues. Through less than a dozen films the roll call of distinguished performances is long indeed: Joseph Cotten, Dorothy Comingore, Ray Collins, Everett Sloane, George Colouris, Agnes Moorehead, Dolores Costello, Anne Baxter, Richard Bennett, Edward G. Robinson, Glenn Anders, Suzanne Cloutier, Charlton Heston, Janet Leigh, Joseph Calleia, Akim Tamiroff, Peter Van Eyck, Michael Redgrave, Suzanne Flon, Katina Paxinou, Romy Schneider, John Gielgud, Keith Baxter, with extraordinarily honorable mention to such limited performers as Tim Holt (as the last of the Ambersons) and Rita Hayworth (as the spectacularly mythic Lady from Shanghai shattered irrevocably in a hall of mirrors, a superb metaphor for the movie career of Orson Welles).

French critics, most notably André Bazin, hailed *Citizen Kane* after the war for its single-take, deep-focus scenes as improvements upon the traditional Hollywood crosscutting (or *champ-contre-champ*) inside a master scene. However, most moviegoers tend to identify Welles stylistically more for his eccentric camera angles and swooping camera movements than for the relative stability of his staging. The world of Orson Welles is the world of the runaway artist who pauses every so often to muse over what he has lost or left behind. Quiet and frenzy alternate in this world, as do nostalgia and adventure. There is stylistic alternation as well between dynamic progressions through the plot and décor and very formal compositions of the characters. Mark Shivas has established a Welles-Hitchcock contrast both thematically and technically with the observation that Welles is concerned with the ordinary feelings of extraordinary people and Hitchcock with the extraordinary feelings of ordinary people. Whereas Welles flourishes in baroque settings, Hitchcock functions in commonplace settings. To a limited extent, at least, Wellesian cinema is as much the cinema of the exhibitionist as Hitchcockian cinema is the cinema of the voyeur.

The Trial deserves a derisory footnote all its own, but with reservations. Since everything Welles had done since *Citizen Kane* and *The Magnificent Ambersons* had been denounced as a betrayal of his talent, it is possible to sympathize with his decision to hurl Kafka at the culture-mongers. The final irony of this absurd situation is that *The Trial* is the most hateful, the most repellent, and the most perverted film Welles ever made. What seemed even to his steadfast admirers a glorious opportunity has dissolved into a fatal temptation. Welles asserts in the prologue that his story has the logic of a dream, but Welles on Kafka, like Mondrian's white on white, is less logical than superfluous, less a dream of something than a dream of a dream of something. Indeed, *The Trial* is in its brilliantly accomplished way as much of a dead end as Minnelli's *Ziegfeld Follies,* which demonstrated that the most hackneyed backstage plot was preferable to no plot at all, and as Resnais's *Last Year at Marienbad,* which demonstrated that ambiguity was less appealing as a subject than as an attitude. Paradoxically, what have always seemed the least meaningful elements of a movie—the surface plot, the apparent subject, the objective background—are also the most necessary. Once a director soars off into time and space without a calendar and an atlas, he loses that force of gravity without which a movie cannot address itself to an audience. By this standard and many others, *Touch of Evil* and *The Lady from Shanghai* are superior to *The Trial.*

The key to the director (as well as *Mr. Arkadin*) is revealed when Orson Welles (alias Gregory Arkadin) tells the story of a frog and a scorpion meeting by a river. When the scorpion asks to ride across the river on the frog's back, the frog demurs: "If I take you on my back, you will sting me, and your sting is fatal." The scorpion responds with a plausible argument: "Where is the logic in that? If I sting you, we both will drown." The frog, a logical creature, then agrees to transport the scorpion, but he no sooner reaches the middle of the river than he feels a deadly sting in his back. "Where is the logic in this?" croaks the dying frog as he begins to sink below the surface. "This is my character," replies the doomed scorpion, "and there is no logic in character."

II.
THE
FAR
SIDE
OF
PARADISE

These are the directors who fall short of the Pantheon either because of a fragmentation of their personal vision or because of disruptive career problems.

ROBERT ALDRICH (1918–   )

FILMS: 1953—The Big Leaguer. 1954—World for Ransom, *Apache, Vera Cruz.* 1955—*Kiss Me Deadly, The Big Knife.* 1956 —Autumn Leaves, *Attack!* 1959—The Angry Hills, Ten Seconds to Hell. 1961—The Last Sunset. 1962—*What Ever Happened to Baby Jane?* 1963—Sodom and Gomorrah. 1964—Four for Texas. 1965—*Hush, Hush . . . Sweet Charlotte.* 1966— *Flight of the Phoenix.* 1967—*The Dirty Dozen.* 1968—The Legend of Lylah Claire. 1969—The Killing of Sister George.

Robert Aldrich has emerged as one of the most strikingly personal directors of the past two decades. His style is notable for its violence even in genres that subsist on violence. His projects have ranged from the elegant escapism of *Vera Cruz* and *Autumn Leaves* to the explicit social protest of *Apache, Attack!,* and *The Big Knife* to the garish gargoyle-watching of *What Ever Happened to Baby Jane?* and *Hush, Hush . . . Sweet Charlotte* to the genuinely democratic treatment of dropouts in *Flight of the Phoenix* and *The Dirty Dozen,* the latter film so commercially successful that it enabled Aldrich to purchase his own movie studio. *Kiss Me Deadly* is perhaps his most perplexing and revealing work, poised as it is on the controversial boundary line between an unfashionable genre and a transcendent attitude toward the genre's moral implications. *Kiss Me Deadly* is not only the best Mickey Spillane screen adaptation; it is also a testament to Aldrich's anarchic spirit.

Except for his baroque sessions with Bette Davis and Joan Crawford, Aldrich can be classified as a moralist in a man's world. His films have a distinctively personal signature, largely through a handful of character players who follow him from film to film. Along with such other underrated genre stylists as Nicholas Ray, Joseph Losey, and Anthony Mann, Aldrich was discovered by European critics long before American reviewers deigned to acknowledge his existence. In recent years his reputation has fluctuated from film to film, but he has achieved a degree of freedom as a producer-director largely on a lucky gamble involving the chemical combustibility of Bette Davis and Joan Crawford in *What Ever Happened to Baby Jane?* Aldrich's direction of his players generally creates a subtle frenzy on the screen, and his visual style suggests an unstable world full of awkward angles and harsh transitions. His films are invariably troubled by intimations of decadence and disorder. The titles of even his lesser films—*World for Ransom, Autumn Leaves, Ten Seconds to Hell, The Last Sunset, Sodom and Gomorrah*—suggest a mood befitting the Decline of the West.

FRANK BORZAGE (1893–1961)

FILMS: 1918—Flying Colors, Until They Get Me, The Gun Woman, Shoes That Danced, Innocents' Progress, Society for Sale, An Honest Man, Who Is to Blame?, The Ghost Flower, The Curse of Iku. 1919—Toton, Prudence of Broadway, Whom the Gods Destroy. 1920—*Humoresque.* 1921—The Duke of Chimney Butte. 1922—Get Rich Quick Wallingford, Bank Day, Silent Shelby, Billy Jim, The Good Provider, Valley of Silent Men, The Pride of Palomar. 1923—Children of Dust, Nth Commandment, Song of Love. 1924—The Age of Desire, Secrets. 1925—The Lady, Daddy's Gone a' Huntin', Wages for Wives, The Circle, Lazybones. 1926—Marriage License, The First Year, The Dixie Merchant, Early to Wed. 1927—*Seventh Heaven.* 1928—*Street Angel.* 1929—*The River, Lucky Star, They Had to See Paris.* 1930—Song o' My Heart, Liliom. 1931—*Bad Girl,* Doctor's Wives, As Young as You Feel. 1932—*A Farewell to Arms,* After Tomorrow, Young America. 1933—*A Man's Castle,* Secrets. 1934—*No Greater Glory, Little Man What Now,* Flirtation Walk. 1935—*Living on Velvet,* Stranded, Shipmates Forever. 1936—*Desire,* Hearts Divided. 1937—*History Is Made at Night, Green Light,* The Big City, Mannequin. 1938—*Three Comrades,* The Shining Hour. 1939—Disputed Passage. 1940—*The Mortal Storm,* Strange Cargo, Flight Command. 1941—Smilin' Through, The Vanishing Virginian. 1942—Seven Sweethearts. 1943—Stage-door Canteen, His Butler's Sister. 1944—Till We Meet Again. 1945—The Spanish Main. 1946—I've Always Loved You, The Magnificent Doll. 1947—That's My Man. 1948—*Moonrise.* 1958—China Doll. 1959—The Big Fisherman.

Frank Borzage was that rarity of rarities, an uncompromising romanticist. Anglo-Saxon film historians have generally underrated Borzage on the assumption that the director's romanticism was a commercially motivated betrayal of realism. Yet, the way of the romanticist is usually much harder than that of the realist. Audiences generally prefer realism, at least on the surface; and intimate love stories have always been box-office poison. On the rare occasions when romanticism seems to be popular, it is usually the false romanticism of Hathaway's *Peter Ibbetson* or Wyler's *Wuthering Heights,* romantic subjects directed coldly by unromantic directors, the coldness disguised in the former instance by the photography of Lee Garmes, and in the latter by the music of Alfred Newman. Borzage never needed dream worlds for his suspensions of disbelief. He plunged into the real world of poverty and oppression, the world of Roosevelt and Hitler, the New Deal and the New Order, to impart an aura to his characters, not merely through soft focus and a fluid camera, but through a genuine concern with the wondrous inner life of lovers in the midst of adversity. His anti-Nazi films—*Little Man, What Now* and *Three Comrades*—were far ahead of their time, emotionally if not politically. Borzage's objection to Hitler was a curious one. What Hitler and all tyrants represented most reprehensibly was an invasion of the emotional privacy of individuals, particularly lovers, those blessed creatures gifted with luminous rapport. *History Is Made at Night* is not only the most romantic title in the history of the cinema but also a profound expression of Borzage's commitment to love over probability. Borzage's cinema is typified by his extraordinary treatment of Janet Gaynor and Margaret Sullavan, actresses with screen personalities molded by Borzage. Jean Arthur and Gail Russell fitted into the Borzage tradition on their first and only tries, and Borzage's actors, notably Spencer Tracy, Charles Boyer, and James Stewart, were made to discard Hollywood's traditionally cynical attitudes toward love. Many of Borzage's projects, particularly toward the end of his career, were indisputably trivial in conception, but the director's personality never faltered, and when the glorious opportunity of *Moonrise* presented itself, Borzage was not stale or jaded. This, if anything, is the moral of the *auteur* theory.

FRANK CAPRA (1897–   )

FILMS: 1926—*The Strong Man.* 1927—*Long Pants*, For the Love of Mike. 1928—That Certain Feeling, So This Is Love, The Matinee Idol, The Way of the Strong, Say It with Sables, Submarine, Power of the Press. 1929—Younger Generation, Donovan Affair, Flight. 1930—Ladies of Leisure, Rain or Shine. 1931—Dirigible, Miracle Woman, *Platinum Blonde.* 1932—Forbidden, *American Madness.* 1933—*Bitter Tea of General Yen, Lady for a Day.* 1934 —*It Happened One Night,* Broadway Bill. 1936—*Mr. Deeds Goes to Town.* 1937—*Lost Horizon.* 1938—*You Can't Take It with You.* 1939—*Mr. Smith Goes to Washington.* 1941—*Meet John Doe.* 1944—Arsenic and Old Lace. 1942–1945—Co-directed seven war documentaries. 1946—*It's a Wonderful Life.* 1948— *State of the Union.* 1950—Riding High. 1951—Here Comes the Groom. 1959—A Hole in the Head. 1961—*Pocketful of Miracles.*

With *Meet John Doe,* Frank Capra crossed the thin line between populist sentimentality and populist demogoguery. Capra's political films—*Meet John Doe, You Can't Take It With You, Mr. Smith Goes to Washington*—had always implied a belief in the tyranny of the majority, but John Doe embodied in Gary Cooper a barefoot fascist, suspicious of all ideas and all doctrines, but believing in the innate conformism of the common man. Capra's Shangri-la Hilton in *Lost Horizon* was an antiintellectual paradise, a rest home for the troubled mind, with even the eternal problems of aging and dying miraculously banished from consideration. At that point, Capra stopped the world and got off. After years of relative inactivity, Capra returned almost triumphantly with the new look in conformity, Frank Sinatra, and a more nervous brand of sentimentality labeled: *Hole in the Head.* In *Pocketful of Miracles,* Capra quoted Pascal to the effect that the heart has its own reasons. Capra's remake of his own *Lady for a Day* was disastrously but touchingly dated.

Capra is a genuine auteur, and there is no mistaking his point of view. The Kaufman and Hart *You Can't Take It with You* on Broadway related the story of an eccentric family that chose to live on the basis of its unconventional impulses. The Capra-Riskin version transformed the eccentric family into a spokesman for all the little people in the world, and perverted the play's stuffy businessman into a bloated shark of Wall Street (a thirties specialty of Edward Arnold) beyond even Eisenstein's power of caricature.

Capra's flair for improvisation was evident throughout his career. This flair made his fortune in *It Happened One Night,* the sleeper of its year and the death knell of the more deliberately expressionistic experiments of Sternberg (*The Scarlet Empress*), Lubitsch (*The Merry Widow*), and Milestone (*Hallelujah, I'm a Bum*). Capra's boisterous humor seemed in tune with the mood of Depression audiences, but there runs through most of his films a somber Christian parable of idealism betrayed and innocence humiliated. The obligatory scene in most Capra films is the confession of folly in the most public manner possible. Indeed, Spencer Tracy's hapless presidential Candidate in *State of the Union* (1948) seems to anticipate George Romney by two decades.

GEORGE CUKOR (1899–)

FILMS: 1930—*The Royal Family of Broadway* (with Cyril Gardner), Grumpy (with Cyril Gardner), Virtuous Sin (with Louis Gasnier). 1931—*Tarnished Lady,* Girls About Town. 1932—*One Hour with You* (directed by Cukor from Lubitsch plan, signed by Lubitsch), *A Bill of Divorcement, What Price Hollywood,* Rockabye. 1933—*Dinner at Eight, Little Women,* Our Betters. 1935—*David Copperfield, Sylvia Scarlett.* 1936—Romeo and Juliet. 1937—*Camille.* 1938—*Holiday,* Zaza. 1939—*The Women.* 1940—*The Philadelphia Story,* Susan and God. 1941—A Woman's Face, Two-Faced Woman. 1942—Her Cardboard Lover. 1943—Keeper of the Flame. 1944—*Gaslight,* Winged Victory. 1948—*A Double Life.* 1949—*Adam's Rib; Edward, My Son.* 1950—A Life of Her Own, Born Yesterday. 1952—The Model and the Marriage Broker, *The Marrying Kind, Pat and Mike.* 1953—*The Actress.* 1954—*A Star Is Born, It Should Happen to You.* 1956—*Bhowani Junction.* 1957—Les Girls, Wild Is the Wind. 1960—*Heller in Pink Tights,*

Let's Make Love, Song Without End (begun and signed by Charles Vidor). 1962—The Chapman Report. 1964—My Fair Lady.

George Cukor's filmography is his most eloquent defense. When a director has provided tasteful entertainments of a high order consistently over a period of more than thirty years, it is clear that said director is much more than a mere entertainer. Mere entertainers seldom entertain for more than five years, and then only intermittently. Even Cukor's enemies concede his taste and style, but it has become fashionable to dismiss him as a woman's director because of his skill in directing actresses, a skill he shares with Griffith, Chaplin, Renoir, Ophuls, Sternberg, Welles, Dreyer, Bergman, Rossellini, Mizoguchi, *ad infinitum, ad gloriam.* Another argument against Cukor is that he relies heavily on adaptations from the stage and that his cinema consequently lacks the purity of the Odessa Steps. This argument was refuted in principle by the late André Bazin. There is an honorable place in the cinema for both adaptations and the non-writer director; and Cukor, like Lubitsch, is one of the best examples of the non-writer auteur, a creature literary film critics seem unable to comprehend. The thematic consistency of Cukor's career has been achieved through a judicious mixture of selection and emphasis. The director's theme is imagination, with the focus on the imaginer rather than on the thing imagined. Cukor's cinema is a subjective cinema without an objective correlative. The husbands never appear in *The Women,* and Edward never appears in *Edward, My Son.* Most critics would argue that this merely proves Cukor's slavish fidelity to his playwrights, but the fact remains that most directors attempt to make plays more "cinematic" by moving outdoors and adding characters and extras. Not Cukor. *Bhowani Junction* and *Heller in Pink Tights* demonstrate that Cukor is fully capable of exploiting exteriors when they serve his purposes. The opening Central Park sequence in *The Marrying Kind* is one of the most graceful exercises in open-air film-making in the history of the cinema, and the corresponding sequence in *It Should Happen to You* is not far behind. Yet, when characters have to thrash out their illusions and problems across the kitchen table, Cukor glides through his interiors without self-conscious reservations about what is "cinematic" and what is not. It is no accident that many of Cukor's characters are thespians of one form or another. John Barrymore and Marie Dressler in *Dinner at Eight,* Ina Claire in *Royal Family of Broadway,* Katharine Hepburn and Cary Grant in *Sylvia Scarlett,* Judy Garland and James Mason in *A Star Is Born,* Jean Simmons in *The Actress,* Marilyn Monroe in *Let's Make Love,* and even Sophia Loren, De Sica's alleged earth mother, in *Heller in Pink Tights.* Even when Cukor's characters do not appear formally behind the footlights, they project an imaginative existence. W. C. Fields is pure ham in *David Copperfield,* and Katharine Hepburn is pure ego in *The Philadelphia Story,* and Cukor is equally sympathetic to the absurdities of both. *Les Girls* is Cukor's *Rashomon,* but where Kurosawa argues that all people are liars, Cukor suggests that all people tell the truth in their fashion. Even when imagination extends to transvestism in *Adam's Rib* and *Sylvia Scarlett,* Cukor retains an indulgent affection for the misguided brashness of Katharine Hepburn. The theme is consistent; the pattern is established. Cukor is committed to the dreamer, if not to the content of the dream. He is a genuine artist.

CECIL B. DE MILLE (1881–1959)

FILMS: 1913—*The Squaw Man.* 1914—The Virginian, The Call of the North, What's His Name, The Man from Home, Rose of the Rancho. 1915—The Girl of the Golden West, The Warrens of Virginia, The Unafraid, The Captive, Wild Goose Chase, The Arab, Chimmie Fadden, Kindling, Maria Rosa, Carmen, Temptation, Chimmie Fadden Out West, *The Cheat.* 1916—The Golden Chance, The Trail of the Lonesome Pine, The Heart of Nora Flynn, The Dream Girl. 1917—Joan the Woman, A Romance of the Redwoods, The Little American, The Woman God Forgot, The Devil Stone. 1918—The Whispering Chorus, Old Wives for New, We Can't Have Everything, Till I Come Back to You, The Squaw Man. 1919—*Don't Change Your Husband,* For Better, for Worse, *Male and Female.* 1920—Why Change Your Wife, Something to Think About. 1921—Forbidden Fruit, The Affairs of Anatol. 1922—Fool's Paradise, Saturday Night, Manslaughter. 1923—Adam's Rib, The Ten Commandments. 1924—Triumph, Feet of Clay. 1925—The Golden Bed, The Road to Yesterday. 1926—The Volga

Boatman. 1927—*The King of Kings.* 1928—The Godless Girl. 1929—Dynamite. 1930—Madame Satan. 1931—The Squaw Man. 1932—*The Sign of the Cross.* 1933—This Day and Age. 1934—Four Frightened People, *Cleopatra.* 1935—*The Crusades.* 1936—*The Plainsman.* 1938—*The Buccaneer.* 1939—*Union Pacific.* 1940—*North West Mounted Police.* 1942—*Reap the Wild Wind.* 1944—The Story of Dr. Wassell. 1947—*Unconquered.* 1949—Samson and Delilah. 1952—*The Greatest Show on Earth.* 1956—The Ten Commandments.

It is inevitable that the mere mention of Cecil B. de Mille will evoke complacent laughter in some quarters, and bristling patriotic speeches in others. If De Mille had the right enemies, he also had the wrong friends. De Mille was neither a primitive like Fuller nor a populist like Capra. Although he appealed to audiences, he never manipulated them. He remained faithful to the literary tradition of Cooper's Leatherstocking Tales and to the dramatic conventions of David Belasco. Griffith, Chaplin, Lubitsch, Murnau, Eisenstein, Ford, Hawks, Capra, Welles, Renoir, Ophuls, and all the others came and went without influencing his style in the slightest. Ironically, his films look much better today than their reputations would indicate. De Mille's cross-reference is Frank Lloyd, and interested or rather disinterested critics might profitably compare De Mille's *Union Pacific* with Lloyd's *Wells Fargo,* or De Mille's *Reap the Wild Wind* with Lloyd's *Rulers of the Sea,* or De Mille's *The Crusades* with Lloyd's *If I Were King.* The comparison in each instance is almost fantastically favorable to De Mille. Where Lloyd's spectacles are dull, heavy, and monotonous; De Mille's are well paced and logically constructed. De Mille relished complications in his narratives, and he may have been the last American director who enjoyed telling a story for its own sake. He may also have been the last Victorian, although the Late George Orwell would probably have held out for Salvador Dali.

BLAKE EDWARDS (1922–   )

FILMS: 1955—Bring Your Smile Along. 1956—He Laughed Last. 1957—*Mr. Cory.* 1958—This Happy Feeling, The Perfect Furlough. 1959—*Operation Petticoat.* 1960—High Time. 1961

—*Breakfast at Tiffany's.* 1962—Experiment in Terror. 1963—
Days of Wine and Roses. 1964—*The Pink Panther, Shot in the
Dark.* 1965—*The Great Race.* 1966—*What Did You Do in the
War, Daddy?* 1967—*Gunn.* 1968—The Party. 1969—Darling
Lili.

Edwards seemed until 1963 to merit only cult recognition. I
wrote at that time: "As Blake Edwards's stock has risen, Richard
Quine's has fallen. Where Edwards has a decisive edge is in the
conviction he applies to a bright, if artificial style. Despite occasional lapses in taste and increasingly frequent bursts of visual
flamboyance, Edwards confirms on a minor scale what Lubitsch
established on a major scale, and that is the correlation of buoy-
ancy with conviction. It follows that Edwards operates most
effectively with the thinly lacquered dramas of *Mr. Cory* and
Breakfast at Tiffany's and the transparently farcical water colors
of *This Happy Feeling, The Perfect Furlough, Operation Petticoat* and *High Time.* In the more realistic black-and-white
worlds of *Experiment in Terror* and *Days of Wine and Roses,* the
removal of the director's rose-colored glasses reveals an unpleasant vision of the plastic forms of urban life."

Since 1963, Edwards has emerged from the ranks of commissioned directors with such personal works as *The Pink Panther,
Shot in the Dark, The Great Race, What Did You Do in the War,
Daddy?* and *Gunn.* His films manage to be funny in spite of repeated violations of the axioms of classical slapstick. (Was it
Proust who said that we say "in spite of" when we mean "because
of"?) One axiom insists that audiences will laugh at a man slip-
ping on a banana peel only if nothing is seriously hurt except his
dignity but that if he fractures his leg the audience will not see
the humor of the situation. Unfortunately for the axiom, Blake
Edwards is one writer-director who has got some of his biggest
laughs out of jokes that are too gruesome for most horror films.

Another axiom is that any farcical pratfall must be constructed from a probable premise. Yet *A Shot in the Dark*
lurches from improbability to improbability without losing its
comic balance. For example, when Peter Sellers inserts a still-
ignited cigarette lighter inside his raincoat, the ensuing slapstick
with smoke and flame is unsatisfactory. Part of the élan of using a

cigarette lighter derives from the courtly symbolism of controlled virility involved in the extinction of the flame of sex. No matter. Edwards leapfrogs over the lighter gag by opening a door in someone's face and sending him out the window, and only the most captious critic has a chance to raise the question of logic. By the same token, the custard-pie sequence in *The Great Race* transcends the psychology of slapstick to qualify as the last spasm of action painting in the Western world.

For a time Edwards seemed to be following in the footsteps of Billy Wilder, with somewhat more visual style and somewhat less verbal crackle. But their paths have diverged. Wilder is a curdled Lubitsch, romanticism gone sour, 78 rpm played at 45, an old wordling from Vienna perpetually sneering at Hollywood as it engulfs him. Edwards is more a new breed, post-Hitler, post-Freud, post-sick-joke, with all the sticky sentimentality of electronic music. The world he celebrates is cold, heartless, and inhuman, but the people in it manage to preserve a marginal integrity and individuality. Edwards has become a stylistic influence in the cinema, and his personality and script dominate Ralph Nelson's *Soldier in the Rain* the way Lubitsch's personality once dominated Cukor's *One Hour with You*.

SAMUEL FULLER (1911–   )

FILMS: 1949—*I Shot Jesse James.* 1950—The Baron of Arizona, *The Steel Helmet.* 1951—*Fixed Bayonets.* 1952—*Park Row.* 1953—*Pickup on South Street.* 1954—Hell and High Water. 1955 —*House of Bamboo.* 1957—*China Gate, Run of the Arrow, Forty Guns.* 1959—The Crimson Kimono. 1960—Verboten! 1961— *Underworld U.S.A.* 1962—*Merrill's Marauders.* 1963—*Shock Corridor.* 1965—The Naked Kiss. 1968—Caine.

Fuller is an authentic American primitive whose works have to be seen to be understood. Seen, not heard or synopsized. His first film, *I Shot Jesse James,* was constructed almost entirely in close-ups of an oppressive intensity the cinema had not experienced since Dreyer's *The Passion of Joan of Arc.* Fuller's script was so compressed that there was no room for even one establishing atmosphere shot or one dramatically irrelevant scene in which characters could suggest an everyday existence. The excitement Fuller arouses in critics sensitive to visual forms is equaled by the horror he arouses in critics of the Left for the lack of social perspective in his films. The cinematic opposition between Right and Left is exemplified in the different approaches of Fuller's *China Gate* and Mankiewicz's *The Quiet American*. Where Fuller thrusts all his political ideas forward with his few characters carrying all the ideological burdens of the Cold War and American-Asian relations, Mankiewicz is always receding from his characters to allow the larger spectacle of the Indo-Chinese masses to serve as a political context. Mankiewicz's adaptation of Greene's personal plot is anecdotal, microcosmic, symbolic. With Fuller, the distinction between the personal plot and its political context evaporates with the first leggy sprawl of Angie Dickinson. Fuller's ideas are undoubtedly too broad and oversimplified for any serious analysis, but it is the artistic force with which his ideas are expressed that makes his career so fascinating to critics who can rise above their political prejudices. Admittedly, it is absurd to attribute the depradations of Indians (*Run of the Arrow*) and neo-Nazis (*Verboten!*) to some universal juvenile delinquency, but Fuller's perversity and peculiarly Old Testament view of retribution carries the day in both instances. It is time the cinema followed the other arts in honoring its primitives. Fuller belongs to the cinema, and not to literature and sociology.

GREGORY LA CAVA (1892–1949)

FILMS: 1924—The New School Teacher, Restless Wives. 1925—Womanhandled. 1926—Let's Get Married, So's Your Old Man, Say It Again. 1927—Paradise for Two, *Running Wild,* Tell It to Sweeney. 1928—The Gay Defender, Feel My Pulse, Half a Bride. 1929—Saturday's Children, Big News. 1930—His First Command. 1931—Laugh and Get Rich, Smart Woman. 1932—Symphony of Six Million, Age of Consent, *The Half-Naked Truth.* 1934 —Affairs of Cellini, What Every Woman Knows. 1935—Private Worlds, *She Married Her Boss.* 1936—*My Man Godfrey.* 1937—

Stage Door. 1939—Fifth Avenue Girl. 1940—Primrose Path. 1941—*Unfinished Business.* 1942—Lady in a Jam. 1947—Living in a Big Way.

Gregory La Cava's best films—*She Married Her Boss, My Man Godfrey, Stage Door,* and *Unfinished Business*—reveal a flair for improvisation and a delicate touch with such expert comediennes as Claudette Colbert, Carole Lombard, Katharine Hepburn, Ginger Rogers, and Irene Dunne. The seduction scene of Irene Dunne and Preston Foster in *Unfinished Business,* like that of Jean Arthur and Joel McCrea in Stevens's *The More the Merrier,* demonstrates the conflict between Hollywood's erotic images and its laundered scripts. Significantly, La Cava was most effective when he could work between the lines of his scenarios and against the conventions of his plots. W. C. Fields credited La Cava with the best comedy mind in Hollywood next to Fields's own, and *Life* magazine once reproduced La Cava's on-the-set sketches for the Billy Rose takeoff in *Unfinished Business.* Of such trifles was the legend of La Cava fashioned. However, the La Cava touch never became as famous as the Lubitsch touch even after the New York Film Critics Circle singled out La Cava's direction of *Stage Door* for an award in 1937. The La Cava touch was mainly touches, whereas the Lubitsch touch expressed a distinctive vision of the world. La Cava's more solemn projects—*What Every Woman Knows, The Affairs of Cellini, Private Worlds,* and *Primrose Path*—suffer from structural deficiencies. He is remembered now for a few interludes of antic desperation in the midst of the Depression.

JOSEPH LOSEY (1909–   )

FILMS: 1948—The Boy with Green Hair. 1950—*The Lawless.* 1951—*The Prowler;* M; *The Big Night.* 1953—Stranger on the Prowl. 1954—The Sleeping Tiger. 1956—Finger of Guilt. 1957—*Time Without Pity.* 1958—The Gypsy and the Gentleman. 1960—*Chance Meeting.* 1962—*The Concrete Jungle.* 1964—*The Servant.* 1965—*These Are the Damned,* Eva. 1966—*King* *and Country, Modesty Blaise.* 1967—*Accident.* 1968—Boom!, Secret Ceremony.

Joseph Losey may not actually thrive on controversy, but he seems to arouse it on every level, from the most vulgar to the most esoteric. Originally an exile from the Hollywood blacklist, he seemed by all indications to belong to the committed Left. In quick succession, he was embraced by a rightist faction in *Cahiers du Cinéma,* enthroned by *Movie,* and repudiated by *Sight and Sound.* Realist critics have always resisted the intensity and sweep of his style, the steady hysteria of his actors, the violence of his plots. By any standards, Losey's is a technique that calls attention to itself or, more properly, to the personal feelings of Joseph Losey.

Losey has spent most of his career on commissioned projects that mixed melodrama with social significance. The movies of his Hollywood period—*The Boy with Green Hair, The Lawless, The Prowler, M,* and *The Big Night*—have gained in interest over the years as the exaggerations of a style have become more expressive of an era. The stage director of Charles Laughton in Bertolt Brecht's *Galileo* and the screen director of Harold Pinter's scripts for *The Servant* and *Accident,* Losey seems always to have aspired beyond the presumed limitations of genre movies. The High Art Game is an understandable temptation to the movie director, particularly in the culturally beleaguered Anglo-American cinema. Indeed, *The Servant* and *Accident* have done more for Losey's general reputation than all his other pictures put together.

Ironically, Losey's personality comes through more clearly and forcefully in such relatively neglected works as *Time Without Pity, Chance Meeting, The Concrete Jungle, King and Country,* and *Modesty Blaise.* Like many directors, Losey seems more effective when he transcends conventions than when he avoids them altogether. Genre movies give him the distancing he needs to writhe expressively on the screen. By contrast, movies about Life and Time and The World seem to make him relatively subdued, functional, and impersonal. Losey's dilemma is not unique. With *Accident,* Losey has escaped the clutches of the cultists to fall into the hands of the snobs. Certainly, nothing could be more fashionable than serving as the house director of the Burtons after Mike Nichols and Franco Zeffirelli. Only time will tell if such fashion will be fatal to Losey's artistic personality.

Losey's best performers are almost invariably male—Van Heflin in *The Prowler,* Dirk Bogarde in *The Sleeping Tiger, The Servant, King and Country, Modesty Blaise,* and *Accident,* Stanley Baker in *Chance Meeting, The Concrete Jungle, Eva,* and *Accident,* Michael Redgrave and Leo McKern in *Time Without Pity,* Patrick McGee in *The Concrete Jungle,* Oskar Werner in *Chance Meeting,* James Fox in *The Servant,* Tom Courtenay in *King and Country,* Terence Stamp in *Modesty Blaise.* There are pleasant enough feminine portrayals in Losey's *œuvre;* Gail Russell in *The Lawless,* Evelyn Keyes in *The Prowler,* Sarah Miles and Wendy Craig in *The Servant,* Viveca Lindfors in *These Are the Damned,* and Vivian Merchant in *Accident* come immediately to mind. But the feminine role in Losey's world is strictly subordinate because of the histrionic hysteria of his actors. Men simply cannot cope with their lives and social institutions, and they crack up with very lyrical results. Meanwhile the women stand by to pick up the pieces. They cope because of their ability to compromise with reality, an ability Losey frankly admires. Unfortunately, the best roles are the least stable. Hence, Losey's actresses are usually denied the great scene-stealing moments of psychic dissolution.

Losey has been criticized for the precision and fluidity of his camera style, but it is through his excesses that he most successfully projects a redeeming sense of humor. When Stanley Baker is jilted at the door by Jeanne Moreau in *Eva,* Losey's steep overhead camera angle makes the humiliation deliciously funny in a nonsadistic way. Losey is playing a joke on his own portentousness. Conversely, *Modesty Blaise* is a more serious enterprise than it seems precisely because of the strenuousness of its levity. Losey is joking about matters concerning the relations of men and women, relations that affect him deeply. There is also in Losey's films time and again that psychic spasm, that futile gesture a character makes to register a personal protest against cosmic injustice. In Losey's world, both sex and politics are out of joint, and if Losey's style is baroque or expressionistic, it is a very nervous baroque or expressionistic. With the disintegration of the male, Yeats's center cannot hold, and anarchy is loosed upon the world.

ANTHONY MANN (1906–1967)

FILMS: 1942—Dr. Broadway, Moonlight in Havana. 1943—Nobody's Darling. 1944—My Best Gal, Strangers in the Night. 1945—The Great Flamarion, Two o'Clock Courage, Sing Your Way Home. 1946—Strange Impersonation, The Bamboo Blonde. 1947—Desperate, Railroaded, *T-Men*. 1948—Raw Deal. 1949—*Reign of Terror, Border Incident, Side Street*. 1950—*Devil's Doorway*, The Furies, *Winchester 73*. 1951—*The Tall Target*. 1952—*Bend of the River*. 1953—*The Naked Spur*, Thunder Bay. 1954—*The Glenn Miller Story*. 1955—*The Far Country, Strategic Air Command, The Man from Laramie*. 1956—*The Last Frontier*, Serenade. 1957—*Men in War*, The Tin Star. 1958—*God's Little Acre, Man of the West*. 1960—Cimarron. 1961—El Cid. 1964—The Fall of the Roman Empire. 1965—The Heroes of Telemark. 1968—A Dandy in Aspic.

Anthony Mann (not to be confused with dreary Daniel and Delbert) directed action movies with a kind of tough-guy authority that never found favor among the more cultivated critics of the medium. His Westerns stand out today as geological excavations of a neglected genre. Writer Philip Yordan once remarked that the ideal film-maker would combine Anthony Mann's exteriors with Nicholas Ray's interiors, the implication being that both Mann and Ray were artistically incomplete.

Back in 1963, I was impressed more with Mann's manner than with his meaning: "Anthony Mann is a style without a theme. His Westerns are distinguished by some of the most brilliant photography of exteriors in the history of the American cinema, and yet it is impossible to detect a consistent thematic pattern in his work. His best films—*Man of the West, The Last Frontier, Men in War, The Naked Spur, Bend of the River*—are directed with psychological intensity and an undercurrent of didacticism. His most didactic film, *Tin Star,* is also one of his weakest. Curiously, Mann's visual style is the American style which most closely resembles that of Antonioni in the literal progression through landscapes from the vegetable to the mineral world as in *Man of the West* and *Il Grido* down to the ultimate decadence of *El Cid* and *L'Eclisse*."

The eight films Mann made with James Stewart are especially interesting today for their insights into the uneasy relationships between men and women in a world of violence and action. Stewart, the most complete actor-personality in the American cinema, is particularly gifted in expressing the emotional ambivalence of the action hero. Mann and Stewart between them suggest that there is more than meets the eye in such reputed potboilers as *Winchester 73, Bend of the River, The Naked Spur, Thunder Bay, The Glenn Miller Story, The Far Country, Strategic Air Command*, and *The Man from Laramie*. Mann's best period lasted little more than a decade between *T-Men* in 1947 and a spread in *Life* magazine for this sleeper and *Man of the West* (in 1958), notable to the general public mainly for Julie London's epochal striptease in a Western. Unfortunately, Universal pictures were seldom taken seriously during this period by anyone except Manny Farber and the French critics, and Mann, like Sirk, was overlooked by the American critical establishment until it was too late for his career to find a firmer footing than obscure cult interest.

LEO MC CAREY (1898–   )

FILMS: 1929—The Sophomore, Red Hot Rhythm. 1930—Let's Go Native, Wild Company, Part Time Wife. 1931—Indiscreet. 1932—The Kid from Spain. 1933—*Duck Soup*. 1934—Six of a Kind, Belle of the Nineties. 1935—*Ruggles of Red Gap*. 1936—The Milky Way. 1937—*The Awful Truth, Make Way for Tomorrow*. 1939—*Love Affair*. 1942—Once Upon a Honeymoon. 1944—*Going My Way*. 1945—*The Bells of St. Mary's*. 1948—Good Sam. 1952—*My Son John*. 1957—*An Affair to Remember*. 1958—Rally Round the Flag, Boys. 1962—Satan Never Sleeps.

Leo McCarey represents a principle of improvisation in the history of the American film. Noted less for his rigorous direction than for his relaxed digressions, McCarey has distilled a unique blend of farce and sentimentality in his best efforts. He has worked with some of the most notable eccentric stars in Hollywood—Laurel and Hardy, the Marx Brothers, Harold Lloyd, Eddie Cantor, Mae West, Victor Moore, and later, and more normally, Cary Grant, Irene Dunne, Charles Boyer, Ingrid Bergman, and Bing Crosby. Jean Renoir once remarked that Leo McCarey understood people better than any other Hollywood director. McCarey's moments may outlive his movies, be it Charles Laughton reciting the Gettysburg Address in *Ruggles of Red Gap* or, even more memorably from that same film, Binnie Barnes teaching Roland Young to play the drums; or Victor Moore saying goodbye to Beulah Bondi in *Make Way for Tomorrow* or Irene Dunne speaking to Maria Ouspenskaya in *Love Affair* or Barry Fitzgerald embracing his mother in *Going My Way* or Cary Grant and Irene Dunne reminiscing about their lost marriage in *The Awful Truth*. After enough great moments are assembled, however, a personal style must be assumed even though it is difficult to describe.

McCarey and Capra seem to go together like ham and eggs. They both started at about the same time in the twenties with the same kind of gag training. They both slipped unobtrusively into the sound era, and didn't hit their stride until the mid-thirties. Both declined in the late forties, virtually faded away in the early fifties, and returned in the late fifties. Both won two Oscars for direction, Capra for *Mr. Deeds Goes to Town* in 1936 and *You Can't Take It with You* in 1938, McCarey for *The Awful Truth* in 1937 and *Going My Way* in 1944. There is on film a record of a thirties Oscar ceremony during which Capra and McCarey playfully wrestled on stage for a golden statuette they both coveted. It is perhaps at that very golden moment that their joint preeminence was officially recognized, a very brief moment before the surge of John Ford and Orson Welles.

VINCENTE MINNELLI (1913–   )

FILMS: 1943—*Cabin in the Sky,* I Dood It. 1944—*Meet Me in St. Louis.* 1945—*The Clock, Yolanda and the Thief.* 1946—

Ziegfeld Follies, Undercurrent. 1948—*The Pirate.* 1949—*Madame Bovary.* 1950—Father of the Bride. 1951—*An American in Paris,* Father's Little Dividend. 1953—*The Bad and the Beautiful,* The Story of Three Loves (Minnelli did Mademoiselle episode with Leslie Caron, Farley Granger, Ethel Barrymore, and Gottfried Reinhardt; the first episode with James Mason and Moira Shearer and the third with Kirk Douglas and Pier Angeli), *The Band Wagon.* 1954 —The Long, Long Trailer; Brigadoon. 1955—*Cobweb,* Kismet. 1956—Lust for Life, Tea and Sympathy. 1957—Designing Woman. 1958—Gigi, *The Reluctant Debutante.* 1959—*Some Came Running.* 1960—Bells Are Ringing, *Home from the Hill.* 1962—*Four Horsemen of the Apocalypse, Two Weeks in Another Town.* 1963—The Courtship of Eddie's Father. 1964—Goodbye Charlie. 1965—The Sand Piper.

Minnelli's reputation has undergone several metamorphoses in a quarter of a century. His Garland-Kelly-Astaire-Charisse-Caron musicals deserve a chapter of their own in any ultimate history of the medium. Minnelli's stylistic flourishes awed even the late James Agee back in the forties, and Stephen Longstreet of the Screenwriters' Guild once attacked the director for distracting audiences from dialogue with fancy camera angles in the 1945 Judy Garland–Robert Walker romance, *The Clock.* Needless to say, no screenwriter today would dare make a comparable objection. *Cabin in the Sky, Meet Me in St. Louis, Yolanda and the Thief,* and *The Pirate* made him the darling of the *Sequence* and *Sight and Sound* generation sparked by Lindsay Anderson, Karel Reisz, Gavin Lambert, and Tony Richardson. This was the period in which his art was more visual than personal, more decorative than meaningful. His Hollywood reputation reached its crest with two curiously depressing musicals, *An American in Paris* and *Gigi.* It suddenly became apparent that Minnelli had an unusual, somber outlook for musical comedy. *The Band Wagon,* his best musical, fitted in with his tendency toward negative thinking as Fred Astaire sang "I Want to Be by Myself " as an unheeding world passed him by and a sympathetic mise-en-scène lyricized loneliness.

A new generation of cinéastes adopted Minnelli for his garish fifties and sixties dramas, most notably *The Bad and the Beautiful, Cobweb, Some Came Running, Home From the Hill, Four*

Horsemen of the Apocalypse, and *Two Weeks in Another Town.* Mark Shivas, Ian Cameron, and V. F. Perkins of *Movie* were particularly perceptive in analyzing Minnelli's dreamlike style with subjects of substance. Unfortunately, the new Minnelli became anathema to most of the Anglo-American critical Establishment, and in 1968 he finds himself exiled back on the musical beat with an intransigent Barbra Streisand.

Nonetheless, the Pirandellian pyrotechnics of *Two Weeks in Another Town,* a self-conscious sequel to his masterpiece on moviemaking, *The Bad and the Beautiful,* summed up his career and the American cinema as a whole with what amounted to Hollywood's final blast at Cinecitta. As a side dividend, *Last Year at Marienbad* and *La Dolce Vita* will never look the same again. Jean-Luc Godard provided a footnote to Minnelli's career by having his protagonist in *Contempt* wear his hat in the bathtub in *un hommage* to Dean Martin from *Some Came Running.* By contrast, François Truffaut exiled Minnelli from the "Politique des Auteurs" by describing him as *"un ésclave."* Truffaut's intolerance toward Hollywood directors has increased markedly since he became their rival instead of their *raisonneur,* but he is especially unfair to a director who has always regarded himself as more of a stylist than an auteur. Furthermore, Minnelli has always required relatively luxurious projects upon which to lavish his taste. If he has a fatal flaw as an artist, it is his naïve belief that style can invariably transcend substance and that our way of looking at the world is more important than the world itself. Critic-film-makers like Godard and Truffaut pay lip service to these doctrines, but they don't really believe them. Only Minnelli believes implicitly in the power of his camera to transform trash into art, and corn into caviar. Minnelli believes more in beauty than in art.

OTTO PREMINGER (1906–   )

FILMS: 1936—Under Your Spell. 1937—Danger—Love at Work. 1943—Margin for Error. 1944—In the Meantime, Darling; *Laura.* 1945—A Royal Scandal, *Fallen Angel.* 1946—Centennial

Summer. 1947—Forever Amber, *Daisy Kenyon*. 1948—That Lady in Ermine (begun and signed by Ernst Lubitsch). 1949—The Fan, *Whirlpool*. 1950—*Where the Sidewalk Ends,* The Thirteenth Letter. 1953—*Angel Face,* The Moon is Blue. 1954—*River of No Return,* Carmen Jones. 1955—The Court-Martial of Billy Mitchell, *The Man with the Golden Arm.* 1957—*Saint Joan.* 1958—*Bonjour Tristesse.* 1959—Porgy and Bess, *Anatomy of a Murder.* 1960 —Exodus. 1962—*Advise and Consent.* 1963—The Cardinal. 1965—*In Harm's Way, Bunny Lake Is Missing.* 1966—Hurry Sundown. 1968—Skidoo!

Laura is Preminger's *Citizen Kane,* at least in the sense that Otto's detractors, like Orson's, have never permitted him to live it down. For his part, Preminger refuses to accept any responsibility whatsoever for the films he directed before *Laura* in 1944. There is admittedly a streak of Foxphorescent giddiness running through the frames of *Under Your Spell* (1936), *Danger—Love at Work* (1937), *Margin for Error* (1943), and *In the Meantime, Darling* (1944). However, Preminger is hardly unique in his disdain for the fruits of his early experience. Fred Zinnemann has never been eager to reminisce about *Kid Glove Killer, Eyes in the Night, Little Mr. Jim,* and *My Brother Talks to Horses.* George Stevens undoubtedly prefers to jump straight to *Alice Adams* without pausing for *Cohens and Kellys in Trouble, Bachelor Bait,* and *Kentucky Kernels.* Vincente Minnelli's mystique does not encompass *I Dood It* any more than Robert Aldrich boasts of *The Big Leaguer,* and Josef von Sternberg would probably prefer to forget his close-up of Grace Moore's tonsils in *The King Steps Out.*

There is no easy moral to draw from the evolution of Preminger's style since he left Fox in the early fifties to become his own producer. Ironically, it was only when Preminger began blowing his own horn from *The Moon Is Blue* onward that his earliest films came into focus. His enemies have never forgiven him for being a director with the personality of a producer. Perhaps they subconsciously resent him for not ruining himself with the excesses of a creative folly. Culture heroes like Sternberg and Stroheim and Ophuls and Welles have acquired, rightly or wrongly, a legendary reputation for profligacy. Preminger's legend is that of the cosmic cost accountant, a ruthless creature who will mangle the muse for the sake of a shooting schedule.

The story is told in the trade of the day Preminger shot the Saint-Newman hilltop scene in *Exodus*. During the last take, the shadow of the boom fell across the couple. It was too late for a retake because the sun had gone. Preminger decided to let the shadow stand rather than return to the location the next day for a retake that would disrupt his shooting schedule. Some finicky aesthetes might write this decision off as sloppy craftsmanship, but for Preminger it is a question of survival. The fact is that he has not enjoyed a major critical and commercial success since *Anatomy of a Murder* in 1959. His frugality, and his frugality alone, has kept him from drowning in a sea of red ink. Almost alone of the new tribe of producer-directors, Preminger has accepted the responsibility of freedom, as well as the lesson of a shrinking market.

But what is the artistic point of all these crass production stories? Or as Dwight Macdonald might put it, what's art to Preminger or Preminger to art? Indeed, serious film criticism of Hollywood movies is always impaled upon the point that Hollywood directors are not profoundly articulate about their alleged art. In this respect, Preminger is not a "good" interview. He will freely concede that more is read into his films by some critics than he consciously put there. He neither abuses his detractors nor embraces his defenders. He seems to enjoy the effect he creates with his outrageous personality, a personality that serves also as a mask. To read all sorts of poignant profundities in Preminger's inscrutable urbanity would seem to be the last word in idiocy, and yet there are moments in his films when the evidence on the screen is inconsistent with one's deepest instincts about the director as a man. It is at these moments that the serenity of his style seems to transcend the limitations of his sensibility.

It is ultimately Preminger's manner, rather than his matter, that should concern us most deeply. Otherwise, his extraordinary eclecticism in subject matter would make him a poor choice indeed for a career analysis. What is one to say of a taste in scripts oscillating between Oscar Wilde and Kathleen Winsor, Bernard Shaw and F. Hugh Herbert, Nelson Algren and Allen Drury, Françoise Sagan and Leon Uris? Thematic consistency is hardly Preminger's hobgoblin. The secret of his style is else-where. One critic has called it fairness, another the ambiguity of objectivity. Its technical correlative is the perversely objective camera viewpoint that keeps his characters in the same frame. Why does Preminger present his spectacle in this way? As he himself explains, he came from the theatre where he was accustomed to looking at drama as a spatial whole. Consequently, his deepest instincts are always opposed to montage. Without an in-bred instinct for cutting, he is not able to execute the movie gags for which Hollywood has developed an original cinematographic language. It follows almost logically that Preminger's projects, more often than not, have a solemn, somber quality. His melo-dramas at Fox, particularly *Laura, Fallen Angel, Whirlpool, Where the Sidewalk Ends,* and his RKO loan-out, *Angel Face,* are all moodily fluid studies in perverse psychology rather than crackling suspense movies. The characters click even as the ac-tion falters. The reviewer in search of crackling melodrama would mark Preminger down as a failure in most of these films, possibly all except *Laura.* Even his comedies are too fluid to en-compass the obligatory reaction shots. *The Moon is Blue* comes out being a little sad, and *Bonjour Tristesse,* far from being a merry Gallic romp, is transformed by Preminger's color/black-and-white duality into a tragedy of time and illusion.

Where Richard Brooks displays a tendency to transform art into trash, Preminger displays a tendency to transform trash into art. His most recent plots have been big, violent, and vulgar. *Exodus, Advise and Consent, The Cardinal, In Harm's Way,* and *Hurry Sundown* are all derived from bloated novels on big sub-jects. Unfortunately, Preminger does not entirely transcend his material on any occasion. Nor does he reshape it sufficiently to his own taste. He is similarly passive with his players. John Wayne and Patricia Neal are as admirable in *In Harm's Way* as Paula Prentiss, Tom Tryon, and Patrick Neal are deplorable. For every John Huston in *The Cardinal* there is unfortunately a Lee J. Cobb in *Exodus.* Where Michael Caine and Jane Fonda are original creations in *Hurry Sundown,* Robert Hooks and Diahann Carroll degenerate into dull stereotypes. Individual scenes can be magnificent—the prison raid in *Exodus,* the shipboard sequences with the President in *Advise and Consent,* the Viennese ballroom scene in *The Cardinal,* and the opening dance scene in *In Harm's Way* invoking in one slowly moving shot the entire Glenn Millerish *Zeitgeist* of the forties. Too often, however, Preminger seems to destroy what he so lovingly creates. This is part of his ambiguity as an artist, a key perhaps to a cynicism far deeper and infinitely more destructive than Billy Wilder's.

Still, every Preminger film, even his most ill-fated, bears the signs of an overall conception and the stigmata of a personal attitude. If a *Centennial Summer* or a *Porgy and Bess* fails of execution, it is not because Preminger lacked a discernible approach toward these musicals, but rather because the various elements in the genre failed to coalesce in terms of the director's conception. By contrast, *Carmen Jones* succeeds on its own questionable terms as the Preminger musical par excellence—drab, austere, and completely depoeticized.

During his career Preminger has moved into direct competition or comparison with other directors. *A Royal Scandal* and *The Fan* pointed up Preminger's relationship to Lubitsch, as did obviously *That Lady in Ermine,* which Preminger finished after Lubitsch's death. Lubitsch is generally given the edge in these sectors and for good reasons. However, it is not entirely fair to Preminger to place him out of his time. As Lubitsch was the unobtrusive cutting of the twenties and thirties, Preminger is the camera movement and long takes of the fifties and sixties. If Lubitsch summed up his time, Preminger was ahead of it in his Fox period. The Lubitsch virtues have disappeared from the cinema, and we are the poorer for it, but Preminger anticipated the conditions that would cause their disappearance. The grace and precision of Lubitsch's sensibility seem out of place in a world consecrated to the most grotesque explosions of the ego. Preminger's impassive gaze—accepting the good with the bad, the beautiful with the ugly, the sublime with the mediocre—is both more appropriate and more merciful.

We are left with a director who has made at least four masterpieces of ambiguity and objectivity—*Laura, Bonjour Tristesse, Advise and Consent,* and *Bunny Lake Is Missing,* a director who sees all problems and issues as a single-take two-shot, the stylistic expression of the eternal conflict, not between right and wrong, but between the right-wrong on one side and the right-wrong on the other, a representation of the right-wrong in all of us as our share of the human condition. In the middle of the conflict stands Otto Preminger, right-wrong, good-bad, and probably sincere-cynical.

NICHOLAS RAY (1911–   )

FILMS: 1949—*They Live by Night,* Knock on Any Door, A Woman's Secret. 1950—*In a Lonely Place,* Born to Be Bad. 1951—Flying Leathernecks, *On Dangerous Ground.* 1952—*The Lusty Men.* 1954—*Johnny Guitar.* 1955—*Run for Cover, Rebel Without a Cause.* 1956—Hot Blood, *Bigger Than Life.* 1957—The True Story of Jesse James. 1958—*Bitter Victory, Wind Across the Everglades,* Party Girl. 1961—*The Savage Innocents,* King of Kings. 1963—55 Days at Peking.

Nicholas Ray has been the cause célèbre of the auteur theory for such a long time that his critics, pro and con, have lost all sense of proportion about his career. Nicholas Ray is not the greatest director who ever lived; nor is he a Hollywood hack. The Truth lies somewhere in between. It must be remembered that *They Live by Night, The Lusty Men, Rebel Without a Cause,* and *Bigger Than Life* are socially conscious films by any standards, and that *Knock on Any Door* is particularly bad social consciousness on the Kramer-Cayatte level. His form is not that impeccable, and his content has generally involved considerable social issues. Ray has always displayed an exciting visual style. For example, if one compares *They Live by Night* with Huston's *The Asphalt Jungle*—and these two films are strikingly similar in mood, theme, and plot—one will notice that where Ray tends to cut between physical movements, Huston tends to cut between static compositions. Ray's style tends to be more kinetic, Huston's more plastic, the difference between dance and sculpture. If Ray's nervous direction has no thematic meaning, he would be a minor director indeed. Fortunately, Ray does have a theme, and a very important one; namely, that every relationship establishes its own moral code and that there is no such thing as abstract morality. This much was made clear in *Rebel Without a Cause* when James Dean and his fellow adolescents leaned back in their seats at the planetarium and passively accepted the proposition that the universe itself was drifting without any frame of reference. Even though Ray's career has been plagued by many frustrations, none of his films lacks some burst of inspiration. *Johnny Guitar* is his most bizarre film, and probably his most personal. Certainly, we can sympathize with Everson and Fenin trying to relate this "Western" to the William S. Hart tradition, and finding Ray lacking; but this is the fallacy of writing about genres. *Johnny Guitar* has invented its own genre. Philip Yordan set out to attack McCarthyism, but Ray was too delirious to pay any heed as Freudian feminism prevailed over Marxist masochism, and Pirandello transcended polemics.

Henri Agel, the French film historian, has linked the romanticism of Nicholas Ray to that of Frank Borzage, and the link is not inapt. The agonizingly adolescent intensity of the lovers in *They Live by Night* (Farley Granger and Cathy O'Donnell) and *Rebel Without a Cause* (James Dean and Natalie Wood) invests the lovers with a privileged aura reminiscent of such Borzage classics as *Seventh Heaven, The River, A Man's Castle, History Is Made at Night,* and *Moonrise.* However, Ray's world is more clouded with moral ambiguity than Borzage's. Ray's characters are inflicted with all the psychic ills of the fifties. Paranoia is provided by Humphrey Bogart at the emotional expense of Gloria Grahame in *In a Lonely Place.* Arthur Kennedy's ingratitude in *The Lusty Men* costs Robert Mitchum his life. Jealousy of Joan Crawford is the murderous motivation of Mercedes McCambridge in *Johnny Guitar;* jealousy and envy of Richard Burton is the murderous motivation of Curt Jurgens in *Bitter Victory.* James Mason suffers from delusions of grandeur in *Bigger than Life,* and Robert Ryan from disillusion with mankind in *On Dangerous Ground.* By contrast, a savage instinct for honor saves two civilized figures of the law (Christopher Plummer and Peter O'Toole) from two of nature's outlaws (Burl Ives and Anthony Quinn) in *Wind Across the Everglades* and *The Savage Innocents* respectively, and—despite the reviewers of the time —impressively. Nicholas Ray's reputation does not depend upon undue rationalization. His films are the indisputable records of a very personal anguish that found artistic expression for little more than a decade.

DOUGLAS SIRK (1900–   )

FILMS: German career (as Detlef Sierk): 1935—April, April; Das Mädchen vom Moorhof, Stutzen der Gesellschaft. 1936—Das Hofkonzert, La Chanson du Souvenir, Schlussakkord. 1937—La Habanera, Zu Neuen Ufern. American career (as Douglas Sirk): 1943—Hitler's Madman. 1944—*Summer Storm.* 1946—*A Scandal in Paris.* 1947—Lured. 1948—Sleep My Love. 1949—Shockproof, Slightly French. 1950—Mystery Submarine. 1951—The First Legion, Thunder on the Hill, The Lady Pays Off, Weekend with Father. 1952—No Room for the Groom, *Has Anybody Seen My Gal?*, Meet Me at the Fair. 1953—*Take Me to Town, All I Desire.* 1954—Taza, Son of Cochise; *Magnificent Obsession,* Sign of the Pagan. 1955—*Captain Lightfoot.* 1956—*All That Heaven Allows,* There's Always Tomorrow, *Battle Hymn.* 1957—*Written on the Wind,* Interlude. 1958—*The Tarnished Angels, A Time to Love and a Time to Die.* 1959—*Imitation of Life.*

Time, if nothing else, will vindicate Douglas Sirk as it has already vindicated Josef von Sternberg. Formal excellence and visual wit are seldom as appreciated at first glance as are the topical sensations of the hour. Yet, *The Defiant Ones* and *On the Beach* are already dead, whereas *Written on the Wind* and *Tarnished Angels* become more impressive with each passing year. Sirk requires no extreme rationalization, and his films require no elaborate defense. The evidence of his style is visible on the screen. It is a personal style, distinct from the impressive technological apparatus of the Universal-MCA-Decca complex. David Miller's *Back Street* and Norman Jewison's *Forty Pounds of Trouble* can serve as decisive cross-references against the theoreticians of studios as auteurs. Even before Sirk came to Universal, he displayed his audacious talent in films like *Summer Storm, A Scandal in Paris,* and *Lured.* The essence of Sirkian cinema is the direct confrontation of all material, however fanciful and improbable. Even in his most dubious projects, Sirk never shrinks away from the ridiculous, but by a full-bodied formal development, his art transcends the ridiculous, as form comments on content. Whereas John Stahl transcended the lachrymose dramas of *Imitation of Life* and *Magnificent Obsession* through the incisiveness of his dark humor. If it be true, as veteran Polish director Aleksander Ford once observed, that the cinema of tomorrow is the cinema of wide screen and color, then Sirk's formal achievements will have helped lead the way into a more sensuous future. Visual style is never an end in itself, and it cannot be ultimately defended except as it relates to a director's taste and sensibility. Any visual style can be mechanically reproduced, but without the linkage to a directorial personality, the effect is indeed mechanical. Sirk's taste is exquisite, and hence, inimitable. One big obstacle to an appreciation of his *œuvre* is an inbred prejudice to what Raymond Durgnat has called the genre of the female weepies as opposed to the male weepies, particularly the kind from Italy that are hailed as "humanist."

GEORGE STEVENS (1905–   )

FILMS: 1933—Cohens and Kellys in Trouble. 1934—Bachelor Bait, Kentucky Kernels. 1935—*Alice Adams*, Laddie, Nitwits, Annie Oakley. 1936—*Swing Time.* 1937—Quality Street, A Damsel in Distress. 1938—Vivacious Lady. 1939—*Gunga Din.* 1940 —Vigil in the Night. 1941—*Penny Serenade.* 1942—*Woman of the Year, The Talk of the Town.* 1943—*The More the Merrier.* 1948—*I Remember Mama.* 1951—*A Place in the Sun.* 1953— *Shane.* 1956—*Giant.* 1959—The Diary of Anne Frank. 1965— The Greatest Story Ever Told.

George Stevens was a minor director with major virtues before *A Place in the Sun,* and a major director with minor virtues after. His instinctive sentimentality has always been intelligently restrained and carefully graded. He served his apprenticeship with Laurel and Hardy two-reelers, and thus learned all the techniques of the slow buildup. Indeed, his dawdling direction of comedy is the slowest in the business. The farcical dénouements of *Vivacious Lady, Woman of the Year, The Talk of the Town,* and *The More the Merrier* now seem interminable despite the behavioral charm of the performers. By contrast, Katharine

Hepburn's incandescent performance in *Alice Adams* remains a tribute to the slow fire of Stevens's direction. Also, *Swing Time* is the best of the Astaire-Rogers musicals, *Gunga Din* the most entertaining of the juvenile Kipling movies, *Penny Serenade* the most honorable of the child-adoption tearjerkers, and *I Remember Mama* the most restrained of the immigrant-family sagas.

All in all, his little movies have outlasted his big ones. The technique of Stevens's American Dream *Sun-Shane-Giant* trilogy that once seemed accomplished now seems labored. *Shane,* particularly, now looks overelaborated in terms of its genre and material, particularly in comparison with the greater spontaneity of Ford and Hawks. Stevens has gained more emotional mileage out of massive slow dissolves than has any other American director, but the emotional linkage of slow dissolves is an effect we now associate more with the thirties than with the fifties. The concentric classicism of the Stevens frame, shot after shot, once looked almost like an official style for national epics. Unfortunately, Stevens ended up looking ponderously old-fashioned in *The Diary of Anne Frank* and *The Greatest Story Ever Told.* What happened to Stevens is that his talent, like that of many of his colleagues, was strained to the breaking point by the massive projects of the fifties. His best days were in the thirties and forties when a movie was just a movie and when any extra care in the direction was conspicuously personal.

ERICH VON STROHEIM (1885–1957)

FILMS: 1918—Blind Husbands. 1919—The Devil's Passkey. 1922—*Foolish Wives,* Merry-Go-Round. 1925—*Greed, The Merry Widow.* 1928—*The Wedding March,* Queen Kelly. 1932—̂ Walking Down Broadway.

Stroheim, like Welles, was often suspected of yielding to the temptation of martyrdom. Film-making, like life, is full of compromises and accommodations, but Stroheim seemed as intransigent on trivial issues as on major ones. What difference did it make, after all, if his royal troops wore the right underwear under their uniforms. Was not this realism carried to idiocy? One might similarly reproach Abel Gance for applying a hundred superimpositions when the audience was aware of only four or five, or Eisenstein for criticizing Korda for not varying the tonality of *Rembrandt* to express the chromatic evolution of the painter as if more than twenty people in the world would get the point. The mark of genius is an obsession with irrelevant detail. Stroheim knew as well as anyone that the commercial exhibition of movies precluded a realistic style that simply accumulated details until the audience was crushed by the sheer weight of the details, but he also understood that realism could not be faked by suggestion or elided by conceptual montage. His films establish a distinction between things as essences and things as appearances.

Stroheim's art is made even more complex by the flamboyant perversity of his personality. A false opposition has been established between Stroheim and Griffith on the grounds of sophistication of film content, but in some ways Stroheim was more Victorian than Griffith, just as cynicism is often more naïve than passion. Perhaps the most remarkable aspect of Stroheim's style is its technical chastity. *The Wedding March,* made in 1928 when Murnau was at the peak of his influence, does not contain a single camera movement. Ultimately, Stroheim's obsessive realism, even in the most romantic settings, anchored his camera to his compositions. Lacking his distinctive personality, his films would have been unbearably literal, and the limitations of his realism would have been more apparent.

However, Stroheim's realism anticipated the sound era in that he established a sense of milieu more through composition than through montage, and also in that he created characterizations less through pantomime than through contextual detail. (His own performances were models of stiff-necked imperturbability, but colorful withal.) Ironically, Stroheim, like Murnau, was to be denied genuine opportunities with the sound film his silent films had heralded.

PRESTON STURGES (1898–1959)

FILMS: 1940—*The Great McGinty, Christmas in July.* 1941 —*The Lady Eve.* 1942—*Sullivan's Travels, The Palm Beach*

Story. 1944—*The Miracle at Morgan's Creek, Hail the Conquering Hero, The Great Moment.* 1947—*Mad Wednesday.* 1948—Unfaithfully Yours. 1949—The Beautiful Blonde from Bashful Bend. 1957—The French They Are a Funny Race.

Acknowledged as the foremost satirist of his time, Preston Sturges enjoyed his greatest vogue between 1940 and 1944, when his pungent wit and frenetic slapstick exploded on such targets as Tammany Hall politics, advertising, American fertility rites, hero and mother worship. Within the context of a Sturges film, a gangster could declare with ringing, heavily accented conviction: "America is a land of great opportunity." An underpaid clerk could rise to fame and fortune by coining the slogan "If you can't sleep, it isn't the coffee. It's the bunk." A sign in a flophouse could remind its denizens: "Have you written to Mother?" Sturges repeatedly suggested that the lowliest boob could rise to the top with the right degree of luck, bluff, and fraud. The absurdity of the American success story was matched by the ferocity of the battle of the sexes. In *The Lady Eve,* when Henry Fonda plaintively confesses, "Snakes are my life," Barbara Stanwyck snaps back, "What a life!" The climax of *Palm Beach Story* finds Rudy Vallee serenading Claudette Colbert's upstairs window while the object of his affections is being seduced by the subject of hers, Joel McCrea.

What distinguishes Sturges from his contemporaries is the frantic congestion of his comedies. The Breughel of American comedy directors, Sturges created a world of peripheral professionals—politicians, gangsters, executives, bartenders, cabdrivers, secretaries, bookies, card sharps, movie producers, doctors, dentists, bodyguards, butlers, inventors, millionaires, and derelicts. These were not the usual flotsam and jetsam of Hollywood cinema, but self-expressive cameos of aggressive individualism. With the determinism of the Sturges plots, these infinitely detailed miniatures served as contingent elements, and it is these elements, and the single-take, multiple viewpoint sequences formally demanded by these elements, that establish the comedies of Preston Sturges as comedy/not tragedy rather than merely comedy/ha ha.

Sturgean comedy was influenced both by the silent antics of Charles Chaplin, Buster Keaton, and Harold Lloyd in the twenties, and by the crackling verbal rhythms of Howard Hawks, Frank Capra, Leo McCarey and Gregory La Cava in the thirties. Sturges contributed to this distinguished tradition mainly through the unusual density of his scripts. His films were noted for the hilarious side effects of character and bit actors. It was not unusual for a gravel-voiced bus driver to use the word "paraphrase" or for a hoodlum to invoke the ruinous symmetry of "Samson and Delilah, Sodom and Gomorrah." A stereotyped performer like Eric Blore was virtually rediscovered savoring the line: "I positively swill in his ale." Similarly, Edgar Kennedy was resurrected from two-reelers to play an inspired bartender reacting to a customer asking for his first drink ever: "Sir, you rouse the artist in me." The Sturges stock company was particularly noted for the contrasting personalities of William Demarest, the eternal roughneck, and Franklin Pangborn, the prissy prune.

Sturges was criticized at his peak by James Agee and Manny Farber for an ambivalence in his work derived from a childhood conflict between a culturally demanding mother and an admired businessman foster father. This unusually Freudian analysis of the director's work, unusual, that is, for its time, sought to explain the incongruity of continental sophistication being challenged by American pragmatism. Sturges himself was seen as an uneasy mixture of savant and wise guy. On the one hand, his extreme literacy, rare among Hollywood screenwriters, enabled him to drop words like "ribaldry" and "vestal" into their proper contexts without a pretentious thud. On the other, he seemed unwilling to develop the implications of his serious ideas. His flair for props and gadgets suited the popularly recalled image of the young inventor of kissproof lipstick.

His reputation today is based mainly on the eight films he directed for Paramount. *The Great McGinty,* a vigorous satire of big-city politics marked by lusty performances from Akim Tamiroff as the Boss and Brian Donlevy as the hobo elevated to governor, was the pilot film of the writer-director movement in Hollywood. Most directors had previously risen from the ranks of studio technicians and stage directors. After Sturges led the way, John Huston, Billy Wilder, Dudley Nichols, Clifford Odets, Nunnally Johnson, Robert Rossen, Samuel Fuller, Frank Tashlin, and Blake Edwards followed from the writer's cubicle to the director's chair. *Christmas in July* lingered over a Depression mood as Dick Powell and Ellen Drew played an engaged couple trying to make ends meet on a combined salary of forty dollars a week. The vagaries of luck and the cruelties of practical jokes developed the plot in a disturbing manner that was later to be recognized as the director's trademark.

The Lady Eve, a sophisticated comedy with Henry Fonda and Barbara Stanwyck, was hailed by *The New York Times* as the best film of 1941. Sturges circumvented the censors with a rowdy blackout technique that began where the more discreet "Lubitsch touch" had left off. (The difference between the Lubitsch smile and the Sturges guffaw is the difference between winking at what is happening behind closed doors and laughing at what happens when the doors are flung open. Lubitsch treated sex as the dessert of a civilized meal of manners; Sturges, more in the American style, served sex with all the courses. Despite its ribaldry and gusto, the Sturges manner was never coarse and tasteless.) An adroit manipulation of mistaken identity aided Sturges in preserving the technical morality of the marriage contract for the oppressive censors of his time. The duet in *The Lady Eve* was later enlarged into the quartet of *Palm Beach Story* in which Joel McCrea, Claudette Colbert, Mary Astor, and Rudy Vallee were perpetually confused and obsessed by the permutations of what Sturges leeringly defined as "Subject A."

Sullivan's Travels, a Swiftian glimpse of Hollywood and its occasional flirtations with social consciousness, is generally considered the most profound expression of the director's personality. Dedicating the film to the world's clowns and mountebanks, Sturges forthrightly defended the muse of comedy against the presumably more serious demands of society. Like Shakespeare's *A Winter's Tale,* the film pivots in one poetic pirouette from the sunny to the somber when an old derelict is trapped in a metal jungle of switch rails, and is unable to avoid an oncoming train.

The Miracle of Morgan's Creek and *Hail the Conquering Hero* represented the director's original vision of small-town America from which Eddie Bracken emerged as a Sturges folk hero. In *Miracle,* Bracken has "greatness thrust upon him" when his frolicsome V-girl sweetheart, Betty Hutton, is thoughtful enough to transcend her disgrace with sextuplets. In *Hero,* Bracken survives the ordeal of a 4-F self-exposed as a false war hero, and again he is redeemed by the generous emotions of his girl friend, Ella Raines. Especially and disturbingly timely was the intense performance of ex-prizefighter Freddie Steele, in the film an orphanage-bred marine hero with a severe mother complex.

After 1944, when he left Paramount to form a short-lived partnership with Howard Hughes, Sturges's career suffered a precipitous decline. His three subsequent Hollywood films were remote from the tastes of their time, and during his long exile in the fifties, his one realized European project, the bilingual *Les Carnets de Major Thompson* (*The French They Are a Funny Race*) was unsuccessful. His present reputation is that of a period director who ultimately lost contact with his audience. Even at the time of his greatest success, he was overshadowed by the emotions aroused by the war and the stylistic revolution introduced with *Citizen Kane.* He received an Academy Award for the script of *The Great McGinty* in 1940, and was nominated twice in 1944 for *The Miracle of Morgan's Creek* and *Hail the Conquering Hero,* though again as a writer rather than as a director.

His directorial style depended more on the pacing of action and dialogue than on visual texture and composition. His canvas was flat, his sense of space shallow. Sturges employed long, uncut, "single-take" scenes to establish the premises of his elaborate scripts, but when he shifted to slapstick, he often cut to reactions before the action had been terminated. His instinct for timing comedy montage made his films the funniest of their era in terms of audience laughter. He was capable of cinematic license with a talking horse or a portrait that changed expressions. When he wanted to speed up the plot, he dispensed with dialogue and let the crisp movement and montage of silent farce fill the screen with hurtling bodies. In *Mad Wednesday,* he went so far as to begin with the last reel of Harold Lloyd's 1925 classic, *The Freshman,* after which he attempted to re-create Lloyd's vertiginous comedy effects with even wilder Sturges variations. As a screenwriter, he had pioneered in the development of the intricate flashback with *The Power and the Glory* in 1933, and his directed scenarios remain models of structural complexity.

KING VIDOR (1894–   )

FILMS: 1913–1918—Short Subjects. 1918—The Turn in the Road. 1919—Better Times, The Other Half, Poor Relations, *The Jack-Knife Man*. 1920—The Family Honor. 1921—The Sky Pilot, Love Never Dies, Conquering the Women; Woman, Wake up. 1922—The Real Adventure, Dusk to Dawn, Alice Adams, Peg o' My Heart. 1923—The Woman of Bronze, Three Wise Fools, Wild Oranges, Happiness. 1924—Wine of Youth, His Hour, Wife of the Centaur. 1925—Proud Flesh, *The Big Parade*, La Bohème. 1926— Bardelys the Magnificent. 1928—*The Crowd, Show People*. 1929 —*Hallelujah!* 1930—Not So Dumb, Billy the Kid. 1931—*Street Scene, The Champ*. 1932—Bird of Paradise, Cynara. 1933—The Stranger's Return. 1934—*Our Daily Bread*, The Wedding Night. 1935—*So Red the Rose*. 1936—The Texas Rangers. 1937— *Stella Dallas*. 1938—*The Citadel*. 1939—*Northwest Passage*. 1940 —Comrade X. 1941—H. M. Pulham, Esq. 1944—An American Romance. 1947—*Duel in the Sun*, On Our Merry Way. 1949— *The Fountainhead*. Beyond the Forest. 1951—Lightning Strikes Twice. 1952—Japanese War Bride, *Ruby Gentry*. 1955—*Man Without a Star*. 1956—*War and Peace*. 1959—Solomon and Sheba.

King Vidor is a director for anthologies. He has created more great moments and fewer great films than any director of his rank. Vidor's is an unusually intuitive talent, less grounded than most in theory. The classics of his humanistic museum period— *The Big Parade, The Crowd, Hallelujah*—are no less uneven or more impressive than the classics of his delirious modern period—*Duel in the Sun, The Fountainhead, Ruby Gentry*.

Vidor's vitality seems ageless, and his plastic force is especially appropriate for partings and reunions, and the visual opposition of individuals to masses, both social and physical. Vidor's is an architectural cinema with none of Lang's determinism or Antonioni's decadence. There are occasions in the cinema when two directors confront the same visual problem and thus provide a convenient cross-reference. Such a cross-reference occurs in Siegel's *Hell Is for Heroes* and Sanders's *War Hunt* when a wounded soldier dies in the midst of his screams as he is being carried to a medic. On a purely technical level, Siegel's treatment is decisively superior in the judicious use of a traveling overhead shot. Similarly, Vidor and Milestone cross each other's path in *The Big Parade* and *All Quiet on the Western Front*. In the Vidor, an enraged American soldier pursues a German into a shell hole. When the American sees that the German is wounded, he is unable to finish the job, but gives his enemy a cigarette instead. In the Milestone, a German soldier bayonets a Frenchman, and then asks his victim's forgiveness. Both scenes are contrived to express human brotherhood, and thereby attack the idea of War. Both scenes involve two figures in a depressed and isolated enclosure. The two-shot is almost mandatory here for both directors because cross-cutting would destroy the meaning of the scene. If two figures are shown in the same frame, a bond is established between them. Cross-cutting would establish separateness and opposition as the point of view changed back and forth. Both Vidor and Milestone understood this much, and thus the issue of montage never arises. Yet, though these scenes are identical in meaning and broadly equivalent in technical execution, the Vidor is both more moving and aesthetically superior to the Milestone. Why? Well, not because the Vidor came first. Most film critics under fifty probably saw the Milestone before they saw the Vidor. Not because Vidor has been arbitrarily designated as a better director than Milestone. One superficial advantage the Vidor possesses is that it is a silent sequence in a silent film, while the Milestone is handicapped by an inexperienced Lew Ayres reciting excessively literary dialogue. The scene in both cases involves soldiers who speak different languages, and so the Milestone imposes a suspension of disbelief unnecessary in the Vidor. The Vidor does not even have to break the continuity of the visual field with titles, and so one of the great advantages of the talkies—their visual continuum—does not help Milestone in this instance.

The personalities of the actors must also be considered somewhat, and in this instance, the advantage is with Vidor. John Gilbert and his German comrade are closer together in age than are

Lew Ayres and a middle-aged Raymond Griffith. The Vidor pair convey more strongly the idea of vital youth wasted in war, while the Milestone pair suggest abstractions of humanity rather than individuals. Ultimately, however, the issue between the two scenes is resolved by the oldest criterion of the cinema, good old camera placement, an aesthetic factor that was as decisive in 1895 as it is today. Vidor moves much closer to his characters, and thus achieves greater dramatic intensity. By staying farther back, Milestone emphasizes the pictorialism of the scene, the frame in which the spectacle unfolds rather than the spectacle itself. Vidor's treatment is more forceful than Milestone's, and hence more emotionally satisfying. We remember the faces of the two protagonists, and not the spectacle as a whole. Thus, in this one sequence, two careers fall into place. Vidor's plasticity versus Milestone's pictorialism. Engagement versus disengagement. An auteur versus a technician. The auteur theory can only record the evidence on the screen. It can never prejudge it. Vidor is superior to Milestone.

RAOUL WALSH (1892–   )

FILMS: 1912—Life of Villa. 1915—The Regeneration, Carmen. 1916—Honor System, Blue Blood and Red, The Serpent. 1917—Betrayed, The Conqueror, The Pride of New York, The Innocent Sinner, Silent Lie. 1918—Woman and the Law, This Is the Life, The Prussian Cur, On the Jump, Every Mother's Son, I'll Say So. 1919—Evangeline, Should a Husband Forgive? 1920—From Now On, The Deep Purple, The Strongest. 1921—The Oath, Serenade. 1922—Kindred of the Dust. 1923—Lost and Found. 1924—The Thief of Bagdad. 1925—East of Suez, The Spaniard. 1926—The Wanderer, The Lucky Lady, The Lady of the Harem, *What Price Glory?* 1927—The Monkey Talks, The Loves of Carmen. 1928—*Sadie Thompson,* The Red Dance, Me Gangster. 1929—Hot for Paris, *In Old Arizona* (with Irving Cummings), *The Cock-Eyed World.* 1930—The Big Trail. 1931—The Man Who Came Back, Women of All Nations, Yellow Ticket. 1932—Wild Girl, Me and My Gal. 1933—Sailor's Luck, The Bowery, Going Hollywood. 1935—Under Pressure, Baby Face Harrington, Every Night at Eight. 1936—Klondike Annie, Big Brown Eyes, Spendthrift. 1937

—You're in the Army Now, When Thief Meets Thief, Artists and Models, Hitting a New High. 1938—College Swing. 1939—St. Louis Blues, *The Roaring Twenties*. 1940—Dark Command, *They Drive by Night*. 1941—*High Sierra, The Strawberry Blonde*, Manpower, *They Died with Their Boots On*. 1942—*Desperate Journey, Gentleman Jim*. 1943—Background to Danger, *Northern Pursuit*. 1944—Uncertain Glory. 1945—*Objective Burma, Salty O'Rourke*, The Horn Blows at Midnight. 1946—*The Man I Love*. 1947—*Pursued, Cheyenne*. 1948—Silver River, *One Sunday Afternoon*, Fighter Squadron. 1949—*Colorado Territory, White Heat*. 1951—Along the Great Divide, *Captain Horatio Hornblower, Distant Drums*. 1952—*Glory Alley, The World in His Arms*, Blackbeard the Pirate. 1953—Sea Devils, *A Lion Is in the Streets, Gun Fury*. 1954—Saskatchewan. 1955—*Battle Cry, The Tall Men*. 1956—The Revolt of Mamie Stover, The King and Four Queens. 1957—*Band of Angels*. 1958—The Naked and the Dead, The Sheriff of Fractured Jaw. 1959—A Private's Affair. 1960—Esther and the King. 1961—Marines, Let's Go.

If the heroes of Ford are sustained by tradition, and the heroes of Hawks by professionalism, the heroes of Walsh are sustained by nothing more than a feeling for adventure. The Fordian hero knows why he is doing something even if he doesn't know how. The Hawksian hero knows how to do what he is doing even if he doesn't know why. The Walshian hero is less interested in the why or the how than in the what. He is always plunging into the unknown, and he is never too sure what he will find there. There is a pathos and vulnerability in Walsh's characters lacking in the more self-contained Ford and Hawks counterparts. Where Ford shifts from the immediacy of the slightly depressed heroic angle to the horizon line of history, and Hawks remains at eye level, Walsh often moves to the slightly elevated angle of the lost child in the big world. One of the most stunning shots of this nature occurs in *Captain Horatio Hornblower* when Walsh's camera recedes and rises slowly to present the lonely image of Gregory Peck, ridiculously gallant in his period costume and yet foreshortened into the lost son of his mother. The *Time* reviewer of *White Heat* has perceptively observed that Raoul Walsh was the only Hollywood director who could have got away with a shot of James Cagney sitting on his mother's lap. The principle of counterpoint operates here. Only the most virile director can effectively project a feminine vulnerability in his characters. Only an actor like Bogart could effectively hold Ava Gardner's dead body in his arms, and wonder aloud why he could never remember the Spanish word for Cinderella. Only a tough actor like Garfield could cry over the death of a friend in *The Breaking Point*. A sensitive actor like Brando was also perceptive enough to hold back his tears at Red Buttons's death in *Sayonara*. The other point that can be made about Walsh is that he has always possessed the necessary technical skills and artistic instincts to bring off the most ambitious physical spectacles. His best films are genuinely exciting, though neither profound nor pretentious. If there is no place in the cinema for the virtues and limitations of Raoul Walsh, there is even less place for an honestly pluralistic criticism.

III.
EXPRESSIVE
ESOTERICA

These are the unsung directors with difficult styles or unfashionable genres or both. Their deeper virtues are often obscured by irritating idiosyncrasies on the surface, but they are generally redeemed by their seriousness and grace.

BUDD BOETTICHER (1916–   )

FILMS: 1944—One Mysterious Night. 1945—The Missing Juror; A Guy, A Gal and a Pal; Escape in the Fog, Youth on Trial. 1948—Assigned to Danger, Behind Locked Doors. 1949—Black Midnight. 1950—Killer Shark, The Wolf Hunters. 1951—*The Bullfighter and the Lady,* The Cimarron Kid. 1952—Red Ball Express, Bronco Buster, Horizons West. 1953—City Beneath the Sea, Seminole, The Man from the Alamo, Wings of the Hawk, East of Sumatra. 1955—*The Magnificent Matador.* 1956—*The Killer Is Loose, Seven Men from Now.* 1957—*Decision at Sundown, The Tall T.* 1958—*Buchanan Rides Alone.* 1959—*Ride Lonesome, Westbound.* 1960—*The Rise and Fall of Legs Diamond, Comanche Station.* 1968—The Carlos Arruzza Story.

Does anyone know where Budd Boetticher is? The last we heard, our gifted friend was on his way to Mexico to make a movie on bullfighting, his third. Be that what it may, Boetticher is one of the most fascinating unrecognized talents in the American cinema. How many admirers of Peckinpah's *Ride the High Country* recognize this film as an attempted summation of the incredibly consistent Boetticher–Randolph Scott–Harry Joe Brown series of Westerns, which from 1956 on, established a new style in the genre? Constructed partly as allegorical Odysseys and partly as floating poker games where every character took turns at bluffing about his hand until the final showdown, Boetticher's Westerns expressed a weary serenity and moral certitude that was contrary to the more neurotic approaches of other directors on this neglected level of the cinema. Similarly, *The Rise and Fall of Legs Diamond* is a minor classic in the perverse *Scarface* tradition. One wonders where directors like Boetticher find the energy and the inspiration to do such fine work, when native critics are so fantastically indifferent that they probably couldn't tell a Boetticher film apart from a Selander or worse. This unyielding taste and dedication is what makes the American cinema so exciting and, at times, so miraculous.

Whatever his action setting, be it the corrida, the covered wagon, or the urban underworld, Boetticher is no stranger to the nuances of *machismo,* that overweening masculine pride that provides both a style and a fatal flaw to his gun-wielding or cape-flourishing characters. Boetticher's films strip away the outside world to concentrate on the deadly confrontations of male antag onists. No audience is required for the final showdown. It is man to man in an empty arena on a wide screen before a very quiet, elemental camera. Elemental but not elementary. Boetticher's timing of action is impeccable. He is not a writer-director like Burt Kennedy or Sam Peckinpah, but he is a much better story-teller.

ANDRE DE TOTH (1900–   )

FILMS: 1944—None Shall Escape, *Dark Waters.* 1947— *Ramrod,* The Other Love. 1948—*Pitfall.* 1949—Slattery's Hurricane. 1951—Man in the Saddle. 1952—Carson City, *Springfield Rifle,* Last of the Comanches. 1953—House of Wax, The Stranger Wore a Gun, Thunder Over the Plains. 1954—Riding Shotgun, Crime-Wave, The Bounty Hunters, Tanganyika. 1955—*The Indian Fighter.* 1957—Monkey on My Back, Hidden Fear. 1959—The Two-Headed Spy, *Day of the Outlaw.* 1960—Man on a String. 1961 —Morgan the Pirate, The Mongols. 1964—Gold for the Caesars. 1968—Play Dirty.

André de Toth's most interesting films reveal an understanding of the instability and outright treachery of human relationships. *Ramrod, Pitfall, Springfield Rifle, The Indian Fighter,* and *Day of the Outlaw* are unusually unpleasant explorations of failed love and trust. The assorted villainies seem more like the natural order of things than like mere contrivances of melodrama. Raymond Burr's soft-spoken Machiavellian schemer in *Pitfall* and Paul Kelly's quietly desperate traitor in *Springfield Rifle* are memorably de Tothian in their adaptability to a world of conflicting interests.

STANLEY DONEN (1924–   )

FILMS: 1949—*On the Town* (with Gene Kelly). 1951—
Royal Wedding. 1952—*Singin' in the Rain* (with Gene Kelly),
Love Is Better than Ever, Fearless Fagan. 1953—*Give a Girl a
Break*. 1954—*Seven Brides for Seven Brothers,* Deep in My Heart.
1955—*It's Always Fair Weather* (with Gene Kelly). 1957—*Funny
Face, The Pajama Game* (with George Abbott), Kiss Them for Me.
1958—*Indiscreet, Damn Yankees.* 1960—Once More with Feel-
ing, Surprise Package, The Grass is Greener. 1963—*Charade.* 1966
—Arabesque. 1968—*Two for the Road*, Bedazzled.

Stanley Donen has always seemed to function best as a hyphen-
ated director. He was dismissed for a time as Gene Kelly's invisible partner on such Golden-Age Metro musicals as *On the
Town, Singin' in the Rain,* and *It's Always Fair Weather.* When
the Metro bubble burst, Donen moved to Warners with *The
Pajama Game* and *Damn Yankees,* two transposed Broadway
musicals seemingly dominated by George Abbott's vigorously
theatrical pacing. Even when Donen received sole directorial
credit, his more notable efforts seemed only marginally personal. *Seven Brides for Seven Brothers,* for example, is stamped
(and stomped) with Michael Kidd's muscular choreography;
Funny Face is graced with Richard Avedon's witty fashion photography. In all these tandem operations, Donen clearly lacks the
stylistic presence of a Vincente Minnelli. As for Donen's relatively personal musicals, *Royal Wedding* and *Give a Girl a
Break* are peculiarly somber affairs with only intermittent
flashes of inspiration, while *Deep in My Heart* is virtually a complete disaster. His nonmusical comedies have been either relent-
lessly trivial (*Love Is Better than Ever, Fearless Fagan*) or nervously oververbalized (*Kiss Them for Me, Once More with Feeling, Surprise Package, The Grass Is Greener*).
    Where Donen has come closest to projecting a personal style is
in *Indiscreet,* a comedy that eventually collapses under the
weight of Norman Krasna's plot indiscretions, but not before
Donen reveals the serious temperament necessary for high com-

edy. His timing is sharp, and he seems at home with an elegant cast; in this instance the height of elegance represented by Cary Grant and Ingrid Bergman. After flirtations with black comedy, op art, and half-baked Hitchcock imitations in *Charade* and *Arabesque,* Donen has found his own road back with *Two for the Road.* The director's serious temperament is well suited to the offbeat casting of Audrey Hepburn with Albert Finney, the stylishly brittle script of Frederic Raphael (*Nothing but the Best, Darling*), and the tinkly romantic score of Henry Mancini. It would seem that if Donen is to be involved in good movies in the future, it will be more as a genial catalyst than as a creative force. Donen seems too much the congenital team player ever to display a marked individuality, and the Donen "touch" remains as elusive as ever. Certainly, *Bedazzled* owes infinitely more of its personal style to Dudley Moore and Peter Cook than to Stanley Donen, whereas a relative newcomer like Joseph McGrath seems already to have stolen Donen's thunder with the psychedelic portions of *Casino Royale* and the more dazzling than *Bedazzled* Dudley Moore capers in *30 Is a Dangerous Age, Cynthia!* Still, if a director acts as a pleasant enough catalyst long enough, he may come to be accepted as a creator if only in the most passive form permitted the claim of creation.

CLIVE DONNER (1926–   )

FILMS: 1956—The Secret Place. 1958—Heart of a Child. 1959—Marriage of Convenience. 1960—The Sinister Man. 1962 —*Some People.* 1964—*The Guest* (*The Caretaker*), Nothing but the Best. 1965—*What's New Pussycat?* 1967—Luv. 1968—Here We Go Round the Mulberry Bush. 1969—Alfred the Great.

Clive Donner has emerged in recent years as a gifted stylist with an eye for contemporaneous detail. He has been particularly fortunate in his writers, notably Frederic Raphael (*Nothing but the Best*), Harold Pinter (*The Caretaker*), Woody Allen (*What's New Pussycat?*), and Murray Schisgal (*Luv*). Donner's scenarists aside, he seems to be emerging as Britain's answer to Vincente

Minnelli. Donner, like Lester, seems to have anticipated the transformation of England from mum to mod. It remains to be seen if the prophet can avoid being swallowed up by his own revolution. With Donner it is not so much a question of aesthetics versus ethics as of decorative complicity versus dramatic conflict. In this sense, the mod mushiness of *Here We Go Round the Mulberry Bush* marks an ominous turn in Donner's career.

ALLAN DWAN (1885–)

FILMS (partial list 1911–1917): 1914—Wildflower, The Straight Road. 1915—A Girl of Yesterday, Jordan Is a Hard Road, The Pretty Sister of Jose, The Dancing Girl, David Harum. 1916— Betty of Greystone, The Habit of Happiness, The Half-Breed, The Good Bad Man, Manhattan Madness, An Innocent Magdalene. 1917 —Panthea, The Fighting Odds. 1918—A Modern Musketeer, Mr. Fix-It, Bound in Morocco, He Comes Up Smiling. 1919—Cheating Cheaters, Soldiers of Fortune, The Dark Star, Getting Mary Married. 1920—Luck of the Irish, A Splendid Hazard, The Forbidden Thing. 1921—The Perfect Crime, A Broken Doll, In the Heart of a Fool, The Scoffer. 1922—The Sin of Martha Queed, Superstition, *Robin Hood.* 1923—Zaza, Glimpses of the Moon, Lawful Larceny, Big Brother. 1924—Her Love Story, Manhandled, A Society Scandal, The Wages of Virtue, Argentine Love. 1925—Night Life in New York, Stage Struck, Coast of Folly. 1926—Sea Horses, Padlocked, Tin Gods, Summer Bachelors. 1927—The Music Master, The Joy Girl; East Side, West Side. 1928—French Dressing, Big Noise. 1929 —*The Iron Mask,* Tide of Empire, Frozen Justice, The Far Call, South Sea Rose. 1930—What a Widow! 1931—Man to Man, Chances, Wicked. 1932—While Paris Sleeps. 1934—The Morning After. 1935—Black Sheep, Beauty's Daughter. 1936—The Song and Dance Man, Human Cargo, High Tension, Fifteen Maiden Lane. 1937—Woman Wise, That I May Live, One Mile from Heaven, Heidi. 1938—Rebecca of Sunnybrook Farm, Josette, *Suez.* 1939— The Three Musketeers, The Gorilla, *Frontier Marshall.* 1940— Sailor's Lady, Young People, Trail of the Vigilantes. 1941—Look Who's Laughing, Rise and Shine. 1942—Friendly Enemies, Here We Go Again. 1943—Around the World. 1944—Abroad with Two Yanks, *Up in Mabel's Room.* 1945—*Brewster's Millions, Getting Gertie's Garter.* 1946—*Rendezvous with Annie.* 1947—Calendar Girl, Northwest Outpost. 1948—The Inside Story, Angel in Exile. 1949—*Sands of Iwo Jima.* 1950—Surrender. 1951—Belle Le Grande, The Wild Blue Yonder. 1952—I Dream of Jeannie, Montana Belle. 1953—Woman They Almost Lynched, Sweethearts on Parade, Flight Nurse. 1954—*Silver Lode,* Cattle Queen of Montana, Passion. 1955—Escape to Burma, Pearl of the South Pacific, *Tennessee's Partner.* 1956—Slightly Scarlet, *Hold Back the Night.* 1957—*The River's Edge, The Restless Breed.* 1958—Enchanted Island. 1961—Most Dangerous Man Alive.

Dwan's career is still being mined for a possibly higher assay of gold to dross. Recent findings—*Silver Lode, The Restless Breed, The River's Edge*—represent a virtual bonanza of hitherto unexplored classics. It is too early to establish any coherent pattern to Dwan's career as a whole, but it may very well be that Dwan will turn out to be the last of the old masters. *Silver Lode* displays a classic circularity of remembered technique, unifying the varied themes of the film by repeating the same images in different contexts. From the Fairbanks period in the silents, to unassuming comedies in the thirties and forties, and to Westerns in the fifties, Dwan has been as active as he has been obscure. Yet, one can recall *Brewster's Millions* and *Rendezvous with Annie* with fond pleasure unprompted by the alleged mystiques of the *auteur* theory. Consequently, there may be much more to be said about Dwan.

TAY GARNETT (1895–   )

FILMS: 1928—Celebrity, *The Spieler.* 1929—Flying Fools, Oh Yeah! 1930—Officer O'Brien, *Her Man.* 1931—Bad Company. 1932—*One Way Passage,* Prestige, Okay America. 1933—Destination Unknown, SOS Iceberg. 1935—China Seas, She Couldn't Take It, Professional Soldier. 1937—Love Is News, *Slave Ship, Stand-In.* 1938—Joy of Living, Trade Winds. 1939—*Eternally Yours.* 1940—Slightly Honorable, *Seven Sinners.* 1941—Cheers for Miss Bishop. 1942—My Favorite Spy. 1943—Bataan, The Cross of Lorraine. 1944—Mrs. Parkington. 1945—*The Valley of Decision.* 1946—*The Postman Always Rings Twice.* 1947—Wild Harvest. 1949—A Connecticut Yankee in King Arthur's

Court. 1950—The Fireball. 1951—Soldiers Three, *Cause for Alarm*. 1952—One Minute to Zero. 1953—Main Street to Broadway. 1954—The Black Knight. 1956—Seven Wonders of the World. 1960—*The Night Fighter*.

Inconsistency is the hobgoblin of Tay Garnett's career, and inconsistency can never be defined satisfactorily. The director of *Her Man, One-Way Passage, The Postman Always Rings Twice,* and *The Night Fighter* stays in the mind despite the lack of an overall pattern in his work. Curiously, the director's fondness for *China Seas* and *The Cross of Lorraine* is as inexplicable as the underground reputations of *Stand-In* and *Cause for Alarm,* but critical values are always topsy-turvy at this level of filmmaking. For the moment, Garnett's ultimate reputation is still unusually elusive. Even as a footnote to Marlene Dietrich's career, the rowdy humor of *Seven Sinners* could tip the scales in the director's favor. The recent loans from the Cinémathèque française of such early Garnetts as *The Spieler* and *Her Man* suggest that Garnett's personality is that of a rowdy vaudevillian, an artist with the kind of rough edges that cause the overcivilized French sensibility to swoon in sheer physical frustration. One of Garnett's most distinguished defenders is the British critic Raymond Durgnat. *Her Man,* according to Durgnat, is superior to Hawks's chilling *A Girl in Every Port* because of, rather than in spite of, Garnett's period sentimentality. What lingers in the mind is James Gleason's knowing comedy relief from the travails of Helen Twelvetrees, the Frankie no less of the Frankie and Johnnie ballad, particularly the wickedly sophisticated bigotry implicit in the muttered exclamation, "There's an octoroon in the kindling." Memorable also in the 1930 *Her Man* are the extraordinarily fluid camera movements that dispel the myth of static talkies, a myth treated as gospel in the official film histories of the period.

SETH HOLT

FILMS: 1959—Nowhere to Go. 1962—*Taste of Fear*. 1964 —*Station Six—Sahara*. 1965—*The Nanny*. 1968—Danger Route.

Seth Holt seemed more promising when he was less accomplished. *The Nanny* fell somewhere between *What Ever Happened to Baby Jane?* and *Die, Die, My Darling* in the gallery of gargoyles. Though Holt is more polished than Aldrich and infinitely more talented than Narizzano, his virtues are things of bits and pieces. Still, there are moments in *Taste of Fear* and *Station Six—Sahara* when it seems that Holt has at least one great picture in him, but where is it and what would it be about?

PHIL KARLSON (1908–)

FILMS: 1944—A Wave, a WAC and a Marine. 1945—There Goes Kelly, G.I. Honeymoon, The Shanghai Cobra. 1946—Live Wires, Swing Parade of 1946, Dark Alibi, Behind the Mask, Bowery Bombshell, Wife Wanted. 1947—Black Gold, Louisiana. 1948—Adventures in Silverado, Rocky, Thunderhoof, Ladies of the Chorus. 1949—The Big Cat. 1950—The Iroquois Trail. 1951—Lorna Doone, Texas Rangers, Mask of the Avenger. 1952—Scandal Sheet, The Brigand. 1953—*99 River Street.* 1954—They Rode West. 1955—*Hell's Island, Tight Spot, Five Against the House, The Phenix City Story.* 1957—*The Brothers Rico.* 1958—*Gunman's Walk.* 1960—*Hell to Eternity,* Key Witness. 1961—The Secret Ways, The Young Doctors. 1962—*Kid Galahad.* 1963—Rampage. 1966—*The Silencers.* 1969—The Wrecking Crew.

Phil Karlson's career has had a peculiar rhythm all its own. He started slowly, and from 1944 through 1952, did little to attract attention. *Ladies of the Chorus* has acquired a retroactive cult composed of some of the admirers of the late Marilyn Monroe in her pristine state, but otherwise nothing much happens until *99 River Street*. Then, in 1955, a Karlson style emerges decisively in *Hell's Island, Tight Spot, Five Against the House,* and *The Phenix City Story,* pictures with more quality than prestige, interestingly ambiguous action heroes ranging from late John Payne to early Brian Keith. *The Brothers Rico* in 1957 is still Karlson's best film; and then a tapering off—*Gunman's Walk, Hell to Eternity, Key Witness, The Young Doctors, Rampage,* and *The Silencers,* the latter the best of the Dean Martin–Matt

Helm takeoffs on the Bond craze, but a deplorable genre all the same, despite Martin's charm and the goofy voluptuousness of Stella Stevens. *Kid Galahad,* Presley's best film since *Flaming Star,* and equally unsuccessful at the box office, represents another oasis in a desert of decline. Karlson may have had bad luck with projects, but the evidence of recession before full recognition is too strong to be denied. Karlson was most personal and most efficient when he dealt with the phenomenon of violence in a world controlled by organized evil. His special brand of lynch hysteria establishes such an outrageous moral imbalance that the most unthinkable violence releases the audience from its helpless passivity. Unfortunately, an American director gets nowhere making films like *The Brothers Rico.* The cosmopolitan genre prejudices are too strong.

JOSEPH H. LEWIS (1900–   )

FILMS: 1937—Courage of the West, Singing Outlaw, International Spy. 1938—The Spy Ring, Border Wolves, The Last Stand. 1940—Two-Fisted Rangers, Blazing Six-Shooters, Texas Stagecoach, The Man from Tumbleweeds, Boys of the City, The Return of Wild Bill, That Gang of Mine. 1941—The Invisible Ghost, Pride of the Bowery. 1942—Arizona Cyclone, Bombs Over Burma, The Silver Bullet, Secrets of a Co-ed, The Boss of Hangtown Mesa, The Mad Doctor of Market Street. 1944—Minstrel Man. 1945—*My Name Is Julia Ross.* 1946—So Dark the Night. 1947—The Swordsman. 1948—The Return of October. 1949—*The Undercover Man, Deadly Is the Female* (or *Gun Crazy*). 1950—Lady Without a Passport. 1952—Retreat, Hell! Desperate Search. 1953—Cry of the Hunted. 1955—*The Big Combo,* A Lawless Street. 1956—The Seventh Cavalry. 1957—*The Halliday Brand.* 1958—Terror in a Texas Town.

Back in the Spring 1962 issue of *Film Culture,* a critic, writing on "The High Forties Revisited," remarked: "If some bright new critic should awaken the world to the merits of Joseph Lewis in the near future, we will have to scramble back to his 1940 record: *Two-Fisted Rangers, Blazing Six-Shooters, Texas Stage-*

coach, The Man from Tumbleweeds, Boys of the City, Return of Wild Bill, and *That Gang of Mine.* Admittedly, in this direction lies madness." Well, madness is always preferable to smugness, and scramble we must because Lewis has been discovered. After several years of Poverty Row, he made *The Minstrel Man,* with Edgar G. Ulmer, no less, as his set designer. Then, in 1945, *My Name Is Julia Ross* became the sleeper of the year. From that point on, the director's somber personality has been revealed consistently through a complex visual style. It would seem that his career warrants further investigation. The director's one enduring masterpiece is *Gun Crazy,* a subtler and more moving evocation of American gun cult than the somewhat overrated *Bonnie and Clyde.* The performances of John Dall and Peggy Cummins in *Gun Crazy* suggest the vitality of the American action movie despite its relative obscurity.

ALEXANDER MACKENDRICK (1912–   )

FILMS: 1950—*Tight Little Island.* 1952—*The Man in the White Suit.* 1953—*The Story of Mandy.* 1954—High and Dry. 1957—*Sweet Smell of Success.* 1965—*A Boy Ten Feet Tall,* A High Wind in Jamaica. 1967—Don't Make Waves. 1969—Mary, Queen of Scots.

Back in 1963, I asked, more rhetorically than realistically: "How much of *Sweet Smell of Success* is attributable to Mackendrick, and how much to Clifford Odets and James Wong Howe? What has happened to Mackendrick's career, and why? We miss Mackendrick without knowing exactly what we are missing."

Mackendrick returned to our attention in 1965, and his career has since followed the curious pattern of sexual sophistication and child-cult cultivation, but it is good to have him back. *A Boy Ten Feet Tall* and *A High Wind in Jamaica* revel in the emotional gusto of tall stories, while *Don't Make Waves* slashes the ethos of the California coast almost as savagely as *Sweet Smell of Success* did for New York. In both instances, the hustle projected by Tony Curtis found its ideal directorial correlative.

ROBERT MULLIGAN (1930–   )

FILMS: 1957—*Fear Strikes Out.* 1960—*The Rat Race,* The Great Impostor. 1961—Come September. 1962—Spiral Road. 1963—To Kill a Mockingbird, Love with the Proper Stranger. 1964 —*Baby, the Rain Must Fall.* 1965—*Inside Daisy Clover.* 1967— *Up the Down Staircase.* 1968—The Stalking Moon. 1969—The Piano Sport. 1970—Good Times, Bad Times.

Back in 1963, I confidently consigned Robert Mulligan to the ranks of the minor disappointments: "François Truffaut to the contrary notwithstanding, Robert Mulligan has struck out on six pitches. To recapitulate, two of the pitches were screwballs (*Fear Strikes Out* and *The Great Impostor*) which broke over the heart of the plate like miniatures of *Citizen Kane.* Two wild blooper pitches (*Come September* and *The Spiral Road*) should never have been swung at in the first place. *To Kill a Mockingbird* was the kind of sweeping literary curve which drives hitters (and directors) back to the minors for more seasoning. *The Rat Race* broke stupidly because that old spitball pitcher Garson Kanin was out there on the mound. Whatever the extenuating circumstances, Mulligan missed every pitch, good and bad. He has yet to make a satisfactory film despite at least two good opportunities. What Mulligan lacks is not technique, but the rudimentary artistic discernment to separate the wheat from the chaff in his material. His direction is unstressed, impersonal, and uncommitted. He never gives his more promising projects the necessary point of view, and he never salvages the impossible projects with the saving grace of humor. Mulligan's direction on every occasion is ultimately too frivolous to justify serious expectations that this competent technician will ever be anything more."

Five years later Mulligan has still not made an entirely satisfactory film, but an accumulation of bits and pieces of lyricism constitutes a vindication of sorts for the director. If Mulligan's movies still suffer from a lack of coherence, they manage nonetheless to establish behavioral beauties. Particularly memorable are the performances of Steve McQueen in *Baby, the Rain Must Fall* and Ellen O'Mara in *Up the Down Staircase.*

GERD OSWALD (1916–)

FILMS: 1956—*A Kiss Before Dying, The Brass Legend.* 1957 —*Crime of Passion, Fury at Showdown, Valerie.* 1958—Paris Holiday, *Screaming Mimi.* 1961—*Brainwashed.* 1966—Agent for H.A.R.M.

Except for such predoomed projects as *Paris Holiday* (with Bob Hope and Fernandel no less) and *Agent for H.A.R.M.,* Gerd Oswald has shown an admirable consistency, both stylistically and thematically, for a director in his obscure position. A fluency of camera movement is controlled by sliding turns and harsh stops befitting a cinema of bitter ambiguity. Oswald's success in imposing a personal style on such otherwise routine Westerns as *The Brass Legend* and *Fury at Showdown* on shooting schedules ranging from five to seven days should serve as an object lesson to young directors who complain that they lack the time to get their films just right. There are paranoiac overtones in all his films, and the anti-Nazi symbolism is never too hard to detect, even in a frontier *Rashomon* like *Valerie.* What is important is that Gerd Oswald has been making distinguished American films that are never reviewed in the fashionable weeklies and monthlies that feed off the fashionable and well-publicized projection-room circuit. Such indifference may be the epitaph for the inspired "sleeper."

ARTHUR PENN (1922–)

FILMS: 1958—*The Lefthanded Gun.* 1962—*The Miracle Worker.* 1965—Mickey One. 1966—The Chase. 1967—*Bonnie and Clyde.*

Bonnie and Clyde has confirmed Penn's position as the American Truffaut, and what I have written in the past about Truffaut applies in some measure to Penn as well: "As an artist, Truffaut is torn between a love for his audience and a fear of emotional facility. As the best-liked director of the *nouvelle vague,* Truffaut is always tempted to be touching. His emotional commitment to and deep involvement with his players and characters generate emotional power with an occasional loss of intellectual perspective." Benton and Newman reportedly offered their script for *Bonnie and Clyde* to Truffaut and Godard, but luckily they obtained Penn instead. However, the tensions between the script and the direction were never fully resolved, and *Bonnie and Clyde* still seems excessively Europeanized for what it is supposed to be.

Nevertheless, for a stage director whose work suffers from an oppressive literalness of effect, Penn has revealed a distinctive flair for the cinema. The intense physicality of the performances in his films serves to counterbalance a strained reading of lines. A director of force rather than grace, Penn may yet reassert the plastic role of the actor in the scheme of things. Be that as it may, *The Lefthanded Gun* remains a tribute to the director's gifts of improvisation.

LOWELL SHERMAN (1885–1934)

FILMS: 1930—Lawful Larceny, The Pay Off. 1931—Bachelor Apartment, Royal Bed, High Stakes. 1932—*The Greeks Had a Word for Them,* Ladies of the Jury, False Faces. 1933—*She Done Him Wrong, Morning Glory,* Broadway Thru a Keyhole. 1934—Born to Be Bad. 1935—Night Life of the Gods.

Lowell Sherman deserves an esoteric niche all his own for the behavioral glories of Katharine Hepburn in *Morning Glory* and Mae West in *She Done Him Wrong.* Both as an actor and as a director, Sherman was gifted with the ability to express the poignancy of male lechery when confronted with female longing. His civilized sensibility was ahead of its time, and the sophistication of his sexual humor singularly lacking in malice.

DONALD SIEGEL (1912–   )

FILMS: 1946—*The Verdict.* 1949—The Big Steal, Night unto Night. 1952—The Duel at Silver Creek, No Time for Flowers. 1953—Count the Hours, China Venture. 1954—*Riot in Cell Block 11, Private Hell 36.* 1955—An Annapolis Story. 1956—*Invasion of the Body Snatchers,* Crime in the Streets. 1957—*Baby Face Nelson.* 1958—Spanish Affair, *The Line-Up,* The Gun Runners. 1959—Hound Dog Man. 1960—Edge of Eternity, Flaming Star. 1962—*Hell Is for Heroes.* 1964—*The Killers.* 1967—Stranger on the Run. 1968—*Madigan,* Coogan's Bluff. 1969—Two Mules for Sister Sara.

Siegel's most successful films express the doomed peculiarity of the antisocial outcast. The director's gallery of loners assimilates an otherwise anomalous group of actors—Neville Brand (*Riot in Cell Block 11*), Steve Cochran (*Private Hell 36*), Mickey Rooney (*Baby Face Nelson*), Eli Wallach (*The Line-Up*), Elvis Presley (*Flaming Star*), Steve McQueen (*Hell Is for Heroes*), Lee Marvin (*The Killers*), Henry Fonda (*Stranger on the Run*), and Richard Widmark (*Madigan*). *Invasion of the Body Snatchers,* one of the few authentic science fiction classics, derives its horror from the systematic destruction of individual feeling by unearthly forces. On another level, *Invasion of the Body Snatchers* evokes wild humor through Siegel's matter-of-fact view of paranoia. Siegel's style does not encompass the demonic distortions of Fuller's, Aldrich's, Losey's, and, to a lesser extent, Karlson's. Siegel declines to implicate the world at large in the anarchic causes of his heroes. Nor does he adjust his compositions to their psychological quirks. The moral architecture of his universe is never undermined by the editing, however frenzied. Nevertheless, the final car chase in *The Line-Up* and the final shoot-up in *Madigan* are among the most stunning displays of action montage in the history of the American cinema. On the negative side, *No Time for Flowers* clearly fails to meet the awesome challenge of Lubitsch's *Ninotchka,* and Audie Murphy's stone-faced virtuousness in *The Gun Runners* seems beyond any director's control. For the present, Siegel seems most assured with the middle-budget action film, and it is to be hoped that he does not become a casualty of Hollywood's excluded middle.

ROBERT SIODMAK (1900–   )

FILMS: 1927—*Menschen am Sonntag.* 1932—Stürme der Leidenschaft. 1933—Le Sexe Faible. 1937—Mister Flow. 1938 —Mollenard. 1939—Pièges. 1941—West Point Widow. 1942 —Fly by Night, My Heart Belongs to Daddy, The Night Before the Divorce. 1943—Someone to Remember, Son of Dracula. 1944—*Phantom Lady,* Cobra Woman, *Christmas Holiday.* 1945— *The Suspect, Uncle Harry.* 1946—*The Spiral Staircase, The Killers, The Dark Mirror.* 1947—Time Out of Mind. 1948—*Cry of the City.* 1949—*Criss Cross,* The Great Sinner, Thelma Jordan. 1950—Deported. 1951—The Whistle at Eaton Falls. 1952—*The Crimson Pirate.* 1954—Le Grand Jeu. 1955—Die Ratten. 1959— L'Affaire Nina B. 1962—Escape from East Berlin. 1963—Magnificent Sinner. 1968—Custer of the West.

Robert Siodmak's Hollywood films were more Germanic than his German ones, and that is as it should be. Why should Germans want to look at Germanic films? Only Americans are suitably impressed by this apparent triumph of form over content. Nevertheless, Siodmak's most successful projects—*Phantom Lady, Christmas Holiday, The Suspect, Uncle Harry, The Spiral Staircase, The Killers*—represent a fortuitous conjunction of such attractive actresses as Ella Raines, Dorothy McGuire, Ava Gardner, and even an absurdly lurid Deanna Durbin, with perverse subjects and expert technicians all whipped together with a heavy Teutonic sauce and served to the customers as offbeat art. After this period, Siodmak's personality, such as it is, becomes less distinctive, and the casual observer might mistake Siodmak's *Cry of the City* as a Dassin, and Dassin's *Brute Force* as a Siodmak. Now, virtually in retrospect, Siodmak evokes the garish Universal lighting of the forties, the music of Miklos Rozsa, Burt Lancaster in his falsely promising debut in *The Killers,* and

Maria Montez at her most deliriously defective in a dual role for *Cobra Woman*. And without Maria Montez we might have been spared Jack Smith's *Flaming Creatures*. However, Siodmak is not to blame for spawning those mutants of the medium, the moviepoids. He merely manipulated Hollywood's fantasy apparatus with taste and intelligence for a studio that has always been more devious than most.

JOHN M. STAHL (1886–1950)

FILMS: 1914–1917: No reliable index. 1918—Wives of Men. 1919—Her Code of Honor, Suspicion, A Woman Under Oath. 1920 —Women Men Forget, Woman in His House. 1921—The Child Thou Gavest Me, Sowing the Wind. 1922—The Song of Life, One Clear Call, Suspicious Wives. 1923—The Wanters, The Dangerous Age. 1924—Husbands and Lovers, Why Men Leave Home. 1925— Fine Clothes. 1926—Memory Lane, The Gay Deceiver. 1927— Lovers, In Old Kentucky. 1931—Seed, *Strictly Dishonorable*. 1932 —*Back Street*. 1933—*Only Yesterday*. 1934—*Imitation of Life*. 1935—*Magnificent Obsession*. 1937—Parnell. 1938—*Letter of Introduction*. 1939—*When Tomorrow Comes*. 1943—*Holy Matrimony, Immortal Sergeant*. 1944—*The Eve of St. Mark, The Keys of the Kingdom*. 1945—*Leave Her to Heaven*. 1947—The Foxes of Harrow, The Walls of Jericho.

John M. Stahl was a neglected pre-Sirkian figure whose career suddenly became illuminated after his death through an accident in film scholarship. A French film historian classified Stahl as a director with only one masterpiece, *Back Street* (1932). A quick recheck of Stahl's career for possible auteur analysis revealed a startling quality of consistency from 1932 on. For the most part, Stahl, like Sternberg and Sirk, was involved with outrageously improbable material. Hence, the disapprobation of the plot-obsessed American critics. *Holy Matrimony,* however, was a success by any standards. *Parnell* was actually one of the more creditable films of Clark Gable, and not the hopeless disaster its reputation would indicate. Stahl's strong point was sincerity and a vivid visual style. Who can forget Gene Tierney on horseback spreading her father's ashes in *Leave Her to Heaven* or Margaret Sullavan having one last tryst with her forgetful lover on the second level of a duplex or Irene Dunne having a somber farewell dinner with hopelessly married Charles Boyer or Andrea Leeds and her *Letter of Introduction* to Adolphe Menjou? Stahl possessed the audacity of Sirk, but not the dark humor. Where Stahl was capable of a straight, reverent treatment of *The Keys of the Kingdom,* Sirk transformed *The First Legion* into a devastating parody of the Jesuits. In *The Eve of St. Mark,* Stahl revealed a profound comprehension of the emotional implications of two-shots as opposed to cross-cutting. At times, Stahl's conception of contrasts was as forceful as Sirk's. In *The Immortal Sergeant,* for example, Henry Fonda is in the desert with a mental image of Maureen O'Hara emerging dripping wet from a swimming pool. This is the cinema of audacity to the point of madness, and yet always preferable to the relative sanity of discretion.

FRANK TASHLIN (1913–)

FILMS: 1952—The First Time, Son of Paleface. 1953—Marry Me Again. 1955—*Artists and Models.* 1956—The Lieutenant Wore Skirts, *Hollywood or Bust, The Girl Can't Help It.* 1957—*Will Success Spoil Rock Hunter.* 1958—Rock-a-bye Baby, Geisha Boy. 1959—Say One for Me. 1960—Cinderfella. 1962—*Bachelor Flat, It's Only Money.* 1963—The Man from the Diners' Club, *Who's Minding the Store?* 1964—*The Disorderly Orderly.* 1966—The Glass Bottom Boat, The Alphabet Murders. 1967—*Caprice.* 1968—The Private Navy of Sgt. O'Farrell.

Back in 1963, I wrote on Tashlin thus: "Peter Bogdanovich and Ian Cameron have analyzed Tashlin's career with great accuracy and perception, and Jean-Luc Godard had already hailed Tashlin as the vanguard of a genuinely modern comedy style in the cinema. What then is the problem with Tashlin? Simply that there is a distinction between what is analyzed and what is directly experienced. In short, Tashlin sounds better than he plays. One can approve vulgarity in theory as a comment on vulgarity, but in practice all vulgarity is inseparable. Tashlin can still be given considerable leeway. An unrecognized comedy director in Hollywood at the present time can hardly write his own ticket, and studio interference is particularly damaging to farce conceptions. Casts are a special problem, also, but the suspicion persists that if Tashlin had not had Jerry Lewis and Jayne Mansfield, he would have invented their equivalents. To ridicule Jayne Mansfield's enormous bust in *Will Success Spoil Rock Hunter* may be construed as satire, indulgent or otherwise, but to ridicule Betsy Drake's small bust in the same film is simply unabashed vulgarity. Although Tashlin is impressively inventive, particularly with gadgets and animals, he has never been sympathetic enough to any of his characters to forego a laugh at their expense. The one possible exception is the sweet, anonymous British girl in *Bachelor Flat,* Tashlin's best film. Ultimately, frenetic farce, however inventive, is self-defeating without a theory of character. Up to now, Tashlin has dealt almost exclusively with caricatures instead of characters, and so unless we are entering an age of robot comedy, the problem of Tashlin will remain a problem of taste."

In five years, Tashlin has become sympathetically obsolete without ever becoming fashionable. What little Tashlin cult interest there was has now shifted almost entirely to Jerry Lewis, actor-director extraordinary. Tashlin himself has been reduced to relatively commissioned projects, and has proved himself time and again stylistically superior to material so odious as to seem an affront to Doris Day in her last filtered days on the screen. Tashlin's little victories, however reassuring to the *Politique,* are ultimately Pyrrhic.

JACQUES TOURNEUR (1904–   )

FILMS: 1931—Tout Ça Ne Vaut Pas L'Amour. 1933—Toto, Pour Etre Aimé. 1934—Les Filles de la Concierge. 1939—They All Come Out, Nick Carter—Master Detective. 1940—Phantom Riders. 1941—Doctors Don't Tell. 1942—*Cat People.* 1943—*I Walked with a Zombie,* The Leopard Man. 1944—Days of Glory,

Experiment Perilous. 1946—*Canyon Passage.* 1947—Out of the Past. 1948—Berlin Express. 1949—Easy Living. 1950—Stars in My Crown, The Flame and the Arrow. 1951—Circle of Danger, Anne of the Indies. 1952—Way of a Gaucho. 1953—Appointment in Honduras. 1955—Stranger on Horseback, *Wichita.* 1956— *Great Day in the Morning,* Nightfall. 1958—*Curse of the Demon,* The Fearmakers. 1959—Timbuktu. 1960—The Giant of Marathon. 1963—The Comedy of Terrors. 1965—War Gods of the Deep.

Jacques Tourneur, son of the late Maurice Tourneur, brings a certain French gentility to the American cinema. At its best, this gentility lifts a Western like *Great Day in the Morning* to a new, unaccustomed level of subdued, pastel-colored sensibility. At its worst, this same gentility drains all the vitality out of a trivial, medieval exercise like *The Flame and the Arrow.* Tourneur's first films for Val Lewton — *The Cat People* and *I Walked with a Zombie* —possessed a subtler dramatic force than those of Wise and Robson. *Out of the Past* is still Tourneur's masterpiece, a civilized treatment of an annihilating melodrama. *Anne of the Indies* and *Way of a Gaucho,* two misguided Fox projects conceived in the last hectic days before Cinemascope, come off much better than anyone had any right to expect despite their intransigent exoticism. *Stranger on Horseback* and *Wichita* lack both excitement and the compensating sensibility of *Great Day in the Morning.* On the commercial downgrade, *Curse of the Demon, The Fearmakers, Timbuktu,* and *The Giant of Marathon* attest to Tourneur's unyielding pictorialism if little else. All in all, Tourneur's career represents a triumph of taste over force.

EDGAR G. ULMER (1900–)

FILMS: 1929—*Menschen am Sonntag* (with Robert Siodmak). 1933—Damaged Lives. 1934—*The Black Cat.* 1937—Green Fields (with Jacob Ben-Ami). 1938—The Singing Blacksmith. 1939 —Moon over Harlem. 1942—Tomorrow We Live. 1943—My Son, the Hero; Girls in Chains, Isle of Forgotten Sins, Jive Junction. 1944—*Bluebeard.* 1945—Strange Illusion, The Strange Woman. 1946—*Detour,* Club Havana, The Wife of Monte Cristo, Her Sister's Secret. 1947—Carnegie Hall. 1948—*Ruthless.* 1949—The Pirates of Capri. 1951—The Man From Planet X, St. Benny the Dip. 1952—Babes in Bagdad. 1955—*Murder Is My Beat, The Naked Dawn.* 1957—Daughter of Dr. Jekyll. 1960—Hannibal, The Amazing Transparent Man, Beyond the Time Barrier. 1961— *L'Atlantide.* 1965—The Cavern.

The French call him *un cinéaste maudit,* and directors certainly don't come any more *maudit.* But yes, Virginia, there is an Edgar G. Ulmer, and he is no longer one of the private jokes shared by auteur critics, but one of the minor glories of the cinema. Here is a career, more subterranean than most, which be signature of a genuine artist. Strictly speaking, most of Ulmer's films are of interest only to unthinking audiences or specialists in mise-en-scène. Yet, anyone who loves the cinema must be moved by *Daughter of Dr. Jekyll,* a film with a scenario so atrocious that it takes forty minutes to establish that the daugher of Dr. Jekyll is indeed the daughter of Dr. Jekyll. Ulmer's camera never falters even when his characters disintegrate. As the executor of the Murnau estate, he is faithful to his trust, and when his material is less impossible, his reflexes are still sharp for the meaningful challenges of *The Black Cat, Bluebeard, Ruthless, Murder Is My Beat, Detour,* and *The Naked Dawn.* That a personal style could emerge from the lowest depths of Poverty Row is a tribute to a director without alibis.

ROLAND WEST (1887–)

FILMS: 1918—De Luxe Annie. 1921—The Silver Lining, Nobody. 1923—The Unknown Purple. 1925—The Monster. 1926 —*The Bat.* 1927—The Dove. 1929—*Alibi.* 1931—Bat Whispers, *Corsair.*

Roland West is one of the forgotten figures of the early thirties. The misty expressionism and delicate feelings of *Corsair* entitle this director to a place in film history. The cigar-chomping stoicism of Ned Sparks reflects West's sensitivity to the softer side of the cynical bootlegging genre. *Alibi* remains to be seen and saved from the limbo of legend.

IV.
FRINGE
BENEFITS

The following directors occupied such a marginal role in the American cinema that it would be unfair to their overall reputations to analyze them in this limited context in any detail, but a few comments may be in order.

MICHELANGELO ANTONIONI (1912–   )

FILMS: Documentaries: 1943–1947—Gente del Po. 1948—
N.U. 1948–1949—L'Amorosa Menzogna, Superstizione. 1949—
Sette Canne un Vestito. 1950—La Funivia del Faloria, La Villa dei
Mostri. 1955—Uomini in Più. Features: 1950—*Cronaca di un
Amore.* 1952—I Vinti. 1952–1953—La Signora Senza Camelie.
1953—Tentato Suicidio (episode in Love in the City). 1955—*Le
Amiche.* 1957—*Il Grido.* 1959–1960—*L'Avventura.* 1960—*La
Notte.* 1961—*L'Eclisse.* 1964—*The Red Desert.* 1966—*Blow-
Up.* 1969—Zabriskie Point.

Antonioni came, saw, and conquered the English-language
market on his very first try. When *Blow-Up* was screened in
Hollywood, the natives chortled with derision. Who was this
Mike Antonioni who thought he could walk in without a shred of
scripting and take over the cultural scene? What the Hollywood
factory workers failed to perceive was the underlying literary
framework of Antonioni's visual doodling. Antonioni had
become adept at exploiting the sentimental pessimism and sensual prying of his age, and the American market was ripe for his
brilliant coup. Ripe to the tune of eight million dollars. In some
ways, Antonioni was more honest in *Blow-Up* than in *La Notte,
Eclipse,* and *The Red Desert,* films in which he sought to graft
Antoniennui onto the world at large. In *Blow-Up,* Antonioni
acknowledged for the first time his own divided sensibility, half
mod and half Marxist. Unlike Fellini, however, Antonioni converted his confession into a genuine movie that objectifies his obsessions without whining or self-pity. As befits the classical tradition of movie-making, *Blow-Up* can be enjoyed by moviegoers
who never heard of Antonioni.

LUIS BUÑUEL (1900–   )

FILMS: 1928—The Fall of the House of Usher, *Un Chien
Andalou.* 1930—*L'Age d'Or.* 1932—*Land Without Bread.* 1947

—Gran Casino. 1949—El Gran Calavera. 1950—*Los Olivados* (The Young and the Damned), Susana. 1951—Daughter of Deceit, A Woman Without Love, Ascent to Heaven. 1952—El Bruto, El Robinson Crusoe. 1953—Wuthering Heights, *Illusion Travels by Streetcar.* 1954—The River and Death. 1955—*The Criminal Life of Archibaldo Cruz.* 1956—La Mort en Ce Jardin. 1958—*Nazarin.* 1959—La fievre monte a El Pao. 1960—The Young One. 1961—*Viridiana.* 1962—*The Exterminating Angel.* 1965—Diary of a Chambermaid, *Simon of the Desert.* 1967—*Belle de Jour.* 1969—La Voie Lactée.

His English-language films—*Robinson Crusoe* and *The Young One*—indicate that he could have been one of Us if he had not hated everything Hollywood stands for. Buñuel had the talent to justify his anger and integrity, but too many people with only anger and integrity think that a brave anti-Hollywood posture will compensate for a lack of talent. It won't. Still, there may come a day when censorship gives up the ghost forever, and Hollywood is thrown to the few audacious spirits in the world, and Buñuel should head the list. Even in 1967, Buñuel's greatest and most beautiful film, the purest expression of surrealism in the history of the cinema, *Belle de Jour,* would probably face less censorship in America than in France.

CLAUDE CHABROL (1930–   )

FILMS: 1958—*Le Beau Serge, Les Cousins.* 1959—*Leda.* 1960—*Les Bonnes Femmes, Les Godelureaux.* 1961—*The Third Lover,* Seven Capital Sins (L'Avarice). 1962—*Ophelia, Landru.* 1964—Le Tigre Aime la Chair Fraiche. 1965—Marie-Chantal Contre le Docteur Kah, Le Tigre Se Parfume à la Dynamite, *Paris vu par . . . Chabrol.* 1966—La Ligne de Demarcation. 1968—The Champagne Murders, The Route to Corinth, *Les Biches.* 1969—La Femme Infidèle.

Claude Chabrol failed to find universality in Universal's *The Champagne Murders,* an exercise in international casting and bilingual shooting. Chabrol belongs in the French cinema as its foremost Hitchcockian, but with a decided Gallic accent.

Chabrol, more than Truffaut and Godard, has followed the Hollywood credo of keeping your hand in even when your heart isn't in it, thus perfecting your craft until the opportunity arrives for practicing your art once more. Ironically, Chabrol had become one of the forgotten figures of the *nouvelle vague* even though he turned out eight very personal and professional feature films while most of his colleagues were still floundering with fragments of films. Films is perhaps less the operative word for Chabrol than movies. Only time will tell if Chabrol's movies will outlive Godard's anticinema.

RENÉ CLAIR (1898–   )

FILMS: 1923—Paris Qui Dort. 1924—*Entr'Acte.* La Fantôme du Moulin Rouge. 1925—Le Voyage Imaginaire. 1926 —La Proie du Vent. 1927—*The Italian Straw Hat.* 1928—Les Deux Timides, La Tour (Documentary). 1930—*Sous les Toits de Paris* (Under the Roofs of Paris). 1931—*Le Million.* 1932—*À Nous la Liberté.* 1933—Quatorze Juillet. 1935—Le Dernier Milliardaire. 1936—*The Ghost Goes West.* 1938—Break the News. 1939—Air Pur (incomplete). 1941—The Flame of New Orleans. 1942—I Married a Witch, Forever and a Day (one episode, replacing Alfred Hitchcock). 1944—It Happened Tomorrow. 1945— *And Then There Were None.* 1947—*Le Silence Est d'Or.* 1950— La Beauté du Diable (Beauty and the Devil). 1952—Les Belles de Nuit (Beauties of the Night). 1956—*Les Grandes Manoeuvres.* 1957—Porte de Lilas (Gates of Paris). 1960—La Française et l'Amour (Love and the Frenchwoman), episode "Le Mariage." 1961 —Tout l'Or du Monde. 1962—Les Quatre Vérité, episode, "Les Deux Pigeons." 1965—Les Fêtes Galantes.

Although Clair made several English-language and Hollywood films, his American period is generally blamed for his decline. The trouble with Clair's American career is that he was typed for fantasy and other fluff, and could never escape his niche. His most successful American film—*And Then There Were None* —confirmed that Clair needed a little realistic vinegar in his material in order to function. Even Agatha Christie's formula murders were preferable to the processions of ghosts and futurities in *I Married a Witch, The Ghost Goes West, It Happened Tomorrow*. Only Dietrich's intransigent corporeality redeemed *The Flame of New Orleans* from the spooky fate of Clair's other films. However, it must be reported honestly that Clair's decline began before he left France for Hollywood's lucre and that Clair never regained his footing back in Paris. *À Nous la Liberté, Le Million, Sous les Toits de Paris, The Italian Straw Hat* retain a certain classic value, but Clair, once too good to be called even the French Lubitsch, now seems more like the French Mamoulian.

RENÉ CLÉMENT (1913–   )

FILMS: 1946—*Le Bataille du Rail,* Le Pére Tranquille. 1947 —*Les Maudits (The Damned).* 1949—*The Walls of Malapaga.* 1950—Le Château de Verre. 1952—*Forbidden Games.* 1954— *Monsieur Ripois (Lovers, Happy Lovers).* 1956—*Gervaise.* 1958 —*This Angry Age.* 1959—*Purple Noon.* 1961—*Quelle Joie de Vivre.* 1963—The Day and the Hour. 1964—*Joy House.* 1966— Is Paris Burning?

The irony of René Clément was that his two best films— *Lovers, Happy Lovers* and *This Angry Age*—were both English-language productions and that Clément, more than such Americanophiles as Melville and Sautet, seemed to possess the necessary pragmatic temperament to become an American director. Unfortunately, since Clément took the plunge, his career has done likewise. The intermittent charm of a *Joy House* cannot compensate for the disastrous dullness of an *Is Paris Burning?*

SERGEI EISENSTEIN (1898–1948)

FILMS: 1924—Strike. 1925—Potemkin. 1927—October (Ten Days That Shook the World). 1929—The General Line. 1931— Que viva Mexico (not completed). 1938—Alexander Nevsky. 1941–1946—Ivan the Terrible, Parts I and II.

The time has come to stop blaming Eisenstein for every excess or inadequacy of montage. As it is, Eisenstein's *Film Form* and *Film Sense* have been almost as misunderstood as Stanislavsky's *An Actor Prepares,* with its legacy of mumbling mummers out of The Method. Furthermore, Eisenstein's montage classics have probably done more harm to American film criticism and film history than any other factor. The totalitarians of the Left embraced Eisenstein and montage as the first step toward brainwashing humanity, but the cinema quickly lent its manipulative social powers to Television. The cinema returned to formal excellence, abandoning the salvation of mankind as a criterion of criticism. Now there is a tendency to dismiss Eisenstein as irrelevant to modern aesthetics, and nothing could be further from the truth.

G. W. PABST (1885-1967)

FILMS: 1923—Der Schatz (The Treasure). 1924—Gräfin Donelli (Countess Donelli). 1925—*Die Freudlose Gasse (The Joyless Street).* 1926—*Geheimnisse Einer Seele (Secrets of a Soul),* Man Spielt Nicht mit der Liebe (Never Play Around with Love). 1927—*Die Liebe der Jeanne Ney (The Love of Jeanne Ney).* 1928 —Begierde (Desire). 1929—*Die Büchse der Pandora (Pandora's Box), Das Tagebuch Einer Verloren (The Diary of a Lost Girl),* Die Weisse Hölle vom Pitz Palu (The White Hell of Pitz Palu) (with Dr. Arnold Fanck). 1930—*Westfront 1918,* Skandal um Eva (Scandal About Eva). 1931—*Die Dreigroschenoper (The Three Penny Opera),* L'Opéra a Quat' Sous (French version of Die Dreigroschenoper), *Kamaradschaft.* 1932—La Tragédie de la Mine (French version of Kamaradschaft), L'Atlantide. 1933—Don Quichotte, Don Quixote (English version), De Haut en Bas, La Nuit. 1934—A Modern Hero. 1936—Mademoiselle Docteur. 1938—Le Drame de Shanghai, L'Esclave Blanche. 1939—Jeunes Filles en Détresse. 1940—Feuertaufe (Baptism of Fire). 1941—Komödianten. 1943 —Paracelsus. 1945—Der Fall Molander (The Molander Affair). 1948—*Der Prozess (The Trial).* 1949—Gehemnisvolle Tiefe. 1952—La Voce del Silenzio. 1953—Cose da Pazzi. 1954—Das

Bekenntnis der Ina Kahr (The Confession of Ina Kahr). 1955—*Der Letzte Akt* (*The Last Ten Days*), Es Geschah am 20. Juli '55 (It Happened on the 20th of July). 1956—Rosen Für Bettina; Durch die Wälder, Durch die Auen.

Pabst is cited here not for his American film *A Modern Hero*, but rather for the retroactive glory of Louise Brooks in *Diary of a Lost Girl* and *Lulu*. The preeminence of Miss Brooks as the beauty of the twenties indicates the classic nature of the cinema, and its built-in machinery for an appeal to the verdict of history.

ROMAN POLANSKI (1933–)

FILMS: Shorts: 1957–1962—Two Men and a Wardrobe, When Angels Fall, The Fat and the Lean, Mammals. 1963—*Knife in the Water*. 1964—Les Plus Belles Escroqueries (Episode in Sketch Film). 1965—*Repulsion*. 1966—Cul-de-Sac. 1967—*The Fearless Vampire Killers*. 1968—*Rosemary's Baby*.

Roman Polanski has introduced a peculiarly European sensibility to the English-language cinema. His early short films were strongly influenced by the empty-world aesthetics of Beckett, Ionesco, and Pinter mixed with Polish cynicism, black humor, and Gothic horror. At his best, Polanski is genuinely unpredictable; at his worst, grievously pretentious. *Repulsion* contains too much undigested clinical material for comfort, but Polanski's handling of Catherine Deneuve anticipates in its perceptiveness Buñuel's definitive diagnosis of the devilish angel in *Belle de Jour*. *Cul-de-Sac* ultimately chokes on its incongruities as a kind of *Waiting for Godot* stranded in a Sir Walter Scott landscape. *The Fearless Vampire Killers* fails as a loving parody of a genre, but not before it has scored its well-calculated coups with a Jewish vampire unintimidated by the traditional malediction of the Cross, and a homosexual vampire rendering into reality one of the most frighteningly hilarious implications of the genre. Polanski's talent is as undeniable as his intentions are dubious.

ROBERTO ROSSELLINI (1906–   )

FILMS: 1936—Dafné (short subject). 1937–1938—Prélude
à l'Après-midi d'un Faune (short subject). 1939—Fantasia Sot-
tomarina, Il Tacchino Prepotente, La Vispa Teresa (short subjects).
1940–1941—Il Ruscello Blanca (short subject). 1941—La Nave
Bianca. 1942—Un Pilota Ritorna. 1943—Desiderio. 1944–1945
—*Open City*. 1946—*Paisan*. 1947–1948—*L'Amore*. 1948—
La Macchina Ammazzacattivi. 1949—*The Flowers of St. Francis*.
1949–1950—Stromboli. 1951–1952—Envy (fifth sketch in The
Seven Deadly Sins). 1952—*Europa 51* (The Greatest Love—released in America in 1954), Dov'e la Libertà. 1953—Ingrid Bergman sketch in We Are the Women, *Viaggio in Italia* (Strangers—released in America in 1955). 1954—Joan at the Stake, Fear. 1957—
India. 1959—*General Della Rovere*. 1960—Era Notte a Roma,
Viva Italia! 1961—*Vanina Vanini*. 1962—Anima Nera. 1963—
First episode in RoGoPaG. 1965—Age of Iron (TV documentary).
1966—*La Prise de Pouvoir par Louis XIV* (TV film released in
theatres abroad).

Rossellini's sublime films with Ingrid Bergman were years ahead
of their time, and are not fully appreciated even today in America. For the record, *Stromboli, The Greatest Love, Strangers,
Fear,* and *Joan at the Stake* constitute one of the most impressively biographical bodies of work in the history of the cinema. It
might be noted also that Rossellennui preceded Antoniennui by
several years.

FRANÇOIS TRUFFAUT (1932–   )

FILMS: Short Subjects: 1954—Une Visite (16 mm.). 1957—
Les Mistons. 1958—Une Histoire d'Eau (with Jean-Luc Godard).
1962—Antoine et Colette (Love at Twenty). Feature Films: 1959—
The Four Hundred Blows. 1960—*Shoot the Piano Player*. 1961—

Jules and Jim. 1964—The Soft Skin. 1966—*Fahrenheit 451.* 1968
—The Bride Wore Black, Stolen Kisses, The Siren of Mississippi.

Truffaut made the jump into the English-language cinema despite his lacking command of the English language. *Fahrenheit 451* is consequently as verbally clumsy as it is visually graceful and emotionally expressive. Truffaut ran for cover back to the womb of the French language, but not before he had demonstrated that there was something irreducibly universal in the cinema of Babel. Truffaut's sympathetically perceptive book on Hitchcock was further proof of this universality up to a point beyond which lurked the misunderstandings of translation and the lost nuances within a culture.

LUCHINO VISCONTI (1906–   )

FILMS: 1942—*Ossessione.* 1948—*La Terra Trema.* 1951—*Bellissima.* 1953—We Are the Women (Anna Magnani episode). 1954—*Senso.* 1957—*White Nights.* 1960—*Rocco and His Brothers.* 1962—*Boccaccio 70* (Romy Schneider episode). 1963—The Leopard. 1965—*Sandra.* 1967—The Stranger.

Luchino Visconti tried to break into the English-language market behind the blocking of Burt Lancaster, he of the broad shoulders and sullen expression. Lampedusa's *The Leopard* deserved much better than Lancaster, but the casting was typical of Visconti's bad luck in these matters. Back in the mid-fifties, Visconti had persuaded Ingrid Bergman and Marlon Brando to appear together in *Senso.* Visconti's casting coup of the decade was blithely vetoed by an Italian producer who preferred and substituted Alida Valli and Farley Granger! Valli was extraordinarily effective and Granger surprisingly so, but the emotional electricity was never turned on. Visconti has never received his due in America largely because his films were always ridiculously delayed in transit. American audiences have never seen *Ossessione* because of difficulties with the James M. Cain estate over the rights to *The Postman Always Rings Twice*. How differently would American highbrows have reacted to neorealism if its first example had been the sexual melodrama of *Ossessione* rather than the dramatic newsreel of Rossellini's *Open City*, and how much jittery photography would we have been spared from naïve Hollywood imitators of Rossellini's wobbly tripod? No one will ever know.

V.
LESS
THAN
MEETS
THE
EYE

These are the directors with reputations in excess of inspirations. In retrospect, it always seems that the personal signatures to their films were written with invisible ink.

JOHN HUSTON (1906–)

FILMS: 1941—*The Maltese Falcon.* 1942—In This Our Life, *Across the Pacific,* Report from the Aleutians (documentary). 1944 —*The Battle of San Pietro* (documentary). 1945—Let There Be Light (documentary). 1948—*The Treasure of the Sierra Madre, Key Largo.* 1949—*We Were Strangers.* 1950—*The Asphalt Jungle.* 1951—*The Red Badge of Courage.* 1952—*The African Queen.* 1953—Moulin Rouge. 1954—*Beat the Devil.* 1956—Moby Dick. 1957—Heaven Knows, Mr. Allison. 1958—The Barbarian and the Geisha, The Roots of Heaven. 1960—The Unforgiven. 1961—The Misfits. 1962—Freud. 1963—The List of Adrian Messenger. 1964—The Night of the Iguana. 1966—The Bible. 1967—Casino Royale, *Reflections in a Golden Eye.* 1969—Sinful Davey, A Walk with Love and Death.

The late James Agee canonized Huston prematurely in a *Life*-magazine auteur piece circa *Treasure of the Sierra Madre.* Agee was as wrong about Huston as Bazin was about Wyler, but Huston is still coasting on his reputation as a wronged individualist with an alibi for every bad movie. If it isn't Jack Warner, it's L. B. Mayer, and if it isn't L. B. Mayer, it's David O. Selznick, and if it isn't David O. Selznick, and if it isn't any of these, it's the whole rotten system of making movies. But who except Huston himself is to blame for the middle-brow banality of *Freud,* a personal project with built-in compromises for the "mass" audience. Huston has confused indifference with integrity for such a long time that he is no longer even the competent craftsman of *The Asphalt Jungle, The Maltese Falcon,* and *The African Queen,* films that owe more to casting coups than to directorial acumen. *Falcon,* particularly, is an uncanny match-up of Dashiell Hammett's literary characters with their visual doubles: Mary Astor, Humphrey Bogart, Sidney Greenstreet, Peter Lorre, and Elisha Cooke, Jr. Only Stendahl's Julien Sorel in search of Gérard Philipe can match *Falcon's* Pirandellian equation. Even in his palmier days, Huston displayed his material without projecting his personality. His technique has always been evasive, his camera often pitched at a standoffish angle away from the heart of the action. *Treasure of the Sierra Madre* and *Beat the Devil,* his two most overrated films, end with howling laughter on the sound track, an echo perhaps of the director laughing at his own feeble jokes.

Huston's dismaying decline notwithstanding, his theme has been remarkably consistent from *The Maltese Falcon* to *Reflections in a Golden Eye.* His protagonists almost invariably fail at what they set out to do, generally through no fault or flaw of their own. Unfortunately, Huston is less a pessimist than a defeatist, and his characters manage to be unlucky without the world being particularly out of joint. Huston's best film, *The Asphalt Jungle,* deals fittingly enough with collective defeat, and even his cast represents an interesting gallery of talented players who did not reach the heights they deserved: Sterling Hayden, the sensitive giant who never made the Wayne-Mitchum-Heston bracket; James Whitmore, who never became the second Spencer Tracy; Jean Hagen, who never obtained the dramatic-pathetic roles her talents demanded; Sam Jaffe, who never won an Oscar; Louis Calhern, who never mounted an adequate Lear although he was tall enough for tragedy; and Marc Lawrence, who never found his niche as the all-purpose villain. Only Marilyn Monroe was sprinkled with stardust after *Asphalt,* and Huston nearly finished her with the casual cruelty of *The Misfits.* The turning point in Huston's career was probably *Moby Dick.* In retrospect, he should have acted Ahab himself and let Orson Welles direct. This was his one gamble with greatness, and he lost, and like the cagey poker player he is, he has been playing it cool and corrupt ever since. *The List of Adrian Messenger,* a case in point, is so corrupt that even a fox hunt is in drag, not to mention *Beat the Devil,* which was consciously (and Capotishly) campy long before camp was even a gleam in Susan Sontag's eye.

As a stylist, Huston has always overloaded the physical with the moral. He never cared for that sissy stuff in drawing rooms where people try to communicate with each other through dialogue. Indeed, Huston's intimate scenes are often staged as if he were playing croquet with a sledgehammer. His antics with the two ridiculously graceful beach boys in *Night of the Iguana* are as false as the breast-thrusting jitterbug routine of the teenager in *The Asphalt Jungle* and all the nonsense with the wild horses in *The Misfits*. Movies are still primarily a dramatic medium, and if you can't establish characters indoors, you're not going to illuminate them with any clarity outdoors. Unfortunately, Huston, unlike Hawks, does not believe sufficiently in the action ethos to enjoy action for its own sake. A director like Cukor may choose to make himself comfortable inside, a director like Hawks outside, a director like Huston nowhere. Ultimately, Huston mistrusts his own dramatic material to the point that he makes excessively meaningful flourishes with the smokily suffused color in *Moulin Rouge* and the severely subdued color in *Reflections in a Golden Eye*. It must have looked good on the drawing board with *Moulin Rouge* color equaling artistic expression and *Reflections in a Golden Eye* colorlessness equaling sexual repression. Very little of the intended effect came through on the screen. Mere technique can never transcend conviction.

ELIA KAZAN (1909–   )

FILMS: 1945—*A Tree Grows in Brooklyn*. 1947—*Boomerang*, The Sea of Grass, Gentleman's Agreement. 1949—*Pinky*. 1950 —*Panic in the Streets*. 1951—*A Streetcar Named Desire*. 1952— *Viva Zapata!* 1953—Man on a Tightrope. 1954—*On the Waterfront*. 1955—*East of Eden*. 1956—Baby Doll. 1957—*A Face in the Crowd*. 1960—*Wild River*. 1961—*Splendor in the Grass*. 1963 —*America America*. 1969—The Arrangement.

Elia Kazan's position seemed dubious in 1963 when I wrote: "The Method of *A Streetcar Named Desire* has finally degenerated into the madness of *Splendor in the Grass*. Kazan's violence has always been more excessive than expressive, more mannered than meaningful. There is an edge of hysteria even to his pauses and silences, and the thin line between passion and neurosis has been crossed time and again. Yet, his brilliance with actors is incontestable. The revolutionary performances of Marlon Brando and the late James Dean are irrevocable, and *East of Eden*, though technically dated, is still a creditable achievement. Kazan's conscious efforts to adjust his personality to the classical forms of Ford (*Pinky, Wild River*) and Eisenstein (*Viva Zapata!*) were commendable if not entirely successful. Unfortunately, his career as a whole reflects an unending struggle between a stable camera and a jittery one. Significantly, his most nervous films—*Man on a Tightrope, Baby Doll,* and *Splendor in the Grass*—are ultimately his weakest. Kazan's gifts can never be written off entirely, but the evidence of decline is overwhelming."

Since 1963, Kazan has made one autobiographical film (*America America*) and written an autobiographical best-selling novel (*The Arrangement*) which he intends to film with Brando in the leading role. With an instinct more dramatic than epic, Kazan is nonetheless drifting into the realm of the epic. His art is more anguished and personal than ever before, less successful but more sympathetic. For the most part, however, it seems that Kazan intends to ignore his limitations rather than transcend them.

DAVID LEAN (1908–   )

FILMS: 1942—*In Which We Serve* (with Noël Coward). 1945 —*Blithe Spirit.* 1946—*Brief Encounter.* 1947—*This Happy Breed, Great Expectations.* 1949—*One Woman's Story.* 1950— Madeleine. 1951—*Oliver Twist.* 1952—*Breaking Through the Sound Barrier.* 1954—*Hobson's Choice.* 1955—*Summertime.* 1957—Bridge on the River Kwai. 1962—Lawrence of Arabia. 1965—Dr. Zhivago.

David Lean was thanking the Motion Picture Academy for his second Oscar back in 1963 while I was writing: "Lean's career has reached the point where the modest virtues of *Brief Encounter* and *Great Expectations* have been inflated with the hot air of *Lawrence of Arabia* and *The Bridge on the River Kwai,* films as pointlessly obscure in their way as that most muddled of all murder mysteries, *Madeleine.* By the time Lean gets around to propounding a question, no one really cares about the answer. The sheer logistics of *Lawrence* and *Kwai* cannot support the luxury of a directorial point of view. Lean is even more of an enigma than Lawrence, but the cinema as an expressive art form is not receptive to enigmas. Now that Lean has been enshrined in the various Academies, whatever artistic sensibility he once possessed is safely embalmed in the tomb of the impersonal cinema. Looking back past the shifting sands of *Lawrence* and the tangled underbrush of *Kwai,* one can fondly remember the tasteful performances of Celia Johnson and Trevor Howard (*Brief Encounter*), Ralph Richardson and Nigel Patrick (*Breaking the Sound Barrier*), John Mills and Brenda de Banzie (*Hobson's Choice*), and Katharine Hepburn (*Summertime*), but these deviations from obfuscation are no longer the measure of a director whose next logical project is a spectacle on the riddle of the Sphinx."

Since 1963, David Lean has labored on but one additional superproduction, *Dr. Zhivago,* a work with more commercial than critical success, a work also of the most impeccable impersonality, and not even an Oscar to show for such self-abnegation. Not that Lean is particularly faithful to Pasternak's extravagant emotions. Lean and his scenarist Robert Bolt are too coldly British for rousing Russian rhetoric. Ultimately, Dr. Zhivago suffers most from too little literary fat and too much visual Lean.

ROUBEN MAMOULIAN (1897–   )

FILMS: 1929—*Applause.* 1931—*City Streets.* 1932—*Dr. Jekyll and Mr. Hyde, Love Me Tonight.* 1933—*Queen Christina,* Song of Songs. 1934—We Live Again. 1935—Becky Sharp. 1936 —*The Gay Desperado.* 1937—High, Wide and Handsome. 1939 —Golden Boy. 1940—The Mark of Zorro. 1941—Blood and Sand. 1942—Rings on Her Fingers. 1948—Summer Holiday. 1957—Silk Stockings.

Mamoulian's tragedy is that of the innovator who runs out of innovations. *Applause* and *City Streets* have been amply honored in the textbooks for helping to break the sound barrier, and *Becky Sharp* is usually cited in any tract on the color film. The obviousness of Mamoulian's technique, like King's in *Tol'able David,* is ideal for anthologies. Unfortunately, while Mamoulian was performing his technical acrobatics, Lubitsch, Vidor, Sternberg, Hawks, and Ford swept into the sound era without breaking their stride. Except for *Applause,* Mamoulian's films date badly. *Love Me Tonight* is imitation Lubitsch with too many camera angles. *High, Wide and Handsome* misapplies Busby Berkeley's crane choreography to the great outdoors, and *The Gay Desperado,* not without its charms, resembles an impersonal operetta. The innovator has become an imitator, and the rest is mediocrity.

JOSEPH L. MANKIEWICZ (1909–   )

FILMS: 1946—Dragonwyck, Somewhere in the Night. 1947 —The Late George Apley, *The Ghost and Mrs. Muir.* 1948— Escape. 1949—*Letter to Three Wives, House of Strangers.* 1950— *No Way Out, All About Eve.* 1951—*People Will Talk.* 1952— *Five Fingers.* 1953—*Julius Caesar.* 1954—*Barefoot Contessa.* 1955—*Guys and Dolls.* 1958—*The Quiet American.* 1959— *Suddenly Last Summer.* 1963—Cleopatra. 1967—The Honey Pot. 1969—Couples, The Bawdy Bard.

The cinema of Joseph L. Mankiewicz is a cinema of intelligence without inspiration. His best films—*All About Eve* and *The Barefoot Contessa*—bear the signature of a genuine auteur. Turn off the sound track, and *The Barefoot Contessa* is closer to Lewin's *Pandora and the Flying Dutchman* than to Ophuls' *Lola Montès.* Mankiewicz' sensibility is decidedly more refined than Lewin's, but his technique is almost as pedestrian. With *Five Fingers,* Mankiewicz set out to prove that he could execute a technical exercise as well as anyone, and he failed honorably. *Cleopatra* and *The Honey Pot* should not be considered the last word on this intelligent American cinéaste because once his limitations are conceded, there is nothing wrong in enjoying his gibes at the Philistines. Mankiewicz' cranky liberalism sometimes gets the better of him, particularly when he wrenches scenes out of their context to inveigh against the evils of farm subsidies (*People Will Talk*) and oil-depletion allowances (*The Barefoot Contessa*). He despises the lechery of fat, greasy plutocrats, the disloyalty of opportunists, and the hypocrisy of moralists, but these commendable attitudes reflect a naïve morality unable to cope with the political hallucinations of Graham Greene (*The Quiet American*) and the sexual traumas of Tennessee Williams (*Suddenly Last Summer*). Although his wit scratches more than it bites, it is undeniable enough to place his area of greatest aptitude somewhere between the brittle worlds imitative of Oscar Wilde (*All About Eve*) and F. Scott Fitzgerald (*The Barefoot Contessa*). His vibrant women—Susan Hayward (*House of Strangers*), Bette Davis, and Anne Baxter (*Eve*), Danielle Darrieux (*Five Fingers*) and Ava Gardner (*Contessa*) —shine with special brilliance from midnight to the three o'clock in the morning of the soul.

LEWIS MILESTONE (1895–   )

FILMS: 1925—Seven Sinners. 1926—The Caveman, The New Klondike. 1927—*Two Arabian Knights*. 1928—The Garden of Eden, *The Racket*. 1929—The Betrayal, New York Nights. 1930 —*All Quiet on the Western Front*. 1931—*The Front Page*. 1932 —*Rain*. 1933—*Hallelujah, I'm a Bum*. 1934—The Captain Hates the Sea. 1935—Paris in Spring. 1936—Anything Goes. *The General Died at Dawn*. 1940—The Night of Nights, *Of Mice and Men*, Lucky Partners. 1941—My Life with Caroline. 1943—Edge of Darkness, The North Star. 1944—The Purple Heart. 1946—*A Walk in the Sun, The Strange Love of Martha Ivers*. 1948—*Arch of Triumph*, No Minor Vices. 1949—The Red Pony. 1950—Halls of Montezuma. 1952—Kangaroo, Les Miserables. 1953—Melba. 1955—They Who Dare. 1959—Pork Chop Hill. 1960—Ocean's Eleven. 1962—Mutiny on the Bounty.

A formalist of the Left, Milestone was hailed as the American Eisenstein after *All Quiet on the Western Front* and *The Front Page*. It is of course possible, though not highly probable, that Eisenstein himself might have ended up directing the Clan in *Ocean's Eleven* if he had remained in Hollywood. Just think of all the opportunities for dialectical montage in Las Vegas! Where else is the naked structure of capitalism so garishly visual? Unfortunately, Milestone's fluid camera style has always been dissociated from any personal viewpoint. The director's cynical detachment is more appropriate to the stylized surfaces of *The General Died at Dawn* and *The Night of Nights* than to the realistic depths of *All Quiet* and *Of Mice and Men.* A propagandist in press releases only, Milestone is almost the classic example of the uncommitted director. From the beginning, his editing was mechanical rather than analytical, and his tracking synthetic rather than expressive. Socially conscious film historians were therefore needlessly agitated by the miscellaneousness of his projects. *Anything Goes* or *The North Star:* What difference does it make? It might be said in Milestone's defense that he has never discriminated against doomed projects like *Rain* and *The Arch of Triumph.* His professionalism is as unyielding as it is meaningless, and not even the seismic eruptions of *Mutiny on the Bounty* can faze him.

CAROL REED (1906–   )

FILMS: 1936—Midshipman Easy, Laburnum Grove. 1937— Talk of the Devil, Bank Holiday. 1938—No Parking, Climbing High, A Girl Must Live, Penny Paradise. 1939—*The Stars Look Down* (1941 in New York), *Night Train* (1940 in New York). 1940 —The Girl in the News, *Kipps,* The Young Mr. Pitt. 1942–1945— Documentaries: The New Lot, The Way Ahead, The True Glory (with Garson Kanin). 1947—*Odd Man Out.* 1949—*Fallen Idol.* 1950—*The Third Man.* 1952—*The Outcast of the Islands.* 1953 —*The Man Between.* 1956—A Kid for Two Farthings, Trapeze. 1958—The Key. 1960—Our Man in Havana. 1963—The Running Man. 1965—The Agony and the Ecstasy. 1968—Oliver!

The decline of Carol Reed since *Outcast of the Islands* is too obvious to be belabored. The director of *Odd Man Out, The Fallen Idol,* and *The Third Man* displayed undeniable talent and feeling at one time, particularly with ensemble acting. His modulated sound tracks seemed impressive in an era when understatement was generally overrated. Similarly, his editing of off-angle compositions produced a misleading impression of visual complexity. Today the technique of even his "golden" period looks too turgid (*Odd Man Out*), too fastidious (*The Fallen Idol*), and too elaborate (*The Third Man*). Nowhere does the director's personality grip the literary themes of F. L. Green, Graham Greene, and Joseph Conrad. From *The Man Between* to that man on the ceiling—*Michelangelo*—Reed steadily lost control of his medium as his feigned objectivity disintegrated into imperviousness. Reed's career demonstrates that a director who limits himself to solving technical problems quickly lapses into the decadence of the inappropriate effect. For example, Reed's fateful camera angles in *The Key* only emphasize the dishonesty of Carl Foreman's script.

Still, Reed's best films seem to have survived their director, particularly in the felicitous charm of Michael Redgrave's *Kipps,* Rex Harrison's agent in *Night Train,* and Emlyn Williams's rogue in the otherwise overrated *The Stars Look Down.* F. J. McCormick in *Odd Man Out* lingers in the mind, as do James Mason and Claire Bloom in *The Man Between,* Ralph Richardson in *Fallen Idol,* and Celia Johnson in *A Kid for Two Farthings.* Perhaps most memorable of all Reed readings is that of Conrad's heroic rhetoric in *Outcast of the Islands* by Trevor Howard and Ralph Richardson. If François Truffaut had understood and appreciated the English language, he would not have been in such a strategic position to write off Carol Reed, as it turned out, prematurely.

WILLIAM WELLMAN (1896–   )

FILMS: 1923—The Man Who Won, Second Hand Love, Big Dan. 1924—-The Vagabond Trail, Cupid's Fireman, Not a Drum Was Heard, The Circus Cowboy. 1926—When Husbands Flirt, The Boob, The Cat's Pajamas, You Never Know Women. 1927—*Wings.* 1928—Legion of Condemned, Ladies of the Mob, *Beggars of Life.* 1929—Chinatown Nights, The Man I Love, Woman Trap. 1930—Dangerous Paradise, Young Eagles, Maybe It's Love, Steel Highway. 1931—*The Public Enemy,* Other Men's Women, Star Witness, Night Nurse, Safe in Hell. 1932—Love is a Racket, *Hatchet Man,* So Big, Purchase Price, The Conquerors. 1933—Frisco Jenny, Central Airport, Lady of the Night, Lilly Turner, College Coach, *Heroes for Sale,* Midnight Mary, *Wild Boys of the Road.* 1934—

Looking for Trouble, Stingaree, *The President Vanishes*. 1935—The Call of the Wild, Robin Hood of El Dorado. 1936—Small Town Girl. 1937—*A Star Is Born, Nothing Sacred*. 1938—Men with Wings. 1939—*Beau Geste, The Light That Failed*. 1940—Reaching for the Sun. 1942—*Roxie Hart*, The Great Man's Lady, Thunder Birds. 1943—*Ox-Bow Incident*, Lady of Burlesque. 1944—Buffalo Bill. 1945—This Man's Navy, *Story of G.I. Joe*. 1946—Gallant Journey. 1947—Magic Town. 1948—The Iron Curtain, Happy Years, The Next Voice You Hear. 1949—*Battleground*. 1950—Across the Wide Missouri, Westward the Women. 1951—*Yellow Sky*. 1952—My Man and I. 1953—Island in the Sky. 1954—*High and the Mighty*, Track of the Cat. 1955—Blood Alley. 1956—*Goodbye, My Lady*. 1958—Darby's Rangers, Lafayette Escadrille.

With Wellman, crudity is too often mistaken for sincerity. What is at issue here is not the large number of bad films he has made, but a fundamental deficiency in his direction of good projects. On parallel subjects, he runs a poorer second to good directors than he should. *The Public Enemy* with Cagney should not be all that inferior to Hawks's *Scarface*, or *Nothing Sacred* with Lombard and Hecht to McCarey's *The Awful Truth*, or *Story of G.I. Joe* with Mitchum and Steele to Ford's *They Were Expendable*. Wellman, like Wyler, Huston, and Zinnemann, is a recessive director, one whose images tend to recede from the foreground to the background in the absence of a strong point of view. *Roxie Hart* is framed like a Sennett primitive without the Sennett pacing. *The Light That Failed* keeps floating back in its frame like a Sunday painting. *The Ox-Bow Incident* looks grotesque today with its painted backdrops treated like the natural vistas in a Ford Western. Again, a Hollywood director cannot be criticized for working with fake sets, but his technique can be called into question if it emphasizes the fakery. With Wellman, as with so many other directors, objectivity is the last refuge of mediocrity.

BILLY WILDER (1906–   )

FILMS: 1942—*The Major and the Minor*. 1943—*Five Graves to Cairo*. 1944—*Double Indemnity*. 1945—*The Lost Weekend*. 1948—The Emperor Waltz, *A Foreign Affair*. 1950—*Sun-*

set Boulevard. 1951—*Ace in the Hole.* 1953—*Stalag 17.* 1954—
Sabrina. 1955—The Seven Year Itch. 1957—Spirit of St. Louis,
Love in the Afternoon. 1958—*Witness for the Prosecution.* 1959—
Some Like It Hot. 1960—*The Apartment.* 1961—One, Two,
Three. 1963—Irma La Douce. 1964—*Kiss Me Stupid.* 1966—
The Fortune Cookie. 1969—Sherlock Holmes.

Billy Wilder is too cynical to believe even his own cynicism. Toward the end of *Stalag 17,* William Holden bids a properly cynical adieu to his prison-camp buddies. He ducks into the escape
tunnel for a second, then quickly pops up, out of character, with
a boyish smile and a friendly wave, and then ducks down for
good. Holden's sentimental waste motion in a tensely timed
melodrama demonstrates the cancellation principle in Wilder's
cinema. For example, the director's irresponsible Berlin films —
A Foreign Affair and *One, Two, Three*—have been wrongly
criticized for social irresponsibility. This is too serious a charge
to level at a series of tasteless gags, half anti-Left and half anti-
Right, adding up to Wilder's conception of political sophistication. Even his best films—*The Major and the Minor, Sunset
Boulevard, Stalag 17,* and *Some Like It Hot*—are marred by
the director's penchant for gross caricature, especially with peripheral characters. All of Wilder's films decline in retrospect because of visual and structural deficiencies. Only Laughton's
owlish performance makes *Witness for the Prosecution* look like
the tour de force it was intended to be, and only Jack Lemmon
keeps *The Apartment* from collapsing into the cellar of morbid
psychology. Wilder deserves full credit for these performances,
and for many of the other felicities that redeem his films from the
superficial nastiness of his personality. He has failed only to the
extent that he has been proved inadequate for the more serious
demands of middle-class tragedy (*Double Indemnity*) and social
allegory (*Ace in the Hole*). A director who can crack jokes about
suicide attempts (*Sabrina* and *The Apartment*) and thoughtlessly
brutalize charming actresses like Jean Arthur (*Foreign Affair*)
and Audrey Hepburn (*Sabrina*) is hardly likely to make a coherent film on the human condition.

    If Billy Wilder's stock has risen slightly in recent years with
the escalation of satiric savagery in *Kiss Me Stupid* and *The For-*

tune Cookie, it is not so much because of the films themselves, but rather because Wilder has chosen to remain himself while almost everyone else has been straining to go mod. Curiously, Wilder seems to have completely abandoned the Lubitsch tradition he upheld ever so briefly with *Love in the Afternoon,* an Audrey Hepburn vehicle not without its cruelties toward agingly jaded Gary Cooper, but not without its beauties as well.

WILLIAM WYLER (1902–   )

FILMS: 1926—Lazy Lightning, Stolen Ranch. 1927—Blazing Days, Hard Fists, Straight Shootin', The Border Cavalier, Desert Dust. 1928—Thunder Riders, Anybody Here Seen Kelly? 1929—The Shakedown, Love Trap. 1930—*Hell's Heroes,* The Storm. 1932—*A House Divided,* Tom Brown of Culver. 1933—Her First Mate, *Counsellor at Law.* 1935—The Good Fairy, *The Gay Deception.* 1936—Come and Get It (with Howard Hawks), *Dodsworth,* These Three. 1937—*Dead End.* 1938—*Jezebel.* 1939—*Wuthering Heights.* 1940—*The Letter,* The Westerner. 1941—*The Little Foxes.* 1942—Mrs. Miniver. 1943–1945—The Memphis Belle, The Fighting Lady (documentaries). 1946—*The Best Years of Our Lives.* 1949—The Heiress. 1951—*Detective Story.* 1952—Carrie. 1953—*Roman Holiday.* 1955—The Desperate Hours. 1956—*Friendly Persuasion.* 1958—The Big Country. 1959—Ben Hur. 1962—The Children's Hour. 1965—*The Collector.* 1966—How to Steal a Million. 1968—Funny Girl.

Back in 1963, I denounced a career that was inflating without expanding: "There is something poetically just in the announcement that William Wyler will direct *Sound of Music,* the *Ben Hur* of Broadway musicals, for Darryl F. Zanuck. If ever there were a prescription for elephantiasis, this is it. A French hack director once expressed his admiration for Wyler as 'the style without a style.' Precisely. *The Little Foxes* owes more to Toland's camera than to Wyler's direction, and *The Letter* still reverberates somewhat with the repressed passion of Bette Davis and James Stephenson. Otherwise, Wyler's career is a cipher as far as personal direction is concerned. What has become increasingly apparent in retrospect is a misanthropic tendency in Wyler's technique, particularly with romantic material like *Wuthering Heights* and *Roman Holiday*. It would seem that Wyler's admirers have long mistaken a lack of feeling for emotional restraint."

As it turned out, Robert Wise, and not William Wyler, directed *Sound of Music* with such straight-faced sobriety that this oversized marshmallow broke all box-office records. For his part, Wyler redeemed his reputation somewhat with *The Collector,* a project for which his meticulous craftsmanship was ideally suited. Welles has called Wyler not inaptly the great producer among directors. No matter. Wyler is back beating on the door of the bonanza musical with Barbra Streisand, no less, in *Funny Girl*. It is as if *The Collector* were an unforeseen interlude in the director's inevitably dismal destiny.

FRED ZINNEMANN (1907–   )

FILMS: Short Subjects: 1938—A Friend Indeed, The Story of Dr. Carver, That Mothers Might Live, Tracking the Sleeping Death, They Live Again. 1939—Weather Wizards, While America Sleeps, Help Wanted!, One Against the World, The Ash Can Fleet, Forgotten Victory. 1940—The Old South, The Way in the Wilderness, The Great Meddler. 1941—Forbidden Passage, Your Last Act. 1942—The Lady or the Tiger? Features: 1935—Waves. 1942—Kid Glove Killer, Eyes in the Night. 1944—The Seventh Cross. 1946—Little Mr. Jim. 1947—My Brother Talks to Horses. 1948—*The Search*. 1949—*Act of Violence*. 1950—*The Men*. 1951—*Teresa*. 1952—*High Noon*, The Member of the Wedding. 1953—*From Here to Eternity*. 1955—Oklahoma! 1957—*A Hatful of Rain*. 1959—*The Nun's Story*. 1960—The Sundowners. 1963—Behold a Pale Horse. 1966—*A Man for All Seasons*.

Fred Zinnemann's career reflects the rise and fall of the realist aesthetic in Hollywood. He directed the first screen performances of Montgomery Clift (*The Search*) and Marlon Brando (*The Men*). His looseness and gentleness with actors contributed to the nice-guy image one does not usually associate with realists in Hollywood. Zinnemann is hardly a Stroheim. Indeed, his neatness and decorum constitute his gravest artistic defects. *The Search, Act of Violence, The Men,* and *Teresa* represented a period of promise. These films were not entirely devoid of modest virtues even though they were ultimately compromised by sentimental formulas. It is the payoff films—*High Noon, From Here to Eternity, The Nun's Story,* and *A Man for All Seasons*—that most vividly reveal the superficiality of Zinnemann's personal commitment. At its best, his direction is inoffensive; at its worst, it is downright dull. Zinnemann has finally settled down to being a semirealist, stepping gingerly around such subgenres as the moralistic melodrama (*Act of Violence*), the anti-populist anti-Western (*High Noon*), the empty sidewalk stage adaptation (*Member of the Wedding, A Hatful of Rain*), the pig-pen musical (*Oklahoma!*), and the painless political allegory (*Behold a Pale Horse*). By draining every subject and every situation of any possible emotional excitement, Fred Zinnemann is now widely considered in academic circles as the screen's most honest director. Besides, he has two Oscars and four scrolls from the New York Film Critics Circle. His inclusion in any objective history of the American cinema is mandatory, but his true vocation remains the making of antimovies for antimoviegoers. Even the realism that once served as his rationale seems to have been displaced in fashionable circles by newfangled notions of stylization and distancing. No matter. Fred Zinnemann will plod on with all the solid virtues of the vestryman and the modest countenance of the truth-seeker. Perhaps there is not in Zinnemann enough of the redeeming outrageousness of the compulsive entertainer. In cinema, as in all art, only those who risk the ridiculous have a real shot at the sublime.

VI.
LIGHTLY
LIKABLE

These are talented but uneven directors with the saving grace of unpretentiousness.

BUSBY BERKELEY (1895–   )

FILMS: 1935—*Gold Diggers of 1935*, Bright Lights, I Live for Love. 1936—Stagestruck. 1937—The Go-Getter, Hollywood Hotel. 1938—Men Are Such Fools, Garden of the Moon, Comet over Broadway. 1939—They Made Me a Criminal, *Babes in Arms*, Fast and Furious. 1940—Strike Up the Band, Forty Little Mothers. 1941 —Babes on Broadway, Blonde Inspiration. 1942—*For Me and My Gal.* 1943—The Gang's All Here. 1948—Cinderella Jones. 1949—*Take Me Out to the Ball Game.*

Busby Berkeley is a name that conjures up a certain form of spectacle in Hollywood musicals of the thirties. Although Berkeley's choreographic and directorial contributions span a period of over thirty years, his maximum influence was exerted mainly through the series of *Gold Digger* movies. It is customary for film historians to assume that Busby Berkeley's style of mass choreography and aerial cinematography were completely eclipsed by the relative grace and simplicity of the Fred Astaire-Ginger Rogers musicals. Actually, Berkeley and Astaire both overlapped and coexisted as stylistic alternatives for the Hollywood musical to follow. At his best, Berkeley's spectacle effects possessed a giddy, vertiginous, disorienting charm. If his musical numbers were larger than life, it was because he found Hollywood sound stages less constricting than the Broadway boards. Berkeley's vitality and ingenuity transcended the limitations of his sensibility, and he bequeathed to posterity an entertaining record of the audacity of an escapist era.

As a choreographer from the crane, Berkeley scrawled a kind of skywriting signature clearly visible from the sound stages of *42nd Street* (1933) to the circus grounds of *Jumbo* (1962). As a moderately entertaining director, he held the fort for the musical between the end of the Astaire-Rogers cycle and the beginning of the Minnelli-Donen-Kelly period. He can claim some of the credit for the spectacular evolution of Judy Garland and Gene Kelly into the titans of the Metro musical. If some of his socialized floral patterns do indeed look a bit naïve and prematurely anti-Astairish today, they did have their time and place in the depths of the Depression when the difference between quality and quantity did not seem too important. Taken as a whole, Berkeley's contributions deserve better than being consigned to the sniggerings of Camp followers. Busby Berkeley deserves enduring respect as the Méliès of the Musical.

My most poignant recollection of Berkeleyana is the "Lullaby of Broadway" number from *The Gold Diggers of 1935.* For years and years I retained the image of a playgirl plunging to her death from a skyscraper ballroom, and then the lingering contemplation of an empty apartment with a hungry kitten waiting to be fed and outside somewhere a chorus singing "Good night, baby" as if perchance to die was but to dream of a lullaby as a requiem mass. *The Gold Diggers of 1935* revisited turned out to be a long prologue, by turns cynical and fatuous, to a very short production number as a show within a show. I had almost begun to doubt my moviegoing memory when suddenly the playgirl plunged to her death and the traveling camera lingered over an empty apartment, and the lullaby engulfed the screen once more as it had once long ago in the darkest days of the Depression. The magic of Busby Berkeley had been miraculously reconfirmed.

HENRY CORNELIUS (1913–1958)

FILMS: 1949—*Passport to Pimlico.* 1951—The Galloping Major. 1954—*Genevieve.* 1955—I Am a Camera. 1960—Next to No Time.

He will be best remembered for *Genevieve,* a luminous comedy of the outdoors, a film glowing with a Defoe-like sense of property. Cornelius was a comic potentiality cut short by death; and, like many of the more colorful contributors to the British cinema, he was not British himself.

JOHN CROMWELL (1888–   )

FILMS: 1929—*Close Harmony, Dance of Life.* 1930—*Street of Chance,* The Texan, For the Defense, Tom Sawyer. 1931—Scandal Sheet, Unfaithful, Vice Squad, Rich Man's Folly. 1932—World and the Flesh. 1933—Sweepings, Silver Cord, Double Harness, Ann Vickers. 1934—This Man Is Mine, Spitfire, *Of Human Bondage,* The Fountain. 1935—Village Tale, Jalna, I Dream Too Much. 1936 —Little Lord Fauntleroy, To Mary with Love, Banjo on My Knee. 1937—*The Prisoner of Zenda.* 1938—Algiers. 1939—*Made for Each Other,* In Name Only, Abe Lincoln in Illinois. 1940—Victory. 1941—*So Ends Our Night.* 1942—*Son of Fury.* 1944—*Since You Went Away.* 1945—*The Enchanted Cottage.* 1946—*Anna and the King of Siam.* 1947—Dead Reckoning, Night Song. 1950 —*Caged,* The Company She Keeps. 1951—The Racket. 1958— *The Goddess.* 1961—A Matter of Morals. 1963—*The Scavengers.*

From Nancy Carroll (*Close Harmony*) to Kim Stanley (*The Goddess*), the motto of Cromwell's cinema has been *cherchez la femme.* Whether by luck or design, his eclectic career has been redeemed by the iconographical contributions of Irene Dunne, Katharine Hepburn, Bette Davis, Madeleine Carroll, Mary Astor, Carole Lombard, Betty Field, Margaret Sullavan, Gene Tierney, Jennifer Jones, and Dorothy McGuire. Fortunately, Cromwell's formal deficiencies seldom obscure the beautiful drivers of his vehicles. Cromwell may be remembered ultimately as the perfect director for David O. Selznick, himself a noted connoisseur of feminine beauty. If Cromwell's career be but a footnote to film history, a footnote should be appended to that footnote for the curious sado-masochistic relationship between Hope Emerson and Eleanor Parker in *Caged,* that minor classic of repression.

MICHAEL CURTIZ (1888–1962)

FILMS: 1927—Moon of Israel, The Third Degree, A Million Bid, The Desired Woman, Good Time Charlie. 1928—Tenderloin. 1929—Noah's Ark, Glad Rag Doll, Madonna of Avenue A, Hearts in Exile. 1930—Mammy, Under a Texas Moon, The Matrimonial Bed. 1931—River's End, Bright Lights, God's Gift to Women, Soldier's Plaything. 1932—Woman from Monte Carlo, Strange Love of Molly Louvain, Doctor X, *Cabin in the Cotton.* 1933—*20,000 Years in Sing Sing,* History of the Wax Museum, The Keyhole, Private Detective 62, Goodbye Again, Kennel Murder Case, Female. 1934—Mandalay; Jimmy, the Gent; The Key, Brutal Agent. 1935 —Case of the Curious Bride, *Black Fury,* Front Page Woman, Little Big Shot, *Captain Blood.* 1936—The Walking Dead, Stolen Holiday, *Charge of the Light Brigade.* 1937—*Kid Galahad,* Mountain Justice, The Perfect Specimen. 1938—Gold Is Where You Find It, *The Adventures of Robin Hood* (with William Keighley), *Four Daughters,* Four's a Crowd, *Angels with Dirty Faces.* 1939— *Dodge City, Daughters Courageous, The Private Lives of Elizabeth and Essex, Four Wives.* 1940—Virginia City, *The Sea Hawk, Santa Fe Trail.* 1941—*The Sea Wolf,* Dive Bomber. 1942—*Casablanca, Yankee Doodle Dandy,* Captains of the Clouds. 1943—Mission to Moscow, This Is the Army. 1944—Passage to Marseilles, Janie. 1945—Roughly Speaking, *Mildred Pierce.* 1946—Night and Day. 1947—Life with Father, The Unsuspected. 1948—Romance on the High Seas. 1949—*Flamingo Road,* My Dream Is Yours, The Lady Takes a Sailor. 1950—*The Breaking Point,* Bright Leaf. 1951—Jim Thorpe—All-American, *Force of Arms,* I'll See You in My Dreams. 1952—The Will Rogers Story, The Jazz Singer. 1954 —The Boy from Oklahoma, The Egyptian, White Christmas. 1955 —We're No Angels. 1956—The Scarlet Hour, The Vagabond King, The Best Things in Life Arc Free. 1957—The Helen Morgan Story. 1958—The Proud Rebel, King Creole. 1959—The Hangman, The Man in the Net. 1960—The Adventures of Huckleberry Finn, A Breath of Scandal. 1961—Francis of Assisi, The Comancheros.

Perhaps more than any other director, Curtiz reflected the strengths and weaknesses of the studio system in Hollywood. This most amiable of Warners' technicians faithfully served the studio's contract players from Dolores Costello to Doris Day. When one speaks of a typical Warners' film in the thirties and forties, one is generally speaking of a typical Curtiz film of those periods. He directed many of Bette Davis's lesser bread-and-butter vehicles, and shared the Errol Flynn cycle with Raoul Walsh. He guided James Cagney (*Yankee Doodle Dandy*) and Joan Crawford (*Mildred Pierce*) to Oscars, and saw the Lane sisters through the Depression. He helped project the memorably anarchic personalities of Cagney, Bogart, Garfield, and Muni in between other less memorable projects. After *Force of Arms,* his career went to the dogs. If many of the early Curtiz films are hardly worth remembering, none of the later ones are even worth seeing. What the collapse of studio discipline meant to Curtiz and to Hollywood was the bottom dropping out of routine film-making. The director's one enduring masterpiece is, of course, *Casablanca,* the happiest of happy accidents, and the most decisive exception to the auteur theory.

HARRY D'ARRAST (1897–1968)

FILMS: 1927—Service for Ladies, *A Gentleman of Paris,* Serenade. 1928—Magnificent Flirt, *Dry Martini.* 1930—*Raffles, Laughter.* 1933—*Topaze.* 1935—The Three Cornered Hat.

His wit was said to be as dry as his own *Dry Martini.* One of the more colorful directors of the late twenties and early thirties, Harry D'Arrast expressed some of the elegance of his time with grace and charm. *Laughter* and *Topaze,* seen today, seem fragile and vulnerable exceptions to the boisterousness of mass taste.

DELMER DAVES (1904–   )

FILMS: 1943—Destination Tokyo. 1944—The Very Thought of You, Hollywood Canteen. 1945—Pride of the Marines. 1947—*The Red House, Dark Passage.* 1948—To the Victor. 1949—A Kiss in the Dark, Task Force. 1950—*Broken Arrow.* 1951—Bird of Paradise. 1952—Return of the Texan. 1953—Treasure of the Golden Condor, Never Let Me Go. 1954—Demetrius and the Gladiators, Drum Beat. 1956—Jubal, *The Last Wagon.* 1957—*3:10 to Yuma.* 1958—*Cowboy,* Kings Go Forth, The Badlanders. 1959—The Hanging Tree, *A Summer Place.* 1961—Parrish, Susan Slade. 1963—Spencer's Mountain. 1964—*Youngblood Hawke.* 1965—The Battle of the Villa Fiorita.

If you have no kind thoughts for the authoritative absurdities of *Dark Passage, The Red House, A Summer Place, Rome Adventure* and *Youngblood Hawke,* read no further. Delmer Daves is the property of those who can enjoy stylistic conviction in an intellectual vacuum. The movies of Delmer Daves are fun of a very special kind. Call it Camp or call it Corn. The director does not so much transcend his material as mingle with it.

EDMUND GOULDING (1891–1959)

FILMS: 1925—Sun-Up; Sally, Irene and Mary. 1926—Paris. 1927—Women Love Diamonds. 1928—Love, The Trespasser, Paramount on Parade, Devil's Holiday. 1931—Reaching for the Moon, Night Angel. 1932—*Grand Hotel,* Blondie of the Follies. 1934—Riptide. 1935—The Flame Within. 1937—That Certain Woman. 1938—*White Banners, The Dawn Patrol.* 1939—*Dark Victory, We Are Not Alone, The Old Maid.* 1940—Till We Meet Again. 1941—*The Great Lie.* 1943—*The Constant Nymph, Claudia.* 1946—Of Human Bondage, *The Razor's Edge.* 1947— *Nightmare Alley.* 1949—Everybody Does It. 1950—*Mr. 880.* 1952—We're Not Married. 1953—Down Among the Sheltering Palms. 1956—*Teen Age Rebel.* 1958—Mardi Gras.

Goulding's career, like his talent, was discreet and tasteful. A vehicle director with something extra, he lent his most threadbare projects a feeling of concern. His best films—*Grand Hotel, The Constant Nymph, Claudia, The Razor's Edge,* and *Nightmare Alley*—are seldom attributed to him. *Grand Hotel* won an Academy Award in a year when he was not even nominated for direction. His remakes—*The Dawn Patrol* and *Till We Meet Again*—were markedly but not disgracefully inferior to the originals of Hawks and Garnett (*One-Way Passage*). Even when he remade his Gloria Swanson vehicle (*The Trespasser*) into a Bette Davis vehicle (*That Certain Woman*), he did not gain or lose much in the process. Plus and minus all the way down the line. *Dark Victory, The Old Maid,* and *The Great Lie* are afflicted by George Brent and excessive melodrama, but they are still much closer to Wyler's Davis counterparts, *Jezebel, The Letter,* and *The Little Foxes,* than anyone would have suspected at the time. Goulding not only enhanced his actresses—Greta Garbo, Bette Davis, Dorothy McGuire, Joan Fontaine, Gene Tierney—but also his supporting actresses—Geraldine Fitzgerald, Jane Bryan, Mary Astor, Anne Baxter, the latter two winning Oscars, and who can forget Marilyn Monroe in a bathing suit in *We're Not Married*?

BYRON HASKIN (1899–   )

FILMS: 1927—Matinee Ladies, Irish Hearts, Ginsberg the Great. 1928—The Siren. 1947—*I Walk Alone*. 1948—Man-Eater of Kumaon. 1949—*Too Late for Tears*. 1950—Treasure Island. 1951—Tarzan's Peril, Warpath, Silver City. 1952—The Denver and the Rio Grande. 1953—The War of the Worlds, His Majesty O'Keefe. 1954—*The Naked Jungle*. 1955—Long John Silver, Conquest of Space. 1956—The First Texan, The Boss. 1958 —From the Earth to the Moon. 1959—Little Savage. 1960—September Storm. 1961—*Armored Command*. 1963—Captain Sinbad. 1964—Robinson Crusoe on Mars.

Byron Haskin's directorial career has seemed so incidental to the processes of personal expression in an impersonal industry that he must be praised indeed for as many as four achievements that linger in the memory, namely, *I Walk Alone, Too Late for Tears, The Naked Jungle,* and *Armored Command,* genre films all with unexpected deposits of feeling and comedy.

HENRY HATHAWAY (1898–   )

FILMS: 1933—Wild Horse Mesa, Heritage of the Desert, Under the Tonto Rim, Sunset Pass, Man of the Forest, To the Last Man. 1934—*Come on Marines,* Last Round-Up, Thundering Herd, *The Witching Hour,* Now and Forever. 1935—*Lives of a Bengal Lancer, Peter Ibbetson.* 1936—*Trail of the Lonesome Pine;* Go West, Young Man. 1937—*Souls at Sea.* 1938—*Spawn of the North.* 1939—The Real Glory. 1940—Johnny Apollo, Brigham Young. 1941—*The Shepherd of the Hills, Sundown.* 1942—Ten Gentlemen from West Point, *China Girl.* 1944—*Home in Indiana, Wing and a Prayer.* 1945—Nob Hill, *The House on 92nd Street.*

1946—*The Dark Corner, 13 Rue Madeleine.* 1947—*Kiss of Death.* 1948—*Call Northside 777.* 1949—Down to the Sea in Ships. 1950—The Black Rose. 1951—*You're in the Navy Now, Rawhide, 14 Hours, The Desert Fox.* 1952—*Diplomatic Courier.* 1953—*Niagara,* White Witch Doctor. 1954—Prince Valiant, Garden of Evil. 1955—The Racers. 1956—The Bottom of the Bottle, 23 Paces to Baker Street. 1957—Legend of the Lost. 1958— *From Hell to Texas.* 1959—Woman Obsessed. 1960—*Seven Thieves, North to Alaska.* 1963—How the West Was Won (with John Ford and George Marshall). 1964—Circus World. 1965— *The Sons of Katie Elder.* 1966—*Nevada Smith.* 1968—5 Card Stud. 1969—True Grit.

Henry Hathaway is a director without complexes or neuroses even when his material is saturated with these modern accouterments. The lunacies of *14 Hours* and *Niagara* are treated with the grotesque straightforwardness of the action genre. The conventional distinctions between realism and romanticism are irrelevant to Hathaway's career. The legendary romanticism of *Peter Ibbetson* can now be clearly traced to Lee Garmes's camera, and the semidocumentary surfaces of *The House on 92nd Street, 13 Rue Madeleine,* and *Call Northside 777* can be dismissed as a passing fancy of the American cinema. Hathaway's charm consists chiefly of minor virtues, particularly a sense of humor, uncorrupted by major pretensions, but this charm is also a limiting factor. The professional detractors of Ford and Hawks almost invariably attempt to palm off Hathaway as a reasonable facsimile, but such a comparison is patently absurd. Hathaway has directed many likable films—*The Witching Hour, The Lives of a Bengal Lancer, Spawn of the North, Shepherd of the Hills, China Girl, From Hell to Texas,* and *North to Alaska.* Even *The Dark Corner,* a poor man's *Laura,* and *The Kiss of Death,* a conformist gangster film, have their merits. Unfortunately, Hathaway has directed, however amiably, too many clinkers. On balance, Hathaway has had a creditable career on Hollywood's roulette wheel, but nothing approaching the high plateau of Ford and Hawks. He is probably closer to Wellman, though Hathaway is neater and less pretentious.

GARSON KANIN (1912–   )

FILMS: 1938—*A Man to Remember*, Next Time I Marry.
1939—*The Great Man Votes, Bachelor Mother.* 1940—*My
Favorite Wife*, They Knew What They Wanted. 1941—*Tom, Dick
and Harry.* 1945—The True Glory (with Carol Reed). 1969—
Where It's At.

As a playwright, Kanin tended to imitate George S. Kaufman.
His direction of film comedies derived from Capra and McCarey
to such an extent that *Cahiers du Cinéma* once erroneously
listed Kanin's *My Favorite Wife* as a McCarey film. Even so, his
work is not without charm and talent. However, his major contribution to the American cinema consists of the inventive scripts
he provided George Cukor for the glorious Judy Holliday cycle
of psychological comedies.

BURT KENNEDY (1923–   )

FILMS: 1961—The Canadians. 1964—*Mail Order Bride.*
1965—*The Rounders.* 1966—*The Money Trap*, The Return of the
Seven. 1967—*Welcome to Hard Times*, The War Wagon. 1968—
The Good Guys and the Bad Guys. 1969—Young Billie
Young.

Burt Kennedy wrote the scripts for some of Budd Boetticher's
best Westerns, but Kennedy's directorial style seems more dis-
cursive and less dramatic than Boetticher's. There is also more
realistic and psychological clutter in Kennedy's mise-en-scène
than in Boetticher's. Kennedy's directorial career has suffered
from one false start (*The Canadians*) and six rides in almost as
many directions. *Mail Order Bride* and *The Rounders* were low-
key folksy exercises on the sexual mores of the New West. *The
Money Trap* was unexpectedly poetic in its evocation of forties
fakery and urban melodrama. *Welcome to Hard Times* rattled in
its hard formal frame as a perverse statement of violence and

sexuality in the allegorical West. The least personal of Kennedy's films were *The War Wagon,* a frolicsome vehicle for John Wayne and Kirk Douglas, and *The Return of the Seven,* a dried-up reprise of *The Magnificent Seven* of John Sturges. Kennedy's best films have been aided in no small measure by the weather-beaten talent and iconography of Glenn Ford, Henry Fonda, Rita Hayworth, Ricardo Montalban and Aldo Ray. An interestingly talented writer-director, Kennedy seems to direct his ideas somewhat too tightly and schematically at the expense of the natural flow of his narrative. Even at its best, Kennedy's direction seems too strained for his scenario.

ALEXANDER KORDA (1893–1956)

FILMS: HUNGARIAN PERIOD: 1916—Egy tiszti Kardbojt, Feher éjszakak, Vergödö szivek, Nagymama, Mesek az Ivógepröl, Egymillio fontos bankó. 1917—Magnas Miska, A Kétszivü férfi, Szent Pter Esernyöje, A Gölyakalifa, Magia, Faun, Harrison and Harrison, A Kétlelku Asszony. 1918—Az Aranyembrr, Mary Ann, Se Ki se be. 1919—Ave Caesar, Feher Rosza, A 111-es, Yamata. AUSTRIAN AND GERMAN PERIOD: 1920—Seine Majestät das Bettlekind. 1922—Herren der Meere, Eine Versunkene Welt, Samson und Dalila. 1923—Der Unbekannte Morgen. 1924—Jedermanns Frau, Tragödie in Hause Habsbourg. 1925—Der Tänzer meiner Frau. 1926—Madame wünscht keine Kinder. AMERICAN PERIOD: 1926—The Stolen Bride. 1927—*The Private Life of Helen of Troy,* Night Watch. 1928—The Yellow Lily. 1929—Love and the Devil, The Squall, Her Private Life. 1930—Women Everywhere, The Princess and the Plumber. FRENCH PERIOD: 1931—Rive Gauche, *Marius.* BRITISH PERIOD: 1931—Service for Ladies. 1932—Wedding Rehearsal. 1933—The Girl from Maxim's, *The Private Life of Henry VIII.* 1934—The Private Life of Don Juan. 1936—*Rembrandt.* 1940—Conquest of the Air. 1941—*Lady Hamilton.* 1945—*Vacation From Marriage.* 1947—An Ideal Husband.

Alexander Korda represented and indeed virtually created the Tradition of Quality in the British Cinema. He was generally underrated by the Marxist film historians because his unyielding gentility seemed an affront to the documentary movement. The fact remains that under his direction, Raimu and Pierre Fresnay in *Marius* and Charles Laughton in *The Private Life of Henry VIII* and *Rembrandt* provided some of the greatest and lustiest acting in the history of the cinema. When Korda is accused of excessive gentility, it might be well to remember that Bertolt Brecht himself derived the idea of his *Galileo* from the spectacle of Charles Laughton's tossing away his chewed-out chicken bones in *Henry VIII*.

ZOLTAN KORDA (1895–   )

FILMS: 1935—Sanders of the River, Forget Me Not. 1937— *Elephant Boy,* Revolt in the Desert. 1938—Drums. 1939—*Four Feathers.* 1942—Jungle Book. 1943—*Sahara.* 1945—Counter-Attack. 1947—*The Macomber Affair,* A Woman's Vengeance. 1952—*African Fury* (Cry the Beloved Country). 1956—Storm Over the Nile.

He directed Paul Robeson and Canada Lee in Africa, and Sabu somewhere in Sabuland. He manned the most far-flung outposts of the British Empire. *Sahara* was the first film to popularize the spirit of the United Nations; and who can forget Ralph Richardson, C. Aubrey Smith, June Duprez, and the Fuzzy-Wuzzies in *Four Feathers*? He also directed the best stretch of Hemingway ever put on the screen (*The Macomber Affair*) and some of the most literate dialogue of Aldous Huxley (*A Woman's Vengeance*). Still, his career is longer on quality than personality, and it remains difficult to define him.

MITCHELL LEISEN (1898–   )

FILMS: 1933—Cradle Song. 1934—Death Takes a Holiday, Murder at the Vanities. 1935—Behold My Wife, Four Hours to Kill, *Hands Across the Table.* 1936—Thirteen Hours by Air, Big Broadcast of 1937. 1937—*Swing High, Swing Low; Easy Living.* 1938—Big Broadcast of 1938, Artists and Models Abroad. 1939— *Midnight.* 1940—*Remember the Night,* Arise My Love. 1941—I

Wanted Wings, *Hold Back the Dawn*. 1942—The Lady Is Willing; Take a Letter, Darling. 1943—No Time for Love. 1944—*Lady in the Dark*, Frenchman's Creek, Practically Yours. 1945—Masquerade in Mexico. 1946—*Kitty, To Each His Own*, Suddenly It's Spring. 1947—*Golden Earrings*, Dream Girl. 1949—Bride of Vengeance, Song of Surrender. 1950—No Man of her Own, Captain Carey, U.S.A. 1951—*The Mating Season;* Darling, How Could You? 1952—Young Man with Ideas. 1953—Tonight We Sing. 1955—Bedeviled. 1957—The Girl Most Likely. 1967—Spree!

When Mitchell Leisen began at Paramount, the art was supplied by Lubitsch and Sternberg, and the junk by almost everyone else. Leisen occupied a middle position in the late thirties and early forties with such stylish productions as *Easy Living, Midnight, Remember the Night, Hold Back the Dawn,* and *Lady in the Dark.* The promotion of Preston Sturges and Billy Wilder from writers' cubicles to directors' chairs in the forties probably contributed to Leisen's decline. He soon found himself in the unenviable position of an expert diamond cutter working with lumpy coal. Yet, even the trivialities of *Kitty, Golden Earrings* and *The Mating Season* are not entirely devoid of directorial niceties.

MERVYN LE ROY (1900–)

FILMS: 1927—No Place to Go. 1928—Flying Romeos, Harold Teen. 1929—Naughty Baby, Hot Stuff, Broadway Daddy. 1930—Little Johnny Jones, Playing Around, Show Girl in Hollywood, Numbered Men, Broken Dishes, Top Speed, *Little Caesar.* 1931—Broad Minded, Too Young to Marry, *Five Star Final,* Local Boy Makes Good, Tonight or Never. 1932—*I Am a Fugitive from a Chain Gang,* High Pressure, Heart of New York, *Two Seconds,* Big City Blues, Three on a Match. 1933—*Hard to Handle,* Tugboat Annie, Elmer the Great, *Gold Diggers of 1933,* The World Changes. 1934—Heat Lightning, *Hi Nellie,* Happiness Ahead, *Sweet Adeline.* 1935—Oil for the Lamps of China, Page Miss Glory, I Found Stella Parish. 1936—Anthony Adverse, Three Men on a Horse. 1937—The King and the Chorus Girl, *They Won't Forget.* 1938—Fools for Scandal. 1940—*Waterloo Bridge, Escape.* 1941—*Blossoms in the Dust,* Unholy Partners. 1942—*Random Harvest, Johnny Eager.*

1943—Madame Curie. 1946—Without Reservations. 1948—Homecoming. 1949—In the Good Old Summertime, Any Number Can Play; East Side, West Side. 1951—Quo Vadis. 1952—Lovely to Look At, Million Dollar Mermaid. 1953—Latin Lovers. 1954—Rosemarie. 1955—Strange Lady in Town, *Mr. Roberts* (with John Ford). 1956—*The Bad Seed,* Toward the Unknown. 1958—No Time for Sergeants, Home Before Dark. 1959—The FBI Story. 1960—Wake Me When It's Over. 1961—The Devil at 4 o'Clock, A Majority of One. 1962—*Gypsy.* 1963—Mary, Mary. 1966—Moment to Moment. 1969—Downstairs at Ramsey's. 1970—The Thirteen Clocks.

From *Little Caesar* to *Gypsy,* Le Roy has converted his innate vulgarity into a personal style. As long as he is not mistaken for a serious artist, Le Roy can be delightfully entertaining. Divested of a spurious social consciousness, *I Am a Fugitive from a Chain Gang* and *They Won't Forget* are as much fun as *Waterloo Bridge* and *Random Harvest.* For all the jokes made about *Quo Vadis,* Le Roy's feeling for spectacle is clearly superior to Wyler's in the unendurable *Ben Hur.* His *Little Caesar* is feeble next to Hawks's *Scarface,* and his *Little Women* are far littler than Cukor's, but you can't have everything. His direction of Conrad Veidt and Norma Shearer in *Escape* and the haunting presence of Irene Dunne in *Sweet Adeline* make up for any numbers of clinkers.

FRANKLIN SCHAFFNER (1920–   )

FILMS: 1963—The Stripper. 1964—*The Best Man.* 1965—*The War Lord.* 1968—Planet of the Apes. 1968—The Double Man.

The great commercial irony of Franklin Schaffner's career is that his silliest project—*Planet of the Apes*—will make more money than all his three other more serious projects put together. However, even the financially fruitful monkeyshines of *Planet of the Apes* are not too high a price to pay for maintaining Schaffner's place in a film industry that has not given his talents the opportunities they deserve. An alumnus of the Philco-Westinghouse "Golden Age" of television drama, Schaffner was particularly successful with the histrionic demands of *The Best Man,* and particularly sympathetic for his unrewarded ambitiousness with *The War Lord,* a film that dared to treat romantic heterosexual love as a sacred subject worthy of epic consideration.

GEORGE SIDNEY (1916–   )

FILMS: 1941—Free and Easy. 1942—Pacific Rendezvous. 1943—Pilot No. 5 . . . , Thousands Cheer. 1944—Bathing Beauty. 1945—*Anchors Aweigh.* 1946—The Harvey Girls, Holiday in Mexico. 1947—Cass Timberlane. 1948—*The Three Musketeers.* 1949—The Red Danube. 1950—*Annie Get Your Gun,* Key to the City. 1951—*Show Boat.* 1952—*Scaramouche.* 1953—*Kiss Me Kate.* 1955—Jupiter's Darling. 1956—*The Eddie Duchin Story.* 1957—*Jeanne Eagels,* Pal Joey. 1960—*Who Was That Lady?,* Pepe. 1963—*Bye Bye Birdie.* 1966—*The Swinger.* 1968—Half a Six-pence.

Alongside Sidney, Le Roy looks like a Bressonian director. It can be argued that Sidney has ruined more good musicals with more gusto than any director in history, but who else has directed Esther Williams and Kim Novak in their opulent periods with such a straight face? There is a point at which brassiness, vulgarity, and downright badness become virtues, and Sidney approached that point in *Scaramouche* and *Jeanne Eagels,* and was not too far behind with *The Three Musketeers* and *The Eddie Duchin Story.* Of course, *Kiss Me Kate* was regrettable, and *Pal Joey* was unforgivable, but Sidney has kept his hand in even when it seemed time and again that the musical gravy train had reached the last stop. Sidney's ability to shift gears after such disasters as *Holiday in Mexico, Jupiter's Darling,* and *Pepe* is a tribute to his tenacity. After all, every aesthete in New York, London, and Paris wants to make a musical, but Sidney just keeps making them by default. Ultimately, Sidney may deserve a footnote in film history as the only director to appreciate Ann-

Margret in such culturally disreputable frolics as *Bye Bye Birdie* and *The Swinger.*

ANDREW L. STONE (1902–)

FILMS: 1928—Two o'Clock in the Morning, Liebenstraum. 1930—Sombras de Gloria. 1932—Hell's Headquarters. 1938—Stolen Heaven, Say It in French. 1939—The Great Victor Herbert. 1941—The Hard-Boiled Canary. 1943—Stormy Weather, Hi Diddle Diddle. 1944—Sensations of 1945. 1950—Highway 301. 1952—Confidence Girl, *The Steel Trap.* 1955—*The Night Holds Terror.* 1956—*Julie.* 1958—*Cry Terror,* The Decks Ran Red. 1960—*The Last Voyage.* 1962—*The Password Is Courage.* 1964—Never Put It in Writing. 1965—The Secret of My Success.

Since *The Steel Trap,* Andrew Stone and his fantastically helpful wife-editor have evolved a materialism without a dialectic, a form of film-making for those who brood over movie "boners." A tree is a tree to the Stones, but they don't shoot it in Griffith Park. If they want to blow up a train, they blow up a real train. If they want to sink an ocean liner, they sink a real ocean liner. This literal approach to catastrophes is pleasantly naïve in this neurotic age when everyone is afraid of his shadow and when what is truly frightening about things is not their essence but their appearance. One sobering deduction: If the Stones had made *On the Beach,* none of us would be around now to review it.

CHARLES WALTERS

FILMS: 1947—*Good News.* 1948—*Easter Parade.* 1949—*The Barkleys of Broadway.* 1950—*Summer Stock.* 1951—Three Guys Named Mike, Texas Carnival. 1952—The Belle of New York. 1953—*Lilli, Torch Song.* 1955—The Glass Slipper, *The Tender Trap.* 1956—High Society. 1957—Don't Go Near the Water. 1959—*Ask Any Girl.* 1960—*Please Don't Eat the Daisies.* 1961—Two Loves. 1962—*Jumbo.* 1964—The Unsinkable Molly Brown. 1966—Walk, Don't Run.

The late H. L. Mencken used to boast that he had never seen a movie, but toward the end of his life, this irascible cynic was induced to see *Lilli,* and he loved it! Charles Walters produces this effect almost inexplicably with the most dubious material. His sensibility is pitched at a certain level of fakery and remains there consistently. If the adjective "nice" could be defined with any precision, it would apply to most of his films. At the very least, his films almost invariably turn out being more entertaining than their subject and title would indicate. Walters is often too arch and affected for comfort, but his direction of players is never lacking in knowledgeable subtlety.

JAMES WHALE (1896–1957)

FILMS: 1930—*Journey's End.* 1931—*Waterloo Bridge, Frankenstein.* 1932—Impatient Maiden, *The Old Dark House.* 1933—The Kiss Before the Mirror, *The Invisible Man,* By Candlelight. 1934—*One More River.* 1935—*The Bride of Frankenstein,* Remember Last Night? 1936—*Show Boat.* 1937—The Road Back, The Great Garrick. 1938—*Sinners in Paradise,* Wives Under Suspicion, Port of Seven Seas. 1939—*The Man in the Iron Mask.* 1940—Green Hell. 1941—They Dare Not Love. 1949—Hello Out There (never released).

James Whale's career has been somewhat submerged by the Karloff cult. John Grierson managed to talk about *Frankenstein* without even mentioning Whale, but connoisseurs of horror films know that the real gem of the series was *The Bride of Frankenstein* with Whale's bizarre camera angles battling Ernest Thesiger's fruity performance for attention. Whale's overall career reflects the stylistic ambitions and dramatic disappointments of an expressionist in the studio-controlled Hollywood of the thirties.

VII.
STRAINED
SERIOUSNESS

These are talented but uneven directors with the mortal sin of pretentiousness. Their ambitious projects
tend to inflate rather than expand.

RICHARD BROOKS (1912–   )

FILMS: 1950—Crisis. 1951—The Light Touch. 1952—*Deadline U.S.A.* 1953—Battle Circus, Take the High Ground. 1954—*The Last Time I Saw Paris.* 1955—*Blackboard Jungle.* 1956—*The Last Hunt,* The Catered Affair. 1957—Something of Value. 1958—The Brothers Karamazov, *Cat on a Hot Tin Roof.* 1960—*Elmer Gantry.* 1962—*Sweet Bird of Youth.* 1964—Lord Jim. 1966—*The Professionals.* 1967—*In Cold Blood.*

Richard Brooks is attracted to violent subjects, but his direction lacks the force to express them. His punches are seen but not felt, and his films consequently lack any lasting impact. The director's superficiality is applied impartially to Dostoyevsky and Chayefsky, Tennessee Williams and Robert Ruark, Sinclair Lewis and Evan Hunter. Brooks's sub-Proustian visualization in *Sweet Bird of Youth* and his facile Freudianizing for *In Cold Blood* are particularly damning proofs of an imagination more shallow than fallow. There has to be something wrong with an artist who searches for the kind of material he knows he will shamefully compromise. Although most of his films display something of value on first viewing, none can take the high ground in retrospect. However, there are moments in *The Last Hunt* and *The Professionals* when Brooks seems to be projecting a prophetic disillusion with individualism and liberalism in America. The conception is provocative, but the execution is excessively rhetorical. As one of the breed of writer-directors, Brooks has a bad habit of saying what he means without showing what he feels.

JACK CLAYTON (1921–   )

FILMS: 1959—*Room at the Top.* 1961—*The Innocents.* 1964—The Pumpkin Eater. 1967—Our Mother's House.

Jack Clayton represents the last word in academic direction. Every project must find its appropriate style. *Room at the Top* was nervously angry-young-mannish, *The Innocents* fluidly Jamesian, *The Pumpkin Eater* palpitatingly Pinteresque, and *Our Mother's House* Gothically Dickensian. The only Clayton constant is impersonality, but such studied impersonality seems out of date.

JULES DASSIN (1911–)

FILMS: 1942—Nazi Agent, The Affairs of Martha, Reunion in France. 1943—Young Ideas. 1945—A Letter for Evie. 1946—Two Smart People. 1947—*Brute Force.* 1948—*The Naked City.* 1949—*Thieves' Highway.* 1950—*Night and the City.* 1956—*Rififi.* 1958—He Who Must Die. 1960—*Never on Sunday.* 1962—Phaedra. 1964—*Topkapi.* 1966—10:30 P.M. Summer. 1968—Survival! 1969—Up Tight!

Confronting a career that verges on the grotesque, one might say that it is easier to drive a director out of Hollywood than to drive Hollywood out of a director. Dassin's softheaded social consciousness has never obscured his minor talents. After the lumpy proletarianism of *He Who Must Die,* the ludicrous escapades of *Never on Sunday* and *Phaedra* seem more appropriate to the delirious director of *Brute Force* and *Night and the City.* If the works of Dassin's Mercourial period are not particularly mercurial, neither is much of the other transatlantic cinema that presumes to graft European intellectualism to American intelligence. Dassin remains a lively director in a minor key, and it is difficult to understand today why anything more was ever expected of him. For the record, Dassin's most famous films, *The Naked City* and *Rififi,* are among his lesser works.

RICHARD FLEISCHER (1916–)

FILMS: 1946—Child of Divorce. 1947—Banjo. 1948—*So This Is New York.* 1949—Make Mine Laughs, The Clay Pigeon,

Follow Me Quietly, Trapped. 1950—Armored Car Robbery. 1952 —*The Narrow Margin*, The Happy Time. 1953—Arena. 1954— 20,000 Leagues Under the Sea. 1955—*Violent Saturday, The Girl on the Red Velvet Swing.* 1956—*Bandido*, Between Heaven and Hell. 1958—*The Vikings.* 1959—*These Thousand Hills, Compulsion.* 1960—Crack in the Mirror. 1961—The Big Gamble. 1962— Barabbas. 1966—Fantastic Voyage. 1967—Dr. Dolittle. 1968— The Boston Strangler.

Responsible critics have advanced Fleischer as a candidate for Walsh's laurels in the adventure category. Since *The Narrow Margin*, Fleischer's career has sputtered, alas, at less than 50 percent efficiency. That is, even if the director be given the benefit of the doubt for *Violent Saturday, The Girl on the Red Velvet Swing, Bandido, The Vikings,* and *These Thousand Hills.* On the theory that a director must be judged by all his films rather than by his more bearable ones, the burden of proof falls on Fleischer's champions. *Crack in the Mirror* alone would be sufficient to disqualify most directors from serious consideration. As for *Compulsion*, the subject is still in search of an abler director. More damning to Fleischer's reputation is the striking vapidity of *The Happy Time*, the Dunne-like turgidity of *Between Heaven and Hell,* the elaborate pointlessness of *The Big Gamble,* and the muddled mindlessness of the *Fantastic Voyage.* Fleischer does get some points for his strenuous efforts in the physical cinema, an addiction perhaps inherited from his cartoonist father, Max Fleischer, whose *Gulliver's Travels* failed to dent the Disney monopoly back in 1939.

BRYAN FORBES (1926–   )

FILMS: 1962—Whistle Down the Wind. 1963—The L-Shaped Room. 1964—*Seance on a Wet Afternoon.* 1965—*King Rat.* 1966—*The Wrong Box.* 1967—The Whisperers. 1968— Deadfall. 1969—The Madwoman of Chaillot.

The Whisperers is an apt title for a Bryan Forbes project. Indeed, the world of Bryan Forbes is one of wisps and whispers. *Whistle Down the Wind* was muted allegory, *The L-Shaped*

Room muted soap opera, *Seance on a Wet Afternoon* muted melodrama, *King Rat* muted adventure, and *The Wrong Box* muted slapstick. Always nibbling at nuances, always straining for subtlety, never quite breaking an egg to make an omelet, never quite exploding a theme into dramatic excitement, Forbes perpetually pursues the anticliché only to arrive at anticlimax.

JOHN FRANKENHEIMER (1930–   )

FILMS: 1957—*The Young Stranger.* 1961—*The Young Savages.* 1962—*All Fall Down,* Birdman of Alcatraz, *The Manchurian Candidate.* 1964—Seven Days in May. 1965—The Train. 1966—Seconds, *Grand Prix.* 1968—The Fixer. 1969—The Gypsy Moths.

A director of parts at the expense of the whole, Frankenheimer betrays his television origins by pumping synthetic technique into penultimate scenes as if he had to grab the audience before the commercial break. The selective eclecticism of his first film, influenced as it was by Stevens and Reed, has degenerated into an all-embracing academicism, a veritable glossary of film techniques. A director capable of alternating shock cuts and slow dissolves is obviously sweating over his technique. Instead of building sequences, Frankenheimer explodes them prematurely, preventing his films from coming together coherently. Until *The Manchurian Candidate,* it was difficult to differentiate between the contradictions in the director's style and the confusion inherent in his material. The vaguely environmental focus on delinquency, criminality, libertinism, and hypocrisy in *The Young Stranger, The Young Savages, All Fall Down,* and *Birdman of Alcatraz* suggested a modern form of social consciousness in search of more sophisticated means of expression. But with George Axelrod's efficient blueprint for a modern thriller, Frankenheimer simply bungled the assignment by dawdling over the motivations of intermediate sequences. When a director flunks the kind of technical exercise a Gerd Oswald or a Blake Edwards would have passed with honors, it becomes difficult to honor his more serious aspirations. Ironically, Frankenheimer's stylistic eclecticism was ideally suited to the monstrous challenge of *Grand Prix,* a multimedia movie to make the most captious critic speed-struck and carsick.

SIDNEY J. FURIE (1933—   )

FILMS: 1961—The Snake Woman, Doctor Blood's Coffin, During One Night, Three on a Spree. 1962—The Young Ones. 1963 —The Boys, The Leather Boys. 1964—Wonderful Life. 1965— The Ipcress File. 1966—The Appaloosa. 1967—The Naked Runner. 1969—The Lawyer.

Sidney J. Furie may be the most obsessively clinical of modern directors. *The Ipcress File* is rather antiseptic in its anti-Bond mannerisms, but its father-fixation ending with its psychically battered hero in the position of choosing which pater to perforate adds a new dimension to the sick cinema. From the black leather jackets of *The Leather Boys* to Marlon Brando's Indian blanket in *The Appaloosa,* Furie seems to elevate fabric fetishism into a personal style. Furie's films are more interesting visually than dramatically, but if *The Naked Runner* be any indication of development, his work is becoming less affecting and more affected.

NORMAN JEWISON

FILMS: 1962—40 Pounds of Trouble. 1963—The Thrill of It All. 1964—Send Me No Flowers. 1965—The Art of Love, *The Cincinnati Kid.* 1966—The Russians Are Coming. 1967—*In The Heat of the Night.* 1968—The Thomas Crown Affair. 1969—Gaily, Gaily. 1971—Fiddler on the Roof.

Norman Jewison has been guided from the very beginning of his career by a commendable desire to escape from the confines of a studio set to the great outdoors of reality. After all, cinema should move, and preferably outdoors. As a director of actors,

Jewison is reasonably good with good people—Steve Mc-
Queen, Tuesday Weld, and Edward G. Robinson in *The Cincinnati Kid,* Alan Arkin in *The Russians Are Coming,* Sidney
Poitier and Rod Steiger for *In the Heat of the Night.* Unfortunately, Jewison's films suffer from the director's compulsion to
be strenuously cinematic. Jewison does not so much direct as
overdirect and too often to diminishing returns. The historical
timing of such projects as *The Russians Are Coming* and *In the
Heat of the Night* has been so fortuitous that Jewison has found
himself somewhat undeservedly at the top of the heap.

STANLEY KUBRICK (1928–   )

FILMS: 1953—Fear and Desire. 1955—Killer's Kiss. 1956
—*The Killing.* 1957—*Paths of Glory.* 1960—Spartacus. 1962—
Lolita. 1964—*Dr. Strangelove* 1968—2001: A Space Odyssey. 1971
—Napoleon.

Back in 1963, I wrote off Kubrick thus: "His métier is projects
rather than films, publicité rather than cinéma. He may wind up
as the director of the best coming attractions in the industry, but
time is running out on his projected evolution into a major artist.
His unfortunate tendency to misapply Ophulsian camera movements to trivial diversions, and his increasing reluctance to express an apparently perverse personality, suggest that his career
is at a standstill of his own devising. *Lolita* is his most irritating
failure to date. With such splendid material, he emphasized the
problem without the passion, the badness without the beauty, the
agony without the ecstasy. What doth it avail a director if a
project be presold to the whole world and he loseth his soul?"
    In the five years since 1963, Kubrick has made two films—
Dr. Strangelove and *2001: A Space Odyssey.* All in all, he has
directed six films in a dozen years. (*Fear and Desire* and *Killer's
Kiss* can be written off as strained experiments.) The very fact
that he makes few films seems to confirm his stature among his
champions. There is supposedly too much care and integrity in
Kubrick to make him work more often. *Dr. Strangelove* clicked

with most sophisticates largely because its irreverence seemed modish at the time and also because some of Terry Southern's lines punctuated the proceedings with the kind of belly laughs Vladimir Nabokov's lines lacked in *Lolita*. Still, the failure of *Lolita* seems more interesting and more personal in retrospect than the success of *Dr. Strangelove*. After the satiric alienation of *Dr. Strangelove,* Kubrick spent five years and ten million dollars on a science-fiction project so devoid of life and feeling as to render a computer called Hal the most sympathetic character in a jumbled scenario. *2001: A Space Odyssey* also confirms Kubrick's inability to tell a story on the screen with coherence and a consistent point of view. Kubrick's tragedy may have been that he was hailed as a great artist before he had become a competent craftsman. However, it is more likely that he has chosen to exploit the giddiness of middle-brow audiences on the satiric level of *Mad* magazine. Ultimately, Stanley Kubrick shares with Claude Lelouch a naïve faith in the power of images to transcend fuzzy feelings and vague ideas. The ending of *2001* qualifies in its oblique obscurity as Instant Ingmar.

RICHARD LESTER (1932–   )

FILMS: 1962—Ring-A-Ding Rhythm. 1964—*A Hard Day's Night*. 1965—The Knack . . . and How to Get It, *Help!* 1966—A Funny Thing Happened on the Way to the Forum. 1967—How I Won the War. 1968—Petulia. 1969—From the Hip, The Bed Sitting Room.

Richard Lester is the most fragmented director this side of Jean-Luc Godard, and his fragmentation is becoming increasingly irritating. He was mistaken at first for the long-awaited satirist of television commercials, but he has degenerated into the servant of the form, though not of course of the content, of these same commercials. From the highwater mark of *A Hard Day's Night,* he has fallen to the piecemeal polemics of *How I Won the War*. It is now clear that one Beatle close-up is worth a thousand Lester cutups.

ALBERT LEWIN (1894–1968)

FILMS: 1942—*The Moon and Sixpence.* 1945—*The Picture of Dorian Gray.* 1947—The Private Affairs of Bel Ami. 1951— *Pandora and the Flying Dutchman.* 1954—Saadia. 1957—The Living Idol.

Jean Renoir said it all when he observed that Albert Lewin was too much of a theoretician. There is an ironic moment in *Pandora and the Flying Dutchman,* Lewin's most memorable film, when Ava Gardner has just defaced James Mason's painting of her, and the doomed painter declares that the desecration introduces the element of accident to his art. Would that there were more room for accident in Lewin's clogged literary narrations and his naïve conception of refinement in the cinema, a refinement that presumes to vulgarize Wilde, De Maupassant, and even Somerset Maugham for the sake of bringing kulchur to the masses. Still, Lewin's cultural evangelism is less offensive than most, and there are even moments of cinematic lucidity in the midst of all his literary elucidation. George Sanders was the Lewin actor par excellence, bored, cynical, decadent, and a bit threadbare. The most memorable face in the Lewin gallery is Hurd Hatfield's as Dorian Gray, a casting coup that Oscar Wilde would have applauded. It is in the surface snobbery of Hatfield's face that Lewin's sensibility can best be measured.

SIDNEY LUMET (1924–   )

FILMS: 1957—*Twelve Angry Men.* 1958—Stage Struck. 1959—*That Kind of Woman,* The Fugitive Kind. 1962—*View from the Bridge, Long Day's Journey into Night.* 1964—Fail Safe. 1965—*The Pawnbroker, The Hill.* 1966—*The Group.* 1968— *Bye Bye Braverman,* The Appointment. 1969—The Sea Gull.

At its best, Lumet's direction is efficiently vehicular but pleasantly impersonal. Sophia Loren and Tab Hunter come off much better in *That Kind of Woman* than do the stronger-willed Anna Magnani and Marlon Brando in *The Fugitive Kind.* The moral is clear. Those who would be led, Lumet will guide. Those who would lead, Lumet will follow. He lacks the necessary temperament of a tyrant on the set, but insists on remaining a constitutional monarch. When his subjects are responsible, as in *Long Day's Journey into Night,* his services are valuable. In most other instances, only his innate good taste saves him from utter mediocrity.

Lumet has tended to be a more venturesome producer-director in the past five years, and though his films are invariably flawed, the very variety of the challenges constitutes a kind of entertainment. *Fail Safe* is funnier unintentionally than *Dr. Strangelove* is intentionally, but there is something manically impressive about Lumet's direction of Walter Matthau and Fritz Weaver. *The Pawnbroker* might have been subtitled *Harlem Mon Amour* if Lumet were capable of regarding the pretentiousness of the project with any humor, but the masochism of *The Pawnbroker,* like the sadism of *The Hill,* depends for its execution upon a humorless temperament. *The Deadly Affair* is a dismal exercise except for the bright cameos of Harry Andrews and Lynn Redgrave; *The Group* is at best well-modulated mediocrity, and *Bye Bye Braverman* as courageous in its conception as it is vulgar in its execution, but here too Joseph Wiseman and Sorrell Brooke are marvelous, and George Segal ultimately affecting. Unfortunately, Lumet shows no sign of ever rising above the middle-brow aspirations of his projects to become the master rather than the mimic of the current trend away from Hollywood.

KAREL REISZ (1926–   )

FILMS: 1961—*Saturday Night and Sunday Morning.* 1964—Night Must Fall. 1966—*Morgan!* 1968—Isadora.

Karel Reisz has moved from the kitchen-sink mannerisms of *Saturday Night and Sunday Morning* to the mod mannerisms of

Morgan! without missing a beat. *Night Must Fall* is a disaster that can be charitably forgotten, *Isadora* a future prospect that can be eagerly anticipated. Reisz may be remembered ultimately as the screen Pygmalion to Vanessa Redgrave's Galatea, a Galatea moreover who is as effectively mannered for Reisz as she is as excruciatingly mannered for everyone else.

TONY RICHARDSON (1928–   )

FILMS: 1959—Look Back in Anger. 1960—The Entertainer. 1961—Sanctuary. 1962—*A Taste of Honey, The Loneliness of the Long Distance Runner.* 1963—*Tom Jones.* 1965—The Loved One. 1966—Mademoiselle. 1967—The Sailor from Gibraltar. 1968—The Charge of the Light Brigade. 1969—Laughter in the Dark.

Tony Richardson has become the most prolific and the most prosperous of the *Sight and Sound* crop of directors, and ultimately the least respected. His authors have included Osborne, Faulkner, Delaney, Sillitoe, Duras, Fielding, and Waugh, his players Burton, Bloom, Olivier, Da Banzie, Plowright, Evans, Finney, Bates, Tushingham, Melvin, Courtenay, Redgrave (Michael), Redmond, Fox, York, Cilento, Steiger, Morse, Moreau, Bannen, and many others of exceptional talent. Curiously, Richardson is as effective a stage director as he is ineffective a screen director. With all the talent at his disposal, it is not surprising that most of his films have a few stirring moments. By any standard, his career has gone downhill since *Tom Jones,* but even in such highly regarded clusters of bits and pieces as *A Taste of Honey* and *The Loneliness of the Long Distance Runner,* Richardson's direction lacks any genuinely unifying force or conviction.

ROBERT ROSSEN (1908–1966)

FILMS: 1947—*Johnny O'Clock, Body and Soul.* 1949—*All the King's Men.* 1951—The Brave Bulls. 1955—Mambo. 1956—

Alexander the Great. 1957—Island in the Sun. 1959—They Came to Cordura. 1961—*The Hustler*. 1964—*Lilith*.

Back in 1963, I wrote of Rossen: "For all their seriousness of purpose, Rossen's films prove only that aspiration is no substitute for inspiration. A moralizer rather than a moralist, the director is always trying to say more than his technique can express. His characters consequently have a tendency to run down after talking themselves out. In all fairness to the director, it must be recorded that Rossen lost four years at a time when his work still seemed promising. (*Mambo* can be charged off to McCarthy.) In retrospect, however, the dreariness of Rossen's direction is remarkably consistent. *All the King's Men* is more pretentious than Walsh's *A Lion Is in the Streets,* but less forceful and less coherent. Similarly, *The Brave Bulls* is more grandiloquent than Boetticher's *The Bullfighter and the Lady,* but less personal and less moving. The point is that Rossen had stronger literary material to begin with, but then dissipated his advantage over Walsh and Boetticher in the transition from script to screen. To compensate for the lack of a visual style, Rossen picks at his characters in the name of psychological realism. Huey Long, Alexander the Great, and the Hustler meet on the same ignoble plane to engage in bizarre intrigues. The low point of psychological (and physiological) realism in the American cinema was probably reached in *They Came to Cordura* when contrite Rita Hayworth sacrificed herself to villainous Van Heflin so that Gary Cooper could get a safe night's sleep. The scabrousness of this intrigue only enhances the power and glory of a similar gambit in Hawks' *Red River*."

Robert Rossen made only one additional film—*Lilith*—before his death, and it was a failure according to the critical consensus, but it somehow upgraded Rossen's reputation as an artist with more feeling than facility. Rossen was never a natural, but *Lilith* was his noblest and most lyrical failure. *Lilith* is closer to the ridiculous at its worst than to the sublime at its best, but Rossen did take the risk of being ridiculed for the sake of Jean Seberg's ambiguous beauty. If Rossen had never been overrated, he would now be due for cultish rediscovery for *Body and Soul, All the King's Men, Johnny O'Clock, The Hustler,* and, above all, *Lilith.*

JOHN SCHLESINGER

FILMS: 1962—A Kind of Loving. 1963—*Billy Liar.* 1965—*Darling.* 1967—Far from the Madding Crowd. 1969—Midnight Cowboy.

John Schlesinger has not yet fully arrived in his permanent position in film history; but, come what may, he will deserve at the very least a footnote as the discoverer of Julie Christie. Originally one of the wave of working-class subject directors, Schlesinger came into his own with *Darling,* Britain's answer to *La Dolce Vita,* and one of the key works in the evolution of the swinging cinema. Schlesinger represents a new blend of pragmatism and experimentation in film making. He is particularly skilled in the direction of dialogue. Dirk Bogarde and Lawrence Harvey in *Darling,* Tom Courtenay in *Billy Liar,* Alan Bates in *A Kind of Loving* and *Far from the Madding Crowd,* Peter Finch and Terence Stamp in *Crowd* constitute a gallery of inspired performances and an index of the enormous supply of gifted British actors available to the English-speaking cinema. Unfortunately, Schlesinger lacks the directorial coherence to tie together his intermittent inspirations.

JOHN STURGES (1911–   )

FILMS: 1946—The Man Who Dared, Shadowed. 1947—Alias Mr. Twilight, For the Love of Rusty, Keeper of the Bees. 1948—Best Man Wins, Sign of the Ram. 1949—*The Walking Hills.* 1950—*Mystery Street,* The Capture, The Magnificent Yankee, Right Cross. 1951—*Kind Lady, The People Against O'Hara,* It's a Big Country. 1952—The Girl in White. 1953—Jeopardy, Fast Company, *Escape from Fort Bravo.* 1955—*Bad Day at Black Rock,* Underwater, The Scarlet Coat. 1956—*Backlash.* 1957—Gunfight at the O.K. Corral. 1958—The Old Man and the Sea, The Law and Jake Wade. 1959—*Last Train from Gun Hill,* Never So Few. 1960 —*The Magnificent Seven.* 1961—By Love Possessed. 1962—

Sergeants Three. 1963—*The Great Escape,* A Girl Named Tamiko. 1965—The Satan Bug, The Hallelujah Trail. 1967—*The Hour of the Gun.* 1969—Marooned.

Long before *The Magnificent Seven,* John Sturges seemed to be striving, albeit unconsciously, to become the American Kurosawa, tortured, humorless, and self-consciously social. Come to think of it, is there much difference between Spencer Tracy's karate crusade in *Bad Day at Black Rock* and Toshiro Mifune's samurai swordplay in *Yojimbo*? If Kurosawa has an advantage here, it is because his personality is more attuned to violence and misanthropy. Unfortunately, it is hard to remember why Sturges's career was ever considered meaningful. How naïve it was, for example, to deduce that Sturges had solved the problems of Cinemascope by his allegorical groupings in the aforementioned *Bad Day at Black Rock.* Even in the era of *Mystery Street, The People Against O'Hara,* and *Escape From Fort Bravo,* the director's easily acquired reputation as an expert technician was incomprehensible. Where Daves attracts attention with his debasing crane, Kubrick with his meaningless tracks, and Wise with the IBM perforations of his montage, Sturges's stock-in-trade for superficial visual analysis is the wasteful pan. The fact that *The Great Escape* is as successful as *The Hallelujah Trail* is unsuccessful indicates not only that Steve McQueen is a more persuasive personality than Burt Lancaster but also that Sturges should work exclusively in the serious if not solemn action genre.

ROBERT WISE (1914—   )

FILMS: 1944—*Curse of the Cat People,* Mlle. Fifi. 1945— *The Body Snatcher,* A Game of Death. 1946—Criminal Court. 1947—Born to Kill. 1948—Mystery in Mexico, Blood on the Moon. 1949—*The Set-Up.* 1950—Two Flags West, Three Secrets. 1951—The House on Telegraph Hill, *The Day the Earth Stood Still.* 1952—The Captive City, Something for the Birds. 1953—Destination Gobi, The Desert Rats, So Big. 1954—*Executive Suite.* 1955 —Helen of Troy. 1956—Tribute to a Bad Man, *Somebody Up There Likes Me.* 1957—This Could Be the Night, Until They Sail.

1958—Run Silent, Run Deep; *I Want to Live.* 1959—*Odds Against Tomorrow.* 1961—*West Side Story* (with Jerome Robbins). 1962—Two for the Seesaw. 1963—The Haunting. 1965—*The Sound of Music.* 1966—The Sand Pebbles. 1968—Star!

Robert Wise was marked as a director to watch very early in his career. Among Val Lewton alumni, he occupies a middle position between Jacques Tourneur at the top and Mark Robson at the bottom. His temperament is vaguely liberal, his style vaguely realistic; but after *The Sound of Music* and *The Sand Pebbles,* the stylistic signature of Robert Wise is indistinct to the point of invisibility. Even the unity-of-time experiment of *The Set-Up* and the click-clack cutting of *Executive Suite* seem to belong in another era entirely. Although montage is not out, as Bazin had once proclaimed, academic montage can no longer function as an adequate means of expression even for the cutter of *Citizen Kane* and *The Magnificent Ambersons.* What has happened to Wise in the fifties and sixties has happened to most technicians without a strong personality. The strained techniques of *Odds Against Tomorrow, Two for the Seesaw,* and *The Haunting* are more elaborate than expressive. For example, the split-screen conception borrowed from the stage version of *Two for the Seesaw* actually defeats the mood of the story. When two people are shown in the same frame, their loneliness is not being expressed visually. Still, Wise's conscientious craftsmanship is something of a virtue in these days of giddy chaos. The commercial success of *The Sound of Music* is a tribute to Wise's ability to treat the most sentimental material with a straight face.

VIII.
ODDITIES,
ONE-SHOTS,
AND
NEWCOMERS

These are the eccentrics, the exceptions and the expectants, the fallen stars and the shooting stars. They defy more precise classification by their very nature.

LINDSAY ANDERSON

FILMS: 1963—*The Sporting Life.* 1966—The White Bus. Short Subjects: Thursday's Children, O Dreamland. 1968—If.

Lindsay Anderson came to the cinema with a reputation as a controversial critic scornful of both Philistinism and dandyism. He has been associated with such oversimplified catchwords as "commitment" and "Free Cinema," but he has striven in *This Sporting Life* and *The White Bus* to express a subtle, supple, and highly individualized sensibility. Nonetheless there has been a tendency to lump Lindsay Anderson together with Karel Reisz, Tony Richardson, John Schlesinger, Jack Clayton, and Desmond Davis in the school of so-called British realism. Anderson, like his French counterparts swept ashore on the "New Wave," disdains such facile categories as mere journalistic conveniences. Both as critic and film-maker, he has remained skeptical of the alleged glories of improvisation. He believes firmly in the value of preparation both with scripts and performers, and he is not ashamed of adapting a novel to the screen. When he was the leading luminary of the *Sequence-Sight-and-Sound* generation of the late forties and early fifties, he revealed a taste capable of embracing simultaneously the works of John Ford, Jean Cocteau, and Vincente Minnelli. He has directed many plays, and has otherwise remained in the forefront of the New Look in British culture. It may be that Anderson is more a critical influence than a creative force. In this, Lindsay Anderson resembles such French critic-creators as Eric Rohmer and Jacques Rivette.

GEORGE AXELROD (1922—   )

FILMS: 1966—*Lord Love a Duck.* 1968—The Secret Life of an American Wife.

George Axelrod had been involved as a controversial middleman between Max Shulman and Leo McCarey on *Rally Round the*

Flag, Boys! and between Truman Capote and Blake Edwards on *Breakfast at Tiffany's.* Axelrod, like Paddy Chayefsky, found the role of writer-producer peculiarly frustrating in an industry oriented more and more toward the director. *Lord Love a Duck* was Axelrod's opportunity to fall flat on his face, but he proved to be surprisingly adept at rendering his own very personal comic vision. Tuesday Weld under Axelrod's direction captured all the sweetness of Nabokov's *Lolita* so lacking in Kubrick's sour direction of Sue Lyon. In addition, Axelrod's zany direction of Roddy Macdowall, Martin West, Lola Albright, and Ruth Gordon revealed a variety of tone and mood hitherto unexpressed in his writing for Broadway and Hollywood.

JOHN BOORMAN

FILMS: 1965—Having a Wild Weekend. 1967—*Point Blank.* 1968—Hell in the Pacific. 1969—Rosencrantz and Guildenstern Are Dead.

John Boorman's sense of architecture in *Point Blank* is stunning, and the curiously bleak rather than cool intermingling of morality, sexuality, and violence makes *Point Blank* more edifying than either *Bonnie and Clyde* or *The Graduate.* There is a bit too much jazzy crosscutting à la Resnais, and Boorman often wallows in an effect, but his direction of Lee Marvin and Angie Dickinson make him a director to watch. Even if *Point Blank* should turn out to be a one-shot for its director, it would deserve lasting admiration for treading over the slick surfaces of evil with the squeaky shoes of morality.

MARLON BRANDO (1924–   )

FILM: 1961—One-Eyed Jacks.

For all his decadent narcissism and self-indulgence, Brando remains one of the most fascinating actors in the cinema. If he has reached the point where he is unable to or unwilling to take strong direction, self-direction would seem a wiser course than weak direction. *One-Eyed Jacks* is quite charming in a disorganized sort of way, with Brando's Western hero closer to Heathcliff than to Hopalong Cassidy, but *The Ugly American,* under Ken Englund's subservient direction, is completely worthless.

PETER BROOK (1912–)

FILMS: 1953—The Beggar's Opera. 1960—Moderato Cantabile. 1962—*Lord of the Flies.* 1967—*Marat / Sade.* 1968—Tell Me Lies.

Peter Brook is interesting mainly as an emissary traveling freely and frequently between the modern theatre and the modern cinema. His films serve as extensions of his ideas about the ultimate direction and destination the cinema must follow. *Moderato Cantabile* is an exercise in languorous introspection of the Resnais–*Hiroshima Mon Amour* school. *The Lord of the Flies* is an expedition in search of inspired improvisation. Brook himself remains a stimulating and articulate spokesman for the growing interdependence of the theatre and the motion picture.

Marat / Sade and *Tell Me Lies* represent Brook's unsuccessful attempts to transpose the theatre of cruelty to the screen without any appreciable formal or intellectual erosion. Unfortunately, Brook has always been more intellectually provocative than artistically successful. *The Beggar's Opera, Moderato Cantabile, Lord of the Flies,* and *Marat / Sade* all looked better on the drawing board than on the screen despite impressive castings and performances of such as Olivier, Belmondo, Moreau, McGee, (Ian) Richardson, and the little boy who played Piggy. Brook seems to have used up all his artistic options from the extreme determinism of *Moderato Cantabile* to the extreme improvisation of *Lord of the Flies,* but *Tell Me Lies* provides an entirely new set of cinematic conceptions that miscarry in the messiest ways imaginable.

JOHN CASSAVETES (1929–   )

FILMS: 1961—Shadows. 1962—Too Late Blues, A Child Is Waiting. 1968—Faces. 1969—Husbands.

John Cassavetes remains an unresolved talent, not entirely happy with the Establishment or against it. His direction, like his acting, hovers between offbeat improvisation and blatant contrivance. Somehow his timing always seems to be off a beat or two even when he understands what he is doing. Too much of the time he is groping when he should be gripping. At his best, however, he makes emotional contact with his material, and transforms his humblest players into breathing, feeling beings.

JAMES CLAVELL (1925–   )

FILMS: 1959—Five Gates to Hell. 1960—Walk Like a Dragon. 1967—To Sir, With Love. 1968—Where's Jack?

James Clavell teeters on the thin line between ideas and gimmicks as a writer and/or director of unusual subjects. He seems particularly attracted to interracial problem parables (*Walk Like a Dragon; To Sir, With Love*) and military adventure allegories (*Five Gates to Hell, The Great Escape, King Rat*). The latter two films are among the most effective entertainments dispensed respectively by directors John Sturges and Bryan Forbes. Clavell's own direction ranges from sub-Fuller (*Hell, Dragon*) to super-Kramer (*To Sir*).

HAROLD CLURMAN (1901–   )

FILM: 1946—Deadline at Dawn.

Back when the Group Theatre was camped in Hollywood, Clurman came up with a film that today resembles nothing so much as a parody of poetic social consciousness. Yet there, in the middle of all the fakery, was Susan Hayward, pure Brooklyn and pure Hollywood, and infinitely more real and lasting than the WPA.

FRANCIS FORD COPPOLA (1939–)

FILMS: 1962—Dementia. 1967—*You're A Big Boy Now*. 1968—Finian's Rainbow. 1969—The Rain People.

Francis Ford Coppola is probably the first reasonably talented and sensibly adaptable directorial talent to emerge from a university curriculum in film-making. *You're A Big Boy Now* seemed remarkably eclectic even under the circumstances. If the direction of Nichols on *The Graduate* has an edge on Coppola's for *Big Boy*, it is that Nichols borrows only from good movies whereas Coppola occasionally borrows from bad ones. Curiously, Coppola seems infinitely more merciful to his grotesques than does anything-for-an-effect Nichols. Coppola may be heard from more decisively in the future.

ROGER CORMAN (1926–)

FILMS: 1955—Apache Woman, The Intruder, Five Guns West. 1957—Not of This Earth, Attack of the Crab Monsters, Teenage Doll, Sorority Girl. 1958—War of the Satellites, I, Mobster. 1959—A Bucket of Blood. 1960—The House of Usher. 1961—The Pit and the Pendulum. 1962—Premature Burial, I Hate Your Guts, Poe's Tales of Terror, Tower of London. 1963—*The Raven*, The Young Racers, The Haunted Palace, *"X" The Man with the X-Ray Eyes*. 1964—*The Masque of the Red Death*, The Secret Invasion. 1966—*The Wild Angels*. 1967—*The St. Valentine's Day Massacre*, The Trip.

Roger Corman's outstanding achievement to date is *The Masque of the Red Death*, but on the whole he seems much stronger visually than dramatically. His acting is usually atrocious, and his feeling for dialogue uncertain. It is quite possible that he is miscast, like Mankiewicz, Wyler, and Wise, as a director, when he would be much more effective as a producer.

DESMOND DAVIS

FILMS: 1964—*Girl With Green Eyes.* 1966—The Uncle, Time Lost and Time Remembered (I Was Happy Here). 1967—Smashing Time. 1969—A Nice Girl Like Me.

Desmond Davis has been sliding downhill since *Girl With Green Eyes,* itself a curious blend of folk caricature and *nouvelle vague* artiness. There is a distinctive sensibility at work in his films, but his means of expression are too muddled and pretentious. The idea of pairing Rita Tushingham and Lynn Redgrave in *Smashing Time* should have been resisted at all costs, and it is a measure of the director's excess that he should flaunt the frightening antisexual implications of this oddest of odd couples.

THEODORE J. FLICKER

FILMS: 1964—The Troublemaker. 1967—The President's Analyst.

Theodore J. Flicker is one of the few exemplars of the New Yorkish cabaret sensibility at large in Hollywood. Flicker seems aware of the pitfalls of excessively satiric conceptions, perhaps too aware. He seems overly conscious of the risks of audacity and insufficiently receptive to the opportunities. His gibes at J. Edgar Hoover and the CIA in *The President's Analyst* were welcome, but he seems too much of the time to be working the high trapeze of irreverence with the net of conformist calculation.

BERNARD GIRARD

FILM: 1966—*Dead Heat on a Merry-Go-Round.* 1969—The Mad Room.

Bernard Girard has made an interesting debut as writer-director of *Dead Heat on a Merry-Go-Round,* but it is difficult to imagine where he can go from here. *Dead Heat* seems complete and definitive as the expression of a chilling sophistication in the treatment of the big caper genre. There is something so inhuman in the directorial attitude revealed that *Dead Heat* seems like a dead end.

ROBERT GIST

FILM: 1966—An American Dream.

An American Dream can be described with some affection as the worst picture of its year because of the hilarious misalliance of Mailer and Hollywood. Robert Gist's direction lingers in the mind in spite of, or perhaps because of, this very misalliance. His stylistic conviction deserves another chance with less intransigent material.

CURTIS HARRINGTON

FILMS: 1942–1955—Fall of the House of Usher, Crescendo, Renascence, Fragment of Seeking, Picnic, On the Edge, Dangerous Houses, The Assignation, The Wormwood Star (Experimental Shorts). 1961—Night Tide. 1966—Queen of Blood. 1967— Games.

Curtis Harrington is the most consciously Sternbergian of the cinéastes of the sixties, and his films reflect the triumph of décor over drama. *Games* comes closest to bridging the gap between the hopelessly self-indulgent symbolism of *Night Tide* and the very conventional attitude Harrington brings to the working out of his plots. Harrington probably needs most a producer like the late Val Lewton. Up to now, however, his films have lacked the finer instincts of Sternberg's. Harrington's glossy surfaces have the feel of Sternberg, but not the feelings.

HARVEY HART

FILMS: 1965—*Bus Riley's Back in Town,* Dark Intruder. 1968 —The Sweet Ride.

Harvey Hart and his Canadian colleagues—Jewison, Furie, Narizzano, Hiller, et al.—seem stronger on technique than personality. Nonetheless Hart's direction of *Bus Riley's Back in Town* almost transcended the egregiousness of William Inge's maudlin memories of the Middle West.

BEN HECHT (1893–1964) &
CHARLES MACARTHUR (1895–1956)

FILMS: 1934—*Crime Without Passion.* 1935—Once in a Blue Moon, *The Scoundrel.* 1936—Soak the Rich. Hecht is credited with direction of three other films without MacArthur: 1940— *Angels Over Broadway* (with Lee Garmes). 1946—Specter of the Rose. 1952—Actors and Sin.

Ben Hecht and Charles MacArthur decided to beat Hollywood at its own game with their own special brand of Broadway sophistication. Together with Noel Coward, they fashioned in *The Scoundrel* the most entertaining exposure of Broadway's notion of sophistication ever filmed. Hecht and MacArthur were a great deal of fun, but they seem even more frivolous today than many of the Hollywood characters they ridiculed.

HOWARD HUGHES (1905–   )

FILMS: 1930—Hell's Angels. 1943—The Outlaw.

Hughes has been caricatured and vilified from *The Barefoot Contessa* to *The Carpetbaggers.* He has been accused of destroying the American career of Jean Simmons, and of rejecting Bette Davis as an actress because she lacked sex appeal. The fact remains that his record as a director and a producer is far more interesting than his lurid reputation would indicate. Anyone who has produced *Scarface, Jet Pilot, Mad Wednesday, Angel Face,* and *Two Arabian Knights* cannot be all bad. To his credit, Hughes has never been as sanctimonious about his "art" as have those revered oracles of mediocrity, Samuel Goldwyn and Dore Schary. At the very least, Hughes is entitled to a sociological footnote for sponsoring the bosom craze that swept the world through Jane Russell's sullen bustiness in *The Outlaw.* (Two good reasons why every red-blooded American boy should see this movie are self-evident; the third exploded over Hiroshima in 1945.)

GENE KELLY (1912–   )

FILMS: With Stanley Donen: 1949—*On the Town.* 1952—*Singin' in the Rain.* 1955—*It's Always Fair Weather.* Solo: 1956—Invitation to the Dance. 1957—The Happy Road. 1958—Tunnel of Love. 1962—Gigot. 1967—Guide for the Married Man. 1969—Hello, Dolly.

The charm and brilliance of Gene Kelly's dancing has not carried over to his direction since the dissolution of his partnership with Donen. If Donen has since diminished, Kelly has completely disintegrated. Kelly's potentialities as a straight actor were never fully developed, and the Metro musical died before his musical ideas had been fully expressed. *Invitation to the Dance* was an uneasy mixture of Hollywood formulas and European pretensions, and *Gigot* was pure slop out of the gutters of an expatriate's Paris. Yet, *Singin' in the Rain* can never be tarnished by the subsequent derelictions of its participants.

BUZZ KULIK (1923–   )

FILMS: 1961—The Explosive Generation. 1963—*The Yellow Canary.* 1964—Ready for the People. 1967—*Warning Shot.* 1968—Sergeant Ryker, Villa Rides!, The Riot.

Buzz Kulik reveals an interesting glimmer of intelligence in *The Yellow Canary* and *Warning Shot*. He is from television, perhaps too much so. *Sergeant Ryker* has created considerable ill will by charging first-run movie prices for an attraction so obviously designed for television that the audience can almost see the test patterns.

CHARLES LAUGHTON (1899–1962)

FILM: 1955—*The Night of the Hunter.*

Rumor has it that the final shooting script of *The Night of the Hunter* was one-third Laughton, one-third James Agee, and one-third Davis Grubb. Be that what it may, *The Night of the Hunter* displays a striking visual style, almost semi-Germanic Griffith, which is completely lacking in the Huston-Agee-Forester *The African Queen* and the Windust-Agee-Crane *The Bride Came to Yellow Sky*. Moral: Directors, not writers, are the ultimate auteurs of the cinema, at least of cinema that has any visual meaning and merit.

IRVING LERNER (1909–   )

FILMS: 1954—Man Crazy. 1958—Edge of Fury, *Murder by Contract.* 1959—City of Fear. 1960—Studs Lonigan. 1963—Cry of Battle.

Murder by Contract is a minor classic of murderous understatement, and is all that need be said about Irving Lerner's career. Perhaps it is a mistake to treat films like *Murder by Contract* as means to an end or as overtures to grand operas. A director, like any artist, may have but one good work in his system. Often the promising work turns out to be the ultimate work, and *Murder by Contract* seems to fall into that category.

IDA LUPINO (1918–)

FILMS: 1949—Not Wanted. 1950—Outrage, Never Fear. 1951—Hard, Fast and Beautiful. 1953—The Bigamist, The Hitch-Hiker. 1965—The Trouble with Angels. Note: *Not Wanted* was actually directed by Elmer Clifton, but Ida Lupino produced and wrote the screenplay and presumably served her technical apprenticeship with the silent-movie veteran.

Ida Lupino's directed films express much of the feeling if little of the skill which she has projected so admirably as an actress. But while we are on the subject: Lillian Gish, that actress of actresses, once directed a film (*Remodeling Her Husband*—1921), and declared afterward that directing was no job for a lady. Simone de Beauvoir would undoubtedly argue the contrary, but relatively few women have put the matter to the test. Dorothy Arzner, Jacqueline Audrey, Mrs. Sidney Drew, Lilian Ducey, Julia Crawford Ivers, Frances Marion, Vera McCord, Frances Nordstrom, Mrs. Wallace Reid, Lois Weber, and Margery Wilson come to mind as little more than a ladies' auxiliary. (The unwary historian might also include such certified males as Monta Bell and Marion Gering). A special footnote must be devoted to the widow of Alexander Dovjenko, particularly for such séance productions as *Poem from the Sea* and *Years of Fire*. A longer and considerably more controversial footnote would be devoted to Leni Riefenstahl, more for the relative objectivity of her *Olympiad* than for the blatant contrivance of *Triumph of the Will*. The jury is still out on Vera Chytilova, Shirley Clarke, Juleen Compton, Joan Littlewood, Nadine Trintignant, Agnes Varda, and Mai Zetterling.

ROBERT MONTGOMERY (1904–)

FILMS: 1946—Lady in the Lake. 1947—*Ride the Pink Horse*. 1949—*Once More, My Darling*. 1950—Eye Witness. 1960 —Gallant Hours.

Robert Montgomery always admired James Cagney's acting, and Cagney always admired Montgomery's, but neither actor received the direction he deserved, except on the rarest occasions, Montgomery with Hitchcock (*Mr. and Mrs. Smith*) and Ford (*They Were Expendable*), Cagney with Walsh (*White Heat*) and Ray (*Run for Cover*). Montgomery directed Cagney in *Gallant Hours* period. Otherwise, Montgomery achieved some notoriety with his subjective camera in *Lady in the Lake*, coaxed a memorable performance out of Wanda Hendrix in *Ride the Pink Horse*, executed a charming *champ-contre-champ* joke in *Once More, My Darling*; and went to Britain to make *Eye Witness*, a film not entirely devoid of merit.

MIKE NICHOLS (1931–   )

FILMS: 1967—Who's Afraid of Virginia Woolf ? 1968—*The Graduate.* 1969—Catch-22.

Everything Mike Nichols has touched on stage and screen has turned to gold if not glory. Why then do there remain little pockets of cultural resistance to his magical manipulation? He was criticized, perhaps unjustly, for taking *Virginia Woolf* out of doors into shivering cinematic reality. Richard Burton gave a good performance; Elizabeth Taylor was monotonously shrill; Sandy Dennis was excruciatingly mannered; George Segal was excessively bland. The film seemed to preen itself on its honesty. But why were the settings so expressively sloppy? Was this an example of the subtlety that Nichols was bringing to Hollywood? Many critics thought so. The public thought so. Mike Nichols stood up to receive the directorial award from the Directors Guild of America, but the calling of his name turned out to be a mistake. Fred Zinnemann, a director infinitely duller and more "honest" than Nichols, was tapped for the dry-as-dust academics of *A Man for All Seasons*.

Whereas Nichols merely transferred *Virginia Woolf*, he transcended *The Graduate*. Nichols was not cashing in on the Burtons and Edward Albee with *The Graduate*. Anne Bancroft,

Dustin Hoffman, and Katherine Ross had little marquee value of their own, and Charles Webb's novel little presold potency. Nichols had turned the trick with a neatly eclectic style borrowed from directors as disparate as Federico Fellini and George Stevens, Ingmar Bergman and Richard Lester, Michelangelo Antonioni and Orson Welles. His supporting actors were dreadfully caricatured. The suspicion persisted in shamefully skeptical circles that Nichols was more a tactician than a strategist and that he won every battle and lost every war because he was incapable of the divine folly of a personal statement. No American director since Orson Welles had started off with such a bang, but Welles had followed his own road, and that made all the difference. Nichols seems too shrewd ever to get off the main highway. His is the cinema and theatre of complicity. And the customer is always right except in the long view of eternity.

CHRISTIAN NYBY

FILMS: 1951—*The Thing.* 1965—Operation C.I.A. 1967—First to Fight.

The Thing, with its understandable traces of Producer Howard Hawks and its unearthly traces of uncredited Orson Welles, remains an inexplicable incident in Nyby's otherwise negligible career.

ROBERT PARRISH (1916–   )

FILMS: 1951—The Mob, *Cry Danger.* 1952—Assignment Paris, My Pal Gus. 1953—Shoot First. 1955—*The Purple Plain,* Lucy Gallant. 1957—*Fire Down Below.* 1958—Saddle the Wind. 1959—*The Wonderful Country.* 1963—In the French Style. 1965 —Up from the Beach. 1967—The Bobo. 1968—Duffy. 1969—Doppelganger.

The Purple Plain stands out in the above list like a pearl among swine. What burst of Buddhist contemplation was responsible for such a haunting exception to such an exceptionable career? Apart from *The Purple Plain,* the films of Robert Parrish belong to a director who craves anonymity.

SAM PECKINPAH (1926–   )

FILMS: 1962—The Deadly Companions, *Ride the High Country.* 1965—*Major Dundee.* 1968—The Wild Bunch.

Ride the High Country was considered the sleeper of its year, but was it? At first glance, the film represented a fusion of the Boetticher-Scott and Tourneur-McCrea traditions, but then it turned out that its director grudgingly accepted Randolph Scott and Joel McCrea and the myths they incarnated simply for the sake of daubs of atmospheric realism from Peckinpah's palette. *Ride the High Country* is thus in retrospect something new in anti-Westerns. The trials and tribulations of *Major Dundee* confirmed the pattern of Peckinpah's ambitions. Since Peckinpah considers himself too intellectual to tell a story, it remains to be seen whether he will be forceful enough to develop a theme.

FRANK PERRY (1930–   )

FILMS: 1962—*David and Lisa.* 1963—Ladybug, Ladybug. 1968—*The Swimmer,* Trilogy. 1969—Last Summer.

David and Lisa brought fame and fortune to Frank and Eleanor Perry, and everyone said it was a case of a good script awkwardly directed because Frank Perry had never directed a movie before, and it is generally assumed that direction is more a craft than an art as writing is more an art than a craft. Actually, *David and Lisa* is rather awkwardly written and rather interestingly directed. Despite the disaster of *Ladybug, Ladybug,* it would seem that more may be heard from the Perrys before *David and Lisa* is written off once and for all as a one-shot. At the very least, Perry deserves attention for the disciplined performances of Keir Dullea and Janet Margolin.

ABE POLONSKY

FILMS: 1948—*Force of Evil*. 1968—Willie Boy.

William Pechter's astute analysis of Polonsky's career in the Spring 1962 issue of *Film Quarterly* confirms that Polonsky's influence was decisive over Rossen's in Garfield's companion vehicle, *Body and Soul*. Polonsky, along with Chaplin and Losey, remains one of the great casualties of the anti-Communist hysteria of the fifties. *Force of Evil* stands up under repeated viewings as one of the great films of the modern American cinema, and Garfield's taxicab scene with Beatrice Pearson takes away some of the luster from Kazan's Brando-Steiger tour de force in *On the Waterfront*.

STUART ROSENBERG

FILMS: 1960—*Murder Inc.* (with Burt Balaban). 1961— Question 7. 1967—*Cool Hand Luke*. 1968—The April Fools. 1969 —The Lenny Bruce Story.

Stuart Rosenberg has had an intermittent movie career in between piling up prestigious credits in television. *Cool Hand Luke* is his most striking achievement to date and one of many recent manifestations of a tendency in the American cinema to use visual virtuosity as an end in itself. *Point Blank, Bonnie and Clyde,* and *In the Heat of the Night* are other examples of films that undercut the conventions of their genres by escaping the controlled studio environments in which the conventions were carefully contrived in terms of light and shadow. Rosenberg, like Boorman (*Point Blank*), Penn (*Bonnie and Clyde*), and Jewison (*In the Heat of the Night*) tends to a certain stylistic eclecticism in rendering scripts that strive very consciously for a Europeanized ambiguity. For all its effectiveness as entertainment, *Cool Hand Luke* seems too histrionic and exhibitionistic for comfort. What is wrong with *Cool Hand Luke* seems less a matter of compromise than miscalculation. Even in the midst of monumental mistakes, Rosenberg's direction is capable of tasteful touches. Nothing, particularly the villainy, ever gets completely out of hand.

ELLIOT SILVERSTEIN

FILMS: 1962—Belle Sommers. 1965—*Cat Ballou*. 1967—*The Happening*. 1969—A Man Called Horse.

Elliot Silverstein's directorial career virtually came out of nowhere with *Cat Ballou*. (*Belle Sommers* was not exactly nowhere, at least not in terms of quality, but Silverstein himself has preferred to begin his official career with *Cat Ballou* much as Preminger begins with *Laura,* Stevens with *Alice Adams* and Zinnemann with *The Search.*) *Cat Ballou* won an Oscar for Lee Marvin and the ire of serious admirers of the Western, a genre that traditionally defies parody and satire. Silverstein then stubbed his toe on *The Happening,* a generation-gap kidnaping comedy-melodrama that was as underrated by the reviewers as *Cat Ballou* was overrated. What is most distinctive about Silverstein's directorial personality is not so much a smart-alecky attitude toward his material as a penchant for Jewish humor in the unlikeliest situations.

ALEXANDER SINGER (1932–   )

FILMS: 1961—*Cold Wind in August*. 1964—Psyche 59. 1965—Love Has Many Faces.

Alexander Singer's screen subjects have become increasingly sordid, and his career increasingly dubious. *Cold Wind in August* still sparkles with Lola Albright's distinctively hip brand of sensuality. Singer was almost as adept with Patricia Neal and Samantha Eggar in *Psyche 59,* but the fading stars and starlets of *Love Has Many Faces* —Lana Turner, Ruth Roman, and Virginia Grey —take the director into the dreaded country of camp. The suspicion persists that Singer is better than his material, but that there is something in the very worst material that attracts his attention. Curiously, Lana Turner, Ruth Roman, and Virginia Grey, and their assorted gigolos are more affecting than they have any right to be. Perhaps Singer has become the poet of the rejected woman while commercially exploiting the subject of the fallen woman.

JACK SMIGHT (1926–   )

FILMS: 1964—I'd Rather Be Rich. 1965—The Third Day. 1966—Harper, *Kaleidoscope.* 1968—The Secret War of Harry Frigg, *No Way to Treat a Lady,* The Illustrated Man. 1969—Rabbit, Run.

Jack Smight's directorial career has been settling into an interesting pattern. *Harper, Kaleidoscope,* and *No Way to Treat a Lady* are very weakly directed on the action and suspense levels. *Lady* is particularly unbelievable whenever New York City is integrated into the action as an exterior set. The same police car hurtles down the same academically neonized corridor of Forty-second Street three times in succession like a recurring refrain in a visual verse by Cocteau. Where Smight excels is in the tensions and humors of offbeat relationships enacted by Paul Newman and Arthur Hill in *Harper,* Susanna York, Clyde Revill, and Murray Melvin in *Kaleidoscope,* and George Segal and Lee Remick in *No Way to Treat a Lady.*

PETER TEWKSBURY

FILMS: 1964—*Sunday in New York,* Emil and the Detectives. 1967—Doctor, You've Got to Be Kidding. 1968—Stay Away, Joe.

Peter Tewksbury's direction is invariably more graceful than his material deserves. *Sunday in New York* was cursed with Norman Krasna's nasty plot contrivances despite the pleasant casting of Jane Fonda, Cliff Robertson, and Rod Taylor, not to mention the moderately miraculous metamorphosis of Jo Morrow from plump ingenue to sleek siren. *Emil and the Detectives* may have been handicapped somewhat by the demands of the Disney Organization, and *Doctor, You've Got to be Kidding* by one's preconceptions about Sandra Dee. Still, Tewskbury has persevered with his pleasantness, and such perseverance should be both recorded and rewarded.

PETER WATKINS (1937–)

FILMS: 1967—The War Game, Privilege.

Peter Watkins would become the Cromwell of film directors if he were given half a chance, and he has been given at least one and a half chances. *The War Game* represents for some the triumph of content over form, for others the triumph of paranoia over perception. *Privilege* manages to be more hysterical than *The War Game* with less provocation. Watkins seems to feel strongly and deeply about the state of the world, but he is so lacking in humor and balance and distance that he would probably wail and whine in Paradise itself. Significantly fallacious is his insistence that Paul Jones's natural charm as a singer and performer be suppressed for the sake of the theme.

JOHN WAYNE (1907–)

FILMS: 1960—The Alamo. 1968—The Green Berets.

Rumor has it that the old master himself, John Ford, directed some of *The Alamo*. Nevertheless, Wayne's epic style reveals enough individual visual beauties amid the oratorical bombast to encourage another try on a less pretentious scale. Unfortunately, *The Green Berets* seems like another trap.

JACK WEBB (1920–   )

FILMS: 1954—Dragnet. 1955—*Pete Kelley's Blues.* 1957—The D.I. 1959— –30–. 1961—The Last Time I Saw Archie.

Jack Webb's directed movies are rather peculiar manifestations of the techniques of his television series—*Dragnet.* Enormous close-ups of faces with clipped, understated dialogue, visual shouting combined with verbal whispering. The movies never clicked with the critics or the public, possibly because Webb's style was too controlled for the little he had to say.

PAUL WENDKOS

FILMS: 1957—*The Burglar.* 1958—*The Case Against Brooklyn,* Tarawa Beachhead. 1959—Gidget, *Face of a Fugitive,* Battle of the Coral Sea. 1960—Because They're Young. 1961—*Angel Baby,* Gidget Goes Hawaiian. 1963—Gidget Goes to Rome. 1966 —Johnny Tiger. 1968—Guns of the Magnificent Seven, Attack on the Iron Coast. 1969—Hellboats.

Paul Wendkos is teetering somewhere between Arthur Penn and John Frankenheimer, with frequent detours to the *Gidget* genre. His ideas about the relationship between form and content are still scrambled, and his career thus far is consistent only in its inconsistency. Perhaps Welles is a dangerous influence on any young director. Welles can get away with a lot more than can his most devout disciples because the power of Welles's personality holds the most varied forms in some meaningful context. However, it would be a mistake to strike too Faustian a tone with Wendkos. The *Gidget* movies are not all that bad, and *The Burglar* and *Angel Baby* are not all that good.

CORNELL WILDE (1915–   )

FILMS: 1956—*Storm Fear.* 1957—The Devil's Hairpin. 1958 —Maracaibo. 1963—Sword of Lancelot. 1966—*The Naked Prey.* 1967—*Beach Red.* 1969—The Raging Sea.

Cornell Wilde's first film, *Storm Fear,* was notable for its half-baked intensity and the actor-director's bizarre imitation of Marlon Brando after years of having other directors exploit Wilde's expressionless good looks. Wilde's turnabout was comparable to Dick Powell's at that moment when the sappiest tenor of the thirties became one of the toughest private eyes of the forties. Wilde's most recent efforts—*The Naked Prey* and *Beach Red* —are nothing if not ambitious. Wilde is still too bland as both actor and director to be given major consideration, but he docs reveal a modestly likable personality in over its head with themes oversized for the talent and skill available.

MICHAEL WINNER (1935–   )

FILMS: 1966—You Must Be Joking!, The Girl Getters. 1967 —The Jokers. 1968—I'll Never Forget What's 'Is Name.

Michael Winner gives conformity a mod look in *The Girl Getters, The Jokers,* and *I'll Never Forget What's 'Is Name.* Winner's films condemn and ridicule the very youthful spirit they exploit. *The Girl Getters* is condescending to young people, *The Jokers* malicious, and *I'll Never Forget What's 'Is Name* destructively cynical. Winner's films manage to be slick and messy at the same time. There are intimations in *What's 'Is Name* of Ingmar Bergman's *Wild Strawberries,* but with Winner there are only sour raspberries.

BUD YORKIN (1926–   )

FILMS: 1963—Come Blow Your Horn. 1965—Never Too Late. 1967—*Divorce American Style*. 1968—Inspector Clouseau. 1969—Two Times Two.

Bud Yorkin served his apprenticeship with two Broadway comedies that gave tastelessness and vulgarity new dimensions. After *Come Blow Your Horn* and *Never Too Late,* the only possible direction was up, but *Divorce American Style* turned out to be surprisingly effective entertainment on its own terms, and Yorkin displayed a commendable sense of timing in his set comedy scenes.

IX.
SUBJECTS
FOR
FURTHER
RESEARCH

These are the directors whose work must be more fully evaluated before any final determination of the American cinema is possible. There may be other unknown quantities as well, but this list will serve for the moment as a reminder of the gaps.

CLARENCE BROWN (1890–)

FILMS: 1920—The Great Redeemer. 1922—The Light in the Dark. 1923—Don't Marry for Money, The Acquittal. 1924—The Signal Tower, Butterfly. 1925—Smouldering Fires, The Eagle, *The Goose Woman.* 1926—Kiki, *Flesh and the Devil.* 1928—Trail of '98. 1929—Woman of Affairs, Wonder of Women, Navy Blues. 1930—*Anna Christie, Romance.* 1931—Inspiration, A Free Soul, Possessed. 1932—*Emma,* Letty Lynton: The Son-Daughter. 1933 —Looking Forward, Night Flight. 1934—Sadie McKee, Chained. 1935—Anna Karenina, *Ah Wilderness!* 1936—Wife Versus Secretary, The Gorgeous Hussy. 1937—Conquest. 1938—Of Human Hearts. 1939—Idiot's Delight, The Rains Came. 1940—Edison, the Man. 1941—Come Live with Me, They Met in Bombay. 1943 —The Human Comedy. 1944—The White Cliffs of Dover. 1945 —*National Velvet.* 1946—*The Yearling.* 1947—Song of Love. 1949—*Intruder in the Dust.* 1950—To Please a Lady. 1951— Angels in the Outfield, When in Rome. 1952—Plymouth Adventure.

Clarence Brown's career is not without a certain amiability in its evolution from German Expressionism (*Flesh and the Devil*) to American Gothic (*Intruder in the Dust*). His best films are usually his most modest—*Anna Christie, Ah Wilderness!, National Velvet,* and *Emma.* His main claim to fame is that he was Garbo's favorite and most frequent director, but none of his efforts attained the peaks of *Ninotchka* (Ernst Lubitsch), *Camille* (George Cukor), and *Queen Christina* (Rouben Mamoulian).

TOD BROWNING (1882–)

FILMS: 1918—Which Woman, The Deciding Kiss, The Eyes of Mystery, Revenge, The Legion of Death. 1919—Unpainted Woman, Wicked Darling, Exquisite Thief, Set Free, Brazen Beauty, Petal on the Current. 1920—The Virgin of Stamboul, Bonnie, Bonnie Lassie. 1921—Outside the Law, No Woman Knows. 1922—

The Wise Kid, Man Under Cover, Under Two Flags. 1923—Drifting, White Tiger, The Day of Faith. 1924—The Dangerous Flirt. 1925—*The Unholy Three*, The Mystic, Dollar Down, Silk Stocking Sal. 1926—The Road to Mandalay, The Black Bird. 1927—The Show, The Unknown, London After Midnight. 1928—Big City. 1929—East Is East, Thirteenth Chair. 1930—Paid. 1931—*Dracula*, Iron Man. 1932—*Freaks*. 1933—Fast Workers. 1935—Mark of the Vampire. 1936—*The Devil-Doll*. 1939—Miracles for Sale.

The morbid cinema of Tod Browning seems to have been ahead of its time on some levels and out of its time on others. *Freaks* is memorable chiefly because of its impassive confrontation of the most monstrous deformities. By contrast, *Dracula* seems dully static in its elaborate expressionism. On a purely technical level, Browning seems less talented than Whale, not to mention Murnau (*Nosferatu*) and Dreyer (*Vampyr*) on the sublime level of obsessional horror. However, Browning's career is more meaningful than Whale's in terms of a personal obsession. Also, *Freaks* may be one of the most compassionate movies ever made.

JAMES CRUZE (1884–   )

FILMS: 1919—Roaring Road, The Dub, Alias Mike Moran, Too Many Millions, You're Fired, Love Burglar. 1920—Hawthorne of the U.S.A., The Lottery Man, Mrs. Temple's Telegram, An Adventure in Hearts, Terror Island, What Happened to Jones. 1921—The Dollar a Year Man, Food for Scandal, Always Audacious, Charm School. A Full House, Crazy to Marry. 1922—One Glorious Day, Is Matrimony a Failure, The Dictator, The Old Homestead, Thirty Days. 1923—*The Covered Wagon, Hollywood, Ruggles of Red Gap*, To the Ladies. 1924—The Garden of Weeds, The Fighting Coward, The City that Never Sleeps, The Enemy Sex, *Merton of the Movies*. 1925—The Goose Hangs High, *Beggar on Horseback*, Welcome Home, Marry Me, The Pony Express. 1926—Mannequin, The Waiter from the Ritz, Old Ironsides. 1927—We're All Gamblers, On to Reno, The City, Gone Wild. 1928—Red Mark, Excess Baggage, Mating Call. 1929—Man's Man. 1930—Once a Gentleman, Great Gabbo, She Got What She Wanted. 1931—Salva-

tion Nell. 1932—*Washington Merry-Go-Round,* If I Had a Million.
1933—Sailor Be Good, Racetrack, *I Cover the Waterfront,* Mr.
Skitch. 1934—*David Harum,* Their Big Moment. 1935—Helldorado, Two Fisted. 1936—*Sutter's Gold.* 1937—The Wrong Road.
1938—Prison Nurse, Gangs of New York, Come On Leathernecks.

James Cruze has been saddled with the epic reputation of *The
Covered Wagon,* one of the most disappointing of all "great classics." The evidence in *The Covered Wagon* and elsewhere suggests a rather lively if somewhat coarse sense of humor hindered
to some degree by a very crude visual style. Cruze looked very
old-fashioned throughout the thirties, but today such interesting
museum pieces as *I Cover the Waterfront, David Harum,* and
even the catastrophic *Sutter's Gold* seem endearingly dated.

PAUL FEJOS (1898–   )

FILMS: HUNGARIAN PERIOD: 1920—The Black Captain, Pan,
Hallucination. 1921—Le Revenant. 1923—The Rose of Eggert.
HOLLYWOOD PERIOD: 1928—Last Moment, Lonesome. 1929—
Broadway, The Last Performance. EUROPEAN PERIOD: 1932—Fan-
tomas, Marie, The Condemned Balaton. 1933—Sonnenstrahl, Les
Millions en Fuite. 1935—Prisoners, Le Hors la Loi, The Golden
Smile. 1938—A Handful of Rice (Ceylonese documentary).

Fejos is a mysterious figure in the American cinema. He is regarded much more highly in France, both for *Lonesome* and for
the European version of George Hill's *The Big House.* He left
Hollywood at about the time of the sound changeover, and later
found his way back to his native Hungary. *Lonesome* is a rather
curious relic of Hollywood's changeover from eloquently expressive silence to coarse and clumsy sound. Many film historians
were traumatized by the heartbreaking superiority of the last
silents to the first talkies, and we are conditioned to invidious
comparisons between the unpopular virtuosity of, say, *Docks of
New York* as opposed to the popular vulgarity of, say, *The Singing Fool. Lonesome,* however, carried the contrast to the point of
schizophrenia. A tender love story in its silent passages, *Lonesome* becomes crude, clumsy, and tediously tongue-tied in its

"talkie" passages added to the finished film to make it that hybrid monstrosity of the period, a part-talkie. We know now that sound was as desirable as it was inevitable, but after seeing and hearing *Lonesome,* it is possible to appreciate the depth of an aesthete's despair at a time when the medium seemed a mess.

SIDNEY FRANKLIN (1893–   )

FILMS: 1918—The Safety Curtain, Her Only Way, The Babes in the Woods, Treasure Island, Aladdin and the Wonderful Lamp, Jack and the Beanstalk, Six Shooter Andy, The Bride of Fear, Confession. 1919—Fan Fan, Probation Wife, Heart of Wetona, Forbidden City, Ali Baba and the Forty Thieves. 1920—The Heart of the Hills, The Hoodlum, Two Weeks. 1921—Not Guilty, Courage, Unseen Forces. 1922—The Primitive Lover, Smilin' Through, The Beautiful and the Damned, East Is West. 1923—Dulcy, Brass, Tiger Rose. 1924—Her Night of Romance. 1925—Learning to Love, Her Sister from Paris. 1926—Beverly of Graustark, The Duchess of Buffalo. 1928—The Actress. 1929—Wild Orchids, Last of Mrs. Cheney, Devil May Care. 1930—Lady of Scandal, A Lady's Morals, Soul Kiss. 1931—*The Guardsman, Private Lives.* 1933—Reunion in Vienna. 1934—Barretts of Wimpole Street. 1935—*The Dark Angel.* 1937—*The Good Earth.* 1957—The Barretts of Wimpole Street.

Sidney Franklin was a director dear to the heart of the legendary Irving J. Thalberg. Franklin was slow, deliberate, conscientious, and dull as were most of the Thalberg-Franklin productions. Perhaps the peak year was 1931 with Lunt and Fontanne transcribing Molnar's *The Guardsman* and Montgomery and Shearer doing the same for Coward's *Private Lives.* This was the era of Hollywood's most Anglicized gentility. We shall never see its equal again.

WILLIAM K. HOWARD (1899–   )

FILMS: 1921—What Love Will Do. 1922—Extra, Extra, Deserted at the Altar, Danger Ahead. 1923—Lucky Dan, The Fourth

Musketeer, Captain-Fly-By-Night, Let's Go. 1924—The Border Legion, East of Broadway, The Torrent. 1925—Code of the West, The Light of Western Stars, The Thundering Herd. 1926—Volcano, Red Dice, Bachelor Brides, Gigolo. 1927—*White Gold*, The Main Event. 1928—Ship Comes In, River Pirate. 1929—Christina, *The Valiant*, Love, Live and Laugh. 1930—Good Intentions, Scotland Yard. 1931—Don't Bet on Women, *Transatlantic*, Surrender. 1932 —Trial of Vivienne Ware, First Year, Sherlock Holmes. 1933— *Power and the Glory*. 1934—Cat and the Fiddle, This Side of Heaven, Evelyn Prentice. 1935—*Vanessa—Her Love Story*, Rendezvous, *Mary Burns—Fugitive*. 1936—*The Princess Comes Across*. 1937—*Fire Over England*, Murder on Diamond Row. 1939 —*Back Door to Heaven*. 1940—Money and the Woman. 1941— Bullets for O'Hara. 1942—Klondike Fury. 1943—Johnny Come Lately. 1944—When the Lights Go On Again. 1946—A Guy Could Change.

William K. Howard has a deserved reputation for individualistic intransigence. *White Gold, The Valiant, Power and the Glory, Mary Burns—Fugitive,* and *Back Door to Heaven* show the signs of a very personal touch. Unfortunately, Howard's films do not display the degree of talent necessary to overcome the problems of a difficult temperament. Film historians talk about the studio system and its effect on the greatest talents, but it is the intermediate talent that suffered the most, specifically the directors, like Howard, who were good, but not quite good enough.

REX INGRAM (1892–   )

FILMS: 1918—His Robe of Honor, Humdrum Brown. 1920 —Shore Acres, Under Crimson Skies, The Day She Paid. 1921— *The Four Horsemen of the Apocalypse*, Hearts are Trumps, The Conquering Power. 1922—Turn to the Right, *Prisoner of Zenda*, Trifling Women. 1923—Where the Pavement Ends, *Scaramouche*. 1924—The Arab. 1926—Mare Nostrum, The Magician. 1927— A Garden of Allah. 1929—Three Passions. 1932—Baroud.

Rex Ingram is one of the forgotten directors of the film societies. His reputation, like Sternberg's, suffers from the charge of excessive pictorialism. Only a resurrection of his work can confirm the validity of the judgment. *The Four Horsemen of the Apocalypse* alone justifies a revaluation.

HENRY KING (1888–   )

FILMS: 1912–1917—Short features for Lubin, Pathé, General Film Company, and Mutual. 1919—23½ Hours Leave, A Fugitive from Matrimony, Haunting Shadows. 1920—The White Dove, Uncharted Channels, One Hour Before Dawn, Help Wanted —Male, Dice of Destiny. 1921—When We Were 21, Mistress of Shenstone, Salvage, The Sting of the Lash, *Tol'able David*. 1922— The Seventh Day, Sonny, The Bond Boy, Fury. 1923—*The White Sister*. 1924—*Romola*. 1925—Sackcloth and Scarlet, Any Woman, *Stella Dallas*. 1926—Partners, *The Winning of Barbara Worth*. 1927—The Magic Flame. 1928—The Woman Disputed (Codirected with Sam Taylor). 1929—She Goes to War. 1930— Hell Harbor, Eyes of the World, *Lightnin'*. 1931—Merely Mary Ann, *Over the Hill*. 1932—The Woman in Room 13. 1933—*State Fair*, I Loved You Wednesday. 1934—Carolina, Marie Galante. 1935—*One More Spring, Way Down East*. 1936—The Country Doctor, Ramona. 1937—*Lloyd's of London*, Seventh Heaven. 1938 —*In Old Chicago, Alexander's Ragtime Band*. 1939—*Jesse James*, Stanley and Livingstone. 1940—Little Old New York, Maryland, Chad Hanna. 1941—A Yank in the RAF, Remember the Day. 1942 —The Black Swan. 1944—*The Song of Bernadette*, Wilson. 1945 —A Bell for Adano. 1946—*Margie*. 1947—The Captain from Castile. 1948—Deep Waters. 1949—The Prince of Foxes. 1950 —*Twelve o'Clock High, The Gunfighter*. 1951—I'd Climb the Highest Mountain. 1952—David and Bathsheba, *Wait Till the Sun Shines Nellie*, The Gift of the Magi episode in O. Henry's Full House, The Snows of Kilimanjaro. 1954—King of the Khyber Rifles. 1955 —Untamed, *Love Is a Many Splendored Thing*. 1956—Carousel. 1957—The Sun Also Rises. 1958—The Bravados. 1959—This Earth Is Mine. 1962—Tender Is the Night.

Would film history have been radically altered if Henry King had directed *The Grapes of Wrath* and John Ford *Jesse James,* instead of vice versa? Not likely. Ford lifted a Western like *Stagecoach* above its customary level of significance, whereas King muffed such fashionably liberal opportunities as *Wilson* and *A Bell for Adano*. The careers of Ford and King run a somewhat parallel course at Fox. Both directed Will Rogers; both did versions of *Lightnin'*, Ford in 1925, King in 1930; both dealt sincerely with rustic themes until that fateful day in 1935 when Variety headlined: STICKS NIX HICKS PIX. Henry King's place in the history books is attributable almost entirely to the happy accident of Pudovkin's admiration of *Tol'able David* with its broad strokes of expressive villainy. *Stella Dallas, The Winning of Barbara Worth, State Fair, In Old Chicago, The Song of Bernadette, Margie, Twelve o'Clock High*, and even *Love Is a Many Splendored Thing* and *The Bravados* are likable enough in their plodding intensity, but not quite forceful enough to compensate for the endless footage of studio-commissioned slop which King could never convert into anything personal or even entertaining. The one film for which he will probably be remembered longest is *The Gunfighter*, the most charming of the handle-bar-mustache anti-Westerns. But even at his best, King tended to be turgid and rhetorical in his storytelling style.

MALCOLM ST. CLAIR (1897–   )

FILMS: 1925—On Thin Ice, Are Parents People, The Trouble with Wives, After Business Hours. 1926—*The Grand Duchess and the Waiter*, Good and Naughty, *A Woman of the World, A Social Celebrity, The Show-Off*, The Popular Sin. 1927—Knockout Reilly, Breakfast at Sunrise. 1928—Gentlemen Prefer Blondes, Sporting Goods, Beau Broadway, Fleet's In. 1929—Canary Murder Case, Side Street, Night Parade. 1930—Montana Moon, Dangerous Nan [*sic*] McGrew, Remote Control, Boudoir Diplomat. 1933—Goldie Gets Along. 1934—Olsen's Big Moment. 1936—Crack-Up. 1937—Time Out for Romance, Born Reckless, She Had to Eat, Dangerously Yours. 1938—A Trip to Paris, Safety in Numbers. 1939—Down on the Farm, Quick Millions. 1940—Young As You Feel, Meet the Missus. 1942—The Bashful Bachelor, The Man in the Trunk, Over My Dead Body. 1943—Two Weeks to Live, Jitterbugs, The Dancing Masters. 1944—The Big Noise. 1945—The Bull Fighters. 1948—Arthur Takes Over, Fighting Back.

St. Clair's silent films, particularly *The Grand Duchess and The Waiter* and *A Social Celebrity*, fizzed, and his sound films fizzled. It was as simple and as tragic as that.

VICTOR SEASTROM (VICTOR SJÖSTRÖM) (1879–1960)

FILMS: 1912—Trädgårdsmästaren (False Alarm), Ett Hemligt Giftermäl (A Secret Marriage), En Sommarsaga (A Tale of Summer), Lady Marions Sommarflirt (Lady Marion's Summer Romance), Det Var I Maj (It Was in May), Aktenskapsbyrän (The Marriage Bureau), Löjen Och Tärar (Laughter and Tears). 1913—Blodets Röst (The Voice of Blood), Ingebord Holm, Livets Konflikter (Life's Conflicts), Prästen (The Pastor), Kärlek Starkare Än Hat (Love Is Stronger Than Hate), Halvblod (Mixed Blood), Miraklet (The Miracle), Strejken (The Strike). 1914—Dömen Icke (Judge Not), Bra Flicka Reder Sig Själv (A Brave Girl Should Solve Her Problems by Herself), Sonad Skuld (Payment for Error), Högfjällets Dotter (Girl of the Snow), Hjärtan Som Mötas (Hearts According to Fashion), Gatans Barn (Children of the Street). 1915—Ev av de Mänga (One Among Many), Landshövdingens Dottrar (The Governor's Daughters), Skomakare Bliv Vid Din Läst (To Each His Calling), Judaspengar (The Wages of Judas), Skepp Som Mötas (The Meeting of Ships), I Prövningens Stund (The Hour of Trial), Havsgamar (The Scavengers of the Sea), Hon Segrade (She Triumphs). 1916—Therese, Dödskyssen (The Strange Adventure of the Engineer Lebell), Terje Vigen. 1917—*Berg-Ejvind Och Hans Hustru* (*The Outlaw's Wife*), Tosen Frän Stormyrtorpe. 1918—*Ingmarssonerna* (I) (The Voice of the Ancestors), *Ingmarssonerna* (II) (The Voice of the Ancestors). 1919—Klostret I Sendomir (The Monastery of Sendomir), *Karin Ingsmarsdotter*, Hans Näds Testamente. 1920—*Körkarlen* (*The Phantom Carriage*), Mästerman (Master Samuel). 1921—Vem Dömer? (Trial by Fire). 1922—Omringade Huset. 1923—Eld Omborg. 1924—Name the Man, *He Who Gets Slapped*. 1925—Confessions of a Queen, *The Tower of Lies*. 1926—*The Scarlet Letter*. 1928—*The Divine Woman, The Wind,* Masks of the Devil. 1930—A Lady to Love, Markurells I Wadköping, Väter und Söhne (German Version of Markurells I Wadköping). 1937—Under the Red Robe.

It is possible that Victor Seastrom was the world's first great director, even before Chaplin and Griffith. Seastrom and Stiller stand at that odd confluence of Scandinavian air and sky later to give artistic life to Dreyer and Bergman. Seastrom's American career is peculiarly uneven, *The Wind* standing up much better today than *The Scarlet Letter*. It is as if when Seastrom left Sweden, his artistic soul couldn't breathe. There was not enough air on the Hollywood sound stages.

MAURICE TOURNEUR (1876–   )

FILMS: 1914—Mother, The Man of the Hour, The Wishing Ring, The Pit. 1915—Alias Jimmy Valentine, The Cub, Trilby, The Ivory Snuff Box, A Butterfly on the Wheel. 1916—The Pawn of Fate, The Hand of Peril, The Closed Road, The Rail Rider, The Velvet Paw. 1917—A Girl's Folly, The Whip, *The Pride of the Clan,* The Poor Little Rich Girl, The Undying Flame, The Law of the Land, Exile, Barbary Sheep, The Rise of Jennie Cushing. 1918— Rose of the World, A Doll's House, The Blue Bird, Prunella, Sporting Life, Woman. 1919—The White Heather, The Broken Butterfly, The Life Line. 1920—My Lady's Garter, Treasure Island, The Great Redeemer, The White Circle, Deep Waters, *The Last of the Mohicans.* 1921—The Bait, *The Foolish Matrons.* 1922—Lorna Doone. 1923—While Paris Sleeps, The Christian, The Isle of Lost Ships, The Brass Bottle, Jealous Husbands. 1924—Torment, The White Moth. 1925—Never the Twain Shall Meet, Sporting Life, Clothes Make the Pirate. 1926—Aloma of the South Seas, Old Loves and New, The Mysterious Island. EUROPEAN PERIOD: 1927— L'Équipage. 1929—Das Schiff der Verloren. 1930—Accusée Levez-Vous. 1931—Maison de Danses, Partir! 1932—Au Nom de la Loi, Les Gaîtés de l'Escalron. 1933—Les Deux Orphelines, Obsession. 1934—Le Voleur. 1935—Justin de Marseille, Königsmark. 1936—Samson, Avec le Sourire. 1938—Le Patriote, Katia. 1940—Volpone. 1941—Péchés de Jeunesse, Mam'zelle Bonaparte. 1942—La Main du Diable. 1943—La Val d'Enfer, Cécile Est Morte. 1947—Apres d'Amour. 1948—L'Impasse des Deux Anges.

Maurice Tourneur's early American films still remain to be explored in depth. Off the startling evidence of *The Last of the Mohicans* and Barbara Bedford's expressively perverse performance therein, it would seem that Tourneur is one of the leading stylists of the period, if not actually in a class by himself.

X.
MAKE
WAY
FOR
THE
CLOWNS!

These are the most conspicuous of the nondirectorial auteurs, and, as such, they cannot be subsumed under any directorial style. They are ultimately the funniest footnotes to the auteur theory.

W. C. FIELDS (1879–1946)

FILMS: 1915—Pool Sharks. 1925—Janice Meredith, *Sally of the Sawdust* (directed by D. W. Griffith). 1926—It's the Old Army Game (A. Edward Sutherland), That Royle Girl (D. W. Griffith), So's Your Old Man (Gregory La Cava). 1927—*Running Wild* (Gregory La Cava), Two Flaming Youths (John Waters), The Potters (Fred Newmeyer). 1928—Tillie's Punctured Romance (A. Edward Sutherland), Fools for Luck (Charles F. Reisner). 1930—*The Golf Specialist* (Monte Brice), Her Majesty Love (William Dieterle). 1932—*The Dentist* (Leslie Pierce), If I Had a Million (Eddie Cline), *Million Dollar Legs* (Eddie Cline), International House. 1933—*The Barber Shop* (Arthur Ripley), *The Fatal Glass of Beer* (Arthur Ripley), The Pharmacist (Arthur Ripley), Alice in Wonderland (Norman McLeod), Tillie and Gus (Francis Martin). 1934—*Six of a Kind* (Leo McCarey), You're Telling Me (Erle Kenton), Mrs. Wiggs of the Cabbage Patch (Norman Taurog), It's a Gift (Norman Taurog), The Old-Fashioned Way (William Beaudine), Mississippi (A. Edward Sutherland), *The Man on the Flying Trapeze* (Clyde Bruckman), *David Copperfield* (George Cukor). 1936—Poppy (A. Edward Sutherland). 1938—The Big Broadcast of 1938 (Mitchell Leisen). 1939—You Can't Cheat an Honest Man (George Marshall), 1940—*The Bank Dick* (Eddie Cline), My Little Chickadee (Eddie Cline). 1941—Never Give a Sucker an Even Break (Eddie Cline). 1942—Tales of Manhattan (Julien Duvivier). 1944—Follow the Boys (A. Edward Sutherland), Song of the Open Road (S. Sylvan Simon). 1945—Sensations of 1945 (Andrew Stone).

The vogue for W. C. Fields is concerned more with the comedian's astringent personality than with any particular form of cinema. W. C. Fields is enjoyed as a critical reaction against the prevailing saccharinity of the American cinema, or at least that part of the American cinema that is sufficiently inane to justify the wildest Fieldsian frenzies against Man and Woman. A combined misanthrope and misogynist, Fields virtually demolished the mythology of the American family in the opening reels of his most successful screen incarnation, *The Bank Dick*. Fields was especially appealing when he was bullying little children who had it all too much their own way on the screen in the thirties and forties. Less successful was Fields' one appearance with Mae West in *My Little Chickadee*. West brought out all the wizened, infantile sexlessness of Fields, and the pairing was more funny/ peculiar than funny/ha ha.

The Fields enthusiasts have amassed a considerable literature on their unheroic hero. The standard line about Fields was that he had the grace of a juggler, but few of his sight gags bear comparison with the more distinctively Fieldsian throwaway delivery of comic lines. With a talent more verbal than visual, it is difficult to appreciate the success of W. C. Fields in the silent cinema, but the fact remains that he functioned with comic effectiveness for silent directors as disparate as D. W. Griffith (*Sally of the Sawdust*) and Gregory La Cava (*Running Wild*). Some of his best comedy shorts were directed by Arthur Ripley. My favorite Fields line occurs on a golf course where, after he expresses the wish that his caddy lose a toenail, Fields hastily assures his female companion: "I was only fooling and pretending." The double disclaimer issues from Fields' lips with all the comic irony of Shakespeare's "Honest, honest Iago" from Othello's. All in all, Fields was a monstrous outgrowth of American Puritanism, and not even Dickens could have imagined such deviously and intransigently petty malice in any human being.

JERRY LEWIS (1928–   )

FILMS: DEAN MARTIN PERIOD: 1949—My Friend Irma (George Marshall). 1950—My Friend Irma Goes West (Hal Walker). 1951 —At War with the Army (Hal Walker), That's My Boy (Hal Walker). 1952—Sailor Beware (Hal Walker), Jumping Jacks (Norman Taurog). 1953—*The Stooge* (Norman Taurog), Scared Stiff (George Marshall), The Caddy (Norman Taurog). 1954—Money from Home (George Marshall), Living It Up (Norman Taurog), Three-Ring Circus (Joseph Pevney). 1955—You're Never Too Young (Norman Taurog), *Artists and Models* (Frank Tashlin). 1956 —Pardners (Norman Taurog), *Hollywood or Bust* (Frank Tashlin). SOLO PERIOD: 1957—The Delicate Delinquent (Don McGuire), The Sad Sack (George Marshall). 1958—Rock-a-Bye Baby (Frank Tashlin), The Geisha Boy (Frank Tashlin). 1959—Don't Give Up the Ship (Norman Taurog). 1960—Visit to a Small Planet (Norman Taurog), *The Bellboy* (Jerry Lewis), Cinderfella (Frank Tashlin). 1961—The Ladies' Man (Jerry Lewis), *The Errand Boy* (Jerry Lewis). 1962—*It's Only Money* (Frank Tashlin). 1963—*The Nutty Professor* (Jerry Lewis), Who's Minding the Store (Frank Tashlin). 1964—*The Patsy* (Jerry Lewis), The Disorderly Orderly (Frank Tashlin). 1965—The Family Jewels (Jerry Lewis), Boeing Boeing (John Rich). 1966—*Three On a Couch* (Jerry Lewis), Way . . . Way Out (Gordon Douglas). 1967—The Big Mouth (Jerry Lewis). 1968—Don't Raise the Bridge, Lower the River (Jerry Pasis).

If in this period of film history and polemics, I choose to take a stand *against* Jerry Lewis, I do so with certain preliminary qualifications. First, unlike some of my American colleagues, I think Jerry Lewis is worth discussing seriously as a bone of contention between American and French criticism. The principle involved in this instance is one of total cinema. What I always hoped the auteur theory would contribute to the American film scene was an expanding vision of the cinema as far as the eye of the beholder could see.

Second, Jerry Lewis cannot be considered an exclusively Cahierist cult figure. Lewis seems to be generally popular in France, and his strongest champions are to be found on the staff of *Positif,* a publication perpetually at war with *Cahiers.* (We will not speak here of a *Positif* critic who so resembles Jerry Lewis that hero-worship verges on narcissism.) Therefore, there are many arguments cited for Jerry Lewis undreamed of in the *Cahiers* aesthetic. The fact remains that Lewis has been blessed with French paradoxes and rationalizations denied to merely mortal *metteurs en scène* like Blake Edwards and Clive Donner. Serge Daney's elaborate analysis of the Edwardian cartoon fallacy in *The Great Race* would seem to pertain more appropriately to Jerry Lewis and his mentor, Frank Tashlin. It was Tashlin, after all, who started out as a cartoonist, not Edwards, and if anything distinguishes the Edwardian style, it is a cool, TV deadpan, verbal wit. I can think of a dozen Tashlin-Lewis gags that consist of contorting the human body into positions of linear distortion beyond muscular reality. The basic Edwards gag on the contrary denies its heroes the ability to transcend their physical limitations. Even when the Edwards characters wear animal masks, they retain their poise and sangfroid. Recall the climax of *The Pink Panther*, and compare it with the much admired (by the French) sequence in *The Patsy* where Hans Conried's hammy music teacher demolishes a room and inverts Jerry Lewis's Valentino eyebrows through the seismic acoustics of singing scales. Which of these two sequences owes more to the cartoon? The disinterested observer can make his own choice. Lest this point be misconstrued as unmotivated rationalization, let me add that I think *The Pink Panther, A Shot in the Dark,* and *What Did You Do in the War, Daddy?* are funnier than all the Lewis-Tashlin movies put together, but such a judgment leads to more complex considerations.

I have the impression that French critics see more in Lewis than mere comedy/ha-ha and that therefore the complaint that Lewis does not get all that many laughs is somewhat beside the point. The French critics often use Lewis as a club against American critics. In addition to the traditional argument about Americans being obtuse when it comes to analyzing their own art, there is the more cogent ploy about comedians and clowns being culturally underrated in their own time and place. Look at Chaplin, Keaton, Laurel and Hardy, and so on, the argument goes. How valid is this argument? Somewhat. Yet look at Wheeler and Woolsey and the Ritz Brothers. They look even worse in retrospect than they did at the time. However, until movies came along, clowns and comedians lacked any medium which could preserve their performances. There were legends and traditions, but no objective way of checking up on them, and there is consequently no verifiable classical criticism on performers. Who knows for sure how good David Garrick was or how adept Shakespeare's clowns? We of the cinema have to make up our own criteria as we go along, and our task is not made easier by the proliferation of categories. Jerry Lewis, for example, is not judged merely as a comic performer but as a comic creator. Cocteau has already been mentioned, and Molière cannot be far behind. Some skeptical observations on Lewis as an artist are therefore in order.

1. Jerry Lewis has become conscious, even self-conscious, about his own art. The Pirandellian ending of *The Patsy* is proof

enough of expanding ambitiousness. That the ending doesn't come off indicates that Lewis's aspiration now exceeds his ability.

2. There is a chasm between Lewis's verbal sophistication in nightclubs and sometimes on television and his simpering simple-mindedness on the screen. The problem of Lewis is thus similar to the problem of Danny Kaye in developing a screen character consistent with the character of a manic entertainer, a Golem, no less, of grotesque comic energy. It follows that Americans would be more conscious of this split in Lewis than the French would be. Similarly, the people in the front row of the Paramount knew the moment that Danny Kaye was permanently corrupted by Royalty in the Palladium. It was that moment when Kaye reverently displayed Harry Lauder's walking stick. The wild boy from Brooklyn had gone posh, and that was the end of his frenzy and his timing. The Queen Mother had turned him into a national shrine.

3. The fact that Lewis lacks verbal wit on the screen doesn't particularly bother the French, who then patiently explain to us what we are missing in Sacha Guitry, which, in turn, is what they are missing in Preston Sturges, particularly in his Paramount Period.

4. It would be presumptuous of Americans to tell the French that Maurice Chevalier represents their national soul. Similarly, it is presumptuous to claim that Lewis's screen experiences represent something profound about America. If Lewis cannot make American audiences respond to his films, he is living on borrowed time appealing to the intellectual authority of the French.

5. Lewis appeals to unsophisticated audiences in the sticks and to ungenteel audiences in the urban slums; he is bigger on Forty-second Street, for example, than anyplace else in the city. Most urban reviewers limit even his most ambitious efforts to the most routine reviews, and the weekly and monthly reviewers barely acknowledge his existence. Little distinction is made between the films he or Tashlin directs and the potboilers turned out by Douglas and Taurog and Rich, and so on. This is one argument for the completeness of French criticism.

6. Throughout his screen career Lewis has played the innocent with themes of effeminacy and transvestism. During his

partnership with Dean Martin, Lewis played the old Ginger Rogers role in a remake of *The Major and the Minor,* the old Carole Lombard role in a remake of *Nothing Sacred* and the old Betty Hutton role in a remake of *The Miracle of Morgan's Creek.* Only recently Lewis himself parodied one of the songs from *West Side Story* by beginning the first bars thus: "Maria, I know a guy named Maria." This kind of borscht-circuit hipsterism puts a different construction on the screen simpleton on whom Lewis lavishes so much sentimentality with so much apparent affection. If he is not playing down to his audience, he is playing down to himself, and all for the dubious dividends of "universality."

7. Martin and Lewis were something unique in comedy teams. Most comedy teams—the Marx Brothers, Laurel and Hardy, Abbott and Costello, even the Beatles—have a certain internal cohesion that unites them against the world outside. That is to say that members of a comedy team have more in common with each other than with anyone else. Martin and Lewis, at their best—and that means not in any of their movies—had a marvelous tension between them. The great thing about them was their incomparable incompatibility, the persistent sexual hostility, the professional knowingness they shared about the cutthroat world they were in the process of conquering. I think of them as they were the night they chased Bob Hope and Bing Crosby off the stage. The atmosphere reeked with the odor of rotting royalty being overthrown by the new Zanies, or the night they pretended to be thrown off the stage by Tony Martin and Joe Louis, and they were on top of the world. If *The Nutty Professor* is Jerry Lewis's best picture, it is largely because of the recreation of Dean Martin in the Hyde-like Buddy Love, and the subsequent rebirth of the Martin-Lewis tension. (*The Nutty Professor* was not handicapped by Victor Young's lovely melody for *The Uninvited* ["Stella by Starlight"] nor by the starlit Stella Stevens the song seemed to caress.)

8. The argument about laughs is irrelevant because laughter is less decisive in this instance than love. The French critics love Jerry Lewis. Many Americans do not.

9. Lewis can be criticized for the weakness of his narrative

bridges between his big comedy sequences. *The Family Jewels* is badly acted throughout, but particularly in the setting-up scenes. Never trust an art or an artist lacking in a passion for detail.

10. This brings up the question of the feature-length film as the proper vehicle for farce with continuous belly laughs. The late James Agee commemorated the Chaplin one- and two-reelers in his classic essay on comedy. Rudi Blesch prefers the shorter Keaton features to the longer ones in his excellent biography of Buster. Laurel and Hardy were better in short features than long ones, and so the argument goes. Perhaps belly laughs are not enough to sustain a feature-length film. Screen farce, like screen pornography, may involve culturally embarrassing examinations of audience metabolism and endurance, examinations which may explain why modern audiences are seldom moved as emotionally as they think guiltily they ought to be by the five-act tragedies of Shakespeare. For Lewis, this may mean a renewed attention to plots, dialogue, and, above all, grading.

11. When Lewis decides he has something to say, it comes out conformist, sentimental and banal. He was quite funny laughing at Hedda Hopper's hat in *The Patsy,* but then he has to go spoil it all by letting dear Hedda make a speech about the importance of being sincere in Hollywood. The clown's speech in *The Family Jewels* might have been conceived in the mind of any smug superpatriot as a sermon on what showbiz folk owe dear old Uncle Sam. The point here is not Lewis's politics, but rather his sanctimoniousness. A John Ford can celebrate the bitter glories of established orders, but the man and the message are one, and the style expresses the essential unity of what Ford is and what he says. Lewis's sentimentality is not only embarrassingly tinny in this admittedly sublime context. It is self-righteous as well.

12. Still, it is unfair to say that Jerry Lewis takes himself too seriously to pretend otherwise. Nor can the French be blamed for ruining him as a comedian. He had nowhere to go but up, and his post-highbrow ones are clearly superior to his pre-highbrow ones. The trouble is that he has never put one brilliant comedy together from fade-in to fade-out. We can only wait and hope, but the suspicion persists that the French are confusing talent with genius.

HAROLD LLOYD (1893–)

FILMS: 1916–1919: More than 100 one- and two-reelers. 1919: (2-reelers) Bumping into Broadway, Captain Kidd's Kids, From Hand to Mouth, His Royal Slyness. 1920: (2-reelers) Haunted Spooks, An Eastern Westerner, High and Dizzy, Get Out and Get Under; Number, Please. 1921: (3-reelers) Now or Never, Among Those Present, I Do, Never Weaken. Features: 1921—A Sailor-Made Man (Fred Newmeyer). 1922—*Grandma's Boy* (Fred Newmeyer), Dr. Jack (Fred Newmeyer). 1923—*Safety Last* (Fred Newmeyer and Sam Taylor), Why Worry? (Newmeyer and Taylor). 1924 —*Girl Shy* (Newmeyer and Taylor), Hot Water (Newmeyer and Taylor). 1925—*The Freshman* (Newmeyer and Taylor). 1926— For Heaven's Sake (Sam Taylor). 1927—The Kid Brother (Ted Wilde). 1928—*Speedy* (Ted Wilde). 1929—Welcome Danger (Clyde Bruckman). 1930—Feet First (Clyde Bruckman). 1932— Movie Crazy (Clyde Bruckman). 1934—The Cat's Paw (Sam Taylor). 1936—*The Milky Way* (Leo McCarey). 1938—Professor Beware (Elliott Nugent). 1947—*Mad Wednesday* (Preston Sturges).

Harold Lloyd has never achieved the critical eminence of Chaplin and Keaton, although *The Freshman* is one of the authentic comedy classics of the American screen. Lloyd has always seemed less universal than Chaplin, less starkly American than Keaton, less individualistic than both. With Chaplin and Keaton we feel that we shall never see their like again. Lloyd's spiritual facsimile is an even-money bet to turn up at the next convention of the Shriners, the Rotarians, or the Elks.

Lloyd's golden age was almost exclusively in the silents. From *Grandma's Boy* to *Speedy,* Lloyd fulfilled the wildest success fantasies of the so-called Jazz Age. He was less effective in the sound era, and even the very special gifts of Preston Sturges were unable to resurrect Lloyd as a comic favorite in *Mad Wednesday.* Audiences were somewhat baffled and put off by this zany optimist with more energy than charm. Lloyd is hardly the only comedian who failed to cross the sound barrier. Keaton's fall was even more precipitous, and Langdon virtually disappeared.

(Laurel and Hardy are a special case in that their sound personalities represent no particular break with their silent personalities. It is as if the coming of sound were incidental to two careers that were more specialized and limited than those of the more classic clowns. In a sense, Laurel and Hardy brought up the rear in the fullest anal sense, and they never seriously challenged the triumvirate of Chaplin, Keaton, and Lloyd in one era, or the Marx Brothers in another. In the end, they were eclipsed by one of the most minor of all comedy teams, Abbott and Costello.)

Lloyd was something else again. His fall was only partly one of inspiration. His comic type simply became obsolete after the Crash. The aggressive values he had embodied in the giddy twenties seemed downright irresponsible in the hung-over thirties. Lloyd's face did not gain in wisdom or pathos or resignation as it aged. It seemed as smug and complacent in the end as it had in the beginning. The fact that Lloyd never lost his money, but remained as rich as Croesus may have contributed to the absence of pain in his features. Lloyd never even seemed to get old. Money and optimism had cushioned him irrevocably against the metaphysical shock registered in the tortured expressions of Chaplin and Keaton in the dressing-room scene of *Limelight*.

THE MARX BROTHERS (Groucho–1895–   ) (Harpo–1893–1967) (Chico–1891–1961)

FILMS: 1929—*The Cocoanuts* (Robert Florey and Joseph Santley). 1930—*Animal Crackers* (Victor Heerman). 1931—*Monkey Business* (Norman McLeod). 1932—*Horse Feathers* (Norman McLeod). 1933—*Duck Soup* (Leo McCarey). 1935—*A Night at the Opera* (Sam Wood). 1937—A Day at the Races (Sam Wood). 1938—Room Service (William A. Seiter). 1939—At the Circus (Edward Buzzell). 1940—Go West (Edward Buzzell). 1941 —The Big Store (Charles Reisner). 1946—A Night in Casablanca (Archie L. Mayo). 1949—Love Happy (David Miller).

The Marx Brothers so completely dominated the slapstick scene in the early sound era that few moviegoers mourned the demise of pantomime. Except for Leo McCarey's relatively integrated

Duck Soup, the Marx Brothers burrowed from within an invariably mediocre mise-en-scène to burst upon the audience with their distinctively anarchic personalities. They were a welcome relief not only from the badness of their own movies but also from the badness of most of the movies around them. Except for Groucho's bad habit of doing double and triple takes after every bon mot to give his audience a chance to laugh, the Marx Brothers have worn reasonably well in the three decades since they burned themselves out somewhere between *A Night at the Opera* and *A Day at the Races*. Their more intellectual admirers have compared them with everyone from the Brothers Karamazov to the Beatles. A case can be made for Gróucho as Ivan, Harpo as Aloysha, and Chico as Dmitri. Groucho, the skeptic of the sound track, was often pitted against Harpo's Fool of silence. The highbrows laughed louder at Groucho, but they smiled more sweetly at Harpo. The Fool fell in more easily with the lingering aesthetic guilt over the demise of the silent film. There were really only three Marx Brothers. Zeppo and Gummo never counted, and Alan Jones was never anything more than one of Irving J. Thalberg's stray tenors. However, Groucho was aided in no small measure by the exquisite dignity and self-abasement of Margaret Dumont, one of the greatest character comediennes in the history of the screen. Groucho's confrontations with Miss Dumont seem much more the heart of the Marxian matter today than the rather loose rapport among the three Brothers themselves.

The limiting factor of the Marx Brothers is their failure to achieve the degree of production control held by Chaplin throughout his career, and Keaton and Lloyd in the silent era. The Marx Brothers often had to sit by in compliant neutrality while the most inane plot conventions were being developed. *Monkey Business*, particularly, suffers from a studio-grafted gangster intrigue in mock imitation of the gangster films of the time. It may seem trivial that Chaplin, Keaton, and Lloyd were always trying to get the girl, whereas the Marx Brothers were trying to get the girl for whatever straight man happened to be around at the time, but that is what made Chaplin, Keaton, and Lloyd major and the Marx Brothers minor.

Nonetheless, the best bits of the Marx Brothers were as funny as anything the sound film has produced. For starters, there is Groucho's land auction in *The Cocoanuts,* Harpo's and Chico's bridge game in *Animal Crackers,* Harpo's madness with the passports and the puppets in *Monkey Business,* Harpo's and Groucho's bunny-nightcap confrontation in the magical mirror of *Duck Soup,* and the stateroom scene in *A Night at the Opera.* On the other side of the ledger were a profusion of piano and harp solos, bad puns from Groucho and Chico, and, toward the end, the desecrations of B-picture budgets and shooting schedules. As for the comparison between the Marx Brothers and the Beatles, the Marx Brothers, to borrow Priestley's phrase, tried to be mad in a sane world, whereas the Beatles try to be sane in a mad world.

MAE WEST (1892–)

FILMS: 1932—Night After Night. 1933—*She Done Him Wrong, I'm No Angel.* 1934—*Belle of the Nineties.* 1935—*Goin' to Town.* 1936—*Klondike Annie;* Go West, Young Man. 1937—Every Day's a Holiday. 1940—My Little Chickadee. 1943—The Heat's On.

The sad story of Mae West is that she was done in by the blue-noses. Social historians have designated 1934 as the censor-ridden year that marked the transition from Anita Loos to Louisa May Alcott, from Big Mama to *Little Women,* from such boisterous nymphs as Mae West and Jean Harlow to such bristling nymphets as Shirley Temple and Deanna Durbin. Even before 1934, however, the unexpurgated Mae West was somewhat too salty for the screen. No movie audience shared a stage audience's delight over such a provocative query as "Are you packin' a rod or are you just glad to see me?" The movies were never the ideal medium for such bawdy Broadway clowns as Miss West, Bobby Clark, Jimmy Savo, and a horde of burlesque lechers and Borscht Circuit fag-imitators.

Mae West was at her best under Lowell Sherman's perceptive direction in *She Done Him Wrong* with Cary Grant as her perfect foil. For the rest, her career was a patchwork of bits and lines and scenes. Calling her the Tom Mix of the boudoir, John Grierson praised the emotional resiliency of a line like "Beulah, peel me a grape" as a preferable example for young girls than Greta Garbo's literally dying for love in *Camille*. A life preserver in World War II was named after Mae West, possibly in recognition of the fact that she was one of the few stars of the leg-conscious thirties with more impressive measurements from east to west than from north to south. (Only Lupe Velez comes to mind as a contemporaneous competitor to Mae West in the comic amplitude of her bosom.) The leering image of Mae West complete with an IBM eye inspection of a man's Priapean potentialities is part of the iconography of the thirties.

In a way, Mae West's brand of fun was infinitely more innocent when it was considered infinitely more wicked. The censors were at least gallant enough to treat her conceits as dangerous symptoms of a too healthy heterosexuality. The tendency nowadays is to smile indulgently at the familiar accents of a female impersonator who just happened to be a woman on the side. (Vide Shirley Clarke's *Jason* for the ultimate corruption of the West legend.) The thirties were surprisingly full of fruity character comedians and gravel-voiced bulldyke character comediennes, but it was always played so straight that when Franklin Pangborn or Cecil Cunningham went into their routines, it was possible to laugh without being too sophisticated. Only in retrospect have we come to realize how much depravity lurked under the surface of Hollywood's wholesomeness.

XI.
MISCELLANY

MICHAEL ANDERSON (1920–   )

FILMS: 1952—Waterfront Women. 1955—The Dam Busters, Will Any Gentleman? 1956—1984, Around the World in 80 Days. 1957—Battle Hell (Yangtse Incident). 1958—Chase a Crooked Shadow. 1959—Shake Hands with the Devil, *The Wreck of the Mary Deare*. 1960—All the Fine Young Cannibals. 1961—The Naked Edge. 1964—Flight from Ashiya, Wild and Wonderful. 1965—Operation Crossbow. 1966—*The Quiller Memorandum*.

Michael Anderson's career is so undistinguished until *The Quiller Memorandum* that two conclusions are unavoidable, one that Harold Pinter was the true auteur of *The Quiller Memorandum,* and two that Pinter found in Anderson an ideal metteur en scène for his (Pinter's) very visual conceits. The fact that Michael Anderson was also the director of the much-applauded *Around the World in 80 Days* does not deserve even the dignity of a footnote.

LASLO BENEDEK (1907–   )

FILMS: 1948—The Kissing Bandit. 1949—Port of New York. 1951—Death of a Salesman. 1952—Storm Over the Tiber. 1954—*The Wild One*, Bengal Brigade. 1957—Affair in Havana. 1962—Malaga. 1966—Namu, the Killer Whale.

The Wild One stands out in the list of Laslo Benedek's credits like a beacon in the darkness. The raffish motorcyclists incarnated in the images of Marlon Brando and Lee Marvin have entered the mythology of the cinema. By contrast, *Death of a Salesman* was atrociously directed away from the expressionistic pseudotragedy of Arthur Miller and Elia Kazan on Broadway to the relatively realistic pseudopathology of Hollywood.

JOHN BRAHM (1893–   )

FILMS: 1935—Scrooge. 1936—The Last Journey. 1937—Broken Blossoms, Counsel for Crime. 1938—Penitentiary, Girl's School. 1939—Let Us Live, Rio. 1940—Escape to Glory. 1941—Wild Geese Calling. 1942—The Undying Monster. 1943—Tonight We Raid Calais, Wintertime. 1944—*The Lodger, Guest in the House.* 1945—*Hangover Square.* 1946—*The Locket.* 1947—*The Brasher Doubloon,* Singapore. 1951—The :Thief of Venice. 1952—The Miracle of Our Lady of Fatima, Face to Face (with Bretaigne Windust). 1953—The Diamond Queen. 1954—The Mad Magician, Die Goldene Pest. 1955—Special Delivery, Bengazi. 1956–1967—Approximately 150 TV films. 1967—Hot Rods to Hell.

John Brahm began his career with conscientious imitations of D. W. Griffith (*Broken Blossoms*) and Fritz Lang (*Let Us Live*). He hit his stride in the forties with a series of mood-drenched melodramas—*The Lodger, Guest in the House, Hangover Square, The Locket, The Brasher Doubloon.* His quiet virtues of visual tastefulness and dramatic balance were unable to sustain his career. He remains a minor example of the studio director cast adrift with the collapse of the studio system.

JACK CONWAY (1887–   )

FILMS: 1918—Bond of Fear, Because of a Woman, Little Red Decides, Her Decision, You Can't Believe Everything. 1919—Diplomatic Mission, Desert Law. 1920—Riders of the Dawn, Lombardi, Ltd. 1921—Dwelling Place of Light, Money Changers, The Spenders, The U.P. Trail, The Kiss, A Daughter of the Law. 1922—Step On It, A Parisian Scandal, The Millionaire, Across the Dead Line, Another Man's Shoes, Don't Shoot, The Long Chance. 1923—The Prisoner, Sawdust, Quicksands, What Wives Want, Trimmed in Scarlet, Lucretia Lombard. 1924—The Trouble Shooter, The Heart Buster. 1925—The Roughneck, The Hunted Woman, The Only

Thing. 1926—Brown of Harvard, Soul Mates. 1927—The Understanding Heart, Twelve Miles Out, Quicksands. 1928—Smart Set, Bringing Up Father, While the City Sleeps. 1929—Alias Jimmy Valentine, Our Modern Maidens, Untamed. 1930—They Learned About Women, Unholy Three, New Moon. 1931—Easiest Way, Just a Gigolo. 1932—*Arsene Lupin,* But the Flesh Is Weak, *Red Headed Woman.* 1933—Hell Below, The Nuisance, Solitare Man. 1934—*Viva Villa!,* The Girl from Missouri, The Gay Bride. 1935 —One New York Night, *A Tale of Two Cities.* 1936—*Libeled Lady.* 1937—Saratoga. 1938—*A Yank at Oxford,* Too Hot to Handle. 1939—Let Freedom Ring, Lady of the Tropics. 1940— Boom Town. 1941—Love Crazy, Honky Tonk. 1942—Crossroads. 1943—Assignment in Brittany. 1944—Dragon Seed. 1947— High Barbaree, The Hucksters. 1948—Julia Misbehaves.

Jack Conway was submerged in the Metro studio system, and few of his films are worth mentioning even in passing, but there are moments of enchantment in *Arsene Lupin, Red Headed Woman, Viva Villa!, A Tale of Two Cities, Libeled Lady,* and *A Yank at Oxford.* Most of the enchantment can be attributed to such acting luminaries as John Barrymore, Jean Harlow, Ronald Colman, Wallace Beery, and the very early Vivien Leigh in *A Yank at Oxford.*

HUBERT CORNFIELD (1929–   )

FILMS: 1955—Sudden Danger. 1957—Lure of the Swamp. 1958—Plunder Road. 1959—The Third Voice. 1961—Angel Baby (with Paul Wendkos). 1962—Pressure Point. 1968—The Night of the Following Day.

Hubert Cornfield's career seems to have been blighted after a disagreement with producer Stanley Kramer over *Pressure Point.* Cornfield seemed to be striving for a Europeanized elegance of form even when his scripts seemed too sordid for serious consideration. It remains to be seen whether Cornfield can return to the scene with any semblance of unity of style and content.

WILLIAM DIETERLE (1893–)

FILMS: 1929—Behind the Altar. 1931—Der Tanz Geht Weiter, *Last Flight, Her Majesty Love.* 1932—Man Wanted, Jewel Robbery, The Crash, Six Hours to Live, Scarlet Dawn, Lawyer Man. 1933—Grand Slam, Adorable, Devils in Love, Female, From Headquarters. 1934—Fashions of 1934, Fog over Frisco, Madame Du Barry, The Firebird. 1935—Secret Bride, Dr. Socrates, A Midsummer Night's Dream, The Story of Louis Pasteur, Concealment, Men on Her Mind. 1936—The White Angel, Satan Met a Lady. 1937—The Great O'Malley, Another Dawn, Life of Emile Zola. 1938—Blockade. 1939—Juarez, Hunchback of Notre Dame. 1940—The Story of Dr. Ehrlich's Magic Bullet, A Dispatch from Reuters. 1941—*All That Money Can Buy* (Here Is a Man). 1942—Syncopation, *Tennessee Johnson.* 1944—Kismet, *I'll Be Seeing You.* 1945—*Love Letters,* This Love of Ours. 1946—The Searching Wind. 1948—The Accused, Portrait of Jenny. 1949—Rope of Sand. 1950—Paid in Full, *Dark City,* September Affair. 1951—Peking Express, Red Mountain. 1952—*Boots Malone,* The Turning Point. 1953—Salome, Volcano. 1954—Elephant Walk. 1956—Magic Fire. 1957—Omar Khayyam.

William Dieterle seemed less interesting than Michael Curtiz in his (Dieterle's) Warners period and less interesting than Billy Wilder in his (Dieterle's) Paramount period. *All That Money Can Buy,* his most successful work, seems somewhat extraneous to his career. *The Last Flight* evokes tender memories of Helen Chandler and bizarre memories of a bowdlerized version of Hemingway's *The Sun Also Rises. Love Letters* is dominated by the nervous emotionalism of Jennifer Jones, Ayn Rand, Lee Garmes, and Victor Young. But Dieterle was around on the set when many interesting things happened over the years, and it is reasonable to assume that he had something to do with them.

ROY DEL RUTH (1895–)

FILMS: 1925—Eve's Lover, Hogan's Alley. 1926—Three Weeks in Paris, The Man Upstairs, The Little Irish Girl, Footloose

Widows, Across the Pacific. 1927—Wolf's Clothing, The First Auto, If I Were Single, Ham and Eggs at the Front. 1928—Five and Ten Cent Annie, Powder My Back, The Terror, Beware of Bachelors. 1929—Conquest, Desert Song, The Hottentot, Gold Diggers of Broadway, Aviator. 1930—Hold Everything, Second Floor Mystery, Three Faces East, Life of the Party. 1931—My Past, Divorce Among Friends, Maltese Falcon, Larceny Lane, Side Show, Blonde Crazy. 1932—*Taxi,* Beauty and the Boss, Winner Take All, *Blessed Event.* 1933—Employees' Entrance, Mind Reader, Little Giant, Bureau of Missing Persons, Captured, *Lady Killer.* 1934—Bulldog Drummond Strikes Back, Upper World, Kid Millions. 1935—Folies Bergere, *Broadway Melody of 1936,* Thanks a Million. 1936—It Had to Happen, Private Number, Born to Dance. 1937—On the Avenue, *Broadway Melody of 1938.* 1938—Happy Landing, My Lucky Star. 1939—Tail Spin, The Star Maker, Here I Am a Stranger. 1940—He Married His Wife. 1941—Topper Returns, The Chocolate Soldier. 1942—Maisie Gets Her Man. 1943—Du Barry Was a Lady. 1944—Broadway Rhythm, Barbary Coast Gent. 1947—It Happened on Fifth Avenue. 1948—The Babe Ruth Story. 1949—Red Light, Always Leave Them Laughing. 1950—The West Point Story. 1951—On Moonlight Bay, Starlift. 1952—About Face, Stop, You're Killing Me. 1953—Three Sailors and a Girl. 1954—Phantom of the Rue Morgue. 1959—The Alligator People.

Roy Del Ruth, like Mervyn LeRoy, switched in the mid-thirties from the hard-boiled world of *Taxi, Blessed Event,* and *Lady Killer* to the gilded musical stage of *Broadway Melody of 1936* and *Broadway Melody of 1938.* On the whole, however, Roy Del Ruth seemed more a trend follower than a trend setter.

GORDON DOUGLAS (1909–   )

FILMS: 1936—General Spanky. 1939—Zenobia. 1940—Saps at Sea. 1941—Road Show, Broadway Limited, Niagara Falls. 1942—The Devil with Hitler, The Great Gildersleeve. 1943—Gildersleeve's Bad Day, Gildersleeve on Broadway. 1944—A Night of Adventure, Gildersleeve's Ghost, Girl Rush, The Falcon in Hollywood. 1945—First Yank into Hollywood. 1946—San Quentin, Dick Tracy vs. Cueball. 1948—The Black Arrow, If You Knew

Susie, Walk a Crooked Mile. 1949—The Doolins of Oklahoma, Mr. Soft Touch. 1950—The Nevadan, The Fortunes of Captain Blood, Rogues of Sherwood Forest, *Kiss Tomorrow Goodbye,* Between Midnight and Dawn, The Great Missouri Raid. 1951—*Only the Valiant,* I Was a Communist for the FBI, *Come Fill the Cup.* 1952— Mara Maru, The Iron Mistress. 1953—She's Back on Broadway, The Charge at Feather River, So This Is Love. 1954—*Them, Young at Heart.* 1955—The McConnell Story, Sincerely Yours. 1957— Santiago, The Big Land, Bombers B-52. 1958—Fort Dobbs, The Fiend Who Walked the West. 1959—Up Periscope, Yellowstone Kelly. 1961—Gold of the Seven Saints, *The Sins of Rachel Cade,* Claudelle Inglish. 1963—Call Me Bwana. 1964—Robin and the 7 Hoods, Rio Conchos. 1965—*Sylvia, Harlow.* 1966—Stagecoach, Way . . . Way Out. 1967—*Tony Rome.* 1968—The Detective, The Lady in Cement.

Gordon Douglas could be dismissed as an efficient technician without too noticeable a personal style, *Kiss Tomorrow Goodbye, Only the Valiant, Come Fill the Cup, Them, Young at Heart,* and *Tony Rome* to the contrary. However, a director who has lived through Liberace (*Sincerely Yours*) deserves all our compassion, particularly when he didn't shirk his job despite the utmost provocation.

PHILIP DUNNE (1908–)

FILMS: 1955—*Prince of Players,* The View From Pompey's Head. 1956—*Hilda Crane,* Three Brave Men. 1958—Ten North Frederick, In Love and War. 1959—Blue Denim. 1961—Wild in the Country. 1962—Lisa. 1966—Blindfold.

Philip Dunne was a prolific and successful screenwriter at Fox with scripts for John Ford (*How Green Was My Valley*), Joseph L. Mankiewicz (*The Ghost and Mrs. Muir*), Elia Kazan (*Pinky*), and Jacques Tourneur (*The Way of a Gaucho*) among many others. Dunne made his directorial debut with *Prince of Players,* the project of an ambitious sensibility. Unfortunately, the public was not electrified by Richard Burton as Edwin Booth. Perhaps it was waiting subconsciously for Burton's Antony to cross the Rubicon of stardom after a tryst on the Tiber. Perhaps the casting of Maggie MacNamara opposite Burton was too much of a handicap. Dunne's civilized taste flickered briefly in the exquisite expressions of Jean Simmons in *Hilda Crane*. The rest is leaden and laborious.

VICTOR FLEMING (1883–1949)

FILMS: 1920—When the Clouds Roll By, The Mollycoddle. 1921—Mamma's Affair. 1922—Woman's Place, Red Hot Romance, Lane That Had No Turning, Anna Ascends. 1923—Dark Secrets, Law of the Lawless, To the Last Man, Call of the Canyon. 1924—Empty Hands, The Code of the Sea. 1925—A Son of His Father, Adventure, The Devil's Cargo, Lord Jim. 1926—Blind Goddess, Mantrap. 1927—Rough Riders, *Way of All Flesh*, Hula. 1928—Abie's Irish Rose, The Awakening. 1929—Wolf Song, *The Virginian*. 1930—Common Clay, Renegades. 1931—Around the World in 80 Minutes. 1932—The Wet Parade, *Red Dust*. 1933—White Sister, *Bombshell*. 1934—*Treasure Island*. 1935—*Reckless*, The Farmer Takes a Wife. 1937—*Captains Courageous*. 1938—Test Pilot. 1939—*The Wizard of Oz, Gone with the Wind*. 1941—Dr. Jekyll and Mr. Hyde. 1942—Tortilla Flat. 1943—*A Guy Named Joe*. 1945—Adventure. 1948—Joan of Arc.

Fleming's work has a Jekyll and Hyde quality of its own. Within the same year, Jekyll could turn out the raucously entertaining *Bombshell* while Hyde was being heavy-handed with *White Sister*. Or is it simply the law of accidents that explains the superiority of *Treasure Island, Captains Courageous,* and *A Guy Named Joe* over *The Virginian, Test Pilot,* and *Tortilla Flat*? Fleming's most popularly remembered films, *Gone with the Wind* and *The Wizard of Oz,* seem extraneous to his career, and such creditable efforts as *Red Dust* and *Reckless* were magnificently remade by Ford (*Mogambo*) and Sirk (*Written on the Wind*), and significantly improved in the process. His last films, *Adventure* and *Joan of Arc* were disastrous failures, yet with somewhat more merit than their reputations would indicate. This mysterious figure probably expressed more of Hollywood's contradictions than did most of his colleagues. Yet, aside from Cukor, he was the only Metro director who could occasionally make the lion roar.

Gone with the Wind is one of the notable exceptions to the notion of directorial authorship. Fleming was actually hired for the job because Clark Gable resented the care George Cukor took with the performances of the ladies in the cast. Some of George Cukor's scenes remain in the film. It can be argued also that David O. Selznick, Ben Hecht, and William Cameron Menzies were particularly influential in the shape the film finally took. That *Gone with the Wind* succeeded as entertainment is due largely to the inspired casting of Vivien Leigh as Scarlett O'Hara. That it failed as personal art is due to the incessant interference with a project that was always too big to be controlled by a single directorial style.

JACK GARFEIN (1930–)

FILMS: 1957—The Young One. 1961—Something Wild.

One of the last and least of Kazan's imitators, Garfein attracted some attention with his first film, and then dispelled any incipient hopes with his second. His style, such as it is, consists of little more than contrived hysteria. Until anger is considered an adequate substitute for talent, Garfein's status will remain dubious.

STUART HEISLER (1894–)

FILMS: 1940—*The Biscuit Eater.* 1941—The Monster and the Girl, Among the Living. 1942—The Remarkable Andrew, *The Glass Key.* 1945—Along Came Jones. 1946—Blue Skies. 1947— *Smash-Up, The Story of a Woman.* 1949—*Tulsa,* Tokyo Joe. 1950 —Chain Lightning, *Storm Warning.* 1951—Journey Into Light. 1952—*Island of Desire.* 1953—*The Star.* 1954—Beachhead, This Is My Love. 1955—I Died a Thousand Times. 1956—The Lone Ranger, The Burning Hills. 1962—Hitler.

Stuart Heisler's career lacks any overall coherence or control, and some of his projects sound more outrageous than they actually are, but he has had moments of insight and charm scattered like loose beads on a sawdust-covered floor. Conventional film historians would probably single him out for *The Biscuit Eater* and *The Glass Key* in his early Paramount period, but he seemed more interesting directing the mature sexuality of Ginger Rogers in *Storm Warning,* Linda Darnell in *Island of Desire,* Susan Hayward in *Tulsa,* and Bette Davis in *The Star,* projects light years beyond such doomed dada as *The Lone Ranger* and *Hitler.*

STANLEY KRAMER (1913–   )

FILMS: 1955—Not As a Stranger. 1957—The Pride and the Passion. 1958—*The Defiant Ones.* 1959—On the Beach. 1960—Inherit the Wind. 1961—Judgment at Nuremberg. 1963—It's a Mad, Mad, Mad, Mad World. 1965—Ship of Fools. 1967—Guess Who's Coming to Dinner? 1969—The Secret of Santa Vittoria.

If Stanley Kramer had not existed, he would have had to have been invented as the most extreme example of thesis or message cinema. Unfortunately, he has been such an easy and willing target for so long that his very ineptness has become encrusted with tradition. He will never be a natural, but time has proved that he is not a fake.

JOSHUA LOGAN (1908–   )

FILMS: 1938—I Met My Love Again (with Arthur Ripley). 1956—*Picnic, Bus Stop.* 1957—Sayonara. 1958—South Pacific. 1960—*Tall Story.* 1961—Fanny. 1964—Ensign Pulver. 1967—Camelot. 1969—Paint Your Wagon.

The promise of *Picnic,* long since betrayed as far as Joshua Logan is concerned, can be attributed to Jo Mielziner's coherent principles of set design. Logan's main function now consists of transporting Broadway's tastelessness to the cinema. The unspeakable quartet of *Sayonara, South Pacific, Fanny,* and *Camelot* invests the director's vulgarity with cosmic dimensions. The last hope of the cinema is that Mr. Logan finds Broadway more congenial and stays there. Unfortunately, the most obscenely lit scrim curtain is no adequate substitute for camera filters and slobbering close-ups, and who can deny a director his addictions?

DAVID MILLER (1905–   )

FILMS: 1941—*Billy the Kid.* 1942—Sunday Punch, Flying Tigers. 1949—Top o' the Morning, *Love Happy.* 1950—Our Very Own. 1951—Saturday's Hero. 1952—*Sudden Fear.* 1954—Twist of Fate. 1955—Diane. 1956—The Opposite Sex. 1957—*The Story of Esther Costello.* 1959—Happy Anniversary. 1960—*Midnight Lace.* 1961—Back Street. 1962—*Lonely Are the Brave.* 1963—Captain Newman, M.D. 1968—Hammerhead.

How a David Miller cult ever got started is one of the unsolved mysteries of underground criticism. Miller's *Billy the Kid* was actually superior to Vidor's without being particularly distinguished in its own right. *Flying Tigers* proved that no one could plagiarize from Hawks's *Only Angels Have Wings* without equaling the master, *Love Happy* that the Marx Brothers have always needed Leo McCarey and a good script, *The Opposite Sex* that George Cukor was indeed inimitable, and *Back Street* that Douglas Sirk was indeed irreplaceable. Not much is left after the parrot pictures are removed. *Sudden Fear* and *Midnight Lace* are ambitious lady-in-distress thrillers, more aggravating than suspenseful. *The Story of Esther Costello* is notable only for the Rossano Brazzi shock treatment, and *Lonely Are the Brave* is worth mentioning only for the presumption of its producer-star, the estimable Kirk Douglas, who deigned to give discriminating American audiences an honest-to-goodness art film from Hollywood, and then found us all unworthy of the privilege. The basic question remains: Who is David Miller?

JEAN NEGULESCO (1900–)

FILMS: 1941—Singapore Woman. 1944—*The Mask of Dimitrios*, The Conspirators. 1946—*Three Strangers*, Nobody Lives Forever. 1947—*Humoresque, Deep Valley*. 1948—*Road House, Johnny Belinda*. 1949—The Forbidden Street. 1950—Under My Skin, Three Came Home, The Mudlark. 1951—*Take Care of My Little Girl*. 1952—Phone Call From a Stranger, Lydia Bailey, Lure of the Wilderness, O. Henry's Full House. 1953—Titanic, How to Marry a Millionaire. 1954—Three Coins in the Fountain, Woman's World. 1955—Daddy Long Legs, The Rains of Ranchipur. 1957—Boy on a Dolphin. 1958—The Gift of Love, A Certain Smile. 1959—Count Your Blessings, The Best of Everything. 1962—Jessica. 1964—The Pleasure Seekers.

Jean Negulesco's career can be divided into two periods labeled B.C. and A.C. or Before Cinemascope and After Cinemascope. *The Mask of Dimitrios, Three Strangers, Humoresque, Deep Valley, Road House, Johnny Belinda* and *Take Care of My Little Girl* are all Before Cinemascope, and all rather competently and even memorably made. Everything After Cinemascope is completely worthless. Negulesco's is the most dramatic case of directorial maladjustment in the fifties.

JOSEPH M. NEWMAN (1909–)

FILMS: 1942—Northwest Rangers. 1945—Diary of a Sergeant. 1948—Jungle Patrol. 1949—The Great Dan Patch, Abandoned. 1950—*711 Ocean Drive*. 1951—Lucky Nick Cain, The Guy Who Came Back, Love Nest, Smoke Jumpers. 1952—Red Skies of Montana, *The Outcasts of Poker Flat*, Pony Soldier. 1953—Dangerous Crossing. 1954—*The Human Jungle*. 1955—This Island Earth, Kiss of Fire. 1956—Flight to Hong Kong. 1957—Death in Small Doses. 1958—Fort Massacre. 1959—The Gunfight at Dodge City, The Big Circus, Tarzan, The Ape Man. 1961—*King of* *the Roaring Twenties—The Story of Arnold Rothstein,* A Thunder of Drums, The George Raft Story, Twenty Plus Two.

Newman nags the critical conscience as an action director with a soft touch and a soupçon of subtlety. The flickering intelligence of Edmond O'Brien in *711 Ocean Drive,* Dale Robertson in *Outcasts of Poker Flat,* Gary Merrill in *The Human Jungle,* and David Janssen in *King of the Roaring Twenties* lingers in the mind long after their inane intrigues have been forgotten. Most memorable of all are the remarkably subdued performances of Mickey Rooney and Jack Carson in *King of the Roaring Twenties.*

ELLIOTT NUGENT (1901–)

FILMS: 1929—Wise Girls. 1932—*The Mouthpiece, Life Begins.* 1933—Whistling in the Dark, *Three-Cornered Moon,* If I Were Free. 1934—Two Alone, Strictly Dynamite, She Loves Me Not. 1935—Love in Bloom, Enter Madame, College Scandal, Splendour. 1936—And So They Were Married, Wives Never Know. 1938—It's All Yours, Professor Beware, Give Me a Sailor. 1939—Never Say Die, *The Cat and the Canary.* 1941—Nothing But the Truth. 1942—The Male Animal. 1943—The Crystal Ball. 1944—*Up in Arms.* 1947—My Favorite Brunette, Welcome Stranger. 1948—My Girl Tisa. 1949—*The Great Gatsby,* Mr. Belvedere Goes to College. 1950—The Skipper Surprised His Wife. 1951—My Brother the Outlaw. 1952—Just For You.

Elliott Nugent has left such a pleasant memory of his stage performances in *The Male Animal* and *The Voice of the Turtle* that it is reasonable to assume that his acting personality can be correlated with some of the subtler touches of directing in *The Mouthpiece, Three-Cornered Moon,* and *The Cat and the Canary.* It is reasonable to assume also that his heart remained in the theatre, and that his position in the cinema is understandably marginal.

ARCH OBOLER (1909–   )

FILMS: 1945—Bewitched. 1946—The Arnelo Affair. 1950 —*Five*. 1952—Bwana Devil. 1953—The Twonky. 1961—One Plus One.

Arch Oboler came to Hollywood out of the radio tube, but he never showed the visual flair of Orson Welles. His name still reverberates from the "Lights Out" radio series I heard in my childhood. Hence, he is included if only as a reminder of the vanished mystique of radio in the motion picture industry.

RICHARD QUINE (1920–   )

FILMS: 1951—On the Sunny Side of the Street, Purple Heart Diary. 1952—Sound Off, Rainbow 'Round My Shoulder. 1953— All Ashore, Siren of Bagdad, Cruisin' Down the River. 1954— *Drive a Crooked Road, Pushover*, So This Is Paris. 1955—*My Sister Eileen*. 1956—*Solid Gold Cadillac*. 1957—*Full of Life*, Operation Madball. 1958—Bell, Book and Candle. 1959—It Happened to Jane. 1960—*Strangers When We Meet*, The World of Suzie Wong. 1962—The Notorious Landlady. 1964—Paris When It Sizzles, Sex and the Single Girl. 1965—How to Murder Your Wife, *Synanon*. 1967—Oh Dad, Poor Dad, Mamma's Hung You in the Closet and I'm Feelin' So Sad, *Hotel*. 1969—A Talent for Loving.

Richard Quine's early Columbia films possessed a discreet charm that seemed promising as late as 1957 with *Operation Madball*. The promise has never been fulfilled. At best, Quine has functioned as an inoffensive imitator of his betters. *Pushover* is a poor man's *Double Indemnity*. *Solid Gold Cadillac* and *Full of Life* are pale copies of Cukor's *It Should Happen to You* and *The Marrying Kind* respectively. Quine's comedy technique for *The Notorious Landlady, How to Murder Your Wife,* and *Sex and the Single Girl* was already ineffectively strenuous before the ultimate disaster of *Oh Dad, Poor Dad, Mamma's Hung You in the*

Closet and I'm Feelin' So Sad. Quine seems more at home with the lower-key seriousness of *Synanon, Hotel,* and *Strangers When We Meet.*

LESLIE STEVENS (1924–   )

FILMS: 1960—Private Property. 1962—Hero's Island.

Leslie Stevens achieved some notice and notoriety with *Private Property,* a film that seems more ambitious than it is. Ted McCord was hired to shoot people through brandy snifters with such affected artiness that McCord should have known better even if Stevens didn't. All that lingers in the mind from *Private Property* is Stevens's flair for feelthy fetishism and the hauntingly stupid blonde beauty of the late Kate Manx, Stevens's wife and garish Galatea. *Hero's Island* is best left to the more esoteric film historians.

EDWARD SUTHERLAND (1895–   )

FILMS: 1925—Wild, Wild Susan, Coming Through, A Regular Fellow. 1926—It's the Old Army Game, Behind the Front, We're in the Navy Now. 1927—Love's Greatest Mistake, Fireman Save My Child, Figures Don't Lie. 1928—Tillie's Punctured Romance, Baby Cyclone, Number Please. 1929—*Close Harmony, Dance of Life,* Fast Company, The Saturday Night Kid, Pointed Heels. 1930—Burning Up, Paramount on Parade, *Social Lion,* Sap from Syracuse. 1931—Gang Buster, June Moon, Up Pops the Devil, Palmy Days. 1932—Sky Devils, Mr. Robinson Crusoe, Secrets of the French Police. 1933—Murders in the Zoo, International House, Too Much Harmony. 1935—*Mississippi,* Diamond Jim. 1936—*Poppy.* 1937—Champagne Waltz, Every Day's a Holiday. 1939—The Flying Deuces. 1940—The Boys from Syracuse, Beyond Tomorrow, One Night in the Tropics. 1941—The Invisible Woman, Nine Lives Are Not Enough, Steel Against the Sky. 1942—Sing Your Worries Away, Army Surgeon, The Navy Comes Through. 1943—Dixie. 1944—Follow the Boys, Secret Command. 1945—Having Wonderful Crime. 1946—Abie's Irish Rose.

Sutherland's career seemed consistently anachronistic through the thirties and forties, and *Abie's Irish Rose* ended things with a toppling down rather than a tapering off. Nonetheless Sutherland remains interesting as an active transitional figure through the switchover to sound. A taste for the Paramount musical of that era is required for any reconsideration of Sutherland's career.

BURT TOPPER

FILMS: 1958—Hell Squad, War Hero. 1959—Tank Commandos, Diary of a High School Bride. 1964—War Is Hell, The Strangler.

Burt Topper has been discovered by *Cahiers du Cinéma* as one of its little jokes on American film scholarship at the Midi-Minuit level. The joke is wearing thin at a time when American films are consistently reviled in the pages of *Cahiers* all the better to sing the praises of the New Albanian Cinema.

W. S. VAN DYKE (1899–   )

FILMS: 1918—Men of the Desert, Gift O' Gab. 1919—Lady of the Dugout. 1922—According to Hoyle, Boss of Camp No. 4, Forget Me Not. 1923—Little Girl Next Door, Miracle Workers, Loving Lies, You Are in Danger. 1924—Half-a-Dollar Bill. 1925 —The Beautiful Sinner, Gold Heels, Hearts and Spurs, The Trail Rider, The Ranger of the Big Pines, The Timber Wolf, The Desert's Price. 1926—The Gentle Cyclone, War Paint. 1927—Winners of the Wilderness, California, Heart of the Yukon, Eyes of the Totem, Foreign Devils, Spoilers of the West. 1928—Wyoming, Under Black Eagle, *White Shadows of the South Seas.* 1929—The Pagan. 1931—*Trader Horn,* Never the Twain Shall Meet, Guilty Hands, Cuban Love Song. 1932—*Tarzan, The Ape Man;* Night World. 1933—Penthouse, *Eskimo, Prizefighter and the Lady.* 1934— Laughing Boy, Manhattan Melodrama, *The Thin Man,* Hide-Out.

1935—Forsaking All Others, Naughty Marietta, I Live My Life. 1936—Rose Marie, San Francisco, His Brother's Wife, The Devil Is a Sissy, Love on the Run, *After the Thin Man*. 1937—Personal Property, They Gave Him a Gun, Rosalie. 1938—*Marie Antoinette*, Sweethearts. 1939—Stand Up and Fight, It's a Wonderful World, Andy Hardy Gets Spring Fever, Another Thin Man. 1940—I Take This Woman, I Love You Again, Bitter Sweet. 1941—Rage in Heaven, The Feminine Touch, Shadow of the Thin Man, Dr. Kildare's Victory. 1942—I Married an Angel, Cairo, Journey for Margaret.

Woody Van Dyke made more good movies than his reputation for carelessness and haste would indicate. Perhaps carelessness and haste are precisely the qualities responsible for the breezy charm of *Trader Horn, Tarzan, The Ape Man; Prizefighter and the Lady, The Thin Man, After The Thin Man,* and even the much-maligned *Marie Antoinette*.

DON WEIS (1922–   )

FILMS: 1951—It's a Big Country (with Richard Thorpe, John Sturges, Charles Vidor, Clarence Brown, Don Hartman, William Wellman), Bannerline. 1952—Just This Once, You for Me. 1953—*I Love Melvin*, Remains to Be Seen, A Slight Case of Larceny, *The Affairs of Dobie Gillis,* Half a Hero. 1954—*The Adventures of Hajji Baba.* 1956—Ride the High Iron. 1959—*The Gene Krupa Story.* 1963—*Critic's Choice.* 1964—Looking for Love, Pajama Party. 1965—Billie. 1966—Ghost in the Invisible Bikini.

The Don Weis cultists in Britain and France are not normally frivolous, but just this once it remains to be seen. Beyond the graceful nonsense of *The Affairs of Dobie Gillis* and *The Adventures of Hajji Baba,* it is difficult to discern any stylistic or thematic pattern in a career longer on commission than on conviction. What Weis lacks more than anything else is one eye-popping masterpiece for the objectively inclined American noncultists.

TERENCE YOUNG (1915–   )

FILMS: 1949—One Night with You, *Corridor of Mirrors,* Woman Hater. 1951—They Were Not Divided. 1952—The Valley of the Eagles. 1953—The Frightened Bride. 1954—The Paratrooper (Red Beret). 1955—That Lady. 1956—Safari, Storm Over the Nile. 1957—Zarak, Action of the Tiger. 1958—Tank Force. 1962—Black Tights. 1963—*Dr. No.* 1964—*From Russia With Love.* 1965—The Amorous Adventures of Moll Flanders, *Thunderball.* 1966—The Dirty Game, The Poppy Is Also a Flower. 1967 —*Wait`Until Dark.* 1968—Mayerling.

Terence Young did the best of the Bonds, *Wait Until Dark,* and the curiously memorable, baroque, and unoriginal *Corridor of Mirrors.* He seems at home with the sweet lyricism of death, but his overall career is staggeringly undistinguished. Nonetheless, he seems to have come into his own, at least commercially.

AFTERWORD: THE AUTEUR THEORY REVISITED

One would think that after so many years of furious controversy there would be no need for another article on the auteur theory. Yet all sorts of scholarly books and articles continue to disseminate an astounding amount of misinformation on the origin and evolution of auteurism. What to do? Having been officially credited or blamed for bringing the words *auteur, auteurism,* and *auteurist* into the English language, I seem to be stuck with these tar-baby terms for the rest of my life. My own previous writings on the subject have been compiled in *The Primal Screen,* a little read volume that came out in 1973. "Notes on the Auteur Theory in 1962" first appeared in *Film Culture,* "Notes on the Auteur Theory in 1970" followed in *Film Comment,* and so now in 1977 a pattern of periodicity seems to justify my current endeavor. Also, auteurism seems to have become a scapegoat for just about every cultural affliction associated with the cinema.

For example, Gore Vidal (in the April *American Film*) associates auteurism with the deification of directors over writers in the moviemaking process. Speaking of Renoir's "great heist" of *The Southerner,* Vidal explains: "Renoir was a man who had great trouble speaking English, much less writing it, and the script was written by William Faulkner. According to Zachary Scott, who acted in it, Faulkner really liked the script and would have been pleased to have had the credit. But Renoir so muddled the business that the credit finally read: 'Screenplay by Jean Renoir.' "

Unfortunately, Vidal neglects to mention that *The Southerner* was adapted from a novel entitled *Hold Autumn in Your*

Hand by George Sessions Perry, the forgotten man in the anti-Renoir, pro-Faulkner anecdote. Who was George Sessions Perry? I have no idea, and neither, apparently, does Vidal. He is (or was) a veteran of the vast army of virtually anonymous authors who have supplied so many of the stories on the screen. Vidal's anecdote implies that Faulkner thought up the story of *The Southerner* all by himself, and Renoir then stole the script and "muddled" it, whatever that means. The anecdote loses something, if Faulkner is revealed as the middleman in the screenwriting process. Until Vidal is prepared to research how much Faulkner's script owes to Perry's novel, the indictment of Renoir as a plagiarist must be thrown out for lack of evidence. Besides, Renoir's reputation does not rest excessively on *The Southerner* any more than Faulkner's reputation rests on his screenplays, credited or uncredited.

Both Renoir and Faulkner must be evaluated in terms of the total context of their careers. This is one of the basic assumptions of auteurism, one that we have always taken for granted in literature, music, and the fine arts, but one that came very late to cinema because of the lack of archival facilities. Hence, film history existed long before there were qualified historians to appraise it. It might be said that the early auteurists discovered so many lost and forgotten treasures in the cinematheques that a theory of history was thrust upon them. They then suggested thematic and stylistic hypotheses which they sought to establish with the proof of a pattern of achievement. But movies were still alive and kicking, and individual careers were still evolving. Some auteurists had placed their bets on Hawks and Hitchcock, others on Renoir and Rossellini. Violent debates ensued between the partisans of Mizoguchi and Kurosawa, Dreyer and Bergman, Antonioni and Fellini, Walsh and Losey. No auteurist completely agreed with any other.

"The auteur theory itself," I wrote back in 1962, "is a pattern theory in constant flux." Despite all my disclaimers, qualifications, and reservations, however, a composite image of the auteurist emerged in anti-auteurist writings. Auteurists were invariably male (at least according to Pauline Kael). They never bathed because it took time away from their viewing of old movies. They shared a preposterous passion for Jerry Lewis. They preferred trash to art. They encouraged the younger generation not to read books.

Vidal himself seeks to establish a dialectical confrontation between the word and the image: "Movies are stories; only writers can tell stories. So the wrong people are making the movies." It might be argued by the defenders of directors that movies are stories told primarily through pictures, or, at least, movies *should* be stories told primarily through pictures. Vidal has an answer for that, too: "We do need the cameraman, the editor. But above all we need the script."

Vidal's position is not particularly audacious for Hollywood. One can imagine the ghosts of the old Hollywood moguls nodding in agreement with Vidal's summary dismissal of directors. All you need to make a good movie is a good story. Everybody on the Bel Air circuit knows *that*. A few years ago *Esquire* published a screenplay entitled *Two-Lane Blacktop* with a come-on across the cover to the effect that this was going to be the best movie of the year. When the critics and public failed to concur with *Esquire*'s prediction, the magazine sheepishly shifted the blame to director Monte Hellman, accusing him of being an auteur. Actually, *Two-Lane Blacktop* was not a bad movie. Choking on the exhaust fumes of the more vulgar and more violent *Easy Rider,* it never caught on at the box office with its subtly modernist malaise, and a brilliant performance by Warren Oates was wasted. This is one of the problems in resolving arguments between auteurists and anti-auteurists: The two sides can never agree entirely on what is good and what is bad. In opposition to the horror stories of Gore Vidal and Rex Reed, there is even a small cult for the movie version of *Myra Breckenridge.*

If one were to examine the pertinent texts of the fifties, the sixties, or the seventies, one would be hard put to find a single generalization in auteurist criticism sweeping enough to justify the simplistic attacks made against it. For one thing, auteurism did not evolve in a vacuum. In the beginning, particularly, its preoccupation with visual structure and personal style was largely a reaction against the sloganized vocabulary of social significance and socialist realism. The open-minded and open-hearted French attitude toward myth and genre enable a new generation of American critics to rediscover and reclaim the American cinema. Suddenly there was credit to parcel out for Hollywood's long despised output, whereas before the auteurists there was only blame. After years on the front lines, my own attitude to the auteurist controversy may have been summed up in the defiant words sung by the late Edith Piaf: *"Non, non, je ne regrette rien."*

Still, if I had to do it all over again, I would reformulate the auteur theory with a greater emphasis on the tantalizing mystery of style than on the romantic agony of the artists. Why, I wondered back in the mid-fifties, had so many Hollywood movies endured as classics despite the generalized contempt of the highbrows? The auteur theory turned out to be a very workable hypothesis for this task of historical reevaluation. But I was never all that interested in the clinical "personalities" of directors, and I have never considered the interview as one of the indispensable weapons in my critical arsenal.

The interview is an autonomous art form like any other, and it follows that directors who give good interviews do not necessarily make good movies, and directors who give bad interviews do not necessarily make bad movies. I am, if anything, anti-interview in that I believe that a director's formal utterances (his films) tell us more about his artistic personality than do his informal utterances (his conversations).

That is why I was far more strongly influenced by the cinematheque-oriented critics on *Cahiers du Cinéma* before 1960 than the tape-recorder interviewers on *Cahiers du Cinéma* after 1960. It is not a question simply of Truffaut, Godard, Chabrol, Rohmer, Rivette, Valcroze, and others validating their pre-1960 critiques with their post-1960 filmmaking. I doubt that Gore Vidal has any notion of what Truffaut was writing about back in 1954 when Truffaut first articulated *La Politique des Auteurs* as an attack on the tradition of quality in the French cinema. Godard's translated criticism has merely mystified even his most determined American admirers. Having published twelve editions of *Cahiers du Cinéma in English* between 1965 and 1967, I can testify that many of my French-speaking acquaintances in America were frequently unable to decipher the cryptic pronouncements of *Cahiers*.

Indeed, few people seem to be aware that my original article on the auteur theory was largely an examination of André Bazin's critique of *La Politique des Auteurs*. Vidal lumps together all French film critics into one monolithic auteurist block as if *Cahier*ism was a national vice. Yet *Cahiers* never sold more than fifteen thousand copies of any monthly issue, and its opinions were violently opposed by other specialized French film publications, most notably and most persistently by *Positif,* which made a point of preferring Huston to Hitchcock, and Fellini to Rossellini. For every Bazin in French film criticism there were a dozen French Bosley Crowthers and Siegfried Kracauers. One did not have to be an auteurist or a *Cahier*ist to adore Jerry Lewis. He happened to be a very catholic French taste. In fact, the most prominent of the Lewis lovers were on the staff of *Positif.*

Similarly, the auteurists of the fifties and sixties did not introduce the cult of the director. Dwight Macdonald and John Grierson were writing very knowledgeably about Hollywood directors back in the early thirties. The great majority of film histories around the world have been organized in terms of the collected works of individual directors. If, as Vidal implies, all that auteurism represents is an emphasis on directors, this so-called theory should be banished for its banality.

A great deal of confusion has been caused by the assumption that auteurism was inseparably linked with the personal tastes of individual critics. Since I was one of the first two American auteurists (along with the late Eugene Archer), I must bear a large part of the blame for this confusion. Let me state at this point, albeit belatedly, that auteurism and Sarrisism are not identical. Both, I hope, have been evolving over the past quarter of a century on a widening front of scholarly activity. Along the way, certain tendencies have clustered around auteurism to form a basis for discussion. Among these tendencies have been the antimontage writings of André Bazin, the many French meditations on mise-en-scène, Lawrence Alloway's celebrations of pop art, and Peter Wollen's valiant efforts to reconcile auteurism with semiotics. Some of these formulations conflicted with others to such an extent that alleged auteurists were often at each other's throats. I have written extensively on many of these internal conflicts, and I have no desire to rehash them now. What I propose instead is a report on the theoretical fallout from the polemical explosions of the past. An attempt will be made to add historical perspective to auteurism, and emerge with a usable residue of critical theory for 1977.

Bazin's most striking contribution to film aesthetics was the restoration of interest in the integrity of the visual field. If he did not actually demolish the montage theories of Eisenstein, Pudovkin, Kuleshov, and Vertov, he did succeed in reducing these theories from imperatives to options. Bazin's writings were never systematic enough or comprehensive enough to establish new imperatives, and there is little indication that he ever wished to establish a new orthodoxy to replace the old. But he did change the way many critics looked at motion pictures. No longer was the ambiguity of the individual image disdained for the dialectical conflict between successive images. Examining both the deep focus shots in *Citizen Kane* and the slow pans in *Open City,* Bazin managed to link these two otherwise dissimilar films in a very ingenious concept of optical realism.

When Bazin's writings first began to filter across the Atlantic in the mid-fifties, the American cinema was in the midst of a formal crisis with wide screens. Most American reviewers either ignored the width altogether or dealt with it in isolation from the script. Wide-screen color canvases like *East of Eden* and *Rebel Without a Cause* were reviewed in America as if they were small-screen, black-and-white Philco Television Playhouse productions like *Marty.* I recall Claude Chabrol's attack on my review of *East of Eden* as *"ennuyeux."* He was right to the extent that my critique did not do justice to the film's emotional sweep encompassed in tilted, distended compositions.

American movies are often discriminated against in America because the ear takes precedence over the eye. By contrast, the French were able to provide a detailed visual analysis of Ameri-

can movies precisely because they were undistracted by the dialogue. To an American ear *Rebel Without a Cause* is still
gravely flawed by its undigested clinical dialogue. But one
would have to be blind to fail to realize that Ray has transcended the tedious social worker rhetoric of the film with a
succession of striking initiatory ceremonies all filmed with profound splendor. And it is to our everlasting disgrace that the
French understood James Dean on a mythic level long before
we did. Similarly, they understood how deeply Alfred Hitchcock's *Vertigo* had influenced Alain Resnais's and Alain Robbe-
Grillet's *Last Year at Marienbad.* While the New York critics
were honoring Stanley Kramer's *The Defiant Ones,* the *Cahiers*
critics were cheering Orson Welles's *Touch of Evil.* Obviously,
their eyes were quicker than our ears.

Although in the long run they could not have the last word
on the American cinema, they gave many of us the first glimpse
of this elusive entity. American film criticism has not been the
same since. There was a time when movies were judged almost
entirely in terms of an absolute fidelity to social reality. Good
intentions alone were too often considered the paving stones to
heaven. By establishing the notion of individual creation in even
the Hollywood cinema, the French shifted the critical emphasis
away from the nature of content to the director's attitude
toward content.

This attitude was expressed through a somewhat mystical
process called mise-en-scène, defined perhaps most eloquently
by French critic-director Alexandre Astruc: "But Mizoguchi
knows well that, after all, it is not very important for his film to
turn out well; he is more concerned with knowing whether the
strongest bonds between himself and his characters are those of
tenderness or contempt. He is like the viewer who sees the reflection of pleasure on the features of the one he watches, even
though he also knows quite well that it is not this reflection
alone which he is seeking but perhaps quite simply the tedious
confirmation of something he has always known but cannot
refrain from verifying. So I consider mise-en-scène as a means
of transforming the world into a spectacle given primarily to

oneself—yet what artist does not know instinctively that what is seen is less important than the way of seeing, or of a certain way of needing to see or be seen."

As I wrote some years ago, I would suggest a definition of mise-en-scène that includes all the means available to a director to express his attitude toward his subject. This takes in cutting, camera movement, pacing, the direction of players and their placement in the decor, the angle and distance of the camera, and even the content of the shot. Mise-en-scène as an attitude tends to accept the cinema as it is and enjoy it for what it is—a sensuous conglomeration of all the other arts.

Bazin, Astruc, and Roger Leehardt caused a ferment in film aesthetics by demystifying so-called "pure" cinema. There was no such entity, they insisted. We could now discuss hitherto verboten subjects as adaptations without placing surgical masks over our faces. What were once considered germs from the other arts were now treated as vitamins. Hence, whereas Agee worried that Olivier's film treatment of *Henry V* was not truly cinematic, Bazin applauded Olivier for honoring cinema by honoring theater.

The French critics tended to brush aside the distinctions between cinema as a medium and cinema as an art form. "The cinema is everything," Godard declared. And he meant it. Every scrap of film was grist for his sensibility. The cinema was no longer a holy temple to which only certain sanctified works were admitted. Cinema was to be found on every movie screen in the world, and Hollywood movies were no less cinematic than anything else. There was still room for disagreement in this new critical climate, but the disputes were couched in terms more relative than absolute.

About the time that auteurism was swimming across the English Channel to London's moviemanes, and across the Atlantic to New York's film cultists, pop art exploded all across the cultural landscape, and nothing has seemed the same since. The two movements converged uneasily in the sixties in such multifaceted artifacts as Richard Lester's *A Hard Day's Night* with the Beatles, John Boorman's *Having a Wild Weekend* with the Dave Clark Five, Jean-Luc Godard's *One Plus One* with the

Rolling Stones, the experimental kinetics of Frank Zappa, and the personal appearances on film of Bob Dylan.

Lawrence Alloway, who had coined the term "pop art," proposed "a criticism of movies as a pop art which can have a critical currency beyond that of footnotes and preposterous learning." Alloway thereby came into conflict with the scholarly tendencies of auteurism. The terms in which he defined the cinema—whether as "the index of a Baudelairean art of modern life" with "modernity" defined by Baudelaire as "that which is ephemeral, fugitive, contingent upon the occasion" or as "the art synthesis proposed by Wagner, the total work to which all arts contribute"—were terms that pertained more to sociological criticism than to auteurist criticism. For the hard-core auteurists, the hitherto despised Hollywood movies could be judged as high art. For Alloway, high art had been supplanted by pop art, and new forms of judgment were required. Alloway's stress on the topicality and expendability of movies as consumer products was not without a certain ironic condescension toward the medium. By contrast, most auteurists tended to view movies as sacred relics of a spiritual medium. Their tone was reverent and, hence, vulnerable. Their only excuse (and mine) was that they thought that they were writing only for other believers.

No one to my knowledge has ever commented on the Kierkegaard quotation from *Either/Or* with which I introduced my 1962 auteur article: "I call these sketches shadowgraphs, partly by the designation to remind you at once that they derive from the darker side of life, partly because like other shadowgraphs they are not directly visible. When I take a shadowgraph in my hand, it makes no impression on me, and gives me no clear conception of it. Only when I hold it up opposite the wall, and now look not directly at it, but at that which appears on the wall, am I able to see it. So also with the picture which does not become perceptible until I see through the external. This external is perhaps quite unobtrusive but not until I look through it do I discover that inner picture which I desire to show you, an inner picture too delicately drawn to be outwardly visible, woven as it is of the tenderest moods of the soul."

Kierkegaard's "inner picture" eventually found its way into my essay as "interior meaning," a term that gave me a great deal of trouble at the time, but one that has since come to define what all serious film criticism seeks to discover. Auteurism has less to do with the way movies are made than with the way they are elucidated and evaluated. It is more a critical instrument than a creative inspiration. Peter Wollen has suggested the hypothetical nature of the enterprise, and I will go along with that. The cinema is a deep, dark mystery that we auteurists are attempting to solve. It is a labyrinth with a treacherous resemblance to reality. I suppose that the difference between auteurists and structuralists is the difference between knowing all the questions before finding the answers, and knowing all the answers before formulating the questions.

At this late date I am prepared to concede that auteurism is and always has been more a tendency than a theory, more a mystique than a methodology, more an editorial policy than an aesthetic procedure. Contrary to anti-auteurist legends, auteurist critics around the world are an unruly lot. For the most part, they do not describe themselves as auteurists. They are content to describe the stylistic and thematic epiphanies of their favorite auteurs.

DIRECTORIAL CHRONOLOGY 1915–1967

The directorial chronology between 1915 and 1928 does not purport to be an authoritative critical valuation. This chronology consists simply of (a) authenticated classics and (b) the films of directors whose work in the sound era is of some interest. There are too many gaps in silent film scholarship at this time for a definitive stand. Conversely, the directorial chronology between 1929 and 1967 represents a weighted critical valuation.

1915

D. W. GRIFFITH—*The Birth of a Nation.*

CHARLES CHAPLIN—His New Job, A Night Out, The Champion, In the Park, The Jitney Elopement, By the Sea, The Tramp, Work, A Woman, The Bank, Shanghaied, A Night at the Show.

CECIL B. DE MILLE—*The Cheat,* The Girl of the Golden West, The Warrens of Virginia, The Unafraid, The Captive, Wild Goose Chase, The Arab, Chimmie Fadden, Kindling, Maria Rosa, Carmen, Temptation, Chimmie Fadden Out West.

ALLAN DWAN—A Girl of Yesterday, Jordan Is a Hard Road, The Pretty Sister of Jose, The Dancing Girl, David Harum.

RAOUL WALSH—The Regeneration, Carmen.

1916

D. W. GRIFFITH—*Intolerance.*

CHARLES CHAPLIN—*The Rink, One A.M., The Pawnshop,* Carmen, Police, The Floorwalker, The Fireman, The Vagabond, The Count, Behind the Screen.

ALLAN DWAN—Manhattan Madness, The Half-Breed, The Good Bad Man, An Innocent Magdalene, Betty of Greystone, The Habit of Happiness.

CECIL B. DE MILLE—The Golden Chance, The Trail of the Lonesome Pine, The Heart of Nora Flynn, The Dream Girl.

RAOUL WALSH—Honor System, Blue Blood and Red, The Serpent.

1917

CHARLES CHAPLIN—*Easy Street, The Immigrant, The Cure, The Adventurer.*

ALLAN DWAN—Panthea, The Fighting Odds, His Excellency, the Governor.

CECIL B. DE MILLE—Joan the Woman, A Romance of the Redwoods, The Little American, The Woman God Forgot, The Devil Stone.

RAOUL WALSH—Betrayed, The Conqueror, The Pride of New York, The Innocent Sinner, Silent Lie.

JOHN FORD—Straight Shooting, The Secret Man, A Marked Man, Bucking Broadway.

MAURICE TOURNEUR—The Pride of the Clan.

1918

D. W. GRIFFITH—*Hearts of the World,* The Great Love, The Greatest Thing in Life.

CHARLES CHAPLIN—*Shoulder Arms, A Dog's Life,* The Bond.

ALLAN DWAN—A Modern Musketeer, Mister Fix-It, Bound in Morocco, He Comes Up Smiling.

CECIL B. DE MILLE—The Squaw Man, Old Wives for New, We Can't Have Everything, Till I Come Back to You, The Whispering Chorus.
ERICH VON STROHEIM—Blind Husbands.
KING VIDOR—The Turn in the Road.
FRANK BORZAGE—Flying Colors, Until They Get Me, The Gun Woman, Shoes That Danced, Innocent's Progress, Society for Sale, An Honest Man, The Ghost Flower, The Curse of Iku, Who Is to Blame?
JOHN FORD—Phantom Riders, Wild Women, Thieves' Gold, The Scarlet Drop, Hell Bent, Delirium, A Woman's Fool, Three Mounted Men.
RAOUL WALSH—Woman and the Law, This Is the Life, The Prussian Cur, On the Jump, Every Mother's Son, I'll Say So.
JOHN STAHL—Wives of Men.

1919

D. W. GRIFFITH—*True Heart Susie, Broken Blossoms,* The Girl Who Stayed at Home, A Romance of Happy Valley, Scarlet Days, The Greatest Question, The Fall of Babylon, The Mother and the Law.
CHARLES CHAPLIN—*Sunnyside,* A Day's Pleasure.
KING VIDOR—*The Jack Knife Man,* Better Times, The Other Half, Poor Relations.
ERICH VON STROHEIM—The Devil's Passkey.
ALLAN DWAN—Cheating Cheaters, Soldiers of Fortune, Sahara, The Dark Star, Getting Mary Married.
RAOUL WALSH—Evangeline, Should a Husband Forgive?
CECIL B. DE MILLE—Don't Change Your Husband, For Better for Worse, Male and Female.
JOHN FORD—Roped, A Fight for Love, The Fighting Brothers, Bare Fists, The Gun Packers, Riders of Vengeance, The Last Outlaw, The Outcasts of Poker Flat, Ace of the Saddle, Rider of the Law, A Gun Fightin' Gentleman, Marked Men.
FRANK BORZAGE—Toton, Prudence of Broadway, Whom the Gods Destroy.
JOHN STAHL—Her Code of Honor, Suspicion, Woman Under Oath.

1920

MAURICE TOURNEUR—*The Last of the Mohicans.*
D. W. GRIFFITH—*Way Down East,* The Love Flower, The Idol Dancer.
FRANK BORZAGE—Humoresque.
ALLAN DWAN—Luck of the Irish, A Splendid Hazard, The Forbidden Thing.
KING VIDOR—The Family Honour.
JOHN FORD—The Prince of Avenue A, The Girl in Number 29, Hitchin' Posts, Just Pals.
RAOUL WALSH—From Now On, The Deep Purple, The Strongest.
CECIL B. DE MILLE—Why Change Your Wife, Something to Think About.
JOHN STAHL—Women Men Forget, Woman in His House.

1921

CHARLES CHAPLIN—*The Kid, The Idle Class.*
D. W. GRIFFITH—*Dream Street.*
KING VIDOR—The Sky Pilot, Love Never Dies, Conquering the Women; Woman, Wake Up.
REX INGRAM—The Four Horsemen of the Apocalypse.
FRANK BORZAGE—The Duke of Chimney Butte.
ALLAN DWAN—The Perfect Crime, A Broken Doll, In the Heart of a Fool, The Scoffer.
MAURICE TOURNEUR—The Foolish Matrons.
CECIL B. DE MILLE—The Affairs of Anatol, Forbidden Fruit.

RAOUL WALSH—The Oath, Serenade.
JOHN FORD—The Big Punch, The Freeze-Out, The Wallop, Desperate Trails, Action, Sure Fire, Jackie.
LEO MC CAREY—Society Secret.
JOHN STAHL—The Child Thou Gavest Me, Sowing the Wind.

1922
ROBERT FLAHERTY—*Nanook of the North.*
CHARLES CHAPLIN—*The Pilgrim, Pay Day.*
D. W. GRIFFITH—*Orphans of the Storm,* One Exciting Night.
ERICH VON STROHEIM—*Foolish Wives,* Merry-Go-Round.
FRED NEWMEYER—*Grandma's Boy* (Harold Lloyd).
REX INGRAM—Prisoner of Zenda.
ALLAN DWAN—Robin Hood, The Sin of Martha Queed, Superstition.
KING VIDOR—Peg O' My Heart, Alice Adams, The Real Adventure, Dusk to Dawn.
FRANK BORZAGE—Get-Rich-Quick Wallingford, Back Pay, Silent Shelby, Billy Jim, The Good Provider, Valley of Silent Men, The Pride of Palomar.
JOHN FORD—Little Miss Smiles, Silver Wings, The Village Blacksmith.
RAOUL WALSH—Kindred of the Dust.
CECIL B. DE MILLE—Fool's Paradise, Saturday Night, Manslaughter.
JOHN STAHL—The Song of Life, One Clear Call, Suspicious Wives.

1923
CHARLES CHAPLIN—*A Woman of Paris.*
BUSTER KEATON—*The Three Ages, Our Hospitality.*
D. W. GRIFFITH—*The White Rose.*
JAMES CRUZE—*Hollywood,* Covered Wagon, Ruggles of Red Gap.
ERNST LUBITSCH—Rosita.
KING VIDOR—Wild Oranges, Three Wise Fools, The Woman of Bronze, Happiness.
FRED NEWMEYER and SAM TAYLOR—Safety Last (Harold Lloyd).
REX INGRAM—Scaramouche.
FRANK BORZAGE—Nth Commandment, Children of Dust, Song of Love.
JOHN FORD—Cameo Kirby, Three Jumps Ahead, The Face on the Bar-room Floor.
ALLAN DWAN—Zaza, Glimpses of the Moon, Lawful Larceny, Big Brother.
CECIL B. DE MILLE—Adam's Rib, The Ten Commandments.
RAOUL WALSH—-Lost and Found on a South Sea Island.
JOHN STAHL—The Wanters, The Dangerous Age.

1924
ERNST LUBITSCH—*The Marriage Circle, Forbidden Paradise,* Three Women.
BUSTER KEATON—*Sherlock Junior, The Navigator.*
JOHN FORD—The Iron Horse, Hoodman Blind, North of Hudson Bay, Hearts of Oak.
D. W. GRIFFITH—America.
RAOUL WALSH—The Thief of Bagdad.
KING VIDOR—Wine of Youth, His Hour, Wife of the Centaur.
FRED NEWMEYER and SAM TAYLOR—Girl Shy (Harold Lloyd), Hot Water (Lloyd).
VICTOR SEASTROM—He Who Gets Slapped.
ALLAN DWAN—Her Love Story, Manhandled, A Society Scandal, The Wages of Virtue, Argentine Love.
FRANK BORZAGE—Secrets, The Age of Desire.

CECIL B. DE MILLE—Triumph, Feet of Clay.
JOHN STAHL—Husbands and Lovers, Why Men Leave Home.

1925

CHARLES CHAPLIN—*The Gold Rush.*
KING VIDOR—*The Big Parade,* La Boheme, Proud Flesh.
ERNST LUBITSCH—Lady Windermere's Fan, Kiss Me Again.
ERICH VON STROHEIM—Greed, The Merry Widow.
BUSTER KEATON—Go West, Seven Chances.
D. W. GRIFFITH—Sally of the Sawdust, Isn't Life Wonderful, The Royle Girl.
JOSEF VON STERNBERG—The Salvation Hunters.
FRED NEWMEYER and SAM TAYLOR—The Freshman (Harold Lloyd).
HERBERT BRENON—A Kiss for Cinderella, Peter Pan.
JAMES CRUZE—Beggar on Horseback.
HENRY KING—Stella Dallas, Romola.
VICTOR SEASTROM—The Tower of Lies.
SVEND GADE—Siege.
TOD BROWNING—The Unholy Three.
JOHN FORD—Lightnin', Kentucky Pride, The Fighting Heart, Thank You.
FRANK BORZAGE—The Lady, Daddy's Gone a'Hunting, Wages for Wives, The Circle, Lazybones.
RAOUL WALSH—East of Suez, The Spaniard.
ALLAN DWAN—Night Life in New York, Stage Struck, Coast of Folly.
CECIL B. DE MILLE—The Road to Yesterday, The Golden Bed.
JOHN STAHL—Fine Clothes.
ALFRED HITCHCOCK—The Pleasure Garden.

1926

BUSTER KEATON—*The General,* Battling Butler.
ERNST LUBITSCH—*So This is Paris.*
ROBERT FLAHERTY—Moana.
JOSEF VON STERNBERG—The Exquisite Sinner, The Sea Gull.
FRANK CAPRA—The Strong Man.
ALFRED HITCHCOCK—The Lodger, The Mountain Eagle.
RAOUL WALSH—What Price Glory?, The Wanderer, The Lucky Lady, The Lady of the Harem.
KING VIDOR—Bardelys the Magnificent.
MALCOLM ST. CLAIR—The Grand Duchess and the Waiter, A Woman of the World.
HERBERT BRENON—Beau Geste.
CLARENCE BROWN—Flesh and the Devil.
JOHN FORD—Three Bad Men, The Shamrock Handicap, The Blue Eagle.
HOWARD HAWKS—Fig Leaves, The Road to Glory.
FRANK BORZAGE—The First Year, Marriage License, Early to Wed, The Dixie Merchant.
D. W. GRIFFITH—The Sorrows of Satan.
ALLAN DWAN—Tin Gods, Summer Bachelors, Sea Horses, Padlocked.
CECIL B. DE MILLE—The Volga Boatmen.
JOHN STAHL—Memory Lane, The Gay Deceiver.
GREGORY LA CAVA—Woman Handled.

1927

JOSEF VON STERNBERG—*Underworld.*
F. W. MURNAU—*Sunrise.*
KING VIDOR—*The Crowd,* The Patsy.
FRANK BORZAGE—Seventh Heaven.
ERNST LUBITSCH—The Student Prince.
BUSTER KEATON—College.

FRANK CAPRA—Long Pants, For the Love of Mike.
ALFRED HITCHCOCK—The Ring, Easy Virtue, Downhill.
RAOUL WALSH—The Loves of Carmen, The Monkey Talks.
JOHN FORD—Upstream.
HOWARD HAWKS—Paid to Love, The Cradle Snatchers.
CECIL B. DE MILLE—The King of Kings.
VICTOR FLEMING—The Way of All Flesh.
GREGORY LA CAVA—Running Wild.
MAURITZ STILLER—Hotel Imperial.
HARRY D'ARRAST—The Gentleman from Paris.
PAUL LENI—The Cat and the Canary.
LEWIS MILESTONE—Two Arabian Knights.
ALLAN DWAN—The Music Master, Joy Girl; East Side, West Side.
JOHN STAHL—Lovers, In Old Kentucky.
HERBERT BRENON—Sorrell and Son.
ALEXANDER KORDA—The Private Life of Helen of Troy.

1928

CHARLES CHAPLIN—*The Circus.*
JOSEF VON STERNBERG—*The Last Command, Docks of New York,* The Dragnet.
BUSTER KEATON—Steamboat Bill Junior, The Cameraman.
HOWARD HAWKS—A Girl in Every Port, The Air Circus, Fazil.
ERICH VON STROHEIM—The Wedding March, Queen Kelly.
PAUL LENI—The Man Who Laughs.
ERNST LUBITSCH—The Patriot.
KING VIDOR—Show People.
FRANK BORZAGE—Street Angel.
VICTOR SEASTROM—The Wind, The Divine Woman.
F. W. MURNAU—The Four Devils.
VICTOR SCHERTZINGER—Forgotten Faces.
HARRY D'ARRAST—Dry Martini.
ANTHONY ASQUITH—Shooting Stars.
D. W. GRIFFITH—The Battle of the Sexes, Drums of Love.
ALFRED HITCHCOCK—The Farmer's Wife, The Manxman, Champagne.
JOHN FORD—Four Sons, Mother Machree, Hangman's House, Napoleon's Barber, Riley the Cop.
RAOUL WALSH—Sadie Thompson, The Red Dance; Me, Gangster.
TAY GARNETT—The Spieler, Celebrity.
HERBERT BRENON—Laugh, Clown, Laugh.
LEWIS MILESTONE—The Racket.
ALLAN DWAN—French Dressing, Big Noise.
CECIL B. DE MILLE—The Godless Girl.

1929

KING VIDOR—Hallelujah!, Not So Dumb.
ERNST LUBITSCH—The Love Parade, Eternal Love.
JOSEF VON STERNBERG—Thunderbolt, The Case of Lena Smith.
ALFRED HITCHCOCK—Blackmail.
FRANK BORZAGE—The River, Lucky Star, They Had to See Paris.
ROLAND WEST—Alibi.
ROUBEN MAMOULIAN—Applause.
PAUL FEJOS—Lonesome.
JACQUES FEYDER—The Kiss.
JOSEPH SANTLEY and ROBERT FLOREY—The Cocoanuts (The Marx Brothers).
D. W. GRIFFITH—Lady of the Pavements.
HOWARD HAWKS—Trent's Last Case.
JOHN FORD—Strong Boy, The Black Watch, Salute.

RAOUL WALSH—The Cockeyed World, In Old Arizona (with Irving Cummings).
CECIL B. DE MILLE—Dynamite.
ALLAN DWAN—The Iron Mask, Tide of Empire, Frozen Justice, The Far Call, South Sea Rose.
FRANK CAPRA—Flight, The Donovan Affair.
LEO MC CAREY—The Sophomore, Red Hot Rhythm.
PAUL LENI—The Last Warning.
TAY GARNETT—Flying Fools, Oh Yeah!
REX INGRAM—Three Passions.
DAVID BUTLER—Sunny Side Up.
HARRY BEAUMONT—The Broadway Melody.
VICTOR FLEMING—The Virginian.
ALFRED E. GREEN—Disraeli.
EDWARD SUTHERLAND—Close Harmony, Dance of Life, Fast Company, Saturday Night Kid, Pointed Heels.

1930

JOSEF VON STERNBERG—*Morocco, The Blue Angel.*
D. W. GRIFFITH—*Abraham Lincoln.*
HOWARD HAWKS—*The Dawn Patrol.*
JOHN FORD—Men Without Women, Up the River, Born Reckless.
F. W. MURNAU—City Girl (Our Daily Bread).
ALFRED HITCHCOCK—Murder, Juno and the Paycock.
ERNST LUBITSCH—Monte Carlo, Paramount on Parade (with Edmund Goulding, Rowland V. Lee, Victor Schertzinger, Dorothy Arzner, Otto Brower, Victor Heerman, Edwin Knopf, Lothar Mendes, Edward Sutherland, and Frank Tuttle.
GEORGE CUKOR—The Royal Family of Broadway (with Cyril Gardner), Grumpy (with Cyril Gardner).
LEWIS MILESTONE—All Quiet on the Western Front.
TAY GARNETT—Her Man, Officer O'Brien.
GEORGE HILL—The Big House, Min and Bill.
HOWARD HUGHES—Hell's Angels.
HARRY D'ARRAST—Raffles, Laughter.
CLARENCE BROWN—Anna Christie, Romance.
KING VIDOR—Billy the Kid.
FRANK BORZAGE—Song o' My Heart, Liliom.
RAOUL WALSH—The Big Trail.
CECIL B. DE MILLE—Madame Satan.
JOHN CROMWELL—Street of Chance.
JAMES WHALE—Journey's End.
VICTOR HEERMAN—Animal Crackers (The Marx Brothers).
FRANK CAPRA—Ladies of Leisure, Rain or Shine.
LEO MC CAREY—Let's Go Native, Wild Company, Part Time Wife.
JOHN STAHL—A Lady Surrenders.
MERVYN LEROY—Little Johnny Jones, Playing Around, Show Girl in Hollywood, Numbered Men, Broken Dishes, Top Speed, Little Caesar.
WILLIAM WYLER—Hell's Heroes.
HERBERT BRENON—The Case of Sergeant Grischa.
EDWARD SUTHERLAND—Social Lion.
ROBERT MILTON—Outward Bound.

1931

CHARLES CHAPLIN—*City Lights*
F. W. MURNAU—*Tabu* (with Robert Flaherty).
JOSEF VON STERNBERG—*An American Tragedy, Dishonored.*
KING VIDOR—Street Scene, The Champ.

HOWARD HAWKS—The Criminal Code.
D. W. GRIFFITH—The Struggle.
ERNST LUBITSCH—The Smiling Lieutenant.
FRANK BORZAGE—Bad Girl, Doctors' Wives, As Young as You Feel.
JOHN FORD—Arrowsmith, The Seas Beneath, The Brat.
GEORGE CUKOR—Tarnished Lady, Girls About Town.
LEWIS MILESTONE—The Front Page.
CECIL B. DE MILLE—The Squaw Man.
FRANK CAPRA—Dirigible, The Miracle Woman, Platinum Blonde.
ROLAND WEST—The Bat Whispers, Corsair.
ALFRED HITCHCOCK—The Skin Game.
LEO MC CAREY—Indiscreet.
JOHN STAHL—Seed, Strictly Dishonorable.
ROUBEN MAMOULIAN—City Streets.
ROWLAND BROWN—Quick Millions.
JAMES WHALE—Frankenstein, Waterloo Bridge.
WILLIAM WELLMAN—The Public Enemy, Other Men's Women, Star Witness,
    Night Nurse, Safe in Hell.
SIDNEY FRANKLIN—The Guardsman, Private Lives.
MERVYN LEROY—Five Star Final.
WILLIAM WYLER—A House Divided.
NORMAN TAUROG—Skippy.
NORMAN MC LEOD—Monkey Business (The Marx Brothers).
WESLEY RUGGLES—Cimarron.
TOD BROWNING—Dracula.
WILLIAM DIETERLE—The Last Flight.

   1932
HOWARD HAWKS—*Scarface,* The Crowd Roars, Tiger Shark.
JOSEF VON STERNBERG—*Shanghai Express,* Blonde Venus.
ERNST LUBITSCH—*Trouble in Paradise,* One Hour With You, The Man I Killed,
    If I Had a Million (with James Cruze, Norman Taurog, Stephen Roberts,
    Norman Z. McLeod, William Seiter, and Bruce Humberstone).
FRANK BORZAGE—A Farewell to Arms, After Tomorrow, Young America.
GEORGE CUKOR—A Bill of Divorcement, What Price Hollywood, Rockabye.
JOHN FORD—Air Mail, Flesh.
ALFRED HITCHCOCK—East of Shanghai.
CECIL B. DE MILLE—The Sign of the Cross.
TAY GARNETT—One Way Passage.
JOHN STAHL—Back Street.
FRANK CAPRA—American Madness, Forbidden.
LEO MC CAREY—The Kid from Spain.
EDMUND GOULDING—Grand Hotel.
ROUBEN MAMOULIAN—Dr. Jekyll and Mr. Hyde, Love Me Tonight.
MERVYN LEROY—I Am a Fugitive from a Chain Gang, High Pressure, Heart of
    New York, Two Seconds, Big City Blues, Three on a Match.
ALLAN DWAN—While Paris Sleeps.
ROWLAND BROWN—Hell's Highway.
W. S. VAN DYKE—Tarzan, The Ape Man.
EDWARD F. CLINE—Million Dollar Legs.
JAMES WHALE—The Invisible Man.
TOD BROWNING—Freaks.
RICHARD BOLESLAWSKI—Rasputin and the Empress.
GREGORY LA CAVA—The Half Naked Truth.
VICTOR FLEMING—Red Dust.
JAMES CRUZE—Washington Merry-Go-Round.
LEWIS MILESTONE—Rain.

LOWELL SHERMAN—The Greeks Had a Word for Them.
EDWARD L. CAHN—Law and Order.
ROY DEL RUTH—Blessed Event.
IRVING PICHEL—The Most Dangerous Game.
WILLIAM WELLMAN—The Hatchet Man.
KARL FREUND—The Mummy.
ELLIOTT NUGENT—The Mouthpiece, Life Begins.
CLARENCE BROWN—Emma.
GEORGE FITZMAURICE—As You Desire Me.

1933

ERNST LUBITSCH—*Design for Living.*
GEORGE CUKOR—*Dinner at Eight,* Little Women, Our Betters.
FRANK BORZAGE—*A Man's Castle,* Secrets.
FRANK CAPRA—Lady for a Day, The Bitter Tea of General Yen.
LEO MC CAREY—Duck Soup.
LEWIS MILESTONE—Hallelujah, I'm a Bum!
JOHN FORD—Doctor Bull, Pilgrimage.
SERGEI EISENSTEIN—Thunder Over Mexico.
HOWARD HAWKS—Today We Live.
ROUBEN MAMOULIAN—Queen Christina, The Song of Songs.
JOHN STAHL—Only Yesterday.
MERVYN LEROY—Gold Diggers of 1933, Hard to Handle.
VICTOR FLEMING—Bombshell.
LOWELL SHERMAN—She Done Him Wrong, Morning Glory.
ROWLAND V. LEE—Zoo in Budapest.
MERRIAM C. COOPER and ERNEST SCHOESDACK—King Kong.
ALEXANDER KORDA—The Private Life of Henry VIII.
HARRY D'ARRAST—Topaze.
ELLIOTT NUGENT—Three-Cornered Moon.
JAMES CRUZE—I Cover the Waterfront.
WILLIAM K. HOWARD—The Power and the Glory.
LLOYD BACON—Forty-second Street, The Picture Snatcher, Footlight Parade.
HENRY KING—State Fair.
WILLIAM WYLER—Counsellor at Law.
FRANK LLOYD—Cavalcade, Berkeley Square.
WILLIAM WELLMAN—Heroes for Sale.

1934

HOWARD HAWKS—*Twentieth Century,* Viva Villa! (with Jack Conway).
JOSEF VON STERNBERG—*The Scarlet Empress.*
ROBERT FLAHERTY—*Man of Aran.*
JOHN FORD—The Lost Patrol, Judge Priest, The World Moves On.
FRANK BORZAGE—Little Man, What Now?, No Greater Glory.
ERNST LUBITSCH—The Merry Widow.
FRANK CAPRA—It Happened One Night, Broadway Bill.
KING VIDOR—Our Daily Bread.
CECIL B. DE MILLE—Cleopatra, Four Frightened People.
JOHN STAHL—Imitation of Life.
EDGAR G. ULMER—The Black Cat.
LEO MC CAREY—Belle of the Nineties, Six of a Kind.
G. W PABST—A Modern Hero.
JAMES CRUZE—David Harum.
VICTOR FLEMING—Treasure Island.
VICTOR SCHERTZINGER—One Night of Love.
JOHN CROMWELL—Of Human Bondage.
HENRY HATHAWAY—The Witching Hour.

MARK SANDRICH—The Gay Divorcee.
MERVYN LEROY—Sweet Adeline, Hi Nellie.
W. S. VAN DYKE—The Thin Man.
GREGORY LA CAVA—What Every Woman Knows, The Affairs of Cellini.
PAUL CZINNER—Catherine the Great.
BASIL DEAN—The Constant Nymph.
JAMES WHALE—One More River.
HAROLD YOUNG—The Scarlet Pimpernel.
ALEXANDER HALL—Little Miss Marker.
BEN HECHT and CHARLES MAC ARTHUR—Crime Without Passion.
NORMAN TAUROG—It's a Gift, Mrs. Wiggs of the Cabbage Patch.

1935

JOSEF VON STERNBERG—*The Devil is a Woman*, Crime and Punishment.
JOHN FORD—*Steamboat 'Round the Bend, The Whole Town's Talking*, The Informer.
ALFRED HITCHCOCK—*The 39 Steps, The Man Who Knew Too Much.*
LEO MC CAREY—Ruggles of Red Gap.
GREGORY LA CAVA—She Married Her Boss, Private Worlds.
GEORGE STEVENS—Alice Adams.
HOWARD HAWKS—Barbary Coast.
GEORGE CUKOR—Sylvia Scarlett, David Copperfield.
FRANK BORZAGE—Living on Velvet.
KING VIDOR—So Red the Rose.
JOHN STAHL—The Magnificent Obsession.
CECIL B. DE MILLE—The Crusades.
HENRY HATHAWAY—Peter Ibbetson, Lives of a Bengal Lancer.
BEN HECHT and CHARLES MAC ARTHUR—The Scoundrel, Once in a Blue Moon.
MARK SANDRICH—Top Hat, Follow the Fleet.
VICTOR FLEMING—Reckless.
JAMES WHALE—Bride of Frankenstein.
WESLEY RUGGLES—The Gilded Lily.
FRANK LLOYD—Mutiny on the Bounty.
ROUBEN MAMOULIAN—Becky Sharp.
MICHAEL CURTIZ—Captain Blood, Black Fury.
WILLIAM K. HOWARD—Mary Burns—Fugitive.
BUSBY BERKELEY—Gold Diggers of 1935.
SAM WOOD—A Night at the Opera (The Marx Brothers).
WILLIAM WYLER—The Gay Deception, The Good Fairy.
CLARENCE BROWN—Ah, Wilderness; Anna Karenina.
ROY DEL RUTH—Broadway Melody of 1936.
TOM CONWAY—A Tale of Two Cities.
ALFRED E. GREEN—Dangerous.
CLYDE BRUCKMAN—The Man on the Flying Trapeze.
EDWARD SUTHERLAND—Mississippi, Diamond Jim.

1936

CHARLES CHAPLIN—*Modern Times.*
ALFRED HITCHCOCK—*Secret Agent.*
GREGORY LA CAVA—*My Man Godfrey.*
JOHN FORD—The Prisoner of Shark Island, Mary of Scotland, The Plough and the Stars.
HOWARD HAWKS—Ceiling Zero, The Road to Glory, Come and Get It (with William Wyler).
FRITZ LANG—Fury.
FRANK CAPRA—Mr. Deeds Goes to Town.
KING VIDOR—The Texas Rangers.

CECIL B. DE MILLE—The Plainsman.
FRANK BORZAGE—Desire.
LEO MC CAREY—The Milky Way.
GEORGE STEVENS—Swing Time.
LEWIS MILESTONE—The General Died at Dawn, Anything Goes.
GEORGE CUKOR—Romeo and Juliet.
JOSEF VON STERNBERG—The King Steps Out.
WILLIAM WYLER—Dodsworth, These Three.
RAOUL WALSH—Klondike Annie, Big Brown Eyes.
RENE CLAIR—The Ghost Goes West.
ALEXANDER KORDA—Rembrandt.
ROUBEN MAMOULIAN—The Gay Desperado.
HENRY HATHAWAY—The Trail of the Lonesome Pine; Go West, Young Man.
MICHAEL CURTIZ—Charge of the Light Brigade.
JACK CONWAY—Libeled Lady.
JAMES WHALE—Show Boat.
ALFRED SANTELL—Winterset.
W. S. VAN DYKE—The Great Ziegfeld, San Francisco, After the Thin Man.
DOROTHY ARZNER—Craig's Wife.
LOTHAR MENDES—The Man Who Could Work Miracles.
WILLIAM DIETERLE—The Story of Louis Pasteur.
ARCHIE MAYO—The Petrified Forest.
WILLIAM CAMERON MENZIES—Things to Come.
JAMES CRUZE—Sutter's Gold.
E. A. DUPONT—A Son Comes Home.
TOD BROWNING—The Devil-Doll.
CLARENCE BROWN—Wife Versus Secretary.

1937
ERNST LUBITSCH—*Angel.*
FRITZ LANG—*You Only Live Once.*
FRANK BORZAGE—*History is Made at Night,* Green Light, Mannequin, The Big
   City.
ALFRED HITCHCOCK—Sabotage.
JOHN FORD—The Hurricane, Wee Willie Winkie.
LEO MC CAREY—The Awful Truth, Make Way for Tomorrow.
GEORGE CUKOR—Camille.
KING VIDOR—Stella Dallas.
FRANK CAPRA—Lost Horizon.
GREGORY LA CAVA—Stage Door.
GEORGE STEVENS—Quality Street, A Damsel in Distress.
JOHN STAHL—Parnell.
TAY GARNETT—Slave Ship, Stand In, Love Is News.
MITCHELL LEISEN—Easy Living; Swing High, Swing Low.
JOHN CROMWELL—The Prisoner of Zenda.
RICHARD THORPE—Night Must Fall.
WILLIAM WELLMAN—A Star Is Born, Nothing Sacred.
VICTOR FLEMING—Captains Courageous.
WESLEY RUGGLES—I Met Him in Paris, True Confession.
MERVYN LEROY—They Won't Forget.
MARK SANDRICH—Shall We Dance?
HENRY HATHAWAY—Souls at Sea.
MICHAEL CURTIZ—Kid Galahad.
ZOLTAN KORDA—Elephant Boy.
JAMES WHALE—The Road Back.
WILLIAM WYLER—Dead End.
WILLIAM DIETERLE—The Life of Emile Zola.

HENRY KOSTER—Three Smart Girls, 100 Men and a Girl.
NORMAN MC LEOD—Topper.
ALEXANDER HALL—Exclusive.
ROUBEN MAMOULIAN—High, Wide, and Handsome.
SIDNEY FRANKLIN—The Good Earth.

1938

GEORGE CUKOR—*Holiday*, Zaza.
HOWARD HAWKS—*Bringing up Baby*.
FRANK BORZAGE—*Three Comrades*, The Shining Hour.
ALFRED HITCHCOCK—The Girl Was Young, The Lady Vanishes.
ERNST LUBITSCH—Bluebeard's Eighth Wife.
JOHN FORD—Submarine Patrol, Four Men and a Prayer.
FRITZ LANG—You and Me.
KING VIDOR—The Citadel.
FRANK CAPRA—You Can't Take It With You.
ANTHONY ASQUITH and LESLIE HOWARD—Pygmalion.
CECIL B. DE MILLE—The Buccaneer.
GEORGE STEVENS—Vivacious Lady.
JOHN STAHL—Letter of Introduction.
HENRY HATHAWAY—Spawn of the North.
MICHAEL CURTIZ—Angels with Dirty Faces, Four Daughters, The Adventures of
   Robin Hood (with William Keighley).
GARSON KANIN—A Man to Remember, Next Time I Marry.
MARK SANDRICH—Carefree.
RICHARD WALLACE—The Young in Heart.
WILLIAM WYLER—Jezebel.
JOHN CROMWELL—Algiers.
WILLIAM DIETERLE—Blockade.
WESLEY RUGGLES—Sing You Sinners.
W. S. VAN DYKE—Marie Antoinette.
HENRY KING—Alexander's Ragtime Band.
JULIEN DUVIVIER—The Great Waltz.
TIM WHELAN—Divorce of Lady X, Action for Slander.
ERICH POMMER—The Beachcomber.
VICTOR SAVILLE—South Riding.
MICHAEL POWELL—The Edge of the World.
ANATOLE LITVAK—The Sisters.
NORMAN TAUROG—Boys Town.
EDMUND GOULDING—The Dawn Patrol, White Banners.
LLOYD BACON—A Slight Case of Murder.

1939

JOHN FORD—*Stagecoach, Young Mr. Lincoln*, Drums Along the Mohawk.
HOWARD HAWKS—*Only Angels Have Wings*.
ERNST LUBITSCH—*Ninotchka*.
LEO MC CAREY—*Love Affair*.
FRANK CAPRA—*Mr. Smith Goes to Washington*.
GEORGE CUKOR—The Women.
ALFRED HITCHCOCK—Jamaica Inn.
JOSEF VON STERNBERG—Sergeant Madden.
RAOUL WALSH—The Roaring Twenties, St. Louis Blues.
KING VIDOR—Northwest Passage.
CECIL B. DE MILLE—Union Pacific.
GEORGE STEVENS—Gunga Din.
VICTOR FLEMING—Gone with the Wind, The Wizard of Oz.
WILLIAM WYLER—Wuthering Heights.

JOHN STAHL—When Tomorrow Comes.
MITCHELL LEISEN—Midnight.
GARSON KANIN—Bachelor Mother, The Great Man Votes.
GREGORY LA CAVA—Fifth Avenue Girl.
EDMUND GOULDING—Dark Victory, The Old Maid, We Are Not Alone.
GEORGE MARSHALL—Destry Rides Again, You Can't Cheat an Honest Man.
WILLIAM K. HOWARD—Back Door to Heaven.
JAY THEODORE REED—What a Life!
ALLAN DWAN—Frontier Marshal.
JOHN CROMWELL—Made for Each Other, In Name Only.
MICHAEL CURTIZ—Dodge City, Daughters Courageous, The Private Lives of Elizabeth and Essex, Four Wives.
ZOLTAN KORDA—Four Feathers.
ROY KELLINO—I Met a Murderer.
BUSBY BERKELEY—Babes in Arms.
VICTOR SCHERTZINGER—The Mikado.
MICHAEL POWELL—The Spy in Black.
WILLIAM DIETERLE—Juarez, Hunchback of Notre Dame.
ANATOLE LITVAK—Confessions of a Nazi Spy.
JOHN FARROW—Five Came Back, Full Confession.
WESLEY RUGGLES—Invitation to Happiness.
GREGORY RATOFF—Intermezzo.
LEWIS SEILER—Dust Be My Destiny.
SAM WOOD—Goodbye, Mr. Chips.

1940

CHARLES CHAPLIN—*The Great Dictator.*
ERNST LUBITSCH—*The Shop Around the Corner.*
HOWARD HAWKS—His Girl Friday.
FRANK BORZAGE—The Mortal Storm, Strange Cargo, Flight Command.
ALFRED HITCHCOCK—Rebecca, Foreign Correspondent.
JOHN FORD—The Grapes of Wrath, The Long Voyage Home.
TAY GARNETT—Seven Sinners, Slightly Honorable.
PRESTON STURGES—The Great McGinty, Christmas in July.
GEORGE CUKOR—The Philadelphia Story, Susan and God.
CECIL B. DE MILLE—Northwest Mounted Police.
WILLIAM WYLER—The Letter.
FRITZ LANG—The Return of Frank James.
RAOUL WALSH—They Drive By Night, The Dark Command.
CAROL REED—Night Train, The Stars Look Down.
GEORGE STEVENS—Vigil in the Night.
LUDWIG BERGER, MICHAEL POWELL, and TIM WHELAN—The Thief of Bagdad.
ROBERT Z. LEONARD—Pride and Prejudice.
MITCHELL LEISEN—Remember the Night; Arise, My Love.
LEWIS MILESTONE—Of Mice and Men, The Night of Nights, Lucky Partners.
GREGORY LA CAVA--The Primrose Path.
GARSON KANIN—My Favorite Wife, They Knew What They Wanted.
MICHAEL CURTIZ—The Sea Hawk, Virginia City, Santa Fe Trail.
BUSBY BERKELEY—Strike Up the Band.
EDWARD F. CLINE—The Bank Dick, My Little Chickadee, The Villain Still Pursued Her.
JOHN CROMWELL—Victory.
RICHARD THORPE—The Earl of Chicago.
LEE GARMES and BEN HECHT—Angels Over Broadway.
VICTOR SCHERTZINGER—Rhythm on the River, Road to Singapore.
WILLIAM DIETERLE—Doctor Ehrlich's Magic Bullet, A Dispatch From Reuters.
ANATOLE LITVAK—City for Conquest, All This and Heaven Too, Castle on the Hudson.

SAM WOOD—Our Town, Kitty Foyle.
WESLEY RUGGLES—Arizona, Too Many Husbands.
GEORGE MARSHALL—When the Daltons Rode.
TIM WHELAN—Sidewalks of London.
HAL ROACH and D. W. GRIFFITH—One Million B.C.

1941
ORSON WELLES—*Citizen Kane.*
JOSEF VON STERNBERG—*The Shanghai Gesture.*
ALFRED HITCHCOCK—*Suspicion,* Mr. and Mrs. Smith.
JEAN RENOIR—*Swamp Water.*
JOHN FORD—*How Green Was My Valley,* Tobacco Road.
FRITZ LANG—*Man Hunt,* Western Union.
HOWARD HAWKS—Sergeant York, Ball of Fire.
RAOUL WALSH—High Sierra, The Strawberry Blonde, They Died With Their Boots On, Manpower.
PRESTON STURGES—The Lady Eve.
JOHN HUSTON—The Maltese Falcon.
GEORGE STEVENS—Penny Serenade.
GEORGE CUKOR—A Woman's Face, Two-Faced Woman.
KING VIDOR—H. M. Pulham, Esq.
ERNST LUBITSCH—That Uncertain Feeling.
WILLIAM WYLER—The Little Foxes.
FRANK CAPRA—Meet John Doe.
RENE CLAIR—The Flame of New Orleans.
GREGORY LA CAVA—Unfinished Business.
MITCHELL LEISEN—Hold Back the Dawn, I Wanted Wings.
EDMUND GOULDING—The Great Lie.
ALEXANDER HALL—Here Comes Mr. Jordan, Bedtime Story, This Thing Called Love.
WILLIAM DIETERLE—All That Money Can Buy.
ALLAN DWAN—Rise and Shine, Look Who's Laughing.
GABRIEL PASCAL—Major Barbara.
ALEXANDER KORDA—That Hamilton Woman.
ROBERT STEVENSON—Back Street.
GARSON KANIN—Tom, Dick and Harry.
CHARLES VIDOR—Ladies in Retirement.
JOHN CROMWELL—So Ends Our Night.
MICHAEL CURTIZ—The Sea Wolf, Dive Bomber.
HENRY HATHAWAY—The Shepherd of the Hills, Sundown.
GEORGE MARSHALL—Texas.
BRUCE HUMBERSTONE—I Wake Up Screaming.
IRVING RAPPER—Shining Victory.
SAM WOOD—The Devil and Miss Jones.

1942
ORSON WELLES—*The Magnificent Ambersons,* Journey Into Fear (with Norman Foster).
ERNST LUBITSCH—*To Be or Not To Be.*
ALFRED HITCHCOCK—Saboteur.
PRESTON STURGES—Sullivan's Travels, The Palm Beach Story.
RAOUL WALSH—Gentleman Jim, Desperate Journey.
MICHAEL CURTIZ—Casablanca, Yankee Doodle Dandy.
CECIL B. DE MILLE—Reap the Wild Wind.
JACQUES TOURNEUR—The Cat People.
BILLY WILDER—The Major and the Minor.
GEORGE STEVENS—Woman of the Year, Talk of the Town.
JOHN HUSTON—Across the Pacific, In This Our Life.

LEO MC CAREY—Once Upon a Honeymoon.
RENE CLAIR—I Married a Witch.
FRANK BORZAGE—Seven Sweethearts.
DAVID LEAN and NOEL COWARD—In Which We Serve.
ALBERT LEWIN—The Moon and Sixpence.
MERVYN LEROY—Random Harvest, Johnny Eager.
HENRY HATHAWAY—China Girl, Ten Gentlemen From West Point.
ALLAN DWAN—Friendly Enemies, Here We Go Again.
WILLIAM WYLER—Mrs. Miniver.
WILLIAM WELLMAN—Roxie Hart.
SAM WOOD—Kings Row, Pride of the Yankees.
MICHAEL POWELL and EMERIC PRESSBURGER—One of Our Aircraft Is Missing.
STUART HEISLER—The Glass Key.
FRANK TUTTLE—This Gun for Hire.
IRVING RAPPER—Now Voyager, The Gay Sisters.

1943

ALFRED HITCHCOCK—*Shadow of a Doubt.*
FRITZ LANG—*Hangmen Also Die.*
HOWARD HAWKS—*The Air Force.*
ERNST LUBITSCH—Heaven Can Wait.
JEAN RENOIR—This Land Is Mine.
JOHN STAHL—Holy Matrimony, The Immortal Sergeant.
H. C. POTTER—Mr. Lucky.
JACQUES TOURNEUR—I Walked With a Zombie, The Leopard Man.
GEORGE CUKOR—Keeper of the Flame.
FRANK BORZAGE—Stage Door Canteen, His Butler's Sister.
DOUGLAS SIRK—Hitler's Madman.
VINCENTE MINNELLI—Cabin in the Sky, I Dood It.
GEORGE STEVENS—The More the Merrier.
RAOUL WALSH—Northern Pursuit, Background to Danger.
BILLY WILDER—Five Graves to Cairo.
EDMUND GOULDING—Claudia, The Constant Nymph.
RICHARD ROSSEN—Corvette K-225.
VICTOR FLEMING—A Guy Named Joe.
RICHARD WALLACE—The Fallen Sparrow.
ZOLTAN KORDA—Sahara.
CLARENCE BROWN—The Human Comedy.
WILLIAM WELLMAN—The Ox-Bow Incident.
JULIEN DUVIVIER—Flesh and Fantasy.
VINCENT SHERMAN—The Hard Way, Old Acquaintance.
MARK ROBSON—The Seventh Victim, The Ghost Ship.
RAY ENRIGHT—Gung Ho!
LEWIS MILESTONE—The North Star.
IRVING PICHEL—The Moon Is Down.
HERBERT WILCOX—Lassie Come Home.
SAM WOOD—For Whom the Bell Tolls.
MARK SANDRICH—So Proudly We Hail.
NORMAN KRASNA—Princess O'Rourke.
HERMAN SHUMLIN—Watch on the Rhine.

1944

OTTO PREMINGER—*Laura.*
PRESTON STURGES—*The Miracle of Morgan's Creek, Hail the Conquering Hero, The Great Moment.*
GEORGE CUKOR—*Gaslight,* Winged Victory.
HOWARD HAWKS—*To Have and Have Not.*

ALFRED HITCHCOCK—Lifeboat.
LEO MC CAREY—Going My Way.
FRANK BORZAGE—Till We Meet Again.
ROBERT SIODMAK—Phantom Lady, Christmas Holiday, Cobra Woman.
VINCENTE MINNELLI—Meet Me in St. Louis.
FRANK CAPRA—Arsenic and Old Lace.
BILLY WILDER—Double Indemnity.
EDGAR G. ULMER—Bluebeard.
JOHN STAHL—The Eve of St. Mark, The Keys of the Kingdom.
ARTHUR RIPLEY—Voice in the Wind.
DOUGLAS SIRK—Summer Storm.
RAOUL WALSH—Uncertain Glory.
KING VIDOR—An American Romance.
CECIL B. DE MILLE—The Story of Dr. Wassell.
JOHN CROMWELL—Since You Went Away.
RENE CLAIR—It Happened Tomorrow.
MITCHELL LEISEN—Lady in the Dark.
JEAN NEGULESCO—The Mask of Dimitrios.
ROBERT WISE—Curse of the Cat People.
ANDRE DE TOTH—Dark Waters.
LEWIS ALLEN—The Uninvited, Our Hearts Were Young and Gay.
WILLIAM CASTLE—When Strangers Marry (Betrayed).
JOHN BRAHM—The Lodger, Guest in the House.
CHARLES VIDOR—Cover Girl, Together Again.
CLIFFORD ODETS—None But the Lonely Heart.
EDWARD DMYTRYK—Murder, My Sweet.
FRED ZINNEMANN—The Seventh Cross.
LEWIS MILESTONE—The Purple Heart.
ROY BOULTING—Thunder Rock.
HENRY KING—The Song of Bernadette, Wilson.
ELLIOTT NUGENT—Up in Arms.

1945
JOHN FORD—*They Were Expendable.*
JEAN RENOIR—*The Southerner.*
FRITZ LANG—*Ministry of Fear,* The Woman in the Window, Scarlet Street.
ALFRED HITCHCOCK—Spellbound.
OTTO PREMINGER—Fallen Angel, A Royal Scandal.
ROBERT SIODMAK—The Suspect, Uncle Harry.
JOHN STAHL—Leave Her to Heaven.
RAOUL WALSH—Salty O'Rourke, Objective Burma, The Horn Blows at Midnight.
LEO MC CAREY—The Bells of St. Mary's.
VINCENTE MINNELLI—The Clock, Yolanda and the Thief.
FRANK BORZAGE—The Spanish Main.
BILLY WILDER—The Lost Weekend.
WILLIAM WELLMAN—Story of G.I. Joe.
ELIA KAZAN—A Tree Grows in Brooklyn.
ALLAN DWAN—Brewster's Millions, Getting Gertie's Garter.
COMPTON BENNETT—The Seventh Veil.
RENE CLAIR—And Then There Were None.
EDGAR G. ULMER—Detour, Strange Illusion.
JOSEPH H. LEWIS—My Name Is Julia Ross.
GUSTAV MACHATY—Jealousy.
ROBERT WISE—The Body Snatcher.
MICHAEL CURTIZ—Mildred Pierce.
CLIVE BROOK—On Approval.

DAVID LEAN—Blithe Spirit.
MICHAEL POWELL and EMERIC PRESSBURGER—The Life and Death of Colonel Blimp.
ALBERT LEWIN—The Picture of Dorian Gray.
ALEXANDER KORDA—Vacation From Marriage.
JOHN BRAHM—Hangover Square.
WILLIAM DIETERLE—Love Letters, I'll Be Seeing You.
GEORGE MARSHALL—Murder, He Says; Incendiary Blonde.
MARK ROBSON—Isle of the Dead.
EDWARD DMYTRYK—Cornered.
HENRY HATHAWAY—The House on 92nd Street.
GEORGE SIDNEY—Anchors Aweigh.
WALTER LANG—State Fair.
HERMAN SHUMLIN—Confidential Agent.
JOHN BAXTER—Love on the Dole.

1946

ALFRED HITCHCOCK—*Notorious.*
HOWARD HAWKS—*The Big Sleep.*
JOHN FORD—*My Darling Clementine.*
JEAN RENOIR—*Diary of a Chambermaid.*
FRANK CAPRA—*It's a Wonderful Life.*
ORSON WELLES—The Stranger.
DOUGLAS SIRK—A Scandal in Paris.
ROBERT SIODMAK—The Killers, The Spiral Staircase, The Dark Mirror.
FRANK BORZAGE—I've Always Loved You, The Magnificent Doll.
ERNST LUBITSCH—Cluny Brown.
FRITZ LANG—Cloak and Dagger.
CAVALCANTI, BASIL DEARDEN, and ROBERT HAMER—Dead of Night.
DAVID LEAN—Brief Encounter.
VINCENTE MINNELLI—Ziegfeld Follies.
RAOUL WALSH—The Man I Love.
WILLIAM WYLER—The Best Years of Our Lives.
ARTHUR RIPLEY—The Chase.
JACQUES TOURNEUR—Canyon Passage.
LEWIS MILESTONE—A Walk in the Sun, The Strange Love of Martha Ivers.
ALLAN DWAN—Rendezvous with Annie, Calendar Girl.
CHARLES VIDOR—Gilda.
EDMUND GOULDING—The Razor's Edge.
JOSEPH H. LEWIS—So Dark the Night.
DON SIEGEL—The Verdict.
LAURENCE OLIVIER—Henry V.
SIDNEY GILLIAT—Notorious Gentleman.
MICHAEL POWELL and EMERIC PRESSBURGER—Stairway to Heaven.
JEAN NEGULESCO—Three Strangers, Nobody Lives Forever, Humoresque.
EDGAR G. ULMER—Her Sister's Secret.
TAY GARNETT—The Postman Always Rings Twice.
JOSEPH L. MANKIEWICZ—Dragonwyck, Somewhere in the Night.
JOHN BRAHM—The Locket.
ROY WILLIAM NEILL—Black Angel.
HAROLD CLURMAN—Deadline at Dawn.
JOHN CROMWELL—Anna and the King of Siam.
GABRIEL PASCAL—Caesar and Cleopatra.
ALFRED E. GREEN—The Jolson Story.
MARK ROBSON—Bedlam.
IRVING RAPPER—Deception.
CURTIS BERNHARDT—Devotion, A Stolen Life.

1947

CHARLES CHAPLIN—*Monsieur Verdoux.*
MAX OPHULS—*The Exile.*
CAROL REED—Odd Man Out.
ANTHONY MANN—T-Men.
JOSEPH LOSEY—The Boy With Green Hair.
KING VIDOR—Duel in the Sun.
JEAN RENOIR—Woman on the Beach.
RAOUL WALSH—Pursued, Cheyenne.
JACQUES TOURNEUR—Out of the Past.
ROBERT ROSSEN—Johnny O'Clock, Body and Soul.
DOUGLAS SIRK—Lured.
FRANK BORZAGE—That's My Man.
JOHN FORD—The Fugitive.
ZOLTAN KORDA—The Macomber Affair, A Woman's Vengeance.
HENRY HATHAWAY—Kiss of Death.
CECIL B. DE MILLE—Unconquered.
OTTO PREMINGER—Daisy Kenyon, Forever Amber.
LEO MC CAREY—Good Sam.
JOHN STAHL—The Foxes of Harrow, The Walls of Jericho.
DAVID LEAN—Great Expectations, This Happy Breed.
MICHAEL POWELL and EMERIC PRESSBURGER—Black Narcissus, I Know Where
    I'm Going.
ROBERT WISE—Born to Kill.
CHARLES WALTERS—Good News.
JULES DASSIN—Brute Force.
ANDRE DE TOTH—Ramrod.
BYRON HASKIN—I Walk Alone.
JOSEPH L. MANKIEWICZ—The Ghost and Mrs. Muir.
ROBERT MONTGOMERY—Ride the Pink Horse.
EDMUND GOULDING—Nightmare Alley.
ELIA KAZAN—Gentleman's Agreement, Boomerang!
EDWARD DMYTRYK—Crossfire.
SIDNEY GILLIAT—Green for Danger.
JEAN NEGULESCO—Deep Valley.
IRVING PICHEL—They Won't Believe Me.
DELMER DAVES—Dark Passage, The Red House.
VINCENT SHERMAN—The Unfaithful.

1948

MAX OPHULS—*Letter From an Unknown Woman.*
ORSON WELLES—*The Lady From Shanghai.*
JOHN FORD—*Fort Apache.*
HOWARD HAWKS—*Red River,* A Song Is Born.
FRANK BORZAGE—*Moonrise.*
JOHN HUSTON—Key Largo, The Treasure of the Sierra Madre.
ABRAHAM POLONSKY—Force of Evil.
FRANK CAPRA—State of the Union.
HENRY HATHAWAY—Call Northside 777.
ALFRED HITCHCOCK—Rope, The Paradine Case.
GEORGE CUKOR—A Double Life.
DOUGLAS SIRK—Sleep, My Love.
VINCENTE MINNELLI—The Pirate.
GEORGE STEVENS—I Remember Mama.
FRITZ LANG—The Secret Beyond the Door.
KING VIDOR—On Our Merry Way.
RAOUL WALSH—Silver River, One Sunday Afternoon, Fighter Squadron.

LAURENCE OLIVIER—Hamlet.
MICHAEL POWELL and EMERIC PRESSBURGER—The Red Shoes.
EDGAR G. ULMER—Ruthless.
ALLAN DWAN—The Inside Story, Angel in Exile.
PRESTON STURGES—Unfaithfully Yours.
CHARLES WALTERS—Easter Parade.
ROUBEN MAMOULIAN—Summer Holiday.
BILLY WILDER—A Foreign Affair, The Emperor Waltz.
ANDRE DE TOTH—Pitfall.
ROBERT SIODMAK—Cry of the City.
JEAN NEGULESCO—Johnny Belinda, Road House.
JOHN FARROW—The Big Clock.
MICHAEL GORDON—Another Part of the Forest, An Act of Murder.
EDWARD LUDWIG—Wake of the Red Witch.
JULES DASSIN—The Naked City.
ALFRED WERKER—He Walked by Night.
RICHARD HAYDEN—Miss Tatlock's Millions.
WALTER LANG—Sitting Pretty.
RALPH THOMAS—The Clouded Yellow.
WILLIAM WELLMAN—Yellow Sky, The Iron Curtain.
LEWIS MILESTONE—Arch of Triumph, No Minor Vices.
ROBERT FLAHERTY—Louisiana Story.
CLAUDE BINYON—The Saxon Charm.
FRED ZINNEMANN—The Search.
ANATOLE LITVAK—The Snake Pit; Sorry, Wrong Number.

1949

JOHN FORD—*She Wore a Yellow Ribbon,* Three Godfathers.
MAX OPHULS—*Caught,* The Reckless Moment.
RAOUL WALSH—*White Heat,* Colorado Territory.
HOWARD HAWKS—I Was a Male War Bride.
KING VIDOR—The Fountainhead, Beyond the Forest.
JOSEPH H. LEWIS—Gun Crazy, Undercover Man.
ANTHONY MANN—Border Incident, Side Street, Reign of Terror.
ALFRED HITCHCOCK—Under Capricorn.
GEORGE CUKOR—Adam's Rib; Edward, My Son.
NICHOLAS RAY—They Live By Night.
JOHN HUSTON—We Were Strangers.
DOUGLAS SIRK—Shockproof, Slightly French.
OTTO PREMINGER—Whirlpool, The Fan.
STANLEY DONEN and GENE KELLY—On the Town.
SAMUEL FULLER—I Shot Jesse James.
VINCENTE MINNELLI—Madame Bovary.
CAROL REED—The Fallen Idol.
JOSEPH L. MANKIEWICZ—A Letter to Three Wives, House of Strangers.
ELIA KAZAN—Pinky.
MICHAEL CURTIZ—Flamingo Road, My Dream Is Yours.
BYRON HASKIN—Too Late for Tears.
FRED ZINNEMANN—Act of Violence.
ROBERT ROSSEN—All the King's Men.
JULES DASSIN—Thieves' Highway.
ROBERT WISE—The Set-Up.
EMLYN WILLIAMS—The Woman of Dolwyn.
CECIL B. DE MILLE—Samson and Delilah.
DON SIEGEL—The Big Steal, Night Unto Night.
CHARLES WALTERS—The Barkleys of Broadway.
PRESTON STURGES—The Beautiful Blonde from Bashful Bend.

CLARENCE BROWN—Intruder in the Dust.
MARK ROBSON—Champion, Home of the Brave.
WILLIAM WELLMAN—Battleground.
WILLIAM WYLER—The Heiress.
ELLIOTT NUGENT—The Great Gatsby.
ROBERT SIODMAK—Criss Cross.
JOHN STURGES—The Walking Hills.
ROBERT MONTGOMERY—Once More, My Darling.
RUDY MATE—D.O.A., No Sad Songs for Me.
STUART HEISLER—Tulsa.
ALFRED WERKER—Lost Boundaries.
TED TATZLAFF—The Window.
TERENCE YOUNG—Corridor of Mirrors.

1950

JOHN FORD—*Wagonmaster, Rio Grande*, When Willie Comes Marching Home.
CAROL REED—*The Third Man.*
JOHN HUSTON—*The Asphalt Jungle.*
OTTO PREMINGER—*Where the Sidewalk Ends.*
JOSEPH LOSEY—The Lawless.
ALFRED HITCHCOCK—Stage Fright.
ANTHONY MANN—Winchester 73, Devil's Doorway, The Furies.
NICHOLAS RAY—In a Lonely Place.
JOSEPH L. MANKIEWICZ—All About Eve, No Way Out.
BILLY WILDER—Sunset Boulevard.
ELIA KAZAN—Panic in the Streets.
JULES DASSIN—Night and the City.
FRITZ LANG—American Guerilla in the Philippines, House by the River.
FRANK CAPRA—Riding High.
SAMUEL FULLER—The Baron of Arizona.
ROBERT HAMER—Kind Hearts and Coronets.
JOHN CROMWELL—Caged.
MICHAEL CURTIZ—The Breaking Point.
GEORGE CUKOR—A Life of Her Own, Born Yesterday.
VINCENTE MINNELLI—Father of the Bride.
CHARLES CRICHTON—The Lavender Hill Mob.
CHARLES WALTERS—Summer Stock.
JOSEPH H. LEWIS—Lady Without a Passport.
JACQUES TOURNEUR—The Flame and the Arrow, Stars in my Crown.
JOHN STURGES—Mystery Street.
GORDON DOUGLAS—Kiss Tomorrow Goodbye.
CYRIL ENDFIELD—Sound of Fury.
WILLIAM DIETERLE—Dark City.
RUDY MATE—Union Station.
MARK ROBSON—My Foolish Heart.
HENRY KING—Twelve O'Clock High, The Gunfighter.
FRED ZINNEMANN—The Men.
ANTHONY ASQUITH—The Winslow Boy.
DELMER DAVES—Broken Arrow.
SIDNEY GILLIAT—State Secret (The Great Manhunt).
RICHARD THORPE—Black Hand, Three Little Words.
JOSEPH M. NEWMAN—711 Ocean Drive.
EDWARD DMYTRYK—Give Us This Day.
STUART HEISLER—Storm Warning.

1951

JEAN RENOIR—*The River.*
ALFRED HITCHCOCK—*Strangers on a Train.*

JOSEPH LOSEY—The Prowler, The Big Night, M.
SAMUEL FULLER—The Steel Helmet, Fixed Bayonets.
ANTHONY MANN—The Tall Target.
RAOUL WALSH—Distant Drums, Captain Horatio Hornblower, Along the Great Divide.
BRETAIGNE WINDUST—The Enforcer.
NICHOLAS RAY—On Dangerous Ground, Flying Leathernecks.
KING VIDOR—Lightning Strikes Twice.
GEORGE STEVENS—A Place in the Sun.
VINCENTE MINNELLI—An American in Paris, Father's Little Dividend.
BUDD BOETTICHER—The Bullfighter and the Lady.
ALLAN DWAN—Belle Le Grande.
PRESTON STURGES—Mad Wednesday.
ELIA KAZAN—A Streetcar Named Desire.
BILLY WILDER—Ace in the Hole.
JOHN STURGES—The People Against O'Hara, Kind Lady.
FRANK CAPRA—Here Comes the Groom.
HENRY KOSTER—No Highway in the Sky.
CHRISTIAN NYBY—The Thing.
JACQUES TOURNEUR—Anne of the Indies, Circle of Danger.
ALBERT LEWIN—Pandora and the Flying Dutchman.
JOSEPH L. MANKIEWICZ—People Will Talk.
DAVID LEAN—Oliver Twist.
JOHN BERRY—He Ran All the Way, Tension.
GORDON DOUGLAS—Come Fill the Cup.
HENRY HATHAWAY—Fourteen Hours, The Desert Fox, You're in the Navy Now, Rawhide.
OTTO PREMINGER—The Thirteenth Letter.
STANLEY DONEN—Royal Wedding.
ANTHONY ASQUITH—The Browning Version.
ROY BAKER—Operation Disaster.
WILLIAM WYLER—Detective Story.
FRED ZINNEMANN—Teresa.
ANATOLE LITVAK—Decision Before Dawn.
JOHN HUSTON—The Red Badge of Courage.
ROBERT WISE—The Day the Earth Stood Still.
LASLO BENEDEK—Death of a Salesman.
MARK ROBSON—Bright Victory.

1952

CHARLES CHAPLIN—*Limelight.*
HOWARD HAWKS—*The Big Sky,* Monkey Business, O'Henry's Full House (with Henry Hathaway, Jean Negulesco, Henry King, and Henry Koster).
JOHN FORD—*The Quiet Man.*
GEORGE CUKOR—The Marrying Kind, The Model and the Marriage Broker, Pat and Mike.
FRITZ LANG—Rancho Notorious, Clash by Night.
KING VIDOR—Ruby Gentry.
ANTHONY MANN—Bend of the River.
JOSEPH L. MANKIEWICZ—Five Fingers.
NICHOLAS RAY—The Lusty Men.
CECIL B. DE MILLE—The Greatest Show on Earth.
DOUGLAS SIRK—Has Anybody Seen My Gal?
STANLEY DONEN and GENE KELLY—Singin' in the Rain.
SAMUEL FULLER—Park Row.
LEO MC CAREY—My Son John.
JOSEF VON STERNBERG—Macao.

RAOUL WALSH—The Lawless Breed, The World in His Arms, Glory Alley, Sea Devils, Blackbeard the Pirate.
CAROL REED—Outcast of the Islands.
ELIA KAZAN—Viva Zapata!
DAVID LEAN—Breaking Through the Sound Barrier.
JOHN HUSTON—The African Queen.
GEORGE STEVENS—Something to Live For.
CHARLES CRICHTON—The Stranger in Between.
GEORGE SIDNEY—Scaramouche.
ALEXANDER MACKENDRICK—The Man in the White Suit.
ROBERT SIODMAK—The Crimson Pirate.
RICHARD BROOKS—Deadline, U.S.A.
FRED ZINNEMANN—High Noon.
ZOLTAN KORDA—Cry, the Beloved Country.
RICHARD FLEISCHER—The Narrow Margin.
MICHAEL POWELL and EMERIC PRESSBURGER—The Small Back Room.
ANDREW STONE—The Steel Trap.
PAT JACKSON—White Corridors.
WILLIAM WYLER—Carrie.
STUART HEISLER—Island of Desire.
DAVID BUTLER—Where's Charlie.
GOTTFRIED REINHARDT—Invitation.
CHARLES MARQUIS WARREN—Hellgate.

1953
ALFRED HITCHCOCK—*I Confess.*
FRITZ LANG—*The Big Heat,* The Blue Gardenia.
DOUGLAS SIRK—*Take Me to Town,* All I Desire.
CAROL REED—*The Man Between.*
JOHN FORD—Mogambo.
HOWARD HAWKS—Gentlemen Prefer Blondes.
OTTO PREMINGER—Angel Face, The Moon Is Blue.
GEORGE CUKOR—The Actress.
VINCENTE MINNELLI—The Bad and the Beautiful, The Bandwagon, The Story of Three Loves (with Gottfried Reinhardt).
RAOUL WALSH—A Lion Is in the Streets, Gun Fury.
SAMUEL FULLER—Pickup on South Street.
GEORGE STEVENS—Shane.
BILLY WILDER—Stalag 17.
ANTHONY MANN—The Naked Spur, Thunder Bay.
WILLIAM WYLER—Roman Holiday.
STANLEY DONEN—Give a Girl a Break.
ALEXANDER MACKENDRICK—The Story of Mandy.
LASLO BENEDEK—The Wild One.
CHARLES WALTERS—Lilli, Torch Song.
PHIL KARLSON—99 River Street.
DON SIEGEL—Count the Hours.
CURTIS BERNHARDT—Miss Sadie Thompson.
RICHARD BROOKS—Take the High Ground, Battle Circus.
HENRY HATHAWAY—Niagara.
JOHN HUSTON—Moulin Rouge.
FRED ZINNEMANN—From Here to Eternity, The Member of the Wedding.
JOSEPH L. MANKIEWICZ—Julius Caesar.
ELIA KAZAN—Man on a Tightrope.
IDA LUPINO—The Hitch-Hiker.
GEORGE SIDNEY—Kiss Me Kate, Young Bess.
DON WEIS—I Love Melvin, The Affairs of Dobie Gillis, Remains To Be Seen.

RUSSELL ROUSE—Wicked Woman.
GEORGE SEATON—Little Boy Lost.

1954

ALFRED HITCHCOCK—*Rear Window*, Dial M for Murder.
JOHN FORD—*The Sun Shines Bright.*
JEAN RENOIR—*The Golden Coach.*
ROBERTO ROSSELLINI—*The Greatest Love.*
LUIS BUNUEL—*The Adventures of Robinson Crusoe.*
NICHOLAS RAY—Johnny Guitar.
GEORGE CUKOR—A Star Is Born, It Should Happen to You.
RENE CLEMENT—Lovers, Happy Lovers.
JOSEF VON STERNBERG—Anatahan.
DON SIEGEL—Riot in Cell Block 11, Private Hell 36.
ELIA KAZAN—On the Waterfront.
OTTO PREMINGER—River of No Return, Carmen Jones.
DOUGLAS SIRK—Magnificent Obsession, Sign of the Pagan; Taza, Son of Cochise.
FRITZ LANG—Human Desire.
JOSEPH L. MANKIEWICZ—The Barefoot Contessa.
ROBERT ALDRICH—Apache, World for Ransom.
SAMUEL FULLER—Hell and High Water.
HENRY CORNELIUS—Genevieve.
ALLAN DWAN—Silver Lode, Cattle Queen of Montana, Passion.
VINCENTE MINNELLI—Brigadoon.
RAOUL WALSH—Saskatchewan.
DAVID LEAN—Hobson's Choice.
STANLEY DONEN—Seven Brides for Seven Brothers.
BYRON HASKIN—The Naked Jungle.
RICHARD BROOKS—The Last Time I Saw Paris.
DON WEIS—The Adventures of Hajji Baba.
ANTHONY MANN—The Glenn Miller Story.
JOHN HUSTON—Beat the Devil.
BILLY WILDER—Sabrina.
ROBERT WISE—Executive Suite.
RICHARD QUINE—Drive a Crooked Road, Pushover, So This Is Paris.
NUNNALLY JOHNSON—Black Widow.
WILLIAM WELLMAN—The High and the Mighty.
GEORGE SEATON—The Country Girl.

1955

ROBERTO ROSSELLINI—*Strangers.*
ALFRED HITCHCOCK—*To Catch a Thief*, The Trouble With Harry.
DOUGLAS SIRK—*Captain Lightfoot.*
ORSON WELLES—*Othello.*
JOHN FORD—*The Long Gray Line*, Mister Roberts (with Mervyn LeRoy).
NICHOLAS RAY—Rebel Without a Cause, Run for Cover.
ROBERT ALDRICH—Kiss Me Deadly, The Big Knife.
FRITZ LANG—Moonfleet.
PHIL KARLSON—The Phenix City Story, Five Against the House, Hell's Island, Tight Spot.
SAMUEL FULLER—House of Bamboo.
ROBERT PARRISH—The Purple Plain.
KING VIDOR—Man Without a Star.
OTTO PREMINGER—The Man With the Golden Arm, The Court Martial of Billy Mitchell.

HOWARD HAWKS—Land of the Pharaohs.
RAOUL WALSH—Battle Cry, The Tall Men.
VINCENTE MINNELLI—The Cobweb, Kismet.
EDGAR G. ULMER—The Naked Dawn, Murder Is My Beat.
ALLAN DWAN—Tennessee's Partner, Pearl of the South Pacific, Escape to Burma.
CHARLES LAUGHTON—The Night of the Hunter.
STANLEY DONEN and GENE KELLY—It's Always Fair Weather.
ELIA KAZAN—East of Eden.
CHARLES WALTERS—The Tender Trap.
FRANK TASHLIN—Artists and Models, The Lieutenant Wore Skirts.
ANTHONY MANN—The Last Frontier, The Man from Laramie, The Far Country, Strategic Air Command.
DAVID LEAN—Summertime.
JOSEPH H. LEWIS—The Big Combo, The Lawless Street.
CHARLES VIDOR—Love Me Or Leave Me.
RICHARD FLEISCHER—Violent Saturday, The Girl in the Red Velvet Swing, Bandido.
JACQUES TOURNEUR—Wichita.
BUDD BOETTICHER—The Magnificent Matador.
ARTHUR LUBIN—Footsteps in the Fog.
JACK WEBB—Pete Kelly's Blues.
JOHN STURGES—Bad Day at Black Rock.
MELVILLE SHAVELSON—Houseboat.
HENRY KING—Love Is a Many Splendored Thing.
WILLIAM WYLER—The Desperate Hours.
RICHARD BROOKS—The Blackboard Jungle.
GEORGE SIDNEY—The Eddy Duchin Story.
DANIEL MANN—The Rose Tattoo.
DELBERT MANN—Marty.
PHILIP DUNNE—Prince of Players.
HALL BARTLETT—Unchained.

1956

JOHN FORD—*The Searchers.*
ALFRED HITCHCOCK—*The Man Who Knew Too Much, The Wrong Man.*
NICHOLAS RAY—Bigger Than Life, Hot Blood.
BUDD BOETTICHER—Seven Men from Now, The Killer Is Loose.
DOUGLAS SIRK—All That Heaven Allows, There's Always Tomorrow, Battle Hymn.
GEORGE CUKOR—Bhowani Junction.
ROBERT ALDRICH—Attack, Autumn Leaves.
DON SIEGEL—Invasion of the Body Snatchers, Crime in the Streets.
STANLEY KUBRICK—The Killing.
FRITZ LANG—While the City Sleeps, Beyond a Reasonable Doubt.
LAURENCE OLIVIER—Richard III.
KING VIDOR—War and Peace.
ALLAN DWAN—Slightly Scarlet, Hold Back the Night.
RAOUL WALSH—A King and Four Queens, The Revolt of Mamie Stover.
VINCENTE MINNELLI—Lust for Life, Tea and Sympathy.
GEORGE STEVENS—Giant.
CECIL B. DE MILLE—The Ten Commandments.
RICHARD BROOKS—The Last Hunt, The Catered Affair.
ALEXANDER MACKENDRICK—The Ladykillers.
GERD OSWALD—Kiss Before Dying, The Brass Legend.
FRANK TASHLIN—The Girl Can't Help It, Hollywood or Bust.
LEWIS FOSTER—The Bold and the Brave.

ROBERT WISE—Somebody Up There Likes Me.
R. G. SPRINGSTEEN—Come Next Spring.
NORMAN PANAMA and MELVIN FRANK—The Court Jester.
ELIA KAZAN—Baby Doll.
JOHN HUSTON—Moby Dick.
JOSHUA LOGAN—Picnic, Bus Stop.
WILLIAM WYLER—Friendly Persuasion.
CAROL REED—A Kid for Two Farthings, Trapeze.
RUSSELL ROUSE—The Fastest Gun Alive.
ARNOLD LAVEN—The Rack.
HARRY KELLER—The Unguarded Moment.
CORNELL WILDE—Storm Fear.
JOSEPH ANTHONY—The Rainmaker.
PHILIP DUNNE—Hilda Crane.
HARRY HORNER—The Wild Party.
DANIEL MANN—I'll Cry Tomorrow.

1957
JOHN FORD—*The Wings of Eagles, The Rising of the Moon.*
SAMUEL FULLER—*Forty Guns,* Run Of the Arrow, China Gate.
JOSEF VON STERNBERG—*Jet Pilot.*
DOUGLAS SIRK—*Written on the Wind,* Interlude.
JEAN RENOIR—*Paris Does Strange Things.*
GEORGE CUKOR—Les Girls, Wild Is the Wind.
OTTO PREMINGER—Saint Joan.
JOSEPH LOSEY—Time Without Pity.
ALEXANDER MACKENDRICK—Sweet Smell of Success.
ALLAN DWAN—The River's Edge, The Restless Breed.
GERD OSWALD—Crime of Passion, Fury at Showdown, Valerie.
BUDD BOETTICHER—The Tall T, Decision at Sundown.
DON SIEGEL—Baby Face Nelson.
ELIA KAZAN—A Face in the Crowd.
RAOUL WALSH—Band of Angels.
VINCENTE MINNELLI—Designing Woman.
LEO MC CAREY—An Affair to Remember.
BLAKE EDWARDS—Mister Cory.
FRANK TASHLIN—Will Success Spoil Rock Hunter?
JOSEPH H. LEWIS—The Halliday Brand.
PHIL KARLSON—The Brothers Rico.
NICHOLAS RAY—The True Story of Jesse James.
STANLEY DONEN—Funny Face, Kiss Them for Me, The Pajama Game (with
    George Abbott).
ANTHONY MANN—Men at War, The Tin Star.
PAUL WENDKOS—The Burglar.
BILLY WILDER—Love in the Afternoon.
ROBERT WISE—This Could Be the Night, Until They Sail.
DAVID LEAN—The Bridge on the River Kwai.
DICK POWELL—The Enemy Below.
ROBERT MULLIGAN—Fear Strikes Out.
DELMER DAVES—3:10 to Yuma, Cowboy.
JOSE FERRER—The Great Man.
DELBERT MANN—The Bachelor Party.
STANLEY KUBRICK—Paths of Glory.
JOHN HUSTON—Heaven Knows, Mr. Allison.
JOHN FRANKENHEIMER—The Young Stranger.
SIDNEY LUMET—Twelve Angry Men.
FRED ZINNEMANN—A Hatful of Rain.

CHARLES WALTERS—Don't Go Near the Water.
GEORGE SIDNEY—Jeanne Eagels, Pal Joey.
MARTIN RITT—Edge of the City.
JACK GARFEIN—The Strange One.
DAVID MILLER—The Story of Esther Costello.

1958

ALFRED HITCHCOCK—*Vertigo.*
ORSON WELLES—*Touch of Evil.*
DOUGLAS SIRK—*A Time to Love and a Time to Die, Tarnished Angels.*
OTTO PREMINGER—*Bonjour Tristesse.*
NICHOLAS RAY—*Wind Across the Everglades, Bitter Victory,* Party Girl.
JOHN FORD—*The Last Hurrah.*
ANTHONY MANN—Man of the West, God's Little Acre.
RENE CLEMENT—This Angry Age.
FRANK BORZAGE—China Doll.
DON SIEGEL—The Line-Up, A Spanish Affair, The Gun Runners.
ARTHUR PENN—The Left Handed Gun.
BUDD BOETTICHER—Buchanan Rides Alone.
RAOUL WALSH—The Naked and the Dead.
ARTHUR RIPLEY—Thunder Road.
IRVING LERNER—Murder by Contract.
VINCENTE MINNELLI—Gigi, The Reluctant Debutante.
JACQUES TOURNEUR—Curse of the Demon.
LEO MC CAREY—Rally Round the Flag, Boys.
GERD OSWALD—Screaming Mimi.
JOSEPH L. MANKIEWICZ—The Quiet American.
STANLEY DONEN—Indiscreet, Damn Yankees (with George Abbott).
JOSEPH H. LEWIS—Terror in a Texas Town.
BLAKE EDWARDS—This Happy Feeling, The Perfect Furlough.
FRANK TASHLIN—Rock-a-bye Baby, Geisha Boy.
PHIL KARLSON—Gunman's Walk.
SIDNEY LUMET—Stage Struck.
ROBERT WISE—I Want to Live.
IRVIN KERSHNER—Stakeout on Dope Street.
JOHN CROMWELL—The Goddess.
DICK POWELL—The Hunters.
HENRY HATHAWAY—From Hell to Texas.
GEORGE MARSHALL—The Sheepman, Imitation General.
PAUL WENDKOS—The Case Against Brooklyn.
RICHARD BROOKS—Cat on a Hot Tin Roof, The Brothers Karamazov.
CAROL REED—The Key.
RONALD NEAME—The Horse's Mouth.
JOHN HUSTON—The Roots of Heaven.
WILLIAM WYLER—The Big Country.
STANLEY KRAMER—The Defiant Ones.
DELBERT MANN—Separate Tables.
DANIEL MANN—Hot Spell.

1959

ALFRED HITCHCOCK—*North by Northwest.*
JOHN FORD—*The Horse Soldiers, Gideon of Scotland Yard.*
DOUGLAS SIRK—*Imitation of Life.*
HOWARD HAWKS—*Rio Bravo.*
OTTO PREMINGER—*Anatomy of a Murder,* Porgy and Bess.
BLAKE EDWARDS—Operation Petticoat.
VINCENTE MINNELLI—Some Came Running.

SAMUEL FULLER—The Crimson Kimono.
BUDD BOETTICHER—Ride Lonesome, Westbound.
ROBERT ALDRICH—The Angry Hills, Ten Seconds to Hell.
FRANK CAPRA—A Hole in the Head.
BILLY WILDER—Some Like It Hot.
DON SIEGEL—Hound Dog Man, Edge of Eternity.
FRANK TASHLIN—Say One for Me.
SIDNEY LUMET—That Kind of Woman.
CHARLES WALTERS—Ask Any Girl.
GEORGE STEVENS—The Diary of Anne Frank.
JACK CLAYTON—Room at the Top.
JOHN STURGES—Last Train from Gun Hill.
ROBERT WISE—Odds Against Tomorrow.
TONY RICHARDSON—Look Back in Anger.
FRED ZINNEMANN—The Nun's Story.
JOSEPH L. MANKIEWICZ—Suddenly Last Summer.
DELMER DAVES—A Summer Place.
JAMES CLAVELL—Five Gates to Hell.
DELBERT MANN—The Middle of the Night.
JOSEPH ANTHONY—Career.
J. LEE THOMPSON—Tiger Bay.
STANLEY KRAMER—On the Beach.
WILLIAM WYLER—Ben-Hur.

1960

ALFRED HITCHCOCK—*Psycho*.
JOHN FORD—*Sergeant Rutledge*.
JOSEPH LOSEY—Chance Meeting.
GEORGE CUKOR—Heller in Pink Tights, Let's Make Love, Song Without End (with Charles Vidor).
OTTO PREMINGER—Exodus.
BUDD BOETTICHER—Comanche Station, The Rise and Fall of Legs Diamond
ELIA KAZAN—Wild River.
BILLY WILDER—The Apartment.
RICHARD BROOKS—Elmer Gantry.
SAMUEL FULLER—Verboten!
VINCENTE MINNELLI—Bells Are Ringing, Home from the Hill.
JOHN STURGES—The Magnificent Seven.
DON SIEGEL—Flaming Star.
ROBERT MONTGOMERY—The Gallant Hours.
ROBERT MULLIGAN—The Rat Race, The Great Impostor.
RAOUL WALSH—Esther and the King.
BLAKE EDWARDS—High Time.
HENRY HATHAWAY—North to Alaska, Seven Thieves.
TAY GARNETT—The Night Fighters.
PHILIP LEACOCK—Take a Giant Step.
STUART ROSENBERG and BURT BALABAN—Murder, Inc.
JOHN HUSTON—The Unforgiven.
PHIL KARLSON—Hell to Eternity, Key Witness.
CHARLES WALTERS—Please Don't Eat the Daisies.
GEORGE SIDNEY—Who Was That Lady?
STANLEY KUBRICK—Spartacus.
HUBERT CORNFIELD—The Third Voice.
JERRY LEWIS—The Bellboy.
RICHARD QUINE—Strangers When We Meet.
RONALD NEAME—Tunes of Glory.
JACK CARDIFF—Sons and Lovers.

JAMES CLAVELL—Walk Like a Dragon.
LESLIE STEVENS—Private Property.
STANLEY DONEN—Once More With Feeling, Surprise Package, The Grass Is Greener.
TONY RICHARDSON—The Entertainer.
JOHN WAYNE—The Alamo.
FRED ZINNEMANN—The Sundowners.
JOSHUA LOGAN—Tall Story.
DANIEL PETRIE—The Bramble Bush.

1961

JOHN FORD—*Two Rode Together.*
BLAKE EDWARDS—*Breakfast at Tiffany's.*
FRANK CAPRA—Pocketful of Miracles.
SAMUEL FULLER—Underworld, U.S.A.
NICHOLAS RAY—The Savage Innocents, The King of Kings.
LUIS BUNUEL—The Young One.
ROBERT MULLIGAN—The Great Impostor.
GERD OSWALD—Brainwashed.
ROBERT ROSSEN—The Hustler.
BYRON HASKIN—Armored Command.
IRVIN KERSHNER—The Hoodlum Priest.
ALEXANDER SINGER—Cold Wind in August.
JEROME ROBBINS and ROBERT WISE—West Side Story.
ANTHONY MANN—El Cid.
ROBERT ALDRICH—The Last Sunset.
RAOUL WALSH—Marines, Let's Go.
MARLON BRANDO—One Eyed Jacks.
JERRY LEWIS—The Ladies' Man.
SETH HOLT—Scream of Fear.
GORDON DOUGLAS—The Sins of Rachel Cade.
ELIA KAZAN—Splendor in the Grass.
KAREL REISZ—Saturday Night and Sunday Morning.
PAUL WENDKOS—Angel Baby.
JACK CLAYTON—The Innocents.
JOSEPH PEVNEY—The Plunderers.
JOSEPH M. NEWMAN—King of the Roaring 20's.
GUY GREEN—The Mark.
JOHN CASSAVETES—Shadows.
CHARLES WALTERS—Two Loves.
PHIL KARLSON—The Young Doctors.
JOHN FRANKENHEIMER—The Young Savages.
JOHN HUSTON—The Misfits.
BILLY WILDER—One, Two, Three.
STANLEY KRAMER—Judgement at Nuremberg.

1962

JOHN FORD—*The Man Who Shot Liberty Valance.*
SAMUEL FULLER—*Merrill's Marauders.*
JOSEPH LOSEY—*The Concrete Jungle.*
VINCENTE MINNELLI—Two Weeks in Another Town, The Four Horsemen of the Apocalypse.
ROBERT ALDRICH—What Ever Happened to Baby Jane?
OTTO PREMINGER—Advise and Consent.
ORSON WELLES—Mister Arkadin.
HOWARD HAWKS—Hatari!
DON SIEGEL—Hell Is for Heroes.

GEORGE CUKOR—The Chapman Report.
FRANK TASHLIN—Bachelor Flat, It's Only Money.
JERRY LEWIS—The Errand Boy.
ARTHUR PENN—The Miracle Worker.
BLAKE EDWARDS—Experiment in Terror.
LEO MC CAREY—Satan Never Sleeps.
STANLEY KUBRICK—Lolita.
SAM PECKINPAH—Ride the High Country, The Deadly Companions.
TONY RICHARDSON—A Taste of Honey, The Loneliness of the Long Distance
    Runner.
DAVID LEAN—Lawrence of Arabia.
JOHN FRANKENHEIMER—The Manchurian Candidate, All Fall Down, Bird Man
    of Alcatraz.
SIDNEY LUMET—Long Day's Journey Into Night, A View from the Bridge.
JOHN CASSAVETES—Too Late Blues.
MERVYN LEROY—Gypsy.
PHIL KARLSON—Kid Galahad.
CHARLES WALTERS—Jumbo.
DAVID MILLER—Lonely Are the Brave.
FRANK PERRY—David and Lisa.
DENIS SANDERS—War Hunt.
RICHARD BROOKS—Sweet Bird of Youth.
ELLIOT SILVERSTEIN—Belle Sommers.
JOHN HUSTON—Freud.
WILLIAM WYLER—The Children's Hour.
BRYAN FORBES—Whistle Down the Wind.
GUY GREEN—Light in the Piazza.
DELMER DAVES—Rome Adventure.
PETER USTINOV——Billy Budd.

   1963
JOHN FORD—*Donovan's Reef*, How the West Was Won (with Henry Hathaway
    and George Marshall).
ALFRED HITCHCOCK—The Birds.
SAMUEL FULLER—Shock Corridor.
OTTO PREMINGER—The Cardinal.
VINCENTE MINNELLI—The Courtship of Eddie's Father.
RALPH NELSON—Soldier in the Rain.
NICHOLAS RAY—55 Days at Peking.
ELIA KAZAN—America America.
ORSON WELLES—The Trial.
JERRY LEWIS—The Nutty Professor.
JOHN CASSAVETES—A Child Is Waiting.
PHIL KARLSON—Kid Galahad, Rampage.
STANLEY DONEN—Charade.
JOHN STURGES—The Great Escape.
GEORGE SIDNEY—Bye, Bye, Birdie.
JOAN LITTLEWOOD—Sparrows Can't Sing.
EDWARD LUDWIG—The Gun Hawk.
BLAKE EDWARDS—Days of Wine and Roses.
ROBERT MULLIGAN—To Kill a Mockingbird, Love With a Proper Stranger.
STEVE SEKELY—The Day of the Triffids.
JACQUES TOURNEUR—The Comedy of Terrors.
ROGER CORMAN—The Raven, "X" The Man With the X-Ray Eyes.
LINDSAY ANDERSON—This Sporting Life.
TONY RICHARDSON—Tom Jones.
JOHN SCHLESINGER—Billy Liar.

CLIFF OWEN—The Wrong Arm of the Law.
DON WEIS—Critic's Choice.
FRANKLIN SCHAFFNER—The Stripper.
FRANK TASHLIN—Who's Minding the Store?, The Man From the Diners' Club.
TERENCE YOUNG—Dr. No.
GEORGE ROY HILL—Toys in the Attic.
BILLY WILDER—Irma La Douce.
JOHN HUSTON—The List of Adrian Messenger.
PETER BROOK—Lord of the Flies.
ADOLFAS MEKAS—Hallelujah the Hills.
PAUL WENDKOS—Gidget Goes to Rome.
ROBERT WISE—The Haunting.
BRIAN FORBES—The L-Shaped Room.
ROBERT ALDRICH—4 For Texas.
ROBERT PARRISH—In the French Style.
LESLIE MARTINSON—PT-109.
HALL BARTLETT—The Caretakers.
PETER GLENVILLE—Term of Trial.

1964
JOSEPH LOSEY—*The Servant.*
HOWARD HAWKS—Man's Favorite Sport.
RICHARD LESTER—A Hard Day's Night.
BLAKE EDWARDS—Pink Panther, A Shot in the Dark.
DONALD SIEGEL—The Killers.
SETH HOLT—Station Six—Sahara.
FRANKLIN SCHAFFNER—The Best Man.
CLIVE DONNER—Nothing But the Best, The Guest.
STANLEY KUBRICK—Dr. Strangelove Or: How I Learned to Stop Worrying And
    Love the Bomb.
ALFRED HITCHCOCK—Marnie.
JOHN FORD—Cheyenne Autumn.
ROGER CORMAN—Masque of the Red Death.
GEORGE CUKOR—My Fair Lady.
VINCENTE MINNELLI—Goodbye Charlie.
BILLY WILDER—Kiss Me Stupid.
SAMUEL FULLER—The Naked Kiss.
FRANK TASHLIN—The Disorderly Orderly.
JERRY LEWIS—The Patsy.
RAOUL WALSH—A Distant Trumpet.
PETER TEWKSBURY—Sunday in New York, Emil and the Detectives.
RENÉ CLÉMENT—Joy House.
BURT KENNEDY—Mail Order Bride.
ARTHUR HILLER—The Americanization of Emily.
JACK CLAYTON—The Pumpkin Eater.
BRIAN FORBES—Seance on a Wet Afternoon.
IRVIN KERSHNER—The Luck of Ginger Coffey.
GEORGE SIDNEY—Viva Las Vegas.
CY ENFIELD—Zulu.
DELMER DAVES—Youngblood Hawke.
CHARLES WALTERS—The Unsinkable Molly Brown.
ALEXANDER SINGER—Psyche '59.
ROBERT STEVENSON—Mary Poppins.
JOHN GUILLERMIN—Guns at Batasi.
SIDNEY LUMET—Fail Safe.
RONALD NEAME—The Chalk Garden.
GEORGE MARSHALL—Advance to the Rear.

MARIO BAVA—Black Sabbath.
PETER GLENVILLE—Becket.
MICHAEL CACOYANNIS—Zorba the Greek.
FRED ZINNEMANN—Behold a Pale Horse.
PAUL HENREID—Dead Ringer.
ROBERT LYNN—Dr. Crippen.
JOHN FRANKENHEIMER—Seven Days in May.
R. G. SPRINGSTEEN—He Rides Tall, Taggart.
GEORGE ROY HILL—The World of Henry Orient.
DOUGLAS HEYES—Kitten With a Whip.
MICHAEL ROEMER—Nothing But a Man.

1965

OTTO PREMINGER—*Bunny Lake Is Missing,* In Harm's Way.
WILLIAM WYLER—The Collector.
JOSEPH LOSEY—These Are the Damned, Eva.
BLAKE EDWARDS—The Great Race.
ROBERT MULLIGAN—Baby, the Rain Must Fall.
CLIVE DONNER—What's New Pussycat?
ALEXANDER MACKENDRICK—A Boy Ten Feet Tall, High Wind in Jamaica.
ELLIOT SILVERSTEIN—Cat Ballou.
ROBERT ALDRICH—Hush . . . Hush . . . Sweet Charlotte.
HARVEY HART—Bus Riley's Back in Town.
ROMAN POLANSKI—Repulsion.
JOHN SCHLESINGER—Darling.
BRIAN FORBES—King Rat.
RICHARD QUINE—Synanon.
FRANKLIN SCHAFFNER—The War Lord.
JACK CARDIFF—Young Cassidy.
SAM PECKINPAH—Major Dundee.
RICHARD LESTER—Help!; The Knack . . . and How to Get It.
JOHN BOORMAN—Having a Wild Weekend.
BURT KENNEDY—The Rounders.
NORMAN JEWISON—The Cincinnati Kid.
SETH HOLT—The Nanny.
SIDNEY LUMET—The Hill, The Pawnbroker.
HOWARD HAWKS—Red Line 7000.
SIDNEY FURIE—The Ipcress File, The Leather Boys.
DAVID LEAN—Doctor Zhivago.
HENRY HATHAWAY—The Sons of Katie Elder.
ALEXANDER SINGER—Love Has Many Faces.
ROBERT WISE—The Sound of Music.
J. LEE THOMPSON—Return From the Ashes.
FRED COE—A Thousand Clowns.
GORDON DOUGLAS—Harlow.
VINCENTE MINNELLI—The Sandpiper.
TONY RICHARDSON—The Loved One.
JACK SMIGHT—The Third Day.
MARTIN RITT—The Spy Who Came in from the Cold.
ARTHUR PENN—Mickey One.
STANLEY KRAMER—Ship of Fools.

1966

JOHN FORD—*Seven Women.*
ALFRED HITCHCOCK—*Torn Curtain.*
MICHELANGELO ANTONIONI—*Blow-up.*
JOSEPH LOSEY—*King and Country,* Modesty Blaise.

FRANÇOIS TRUFFAUT—Fahrenheit 451.
BLAKE EDWARDS—What Did You Do in the War, Daddy?
MICHAEL ANDERSON—The Quiller Memorandum.
BURT KENNEDY—The Money Trap.
ROBERT ALDRICH—The Flight of the Phoenix.
GEORGE AXELROD—Lord Love a Duck.
ROBERT MULLIGAN—Inside Daisy Clover.
KAREL REISZ—Morgan!
ANTHONY MANN—The Heroes of Telemark.
BILLY WILDER—The Fortune Cookie.
ARTHUR PENN—The Chase.
JACK SMIGHT—Kaleidoscope, Harper.
PHIL KARLSON—The Silencers.
SIDNEY LUMET—The Group.
JERRY LEWIS—Three On a Couch.
HENRY HATHAWAY—Nevada Smith.
FRANK TASHLIN—The Glass-Bottom Boat, The Alphabet Murders.
BRIAN FORBES—The Wrong Box.
BERNARD GIRARD—Dead Heat On a Merry-Go-Round.
CORNELL WILDE—The Naked Prey.
WILLIAM WYLER—How to Steal a Million.
MIKE NICHOLS—Who's Afraid of Virginia Woolf?
RICHARD BROOKS—The Professionals.
ROMAN POLANSKI—Cul-de-Sac.
FRED ZINNEMANN—A Man For All Seasons.
IRVIN KERSHNER—A Fine Madness.
GEORGE SIDNEY—The Swinger.
STANLEY DONEN—Arabesque.
RICHARD LESTER—A Funny Thing Happened On the Way to the Forum.
JOHN GUILLERMIN—The Blue Max.
CHARLES WALTERS—Walk, Don't Run.
KENNETH ANGER—Scorpio Rising.
ROBERT GIST—The American Dream.

1967
HOWARD HAWKS—*El Dorado.*
JOHN BOORMAN—Point Blank.
BLAKE EDWARDS—Gunn.
ORSON WELLES—Falstaff.
CHARLES CHAPLIN—A Countess From Hong Kong.
JOSEPH LOSEY—Accident.
ROBERT MULLIGAN—Up the Down Staircase.
ARTHUR PENN—Bonnie and Clyde.
FRANCIS FORD COPPOLA—You're a Big Boy Now.
MIKE NICHOLS—The Graduate.
JOHN HUSTON—Reflections in a Golden Eye.
STUART ROSENBERG—Cool Hand Luke.
BUD YORKIN—Divorce American Style.
OTTO PREMINGER—Hurry Sundown.
NORMAN JEWISON—In the Heat of the Night.
ROBERT ALDRICH—The Dirty Dozen.
STANLEY DONEN—Two For the Road, Bedazzled.
DONN PENNEBAKER—Don't Look Back.
ANDY WARHOL—Bike Boy, The Nude Restaurant.
BURT KENNEDY—Welcome to Hard Times, The War Wagon.
ALEXANDER MACKENDRICK—Don't Make Waves.
JAMES CLAVELL—To Sir, With Love.

ELLIOT SILVERSTEIN—The Happening.
IRVIN KERSHNER—The Flim Flam Man.
ROY BOULTING—The Family Way.
PETER BROOK—Marat/Sade.
TERENCE YOUNG—Wait Until Dark.
GORDON DOUGLAS—Tony Rome.
ROMAN POLANSKI—The Fearless Vampire Killers.
BRIAN FORBES—The Whisperers.
BUZZ KULIK—Warning Shot.
FRANK TASHLIN—Caprice.
JOSEPH L. MANKIEWICZ—The Honey Pot.
CLIVE DONNER—Luv.
CORNELL WILDE—Beach Red.
CURTIS HARRINGTON—Games.
PETER TEWKSBURY—Doctor, You've Got to Be Kidding.
JOHN STURGES—Hour of the Gun.
MARTIN RITT—Hombre.
DON CHAFFEY—One Million Years B.C.
PETER GOLDMAN—Echoes of Silence.
TONY RICHARDSON—Sailor From Gibraltar.
T. C. FRANK—Born Losers.
RICHARD LESTER—How I Won the War.
JOSHUA LOGAN—Camelot.
STANLEY KRAMER—Guess Who's Coming to Dinner?

DIRECTORIAL INDEX TO THE AMERICAN CINEMA

By Michael Schwartz and James R. Prickett

The following index contains every English language film made after 1929 and mentioned in this book. In addition, the authors have culled films from fourteen other sources. They are alphabetized computer style: spaces and punctuation are treated as letters. For example, *No, Not Again* would appear before *Noah's Ark* but after *No Time for Sergeants*. Although this index falls short of our original goal (a listing of every American film ever made), it still should go a long way toward ending the tyranny of randomness plaguing those who spend their time watching movies on television.

1944; Irving Rapper

Adventures of Quentin Durward, The; 1956; Richard Thorpe

Adventures of Robin Hood, The; 1938; Michael Curtiz and William Keighley

Adventures of Sherlock Holmes, The; 1939; Alfred Werker

Adventures of Tom Sawyer; 1938; H. C. Potter and Norman Taurog

Advise and Consent; 1962; Otto Preminger

Affair in Havana; 1957; Laslo Benedek

Affair of the Skin, An; 1963; Ben Maddow

Affair of Trinidad; 1957; Vincent Sherman

Affair to Remember, An; 1957; Leo McCarey

Affairs of Cellini; 1934; Gregory La Cava

Affairs of Dobie Gillis, The; 1953; Don Weis

Affairs of Martha, The; 1942; Jules Dassin

Affairs of Susan, The; 1935; Kurt Neumann

Affairs of Susan, The; 1945; William Seiter

Affectionately Yours; 1941; Lloyd Bacon

African Fury; 1952; Zoltan Korda

African in London, An; 1943; George Pearson

African Queen, The; 1952; John Huston

After Midnight with Boston Blackie; 1943; Lew Landers

After Office Hours; 1935; Robert Z. Leonard

After the Thin Man; 1936; W. S. van Dyke

After Tomorrow; 1932; Frank Borzage

After Tonight; 1933; George Archainbaud

Against All Flags; 1952; George Sherman

Against the Wind; 1948; Charles Crichton

Age of Consent; 1932; Gregory La Cava

Agent 8¾; 1963; Ralph Thomas

Agony and the Ecstasy, The; 1964; Carol Reed

Ah, Wilderness; 1935; Clarence Brown

Aimez-Vous Brahms; 1961; Anatole Litvak

Ain't Misbehaving; 1955; Edward Buzzell

Air Force; 1943; Howard Hawks

Air Mail; 1932; John Ford

Al Capone; 1959; Richard Wilson

Alamo, The; 1960; John Wayne

Albert RN; 1953; Lewis Gilbert

Alexander the Great; 1956; Robert Rossen

Alexander's Ragtime Band; 1938; Henry King

Alfie; 1965; Lewis Gilbert

Alfred the Great; 1968; Clive Donner

Algiers; 1938; John Cromwell

Ali Baba and the Forty Thieves; 1943; Arthur Lubin

Alias Jesse James; 1959; Norman Z. McLeod

Alias Jimmy Valentine; 1929; Jack Conway

Alias Mary; 1935; Kurt Neumann

Alias Mr. Twilight; 1947; John Sturges

Alias Nick Beal; 1949; John Farrow

Alias the Doctor; 1932; Lloyd Bacon

Alibi; 1929; Roland West

Alice Adams; 1935; George Stevens

Alice in Wonderland; 1933; Norman Z. McLeod

All About Eve; 1950; Joseph Mankiewicz

All American, The; 1953; Jesse Hibbs

All Ashore; 1953; Richard Quine

All Fall Down; 1962; John Frankenheimer

All I Desire; 1953; Douglas Sirk

All in Good Time; 1965; John Boulting and Roy Boulting

All My Sons; 1948; Irving Reis

All Night Long; 1961; Basil Dearden

All Over the Town; 1948; Derek Twist

All Quiet on the Western Front; 1930; Lewis Milestone

All That Heaven Allows; 1956; Douglas Sirk

All That Money Can Buy; 1941; William Dieterle

All the Brothers Were Valiant; 1953; Richard Thorpe

All the Fine Young Cannibals; 1958; Michael Anderson

All the King's Horses; 1935; Frank Tuttle

All the King's Men; 1949; Robert Rossen

Dyke
Anthony Adverse; 1936; Mervyn Le Roy
Any Number Can Play; 1949; Mervyn Le Roy
Anything Goes; 1936; Lewis Milestone
Apache; 1954; Robert Aldrich
Apache Woman; 1955; Roger Corman
Apartment, The; 1960; Billy Wilder
Appaloosa, The; 1966; Sidney Furie
Applause; 1929; Rouben Mamoulian
Appointment, The; 1968; Sidney Lumet
Appointment in Honduras; 1953; Jacques Tourneur
Appointment with Danger; 1951; Lewis Allen
Appointment with Venus; 1951; Ralph Thomas
Arabesque; 1966; Stanley Donen
Arabian Nights; 1942; Mario Bava and Henry Levin
Arch of Triumph; 1948; Lewis Milestone
Arena; 1953; Richard Fleischer
Arise My Love; 1940; Mitchell Leisen
Arizona; 1941; Wesley Ruggles
Arizona Cyclone; 1942; Joseph H. Lewis
Arizonian, The; 1935; Charles Vidor
Arkansas Traveler, The; 1938; Alfred Santell
Armored Car Robbery; 1950; Richard Fleischer
Armored Command; 1961; Byron Haskin
Army Surgeon; 1942; Edward Sutherland
Arnelo Affair; 1946; Arch Oboler
Around the World; 1943; Allan Dwan
Around the World in 80 Days; 1956; Michael Anderson
Around the World in 80 Minutes; 1931; Douglas Fairbanks and Victor Fleming
Arouse and Beware; 1940; Leslie Fenton
Arrowsmith; 1931; John Ford
Arruza (Doc); 1963; Budd Boetticher
Arsene Lupin; 1932; Jack Conway
Arsenic and Old Lace; 1944; Frank Capra
Art of Love, The; 1965; Norman Jewison
Arthur Takes Over; 1948; Malcolm St. Clair

Artists and Models; 1937; Raoul Walsh
Artists and Models; 1955; Frank Tashlin
Artists and Models Abroad; 1938; Mitchell Leisen
As You Desire Me; 1932; George Fitzmaurice
As You Like It; 1936; Paul Czinner
As Young as You Feel; 1931; Frank Borzage
As Young as You Feel; 1951; Harmon Jones
Ask a Policeman; 1941; Max Varnel
Ask Any Girl; 1959; Charles Walters
Asphalt Jungle, The; 1950; John Huston
Assassin, The; 1953; Ralph Thomas
Assigned to Danger; 1948; Budd Boetticher
Assignment in Brittany;. 1943; Jack Conway
Assignment Paris; 1952; Robert Parrish
At Gunpoint; 1958; Alfred Werker
At the Circus; 1938; Edward Buzzell
Atlantis the Lost Continent; 1961; George Pal
Atomic City, The; 1952; Jerry Hopper
Atomic Kid, The; 1954; Leslie H. Martinson
Atomic Man, The; 1956; Kenneth Hughes
Attack; 1956; Robert Aldrich
Attack of the Crab Monsters; 1957; Roger Corman
Auntie Mame; 1958; Morton da Costa
Autumn Leaves; 1956; Robert Aldrich
Avenger, The (Murders); 1934; Louis Brooks
Aviator; 1929; Roy del Ruth
Away All Boats; 1956; Joseph Pevney
Awful Truth, The; 1937; Leo McCarey

B.F.'s Daughter; 1948; Robert Z. Leonard
Babbitt; 1934; William Keighley
Babe Ruth Story, The; 1948; Roy del Ruth
Babes in Arms; 1939; Busby Berkeley
Babes in Bagdad; 1952; Edgar G. Ulmer
Babes on Broadway; 1941; Busby Berkeley
Baby Doll; 1956; Elia Kazan
Baby Face Harrington; 1935; Raoul Walsh

Beast with Five Fingers; 1946; Robert Florey

Beat the Devil; 1954; John Huston

Beau Brummel; 1954; Curtis Bernhardt

Beau Geste; 1939; William Wellman

Beautiful Blonde from Bashful Bend, The; 1949; Preston Sturges

Beautiful but Dangerous; 1955; Robert Z. Leonard

Beauty and the Beast; 1962; Edward L. Cahn

Beauty and the Boss; 1932; Roy del Ruth

Beauty for Sale; 1933; Richard Boleslavsky

Beauty Jungle, The; 1964; Val Guest

Beauty Parlor; 1932; Richard Thorpe

Beauty's Daughter; 1935; Allan Dwan

Because of Him; 1946; Richard Wallace

Because They're Young; 1960; Paul Wendkos

Becket; 1964; Peter Glenville

Becky Sharp; 1935; Rouben Mamoulian

Bed of Roses; 1933; Gregory La Cava

Bedazzled; 1968; Stanley Donen

Bedeviled; 1955; Mitchell Leisen

Bedford Incident, The; 1965; James B. Harris

Bedlam; 1946; Mark Robson

Bedside; 1934; Robert Florey

Bedtime Story; 1942; Alexander Hall

Beggar's Opera, The; 1953; Peter Brook

Behind Locked Doors; 1948; Budd Boetticher

Behind the Mask; 1946; Phil Karlson

Behind the Mask; 1960; Brian D. Hurst

Behind the Rising Sun; 1943; Edward Dmytryk

Behold a Pale Horse; 1964; Fred Zinnemann

Behold My Wife; 1935; Mitchell Leisen

Bell for Adano, A; 1945; Henry King

Bell, Book, and Candle; 1958; Richard Quine

Bellboy, The; 1960; Jerry Lewis

Belle le Grande; 1951; Allan Dwan

Belle of New York, The; 1952; Charles Walters

Belle of the Nineties; 1934; Leo McCarey

Belle of the Yukon; 1944; William Seiter

Belle Sommers; 1962; Elliot Silverstein

Bells Are Ringing; 1960; Vincente Minnelli

Bells Go Down, The; 1942; Basil Dearden

Bells of St. Mary's, The; 1945; Leo McCarey

Beloved Brat; 1937; Arthur Lubin

Beloved Enemy; 1936; H. C. Potter

Beloved Infidel; 1959; Henry King

Below Zero (Short); 1930; James Parrott

Ben Hur; 1959; William Wyler

Bend of the River; 1952; Anthony Mann

Bengal Brigade; 1954; Laslo Benedek

Bengal Tiger; 1934; Joe May

Bengazi; 1955; John Brahm

Benjy (Doc); 1951; Fred Zinnemann

Berkeley Square; 1933; Frank Lloyd

Berlin Express; 1948; Jacques Tourneur

Bermuda Affair; 1957; Edward Sutherland

Bespoke Overcoat, The; 1955; Jack Clayton

Best Foot Forward; 1943; Eddie Buzzell

Best Man, The; 1964; Franklin Schaffner

Best Man Wins; 1948; John Sturges

Best of Enemies, The; 1962; Guy Hamilton

Best of Everything, The; 1959; Jean Negulesco

Best Things in Life Are Free, The; 1956; Michael Curtiz

Best Years of Our Lives, The; 1946; William Wyler

Betrayed (When Strangers Marry); 1944; William Castle

Betrayal, The; 1929; Lewis Milestone

Better Tomorrow, A (Doc); 1945; Alexander Hackenschmied

Between Heaven and Hell; 1956; Richard Fleischer

Between Midnight and Dawn; 1950; Gordon Douglas

Between Two Worlds; 1944; Edward A. Blatt

Between Us Girls; 1942; Henry Koster

Beware; 1946; Bud Pollard

Beware My Lovely; 1952; Harry Horner

Beware of Children (No Kidding);

1961; Gerald Thomas
Bewitched; 1945; Arch Oboler
Beyond a Reasonable Doubt; 1956; Fritz Lang
Beyond the Forest; 1949; King Vidor
Beyond the Time Barrier; 1960; Edgar G. Ulmer
Beyond This Place; 1958; Jack Cardiff
Beyond Tomorrow; 1940; Edward Sutherland
Bhowani Junction; 1956; George Cukor
Bible, The; 1966; John Huston
Big Beat, The; 1958; Will Cowan
Big Boodle, The; 1957; Richard Wilson
Big Broadcast, The; 1932; Frank Tuttle
Big Broadcast of 1937; 1936; Mitchell Leisen
Big Broadcast of 1938; 1938; Mitchell Leisen
Big Brown Eyes; 1936; Raoul Walsh
Big Business (Short); 1929; James W. Horne
Big Circus, The; 1959; Joseph M. Newman
Big News; 1929; Gregory La Cava
Big Cage, The; 1933; Kurt Neumann
Big Carnival, The (Ace in the Hole); 1951; Billy Wilder
Big Cat, The; 1949; Phil Karlson
Big Circus, The; 1959; Joseph M. Newman
Big City, The; 1937; Frank Borzage
Big City Blues; 1932; Mervyn Le Roy
Big Clock, The; 1948; John Farrow
Big Combo, The; 1955; Joseph H. Lewis
Big Country, The; 1958; William Wyler
Big Fella; 1938; J. Elder Wills
Big Fisherman, The; 1959; Frank Borzage
Big Gamble, The; 1961; Richard Fleischer
Big Guy, The; 1940; Arthur Lubin
Big Hearted Herbert; 1934; William Keighley
Big Heat, The; 1953; Fritz Lang
Big House, The; 1930; George Hill
Big Jim McLain; 1952; Edward Ludwig
Big Knife, The; 1955; Robert Aldrich
Big Land, The; 1957; Gordon Douglas
Big Leaguer, The; 1953; Robert Aldrich

Big Night, The; 1951; Joseph Losey
Big Noise, The; 1944; Malcolm St. Clair
Big Red; 1962; Norman Tokar
Big Shot, The; 1942; Lewis Seiler
Big Sky, The; 1952; Howard Hawks
Big Sleep, The; 1946; Howard Hawks
Big Steal, The; 1949; Don Siegel
Big Store, The; 1941; Charles Reisner
Big Street, The; 1943; Irving Reis
Big Town Czar; 1939; Arthur Lubin
Big Trail, The; 1930; Raoul Walsh
Big Trees, The; 1952; Felix Feist
Bigamist, The; 1953; Ida Lupino
Bigger than Life; 1956; Nicholas Ray
Bike Boy; 1967; Andy Warhol
Bikini Beach; 1965; William Asher
Bill of Divorcement, A; 1932; George Cukor
Bill of Divorcement, A; 1940; John Farrow
Billy Budd; 1962; Peter Ustinov
Billy Liar; 1963; John Schlesinger
Billy the Kid; 1930; King Vidor
Billy the Kid; 1941; David Miller
Bird of Paradise; 1932; King Vidor
Bird of Paradise; 1951; Delmer Daves
Birdman of Alcatraz; 1962; John Frankenheimer
Birds, The; 1963; Alfred Hitchcock
Birds and the Bees, The; 1956; Norman Taurog
Birth of the Blues; 1941; Victor Schertzinger
Birthday Present, The; 1957; Pat Jackson
Biscuit Eater, The; 1940; Stuart Heisler
Bishop's Wife, The; 1948; Henry Koster
Bitter Creek; 1954; George Waggner
Bitter Harvest; 1963; Peter Graham Scott
Bitter Sweet; 1940; W. S. van Dyke
Bitter Tea of General Yen; 1933; Frank Capra
Bitter Victory; 1958; Nicholas Ray
Black Angel; 1946; Roy William Neill
Black Arrow, The; 1948; Gordon Douglas
Black Castle; 1952; Nathan Juran
Black Cat, The; 1934; Edgar G. Ulmer
Black Cat, The; 1941; Albert S. Rogell
Black Friday; 1940; Arthur Lubin
Black Fury; 1935; Michael Curtiz
Black Gold; 1947; Phil Karlson
Black Gold; 1963; Leslie H. Martinson

Black Hand, The; 1950; Richard Thorpe

Black King, The; 1932; Bud Pollard

Black Knight, The; 1954; Tay Garnett

Black Legion, The; 1936; Archie Mayo

Black like Me; 1964; Carl Lerner

Black Midnight; 1949; Budd Boetticher

Black Narcissus; 1947; Michael Powell and Emeric Pressburger

Black Orchid, The; 1959; Martin Ritt

Black Room; 1935; Roy William Neill

Black Rose, The; 1950; Henry Hathaway

Black Sabbath; 1964; Mario Bava

Black Sheep; 1935; Allan Dwan

Black Sheep of Whitehall, The; 1941; Basil Dearden and Will Hay

Black Shield of Falworth; 1954; Rudolph Mate

Black Sleep, The; 1956; Reginald Le Borg

Black Spurs; 1964; R. G. Springsteen

Black Sunday; 1961; Mario Bava

Black Swan, The; 1942; Henry King

Black Tights; 1962; Terence Young

Black Torment, The; 1964; Robert Hartford-Davis

Black Tuesday; 1955; Hugo Fregonese

Black Watch; 1929; John Ford

Black Waters; 1929; Herbert Wilcox

Black Widow; 1954; Nunnally Johnson

Blackbeard the Pirate; 1952; Raoul Walsh

Blackboard Jungle, The; 1955; Richard Brooks

Blackmail; 1929; Alfred Hitchcock

Blackmail; 1939; H. C. Potter

Blackout; 1950; Robert S. Baker

Blanche Fury; 1947; Marc Allegret

Blaze of Noon; 1947; John Farrow

Blazing Six Shooters; 1940; Joseph H. Lewis

Blessed Event; 1932; Roy del Ruth

Blind Adventure; 1933; Ernest L. Schoesdack

Blind Alibi; 1939; Charles Vidor

Blind Date (Chance Meeting); 1960; Joseph Losey

Blindfold; 1966; Philip Dunne

Blithe Spirit; 1945; David Lean

Blockade; 1938; William Dieterle

Blockheads; 1938; John Blystone

Blonde Bait; 1956; Elmo Williams

Blonde Crazy; 1931; Roy del Ruth

Blonde Inspiration; 1941; Busby Berkeley

Blonde Venus; 1932; Josef von Sternberg

Blondie of the Follies; 1932; Edmund Goulding

Blood Alley; 1955; William Wellman

Blood and Sand; 1941; Rouben Mamoulian

Blood of the Vampire; 1958; Henry Cass

Blood on the Moon; 1948; Robert Wise

Blood on the Sun; 1945; Frank Lloyd

Blossoms in the Dust; 1941; Mervyn Le Roy

Blossoms on Broadway; 1937; Richard Wallace

Blow Up; 1966; Michelangelo Antonioni

Blowing Wild; 1953; Hugo Fregonese

Blue Angel, The; 1930; Josef von Sternberg

Blue Angel, The; 1959; Edward Dmytryk

Blue Denim; 1959; Philip Dunne

Blue Gardenia, The; 1953; Fritz Lang

Blue Lamp, The; 1949; Basil Dearden

Blue Max, The; 1966; John Guillermin

Blue Skies; 1946; Stuart Heisler

Bluebeard; 1944; Edgar G. Ulmer

Bluebeard's Eighth Wife; 1938; Ernst Lubitsch

Blues in the Night; 1941; Anatole Litvak

Bobo, The; 1967; Robert Parrish

Body and Soul; 1931; Alfred Santell

Body and Soul; 1947; Robert Rossen

Body Disappeared, The; 1942; D. Ross Lederman

Body Snatcher, The; 1945; Robert Wise

Bohemian Girl, The; 1936; James W. Horne

Bold and the Brave, The; 1956; Lewis R. Foster

Bombardier; 1942; Richard Wallace

Bombers B-52; 1957; Gordon Douglas

Bombs over Burma; 1942; Joseph H. Lewis

Bombshell; 1933; Victor Fleming

Bondage; 1933; Alfred Santell

Bonjour Tristesse; 1958; Otto Preminger

Bonnie and Clyde; 1967; Arthur Penn

Boom; 1968; Joseph Losey

Boom Town; 1940; Jack Conway

Carve Her Name with Pride; 1958; Lewis Gilbert

Casablanca; 1942; Michael Curtiz

Casanova Brown; 1944; Sam Wood

Casanova's Big Night; 1954; Norman Z. McLeod

Casbah; 1948; John Berry

Case Against Brooklyn, The; 1958; Paul Wendkos

Case of Lena Smith, The; 1929; Josef von Sternberg

Case of the Curious Bride; 1935; Michael Curtiz

Case of the Lucky Legs; 1935; Archie Mayo

Cash McCall; 1960; Joseph Pevney

Casino Royale; 1967; John Huston

Cass Timberlane; 1947; George Sidney

Castle on the Hudson; 1940; Anatole Litvak

Cat and the Canary; 1939; Elliott Nugent

Cat and the Fiddle; 1934; William K. Howard

Cat Ballou; 1965; Elliot Silverstein

Cat on a Hot Tin Roof; 1958; Richard Brooks

Cat People; 1942; Jacques Tourneur

Catered Affair, The; 1956; Richard Brooks

Catherine The Great; 1934; Paul Czinner

Cattle Queen of Montana; 1954; Allan Dwan

Caught; 1949; Max Ophuls

Cause for Alarm; 1951; Tay Garnett

Cavalcade; 1933; Frank Lloyd

Cease Fire; 1953; Owen Crump

Ceiling Zero; 1936; Howard Hawks

Centennial Summer; 1946; Otto Preminger

Central Airport; 1933; William Wellman

Centurions, The; 1966; Mark Robson

Ceremony, The; 1963; Laurence Harvey

Certain Smile, A; 1955; Jean Negulesco

Chad Hanna; 1940; Henry King

Chain Lightning; 1950; Stuart Heisler

Chained; 1934; Clarence Brown

Chalk Garden, The; 1964; Ronald Neame

Challenge, The; 1938; Milton Rosmer

Champ, The; 1931; King Vidor

Champagne Waltz; 1937; Edward Sutherland

Champagne Murders, The; 1968; Claude Chabrol

Champion; 1949; Mark Robson

Chance at Heaven; 1933; William Seiter

Chance Meeting (Blind Date); 1960; Joseph Losey

Chances; 1931; Allan Dwan

Chandu the Magician; 1932; William C. Menzies

Chapman Report, The; 1962; George Cukor

Charade; 1963; Stanley Donen

Charge at Feather River, The; 1953; Gordon Douglas

Charge of the Light Brigade; 1936; Michael Curtiz

Charlie Chan at the Olympics; 1937; H. Bruce Humberstone

Charlie Chan at the Opera; 1936; H. Bruce Humberstone

Charlie Chan at the Race Track; 1936; H. Bruce Humberstone

Charlie Chan at Treasure Island; 1939; Norman Foster

Charlie Chan in Panama; 1940; Norman Foster

Charlie Chan in Reno; 1939; Norman Foster

Charlie's Aunt; 1941; Archie Mayo

Chase, The; 1946; Arthur Ripley

Chase, The; 1966; Arthur Penn

Chase a Crooked Shadow; 1958; Michael Anderson

Chasing Trouble; 1940; Howard Bretherton

Cheaper by the Dozen; 1949; Walter Lang

Cheating Cheaters; 1934; Richard Thorpe

Checkers; 1937; H. Bruce Humberstone

Cheers for Miss Bishop; 1941; Tay Garnett

Cheyenne (The Wyoming Kid); 1947; Raoul Walsh

Cheyenne Autumn; 1964; John Ford

Chicago Deadline; 1949; Lewis Allen

Child Is Born, A; 1940; Lloyd Bacon

Child Is Waiting, A; 1962; John Cassavetes

Child of Divorce; 1946; Richard Fleischer

Children at School (Doc); 1937; Basil Wright

Children of Dreams; 1931; Alan Cros-

Comanche; 1956; George Sherman

Come and Get It; 1936; Howard Hawks and William Wyler

Come Back Little Sheba; 1953; Daniel Mann

Come Fill the Cup; 1951; Gordon Douglas

Come Live with Me; 1941; Clarence Brown

Come Next Spring; 1956; R. G. Springsteen

Come On, The; 1956; Russell Birdwell

Come On Leathernecks; 1938; James Cruze

Come On Marines; 1934; Henry Hathaway

Come September; 1961; Robert Mulligan

Comedy of Terrors, The; 1964; Jacques Tourneur

Comet over Broadway; 1938; Busby Berkeley

Comanche Station; 1960; Budd Boetticher

Comancheros, The; 1961; Michael Curtiz

Command Decision; 1949; Sam Wood

Common Clay; 1930; Victor Fleming

Common Lady, The; 1931; Paul Stein

Common Touch; 1941; John Baxter

Company of Cowards; 1964; George Marshall

Company She Keeps, The; 1950; John Cromwell

Compulsion; 1959; Richard Fleischer

Comrade X; 1940; King Vidor

Concealment; 1935; William Dieterle

Concrete Jungle, The; 1962; Joseph Losey

Condemned; 1929; Wesley Ruggles

Coney Island; 1943; Walter Lang

Confessions of a Nazi Spy; 1939; Anatole Litvak

Confessions of Boston Blackie; 1941; Edward Dmytryk

Confidence Girl; 1952; Andrew L. Stone

Confidential Agent; 1945; Herman Shumlin

Confidential Report (Mister Arkadin); 1962; Orson Welles

Confirm or Deny; 1941; Archie Mayo

Connecticut Yankee; 1931; David Butler

Connecticut Yankee in King Arthur's Court, A; 1949; Tay Garnett

Connection, The; 1960; Shirley Clarke

Conqueror, The; 1955; Dick Powell

Conquerors, The; 1932; William Wellman

Conquest; 1929; Roy del Ruth

Conquest (Marie Walewska); 1937; Clarence Brown

Conquest of Space; 1955; Byron Haskin

Conquest of the Air; 1940; Alexander Korda

Conspirators, The; 1944; Jean Negulesco

Constant Nymph, The; 1943; Edmund Goulding

Contact Man, The; 1949; John Farrow

Convention City; 1933; Archie Mayo

Convict Ninety-Nine; 1938; Max Varnel

Cool Hand Luke; 1967; Stuart Rosenberg

Cool Mikado, The; 1963; Michael Winner

Cool Sound from Hell; 1956; Sidney Furie

Cool World, The; 1963; Shirley Clarke

Copacabana; 1947; Alfred E. Green

Copper Canyon; 1950; John Farrow

Corn Is Green, The; 1945; Irving Rapper

Corridor of Mirrors; 1949; Terence Young

Corsair; 1931; Roland West

Corvette K-225; 1943; Richard Rossen

Cottage on Dartmoor; 1929; Norah Baring and Anthony Asquith

Counsel for Crime; 1937; John Brahm

Counsellor at Law; 1933; William Wyler

Count of Monte Cristo; 1933; Rowland V. Lee

Count the Hours; 1953; Don Siegel

Count Your Blessings; 1959; Jean Negulesco

Counterattack; 1945; Zoltan Korda

Counterfeit Traitor, The; 1961; George Seaton

Countess from Hong Kong, A; 1967; Charles Chaplin

Country Doctor; 1936; Henry King

Country Girl, The; 1954; George Seaton

Country Music Holiday; 1958; Alvin Ganzer

Courage of the West; 1937; Joseph H. Lewis

Court Jester, The; 1956; Norman Pan-

Damn the Defiant; 1962; Lewis Gilbert

Damn Yankees; 1958; Stanley Donen

Damned Don't Cry, The; 1950; Vincent Sherman

Damsel in Distress, A; 1937; George Stevens

Dance, Fools Dance; 1931; Harry Beaumont

Dance of Life; 1929; John Cromwell and Edward Sutherland

Dance with Me, Henry; 1956; Charles T. Barton

Dancing Lady; 1933; Robert Z. Leonard

Dancing Masters, The; 1943; Malcolm St. Clair

Dandy in Aspic; 1968; Anthony Mann

Danger, Love at Work; 1937; Otto Preminger

Danger Signal; 1945; Robert Florey

Dangerous; 1935; Alfred E. Green

Dangerous Age, A; 1956; Sidney Furie

Dangerous Crossing; 1953; Joseph M. Newman

Dangerous Female (The Maltese Falcon); 1931; Roy del Ruth

Dangerous Nan McGrew; 1930; Malcolm St. Clair

Dangerous Number; 1937; Richard Thorpe

Dangerous Paradise; 1930; William Wellman

Dangerously They Live; 1941; Robert Florey

Dangerously Yours; 1933; Frank Tuttle

Dangerously Yours; 1937; Malcolm St. Clair

Dante's Inferno; 1935; Harry Lachman

Darby's Rangers; 1958; William Wellman

Dark Alibi; 1946; Phil Karlson

Dark Angel, The; 1935; Sidney Franklin

Dark at the Top of the Stairs, The; 1960; Delbert Mann

Dark City; 1950; William Dieterle

Dark Command; 1940; Raoul Walsh

Dark Corner, The; 1946; Henry Hathaway

Dark Horse, The; 1932; Alfred E. Green

Dark Intruder; 1965; Harvey Hart

Dark Journey; 1937; Victor Saville

Dark Mirror, The; 1946; Robert Siodmak

Dark Passage; 1947; Delmer Daves

Dark Past, The; 1948; Rudolph Mate

Dark Sands (Jericho); 1937; Thornton Freeland

Dark Victory; 1939; Edmund Goulding

Dark Waters; 1944; Andre de Toth

Darling; 1965; John Schlesinger

Darling, How Could You; 1951; Mitchell Leisen

Darling Lili; 1969; Blake Edwards

Daughter of Dr. Jekyll; 1957; Edgar G. Ulmer

Daughter of Rosie O'Grady, The; 1950; David Butler

Daughter of Shanghai; 1937; Robert Florey

Daughters Courageous; 1939; Michael Curtiz

David and Bathsheba; 1952; Henry King

David and Lisa; 1962; Frank Perry

David Copperfield; 1935; George Cukor

David Harum; 1934; James Cruze

Dawn Patrol, The; 1930; Howard Hawks

Dawn Patrol, The; 1938; Edmund Goulding

Day and the Hour; 1963; René Clément

Day at the Races, A; 1939; Sam Wood

Day of the Arrow; 1965; Sidney Furie

Day of the Outlaw; 1959; Andre de Toth

Day of the Triffids, The; 1963; Steve Sekely

Day Shall Dawn, The; 1959; A. Kardar

Day the Earth Caught Fire; 1962; Val Guest

Day the Earth Stood Still, The; 1951; Robert Wise

Day the World Ended, The; 1956; Roger Corman

Day They Robbed the Bank of England; 1960; John Guillermin

Daybreak; 1932; Jacques Feyder

Daytime Wife; 1939; Gregory Ratoff

Days of Glory; 1944; Jacques Tourneur

Days of Wine and Roses; 1963; Blake Edwards

Dead End; 1937; William Wyler

Dead Heat on a Merry-Go-Round; 1966; Bernard Girard

Wilde

Devil and Daniel Webster; 1941; William Dieterle

Devil and Miss Jones; 1941; Sam Wood

Devil and the Deep; 1932; Marion Gering

Devil at 4 O'clock, The; 1961; Mervyn Le Roy

Devil Dogs of the Air; 1935; Lloyd Bacon

Devil Doll, The; 1936; Tod Browning

Devil Is a Sissy, The; 1936; W. S. van Dyke

Devil Is a Woman, The; 1935; Josef von Sternberg

Devil Makes Three, The; 1952; Andrew Marton

Devil May Care; 1929; Sidney Franklin

Devil Pays Off, The; 1941; John Auer

Devil to Pay, The; 1930; George Fitzmaurice

Devil with Hitler, The; 1942; Gordon Douglas

Devil with Women, A; 1930; Irving Cummings

Devil's Canyon; 1953; Alfred Werker

Devil's Disciple, The; 1959; Guy Hamilton

Devil's Doorway; 1950; Anthony Mann

Devil's in Love; 1933; William Dieterle

Devotion; 1946; Curtis Bernhardt

D.I., The; 1957; Jack Webb

Dial M for Murder; 1954; Alfred Hitchcock

Diamond Head; 1962; Guy Green

Diamond Jim; 1935; Edward Sutherland

Diamond Queen, The; 1953; John Brahm

Diane; 1955; David Miller

Diary of a Chambermaid; 1946; Jean Renoir

Diary of a High School Bride; 1959; Burt Topper

Diary of a Madman; 1963; Reginald Le Borg

Diary of a Sergeant; 1945; Joseph M. Newman

Diary of Anne Frank, The; 1959; George Stevens

Dick Tracy Versus Cueball; 1946; Gordon Douglas

Dimples; 1936; William Seiter

Dinner at Eight; 1933; George Cukor

Diplomaniacs; 1933; William Seiter

Diplomatic Courier; 1952; Henry Hathaway

Dirigible; 1931; Frank Capra

Dirty Dozen, The; 1967; Robert Aldrich

Dirty Game, The; 1966; Christian Jacque and Carlo Lizzani

Disbarred; 1939; Robert Florey

Dishonored; 1931; Josef von Sternberg

Dishonored Lady; 1947; Robert Stevenson

Disobedient; 1954; Charles Frank

Disorderly Orderly, The; 1964; Frank Tashlin

Dispatch from Reuters, A; 1940; William Dieterle

Disputed Passage; 1939; Frank Borzage

Disraeli; 1929; Alfred E. Green

Distant Drums; 1951; Raoul Walsh

Distant Trumpet, A; 1964; Raoul Walsh

Dive Bomber; 1941; Michael Curtiz

Divide and Conquer (Doc); 1943; Frank Capra and Anatole Litvak

Divided Heart, The; 1954; Charles Crichton

Divine; 1935; Max Ophuls

Divine Lady; 1929; Frank Lloyd

Divorce American Style; 1967; Bud Yorkin

Divorce Among Friends; 1931; Roy del Ruth

Dixie; 1943; Edward Sutherland

Dixie Jamboree; 1945; Christy Cabanne

D.O.A.; 1949; Rudolph Mate

Docks of New Orleans; 1948; Derwin Abrahams

Doctor and the Playgirl, The; 1965; William Martin

Doctor at Sea; 1955; Ralph Thomas

Doctor Blood's Coffin; 1960; Sidney Furie

Doctor Broadway; 1942; Anthony Mann

Doctor Bull; 1933; John Ford

Doctor Crippen; 1964; Robert Lynn

Doctor Cyclops; 1940; Ernest L. Schoesdack

Doctor Dolittle; 1967; Richard Fleischer

Doctor Ehrlich's Magic Bullet; 1940; William Dieterle

Duel on the Mississippi; 1955; William Castle

Duffy; 1968; Robert Parrish

Duke Steps Out, The; 1929; James Cruze

During One Night (Night of Passion); 1961; Sidney Furie

Dust Be My Destiny; 1939; Lewis Seiler

Dynamite; 1929; Cecil B. de Mille

Each Dawn I Die; 1939; William Keighley

Eagle and the Hawk, The; 1933; Stuart Walker

Eagle Squadron; 1942; Arthur Lubin

Earl of Chicago, The; 1940; Richard Thorpe

Earth Dies Screaming; 1964; Terence Fisher

Easiest Way; 1931; Jack Conway

East Is East; 1929; Tod Browning

East of Borneo; 1932; George Melford

East of Eden; 1955; Elia Kazan

East of Shanghai; 1932; Alfred Hitchcock

East of Sumatra; 1953; Budd Boetticher

East of the Rising Sun (Malaya); 1949; Richard Thorpe

East of the River; 1940; Alfred S. Green

East Side, West Side; 1949; Mervyn Le Roy

Easter Parade; 1948; Charles Walters

Easy Come, Easy Go; 1947; John Farrow

Easy Living; 1937; Mitchell Leisen

Easy Living; 1949; Jacques Tourneur

Easy to Love; 1934; William Keighley

Easy to Wed; 1946; Edward Buzzell

Easy Way, The (Room for One More); 1952; Norman Taurog

Eddie Cantor Story; 1954; Alfred E. Green

Eddie Duchin Story, The; 1956; George Sidney

Edge of Darkness; 1943; Lewis Milestone

Edge of Eternity; 1960; Don Siegel

Edge of Fury; 1958; Irving Lerner

Edge of Hell; 1956; Hugo Haas

Edge of the City (Man is Ten Feet Tall, A); 1957; Martin Ritt

Edison the Man; 1940; Clarence Brown

Egyptian, The; 1954; Michael Curtiz

Eight Girls in a Boat; 1934; Richard Wallace

Eight Iron Men; 1952; Edward Dmytryk

El Cid; 1961; Anthony Mann

El Dorado; 1967; Howard Hawks

Elephant Boy; 1937; Zoltan Korda and Robert Flaherty

Elephant Walk; 1954; William Dieterle

Elizabeth the Queen (Private Lives of Elizabeth and Essex, The); 1939; Michael Curtiz

Ellery Queen Master Detective; 1940; Kurt Neumann

Elmer Gantry; 1960; Richard Brooks

Elmer the Great; 1933; Mervyn Le Roy

Emil and the Detectives; 1964; Peter Tewksbury

Emma; 1932; Clarence Brown

Emperor Jones, The; 1933; Dudley Murphy

Emperor Waltz, The; 1948; Billy Wilder

Employees Entrance; 1933; Roy del Ruth

Empty Saddles; 1936; Leslie Selander

Enchanted Cottage, The; 1945; John Cromwell

Enchanted Island; 1958; Allan Dwan

End of the Affair, The; 1955; Edward Dmytryk

End of the River, The; 1947; Derek Twist

Enemy General, The; 1960; George Sherman

Enforcer, The; 1951; Bretaigne Windust

Enough to Eat (Doc); 1936; Edgar Anstey

Escape from Devil's Island; 1936; Albert S. Rogell

Escape from San Quentin; 1957; Fred F. Sears

Enter Madame; 1935; Elliott Nugent

Entertainer, The; 1960; Tony Richardson

Erik the Great Illusionist; 1929; Paul Fejos

Errand Boy, The; 1962; Jerry Lewis

Escapade; 1935; Robert Z. Leonard

Escapade; 1955; Philip Leacock

Escape; 1940; Mervyn Le Roy

Escape; 1948; Joseph Mankiewicz

Escape from East Berlin (Tunnel 28); 1962; Robert Siodmak

Farewell to Arms, A; 1957; Charles Vidor

Farmer Takes a Wife, The; 1935; Victor Fleming

Farmer's Daughter, The; 1947; H. C. Potter

Fashions of 1934; 1934; William Dieterle

Fast and Furious; 1939; Busby Berkeley

Fast and Loose; 1930; Fred Newmeyer

Fast Company; 1929; Edward Sutherland

Fast Lady, The; 1963; Ken Annakin

Fast Workers; 1933; Tod Browning

Fastest Gun Alive; 1949; Russell Rouse

Fate Is the Hunter; 1964; Ralph Nelson

Father Brown (The Detective); 1954; Robert Hamer

Father Came Too; 1964; Peter Graham Scott

Father Goose; 1964; Ralph Nelson

Father of the Bride; 1950; Vincente Minnelli

Father Takes a Wife; 1941; J. Hively

Father's Little Dividend; 1951; Vincente Minnelli

FBI Story, The; 1959; Mervyn Le Roy

Fear and Desire; 1954; Stanley Kubrick

Fear Strikes Out; 1957; Robert Mulligan

Fearless Fagan; 1952; Stanley Donen

Fearless Vampire Killers, The; 1967; Roman Polanski

Fearmakers, The; 1958; Jacques Tourneur

Feather in Her Hat, A; 1935; Alfred Santell

Feet First; 1930; Clyde Bruckman

Fellow Americans (Doc); 1942; Garson Kanin

Female; 1933; Michael Curtiz and William Dieterle

Female on the Beach; 1955; Joseph Pevney

Feminine Touch, The; 1941; W. S. van Dyke

Feminine Touch, The; 1955; Pat Jackson

Ferry Cross the Mersey; 1964; Jeremy Summers

Ferry to Hong Kong; 1959; Lewis Gilbert

Feudin' Fools; 1952; William Beaudine

Fever in the Blood; 1950; Vincent Sherman

Fiddlers Three; 1944; Harry Watt

Fiend Who Walked the West, The; 1958; Gordon Douglas

Fiend Without a Face; 1958; Arthur Crabtree

Fiesta; 1947; Richard Thorpe

Fifteen Maiden Lane; 1936; Allan Dwan

Fifth Avenue Girl; 1939; Gregory La Cava

Fifty-Five Days at Peking; 1962; Nicholas Ray

Fighter Squadron; 1948; Raoul Walsh

Fighting Back; 1948; Malcolm St. Clair

Fighting Caravans; 1931; Otto Brower and David Burton

Fighting Kentuckian, The; 1949; George Waggner

Fighting Lady, The (Doc); 1943; William Wyler

Fighting Seabees, The; 1944; Edward Ludwig

Fighting 69th, The; 1940; William Keighley

Fighting Sullivans (The Sullivans); 1944; Lloyd Bacon

Fine Madness, A; 1966; Irvin Kershner

Finger of Guilt; 1956; Joseph Losey

Finger Point, The; 1931; John Francis Dillon

Finian's Rainbow; 1968; Francis Ford Coppola

Fire Down Below; 1957; Robert Parrish

Fire over England; 1936; William K. Howard

Fireball, The; 1950; Tay Garnett

Firebird, The; 1934; William Dieterle

Fireman Save My Child; 1932; Lloyd Bacon

Firefly, The; 1937; Robert Z. Leonard

First Legion, The; 1951; Douglas Sirk

First Love; 1939; Henry Koster

First Texan; 1956; Byron Haskin

First Time, The; 1952; Frank Tashlin

First to Fight; 1967; Christian Nyby

First Weapons; 1950; René Wheeler

First Yank into Hollywood; 1945; Gordon Douglas

First Year; 1932; William K. Howard

Five; 1951; Arch Oboler

Five Against the House; 1955; Phil

Richard Sale

Gentlemen of the Press; 1934; Millard Webb

Gentlemen Prefer Blondes; 1953; Howard Hawks

Gentlemen's Agreement; 1947; Elia Kazan

George Washington Slept Here; 1942; William Keighley

Geronimo; 1962; Arnold Laven

Getting Gertie's Garter; 1945; Allan Dwan

Ghost and Mrs. Muir, The; 1947; Joseph Mankiewicz

Ghost Breakers, The; 1940; George Marshall

Ghost Goes West, The; 1936; René Clair

Ghost Ship, The; 1943; Mark Robson

GI Honeymoon; 1945; Phil Karlson

Giant; 1956; George Stevens

Giant of Marathon, The; 1960; Jacques Tourneur

Gideon of Scotland Yard; 1959; John Ford

Gidget; 1959; Paul Wendkos

Gidget Goes Hawaiian; 1961; Paul Wendkos

Gidget Goes to Rome; 1963; Paul Wendkos

Gift of Love, The; 1958; Jean Negulesco

Gigi; 1958; Vincente Minnelli

Gigot; 1962; Gene Kelly

Gilda; 1946; Charles Vidor

Gilded Lily, The; 1935; Wesley Ruggles

Gildersleeve on Broadway; 1943; Gordon Douglas

Gildersleeve's Bad Day; 1943; Gordon Douglas

Gildersleeve's Ghost; 1944; Gordon Douglas

Girl Can't Help It, The; 1956; Frank Tashlin

Girl Crazy; 1932; William Seiter

Girl Crazy; 1943; Norman Taurog

Girl He Left Behind, The; 1956; David Butler

Girl from Maxim's; 1933; Alexander Korda

Girl From Missouri, The; 1933; Jack Conway

Girl Getters, The; 1966; Michael Winner

Girl Hunters, The; 1963; Roy Rowland

Girl in Every Port, A; 1952; Chester Erskine

Girl in the News, The; 1940; Carol Reed

Girl in the Red Velvet Swing, The; 1955; Richard Fleischer

Girl in White, The; 1952; John Sturges

Girl Missing; 1933; Robert Florey

Girl Most Likely, The; 1957; Mitchell Leisen

Girl Must Live, A; 1938; Carol Reed

Girl Named Tamiko, A; 1962; John Sturges

Girl of the Golden West; 1938; Robert Z. Leonard

Girl Rush; 1944; Gordon Douglas

Girl Was Young, A; 1938; Alfred Hitchcock

Girl With Green Eyes; 1964; Desmond Davis

Girl's School; 1938; John Brahm

Girls About Town; 1931; George Cukor

Girls in Chains; 1943; Edgar G. Ulmer

Girls on the Beach; 1965; William Witney

Give a Girl a Break; 1953; Stanley Donen

Give Me a Sailor; 1938; Elliott Nugent

Give Me Your Eyes; 1942; Sacha Guitry

Give Me Your Heart; 1936; Archie Mayo

Give My Regards to Broadway; 1947; Lloyd Bacon

Give Us This Day; 1950; Edward Dmytryk

Glad Rag Doll; 1929; Michael Curtiz

Glass-Bottom Boat, The; 1966; Frank Tashlin

Glass Cage, The; 1955; Montgomery Tully

Glass Key, The; 1935; Frank Tuttle

Glass Key, The; 1942; Stuart Heisler

Glass Menagerie; 1950; Irving Rapper

Glass Slipper, The; 1955; Charles Walters

Glass Wall, The; 1953; Maxwell Shane

Glass Web, The; 1954; Jack Arnold

Glenn Miller Story, The; 1954; Anthony Mann

Glory Alley; 1952; Raoul Walsh

Glory Brigade, The; 1953; Robert D. Webb

Glory Guys, The; 1965; Arnold Laven

Go into Your Dance; 1935; Archie Mayo

Great Day in the Morning; 1956; Jacques Tourneur
Great Dictator, The; 1940; Charles Chaplin
Great Escape, The; 1963; John Sturges
Great Expectations; 1947; David Lean
Great Flamarion, The; 1945; Anthony Mann
Great Gambini, The; 1937; Charles Vidor
Great Gabbo, The; 1929; James Cruze
Great Garrick, The; 1937; James Whale
Great Gatsby, The; 1949; Elliott Nugent
Great Gildersleeve, The; 1942; Gordon Douglas
Great God Gold; 1935; Arthur Lubin
Great Imposter, The; 1960; Robert Mulligan
Great Jesse James Raid, The; 1953; Reginald Le Borg
Great Lie, The; 1941; Edmund Goulding
Great Locomotive Chase, The; 1956; Francis D. Lyon
Great Lover, The; 1949; Alexander Hall
Great Man, The; 1957; José Ferrer
Great Man Votes, The; 1939; Garson Kanin
Great Man's Lady, The; 1942; William Wellman
Great McGinty, The; 1940; Preston Sturges
Great Missouri Raid, The; 1950; Gordon Douglas
Great Moment, The; 1944; Preston Sturges
Great O'Malley, The; 1937; William Dieterle
Great Race, The; 1964; Blake Edwards
Great Sinner, The; 1949; Robert Siodmak
Great Sioux Uprising, The; 1953; Lloyd Bacon
Great Victor Herbert, The; 1939; Andrew L. Stone
Great Waltz, The; 1938; Julien Duvivier
Great Ziegfeld, The; 1936; Robert Z. Leonard
Greatest Show on Earth, The; 1952; Cecil B. de Mille
Greatest Story Ever Told, The; 1964; George Stevens
Green Berets, The; 1968; John Wayne

Green Eyes; 1934; Richard Thorpe
Green Fields; 1937; Jacob Ben-Ami and Edgar G. Ulmer
Green Glove, The; 1952; Rudolph Mate
Green Goddess, The; 1932; Alfred E. Green
Green Grow the Rushes; 1951; Derek Twist
Green Hell; 1940; James Whale
Green Light; 1937; Frank Borzage
Green Man, The; 1957; Robert Day
Green Mansions; 1958; Mel Ferrer
Green Pastures, The; 1936; Marc Connelly and William Keighley
Greengage Summer, The (Loss of Innocence); 1961; Lewis Gilbert
Greenwich Village Story; 1963; Jack O'Connell
Grip of the Strangler; 1958; Robert Day
Group, The; 1965; Sidney Lumet
Grumpy; 1930; George Cukor and Cyril Gardner
Guardsman, The; 1931; Sidney Franklin
Guess Who's Coming to Dinner; 1967; Stanley Kramer
Guest, The; 1964; Clive Donner
Guest in the House; 1944; John Brahm
Guide for the Married Man; 1967; Gene Kelly
Guilt of Janet Ames, The; 1947; Charles Vidor
Guilty Hands; 1931; W. S. van Dyke
Guinea Pig, The; 1948; John Boulting and Roy Boulting
Gun Battle at Monterey; 1957; Sidney Franklin and Karl K. Hittelman
Gun Crazy; 1949; Joseph H. Lewis
Gun for a Coward; 1957; Abner Biberman
Gun Fury; 1953; Raoul Walsh
Gun Glory; 1957; Roy Rowland
Gun Hawk, The; 1963; Edward Ludwig
Gun Runners, The; 1958; Don Siegel
Gun the Man Down; 1956; Andrew McLaglen
Gun-Slinger, The; 1958; Roger Corman
Gunfight at Dodge City, The; 1959; Joseph M. Newman
Gunfight at the O K Corral; 1957; John Sturges
Gunfighter, The; 1950; Henry King
Gung Ho; 1943; Ray Enright

Edward Sutherland

Having Wonderful Time; 1938; Alfred Santell

He Laughed Last; 1956; Blake Edwards

He Married His Wife; 1940; Roy del Ruth

He Ran All the Way; 1951; John Berry

He Rides Tall; 1964; R. G. Springsteen

He Walked by Night; 1941; Alfred Werker

He Was Her Man; 1934; Lloyd Bacon

He Who Must Die; 1958; Jules Dassin

Hear Me Good; 1957; Don McGuire

Heart of a Child; 1958; Clive Donner

Heart of New York; 1932; Mervyn Le Roy

Heart of the Matter, The; 1954; George More O'Ferrall

Hearts Divided; 1936; Frank Borzage

Hearts in Dixie; 1929; Paul Sloane

Hearts in Exile; 1929; Michaël Curtiz

Heat Lightning; 1934; Mervyn Le Roy

Heat's On, The; 1943; Gregory Ratoff

Heaven Can Wait; 1943; Ernst Lubitsch

Heaven Knows, Mr. Allison; 1957; John Huston

Heavens Above; 1963; John Boulting and Roy Boulting

Heidi; 1937; Allan Dwan

Heiress, The; 1949; William Wyler

Helen Morgan Story, The; 1957; Michael Curtiz

Helen of Troy; 1955; Robert Wise

Hell and High Water; 1954; Samuel Fuller

Hell Bent for Leather; 1960; George Sherman

Hell Below; 1933; Jack Conway

Hell Below Zero; 1954; Mark Robson

Hell Canyon Outlaws; 1957; Paul Landres

Hell Harbor; 1930; Henry King

Hell in the Pacific; 1968; John Boorman

Hell Is a City; 1959; Val Guest

Hell on Frisco Bay; 1955; Frank Tuttle

Hell Squad; 1958; Burt Topper

Hell to Eternity; 1960; Phil Karlson

Hell's Angels; 1930; Howard Hughes

Hell's Five Hours; 1958; Jack L. Copeland

Hell's Headquarters; 1932; Andrew L. Stone

Hell's Heroes; 1930; William Wyler

Hell's Highway; 1932; Rowland Brown

Hell's Island; 1955; Phil Karlson

Hellbent for Glory; 1958; William Wellman

Helldorado; 1935; James Cruze

Heller in Pink Tights; 1960; George Cukor

Hellfire; 1939; R. G. Springsteen

Hellfire Club; 1963; Monty Berman and Robert S. Baker

Hellgate; 1952; Charles Marquis Warren

Hello Dolly; 1968; Gene Kelly

Hello Out There (Never released); 1949; James Whale

Hellzapoppin; 1942; H. C. Potter

Help; 1965; Richard Lester

Helpmates; 1931; James Parrott

Helter Skelter; 1948; Ralph Thomas

Hemingway's Adventures of a Young Man; 1962; Martin Ritt

Henry V; 1945; Sir Laurence Olivier

Her Cardboard Lover; 1942; George Cukor

Her First Mate; 1933; William Wyler

Her Highness and the Bellboy; 1945; Richard Thorpe

Her Majesty Love; 1931; William Dieterle

Her Man; 1930; Tay Garnett

Her Private Life; 1929; Alexander Korda

Her Sister's Secret; 1946; Edgar G. Ulmer

Here Come the Waves; 1944; Mark Sandrich

Here Comes Mister Jordan; 1941; Alexander Hall

Here Comes the Groom; 1951; Frank Capra

Here Comes the Navy; 1934; Lloyd Bacon

Here I Am a Stranger; 1939; Roy del Ruth

Here Is a Man; 1941; William Dieterle

Here We Go Again; 1942; Allan Dwan

Here We Go Round the Mulberry Bush; 1968; Clive Donner

Heritage of the Desert; 1933; Henry Hathaway

Hero's Island; 1963; Leslie Stevens

Heroes for Sale; 1933; William Wellman

Heroes of Telemark; 1966; Anthony Mann

son
Home Sweet Homicide; 1946; Lloyd Bacon
Homecoming; 1948; Mervyn Le Roy
Homely Girl; 1936; Henry Koster
Homicidal; 1961; William Castle
Hondo; 1953; John Farrow
Honey Pot, The; 1967; Joseph Mankiewicz
Honeymoon; 1947; William Keighley
Honeymoon for Three; 1941; Lloyd Bacon
Honeymoon Limited; 1935; Arthur Lubin
Hong Kong Confidential; 1958; Edward L. Cahn
Honky Tonk; 1941; Jack Conway
Honor Among Lovers; 1931; Dorothy Arzner
Hoodlum Priest, The; 1961; Irvin Kershner
Hoodlum Saint, The; 1946; Norman Taurog
Hook, The; 1963; George Seaton
Horizons West; 1952; Budd Boetticher
Horizontal Lieutenant, The; 1962; Richard Thorpe
Horn Blows at Midnight, The; 1945; Raoul Walsh
Horror of Dracula; 1958; Terence Fisher
Horror of It All; 1964; Terence Fisher
Horse Feathers; 1932; Norman Z. McLeod
Horse Soldiers, The; 1959; John Ford
Horse's Mouth, The; 1958; Ronald Neame
Hostage, The; 1956; Harold Huth
Hostages; 1943; Frank Tuttle
Hot Blood; 1956; Nicholas Ray
Hot Enough for June; 1964; Ralph Thomas
Hot for Paris; 1929; Raoul Walsh
Hot Saturday; 1932; William Seiter
Hot Spell; 1958; Daniel Mann
Hot Rods to Hell; 1967; John Brahm
Hot Steel; 1940; Christy Cabanne
Hot Stuff; 1929; Mervyn Le Roy
Hotel Berlin; 1945; Peter Godfrey
Hotel for Women; 1939; Gregory Ratoff
Hotel Imperial; 1939; Robert Florey
Hotel Paradiso; 1966; Peter Glenville
Hotel Sahara; 1951; Ken Annakin
Hottentot, The; 1929; Roy del Ruth
Hound Dog Man; 1959; Don Siegel
Hound of the Baskervilles; 1939; Sid-

ney Lanfield
Hound of the Baskervilles; 1959; Terence Fisher
Hounded (Johnny Allegro); 1949; Ted Tetzlaff
Hounds of Zaroff, The (Most Dangerous Game, The); 1932; Irving Pichel and Ernest L. Schoesdack ·
Hour Before the Dawn, The; 1943; Frank Tuttle
Hour of the Gun; 1967; John Sturges
House by the River; 1950; Fritz Lang
House Divided, A; 1932; William Wyler
House of a Thousand Candles; 1936; Arthur Lubin
House of Bamboo; 1955; Samuel Fuller
House of Connelly, The; 1934; Henry King
House of Fear, The; 1945; Roy William Neill
House of Horror, The; 1929; Benjamin Christensen
House of Rothschild, The; 1934; Alfred Werker
House of Secrets; 1957; Guy Green
House of Strangers; 1949; Joseph Mankiewicz
House of the Seven Hawks, The; 1959; Richard Thorpe
House of Usher, The; 1961; Roger Corman
House of Wax; 1952; Andre de Toth
House of Women; 1962; Walter Doniger
House on 56th Street; 1933; Robert Florey
House on Haunted Hill, The; 1959; William Castle
House on Telegraph Hill, The; 1951; Robert Wise
House on 92nd Street, The; 1945; Henry Hathaway
Houseboat; 1958; Melville Shavelson
How Green Was My Valley; 1941; John Ford
How I Won the War; 1967; Richard Lester
How the West Was Won; 1963; John Ford, Henry Hathaway, and George Marshall
How to Be Very, Very Popular; 1954; Nunnally Johnson
How to Marry a Millionaire; 1953; Jean Negulesco
How to Murder Your Wife; 1964;

Guillermin

I Wonder Who's Kissing Her Now; 1947; Lloyd Bacon

I'd Climb the Highest Mountain; 1951; Henry King

I'd Rather Be Rich; 1964; Jack Smight

I'll Be Seeing You; 1944; William Dieterle

I'll Be Yours; 1947; William Seiter

I'll Cry Tomorrow; 1956; Daniel Mann

I'll Never Forget What's 'Is Name; 1968; Michael Winner

I'll Never Forget You; 1951; Roy Baker

I'll See You in My Dreams; 1951; Michael Curtiz

I'll Take Sweden; 1965; Frederick de Cordova

I'm All Right Jack; 1960; John Boulting

I'm No Angel; 1933; Wesley Ruggles

I'm Nobody's Sweetheart Now; 1940; Arthur Lubin

I've Always Loved You; 1946; Frank Borzage

Ice Cold in Alex (Desert Attack); 1958; J. Lee Thompson

Ice Follies; 1939; Reinhold Schunzel

Ice Palace; 1960; Vincent Sherman

Ideal Husband, An; 1948; Alexander Korda

Identity Unknown; 1945; Walter Colmes

Identity Unknown; 1960; Frank Marshall

Idiot's Delight; 1939; Clarence Brown

Idol, The; 1966; Daniel Petrie

Idol of the Crowds; 1937; Arthur Lubin

If; 1968; Lindsay Anderson

If a Man Answers; 1962; Henry Levin

If I Had a Million; 1930; James Cruze and H. Bruce Humberstone

If I Were Free; 1933; Elliott Nugent

If I Were King; 1938; Frank Lloyd

If You Knew Susie; 1948; Gordon Douglas

Illustrated Man, The; 1968; Jack Smight

Imitation of Life; 1934; John Stahl

Imitation of Life; 1959; Douglas Sirk

Immortal Land, The; 1958; Basil Wright

Immortal Sergeant; 1943; John Stahl

Immortal Story, The; 1968; Orson Welles

Impact; 1949; Arthur Lubin

Impatient Maiden; 1932; James Whale

Imperfect Lady; 1947; Lewis Allen

Importance of Being Earnest, The; 1952; Anthony Asquith

Imposter, The (Strange Confession); 1943; Julien Duvivier

In a Lonely Place; 1950; Nicholas Ray

In Caliente; 1935; Lloyd Bacon

In Cold Blood; 1967; Richard Brooks

In Harm's Way; 1964; Otto Preminger

In Love and War; 1958; Philip Dunne

In Name Only; 1939; John Cromwell

In Old Arizona; 1929; Raoul Walsh and Irving Cummings

In Old California; 1942; William McGann

In Old Chicago; 1938; Henry King

In Old Kentucky; 1935; George Marshall

In Our Time; 1944; Vincent Sherman

In Search of the Castaways; 1961; Robert Stevenson

In the Cool of the Day; 1963; Robert Stevens

In the French Style; 1963; Robert Parrish

In the Good Old Summertime; 1949; Robert Z. Leonard

In the Heat of the Night; 1967; Norman Jewison

In the Meantime Darling; 1944; Otto Preminger

In This Our Life; 1942; John Huston

In Which We Serve; 1942; Noel Coward and David Lean

Incendiary Blonde; 1945; George Marshall

Incident at Phantom Hill; 1966; Earl Bellamy

Incredible Shrinking Man; 1957; Jack Arnold

Incredibly Strange Creatures Who Stopped Living and Became Zombies, The; 1962; Ray Dennis Stecker

Indian Fighter, The; 1955; Andre de Toth

Indiscreet; 1931; Leo McCarey

Indiscreet; 1958; Stanley Donen

Inferno; 1952; Roy Baker

Informer, The; 1935; John Ford

Inherit the Wind; 1960; Stanley Kramer

Inn of the Sixth Happiness, The; 1958; Mark Robson

Innocent Eye, The (Short); 1958; John Schlesinger

Brown and Don Hartman
It's a Date; 1940; William Seiter
It's a Great Feeling; 1949; David Butler
It's a Mad, Mad, Mad, Mad World; 1963; Stanley Kramer
It's a Wonderful Life; 1946; Frank Capra
It's a Wonderful World; 1939; W. S. van Dyke
It's All Yours; 1938; Elliott Nugent
It's Always Fair Weather; 1955; Gene Kelly and Stanley Donen
It's in the Bag; 1944; Richard Wallace
It's Love I'm After; 1937; Archie Mayo
It's Only Money; 1962; Frank Tashlin
Ivanhoe; 1952; Richard Thorpe
Ivy; 1947; Sam Wood

Jack London; 1942; Alfred Santell
Jack the Ripper; 1959; Robert S. Baker and Monty Berman
Jackpot, The; 1950; Walter Lang
Jacqueline; 1956; Roy Baker
Jailhouse Rock; 1957; Richard Thorpe
Jalna; 1935; John Cromwell
Jammin' the Blues; 1945; Gjon Mili
Jamaica Inn; 1939; Alfred Hitchcock
Jane Eyre; 1944; Robert Stevenson
Janie; 1944; Michael Curtiz
Japanese War Bride; 1952; King Vidor
Jazz Singer, The; 1952; Michael Curtiz
Jazzboat; 1960; Kenneth Hughes
Jealousy; 1929; Jean De Limur
Jealousy; 1945; Gustav Machaty
Jeanne Eagels; 1957; George Sidney
Jeopardy; 1953; John Sturges
Jericho (Dark Sands); 1937; Thornton Freeland
Jesse James; 1939; Henry King
Jessica; 1962; Jean Negulesco
Jet over the Atlantic; 1959; Byron Haskin
Jet Pilot; 1957; Josef von Sternberg
Jewel Robbery; 1932; William Dieterle
Jezebel; 1938; William Wyler
Jigsaw; 1962; Val Guest
Jim Thorpe—All American; 1951; Michael Curtiz
Jimmy, The Gent; 1934; Michael Curtiz
Jitterbugs; 1943; Malcolm St. Clair
Jive Junction; 1943; Edgar G. Ulmer
Joan of Arc; 1948; Victor Fleming

Joan of Paris; 1942; Robert Stevenson
Joe Dakota; 1957; Richard Basehart
Joe Macbeth; 1955; Kenneth Hughes
John Goldfarb, Please Come Home; 1964; J. Lee Thompson
John Meade's Woman; 1936; Richard Wallace
John Paul Jones; 1959; John Farrow
Johnny Allegro (Hounded); 1949; Ted Tetzlaff
Johnny Angel; 1945; Edwin L. Marin
Johnny Apollo; 1940; Henry Hathaway
Johnny Belinda; 1948; Jean Negulesco
Johnny Concho; 1956; Don McGuire
Johnny Cool; 1964; William Asher
Johnny Come Lately; 1943; William K. Howard
Johnny Eager; 1942; Mervyn Le Roy
Johnny Guitar; 1954; Nicholas Ray
Johnny Norse; 1964; Don Siegel
Johnny O'Clock; 1947; Robert Rossen
Johnny One-Eye; 1950; Robert Florey
Johnny Stool Pigeon; 1949; William Castle
Johnny Tiger; 1966; Paul Wendkos
Joker Is Wild, The; 1958; Charles Vidor
Jokers, The; 1967; Michael Winner
Jolly Bad Fellow, A; 1964; Don Chaffey
Jolson Sings Again; 1950; Henry Levin
Jolson Story, The; 1946; Alfred E. Green
Josephine and Men; 1955; Roy Boulting
Josette; 1938; Allan Dwan
Journal of a Crime; 1934; William Keighley
Journey, The; 1959; Anatole Litvak
Journey for Margaret; 1942; W. S. van Dyke
Journey into Fear (Signed N. Foster); 1942; Orson Welles
Journey into Light; 1951; Stuart Heisler
Journey to the Lost City; 1960; Fritz Lang
Journey's End; 1930; James Whale
Joy House; 1964; René Clement
Joy of Living; 1938; Tay Garnett
Juarez; 1939; William Dieterle
Jubal; 1956; Delmer Daves
Judge Priest; 1934; John Ford
Judgement at Nuremberg; 1961; Stanley Kramer

Lorna Doone; 1951; Phil Karlson
Loss of Innocence; 1961; Lewis Gilbert
Lost Angel; 1944; Roy Rowland
Lost Boundaries; 1949; Alfred Werker
Lost Command; 1966; Mark Robson
Lost Horizon; 1937; Frank Capra
Lost Lady, The; 1932; William Wellman
Lost Moment, The; 1947; Martin Gabel
Lost Patrol, The; 1934; John Ford
Lost Squadron, The; 1932; George Archainbaud
Lost Weekend, The; 1945; Billy Wilder
Lost World, The; 1960; Irwin Allen
Lottery Bride, The; 1930; Paul Stein
Louisiana; 1947; Phil Karlson
Louisiana Story; 1948; Robert Flaherty
Lovable Cheat, The; 1949; Richard Oswald
Love Affair; 1932; Thornton Freeland
Love Affair; 1939; Leo McCarey
Love and the Devil; 1929; Alexander Korda
Love Before Breakfast; 1936; Walter Lang
Love Crazy; 1941; Jack Conway
Love Happy; 1949; David Miller
Love Has Many Faces; 1964; Alexander Singer
Love in Bloom; 1935; Elliott Nugent
Love in Las Vegas (Viva Las Vegas); 1964; George Sidney
Love in the Afternoon; 1957; Billy Wilder
Love Is a Ball; 1963; David Swift
Love Is a Many Splendored Thing; 1955; Henry King
Love Is a Racket; 1932; William Wellman
Love Is Better Than Ever; 1952; Stanley Donen
Love Is Dangerous; 1933; Richard Thorpe
Love Is Like That; 1933; Richard Thorpe
Love Is News; 1937; Tay Garnett
Love Letters; 1945; William Dieterle
Love Live and Laugh; 1929; William K. Howard
Love Me Forever; 1935; Victor Schertzinger
Love Me or Leave Me; 1934; Charles Vidor
Love Me or Leave Me; 1955; Charles Vidor
Love Me Tender; 1956; Robert D. Webb
Love Me Tonight; 1932; Rouben Mamoulian
Love Nest; 1951; Joseph M. Newman
Love on the Dole; 1940; John Baxter
Love on the Run; 1936; W. S. van Dyke
Love Parade, The; 1929; Ernst Lubitsch
Love Racket, The; 1930; William Seiter
Love Slaves of the Amazon; 1957; Curt Siodmak
Love Trap; 1929; William Wyler
Love Under Fire; 1937; George Marshall
Love with a Proper Stranger; 1963; Robert Mulligan
Loved One, The; 1964; Tony Richardson
Lovely to Look At; 1952; Mervyn Le Roy
Lover Come Back; 1961; Delbert Mann
Lovers, Happy Lovers; 1954; René Clement
Lovers and Lollipops; 1955; Engel Morris and Ruth Orkin
Loves of a Dictator, The; 1935; Victor Saville
Loves of Carmen, The; 1948; Charles Vidor
Lure of the Wilderness; 1952; Jean Negulesco
Luck of Ginger Coffey, The; 1963; Irvin Kershner
Lucky Cisco Kid; 1940; H. Bruce Humberstone
Lucky Ghost; 1941; Jed Buell
Lucky Jim; 1957; John Boulting and Roy Boulting
Lucky Jordan; 1942; Frank Tuttle
Lucky Me; 1954; Jack Donahue
Lucky Nick Cain; 1951; Joseph M. Newman
Lucky Partners; 1940; Lewis Milestone
Lucky Star; 1929; Frank Borzage
Lucretia Borgia; 1935; Abel Gance
Lucy Gallant; 1955; Robert Parrish
Lullaby of Broadway; 1951; David Butler
Lure of the Swamp; 1957; Hubert Cornfield

Me and My Gal; 1932; Raoul Walsh

Me and the Colonel; 1958; Peter Glenville

Meet Boston Blackie; 1941; Robert Florey

Meet Danny Wilson; 1951; Joseph Pevney

Meet John Doe; 1941; Frank Capra

Meet Me at Dawn; 1947; Thornton Freeland

Meet Me at the Fair; 1952; Douglas Sirk

Meet Me in St. Louis; 1944; Vincente Minnelli

Meet Nero Wolfe; 1936; Herbert Biberman

Meet the Missus; 1940; Malcolm St. Clair

Meet the Stewarts; 1942; Alfred E. Green

Meet the Wildcat; 1940; Arthur Lubin

Melancholy Dame; 1929; Octavius Roy Cohen

Melba; 1953; Lewis Milestone

Member of the Wedding, The; 1952; Fred Zinnemann

Memory for Two; 1946; Del Lord

Memphis Belle, The (Doc); 1943; William Wyler

Men, The; 1950; Fred Zinnemann

Men Are Not Gods; 1937; Walter Reisch

Men Are Such Fools; 1938; Busby Berkeley

Men in Exile; 1937; John Farrow

Men in War; 1957; Anthony Mann

Men in White; 1934; Richard Boleslavsky

Men O'War (Short); 1929; Lewis R. Foster

Men of Destiny; 1942; Ray Enright

Men on Her Mind; 1935; William Dieterle

Men with Wings; 1938; William Wellman

Men Without Law; 1937; Lewis Seiler

Men Without Women; 1930; John Ford

Merely Mary Ann; 1931; Henry King

Merrill's Marauders; 1962; Samuel Fuller

Merrily We Go to Hell; 1932; Dorothy Arzner

Merrily We Live; 1938; Norman Z. McLeod

Merry Andrew; 1957; Michael Kidd

Merry Widow, The; 1934; Ernst Lubitsch

Message to Garcia; 1935; George Marshall

Mexicans; 1945; Alfred Santell

Miami Exposé; 1956; Fred F. Sears

Mickey One; 1965; Arthur Penn

Mickey the Kid; 1939; Arthur Lubin

Middle of the Night; 1959; Delbert Mann

Midnight; 1934; Chester Erskine

Midnight; 1939; Mitchell Leisen

Midnight Alibi; 1934; Alan Crosland

Midnight Intruder; 1937; Arthur Lubin

Midnight Lace; 1960; David Miller

Midnight Lady; 1932; Richard Thorpe

Midnight Mary; 1933; William Wellman

Midshipman Easy; 1936; Carol Reed

Midsummer Night's Dream, A; 1935; William Dieterle and Max Reinhardt

Mighty Barnum, The; 1936; Walter Lang

Mighty Joe Young; 1949; Merian C. Cooper and Ernest L. Schoesdack

Mikado, The; 1939; Victor Schertzinger

Mildred Pierce; 1945; Michael Curtiz

Milky Way, The; 1936; Leo McCarey

Million Dollar Legs; 1932; Eddie Cline

Million Dollar Mermaid; 1952; Mervyn Le Roy

Millionairess, The; 1960; Anthony Asquith

Min and Bill; 1930; George Roy Hill

Mind Benders, The; 1963; Basil Dearden

Mind Reader; 1933; Roy del Ruth

Mine Own Executioner; 1947; Anthony Kimmins

Ministry of Fear; 1945; Fritz Lang

Miniver Story, The; 1950; H. C. Potter

Minstrel Man; 1944; Joseph H. Lewis

Miracle, The; 1959; Irving Rapper

Miracle at Morgan's Creek, The; 1944; Preston Sturges

Miracle in Soho; 1957; Julian Amyes

Miracle in the Rain; 1955; Rudolph Mate

Miracle of Our Lady of Fatima, The; 1952; John Brahm

Miracle of the Bells, The; 1948; Irving Pichel

Miracle on 34th Street; 1947; George

Nutty Professor, The; 1963; Jerry Lewis

O Dreamland (Short); 1953; Lindsay Anderson

O. Henry's Full House; 1952; Howard Hawks and Henry King

O'er Hill and Dale; 1931; Basil Wright

O'Shaughnessy's Boy; 1935; Richard Boleslavsky

Objective Burma; 1945; Raoul Walsh

Obliging Young Lady; 1942; Richard Wallace

Obsession; 1934; Maurice Tourneur

Ocean's Eleven; 1960; Lewis Milestone

October Man, The; 1947; Roy Baker

Odd Man Out; 1947; Carol Reed

Odds Against Tomorrow; 1959; Robert Wise

Odette; 1950; Herbert Wilcox

Of Human Bondage; 1934; John Cromwell

Of Human Bondage; 1946; Edmund Goulding

Of Human Bondage; 1963; Kenneth Hughes

Of Human Hearts; 1938; Clarence Brown

Of Mice and Men; 1940; Lewis Milestone

Offbeat; 1960; Cliff Owen

Officer O'Brien; 1930; Tay Garnett

Oh, For a Man; 1930; Hamilton MacFadden

Oh Men, Oh Women; 1957; Nunnally Johnson

Oh, Mister Porter; 1939; Max Varnel

Oh Yeah; 1929; Tay Garnett

Oil for the Lamps of China; 1935; Mervyn Le Roy

OK Roberta; 1934; William Seiter

Okay America; 1932; Tay Garnett

Oklahoma; 1955; Fred Zinnemann

Oklahoma Kid; 1939; Lloyd Bacon

Old Acquaintance; 1943; Vincent Sherman

Old Bones of the River; 1939; Max Varnel

Old Dark House, The; 1932; James Whale

Old Dark House, The; 1963; William Castle

Old Maid, The; 1939; Edmund Goulding

Old Man and the Sea, The; 1958; John Sturges

Old Yeller; 1957; Robert Stevenson

Oliver; 1968; Carol Reed

Oliver Twist; 1951; David Lean

Olsen's Big Moment; 1934; Malcolm St. Clair

Omar Khayyam; 1957; William Dieterle

On Approval; 1944; Clive Brook

On Borrowed Time; 1939; Harold S. Bucquet

On Dangerous Ground; 1951; Nicholas Ray

On Moonlight Bay; 1951; Roy del Ruth

On Our Merry Way; 1947; King Vidor

On the Avenue; 1936; Roy del Ruth

On the Beach; 1959; Stanley Kramer

On the Night of the Fire; 1939; Brian D. Hurst

On the Riviera; 1951; Walter Lang

On the Run; 1963; Robert Tronson

On the Sunny Side; 1942; Harold Schuster

On the Sunny Side of the Street; 1951; Richard Quine

On the Threshhold of Space; 1956; Robert D. Webb

On the Town; 1949; Stanley Donen and Gene Kelly

On the Waterfront; 1954; Elia Kazan

On Velvet; 1938; Widgey Newman

On with the Show; 1929; Alan Crosland

On Your Toes; 1939; Ray Enright

Once a Gentleman; 1930; James Cruze

Once a Thief; 1965; Ralph Nelson

Once in a Blue Moon; 1935; Ben Hecht

Once in a Lifetime; 1932; Russell Mack

Once More with Feeling; 1960; Stanley Donen

Once More, My Darling; 1949; Robert Montgomery

Once upon a Honeymoon; 1942; Leo McCarey

Once upon a Time; 1944; Alexander Hall

One Crowded Night; 1940; Irving Reis

One Desire; 1955; Jerry Hopper

One Foot in Heaven; 1941; Irving Rapper

One Foot in Hell; 1960; James B. Clark

One Hour with You; 1932; George Cukor and Ernst Lubitsch

One Hundred Men and a Girl; 1937;

Over Twenty-One; 1945; Charles Vidor

Overland Stage Riders; 1938; George Sherman

Overlanders, The; 1946; Harry Watt

Ox Bow Incident (Strange Incident); 1943; William Wellman

Pacific Rendezvous; 1942; George Sidney

Pack Up Your Troubles; 1932; George Marshall

Pack Up Your Troubles; 1939; H. Bruce Humberstone

Pagan, The; 1929; W. S. van Dyke

Pagan Love Song; 1950; Robert Alton

Page Miss Glory; 1935; Mervyn Le Roy

Paid; 1930; Sam Wood

Paid in Full; 1950; William Dieterle

Painted Lady, The; 1931; Howard Higgin

Painted Veil, The; 1934; Richard Boleslavsky and W. S. van Dyke

Pajama Game, The; 1957; George Abbott and Stanley Donen

Pal Joey; 1957; George Sidney

Paleface, The; 1948; Norman Z. McLeod

Palm Beach Story, The; 1942; Preston Sturges

Palm Springs Weekend; 1963; Norman Taurog

Palmy Days; 1931; Edward Sutherland

Panama Hattie; 1943; Norman Z. McLeod

Pandora and the Flying Dutchman; 1951; Albert Lewin

Panic Button; 1964; George Sherman

Panic in the Parlor; 1957; Gordon Parry

Panic in the Streets; 1950; Elia Kazan

Panic in the Year Zero; 1962; Ray Milland

Panthers Moon; 1950; George Sherman

Parachute Jumper; 1933; Alfred S. Green

Paradine Case, The; 1947; Alfred Hitchcock

Paradise in Harlem; 1939; Joseph Seiden

Paramount on Parade; 1930; Dorothy Arzner and Otto Brower

Paratrooper, The (Red Beret); 1954; Terence Young

Pardners; 1956; Norman Taurog

Pardon Us; 1931; James Parrott

Paris Bound; 1929; Edward H. Griffith

Paris Blues; 1961; Martin Ritt

Paris Does Strange Things; 1957; Jean Renoir

Paris Holiday; 1958; Gerd Oswald

Paris Honeymoon; 1939; Frank Tuttle

Paris in Spring; 1935; Lewis Milestone

Paris Underground; 1946; Gregory Ratoff

Paris When It Sizzles; 1963; Richard Quine

Park Row; 1952; Samuel Fuller

Parnell; 1937; John Stahl

Parole Fixer; 1940; Robert Florey

Parrish; 1961; Delmer Daves

Part Time Wife; 1930; Leo McCarey

Party, The; 1968; Blake Edwards

Party Girl; 1958; Nicholas Ray

Party's Over, The; 1963; Guy Hamilton

Passage to Marseilles; 1944; Michael Curtiz

Passion; 1954; Allan Dwan

Passport to Hell, A; 1932; Frank Lloyd

Passport to Pimlico; 1948; Henry Cornelius

Password Is Courage, The; 1962; Andrew L. Stone

Pat and Mike; 1952; George Cukor

Patch of Blue, A; 1965; Guy Green

Paths of Glory; 1957; Stanley Kubrick

Patsy, The; 1964; Jerry Lewis

Patterns; 1956; Fielder Cook

Pawnbroker, The; 1965; Sidney Lumet

Pay or Die; 1960; Richard Wilson

Payment on Demand; 1951; Curtis Bernhardt

Pay-Off, The; 1935; Robert Florey

Payroll; 1961; Sidney Hayers

Peace of Britain (Doc); 1936; Paul Rotha

Pearl of the South Pacific; 1955; Allan Dwan

Peeper, The (Peeping Tom); 1960; Michael Powell

Peer Gynt; 1941; David Bradley

Peking Express; 1951; William Dieterle

Penitentiary; 1938; John Brahm

Pennies from Heaven; 1937; Norman Z. McLeod

Penny Paradise; 1938; Carol Reed

Penny Princess; 1951; Val Guest

Penny Serenade; 1941; George Stevens

Penrod and Sam; 1937; William McGann

Penthouse; 1933; W. S. van Dyke

People Against O'Hara, The; 1951; John Sturges

People Will Talk; 1935; Alfred Santell

People Will Talk; 1951; Joseph Mankiewicz

Pepe; 1960; George Sidney

Perfect Day (Short); 1929; James Parrott

Perfect Furlough, The; 1958; Blake Edwards

Perfect Marriage, The; 1946; Lewis Allen

Perfect Specimen, The; 1937; Michael Curtiz

Perfect Strangers; 1950; Bretaigne Windust

Perfect Understanding; 1933; Cyril Gardner

Perilous Journey, A; 1953; R. G. Springsteen

Perils of Pauline; 1947; George Marshall

Personal Column (Lured); 1947; Douglas Sirk

Personal Property; 1937; W. S. van Dyke

Pete Kelly's Blues; 1955; Jack Webb

Peter; 1935; Henry Koster

Peter Ibbetson; 1935; Henry Hathaway

Petrified Forest, The; 1936; Archie Mayo

Petulia; 1968; Richard Lester

Petty Girl; 1950; Henry Levin

Peyton Place; 1957; Mark Robson

Phaedra; 1962; Jules Dassin

Phantom Killers, The; 1943; William Beaudine

Phantom Lady; 1944; Robert Siodmak

Phantom of the Opera, The; 1943; Arthur Lubin

Phantom of the Opera, The; 1954; Roy del Ruth

Phantom of the Opera, The; 1962; Terence Fisher

Phantom of the Rue Morgue; 1954; Roy del Ruth

Phantom Riders; 1940; Jacques Tourneur

Phenix City Story, The; 1955; Phil Karlson

Phffft; 1954; Mark Robson

Philadelphia Story, The; 1940; George Cukor

Phone Call from a Stranger; 1952; Jean Negulesco

Piccadilly; 1929; E. A. Dupont

Piccadilly Incident; 1946; Herbert Wilcox

Pickup; 1951; Hugo Haas

Pickup on South Street; 1953; Samuel Fuller

Picnic; 1956; Joshua Logan

Picture of Dorian Gray, The; 1945; Albert Lewin

Picture Snatcher; 1933; Lloyd Bacon

Pied Piper, The; 1942; Irving Pichel

Pied Piper of Hamelin, The; 1959; Bretaigne Windust

Pieges; 1939; Robert Siodmak

Pigeon That Took Rome, The; 1962; Melville Shavelson

Pigskin Parade; 1936; David Butler

Pilgrimage; 1933; John Ford

Pillow Talk; 1958; Michael Gordon

Pilot No. 5; 1943; George Sidney

Pimpernel Smith; 1942; Leslie Howard

Pin-Up Girl; 1944; H. Bruce Humberstone

Pink Panther, The; 1964; Blake Edwards

Pink String and Sealing Wax; 1945; Robert Hamer

Pinky; 1949; Elia Kazan

Pirate, The; 1948; Vincente Minnelli

Pirates of Capri, The; 1949; Edgar G. Ulmer

Pirates of Tortuga, The; 1961; Robert D. Webb

Pit and the Pendulum, The; 1961; Roger Corman

Pitfall, The; 1948; Andre de Toth

Pittsburgh Kid, The; 1942; Jack Townley

Place in the Sun, A; 1951; George Stevens

Place to Live, A (Doc); 1941; Irving Lerner

Plainsman, The; 1936; Cecil B. de Mille

Planter's Wife, The; 1952; Ken Annakin

Platinum Blonde; 1931; Frank Capra

Platinum High School (Trouble at 16); 1960; Albert Zugsmith

Play Dirty; 1968; Andre de Toth

Play It Cool; 1962; Michael Winner

Planet of the Apes; 1968; Franklin Schaffner

Playboy of the Western World, The; 1962; Brian D. Hurst

Playing Around; 1930; Mervyn Le Roy

Please Believe Me; 1950; Norman Taurog

Please Don't Eat the Daisies; 1960; Charles Walters

Pleasure Cruise; 1933; Frank Tuttle

Pleasure Garden, The; 1954; James Broughton

Pleasure of His Company, The; 1961; George Seaton

Pleasure Seekers, The; 1964; Jean Negulesco

Plough and the Stars, The; 1936; John Ford

Plunder of the Sun; 1953; John Farrow

Plunder Road; 1957; Hubert Cornfield

Plymouth Adventure; 1952; Clarence Brown

Pocketful of Miracles; 1961; Frank Capra

Poe's Tales of Terror; 1962; Roger Corman

Point Blank; 1967; John Boorman

Pointed Heels; 1929; Edward Sutherland

Police Dog; 1955; Derek Twist

Polly of the Circus; 1932; Alfred Santell

Pollyanna; 1960; David Swift

Pony Express; 1953; Jerry Hopper

Pony Soldier; 1952; Joseph M. Newman

Pool of London; 1950; Basil Dearden

Poppy; 1936; Edward Sutherland

Poppy Is Also a Flower, The; 1966; Terence Young

Porgy and Bess; 1959; Otto Preminger

Pork Chop Hill; 1959; Lewis Milestone

Port Afrique; 1956; Rudolph Mate

Port of New York; 1949; Laslo Benedek

Port of Seven Seas; 1938; James Whale

Portrait in Black; 1960; Michael Gordon

Portrait of a Mobster; 1961; Joseph Pevney

Portrait of Jason; 1967; Shirley Clarke

Portrait of Jennie; 1947; William Dieterle

Possessed; 1931; Clarence Brown

Possessed; 1947; Curtis Bernhardt

Postman Always Rings Twice, The;

1946; Tay Garnett

Pot Carriers, The; 1962; Peter Graham Scott

Power, The; 1968; Byron Haskin and George Pal

Powder River; 1953; Louis King

Power and the Glory; 1933; William K. Howard

Practically Yours; 1944; Mitchell Leisen

Prelude to War (Doc); 1942; Frank Capra

Premature Burial, The; 1961; Roger Corman

Presenting Lily Mars; 1943; Norman Taurog

President Vanishes, The; 1934; William Wellman

President's Analyst, The; 1967; Theodore J. Flicker

Pressure Point; 1962; Hubert Cornfield

Prestige; 1932; Tay Garnett

Pretty Baby; 1950; Bretaigne Windust

Preview Murder Mystery; 1936; Robert Florey

Price of Fear, The; 1956; Abner Biberman

Pride and Prejudice; 1940; Robert Z. Leonard

Pride and the Passion, The; 1957; Stanley Kramer

Pride of the Bowery; 1941; Joseph H. Lewis

Pride of the Marines; 1945; Delmer Daves

Pride of the Yankees; 1942; Sam Wood

Prime Minister, The; 1941; Thorold Dickinson

Primrose Path; 1940; Gregory La Cava

Prince and the Pauper, The; 1937; William Keighley

Prince and the Showgirl, The; 1957; Sir Laurence Olivier

Prince of Foxes; 1949; Henry King

Prince of Players; 1955; Philip Dunne

Prince Valiant; 1954; Henry Hathaway

Prince Who Was a Thief; 1951; Rudolph Mate

Princess and the Pirate, The; 1944; David Butler

Princess and the Plumber, The; 1930; Alexander Korda

Princess Comes Across; 1937; William K. Howard

Quiet Man, The; 1952; John Ford
Quick Millions; 1931; Rowland Brown
Quick Millions; 1939; Malcolm St. Clair
Quiet One, The; 1948; Sidney Meyers
Quiller Memorandum, The; 1966; Michael Anderson
Quitter, The; 1934; Richard Thorpe
Quo Vadis; 1951; Mervyn Le Roy

Rabbit Trap, The; 1958; Philip Leacock
Rabbit, Run; 1969; Jack Smight
Racers, The; 1955; Henry Hathaway
Rack, The; 1956; Arnold Laven
Racket, The; 1951; John Cromwell
Racket Busters; 1938; Lloyd Bacon
Racetrack; 1933; James Cruze
Raffles; 1930; Harry D'Arrast and George Fitzmaurice
Raffles; 1939; Sam Wood
Rafter Romance; 1934; William Seiter
Rage in Heaven; 1941; W. S. van Dyke
Rage of Paris, The; 1938; Henry Koster
Raging Sea, The; 1969; Cornell Wilde
Raid, The; 1954; Hugo Fregonese
Railroaded; 1947; Anthony Mann
Rain; 1932; Lewis Milestone
Rain People, The; 1969; Francis Ford Coppola
Rain or Shine; 1930; Frank Capra
Rainbow Jacket, The; 1954; Basil Dearden
Rainbow on the River; 1936; Kurt Neumann
Rainbow over Broadway; 1933; Richard Thorpe
Rainbow Round My Shoulder; 1952; Richard Quine
Rainmaker, The; 1956; Joseph Anthony
Rains Came, The; 1939; Clarence Brown
Rains of Ranchipur, The; 1955; Jean Negulesco
Raintree County; 1957; Edward Dmytryk
Raisin in the Sun, A; 1961; Daniel Petrie
Rally Round the Flag Boys; 1958; Leo McCarey
Ramona; 1936; Henry King
Rampage; 1963; Phil Karlson
Rancho Notorious; 1952; Fritz Lang
Random Harvest; 1942; Mervyn Le Roy

Rango; 1931; Ernest L. Schoesdack
Ransom; 1956; Alex Segal
Rapture; 1965; John Guillermin
Rare Breed, The; 1965; Andrew McLaglen
Rasputin and the Empress; 1932; Richard Boleslavsky
Rat Race, The; 1960; Robert Mulligan
Raven, The; 1935; Louis Friedlander
Raven, The; 1963; Roger Corman
Raw Deal; 1948; Anthony Mann
Raw Wind in Eden; 1958; Richard Wilson
Rawhide (Desperate Siege); 1951; Henry Hathaway
Rawhide Years, The; 1956; Rudolph Mate
Razor's Edge, The; 1946; Edmund Goulding
Reach for Glory; 1963; Philip Leacock
Reach for the Sky; 1956; Lewis Gilbert
Reaching for the Moon; 1930; Edmund Goulding
Reaching for the Sun; 1940; William Wellman
Ready for the People; 1964; Buzz Kulik
Real Glory, The; 1939; Henry Hathaway
Reap the Wild Wind; 1942; Cecil B. de Mille
Rear Window; 1954; Alfred Hitchcock
Rebecca; 1940; Alfred Hitchcock
Rebecca of Sunnybrook Farm; 1932; Alfred Santell
Rebecca of Sunnybrook Farm; 1938; Allan Dwan
Rebel in the Ring; 1964; Jay O. Lawrence
Rebel Without a Cause; 1955; Nicholas Ray
Reckless; 1935; Victor Fleming
Reckless Moment; 1949; Max Ophuls
Recoil; 1963; Paul Wendkos
Red Badge of Courage, The; 1951; John Huston
Red Ball Express; 1952; Budd Boetticher
Red Beret (The Paratrooper); 1954; Terence Young
Red Danube, The; 1949; George Sidney
Red Dust; 1932; Victor Fleming
Red Garters; 1954; George Marshall
Red Headed Woman; 1932; Jack Conway

Right to Live; 1935; William Keighley

Right to Romance; 1933; Alfred Santell

Ring of Spies; 1964; Robert Tronson

Ring of Steel (Doc); 1942; Garson Kanin

Ringer, The; 1952; Guy Hamilton

Rings on Her Fingers; 1942; Rouben Mamoulian

Rio; 1939; John Brahm

Rio Bravo; 1959; Howard Hawks

Rio Conchos; 1964; Gordon Douglas

Rio Grande; 1950; John Ford

Rio Rita; 1942; S. Sylvan Simon

Riot, The; 1969; Buzz Kulik

Riot in Cell Block 11; 1954; Don Siegel

Riptide; 1934; Edmund Goulding

Rise and Fall of Legs Diamond, The; 1960; Budd Boetticher

Rise and Shine; 1941; Allan Dwan

Rising of the Moon, The; 1957; John Ford

Risk, The; 1961; John Boulting and Roy Boulting

Risky Business; 1939; Arthur Lubin

River, The; 1929; Frank Borzage

River, The (Doc); 1938; Pare Lorentz

The River; 1951; Jean Renoir

River Beat; 1953; Guy Green

River of No Return; 1954; Otto Preminger

River's Edge, The; 1957; Allan Dwan

River's End; 1931; Michael Curtiz

Road Back, The; 1937; James Whale

Road House; 1948; Jean Negulesco

Road Show; 1941; Gordon Douglas

Road to Bali, The; 1953; Hal Walter

Road to Glory, The; 1936; Howard Hawks

Road to Hollywood, The; 1933; Bud Pollard

Road to Hong Kong, The; 1962; Norman Panama

Road to Rio; 1948; Norman Z. McLeod

Road to Singapore, The; 1940; Victor Schertzinger

Road to Utopia; 1946; Hal Walker

Road to Zanzibar; 1941; Victor Schertzinger

Roaring Twenties, The; 1939; Raoul Walsh

Robbery Under Arms; 1957; Jack Lee

Robe, The; 1953; Henry Koster

Roberta; 1935; William D. Seiter

Robin and the Seven Hoods; 1964; Gordon Douglas

Robin Hood of El Dorado; 1935; William Wellman

Robinson Crusoe; 1953; Luis Buñuel

Robinson Crusoe on Mars; 1964; Byron Haskin

Rock-A-Bye Baby; 1958; Frank Tashlin

Rockabye; 1932; George Cukor

Rocketship XM; 1950; Kurt Neumann

Rocky; 1948; Phil Karlson

Rocky Mountain; 1950; William Keighley

Rogue Song, The; 1930; Lionel Barrymore

Roger Touhy, Gangster; 1944; Robert Florey

Rogues of Sherwood Forest; 1950; Gordon Douglas

Roman Holiday; 1953; William Wyler

Roman Scandals; 1933; Frank Tuttle

Roman Spring of Mrs. Stone; 1961; J. Quintero

Romance; 1930; Clarence Brown

Romance and Riches; 1937; Alfred Zeisler

Romance of Rosy Ridge; 1947; Roy Rowland

Romance on the High Seas; 1948; Michael Curtiz

Romanoff and Juliet; 1961; Peter Ustinov

Rome Adventure; 1962; Delmer Daves

Rome Express; 1932; Walter Forde

Romeo and Juliet; 1936; George Cukor

Rookery Nook; 1930; Herbert Wilcox

Room at the Top; 1958; Jack Clayton

Room for One More (The Easy Way); 1952; Norman Taurog

Room Service; 1938; William Seiter

Rooney; 1958; George Pollock

Roots of Heaven, The; 1958; John Huston

Rope; 1948; Alfred Hitchcock

Rope of Sand; 1949; William Dieterle

Rosalie; 1937; W. S. van Dyke

Rose Marie; 1936; W. S. van Dyke

Rose of Washington Square; 1939; Gregory Ratoff

Rose Tattoo, The; 1954; Daniel Mann

Roseanna McCoy; 1949; Irving Reis

Rose Marie; 1936; W. S. van Dyke

Rosemarie; 1954; Mervyn Le Roy

Rosemary's Baby; 1968; Roman Polanski

Saturday Night Out; 1963; Robert Hartford-Davis
Saturday's Children; 1929; Gregory La Cava
Saturday's Children; 1940; Vincent Sherman
Saturday's Hero; 1951; David Miller
Savage Innocents, The; 1961; Nicholas Ray
Savage Sam; 1963; Norman Tokar
Saxon Charm, The; 1948; Claude Binyon
Say It in French; 1938; Andrew L. Stone
Say One for Me; 1959; Frank Tashlin
Sayonara; 1957; Joshua Logan
Scandal in Paris, A; 1946; Douglas Sirk
Scandal Sheet; 1931; John Cromwell
Scandal Sheet; 1952; Phil Karlson
Scapegoat, The; 1958; Robert Hamer
Scaramouche; 1952; George Sidney
Scared Stiff; 1953; George Marshall
Scarface; 1932; Howard Hawks
Scarlet Clue, The; 1945; Phil Rosen
Scarlet Coat, The; 1955; John Sturges
Scarlet Dawn; 1932; William Dieterle
Scarlet Empress; 1934; Josef von Sternberg
Scarlet Hour, The; 1956; Michael Curtiz
Scarlet Pimpernel, The; 1933; Harold Young
Scarlet Street; 1945; Fritz Lang
Scavengers, The; 1959; John Cromwell
Scene of the Crime; 1949; Roy Rowland
Scent of Mystery; 1960; Jack Cardiff
School for Scoundrels; 1960; Robert Hamer
School for Secrets; 1946; Peter Ustinov
Scorpio Rising; 1966; Kenneth Anger
Scotland Yard; 1941; Norman Foster
Scotland Yard; 1930; William K. Howard
Scotland Yard Triumphs (One Epis); 1964; Clive Donner
Scoundrel, The; 1935; Charles MacArthur and Ben Hecht
Scream of Fear; 1961; Seth Holt
Screaming Mimi; 1958; Gerd Oswald
Scrooge; 1935; John Brahm
Sea Chase, The; 1955; John Farrow
Sea Devils; 1953; Raoul Walsh
Sea Hawk, The; 1940; Michael Curtiz

Sea of Grass, The; 1947; Elia Kazan
Sea Shall Not Have Them, The; 1953; Lewis Gilbert
Sea Wolf, The; 1941; Michael Curtiz
Sealed Verdict; 1947; Lewis Allen
Seance on a Wet Afternoon; 1964; Brian Forbes
Search, The; 1948; Fred Zinnemann
Searchers, The; 1956; John Ford
Searching Wind, The; 1946; William Dieterle
Seas Beneath, The; 1931; John Ford
Season of Passion; 1961; Leslie Norman
Second Chance; 1953; Rudolph Mate
Second Floor Mystery; 1930; Roy del Ruth
Second Greatest Sex, The; 1955; George Marshall
Second Time Around, The; 1961; Vincent Sherman
Seconds; 1966; John Frankenheimer
Secret Agent; 1936; Alfred Hitchcock
Secret Beyond the Door; 1948; Fritz Lang
Secret Bride; 1935; William Dieterle
Secret Ceremony; 1968; Joseph Losey
Secret Command; 1944; Edward Sutherland
Secret Door, The; 1962; Gilbert L. Kay
Secret Garden, The; 1949; Fred M. Wilcox
Secret Invasion, The; 1964; Roger Corman
Secret Life of an American Wife, The; 1968; George Axelrod
Secret Life of Walter Mitty; 1947; Norman Z. McLeod
Secret of My Success, The; 1965; Andrew L. Stone
Secret of the Chateau; 1935; Richard Thorpe
Secret of the Incas; 1954; Jerry Hopper
Secret Passion, The (Freud); 1962; John Huston
Secret People, The; 1950; Thorold Dickinson
Secret Place, The; 1956; Clive Donner
Secret Service; 1932; J. Walter Ruben
Secret Six, The; 1931; George Hill
Secret War of Harry Frigg; 1968; Jack Smight
Secret Ways, The; 1961; Phil Karlson
Secrets; 1933; Frank Borzage
Secrets of a Co-Ed; 1942; Joseph H.

She Goes to War; 1929; Henry King

She Got What She Wanted; 1930; James Cruze

She Had to Eat; 1937; Malcolm St. Clair

She Knew All the Answers; 1940; Richard Wallace

She Loves Me Not; 1934; Elliott Nugent

She Married Her Boss; 1935; Gregory La Cava

She Wore a Yellow Ribbon; 1949; John Ford

She-Gods of Shark Reef; 1957; Roger Corman

She's Back on Broadway; 1953; Gordon Douglas

Sheepman, The; 1958; George Marshall

Sheik Steps Out, The; 1937; Irving Pichel

Shenandoah; 1965; Andrew McLaglen

Shepherd of the Hills, The; 1941; Henry Hathaway

Sheriff of Fractured Jaw, The; 1958; Raoul Walsh

Sherlock Holmes; 1932; William K. Howard

Sherlock Holmes and the Voice of Terror; 1942; John Rawlins

Shining Hour, The; 1938; Frank Borzage

Ship of Fools; 1965; Stanley Kramer

Ship's Cafe; 1935; Robert Florey

Shipmates Forever; 1935; Frank Borzage

Shock Corridor; 1963; Samuel Fuller

Shock Treatment; 1963; Denis Sanders

Shockproof; 1949; Douglas Sirk

Shoot First; 1953; Robert Parrish

Shoot to Kill; 1960; Michael Winner

Shop Around the Corner, The; 1940; Ernst Lubitsch

Shop Soiled (The Crowded Day); 1954; John Guillermin

Shopworn Angel; 1929; Richard Wallace

Shopworn Angel; 1938; H. C. Potter

Short Cut to Hell; 1956; James Cagney

Shot in the Dark, A; 1964; Blake Edwards

Shotgun; 1955; Leslie Selander

Show Boat; 1936; James Whale

Show Girl in Hollywood; 1930; Mervyn Le Roy

Show Goes On, The; 1935; Kurt Neumann

Show of Shows, The; 1929; John Adolfi

Show Them No Mercy; 1935; George Marshall

Showboat; 1929; Harry Pollard

Showboat; 1936; James Whale

Showboat; 1951; George Sidney

Shrike, The; 1955; José Ferrer

Side Show; 1931; Roy del Ruth

Side Street; 1929; Malcolm St. Clair

Side Street; 1949; Anthony Mann

Sidewalks of London (St. Martin's Lane); 1938; Tim Whelan

Siege at Red River; 1954; Rudolph Mate

Siege of Pinchgut, The; 1958; Harry Watt

Sign of the Cross, The; 1932; Cecil B. de Mille

Sign of the Pagan; 1954; Douglas Sirk

Sign of the Ram; 1948; John Sturges

Silencers, The; 1966; Phil Karlson

Silk Hat Kid; 1935; H. Bruce Humberstone

Silk Stockings; 1957; Rouben Mamoulian

Silver Bullet, The; 1942; Joseph H. Lewis

Silver City; 1951; Byron Haskin

Silver Cord; 1933; John Cromwell

Silver Lode; 1954; Allan Dwan

Silver Queen; 1942; Lloyd Bacon

Silver River; 1948; Raoul Walsh

Sin Takes a Holiday; 1930; Paul Stein

Sin Town; 1942; Ray Enright

Sinbad the Sailor; 1947; Richard Wallace

Since You Went Away; 1944; John Cromwell

Sincerely Yours; 1955; Gordon Douglas

Sinful Davey; 1969; John Huston

Sing Baby Sing; 1936; Sidney Lanfield

Sing Your Way Home; 1945; Anthony Mann

Sing Your Worries Away; 1942; Edward Sutherland

Singapore; 1947; John Brahm

Singapore Woman; 1941; Jean Negulesco

Singer Not the Song, The; 1960; Roy Baker

Singin' in the Rain; 1952; Stanley Donen and Gene Kelly

Singing Blacksmith, The; 1938; Edgar G. Ulmer

Singing Kid, The; 1936; William

Quine

Solitaire Man; 1933; Jack Conway

Solomon and Sheba; 1959; King Vidor

Some Came Running; 1959; Vincente Minnelli

Some Like It Cool; 1961; Michael Winner

Some Like It Hot; 1959; Billy Wilder

Some People; 1962; Clive Donner

Somebody Up There Likes Me; 1956; Robert Wise

Someone to Remember; 1943; Robert Siodmak

Something for the Birds; 1952; Robert Wise

Something of Value; 1957; Richard Brooks

Something to Live For; 1952; George Stevens

Something to Shout About; 1943; Gregory Ratoff

Something to Sing About; 1937; Victor Schertzinger

Something Wild; 1961; Jack Garfein

Somewhere in the Night; 1946; Joseph Mankiewicz

Son of a Sailor; 1933; Lloyd Bacon

Son of Ali Baba; 1953; Kurt Neumann

Son of Dracula; 1943; Robert Siodmak

Son of Flubber; 1963; Robert Stevenson

Son of Frankenstein; 1939; Rowland V. Lee

Son of Fury; 1942; John Cromwell

Son of Kong; 1933; Ernest L. Schoesdack

Son of Paleface; 1952; Frank Tashlin

Son of the Gods; 1930; Frank Lloyd

Son-Daughter, The; 1932; Clarence Brown

Song and Dance Man, The; 1936; Allan Dwan

Song Is Born, A; 1948; Howard Hawks

Song O' My Heart; 1930; Frank Borzage

Song of Bernadette, The; 1944; Henry King

Song of Ceylon; 1934; Basil Wright

Song of Freedom; 1937; J. Elder Wills

Song of Love; 1947; Clarence Brown

Song of Songs; 1933; Rouben Mamoulian

Song of Surrender; 1949; Mitchell Leisen

Song of the Thin Man; 1947; Edward

Buzzell

Song to Remember; 1945; Charles Vidor

Song Without End; 1960; George Cukor and Charles Vidor

Sons and Lovers; 1960; Jack Cardiff

Sons of Katie Elder; 1965; Henry Hathaway

Sophomore, The; 1929; Leo McCarey

Sorority Girl; 1957; Roger Corman

Sorority House; 1939; John Farrow

Sorry Wrong Number; 1948; Anatole Litvak

SOS Iceberg; 1933; Tay Garnett

Soul Kiss; 1930; Sidney Franklin

Souls at Sea; 1937; Henry Hathaway

Souls for Sale (Evils of Chinatown); 1963; Albert Zugsmith

Sound and the Fury, The; 1957; Martin Ritt

Sound of Fury, The; 1950; Cyril Endfield

Sound of Music, The; 1965; Robert Wise

Sound Off; 1952; Richard Quine

South Pacific; 1958; Joshua Logan

South Riding; 1938; Victor Saville

South Sea Rose; 1929; Allan Dwan

Southerner, The; 1945; Jean Renoir

Spanish Affair; 1958; Don Siegel

Spanish Earth, The; 1937; Joris Ivens

Spanish Gardener, The; 1956; Philip Leacock

Spanish Main, The; 1945; Frank Borzage

Spare the Rod; 1961; Leslie Norman

Sparrows Can't Sing; 1963; Joan Littlewood

Spartacus; 1960; Stanley Kubrick

Spawn of the North; 1938; Henry Hathaway

Special Agent; 1935; William Keighley

Special Delivery; 1955; John Brahm

Spectre of the Rose; 1946; Ben Hecht

Spell of the Hypnotist (Fright); 1957; W. Lee Wilder

Spellbound; 1945; Alfred Hitchcock

Spencer's Mountain; 1963; Delmer Daves

Spendthrift; 1936; Raoul Walsh

Spider and the Fly, The; 1951; Robert Hamer

Spider Woman, The; 1944; Roy William Neill

Spiral Road, The; 1962; Robert Mulligan

Time Out of War (Short); 1954; Denis Sanders

Time to Love and a Time to Die, A; 1958; Douglas Sirk

Time Without Pity; 1957; Joseph Losey

Timetable; 1955; Mark Stevens

Tin Pan Alley; 1940; Walter Lang

Tin Star, The; 1957; Anthony Mann

Tingler, The; 1959; William Castle

Titanic; 1953; Jean Negulesco

Titfield Thunderbolt, The; 1953; Charles Crichton

Tip on a Dead Jockey; 1957; Richard Thorpe

To Be a Man; 1962; Irving Lerner

To Be or Not to Be; 1942; Ernst Lubitsch

To Catch a Thief; 1955; Alfred Hitchcock

To Each His Own; 1946; Mitchell Leisen

To Have and Have Not; 1944; Howard Hawks

To Hell and Back; 1955; Jesse Hibbs

To Kill a Mockingbird; 1963; Robert Mulligan

To Mary with Love; 1936; John Cromwell

To Paris with Love; 1955; Robert Hamer

To Please a Lady; 1950; Clarence Brown

To Sir, With Love; 1967; James Clavell

To the Last Man; 1933; Henry Hathaway

To the Victor; 1948; Delmer Daves

Toast of New York; 1937; Rowland V. Lee

Tobacco Road; 1941; John Ford

Today We Live; 1933; Howard Hawks

Together Again; 1944; Charles Vidor

Tokyo File 212; 1951; Dorrell McGowan and Stuart McGowan

Tokyo Joe; 1949; Stuart Heisler

Tom Brown of Culver; 1932; William Wyler

Tom Brown's School Days; 1940; Robert Stevenson

Tom Jones; 1963; Tony Richardson

Tom Sawyer; 1930; John Cromwell

Tom Thumb; 1958; George Pal

Tom, Dick and Harry; 1941; Garson Kanin

Tomorrow and Forever; 1945; Irving Pichel

Tomorrow and Tomorrow; 1932; Richard Wallace

Tomorrow Is Another Day; 1951; Felix Feist

Tomorrow the World; 1944; Leslie Fenton

Tomorrow We Live; 1942; Edgar G. Ulmer

Tonight or Never; 1931; Mervyn Le Roy

Tonight We Raid Calais; 1943; John Brahm

Tonight We Sing; 1953; Mitchell Leisen

Tony Rome; 1967; Gordon Douglas

Too Hot to Handle; 1938; Jack Conway

Too Late Blues; 1962; John Cassavetes

Too Late for Tears; 1949; Byron Haskin

Too Much Harmony; 1933; Edward Sutherland

Too Much Too Soon; 1958; Art Napoleon

Too Young to Love; 1961; Muriel Box

Too Young to Marry; 1931; Mervyn Le Roy

Top Hat; 1935; Mark Sandrich

Top o' the Morning; 1949; David Miller

Top Secret Affair; 1957; H. C. Potter

Top Speed; 1930; Mervyn Le Roy

Topaz; 1969; Alfred Hitchcock

Topaze; 1933; Harry d'Arrast

Topper; 1937; Norman Z. McLeod

Topper Returns; 1941; Roy del Ruth

Topper Takes a Trip; 1938; Norman Z. McLeod

Torch Song; 1953; Charles Walters

Torment; 1949; John Guillermin

Tormented; 1960; Bert I. Gordon

Torn Curtain; 1966; Alfred Hitchcock

Tornado; 1943; William Berke

Torpedo Alley; 1953; Lew Landers

Torrid Zone; 1940; William Keighley

Tortilla Flat; 1942; Victor Fleming

Touch of Evil; 1958; Orson Welles

Touch of Larceny, A; 1959; Guy Hamilton

Toughest Man in Arizona, The; 1953; R. G. Springsteen

Tovarich; 1937; Anatole Litvak

Toward the Unknown; 1956; Mervyn Le Roy

Tower of London; 1940; Rowland V. Lee

Two Against the World; 1932; Archie Mayo

Two Alone; 1934; Elliott Nugent

Two and Two Make Six; 1960; Freddie Francis

Two Before Zero; 1962; William Faralla

Two Black Sheep; 1935; Arthur Lubin

Two Down, One to Go (Doc); 1945; Frank Capra

Two Faces of Dr. Jekyll; 1960; Terence Fisher

Two Fisted; 1935; James Cruze

Two Flags West; 1950; Robert Wise

Two for the Road; 1967; Stanley Donen

Two for the Seesaw; 1962; Robert Wise

Two for Tonight; 1935; Frank Tuttle

Two Guns and a Badge; 1954; Lewis D. Collins

Two in a Taxi; 1941; Robert Florey

Two Left Feet; 1964; Roy Baker

Two Loves; 1961; Charles Walters

Two Men; 1934; John Farrow

Two Mrs. Carrolls, The; 1947; Peter Godfrey

Two O'Clock Courage; 1945; Anthony Mann

Two on the Tiles; 1950; John Guillermin

Two Rode Together; 1961; John Ford

Two Seconds; 1932; Mervyn Le Roy

Two Sinners; 1935; Arthur Lubin

Two Smart People; 1946; Jules Dassin

Two Thousand and One—A Space Odyssey; 1968; Stanley Kubrick

Two Weeks in Another Town; 1962; Vincente Minnelli

Two Weeks to Live; 1943; Malcolm St. Clair

Two Years Before the Mast; 1946; John Farrow

Two-Faced Woman; 1941; George Cukor

Two-Fisted Rangers; 1940; Joseph H. Lewis

Two-Headed Spy, The; 1959; Andre de Toth

Two-Way Stretch; 1961; Robert Day

Twonky, The; 1953; Arch Oboler

Tycoon; 1947; Richard Wallace

Ugly American, The; 1963; George Englund

Uncertain Glory; 1944; Raoul Walsh

Unchained; 1955; Hall Bartlett

Uncle, The; 1966; Desmond Davis

Uncle Harry; 1945; Robert Siodmak

Unconquered; 1947; Cecil B. de Mille

Undead, The; 1958; Roger Corman

Under a Texas Moon; 1930; Michael Curtiz

Under Capricorn; 1949; Alfred Hitchcock

Under Eighteen; 1932; Archie Mayo

Under Fire; 1957; James B. Clark

Under My Skin; 1950; Jean Negulesco

Under Pressure; 1935; Raoul Walsh

Under Pup, The; 1939; Richard Wallace

Under the Red Robe; 1937; Victor Seastrom

Under the Tonto Rim; 1933; Henry Hathaway

Under the Yum Yum Tree; 1963; David Swift

Under Two Flags; 1936; Frank Lloyd

Under Your Spell; 1936; Otto Preminger

Undercover Man, The; 1949; Joseph H. Lewis

Undercurrent; 1946; Vincente Minnelli

Underground; 1930; Anthony Asquith

Undertow; 1949; William Castle

Underwater; 1955; John Sturges

Underworld U.S.A.; 1961; Samuel Fuller

Undying Monster, The; 1942; John Brahm

Unearthly Stranger; 1963; John Krish

Unfaithful; 1931; John Cromwell

Unfaithful, The; 1947; Vincent Sherman

Unfaithfully Yours; 1948; Preston Sturges

Unfinished Business; 1941; Gregory La Cava

Unforgiven, The; 1960; John Huston

Unguarded Moment, The; 1956; Harry Keller

Unholy Garden, The; 1931; George Fitzmaurice

Unholy Partners; 1941; Mervyn Le Roy

Unholy Three, The; 1930; Jack Conway

Unholy Wife; 1957; John Farrow

Uninvited, The; 1944; Lewis Allen

Union Pacific; 1939; Cecil B. de Mille

Union Station; 1949; Rudolph Mate

Unknown Guest; 1943; Kurt Neumann

Voice of Bugle Ann; 1936; Richard Thorpe

Voice of the Turtle; 1948; Irving Rapper

Voice of the World; 1932; Arthur Elton

Volcano; 1953; William Dieterle

Voltaire; 1933; John G. Adolphi

Voodoo Island; 1957; Reginald Le Borg

Von Ryan's Express; 1965; Mark Robson

Wackiest Ship in the Army, The; 1960; Richard Murphy

Wagonmaster; 1950; John Ford

Wagons Roll at Night, The; 1941; Ray Enright

Waikiki Wedding; 1937; Frank Tuttle

Wait Till the Sun Shines Nellie; 1952; Henry King

Wait Until Dark; 1967; Terence Young

Wake Island; 1942; John Farrow

Wake Me When It's Over; 1960; Mervyn Le Roy

Wake of the Red Witch; 1948; Edward Ludwig

Wake Up and Dream; 1934; Kurt Neumann

Wake Up and Dream; 1945; Lloyd Bacon

Wake Up and Live; 1937; Sidney Lanfield

Wakefield Express (Short); 1952; Lindsay Anderson

Walk a Crooked Mile; 1948; Gordon Douglas

Walk, Don't Run; 1966; Charles Walters

Walk East on Beacon; 1952; Alfred Werker

Walk in the Sun (Salerno Beachhead); 1946; Lewis Milestone

Walk like a Dragon; 1960; James Clavell

Walk on the Wild Side; 1962; Edward Dmytryk

Walk Softly Stranger; 1950; Robert Stevenson

Walking Dead, The; 1936; Michael Curtiz

Walking down Broadway; 1932; Erich von Stroheim

Walking Hills, The; 1949; John Sturges

Walking My Baby Back Home; 1953; Lloyd Bacon

Walking on Air; 1946; Aveling Ginever

Walls of Jericho, The; 1947; John Stahl

Waltz of the Toreadors; 1962; John Guillermin

Wanda, Elyse, and Patti; 1944; John Farrow

Wanted for Murder; 1945; Lawrence Huntington

War and Peace; 1956; King Vidor

War Arrow; 1954; George Sherman

War Comes to America (Doc); 1945; Anatole Litvak

War Game, The; 1967; Peter Watkins

War Hero; 1958; Burt Topper

War Hunt; 1962; Denis Sanders

War Is Hell; 1964; Burt Topper

War Lord, The; 1965; Franklin Schaffner

War Lover, The; 1962; Philip Leacock

War of the Satellites; 1959; Roger Corman

War of the Worlds, The; 1953; Byron Haskin

War Wagon, The; 1967; Burt Kennedy

Ware Case, The; 1938; Robert Stevenson

Warlock; 1959; Edward Dmytryk

Warning Shot, The; 1967; Buzz Kulik

Warpath; 1951; Byron Haskin

Washington Merry-Go-Round; 1933; James Cruze

Wasp Woman; 1959; Roger Corman

Watch on the Rhine; 1943; Vincent Sherman and Herman Shumlin

Watch Your Stern; 1960; Gerald Thomas

Waterfront Women; 1952; Michael Anderson

Waterloo Bridge; 1940; Mervyn Le Roy

Wave, The (Doc); 1935; Fred Zinnemann and Muriel Gomez

Wave, A Wac and a Marine, A; 1944; Phil Karlson

Way Ahead, The (Doc); 1942; Carol Reed

Way Down East; 1935; Henry King

Way Down South; 1939; Bernard Vorhaus

Way of a Gaucho; 1952; Jacques Tourneur

Way Out West; 1937; James W. Horne

Way to the Gold, The; 1957; Robert D. Webb

Way to the Stars, The; 1945; Anthony

son
Young Eagles; 1930; William Wellman
Young Hellions (High School Confidential); 1960; Albert Zugsmith
Young Ideas; 1943; Jules Dassin
Young in Heart, The; 1938; Richard Wallace
Young Land, The; 1959; Ted Tetzlaff
Young Lions, The; 1958; Edward Dmytryk
Young Lovers, The; 1949; Ida Lupino
Young Lovers, The; 1954; Anthony Asquith
Young Man with Ideas; 1952; Mitchell Leisen
Young Mister Pitt, The; 1940; Carol Reed
Young Mr. Lincoln; 1939; John Ford
Young Nowheres; 1929; Frank Lloyd
Young One, The; 1960; Luis Buñuel
Young Ones, The; 1961; Sidney Furie
Young People; 1940; Allan Dwan
Young Philadelphians, The; 1959; Vincent Sherman
Young Racers, The; 1963; Roger Corman
Young Savages, The; 1961; John Frankenheimer

Young Stranger, The; 1957; John Frankenheimer
Young Tom Edison; 1940; Norman Taurog
Youngblood Hawke; 1964; Delmer Daves
Younger Generation; 1929; Frank Capra
Your Cheatin' Heart; 1964; Gene Nelson
Your Past Is Showing; 1958; M. Zampi
Youth on Trial; 1945; Budd Boetticher

Zarak; 1957; Terence Young
Zaza; 1938; George Cukor
Zenobia; 1939; Gordon Douglas
Zero Hour; 1957; Hall Bartlett
Ziegfeld Follies; 1946; Vincente Minnelli
Ziegfeld Girl; 1941; Robert Z. Leonard
Zoo in Budapest; 1933; Rowland V. Lee
Zombies, The; 1933; Victor Halperin
Zorba the Greek; 1964; Michael Cacoyannis
Zulu; 1964; Cy Enfield

"Hilarious, brainy, and balanced . . . A trip with Horwitz is as good as it gets."   —*The Charlotte Observer*

"Horwitz's adventures pay illuminating tribute to the great navigator—to Captain Cook himself and to his intrepid eighteenth-century colleagues, including the improbably attractive Sir Joseph Banks. But most of all *Blue Latitudes* offers clear-eyed, vivid, and highly entertaining reassurance that there are still outlandish worlds to be discovered."
            —Caroline Alexander, author of *The Endurance: Shackleton's Legendary Antarctic Expedition*

"*Blue Latitudes* is a rollicking read that is also a sneaky work of scholarship, providing new and unexpected insights into the man who out-discovered Columbus. A terrific book—I inhaled it in one weekend."
            —Nathaniel Philbrick, author of *In the Heart of the Sea*

"One of the best . . . full of humor . . . It is with people that Horwitz excels. As he demonstrated in *Confederates in the Attic*, he has a gift for getting them to open up. A terrific reporter, Horwitz investigates how the places he visits have changed. . . . What he also does, and what makes this book so absorbing, is intersperse among all the details of life today in these far-flung places an elegant running account of Cook's exploits."   —*The New York Times Book Review* (cover)

"Compelling . . . Horwitz is particularly convincing when he's establishing just how harsh a sailor's life could be in the 1700s, why most of them were drunk so much of the time, and why today's mariners have it relatively easy. . . . Remarkable."   —*The Oregonian* (Portland)

"A rewarding and—trust me on this—witty tale of a remarkable explorer who now occupies a controversial place in history because of disease, greed, thievery, and prostitution that followed in his wake . . . Perhaps the highest praise of any book is that it takes you somewhere. Horwitz manages to do this on two levels, mingling history with a humorous travelogue."   —*The Mercury News* (San Jose)

"A swashbuckling history."   —*Newsday*

"An entertaining and rewarding read. Horwitz remains an intriguing sketcher of characters, and there are plenty of aging hippies, burnt-out colonials, and out-and-out oddballs in his path. He's still the master of the targeted anecdote or factoid . . . Charming . . . *Blue Latitudes* stretches from Easter Island to Alaska, from Cape Horn to Indonesia. In Mr. Horwitz's company, it seems all too short a trip."

—*Sunday Star-News*

"Delightful . . . [Horwitz] is an observant traveler, with an eye for both the oddball and the salient. He also has the good sense to enlist the services of a madcap Aussie traveling companion, who is determined to make certain that any journey, to be worth its salt, must include plenty of misadventures."   —*Seattle Post-Intelligencer*

"At once well-researched, gripping, and peppered with humorous passages . . . The book's literary magic comes from mixing information from Horwitz's observations with observations written by Cook himself. . . . *Blue Latitudes* ought to appeal to diverse audiences—those who devour travel books, those who care about the mixed legacy of famous dead white males, and those who treasure memorable writing whatever the subject matter."   —*St. Louis Post-Dispatch*

"Thanks to Horwitz's thorough research—he seems to have read all of Cook's journals, previous biographies, and anthropological studies of the Pacific—naval life and island life come brilliantly alive. . . . Paul Theroux travels the world and finds disappointment; Tony Horwitz finds a cast of colorful characters and history embedded in the land."

—*The Providence Journal*

"A compelling account."   —*Milwaukee Journal Sentinel*

"[Horwitz] weaves his own experiences with those gleaned from Cook's own writings and those of his crew into a fabric dense with the delicious details that keep readers turning pages long past bedtime."

—*Chicago Tribune*

"Filled with history and alive with contrasts."   —*Kirkus Reviews*

"A staggering blend of historical research, character study, sociological analysis, and intriguing tales of travel."   —*The Boston Globe*

"This alternately hilarious, poignant, and insightful book is history for people who don't like history, and a travelogue full of wonder and smart observation, not jaded cynicism. . . . Horwitz succeeds brilliantly in turning the English from stiff icons to flesh-and-blood human beings. The book's constant humor, honesty, and judgment recall his own *Confederates in the Attic* or Bill Bryson's *A Walk in the Woods*. . . . This book will keep you enthralled."

—*The Seattle Times*

"Tony Horwitz has done it again. . . . [With] keen insight, open-mindedness and laugh-out-loud humor, he . . . travel[s] across the globe in search of the memory of Capt. James Cook."

—*San Francisco Chronicle*

"Horwitz has a self-deprecating wit that translates well into print, making him an eloquent Everyman in whatever exotic setting he enters. He is a meticulous observer, a preternaturally gifted student of human nature."

—*The Atlanta-Journal Constitution*

"With prodigious research and a willingness to raise the subject of Captain Cook with anyone, including a drunk, a king, and a girl in a wet T-shirt, Horwitz has managed to muscle a big, sloppy idea into something coherent and fun to read . . . Horwitz reveals the most about Cook by acting like Cook, exploring each place with the same energy and relentless curiosity as the man himself. . . . He one-upped Cook and made it home in one piece."

—*Forbes FYI*

"Horwitz offers an affectionate but convincing defense of the captain as a man driven by a 'stubborn Enlightenment faith in firsthand observation,' and conjures the hero's primal encounters by getting off the beaten path himself."

—*Outside*

"[An] engaging outing . . . Horwitz seamlessly weaves humorous anecdotes from Cook's journals with his own peripatetic observations—and without succumbing to hero worship, he conveys Cook's lifelong romance with traveling to the far reaches of the then-unknown world."

—*Entertainment Weekly*

The Three Great Voyages of Captain James Cook

SIBERIA

ARCTIC CIRCLE

Bering
Strait

Kamchatka
Petropavlovsk

Bering Sea

Aleutian Islands

Unalaska

ASIA

Pacific Ocean

NEW
GUINEA

Christmas Island

INDONESIA

Vanuatu
(New Hebrides)

Cook
Islands

Niue
(Savage Island)

Jakarta
(Batavia)

New
Caledonia

Fiji

AUSTRALIA
(New Holland)

Norfolk
Island

Tonga

Indian Ocean

North Island

TASMANIA
(Van Diemen's Land)

South Island

NEW
ZEALAND

0 Miles   3000

0 Kilometers   3000

Scale at Equator

PICADOR
HENRY HOLT AND COMPANY
NEW YORK

Blue Latitudes

Boldly Going Where
Captain Cook
Has Gone Before

Tony Horwitz

www.picadorusa.com

Picador® is a U.S. registered trademark and is used by
Henry Holt and Company under license from Pan Books Limited.

For information on Picador Reading Group Guides, as well as ordering, please contact the
Trade Marketing department at St. Martin's Press.
Phone: 1-800-221-7845 extension 763
Fax: 212-677-7456
E-mail: trademarketing@stmartins.com

Frontispiece © National Maritime Museum, London

Cartography by Jeffrey L. Ward

Library of Congress Cataloging-in-Publication Data

Horwitz, Tony, 1958–
    Blue latitudes : boldly going where Captain Cook has gone before / Tony Horwitz.
        p.   cm.
    Includes bibliographical references (p. 453).
    ISBN 0-312-42260-1
        1. Cook, James, 1728–1779—Journeys.   2. Voyages around the
    world.   3. Oceania—Discovery and exploration.   4. Horwitz, Tony,
    1958– —Journeys—Oceania.   5. Endeavour II (Ship)   I. Title.

G420.C65 H67 2002
910'.92—dc21   2002024133

First published in the United States by Henry Holt and Company

First Picador Edition: August 2003

10 9 8 7 6 5 4 3 2 1

For Natty, an adventurer at five

CONTENTS

Blue
Latitudes

PROLOGUE:
The Distance Traveled

Ambition leads me not only farther than any other man has been before me, but as far as I think it possible for man to go. —THE JOURNAL OF CAPTAIN JAMES COOK

Just after dark on February 16, 1779, a *kahuna,* or holy man, rode a canoe to His Majesty's Sloop *Resolution,* anchored off the coast of Hawaii. The *kahuna* came aboard with a bundle under his arm. Charles Clerke, the ship's commander, unwrapped the parcel in the presence of his officers. He found "a large piece of Flesh which we soon saw to be Human," Clerke wrote in his journal. "It was clearly a part of the Thigh about 6 or 8 pounds without any bone at all."

Two days before, islanders had killed five of the ship's men on the lava shoreline of Kealakekua Bay, and carried off the bodies. Nothing had been seen of the corpses since. Unsure what to make of the *kahuna*'s grisly offering, Clerke and his men asked whether the rest of the body had been eaten. The Hawaiian seemed appalled by this question. Did Englishmen eat *their* foes?

Hawaiians weren't cannibals, the *kahuna* said. They cut up and cooked the bodies of high chiefs to extract certain bones that possessed godly power. Islanders distributed these remains among their leaders and discarded the flesh. Hence the *kahuna*'s return of the deboned thigh, "which," Clerke wrote, "he gave us to understand was part of our late unfortunate Captain."

James Cook, the *Resolution*'s captain, was one of the five men who had died on shore. There was no way of knowing for certain if this pungent thigh belonged to him. But several days later, the Hawaiians delivered another package, bundled in a feathered cloak. This one contained scorched limbs, a scalp with the ears attached and hair cut short, and two hands that had been scored and salted, apparently to preserve them. Fifteen years earlier, a powder horn had exploded in Cook's right hand, leaving an ugly gash. This "remarkable Cut," one of his lieutenants wrote, remained clearly visible on the severed right hand delivered to the ship.

While the Hawaiians were parceling out Cook's bones among their leaders, the English performed a parallel ritual aboard the *Resolution*. Officers and "gentlemen" divided and sold the captain's clothes and other effects, in accordance with shipboard custom. Two and a half years out from home, in waters no other Europeans had sailed before, the English needed the useful items in the dead captain's kit.

On the evening of February 21, the English put their flags at half-mast, crossed the ship's yards, tolled bells, and fired a ten-gun salute. "I had the remains of Capt Cook committed to the deep," Charles Clerke wrote, "with all the attention and honour we could possibly pay it in this part of the World."

The thirty-seven-year-old Clerke, who had inherited command of the *Resolution* following Cook's death, was himself dying, from tuberculosis. As the ship weighed anchor, he retired to his cabin, turning the quarterdeck over to Lieutenant James King and to the ship's brilliant but testy young master, William Bligh.

"Thus we left Karacacooa bay," King wrote, "a place become too remarkably famous for the very unfortunate & Tragical death of one of the greatest Navigators our Nation or any Nation ever had."

HALF A WORLD away from Kealakekua Bay, in a sodden Yorkshire churchyard, a single headstone honors the family into which James Cook was born. "To Ye Memory of Mary and Mary, Jane and William," the inscription reads, listing siblings who perished by the age of five. The stone also mentions James's older brother, John, who died at the age of twenty-three. A second epitaph commemorates the mother and father of this short-lived brood: "James and Grace Cook were the parents of the celebrated circumnavigator Captain James Cook who was born at Marton Oct. 27th, 1728," the inscription says, "and killed at Owhyhee Dec. 14th, 1779."

The latter date is incorrect; Cook died in Hawaii on February 14. But this simple gravestone speaks more eloquently to the distance Cook had traveled than any of the grand monuments erected in his name. Cook was born just a few miles from his family's grave plot, in a mud-and-thatch hovel: a building type known in the North Riding of Yorkshire as a biggin. Farm animals wandered in and out of the hut's two small rooms. Sacking and meadowsweet, spread on the dirt floor, kept down the damp and odor.

Cook's father worked as a day laborer, close to the bottom of Britain's stratified society. The prospects for a day laborer's son were bleak, even if he survived the harsh conditions that killed most of Cook's siblings in early childhood. Public education didn't exist. There was very little mobility, social or geographic. The world of the rural poor remained what it had been for generations: a day's walk in radius, a tight, well-trod loop between home, field, church, and, finally, a crowded family grave plot.

James Cook didn't just break this cycle; he exploded it. Escaping to sea as a teenager, he became a coal-ship apprentice and joined the Royal Navy as a lowly "able seaman." From there, he worked his way to the upper reaches of the naval hierarchy and won election to the Royal Society, the pinnacle of London's intellectual establishment. Cook's greatest feat, though, was the three epic voyages of discovery he made in his forties—midlife today, closer to the grave in the eighteenth century.

In 1768, when Cook embarked on the first, roughly a third of the world's map remained blank, or filled with fantasies: sea monsters, Patagonian giants, imaginary continents. Cook sailed into this void in a small wooden ship and returned, three years later, with charts so accurate that some of them stayed in use until the 1990s.

On his two later voyages, Cook explored from the Arctic to the Antarctic, from Tasmania to Tierra del Fuego, from the northwest shore of America to the far northeast coast of Siberia. By the time he died, still on the job, Cook had sailed over 200,000 miles in the course of his career—roughly equivalent to circling the equator eight times, or voyaging to the moon. "Owhyhee," a sun-struck paradise unknown to the West before Cook arrived, was as far as a man could go from the drear Yorkshire churchyard he seemed destined at birth to occupy.

Cook not only redrew the map of the world, creating a picture of the globe much like the one we know today; he also transformed the West's image of nature and man. His initial Pacific sail, on a ship called *Endeavour*, was the first of its kind in Britain—a voyage of scientific discovery, carrying trained observers: artists, astronomers, naturalists. The ship's botanists collected so much exotic flora that they expanded the number of known plant species in the West by a quarter. This seeded the modern notion of biodiversity and made possible the discoveries of men such as Charles Darwin, who followed in the *Endeavour*'s path aboard the *Beagle*.

Similarly, the art and writing of Cook and his men, and the native objects they collected, called "artificial curiosities," transfixed the West with images of unfamiliar peoples: erotic Tahitian dancers, Maori cannibals, clay-painted Aborigines. Sailors adopted the Polynesian adornment called tattoo, and words such as "taboo" entered the Western lexicon. A London brothel keeper offered a special night to her clients, featuring "a dozen beautiful Nymphs" performing the ritualized sex Cook had witnessed in Tahiti. Poets and philosophers seized on the South Seas as a liberating counterpoint to Europe. On the other side of the Atlantic, Benjamin Franklin issued an extraordinary order, in the midst of the Revolutionary War, commanding American naval officers to treat Cook and his men as friends rather than foes.

For the lands and peoples Cook encountered, the impact of his voyages was just as profound, and far more destructive. His decade of discovery occurred on the cusp of the Industrial Revolution. The steam engine and spinning jenny emerged as Cook set off on his first Pacific tour; Adam Smith published *The Wealth of Nations* in 1776, as Cook embarked on his last. His explorations opened vast new territories to the West's burgeoning economies and empires, and all that came with them: whalers, missionaries, manufactured goods, literacy, rum, guns, syphilis, smallpox.

Cook, in sum, pioneered the voyage we are still on, for good and ill. "More than any other person," writes the historian Bernard Smith, "he helped to make the world one."

LIKE MOST AMERICANS I grew up knowing almost nothing of Captain Cook, except what I learned in fifth-grade geography class. Though I didn't realize it at the time, I also absorbed his adventures through episodes of *Star Trek*. A suburban kid, growing up in a decade when even the moon had been conquered, I never ceased to feel a thrill at the TV show's opening words: "These are the voyages of the Starship *Enterprise*. Its five-year mission: to explore strange new worlds, to seek out new life and new civilizations, to boldly go where no man has gone before!"

It wasn't until years later that I realized how much *Star Trek* echoed a true story. Captain James Cook; Captain James Kirk. The *Endeavour*; the *Enterprise*. Cook, the Yorkshire farm boy, writing in his journal that he'd sailed "farther than any other man has been before." Kirk, the Iowa farm boy, keeping his own log about boldly going "where no man has gone before!" Cook rowed jolly boats ashore, accompanied by his naturalist, his surgeon, and musket-toting, red-jacketed marines. Kirk "beamed down" to planets with the science officer Mr. Spock, Dr. McCoy, and phaser-wielding, red-jerseyed "expendables." Both captains also set out—at least in theory—to discover and describe new lands, rather than to conquer or convert.

In my twenties, I fell in love with an Australian and followed her to Sydney. Geraldine and I found a house just a few miles from the beach where Cook and his men, landing in 1770, became the first Europeans to visit the east coast of Australia. My new surrounds seemed wondrous but disorienting: the sun blazing in the northern sky, scribbly gums that shed bark instead of leaves, fruit bats squeaking at night in the fig trees. One day at an antiquarian bookshop, I found a copy of Cook's journals and read his own impressions of this strange land over two centuries before me.

"It was of a light Mouse colour and the full size of a grey hound and shaped in every respect like one," Cook wrote of a creature he saw fleetingly near shore. "I would have taken it for a wild dog, but for its walking or running in which it jumped like a Hare or a dear." Unsure what to call this odd beast, Cook referred to it simply as "the animal." Later, he inserted the native word, which he rendered "kanguru." The

Endeavour carried home a skull and skin, the first kangaroo specimen in the West. It resided in a London museum until destroyed in the Blitz during World War II.

Even stranger to Cook and his men were Aborigines, who possessed almost nothing—not even loincloths—yet showed a complete disdain for European goods. To well-born gentlemen aboard the *Endeavour*, this was evidence of native brutishness. Cook took a much more thoughtful and humane view. "Being wholly unacquainted not only with the superfluous but the necessary conveniences so sought after in Europe, they are happy not knowing the use of them," he wrote. "They live in Tranquility which is not disturb'd by the Inequality of Condition."

I returned to these words years later, while reading on the back porch of my house in America. After a decade of circumnavigating the globe as foreign correspondents, Geraldine and I had settled down, bought an old house, planted a garden, had a child. At forty, I'd tired of travel, of dislocation. Part of me wanted to rot, like my porch in Virginia. Then, one lazy summer's day, I picked up my neglected copy of Cook's journals. In Australia, I'd only scanned them. This time I read for days: about human sacrifice and orgiastic sex in Tahiti, charmed arrows and poison fish in Vanuatu, sailors driven mad off Antarctica by "the Melancholy Croaking of Innumerable Penguins." And, at the center of it all, a man my own age, coolly navigating his ship through the most extraordinary perils imaginable.

"One is carried away with the general, grand, and indistinct notion of A VOYAGE ROUND THE WORLD," James Boswell confided to Samuel Johnson after dining with Cook in London. Perched in a cane rocker on my back porch in Virginia, lawn mowers murmuring in the distance, I felt the same impulse. Apart from the coast near Sydney, I'd seen none of the territory Cook explored: Bora-Bora, the Bering Sea, the Great Barrier Reef, Tonga, Kealakekua Bay—the list of alluring destinations seemed endless.

I wondered what these places were like today, if any trace of Cook's boot prints remained. I also wanted to turn the spyglass around. Cook and his men were as exotic to islanders as natives seemed to the English. What had Pacific peoples made of pale strangers appearing from the sea, and how did their descendants remember Cook now?

I wanted to probe Cook, as well. His journals recorded every detail of where he went, and what he did. They rarely revealed why. Perhaps, following in Cook's wake, I could fathom the biggin-born farm boy whose ambition drove him farther than any man, until it killed him on a faraway shore called Owhyhee.

Chapter 1

PACIFIC NORTHWEST:
One Week Before the Mast

Those who would go to sea for pleasure would go to hell
for pastime.   —EIGHTEENTH-CENTURY APHORISM

When I was thirteen, my parents bought a used sailboat, a ten-foot
wooden dory that I christened *Wet Dream*. For several summers, I
tacked around the waters off Cape Cod, imagining myself one of the
whalers who plied Nantucket Sound in the nineteenth century. I read
Moby-Dick, tied a bandanna around my head, even tried my hand at
scrimshaw. This fantasy life offered escape from the fact that I could
barely sail—or caulk, or knot anything except a shoelace. One day,
bailing frantically with a sawed-off milk jug after gashing the *Wet
Dream* against a rock, I found my whaling dream had become real. I
was Ishmael, the *Pequod* sinking beneath me.

This hapless memory returned to me as I studied an application for
a berth on His Majesty's Bark *Endeavour*. An Australian foundation
had built a museum-quality replica of Cook's first vessel and dispatched it around the globe in the navigator's path. At each port, the
ship's professional crew took on volunteers to help sail the next leg and
experience life as eighteenth-century sailors. This seemed the obvious
place to start; if I was going to understand Cook's travels, I first had to
understand *how* he traveled.

The application form asked about my "qualifications and experience," with boxes beside each question, marked yes or no.

> Have you had any blue water ocean sailing experience?
> Can you swim 50 meters fully clothed?
> You will be required to work aloft, sometimes at night in heavy weather. Are you confident of being able to do this?

I wasn't sure what was meant by "blue water ocean." Did it come in other colors? I'd never swum clothed, except once, after falling off the *Wet Dream*. As for working aloft, I'd climbed ladders to scoop leaves from my gutter in Virginia. I checked "yes" next to each question. But the last query gave me pause: "Do you suffer from sea sickness?"

Only when I went to sea. I opted for the box marked "moderate," rather than the "chronic" box, fearing I'd otherwise be judged unfit.

A week later, I received a terse note confirming a berth in early autumn from Gig Harbor, Washington, to Vancouver, British Columbia. The letter came with a "Safety and Training Manual." A page headed "Abandon Ship" offered this helpful tip: "Stay together in waters—**stay calm**." Other pages dealt with "burns and scalds," "sudden serious injury," drowning, and seasickness: "You may feel like you're dying but you will survive." In case you didn't, there was a liability waiver to sign ("I understand and expressly assume these risks and dangers, including death, illness, disease . . .").

The safety tips, at least, were stated in plain English. The training section read like a home appliance manual, badly translated from Korean, with "some assembly required." A typical diagram showed intersecting arrows and loops, allegedly explaining the layout of "Bits & Fife Rail to Fwd. of Mainmast Looking from Starboard Side."

I quickly gave up and spent the weeks until my voyage studying history books instead. Among other things, I learned that the original *Endeavour* was a mirror of the man who commanded it: plain, utilitarian, indomitable. Like Cook, the ship began its career in the coal trade, shuttling between the mine country of the north of England and the docks of east London. Bluff-bowed and wide-beamed, the ninety-seven-foot-long ship was built for bulk and endurance rather than speed or comfort. "A cross between a Dutch clog and a coffin," was how one historian described it.

The tallest of the *Endeavour*'s three masts teetered a vertiginous 127 feet. Belowdecks, the head clearance stooped to four foot six. The *Endeavour*'s flat bottom and very shallow keel—designed so the collier could float ashore with the tide to load and unload coal—made the ship exceptionally "tender," meaning it tended to roll from side to side. "Found the ship to be but a heavy sailer," wrote the ship's botanist, Joseph Banks, "more calculated for stowage, than for sailing." He wrote this in calm seas, two days after leaving England. When the going turned rough, Banks retreated to his cot, "ill with sickness at stomach and most violent headach."

Duly warned, I sampled a seasickness pill on the flight to Seattle. It made me so listless and wobbly that I almost fell down in the aisle. This seemed a bad state in which to work aloft, at night in heavy seas. I flushed the rest of the pills down the airplane toilet.

The pier at Gig Harbor, an hour south of Seattle, teemed with gleaming new yachts. In this sea of sleek fiberglass, the replica *Endeavour* was easy to spot. The original ship had been made almost entirely from grasses and trees—hemp, flax, elm, oak, pine tar—with bits of iron and brass thrown in. The replica appeared much the same. With its sails furled and its masts poking skeletally into the damp air, the vessel looked boxy and brittle, a boat built from matchsticks. At a hundred feet long, it wasn't much bigger than many of the nearby yachts.

A dozen sailors, mostly tanned young Australians in navy-colored work clothes, stood coiling ropes on the dock and bantering in the matey, mocking fashion I knew well from my years in Sydney. "Press-ganged men over there," one sailor said, pointing me to a waterside park. My fellow recruits numbered forty, mostly Americans and Canadians, including six women. Chatting nervously, I was relieved to discover that some of them had little more sailing experience than I did.

Then again, they seemed a fit lot, accustomed to hard labor, or at least hard exercise: construction workers, military veterans, sinewy joggers. "This'll be like a week at a dude ranch," a broad-shouldered carpenter assured me.

A trim, brisk figure strode over from the ship and barked, "Listen up!" This was our captain, Chris Blake, a mild-featured man much shorter than Cook but no less commanding in manner. "We'll get on with a very fast learning curve," he said, handing us over to the ship's first mate, a gruff Englishman named Geoff.

"This will be like going back into the Army, if you've ever been there, with a lot less sleep," Geoff began. "Your straight eight, you're not going to get it on this ship, so when you have a chance to put your head down, do it." He also told us where to put our heads when seasick. "Make friends with one of our plastic buckets and make sure you chuck it over the lee side so you're not wearing your pizza. And no throwing up belowdecks, because you'll have every other person throwing up beside you."

A safety officer followed with a brief talk about abandoning ship. "Hold your nostrils when you jump overboard because it's a long fall and can break your nose," he said. "Blokes, keep your legs crossed when you go over, same reason. Also, try to huddle together in the water. It's not going to save you, but it might give you a few more minutes." Then he warned us about the "gasp reflex." As he explained it: "The water's so cold that you gasp and suck a lot in."

After this orientation, we split into three "watches," each one assigned to a mast and a captain-of-tops, our drill sergeant for the week ahead. My watch was mainmast, by far the tallest of the three, commanded by Todd, a raffishly handsome Australian with a ponytail, earrings, and a red bandanna wrapped round his unshaven neck. "Okay, you scurvy dogs and wenches," he said, "let's start with the slops."

"Slops" was the eighteenth-century term for naval gear. Sailors on the original *Endeavour* wore no prescribed uniform, nor would we dress in period costume. Todd tossed us each a set of brown oilskin pants and jacket. "In Australia they're called Driza-Bone, but we call them Wet-as-a-Bastard. As soon as they get wet they stay that way." He also issued us orange night vests, and safety harnesses that looked like mountain-climbing belts.

Then Todd led us across the ship's deck and down a ladder, or companionway, which plunged to a dark chamber called the mess deck. We squinted at tables roped to the ceiling, as well as vinegar kegs, a huge iron stove, and sea chests that doubled as benches—all packed into a room the size of a suburban den. This cramped cavern would some-how accommodate thirty of us, with the other ten recruits in a small adjoining space.

Todd tossed us canvas hammocks and showed how to lash them to the beams above the tables. We were allotted just fourteen inches' width of airspace per sling, the Navy's prescribed sleeping area in the eighteenth century. "If you don't know knots, tie lots," Todd said, as I struggled to complete a simple hitch. He also showed us how to stow the hammocks, snug and tightly roped, in a netted hold.

Stumbling around the dark deck, colliding with tables and people, and bending almost double when the head clearance plunged to dwarf height, I tried to imagine spending three years in this claustrophobic hole, as Cook's men had. Incredibly, the original *Endeavour* left port with forty more people than we had on board—accompanied by seventeen sheep, several dozen ducks and chickens, four pigs, three cats (to catch rats), and a milk goat that had circled the globe once before. "Being in a ship is being in a jail," Samuel Johnson sagely observed, "with the chance of being drowned."

THE *ENDEAVOUR'S* MISSION was as daunting as the conditions on the ship. Though Ferdinand Magellan had first crossed the Pacific two and a half centuries before, the ocean—covering an area greater than all the world's landmasses combined—remained so mysterious that mapmakers labeled vast stretches of the Pacific *nondum cognita* (not yet known). Cartographers knew so little of the lands within the Pacific that they simply guessed at the contours of coasts: a French chart from 1753, fifteen years before the *Endeavour's* departure, shows dotted shorelines accompanied by the words *"Je suppose."*

One reason for this ignorance was that most of the ships sailing after Magellan followed the same, relatively narrow band of ocean, channeled by prevailing winds and currents, and constrained by poor navigational tools. Also, geography in the early modern era was regarded as proprietary information; navies kept explorers' charts and journals under wraps, lest competing nations use them to expand their own empires.

Not that these reports were very reliable. Magellan's pilot miscalculated the longitude of the Philippines by 53 degrees, an error akin to planting Bolivia in central Africa. When another Spanish expedition stumbled on an island chain in the western Pacific in 1567, the captain believed he'd found the biblical land of Ophir, from which King Solomon shipped gold, sandalwood, and precious stones. Spanish charts, and the navigational skills of those who followed, were so faulty that Europeans failed to find the Solomon Islands again for two centuries. No gold and not much of economic value was ever discovered there.

Pacific adventurers also showed an unfortunate tendency toward abbreviated careers. Vasco Núñez de Balboa, the first European to sight the ocean, in 1513, was beheaded for treason. Magellan set off in 1519 with five ships and 237 men; only one ship and eighteen men made it home three years later, and Magellan was not present, having been speared in the Philippines. Francis Drake, the first English circumnavigator, died at sea of dysentery. Vitus Bering, sailing for the czar, perished from exposure after shipwrecking near the frigid sea now named for him; at the last, Bering lay half-buried in sand, to keep warm, while Arctic foxes gnawed at his sick and dying men.

Other explorers simply vanished. Or went mad. In 1606, the navigator Fernandes de Queirós told his pilot, "Put the ships' heads where they like, for God will guide them as may be right." When God delivered the Spanish ships to the shore of what became the New Hebrides, Fernandes de Queirós founded a city called New Jerusalem and anointed his sailors "Knights of the Holy Ghost."

But the most persistent and alluring mirage of Pacific exploration was *terra australis incognita,* an unknown "south land," first conjured into being by the wonderfully named Roman mapmaker Pomponius Mela. He, like Ptolemy, believed that the continents of the northern hemisphere must be balanced by an equally large landmass at the bottom of the globe. Otherwise, the world would tilt. This appealingly symmetrical notion was embellished by Marco Polo, who claimed he'd seen a south land called Locac, filled with gold and game and elephants and idolators, "a very wild region, visited by few people." Renaissance mapmakers took the Venetian's vague coordinates and placed Locac—also known as Lucach, Maletur, and Beach—far to the south, part of the fabled *terra australis*. The discovery of America only heightened Europeans' conviction that another vast continent, rich in resources, remained to be found.

So things stood in 1768, when London's august scientific group, the Royal Society, petitioned King George III to send a ship to the South Pacific. A rare astronomical event, the transit of Venus across the sun, was due to occur on June 3, 1769, and not again for 105 years. The society hoped that an accurate observation of the transit, from disparate points on the globe, would enable astronomers to calculate the earth's distance from the sun, part of the complex task of mapping the solar system. Half a century after Isaac Newton and almost three centuries after Christopher Columbus, basic questions of where things were—in the sky, as well as on earth—remained unresolved.

The king accepted the society's request, and ordered the Admiralty to fit out an appropriate ship. As commander, the Royal Society recommended Alexander Dalrymple, a distinguished theorist and cartographer who had sailed to the East Indies, and who believed so firmly in the southern continent that he put its breadth at exactly 5,323 miles and its population at fifty million. The Admiralty instead selected James Cook, a Navy officer whose oceangoing experience was limited to the North Atlantic.

On the face of it, this seemed an unlikely choice—and, among some in the establishment, it was unpopular. Cook was a virtual unknown outside Navy circles and a curiosity within. He had spent the previous decade charting the coast of Canada, a task at which he displayed exceptional talent. One admiral, noting "Mr. Cook's Genius and Capacity," observed of his charts: "They may be the means of directing many in the right way, but cannot mislead any." But Cook's rank remained that of second lieutenant, and, as an ill-educated man of low birth, married to the daughter of a dockside tavernkeeper, he didn't fit the mold of the scientific and naval elite.

Cook's bearing was as plain as his background. Though very tall for his day, at several inches over six feet, he was rawboned and narrow. The few surviving portraits show a commanding but austere figure: long straight nose, thin lips, high cheekbones, deep-set brown eyes.

James Boswell described Cook as "a grave, steady man" who possessed "a ballance in his mind for truth as nice as scales for weighing a guinea."

This guarded, meticulous Yorkshireman also faced a mission much more daring than the astronomical voyage requested by the Royal Society. The Lords of the Admiralty dispatched Cook with two sets of orders. One instructed him to proceed to a recently discovered South Pacific island, named for King George, to observe the transit of Venus and survey harbors and bays. "When this Service is perform'd," the orders concluded, "you are to put to Sea without Loss of Time, and carry into execution the Additional Instructions contained in the inclosed Sealed Packet."

These orders, labeled "secret," laid out an ambitious plan for "making Discoverys of Countries hitherto unknown." In particular, Cook was to search unexplored latitudes for the fabled continent of Pomponius Mela and Marco Polo. "Whereas there is reason to imagine that a Continent or Land of great extent, may be found," the orders commanded, "You are to proceed to the southward in order to make discovery of the Continent abovementioned."

In other words, Cook and his men were to voyage to the edge of the known world, then leap off it and sail into the blue.

ON MY FIRST night aboard the replica *Endeavour,* I sat down with my watchmates to a dinner advertised on the galley blackboard as "gruel." This turned out to be a tasty stew, with pie and fruit to follow. It was also a marked improvement on the fare aboard the original *Endeavour.* Before leaving port, Cook complained to the Navy Board that the cook assigned his ship was "a lame infirm man, and incapable of doing his Duty." The board granted his request for a replacement, sending John Thompson, who had lost his right hand. Cook's request for still another man was denied. The Navy gave preference to "cripples and maimed persons" in its appointment of cooks, a fair indicator of its regard for sailors' palates.

"Victualled" for twelve months, the *Endeavour* toted thousands of pounds of ship's biscuit (hardtack), salt beef, and salt pork: the sailors' staples. On alternate days, the crew ate oatmeal and cheese instead of meat. Though hearty—a daily ration packed 4,500 calories—the sailors' diet was as foul as it was monotonous. "Our bread indeed is but indifferent," the *Endeavour*'s botanist, Joseph Banks, observed, "occasioned by the quantity of Vermin that are in it. I have often seen hundreds nay thousands shaken out of a single bisket." Banks catalogued five types of insect and noted their mustardy and "very disagreeable" flavor, which he likened to a medicinal tonic made from stags' horns.

On the replica, we also enjoyed a considerable luxury denied Cook's men: marine toilets and showers tucked discreetly in the forward hold. Up on the main deck, Todd showed us what the original sailors used: holed planks extending from the bow, utterly exposed in every sense. These were called heads, or seats of ease. On Cook's second voyage, an unfortunate sailor was last seen using the heads, from which he fell and drowned.

Once we'd eaten and showered, Todd recommended we head straight for our hammocks. "Call all hands" was scheduled for six A.M., and many of us would have to rise before then for a shift on deck. This was also our last night in port. "Once the rocking and rolling starts," Todd warned, "you may not get much rest."

I hoisted myself into the hammock—and promptly tumbled out the other side. On the second try I managed a mummylike posture, arms folded tightly across my chest. At least I couldn't toss and turn, as I normally do in bed. "I feel like a bat," moaned Chris, the crewman a few inches to my left, his nose almost brushing the ceiling.

To my right, lying with his feet past my head, swung Michael, a man built like Samson. As soon as he fell asleep, his massive limbs spilled out of his hammock and into mine. My face pressed against his thigh; a loglike arm weighed on my ankles. Then a storm came up and the ship started swaying. Michael's oxlike torso thudded against me, knocking my hammock against Chris's and back into Samson's. I felt like a carcass in a meat locker. The ship's timbers also creaked and groaned, adding to the snores and curses of my cabin mates.

At midnight, the watches changed. Crewmen thudded down the companionway and rousted the next shift from their hammocks. Then a woman began sneezing and hacking. "I'm allergic to something down here," she moaned, having woken most of us up, "and I didn't bring any medicine."

I'd just managed a fitful doze when someone poked me hard in the ribs: four A.M. watch. Groggily pulling on my gear, I mustered on deck with several others. We were still near shore and had little to do except make sure that the anchor line didn't tangle. Loitering about the dark, empty ship, I felt oddly like a night guard at a museum.

This gave me a chance to become acquainted with my watch mates. Chris, my hammock neighbor, was a bespectacled psychology professor. Samsonesque Michael worked as a tugboat captain. The fourth member of our night watch, Charlie, had just retired after thirty-two years as a firefighter. "I guess I still need excitement," he said, when I asked why he'd signed on. "So I decided to try adventure travel."

"Adventure torture's more like it," Chris said. "I was lying there all night thinking, 'I volunteered for this? To be straitjacketed?' "

At seven A.M., we were called below for the last sitting of breakfast: porridge and toast with Vegemite, the bitter Australian spread that looks like creosote. "On deck in five minutes!" Todd shouted as soon as we'd sat down. We bolted our food and rushed to stow our hammocks. I'd already forgotten Todd's instructions: roped up, my sling looked bloated and uneven, like a strangled sausage. I crammed it as best I could into the stow hold and lunged up the companionway, thudding my head so hard I almost fell back down the steps.

"Okay," Todd said, clapping his hands. "Now that you're rested and fed, it's time for some hard labor." As far as I could gather, this meant yanking and tying down ropes. "It's Newton's third law, every action has an equal reaction," Todd explained. "You've got to ease on one side of the ship so you can haul on the other. Haul or ease away, either way the order is 'Haul away!' Take the line down the left side of the cleat, then do a figure eight with three turns and run it round the back and loop it. That's called a tugboat hitch." He paused for breath. "Everything clear?"

There were twelve of us on mainmast. I reckoned I could lose myself in the mob, or latch on to someone who knew what he or she was doing. "Stand by for cannon!" shouted a longhaired gunner wearing earmuffs. "Fire in the hole!" He lowered a blowtorch to a small pan of black powder, then stepped away as the cannon expelled a cloud of smoke and wadded newspaper into the damp, foggy air.

The first mate shouted, "Haul away!" and I joined the others in tugging at the thick, heavy ropes. Todd urged us on with an antique gun-crew command: "Two-six heave! Put your back into it! For queen and country!" We yanked another rope, and then another, maneuvering some small part of the impossibly complex rigging. The horizontal yards shifted along the masts, like rotating crucifixes. The first of the ship's twenty-eight sails fluttered from the bowsprit. Rope rained down all around us, twenty miles of rope in all. After an hour of grabbing and tugging, I felt as though I'd been put to the rack.

Four older men wandered up from below, looking rested and relaxed. These were the ship's passengers, who paid a fat sum to occupy private cabins. Like almost everything else on the replica *Endeavour*, their presence hewed to the original. A month before the ship's departure, the Admiralty informed Cook that "Joseph Banks Esq.," a member of the Royal Society and "a Gentleman of Large Fortune, well versed in Natural History," would be accompanying the voyage, along with "his Suite consisting of eight Persons and their Baggage."

Though only twenty-five years old, Banks had inherited a vast estate and paid some £10,000—more than twice what the king contributed to the voyage, and roughly equivalent to a million dollars today—to join the expedition. His entourage on the *Endeavour* included two Swedish naturalists, two artists, two footmen, and two black servants, as well as Banks's greyhound and spaniel. Known collectively as supernumeraries, or the "gentlemen," Banks and his retinue had their own quarters and dined with Cook in the stern's airy "great cabin," far removed from the teeming mess deck.

The supernumeraries on the replica enjoyed similar privileges, including tea served to them in bed in china cups. On deck, they could join in the work if they felt like it. At the moment, none did. "We're just deadweight," joked a burly man who occupied the cabin of the *Endeavour*'s astronomer, Charles Green. "Look it up in the dictionary. 'Deadweight: a vessel's lading when it consists of heavy goods.'" He laughed. "Plus I croak from dysentery during the voyage—Charles Green, I mean."

Eavesdropping on the supernumeraries' banter, I felt a sullen solidarity with my sweating, grunting workmates. Even more than most blue-collar jobs, ours demanded teamwork. If we didn't clutch and release ropes at exactly the same moment, we were quickly pancaked, like losers at a tug-of-war match. Accustomed to spending my workdays alone, a man and his desk, I found it refreshing to labor in a group, in the open air, at hard physical toil.

Then again, we'd only just started. And the task I'd been dreading—going aloft—was about to commence. Todd jumped atop the rail and grabbed the shrouds, vertical lines leading to the masthead that had smaller ropes, called ratlines, strung horizontally between them to create a rope ladder alongside the mast. "Try to keep three points of contact at all times with your feet and hands," Todd said, "and always go up the windward side of the mast so if there's a roll or blow you'll fall onto the deck rather than in the drink."

At first the climbing seemed easy. Freshly tarred, the shrouds were firm and sticky, easy to grasp. After a few minutes, we reached the underside of a platform called the fighting top. To surmount this, we grasped cables called futtock shrouds and did a short but unnerving climb while dangling backward at a 45-degree angle. Then, clutching a bar at the rim of the platform, we hoisted ourselves up and onto the fighting top. A chill wind blew across the platform, making the temperature feel ten degrees cooler than on deck. It was a late September morning in the Pacific Northwest, balmy compared to many of the places Cook went. And we weren't even halfway up the mast. We also had something Cook's men lacked: our safety harnesses, which we attached to a secure line before the next maneuver, called stepping onto the yard.

"Stepping" was a misnomer; we had to tiptoe sideways along a narrow, drooping foot line strung beneath the yard, which ran perpendicular to the mast. Each time a new person stepped on, the line quivered and bounced. I crab-walked to the end, perched over the water. This was the yardarm, from which men sentenced to death at sea were hanged. Just standing on the tightropelike line, leaning my belly against the yard, was unsettling enough. Then came actual labor. Bending awkwardly over the yard, as if flung across a gymnastic beam, we reached down to untie thick knots around the sails. Fumbling with the rope, I tried to focus tightly on my hands rather than let my gaze drift to the blur of water below. At one point I glanced straight ahead at the foremast watch, performing the same task: six protruding rumps, legs dancing spastically on the foot line, arms and torsos lost in a tangle of rope and sail.

When the job was done, we scuttled back to the fighting top, grinning at one another with nervous relief. My hands were shaking from adrenaline or cold, probably both. Dangling backward over the fighting top, I felt with my feet for the futtock shrouds and scrambled down to the deck as quickly as I could. For the first time all day I had a moment to rest, so I settled atop a life raft.

"No sitting on the boats!" a crewman barked. I headed toward the stern and tripped over the ankle-high tiller line, barking my shin and flopping onto the quarterdeck. I'd just got upright when another crewman said, "Mate, I wouldn't stand on that coiled line, unless you want to be hanging up in the rigging by your foot."

Finally finding a safe perch, I slumped on the deck, tired but exhilarated. A hard morning's work completed, a fear partly overcome. (The topmost yard, perched at twice the height of the one we'd just visited, remained to be conquered.) I was hungry and ready for a nap. I glanced at my watch. Only ten o'clock. "Mainmast to cleaning stations!" Todd yelled.

Dispatched below to scrub the galley, I swept the floor, wiped tables, washed dishes. This, at least, I knew how to do. Leaning on my broom, I asked the cook, a New Zealander named Joanna, what was on the lunch menu.

"Food," she replied.

I glanced at the stove. "Gingerbread men?"

"I use a lot of ginger, calms the stomach," she said. "I don't use many other spices. You don't want foods with strong odors, in case they don't stay down."

The first mate charged down the stairs. Trailing his finger under the table I'd just wiped, Geoff barked, "What's all this rubbish here?" I followed him with a cloth. "And what's this, a bloody dust ball?" I swept the floor again. Finishing the inspection, he frowned and said, "I rate this a pass. I expect better next time." As soon as he'd gone, Michael, my Samsonesque watch mate, muttered, "I thought a tugboat was bad, but this is a floating gulag."

Then Geoff's voice bellowed again from deep inside the ship. "Who is hammock fifteen? Hammock fifteen report here immediately!" I wearily ran through the numbers I'd been assigned since coming aboard: muster order, peg number, hammock . . . fifteen. Perhaps, I thought dreamily, the first mate was ordering me back to bed.

Geoff hunched over the hammock storage area with the rest of mainmast gathered round. Before us lay my bedding, which I'd clumsily stowed hours before. Geoff poked at it with his foot, like a detective probing a badly bundled corpse. "We've just got a message," he said, "your mother's not going to be here to make your bed today." While the rest looked on, I fumbled several times before finally stowing the hammock properly.

When Geoff returned to the quarterdeck, Todd gave me a sympathetic pat on the back. "Sit down and relax," he said. "Grab a cup of tea or ten minutes of shut-eye." Most of us raced to the toilets, which we'd been trying to find a moment to use all morning. I'd just reached the front of the line when a cry came from above. "All hands on deck! We've got wind! Hustle!"

This time we manned "sail setting stations," another bewildering cobweb of lines called clews, bunts, and reefs. "The best way to remember which is which," Todd said, "is by saying to yourself, 'Clews, Bunts, Reefs. Can't bloody remember.'" Then the arcane orders started up again. "Hold cro'jack!" "Belay starboard side braces!" "Haul away port bunt!"

Yards shifted; sails tightened and filled. The ship suddenly went silent except for the luffing of sails and the gentle slap of waves against wood. I gazed to starboard and saw Seattle's Space Needle in the distance, rising above a jungle of office towers. Traffic crawled across a bridge. Monday morning and we were free from all that, out here on the water. My spirits lifted.

A mop and bucket thudded against my chest. "Time to swab the deck," Todd said.

THE *ENDEAVOUR* SET sail on August 26, 1768, from Plymouth, the same spot from which the Pilgrims embarked. That day's *London Gazette* gives some flavor of the Hogarthian world the sailors left behind. A front-page story, headlined "A Rogue Dispatched to His Maker," described the hanging and gibbeting of a highwayman as pickpockets worked the jeering crowd. Another item reported on a hangman whipping a thief in the street for stealing two loaves of bread.

There was also a story about a lecture titled "On the Perils of Travel in Tropical Climes," during which a "much traveled Gentleman" caused women to swoon by claiming that natives "believed their gods would be more pleased if they spilled the blood of a white child." Two small items of overseas news made the front page. John Adams, known for his "encouragement of insurgency," was on his way to Boston. And a "Young Genius" by the name of Mozart had been appointed maestro at the age of twelve.

The *Endeavour*'s departure merited only a brief mention. James Cook wrote just as tersely in his own journal. "At 2 pm got under sail and put to sea having on board 94 persons," he wrote. "Sounded and had 50 fathoms Grey sand with small stones and broken shells."

Cook wrote with similar dispassion three weeks later, when he observed: "In heaving the Anchor out of the Boat Mr. Weir Masters mate was carried over board by the Buoy-rope and to the bottom." This is all we learn about the death of Alexander Weir, a thirty-five-year-old Scotsman from Fife. Cook expended as much ink—and expressed more regret—when several dozen chickens washed overboard in a storm the same month.

This seeming callousness reflected the grim reality of eighteenth-century naval life. Fresh poultry was scarce at sea. A drowned man could be easily replaced. On the day of Weir's death, Cook "Impress'd into his Majesty's service"—that is, legally kidnapped—a twenty-year-old sailor from a passing American sloop (Americans were then still British subjects). This man would also die during the voyage, as would thirty-six of the *Endeavour*'s original company of ninety-four. The ship's 40 percent casualty rate wasn't extraordinary for the day; in fact, Cook would later be hailed for the exceptional concern he showed for the health of his crew.

A sailor's life was as anonymous as it was cheap. Most of what's known about the *Endeavour*'s sailors—or "the People," as Cook called them—derives from the sparse details in the ship's muster book. As a group, the crewmen were young, many still in their teens and one aged just twelve. They hailed from all over: east London, Ireland, the Orkneys, New York, Venice, "the Brazils." Some sailors doubled as shipboard tradesmen: barbers, tailors, butchers, poulterers. Once at sea, they rarely appeared in the ship's log as individuals unless they'd been flogged, deserted, or died.

We know much more about the officers, several of whom kept journals. The aptly named John Gore was a trigger-happy American, a seaborne Hawkeye who would prove very skillful at shooting birds, kangaroos, and occasionally people. He had sailed the Pacific twice before and would do so two more times with Cook. Another Pacific veteran, Charles Clerke, was a waggish twenty-seven-year-old who had written a paper published in the Royal Society's journal, claiming that Patagonians in South America were so tall that Europeans reached only to the giants' waists. "At drinking and whoring he is as good as the best of them," one colleague wrote. Clerke would mature into a sober commander by the time he buried his superior off the coast of Hawaii a decade later.

But it is James Cook and the botanist Joseph Banks who dominate the *Endeavour*'s story and give the voyage its most unexpected dimension. The two men were fifteen years apart in age and hailed from opposite ends of the class system: Cook of peasant stock, with little schooling; Banks a nobleman's son, educated at Harrow, Eton, and Oxford. Their characters could hardly have differed more: Cook was a family man and naval careerist, Banks a rakish dilettante who regarded the voyage as a bold version of the traditional ruling-class tour of continental Europe. "Every blockhead does that," he told friends. "My Grand Tour shall be one round the whole globe." Their status on board also seemed a recipe for strife. Cook had absolute command over the ship and its crew, while Banks, who had all but bankrolled the voyage, ruled a small fiefdom of artists, scientists, and servants largely exempt from naval duties and discipline.

Yet the day laborer's son and the landed gentleman would forge one of the great partnerships in the history of exploration, akin to that between Meriwether Lewis and William Clark. Like the two Americans, Cook and Banks possessed complementary talents, and their voluminous day-to-day journals tell the same story through very different eyes. Cook titles his journal *Remarkable Occurences on Board His Majestys Bark Endeavour,* and he leaves out many details of ship life that to him seemed routine. An unsentimental man, accustomed to drawing charts, he surveys even the most exotic scenes with cool objectivity and factual precision.

Banks is chalk to Cook's cheese: opinionated, anecdotal, Romantic, self-revealing. "A genteel young man," Boswell called him, "of an agreeable countenance, easy and communicative, without any affectation." In his journal, Banks writes about his nausea, his bowel pains— even about banging his head while "foolishly" doing exercises in his cabin. He also conveys the awe and terror of launching into the deep in a way that Cook, the middle-aged salt, cannot. Several weeks out from Plymouth, after sailing past Spain, the *Endeavour* swung west across the Atlantic. Cook calmly noted the wind speed and weather. Banks, battling butterflies as well as seasickness, confided in his journal: "Took our leave of Europe for heaven alone knows how long, perhaps for Ever."

ON THE EVENING of my second day aboard the replica, I pulled the "last dog" watch, from 1800 to 2000 hours. This was a pleasant time to be on deck, with the sun setting and my belly warmed by the corn chowder I'd bolted at dinner. It was refreshing to feel genuine appetite bred of hard labor rather than habit. And, for the first time all day, there seemed little to do. Only six sailors were needed to work the helm and keep watch from the bow, leaving the rest of us to idle by the rail. Even the roll of the ship seemed soothing, like a cradle. As the light faded, I closed my eyes.

Todd nudged me awake, his dark features curled in a mischievous grin. "I've got something to perk you up," he said.

"Coffee?"

"Better. Topgallant needs putting to bed." In other words, the sails draped from the topmost yard had to be furled. Todd handed me over to a young Australian deckhand named Jess, my guide to the top of the mast. She started scampering up the shrouds and I followed, climbing beside Charlie the fireman and Chris the professor. This seemed reassuring. Charlie had told me the night before about rescuing a man from a burning building. Chris was a neuroscientist who studied conditioned response and the power of suggestion. Two men with a professional perspective on fear and how to confront it.

Then I noticed that Charlie had stopped midway up the mast, paralyzed by the ship's sudden sway. "At least a fire ladder's solid," he said. The topmost yard lurched far above us, like a drunken pencil. A dizzying glimpse of deck and sea swam below. "I don't know what's worse," Charlie said, "looking up or down."

"Just focus on your hands and concentrate on what you're doing!" Chris shouted, climbing behind us. "If you don't think about falling you won't get dizzy." This sounded like good advice. Except that Chris was clinging to the shrouds so tightly that his hands had gone as white as his face. I parroted a line that Chris had handed us the night before: "Irrational fears go away if you confront them." My voice came out strangled, high-pitched.

"It's a little different when those fears are entirely rational," Chris replied, peering between his legs.

Jess, climbing high above, shot us a withering look. "Come on, you wankers!" she shouted. "You want to do this job in the dark?"

We resumed climbing to the crosstrees, three narrow ribs of wood perched beneath the top yard. Earlier in the day, in full light and calm seas, the much lower and larger fighting top had seemed a relatively secure haven. Now, at dusk, in a brisk wind, this tiny way station felt horribly precarious. Height radically amplifies a ship's motion; a roll that tilts the deck a foot will move the top of the mast five times as much. "Funny, when you're on the deck the ship seems really wide," Chris said, foolishly glancing down again. "Not anymore."

We hooked our safety harnesses, crept along a foot line, and belly flopped over the yard. Furling a sail was much more awkward and tiring than letting it down. Following Jess's lead, we grabbed fistfuls of flapping fabric, bunched the sail against the yard, and reached down for more. I was just getting the hang of it when the ship pitched forward, teetering us over the bow, before swinging back. Then it pitched again. As we raised the sail we had to tie it to the yard. When we practiced this maneuver on deck, it had seemed simple enough: looping a rope under the sail, cinching it tight, then throwing the spare line over one shoulder before edging along the yard to tie up another clot of sail. Now, a hundred feet up, as the ship pitched, the job felt about as easy as roping a steer. The rope became tangled around my neck and under my arm and each time I crept down the foot line the sail I'd just tied up began to sag. "I feel like a stroke victim," Chris said. "My hands can't seem to follow simple mental commands."

He fled to the crosstrees. Jess skipped out along the foot line and deftly corrected our sloppy work. I was well past feeling any shame. "Could you carry me down while you're at it?" I asked, only half in jest.

"No worries, mate." She tied off the last bit of rope. "By the end of the week you'll have done this so many times it'll seem dead easy."

When we reached the deck, my hands were black from the tarred shrouds and bleeding from clutching the ropes too hard. My legs shook. Mostly, though, what I felt was incredulity. Cook's men had performed this harrowing job not simply as a matter of course, without safety gear, but in conditions that made our scamper up the mast seem like a child's pirate game.

"Sleet and Snow froze to the Rigging as it fell and decorated the whole with icicles," Cook wrote of a gale off Antarctica. "Our ropes were like wires, Sails like board or plates of Metal. . . . It required our utmost effort to get a Top-sail down and up; the cold so intense as hardly to be endured." Cook didn't bother to mention that he and much of the crew were laboring against sickness, including severe joint pains from incipient scurvy. Many of Cook's men also suffered from hernias—bursted bellies, as sailors called them.

My only affliction was bone-crushing fatigue. I'd been on my feet for most of the past eighteen hours. When our watch ended, I went straight to my hammock, too tired to wash. Climbing in, I decided the sling wasn't so bad after all. A cocoon almost. Samson hoisted into his, thumping against me. The allergic woman began coughing and sneezing again. Only four more nights and days of this, I thought, drifting straight to sleep.

IF I'D BEEN aboard the original *Endeavour*, the journey ahead would have loomed rather larger: 1,052 days, to be exact, assuming I was among the 60 percent who survived. This was a notion I struggled to wrap my mind around. I'd often felt sorry for myself when flying to and from Australia. Twenty hours in the air! A forced march through movies, meals, and mystery novels. Almost the limit of the modern traveler's endurance. Yet it had taken Cook and his men a year and a half to reach Australia, and almost as long to get home again. The ship crawled at seven or eight knots in ideal conditions, much slower in light wind. And each day on the water unfolded much like the one before, a metronomic routine of watches, scrubbing, furling and unfurling sails. "The sea," landsman Joseph Banks observed, "is certainly an excellent school for patience."

Reading the thousand or so entries in Cook's *Endeavour* journal also brought home Winston Churchill's famous quip about naval tradition: "It's nothing but rum, sodomy and the lash." At the start of the voyage, Cook read his crew the Articles of War, which listed punishable offenses, including drunkenness, "profane Oaths," the "unnatural and detestable sin of buggery or sodomy with man or beast" (in Canada, Cook had twice lashed seamen for attempting this offense), and "stirring up disturbances on account of the Unwholesomness of Victual." It was this last crime that occasioned the first flogging on the *Endeavour*, just three weeks out to sea: twelve lashes each for two sailors who complained about their allowance of beef.

On our first-day tour of the replica, Todd had showed us a canvas bag; inside it was a heavy knotted rope—the cat-o'-nine-tails, so named for the number of its cords and the catlike scratches it left on a man's back. This was also the origin of the phrases "let the cat out of the bag" and "not enough room to swing a cat." The cat came out of the bag with depressing regularity during the *Endeavour*'s long passage to the Pacific. On one day alone, three men were lashed, the last for "not doing his duty in punishing the above two." Before the trip was over, Cook would flog one in four of his crew, about average for eighteenth-century voyages.

If Cook didn't spare the lash, he also didn't stint sailors their most treasured salve: alcohol. The *Endeavour* sailed with a staggering quantity of booze: 1,200 gallons of beer, 1,600 gallons of spirits (brandy, arrack, rum), and 3,032 gallons of wine that Cook collected at Madeira. The customary ration for a sailor was a gallon of beer a day, or a pint of spirits, diluted with water to make a twice-daily dose of "grog." Sailors also mixed beer with rum or brandy to create the debilitating drink known as flip. Cook's notes on individual crewmen include frequent asides such as "more or less drunk every day."

Midway across the Atlantic, the *Endeavour* crossed the equator, an occasion marked with ancient, rum-soaked ritual. From here on, the skies and seasons would reverse, an experience known only to the handful on board who had "crossed the Line" before. For one day, the ship's hierarchy also turned upside down. Veterans of the South Seas conducted a fraternitylike initiation of other crewmen, regardless of their rank. The salts tied novices to a makeshift stool, hoisted them up the main yard, and then plunged them into the sea three times. Any sailor who refused to undergo this dunking had to forfeit four days' allowance of drink.

"This ceremony was performed on about 20 or 30 to the no small deversion of the rest," wrote Cook, who ransomed himself with rum. Those being ducked didn't enjoy themselves quite so much. Some "were almost suffocated," wrote Banks, who paid extra brandy to spare his servants and dogs. That evening, he added, "was spent merrily."

Christmas afforded another occasion for excess. "All good Christians that is to say all hands got abominably drunk so that at night there was scarce a sober man in the ship," Banks wrote. "Wind thank god very moderate or the lord knows what would have become of us." Considering the quantity of booze that sailors consumed on a normal day, it staggers the mind to imagine how much grog the men downed that Christmas.

At Tierra del Fuego, at the bottom of South America, Banks went ashore with a small party to gather plants. The weather turned suddenly frigid and snow began to fall. Banks's two black servants "stupefied themselves" with rum, and stayed behind while the others struggled ahead. By the time a rescue party returned, the two men had died from exposure or alcohol poisoning. Later in the voyage, a man entered the ship's log as having "died at sea of an excess of rum." Some who fell from the ship and drowned undoubtedly did so while drunk.

There wasn't any risk of that happening on the replica *Endeavour*. The ship was alcohol-free, a concession to modern sensibilities about sailing under the influence. "People get a little more upset these days if you lose someone overboard," Captain Blake dryly explained. In three years at sea, only one man had fallen off the replica: a safety officer who slipped while stowing a sail. He was pulled out ten minutes later, frightened but unhurt. Another crewman had fallen from the rigging. Though saved by his harness, he suffered bruises and shock. Rough seas also threw crew around the lower deck, resulting in broken ribs and gashed heads.

Even in calm weather, minor injuries were common: sprains, twists, rope burns. On our second day out, Chris slipped from a rail, tearing a ligament in his knee. Another man badly wrenched his ankle. This meant more work for the rest of us. In theory, the watch system divided the ship's labor into four-hour shifts, with no more than twelve hours a day of work for any sailor. In practice, this clearly defined schedule was subject to change at any moment: if the wind died or gusted, if we had to tack, or if some problem arose that required more than twelve hands on deck. Meals and sleep were prone to similar interruptions. Before long, I stopped watching the clock and stumbled from task to task in a plodding daze.

At some point I found myself winding up the anchor with the capstan, a revolving wood cylinder that eight of us moved by pushing chest-high spokes, around and around, like blindfolded camels grinding grain. It was brute work, set to brute commands: "Heave away!" "Avast!" "Heave and pawl!" Todd interspersed these orders with an off-color chantey, set to the tune of an Australian rugby song: "I wish all the ladies were waves in the ocean, and I was a surfer. / I'd ride them all in motion. / I wish all the ladies were bricks in a pile, and I was a builder. / I'd lay them all in style."

As Todd sang, a Californian named Karen shook her head. "Onshore you'd get fired for sexual harassment singing that," she said, pushing the capstan beside me. "Not that I care out here. I don't care about anything anymore."

"It's like a cult," added a Canadian named John, who was pushing in front of us. "They get you on this ship and use fear and sleep deprivation and lead-based paint fumes until you become a complete automaton."

One task offered relief from this ceaseless toil. At sunset, Todd ordered me to keep watch from the bow. This meant shimmying to the end of the twenty-foot bowsprit and looking for logs, buoys, or small boats. If I saw anything I called out its position to a "runner" at the rail. Lying with my elbows on the bowsprit, the wind gusting past, I felt rather like a figurehead—albeit a ludicrous one, bundled in layers of filthy clothes and a wool cap pulled down around my ears. The original *Endeavour* was so prosaic a ship that it sailed without a figurehead, or even its name painted on the transom.

Settling in, I realized that bow watch suited my temperament much better than tugging ropes, shoving the capstan, or scurrying up the mast as a cog in a mechanism I didn't comprehend. Here, all I had to do was observe, and report on what I saw—not so different from my normal occupation as a journalist. "Buoy, two points to port!" I shouted to the runner, conveying the only breaking news during the contented hour I spent astride the bowsprit.

For several days I'd barely had a moment to gaze out to sea, except in terror from the top of the mast. Now, I watched a porpoise surface and a family of eiders paddle past. Seagulls perched atop seaweed. The water seemed wondrously varied and textured, in one spot dark green and glass-smooth, in another indigo and ruffled, as if pattered by tiny raindrops. At other points, the sea eddied and frothed into whitecaps: miniatures of the snow-covered Cascade Mountains looming off to starboard, slowly turning pink in the setting sun.

COOK HADN'T BEEN quite so awed by the majesty of the Pacific Northwest. By the time he arrived off the west coast of America, midway through his third voyage, he'd become a bit jaded by all the scenery he'd passed during the previous nine years: Antarctic icebergs, Krakatoa's volcano, the fjords of New Zealand. Sighting the coast of present-day Oregon, he wrote of the view: "There was nothing remarkable about it." Nor was Cook impressed by the climate. "The land formed a point, which I called *Cape Foul Weather* from the very bad weather we soon after met with."

Coasting north through squalls, hail, sleet, and snow, Cook searched for a port or even a clear sight of land. Close to where we now sailed, he spotted an opening "which flatered us with hopes of finding a harbour." It proved an illusion, and Cook left behind another disappointed name: Cape Flattery. Later, he neared the Strait of Juan de Fuca, named for a navigator who claimed to have come this way in 1592, and who returned with tales of beautiful islands "rich of gold, Silver, Pearle, and other things." Cook, once again, was foiled by darkness and weather. "We saw nothing like it, nor is there the least probability that iver any such thing exhisted," he wrote of the strait, before departing the present-day United States.

We were much more fortunate. At dawn on our third day out, the ship approached a wide passage between the Olympic Peninsula and Vancouver Island. "There it is, mates," Todd announced. "The Strait of Wanna Puka." The last time the replica had sailed past the Juan de Fuca Strait, half the crew had spent the day hugging "chunder buckets"—plastic pails with smiley faces at the bottom beside the words "You will get better."

The wind quickly picked up and I struggled to keep my balance on deck. But the scenery was lovely, not a sign of humanity, the lonely San Juan Islands just ahead. By now, the first mate's commands had also taken on the pleasantly repetitive rhythm of a caller at a square dance.

"Hold your starboard reef!

"Hold your starboard bunt!

"Belay starboard!"

I still wasn't sure what much of this meant, but I knew what to do: tug and hold weight until someone tied off the line. Only a few people had to flex their minds. The rest of us were just muscle. Even scaling the mast had lost some of its terror. Or rather, the terror made me feel safe; I was so focused on keeping a tight grip and getting the job done that I felt preternaturally alert, like a soldier in combat.

A deep apathy about personal hygiene had also set in. At one point I caught my reflection while polishing brass: three days' scruff on my cheeks, lank hair, red eyes, tar-speckled chin. I looked like a street person, and behaved like one, too. Discovering a Vegemite-smeared crust in my pocket, stashed the day before while dashing from the galley to the deck, I bolted it without shame. During a rare slack moment between watches, I wrapped a rank shirt around my head and sprawled on the nearest patch of deck. At night it was all I could do to peel off two layers of socks.

Eighteenth-century sailors were far more slovenly. They often slept fully clothed, in case they were called on deck during the night. Soap didn't become a Navy provision until 1796. Lice were endemic; maggots, cockroaches, and rats also swarmed the ship. For napkins, sailors used bits of frayed rope, which became so greasy that the men recycled them as candles. Makeshift urinals added to the squalor. Some sailors didn't bother to use them, pissing from the deck through grates to the hold below. On Cook's second voyage, a marine was punished for defecating between decks, and when a ship's cook died from disease, his mates attributed it to his filth: as one put it, "he being so very indolent & dirtily inclined there was no possability of making him keep himself clean, or even to come on Deck to breath the fresh air." Not surprisingly, given this level of hygiene—even among cooks—sailors also suffered from dysentery, a horrible thought given that the only toilets were the dreaded "seats of ease."

Cook fought hard to change sailors' habits. He encouraged them to take cold seawater baths, as he did, and enforced regular cleaning of hammocks, bedding, and clothes, sometimes towing laundry behind the ship. He also used sailcloth to channel fresh air into the lower deck, as well as scrubbing the floors with vinegar and lighting fires of brimstone to clear out the fug. But it was in the realm of diet that Cook made his greatest mark. The *Endeavour* was not only on a voyage of scientific discovery; it was also a laboratory for testing the latest theories and technology, rather as spaceships are today. In particular, Cook and his men became guinea pigs in the Navy's long fight against "the scourge of the sea," otherwise known as scurvy.

The human body can store only about six weeks of vitamin C, and as the supply runs out the hideous symptoms of scurvy appear: lassitude; loose teeth; rotted gums; putrid belching; joint pain; ulcerated skin; the reopening of old wounds and healed fractures; hemorrhaging from the mouth, nose, and lungs; and, ultimately, death. Some eighteenth-century ships lost half their men to scurvy. Also, because of the disease's time cycle, it would often strike much of the crew at once, filling the ship with sick men. This made scurvy as significant an impediment to exploration as sailors' inexact means of calculating longitude.

The Navy suspected that scurvy sprang from a lack of fresh food at sea. But it had failed to adopt the findings of James Lind, a Scottish physician who, fifteen years before the *Endeavour*'s sail, wrote a treatise on scurvy that recommended citrus fruit as a prophylactic. Instead, the Navy's "Sick and Hurt Board" loaded the *Endeavour* with experimental antiscorbutics such as malt wort (a drink), sauerkraut, and "portable soup," a decoction of "vegetables mixed with liver, kidney, heart and other offal boiled to a pulp." Hardened into slabs, it was dissolved into oatmeal or "pease," a pudding of boiled peas.

Cook enforced this diet with fanatical zeal, and with a keen grasp of sailors' psychology. "Such are the Tempers and disposissions of Seamen in general that whatever you give them out of the Common way," he wrote, "it will not go down with them and you will hear nothing but murmurings." At first, the sailors wouldn't touch sauerkraut. Then Cook made it known that the dish was being served each day to the gentlemen and officers, and left the People to decide if they wanted to eat it or not. Before long, every man did. "The Moment they see their Superiors set a Value upon it, it becomes the finest stuff in the World," Cook wrote. He also forbade sailors one of their favorite dishes—biscuits smeared with "slush," or fat skimmings—because he believed it obstructed digestion and blocked "putrid air" in the body.

Cook succeeded in quelling scurvy, though not for the reasons he or the Navy supposed. The antiscorbutics on board were of little or no value. Instead, it appears that Cook's equally dedicated pursuit of fresh food at every port he reached protected his men. "It was the Custom of our Crews to Eat almost every Herb plant Root and kinds of Fruit they Could Possibly Light upon," a sailor wrote, adding that crewmen "knew it was A great Recommendation to be seen Coming on board from A pleasure Jaunt with A Handkerchif full of greens."

Ironically, Cook's later endorsement of malt wort retarded the fight against scurvy. It wasn't until the twentieth century that scientists conclusively determined that a daily dose of a mere ten milligrams of vitamin C was enough to prevent a disease that had killed tens of thousands of sailors.

ON OUR FOURTH night at sea, I was shaken awake for what I assumed was the four A.M. watch. Struggling out of my hammock, I fell to the sharply tilted floor. I glanced at my watch: it was only two o'clock. The ship righted, then rolled again. The thought of getting back in my hammock made me queasy. I went to the galley and found six others, nervously clutching tables. A woman named Sharon was distracting herself by compiling a list of nautical terms that had entered modern slang: "all washed up," "around the horn," "clear the decks," "catch someone's drift," "taken aback" (when sails drive a ship to stern), "scuttlebutt" (a water cask around which sailors gossiped). The rest of us pitched in words we'd learned during the course of the week, such as "three sheets to the wind" (if a ship's sheets, or ropes, are hanging loose, the sails flap and the ship is unsteady; hence, drunk), and "bitter end" (the last piece of an anchor cable, attached to a bitt, or post).

"Pooped," someone said.

"What's that?"

"It's in rough seas, when the water comes over the stern and onto the poop deck."

The galley went silent. We listened to water slosh in the bilge. Dishes rattled in latched cupboards. "Batten down the hatches," Sharon said, adding the phrase to her list.

For once, I was grateful when my shift on deck began. In rough seas, the open air seemed far preferable to the stifling mess deck. Then again, as soon as I climbed the companionway, the wind bounced me from mast to rail and pierced my long johns, jeans, and four layers of shirts and jackets. "Crisp morning," the captain said, giving Todd the course and ducking below.

As luck would have it, my turn at the helm had arrived. This job required two people. One crewman, called "brains," shouted changes in direction, while another, called "muscle," turned the heavy ten-spoked wheel. Working first as muscle, I struggled to keep track of where I was on the wheel while the brains called out, "two spokes to port," or "four spokes to starboard," or "midships," the wheel's original position.

"Brains" was much trickier. I had to keep a simultaneous eye on the faint, bobbing horizon and on a gyrating compass. When the ship strayed more than 5 degrees off course—which it did constantly, in gusts of up to thirty-five knots—I had to judge how much to adjust, at the same time recalling how many spokes we'd already moved to port or starboard.

A 370-ton wooden tub doesn't shift so nimbly as a fiberglass yacht. The ship took half a minute to respond each time I moved the rudder; when it did, I invariably found I'd corrected too much. Then I'd correct the correction, fishtailing too far the other way. I felt as though I was steering a poorly aligned truck on an icy highway. And each time I'd finally got things under control, the captain would pop his head up from below to order a new course, starting the mad skid all over again.

At least the work kept my mind off the rolling seas. At six A.M., handing over the helm, I tripped on a heavy bundle by the rail. A muffled groan came from inside the blanket. A little way on, I passed several hunched figures retching into buckets. Struggling to the bow, I arrived just as the ship pitched into a wave, tossing cold spray in my face. A moment later, Todd lifted my wool cap and shouted in my ear to come back and help brace a spritsail spar. There were no other able bodies available.

Grasping a rope and pulling down with all my weight, I lifted off the deck, swinging like a pirate, until Michael fastened the line. "Do it fast and don't let go," Todd told him, "or else Errol Flynn there will fall back on the deck, crack his head, and die a terrible death."

"Shit happens," Michael said, calmly belaying the rope.

At breakfast, half the members of mainmast stared greenly into their swaying porridge. The rest of us bantered with the obnoxious merriment of the spared. "Eat up," Chris said to one of the stricken. "It'll give you something to do back on deck. Two-six heave."

Todd pitched in with tales of epic vomiting from voyages past. "Someone spewed while aloft and the wind was blowing so hard it went horizontally," he said. Another sailor, dangling from the topmost yard, daintily puked in her hat rather than shower those below. "Unfortunately, she dropped her hat on the way down."

I was surprised to learn that Todd, who had been at sea for three years, sometimes became sick, as did others among the permanent crew. During a gale shortly before our voyage, the *Endeavour* had heeled so sharply that the cannons dipped in the sea and water sloshed over the rails. "Sea legs aren't much good," Todd said, "when your legs are almost in the sea." The most sickening motion, though, was when the ship "corkscrewed," rolling and pitching at the same time. Todd added what was meant to be a consoling footnote. "I've never known anyone to spew for more than three days and three nights."

Midmorning, the wind settled down, and I was ordered below to clean the quarters of the officers and gentlemen. This meant collecting seawater in canvas bags slung over the ship's side, then struggling down a steep ladder to scrub the uneven wood floors. Compared to our quarters, the aft deck felt decadent. The only natural light in the mess deck shafted narrowly down the companionway. Here, sun filtered through a transom and latticed windows. The table in the officers' mess was laid with pewter, china, and cloth napkins. There was more than enough room to swing a cat.

The cabins, though, were six-foot-square hutches, crowded with gimballed beds, sea chests, and chamber pots. Even Cook's cabin felt tiny, with barely enough space for a foldout desk and a chair with shortened legs. Banks, at six foot four, stood several inches longer than his room; he usually left his quarters to his books and dogs, preferring to sling a hammock in the "great cabin." This was where the captain and gentlemen dined and worked. Here, light and air poured through wide sashes opening out both sides of the ship, and to stern. A large table, with chairs lashed to its base, stood at the room's center, surrounded by cupboards, a fireplace, a shelf of nautical and botanical books, and a birdcage with a fake parakeet.

Captain Blake sat at the table, writing in the ship's log. His rendition of the last twelve hours sounded disappointingly tame. The wind had reached "force six," he wrote, referring to the Beaufort Scale, "bringing with it a short sharp sea chop that had some effect on the crew." When we'd finished cleaning, he invited several of us to join him at the table. This wouldn't have happened in Cook's day. Officers and gentlemen kept to the quarterdeck when above, an area off limits to ordinary sailors. Below, they remained separated from the sailors by a party of marines, whose quarters formed a firewall against mutiny. The marines were a sort of seaborne middle class, dining and dwelling apart from both the officers and the People. The *Endeavour* was England in miniature: a hundred men on a hundred-foot ship, decorously maintaining the same divisions at sea that prevailed on land.

"You couldn't be that formal now, even if you wanted to," Blake said. "Not with a crew of Australians. They'd tell you to get stuffed."

Blake, an Englishman born in Nigeria, had gone to sea at fifteen and spent the next three decades working on everything from cargo boats to luxury cruise ships. He possessed the unflappable air of a mariner who had seen all that the sea could throw at him. Even so, the captain confessed that he'd been startled by the experience of piloting the *Endeavour*. "I'm not a romantic," he said, "but you do start to appreciate what they did, and how soft we've become by comparison."

In Cook's day, sailors still relied on much the same tools they'd used for centuries. They calculated the ship's speed with an hourglass and a knotted line draped in the water (hence the term "knots"). They dropped lead lines with tallow at the end to determine the water depth and test the sea's bottom. A relatively new and improved system of sextant, almanac, and lunar tables helped sailors figure out where they were on the globe. All these tasks—performed in an instant today by sonar, radar, and global positioning systems—were not only tricky and time-consuming; they also left little or no margin for error on a ship that was unwieldy, even for its day.

"The *Endeavour* was the Mack truck of the eighteenth century," Blake said. "A beast to maneuver." The replica, like the original, sailed poorly into the wind and slipped steadily sideways in a heavy current or cross breeze. If the replica found itself close to shore in shifty winds or water, Blake could hit the emergency engines, and motor out of trouble. "Cook had to sail out of it or be crushed against rocks," he said. Added to that was the constant anxiety of keeping the ship provisioned with fresh water, firewood, and food.

But what awed Blake most was the *Endeavour*'s mission. For much of the voyage, Cook sailed blind: into uncharted waters, toward unknown lands, through hurricane belts with nothing but clouds to warn of the weather ahead. The only modern experience that seemed remotely analogous was hurtling into space; one NASA shuttle had been named, appropriately, the *Endeavour*. But even this comparison didn't capture the utter vulnerability of Cook's ship. Astronauts have satellite images, contact with Mission Control, and high-tech instruments to bail them out. Cook traveled far beyond the range of any help, without so much as a life raft.

"We throw around words like 'courage' and 'stress' very carelessly today," Blake said. "Anyone who does anything out of the ordinary is a 'hero,' a 'survivor.'" He shook his head. "I don't think many of us could endure a week of what Cook and his men confronted, physically and psychologically, day in and day out, for years at a time."

In one respect, though, Blake envied Cook. The replica *Endeavour* had to keep to a schedule, forcing Blake to spend much of his day watching the clock and calling in his coordinates to the Coast Guard. Cook had a schedule, too, but it was generally measured in seasons. Could he reach the Arctic before winter closed in? Would breadfruit and other foodstuffs still be in season when he reached the tropics?

"We've lost that patience, that sense of chance," Blake said. "I think that's why a lot of people come out on this ship. They feel confined, coddled, time-sick." He laughed. "Either that or they've read too many Patrick O'Brian novels."

The replica's professional sailors were different. Many came from maritime backgrounds and hoped to spend their careers at sea. One was a shipwright's son from the Sydney docks. Others had labored in the merchant marine. Todd, a truckdriver's son who'd spent his teenage years as a lifeguard on Australia's rough Pacific beaches, planned to get a maritime pilot's license. One sailor had decided to stick to historic vessels: his next posting was aboard a replica of an Irish famine ship.

Like Cook's men, the replica's sailors also played as hard as they worked. "There may not be any booze on this ship, but everyone makes up for it on shore," Blake said. "The world's a different place

than it was in Cook's time, but sailors' characters haven't changed all
that much."

THE NEXT DAY, Vancouver's skyline hove into view, set against a
spectacular backdrop of jagged, snowcapped mountains. Cook had
missed this, too. The closest he came was Nootka Sound, off Vancouver Island, where he spent a month provisioning and repairing his gale-
battered ship. For "the People," who had previously enjoyed the
beauty and liberality of Polynesian women, Nootka proved a disappointment. "The women here are quite out of the question," a surgeon's mate, William Ellis, wrote of the lice-ridden, ocher-painted
natives. Not all the crewmen agreed: some scrubbed the women on
deck before bartering for their company.

Our own arrival in Canada was considerably less exotic. On the
morning of our last day at sea, we were assigned an additional job:
turning the lower deck from a working ship into a museum exhibit for
the *Endeavour*'s stay in port. We laid out bowls of plastic sauerkraut,
piles of hardtack, dominoes, and wooden mugs and pitchers. Stringing
a sample hammock, I felt like climbing in and staying in the sling as
part of the exhibit: dead sailor. Among other things, I'd learned that
hammocks doubled as shrouds for those who perished at sea. My
hands were so swollen and raw that I couldn't make a fist or do the
buttons on my shirt. Every limb throbbed. My eyes twitched and
blurred from fatigue.

We went aloft one last time to furl the sails and we stayed on the
yard to enjoy the view as the ship eased into harbor. A replica longboat
pulled alongside, rowed by men in horned helmets, the kind that mock
Vikings drink from. "Ahoy!" they shouted, raising their oars. The
dock was crowded with schoolchildren waving Union Jacks, red-
uniformed Mounties, city officials, and television camera crews. After
just a week on board, I felt unexpectedly proprietorial and proud.

"Fire in the hole!" the gunner yelled, delivering a broadside of
shredded newspaper in the direction of downtown. Then he soberly
approached the helm. "Minimal collateral damage, Captain. We can
still use the pub."

And we did, toting our duffel bags through a seedy district to Fred's

Uptown Tavern. I found myself walking bowlegged and leaning into an imagined swell. I didn't register much else; after two beers, the bar began to sway like the quarterdeck. I blearily exchanged hugs and phone numbers with my watch mates, then found a room on the top floor of a cheap hotel. Falling into the shower, I tried to scrub off the tar stuck in my hair and the grime embedded in every inch of exposed skin—a fraction of the filth the *Endeavour*'s sailors must have acquired in three years at sea. As soon as I closed my eyes, the bed began to pitch and roll, a mattress pinned atop a fifteen-story mast. I'd only been at sea a week, in relatively calm seas. Cook and his men once sailed extreme latitudes for 117 days without touching land. It's a wonder they could still walk when they reached shore.

The next morning I headed to the airport, still wobbly on my feet. As the plane lifted off and wheeled over the harbor, I caught a glimpse of the *Endeavour,* far below. The ship looked like a bath toy, its towering masts no bigger than toothpicks. As the plane rose through the clouds, I eased back my seat, several inches wider than the ship's hammocks.

Just as I slipped into a half-sleep, a voice reeled me in. "This is the first mate," the PA system crackled.

Can't be, I thought. Geoff, ordering us back on deck.

No. Just the cockpit, telling us our altitude and travel time. Flight attendants came down the aisle with drinks. I undid my shoes, idly fingering the laces. Tugboat hitch. Square lashing. Up here, they seemed so simple. The woman in the next seat glanced at me strangely.

"I just got off a ship," I said. "Captain Cook's ship. We had to tie a lot of knots."

She smiled, the way one does at a fanciful child, and put on her headphones.

Chapter 2

TAHITI:

Sic Transit Venus

The alurements of disipation are more than equal to any-
thing that can be conceived.
— CAPTAIN WILLIAM BLIGH, WRITING ABOUT
TAHITI AFTER THE MUTINY ON THE BOUNTY

In late May 1768, two months before the *Endeavour*'s departure from
England, a ship called the *Dolphin* anchored near the mouth of the
Thames. Dispatched two years earlier on a voyage of discovery, the
scurvy-racked vessel had found only one place of consequence: a
mountainous isle in the South Pacific. The wondrous tales told of this
island by the *Dolphin*'s crewmen, and by French sailors who visited
soon after, stirred Western imaginations in ways that still shape our
vision of the Pacific.

The island was temperate and fertile, abounding in everything a man
long at sea might dream of: fruit, fowl, fresh water, and females more
enticing than any in the world, bare-legged and bare-breasted, with
flowers garlanding their jet-black hair. The women lined the beach and
tempted the English with "every lewd action they could think of," one
crewman reported. It was a vision straight out of the Odyssey.

So was the scene that followed. Sailors coupled with native women
on the beach, on the ship's deck, in huts along the shore. The English
gave the women nails: highly prized metal that native men molded into
fishhooks. Before long, the *Dolphin*'s sailors had pried so much iron
from their ship that cleats loosened and two-thirds of the men had to

{42}

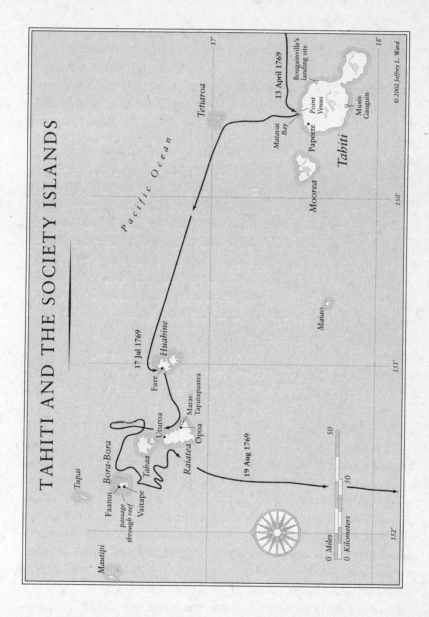

TAHITI AND THE SOCIETY ISLANDS

Mantipi

Tupai

Bora-Bora
Faanui
Vaitape
passage
through reef
Tabaa
Uturoa
Raiatea
Opoa
Marae
Tapupuatea
Fare
Huahine

17 Jul 1769

19 Aug 1769

Pacific Ocean

Tetiaroa

17°

13 April 1769
Bougainville's
landing site
Point
Venus
Matavai
Bay
Papeete
Musée
Gauguin
Tahiti

Moorea

Maiao

150°

151°

152°

18°

0 Miles   50
0 Kilometers   50

© 2002 Jeffrey L. Ward

sleep on the deck, having removed the nails that held up their hammocks. Officers caught one sailor stealing nails and forced him to run the gauntlet, or sprint between two lines of men armed with whips. His mates barely flogged him, and they soon began giving women their shirts instead of nails.

Even the *Dolphin*'s sour, sick commander, Samuel Wallis, eventually succumbed. On his first trip ashore, islanders carried the captain to a hut where young women undressed and massaged him. Wallis found "great benefit" from "the chafing," as he called it, and allowed himself to be dressed in native cloth and attended to by a chief's wife, a large, handsome woman whom Wallis christened "my Princess, or rather Queen." The enchanted captain named the island after King George and sailed off with embraces and "such tenderness of affection and grief, as filled both my heart and my eyes."

Ten months later, on another shore of the island, two French ships arrived under the command of Louis-Antoine de Bougainville, a classicist and gentleman as well as a naval officer. "The young girl negligently allowed her loincloth to fall to the ground," he wrote of a woman who climbed aboard the ship, "and appeared to all eyes as Venus showed herself to the Phrygian shepherd. She had the Goddess's celestial form." A naturalist on board wrote even more rhapsodically about island lovemaking, much of which was public: "Here, modesty and prudery lose their tyranny. The act of procreation is an act of religion; its preludes are encouraged by the voices and songs of the assembled people, and its end is greeted by universal applause."

The French felt as though they'd walked into the pages of Jean-Jacques Rousseau, whose *Discourses* extolling "natural man," uncorrupted by society, were the rage of Parisian salons. "I thought I had been transported to the Garden of Eden," Bougainville wrote of the island's lush interior. "Restfulness, a quiet joy and all the semblances of happiness reign everywhere." Bougainville entertained islanders with a flute-and-violin concert, followed by fireworks. At the end of this ten-day idyll, Bougainville named the island "New Cythera," after the Greek isle where the love goddess Aphrodite emerged from the sea foam. "What a country! What a people!" he exclaimed.

Natives had their own name for the island: O Tahiti. This was

Cook's destination in 1768, and the paradise to which I planned to follow him after setting up base in Australia.

SYDNEY IS HOME to the world's best archive of rare books and manuscripts on Cook. It is also the hometown of my wife, Geraldine, who looked forward to living there with our son while I researched Cook and roamed the Pacific. She found us a row house with a view of the Sydney docks. We'd been there three days when a close friend from our previous stay in Sydney, Roger Williamson, appeared at the door carrying a bottle of wine in each hand. Like most males in Australia, Roger drank too much. Whenever I was with him, I did the same.

Over the first bottle, I shared my plan for traveling in Cook's wake. Over the second, Roger declared that he'd go with me. "I grew up in Yorkshire, like Cook," he said. "I understand the man."

"You'd be a bad influence."

"Very bad. That's the point."

Roger had spent his first twenty-six years in Yorkshire, exactly as Cook had. His mother still lived in Whitby, the port from which Cook first sailed. Roger was also a skilled sailor who spent every free moment on the water.

"It's my trip," I told him. "I'd have to be captain."

"Fine. You can bend me over the boom and flog me. I like being beaten. I'm English."

"Okay," I said, pouring him another glass. "Free-associate. What do you think of when I say 'Captain Cook'?"

"Roast beef, silly wig, funny hat. All that grim-lipped, hunchbacked British sense of duty I came to Australia to escape." He paused. "Also the greatest sailor of all time. I'm an utter poltroon compared to Cook."

"And Tahiti?"

"Coconuts. Swaying hips. Grass skirts. Mostly to do with crumpet."

"Crumpet?"

"Sheilas. Or whatever you call them in America. Warm, willing flesh." Roger had recently separated from his wife and decamped to a dismal flat in downtown Sydney. Crumpet was much on his mind.

"We'll put on wigs and stockings and march onto the beach at Tahiti, like Cook and his men," he went on. "I'd look good in stockings."

This was probably true. Like many English émigrés to Australia, Roger came from pale, pinched working-class stock, but during twenty years in Sydney he'd leisured himself into a handsome, bronzed Aussie. He was tall and broad-shouldered, with sun-streaked blond curls, and blue eyes set in a perpetually tanned face. I rarely saw him out of the Sydney summer uniform: T-shirt, shorts, deck shoes.

"Of course," he said, "I can assure you as a proud Yorkshireman that Cook didn't disgrace himself by rooting the natives. Only filthy sailors did that. They were rough as boots." He chuckled. "You can play Cook."

We finished off the wine. I woke some hours later with a sore head, and lay awake mulling the notion of taking on crew. "Only those associated with the sea can appreciate Cook and his achievements," Horatio Nelson observed. Perhaps Roger could explain some of that to me. At the least, he'd be good company.

The next day, Roger phoned from Melbourne, where he'd gone on business. He worked for a firm that sold books to libraries. It was Roger's job to charm librarians into buying the titles his company peddled. He was good at this, so he had time and money to devote to his sailboat and wine cellar—or to bumming around the Pacific with me.

"It's bloody gray and awful here, like Yorkshire," he said. Most Sydneysiders disdain Melbourne as dull, with dismal weather. "Let's go to Tahiti. Now."

"Not now. It's the wet season there, ninety degrees every day and a hundred and ten percent humidity."

"Yes, it'll be vile. We'll get scrotum rot." Roger laughed. "Don't be a pathetic Yank. You think Cook was put off by a little rain?"

BY THE TIME Cook reached Tahiti in 1769, he'd been sailing west for eight months, the longest ocean passage of his career to that point. He'd endured a chilly reception from the Portuguese in Rio (who suspected the English were smugglers), rounded Cape Horn, and lost five men, including "a good hardy seaman" who had served with him in Canada. "Peter Flower seaman fell over board and before any Assistance could be given him was drown'd," Cook wrote with customary terseness. "In his room we got a Portuguese."

During the ten-week Pacific passage, along a more southerly course than any ship had sailed before, a despairing marine threw himself overboard and drowned. The wine ran out. Banks felt his gums swell and "pimples" form in his mouth: early signs of scurvy. Whatever else Cook might have worried about as he neared the tropics, rain was certainly the least of it.

The *Endeavour* dropped anchor on April 13, 1769, in Tahiti's Matavai Bay, the same inlet the *Dolphin* had visited two years before. Sydney Parkinson, an artist aboard the *Endeavour,* painted a word-picture of the scene: "The land appeared as uneven as a piece of crumpled paper, being divided irregularly into hills and valleys; but a beautiful verdure covered both, even to the tops of the highest peaks."

Several of the *Dolphin*'s men had joined the *Endeavour* and inflamed the crew with tales of the island's bounty. On first landing, however, the English found both food and islanders scarce. "No very agreeable discovery," Cook grumbled, "to us whose Ideas of plenty upon our arrival at this Island was carried to the very highest pitch."

The *Dolphin* veterans insisted that the bay had changed, and it had; an attack by islanders from the interior had driven much of the population away. But exploring a little farther, the English encountered the welcome they'd hoped for. Islanders greeted Cook and Banks with green boughs (a symbol of peace), calling them *tiao,* or friend, and giving them presents of perfumed cloth. Then they escorted several officers and gentlemen to an open longhouse. Women pointed at mats on the ground, "sometimes by force seating themselves and us upon them," Banks wrote. Unlike his French predecessor, the English naturalist saw virtue in privacy. "The houses being intirely without walls, we had not an opportunity of putting their politeness to every test."

Cook, a staid family man, made no mention of this scene. But Banks, a twenty-six-year-old bachelor—albeit a bachelor engaged to a soon-forgotten Englishwoman—pressed on. "I espied among the common croud a very pretty girl with a fire in her eyes," he wrote of a feast later the same day. Beckoning the girl to his side, Banks gave her beads and other trinkets. A jealous chief's wife, seated on the botanist's other flank, plied him with fish and coconut milk. "How this would have ended is hard to say," Banks wistfully reported. At that moment, several of his companions realized they'd been pickpocketed, losing a snuffbox and spyglass. The English angrily demanded the items' return, and eventually got their possessions back—but not before the girl with fire in her eyes had fled.

The next day, as the English set up camp on a promontory Cook named Point Venus, a Tahitian snatched a sentinel's musket. The young officer on duty ordered his men to fire and one of them shot the thief dead. The Quaker artist, Sydney Parkinson, was appalled: "What a pity, that such brutality should be exercized by civilized people upon unarmed ignorant Indians!" Cook explained to the Tahitians "that the man was kill'd for taking away the Musquet and that we still would be friends with them."

How he communicated this concept isn't clear. The *Dolphin* veterans doubtless acted as interpreters, though they knew only a smattering of the local language; the rest had to be conveyed with hand signs. Nor do we hear the Tahitian side of the story. Attempting to divine islanders' thoughts from the English journals is like watching a movie with the volume off; most of what we get are reaction shots. "No sign of forgiveness could I see in their faces, they lookd sulky and affronted," Banks wrote of a later confrontation.

Four days after the English landing, Alex Buchan, a landscape and figure painter in Banks's retinue, died during an epileptic seizure. "His Loss to me is irretrievable," Banks wrote, "my airy dreams of entertaining my friends in England with the scenes that I am to see here are vanished." It fell to Parkinson, a draftsman who specialized in plants and animals, to fill the gap. The artist faced an added challenge: Tahiti's voracious flies. "They eat the painters colours off the paper as fast as they can be laid on," Banks wrote, "and if a fish is to be drawn there is more trouble in keeping them off than in the drawing itself."

Flies and pickpockets aside, the English were enchanted by their surrounds. Wandering inland, Banks found "groves of Cocoa nut and bread fruit trees loaded with a profusion of fruit and giving the most gratefull shade I have ever experienced, under these were the habitations of the people most of them without walls: in short the scene was the truest picture of an arcadia of which we were going to be kings that the imagination can form."

The islanders inspired similar awe. "I never beheld statelier men," wrote Parkinson, who described them as tall, muscular, and tawny, with large black eyes and perfect white teeth. They seemed to possess a natural grace: in their gait, in their manners, in their fluid athleticism when swimming and canoeing. But it was the women who captivated the English most of all. They bathed three times a day in a river near Point Venus, shaved under their arms (as did the men), bedecked their hair with blossoms, and anointed themselves with coconut oil. (Banks, who disliked the oil's smell, nonetheless judged it preferable "to the odoriferous perfume of toes and armpits so frequent in Europe.")

Islanders also displayed as little inhibition with the *Endeavour*'s crew as they had with the *Dolphin*'s. "The women begin to have a share in our Freindship which is by no means Platonick," the ship's master, Robert Molyneux, observed soon after the *Endeavour*'s arrival. He returned to the subject a few weeks later: "The Venereal Disorder made sad work among the People." So sad that more than a third of the crew showed signs of infection.

Cook, always mindful of his men's health, tried to contain the disease's spread by barring infected men from going ashore. "But all I could do was to little purpose for I may safely say that I was not assisted by any one person in ye Ship." Cook also feared for Tahitians, presciently observing that the disease "may in time spread it self over all the Islands in the South Seas, to the eternal reproach of those who first brought it among them."

Who had brought it remained unclear. The *Dolphin*'s crew hadn't reported any cases of venereal disease—or, as Cook and his crew variously termed the illness in their journals, "this filthy distemper," "the fowl disease," "the Pox," "a Clap," "that heavy Curse," and "that greatest plague that ever the human Race was afflicted with." A month before the *Endeavour*'s arrival in Tahiti, Cook's surgeon had checked the men and found only one sailor afflicted; he was barred from contact with Tahitian women. So Cook consoled himself with islanders' reports that the disease had arrived with other European visitors.

The Frenchman, Bougainville, disputed this. He wrote that syphilis was already present when he landed ten months after the *Dolphin*. Hence another chapter in the cross-Channel blame game, whereby the English termed syphilis the French disease and the French referred to it as *le mal Anglais*. To complicate matters, some scholars believe that the sickness wasn't syphilis but yaws, a tropical skin disease that produces symptoms similar to those of venereal disease.

To afflicted islanders, the source of the contagion made little difference. Nor was venereal disease the deadliest consequence of Western contact. When Cook returned to Tahiti in 1773, islanders complained of another scourge, brought by a Spanish ship that had visited in the interim. "They say that it affects the head, throat and stomack and at length kills them," Cook wrote. "They dread it much and were constantly enquiring if we had it." Cook didn't identify this influenzalike ailment, but he wrote that Tahitians called it *Apa no Peppe* (the sickness of Pepe), "just as they call the venereal disease Apa no Britannia or Brit-tanee, notwithstanding they to a man say that it was first communicated by M. de Bougainville."

As Tahiti became a popular port of call in the decades following Cook's visit, other diseases took hold: tuberculosis, smallpox, measles, whooping cough. Alcoholism and internecine warfare, abetted by Western weapons and mercenaries, became rife as well. The toll was catastrophic. In 1774, Cook estimated Tahiti's population at 204,000. By 1865, less than a century after the first European visit, a French census recorded only 7,169 native inhabitants remaining on the island.

ROGER AND I arrived in Tahiti after a ten-hour flight from Sydney to Papeete, the capital of French Polynesia (a French protectorate that includes Tahiti and 117 other islands sprinkled across a swath of the South Pacific roughly the size of Europe). Men in floral shirts strummed ukuleles as we waited for our baggage in a decrepit terminal cooled by ceiling fans. After passing through immigration, we were met by honey-colored women in tight floral dresses cut high up the thigh. They greeted us with wreaths of pink and white hibiscus and signs touting package holidays: "Tahiti Legends," "Pacific Escapes," "Exotismes."

We changed money and found flowered beauties adorning the banknotes. I bought a bottle of mineral water while we waited for a bus to our hotel. The label bore a reproduction of a Gauguin maiden, bare-breasted, in a colorful wrap. The tourist brochures offered similar images of bronzed women in string bikinis. Whatever else might have changed, Tahitians still sold sex as aggressively as they had to the young sailors who landed here in the 1760s.

We woke late the next morning in a hotel at the edge of Papeete. Roger pulled aside the curtains and exulted, "It's just like the pictures! Palm trees, emerald sea, smoky verdant hills!" He opened the door to the balcony and stepped halfway through—only to be blown back, as if by a nuclear flash. "Good God, it's an inferno," he gasped, slumping by the air conditioner.

Rather than hike several miles to the center of town, we stood on the boulevard in front of the hotel, waiting for the local bus service, called *le truck*. A dense clot of mopeds and French sedans motored past, belching lead-fumed exhaust. *Le truck* resembled a cattle car, open-air, with hard, spine-rattling benches. I found myself squeezed between enormous women in shorts, T-shirts, and flip-flops. Almost all the passengers smoked, despite a sign saying *"Defense de Fumer."* No one returned my smile.

The view from *le truck* was just as deflating. Papeete seemed a congested, honking mess, combining Parisian insouciance with Cairo-like infrastructure. Cars double-parked on crumbling sidewalks; motorists plowed through pedestrian crossings; signs toppled from cement-block buildings. We climbed out at Papeete's central market and watched women whisk flies from fruit and fish. Then we wandered up Rue Colette and Rue Paul Gauguin, past peeling shopfronts and eateries called American Wave, Bip-Bop Burger, and Snack La Vague.

"It's an utter shitbox," Roger said, as we took refuge in a café crowded with sweat-stained Frenchmen smoking Gitanes and sipping Pernod. "The architects who designed this town must have been unemployable anywhere else."

No settlement had existed here at the time of the *Endeavour*'s visit. But the traders and whalers who followed Cook to Tahiti chose Papeete's sheltered bay as the island's best port. In 1842, the French seized Tahiti from the British in a bloodless coup and made Papeete the administrative center of their growing Pacific colony. The twentieth century brought devastating cyclones, a German naval bombardment in World War I, and French nuclear tests, which pumped billions of francs and thousands of French soldiers and bureaucrats into Papeete. Rural job seekers followed, swelling the town's population to include more than half of the 220,000 people living in all of French Polynesia. Whatever charm Papeete might once have possessed had long since vanished beneath ferroconcrete, car fumes, and billboards touting second-rate European goods dumped on the Pacific market at ruinous prices.

The only rental car we could find, at almost $100 a day, was a dwarfish box called a Fiat Panda Jolly, barely big enough for Roger to squeeze inside. "Special features—none," he declared, discovering that the car had neither a radio nor a parking brake nor seat belts. We filled the Panda with $5-a-gallon gas and puttered ten miles east to Matavai Bay, the site of the *Endeavour's* anchorage. At one end of the bay lay Point Venus, the peninsula on which Cook built a small fort to enclose his astronomical instruments and house his men when on shore. There was no road sign for the point, just an unmarked turnoff between Venustar Supermarché and a grocery called Chez Faty.

The road ended at a litter-strewn parking lot. Point Venus, the setting of so much Polynesian lore, now spread before us, a swampy peninsula edged by black volcanic sand. In the broiling afternoon sun, the beach looked about as romantic and welcoming as a tar pit. I later learned that producers of the 1962 Marlon Brando film *Mutiny on the Bounty* had imported white sand from America so Matavai Bay would match the Hollywood image of a tropical island.

A weekend crowd spread across the black sand. Most of the sunbathers appeared to be French or *demis,* the local word for islanders of mixed European and Polynesian descent. (French and *demis* make up about a quarter of the population, with Tahitians comprising two-thirds, and the rest mostly Chinese.) Almost all the women were topless.

We found a quiet spot at the end of the beach, beside a woman with two small children. I'd brought a copy of the "Hints" provided to Cook by the Earl of Morton, who was the president of the Royal Society, advising the commander on proper behavior toward islanders. Cook used the "Hints" in formulating the rules of conduct he read aloud to his men before touring Matavai Bay. I decided to do the same.

" 'Exercise the utmost patience and forbearance with respect to the Natives,' " Morton began. " 'Check the petulance of the Sailors, and restrain the wanton use of Fire Arms.' "

"That was roundly ignored," Roger said. "But I promise not to be petulant."

" 'No European Nation has the right to occupy any part of their country,' " I read on, " 'or settle among them without their voluntary consent.' "

Roger nodded and turned to the woman beside us. "Do you mind if we claim your beach for Britain?"

"Excusez-moi?"

In rusty high school French, I told her that we'd come to replay Cook's landing in 1769.

"Where is your boat?" she replied in English.

"It sank," Roger deadpanned. Then he reached into his bag. "Don't be alarmed by what you're about to see."

He pulled out two wigs from a costume shop in Sydney. I'd taken Roger up on his wine-soaked proposal in Sydney that we inaugurate our visit to Matavai Bay as proper Englishmen. However, eighteenth-century naval hairpieces weren't easy to come by. So I'd opted for the next best thing: huge white mops made of an itchy synthetic.

"This is lamentable," Roger said, pulling his on. "It'd fit anyone's head. It'd fit two heads." He climbed into white stockings while I buttoned up knee-length britches. Then I followed him into the warm, shallow water. We gazed up at the majestic green hills, wreathed in clouds. "This is a solemn moment," Roger declared.

He took out the last of our props, a Union Jack. "Made in the Republic of Taiwan," he said, studying the label. Then we waded parallel to the beach, in waist-deep water, with Roger wrapped in the flag. A few children in the water pointed at us and giggled, but their parents, reclining on the beach, barely turned their heads.

"This wig is hot and heavy," Roger complained. "The history books don't mention that." He navigated ashore, steering toward a young *demi* in a bikini thong. Roger spread out the Union Jack and sprawled on top of it. In his wet tights and drooping wig, he looked like an unemployed clown. Roger smiled at the young woman beside us and said, "*Nous sommes les Anglais qui arriver ici* a very long time ago." She shrugged, smeared her bare chest with coconut oil, and lay back on her towel.

I opened Cook's journal and read another of Lord Morton's hints: " 'If a Landing can be effected, whether with or without resistance, it might not be amiss to lay some few trinkets, particularly Looking Glasses upon the Shore.' " Roger reached in our bag: sunscreen, passports, car keys. "We could rip the rearview mirror off the Fiat Panda, if it's got one."

" 'Observe the natural Dispositions of the people,' " Morton continued. " 'The Characters of their Persons, Features, Complection, Dress.' "

Roger glanced at the topless woman on the beach towel beside us. "No great call on the world's fabric here, that's one thing that hasn't changed."

We read awhile longer, until the sun and burning black sand chased us into the woods skirting the beach. Here the crowd was mostly Tahitian, with families playing *boule* or lining up before snack stands. I tried to strike up a conversation with a vendor, asking him, "*Connaissez-vous Capitaine Cook?*" He stared blankly and handed me a Coke.

We walked the rest of Point Venus, trying to reconstruct the narrow promontory described in English maps and journals. A river from which the *Endeavour*'s crew had filled water casks was now a muddy, trash-choked trench. At the approximate site of the fort the English erected, sanitation men raked coconut husks, plastic bottles, Styrofoam, and other refuse into piles and set them alight, filling the air with industrial-smelling smoke.

Farther back from the water stood a tiny stucco lighthouse, with an enigmatic plaque quoting Robert Louis Stevenson: "Great were the feelings of emotion as I stood with my mother by my side and we looked upon the edifice designed by my father when I was sixteen and worked in his office during the summer of 1866." Stevenson's father designed lighthouses in Scotland, and the writer didn't visit Tahiti until 1888, twenty years after a French engineer built the edifice we were looking at.

Also puzzling was a nearby plinth, topped by a cannonball-sized sphere. The pillar's pedestal appeared etched with the points of a compass. Only later did we learn that this was Tahiti's sole memorial to Cook, erected by Britain's Royal Society and Royal Geographical Society in 1901. The plaque had long since fallen off or been stolen, and high weeds had grown up around the shaft.

Much better tended was a large sculpture in the shape of a ship's prow. It commemorated the arrival on March 5, 1797, of emissaries from the London Missionary Society aboard a vessel called the *Duff*. "After years of resistance and indifference the people of Tahiti embraced the gospel," the inscription read, "and, following the path of the setting sun, bore its words to the uttermost islands of the Pacific Ocean." March 5 remained a holiday in French Polynesia, marked by church gatherings and a celebration at Point Venus.

"Cook's forgotten, but these hair shirts get a bloody big monument," Roger grumbled.

As the monument suggested, the missionaries had met with mixed success, at least at first. Seventeen evangelicals, plus five of their wives and three children, disembarked at Tahiti in 1797. Eight missionaries fled on the next boat out, to Sydney. One of the remaining missionaries married a native woman and left the church. The first English child born on the island ran off with a Tahitian chief. "They in general treated our message with a great deal of levity and disregard," one of the missionaries wrote of Tahitians. The churchmen also received a cool reception from Western sailors calling at Tahiti, who feared the Gospel would interfere with their traffic in rum, tobacco, and women.

But reinforcements arrived, including a very determined missionary named William Ellis. Tahiti's alcoholic young king decided to embrace Christianity, and his subjects followed. Before long, the missionaries had imposed their austere creed. They banned "all lascivious songs, games or entertainment," as well as the wearing of flower crowns in church. Island women hid themselves in the all-concealing gowns known as Mother Hubbards. "It was a thousand pities that the Tahitians did not convert Mr. Ellis," wrote Robert Keable, a former English vicar who lived in Polynesia in the early twentieth century.

French influence, mass tourism, and a Tahitian cultural revival in recent decades had gradually eroded the missionaries' grip. The skin on display at Point Venus gave evidence of that. So, too, we were about to discover, did Papeete's nightlife, which recalled the extraordinary scenes that Cook and his men witnessed more than two centuries before us.

SOON AFTER THE *Endeavour*'s arrival, a procession of canoes entered Matavai Bay. One bore the stately woman that Samuel Wallis of the *Dolphin* had called Queen of the island. With great pomp, she presented the English with a hog and bunches of plantains. Cook reciprocated with trinkets. "What seem'd to please her most was a childs Doll which I made her understand was the Picter of my Wife."

That's what Cook wrote at the time. He later deleted this rare flash of humor—and the only mention in his journal of his wife—from the official version he submitted to the Admiralty. J. C. Beaglehole, the greatest of Cook's biographers and the editor of his journals, believes the navigator omitted the doll episode "as unworthy of the dignity of such a document." This instinctive self-censorship has left us an image of Cook that is probably sterner and more formal than he was in person.

Joseph Banks, who felt no such constraint, provides much richer detail of the light, often titillating side of the *Endeavour*'s stay in Tahiti. Of the Queen (whose name was Purea), the botanist wrote that she was "about 40, tall and very lusty, her skin white and her eyes full of meaning." Though married to a chief, she had taken "a hansome lusty young man of about 25" as her lover. Purea also made advances toward Banks, who appears in youthful portraits as a handsome, dark-haired man with full lips and fine clothes adorning his six-foot, four-inch frame (in Tahiti, he wore a white jacket and waistcoat with silver frogs). The botanist rebuffed the Queen, having already attached himself to one of her young attendants, whom he called "my flame."

Whole weeks pass in Banks's journal with barely a mention of botany. Instead, he reports on elaborate feasts, wrestling matches, archery contests, traveling minstrels playing nose flutes, and long hot nights sleeping naked in islanders' homes or beneath the thatched awnings of their canoes. During one such sleepover, Banks awoke to find his clothes had been stolen. No matter; dispatching a Tahitian to recover the garments, Banks wrote, "I heard their musick and saw lights near me; I got up and went towards them." It was a *heiva,* or festival of dance and song.

The next morning, when the Tahitian returned with only part of Banks's wardrobe, Purea gave the botanist native cloth to wear in place of his jacket. "I made a motley apearance," Banks wrote with obvious delight, "my dress being half English and half Indian." Later in his journal, Banks makes passing mention of "a turban of Indian cloth which I wore instead of a hat." Eventually, he went entirely native, joining two women as a performer in a mourning ceremony. "I was next prepard by stripping off my European cloths and putting me on a small strip of cloth round my waist, the only garment I was allowd to have," he wrote. "Neither of the women were a bit more covered than myself. Then they began to smut me and themselves with charcoal and water."

If Cook wrote with an eye to the Admiralty, Banks obviously looked to the drawing rooms of London. But Banks wasn't just a hedonistic fop. Like Richard Burton and T. E. Lawrence, later British travelers who shared Banks's taste for steamy exoticism, the botanist was a sensitive observer whose headlong immersion in native culture gave him access and insights denied less adventurous men. Cook, a keen judge of character, quickly recognized this, and put the botanist in charge of the delicate task of managing trade between the English and Tahitians. "Mr. Banks," Cook wrote, in an uncommon expression of praise for any of the *Endeavour*'s men, "is always very alert upon all occations wherein the Natives are concern'd."

Tahitians seemed as eager to sample English ways as Banks was to taste theirs. As a result, the *Endeavour*'s visit—much longer and more intimate than that of the *Dolphin* or the French ships—became a prolonged feast of mutual discovery. The islanders served the English a local delicacy, roasted dog, which Banks found "a most excellent dish," and Cook declared "next to an English Lamb" in taste. The English invited Tahitians to dine on Western fare and drink to His Majesty's health. "He imitates our manners in every instance," Banks wrote of one chief, "already holding a knife and fork more handily than a Frenchman could learn to do in years."

One night, islanders dragged Banks to the home of a sick, vomiting

man. His family believed the man was dying "in consequence of something our people had given him to eat," Banks wrote. The islanders
presented the botanist with the remains of the man's dinner as evidence. "This upon examination I found to be a Chew of tobacco
which he had begg'd of some of our people, and trying to imitate them
in keeping it in his mouth as he saw them do had chewd it almost to
powder swallowing his spittle." Banks prescribed coconut milk and
the man soon recovered.

The English, for their part, submitted to a strange and painful form
of Tahitian adornment. Natives dipped a sharp comb into the sooty
juice of burnt candlenut and beat the comb's teeth into their skin with
a mallet. "The stain left in the skin, which cannot be effaced without
destroying it, is of a lively bluish purple, similar to that made upon the
skin by gun-powder," wrote the artist, Sydney Parkinson. He and several crewmen "underwent the operation" on their arms, becoming the
first Europeans to adopt the badge of seamen ever since: the tattoo, or,
as the *Endeavour*'s crew rendered the Tahitian word, *tat-tow* or
tataow. (The Tahitians, who had never seen writing, applied the same
word to the strange figures the English inked on paper.)

The English and Tahitians also tried, with limited success, to
explain their beliefs to each other. And so another novel word entered
the Western vocabulary: *tapu,* or "taboo," the intricate system by
which Polynesians ordered the world into sacred and profane. It was
tapu, for instance, for Tahitian women to eat in the presence of men.
"They never gave no other answer but that they did it because it was
right," Cook wrote of his vain attempts at understanding this segrega-
tion. Curiously, a woman might sometimes break this taboo when
alone with English men, "but always took care that her country people
should not know what she had done."

Cook, judging from his journals, was not a pious man. A product of
the eighteenth century Enlightenment, he valued reason above all else,
and showed little patience for what he called "Priest craft" and
"superstition." But the Articles of War, and Lord Morton's "Hints,"
ordained that Cook conduct "divine service" for his men. Banks
invited some Tahitians to attend one such observance at Point Venus.
The Tahitians closely mimicked the English, kneeling and standing,

Banks wrote, and "so much understood that we were about something very serious that they calld to the Indians without the fort to be silent."

Later that same Sunday, at the gate of the English fort, the Tahitians reciprocated by performing a rite of their own. "A young fellow above 6 feet high lay with a little Girl about 10 or 12 years of age publickly before several of our people and a number of the Natives," Cook wrote. He guessed this public copulation was ceremonial, since venerable women stood coaching the young girl "how she should act her part, who young as she was, did not seem to want it." (By "want it," Cook meant that she didn't need instruction.) Cook's description of this scene would be widely popularized in writings about the voyage and create a sensation back home, prompting condemnation by English churchmen and the publication by literary wags of pornographic verse.

Cook later learned that the lovers outside the fort at Point Venus were *Ariori,* a class of Tahitians who devoted themselves to performing erotic songs, dances, and ritual sex. The *Ariori* belonged to a religious sect or fertility cult, one that also required its members to remain free by smothering any children born of their promiscuous unions. Needless to say, this horrified the English. And Cook, while no prude, believed the *Ariori*'s public orgies reflected the general lewdness of the culture. "Both sexes express the most indecent ideas in conversation without the least emotion and they delight in such conversation behond any other. Chastity indeed is but little Valued."

The Tahitians were just as shocked by aspects of their visitors' behavior. Discipline had begun to deteriorate within days of the *Endeavour*'s arrival, and Cook duly punished his sailors; mindful of the *Dolphin*'s experience, he dispensed two dozen lashes, double the usual sentence, to a man who stole nails. When the ship's butcher threatened an island man's wife, the English invited Tahitians to watch the butcher flogged, to demonstrate the severity and evenhandedness of Western justice. "They stood quietly and saw him stripd and fastned to the rigging," Banks wrote of the Tahitian audience, "but as soon as the first blow was given interfered with many tears, begging the punishment might cease a request which the Captn would not comply with."

Cook also ratcheted up his reprisals against native thefts. When a man stole a coal rake from the fort, Cook seized twenty-five fishing canoes loaded with fresh catch. Though the rake was returned, "Captn Cooke thought he had now in his hands an opportunity of recovering all the things which had been stolen," Banks wrote. "He therefore proclaimed to every one that till all the things which had been stolen from us were brought back the boats should not stir."

Banks regarded this punishment as disproportionate and misdirected, "as the Canoes pretty certainly did not belong to the people who had stolen the things." Not only did the islanders fail to return the stolen items, they retaliated by halting all trade of breadfruit and other goods. Cook stubbornly held out for several weeks before finally releasing the canoes.

Mutual incomprehension over notions of property and justice would plague Cook throughout his Pacific voyages. Polynesians, for the most part, lived communally and had few personal possessions. The climate in Tahiti was benign and bountiful; islanders gathered as much fish and fruit as they needed for their immediate wants. If they had extra, they shared it. Extravagant gift giving was—and still is—a point of honor in Polynesia, an expression of how much a host values his visitor.

Given this custom, what were Tahitians to make of a ship stuffed with dazzling surplus? The English helped themselves to fish, fresh water, and other of the island's resources. Why shouldn't the Tahitians help themselves to muskets, tools, watches, and whatever else they could lay their hands on—even the ship's lightning rod and quadrant?

The English, for their part, hailed from a society in which property rights were so sacrosanct that to poach a rabbit was a capital offense. Accustomed to public hangings and the severity of shipboard discipline, young sailors could hardly be expected to show mercy toward nimble-fingered Tahitians. Cook's behavior, however, seems out of character. In almost every other circumstance, he treated natives with tolerance and restraint. Yet the theft of even minor goods unhinged him, and the more it occurred, the harsher his reprisals became. This was, perhaps, Cook's tragic flaw. The cycle of larceny and retribution that began at Tahiti would continue for a decade, until it claimed Cook's own life on a beach almost three thousand miles from Matavai Bay.

THE DANCE SHOW at the Captain Bligh Restaurant began with bare-chested men thumping drums. Lithe women in coconut-shell bras and palm-frond skirts shimmied onto the floor, shaking their hips side to side, fast and furiously. A lone woman followed, stripping off a sarong and performing a sinuous pelvic motion. Men in loincloths came next, opening and closing their legs rapidly, sweat glistening on their bronzed thighs.

"These are some traditional dances of Tahiti," the emcee announced, in French and English. "Now we will see dances from other islands of Polynesia." A woman in a Hawaiian *mu'umu'u* made feathery motions with her fingers. Tongans in ankle-length gowns did various tricks with wooden sticks. The Maori of New Zealand swung balls attached to strings in what seemed like a cheerleader routine. Then, just as the audience's attention began to drift, the half-naked Tahitians returned, thrusting their hips to a pulsing drumbeat.

The message was hard to miss. Tahiti, as its tourist literature proclaimed, was "the Island of Love," a title that none of its neighbors dared challenge. The show, despite its touristy presentation, also gave some inkling of the "indecent dances" Cook and his men described. "You've been at sea for months, you've been lashed, fed filthy food, and haven't seen a woman forever, and never seen one like this," Roger said, his eyes trained on a dancer's undulating hips. "Can you imagine? It's a miracle they didn't all desert."

From the Captain Bligh, we headed to Papeete's waterfront strip of bars and nightclubs: Manhattan Discoteque, Hotel Kon tiki, Paradise Night. Crowded with French soldiers and young Tahitians, the clubs didn't look very enticing. A girl of about fifteen stumbled out of one of the bars and came up to us mumbling something I didn't understand.

"Pardon?"

She reached for my groin. *"Je suck?"*

We wandered away from the water to Rue Colette and found a dance joint called the Kikiriri. Inside the dark bar, couples performed the Tahitian waltz, a fast, close dance in which the men planted their hands low on their partners' buttocks. A few tourists bravely took to the floor and mimicked the Tahitians' motions. "They look like Christmas turkeys, pale and waddling, flapping their wings," Roger observed. He ordered another glass of overpriced *vin ordinaire*. "Two days in this place and I already feel a tremendous sense of racial inferiority. I'll never look at a white woman again. And I don't stand a chance with the locals."

"We could try the men."

"What?"

I led Roger down Rue des Ecoles to a place I'd read about in our tourist guide, called the Piano Bar. Cook and his men had written about the masculine quality of some Polynesian women, and noted islanders of mixed or ambiguous gender. These were probably *mahu*, Tahitian boys raised as girls, wearing women's clothes and performing traditionally female tasks. *Mahu* remained a strong presence in Tahiti, nowhere more so than at the Piano Bar, Papeete's premier transvestite club.

"Think of it as research," I said, dragging Roger past the jolly eunuchlike bouncers at the door. Inside, we found a table beside the dance floor, which was crowded with couples performing the same, groin-grinding waltz we'd seen at the Kikiriri. Except that many of these dancers were tall and broad-shouldered, wearing pink lamé miniskirts, halter tops, and high-heeled pumps.

We'd arrived on a special night: an annual beauty contest to elect a new Miss Piano Bar. Five contestants in long sequined dresses and strapless black gowns appeared. An emcee sang "Queen of the Night" as the contestants sashayed around the floor to loud hoots from the audience. Half of Papeete seemed to have crowded into the bar, including a tall, elegant beauty who squeezed into a chair beside Roger, smiling and rubbing his thigh.

"Bloke or sheila?" Roger whispered to me.

"Bloke, I think."

Roger shrugged. "I like it here. At least I feel challenged."

The contestants reappeared in bathing suits: high-cut, one-piece costumes exposing smooth backs, slim arms and legs, and what looked like cleavage. "Perfect skin, glossy hair, exquisite thighs," Roger said. "If they were girls, they'd be fantastic."

An evening-wear competition and talent contest followed. Samantha, a six-foot-two stunner, won the beauty contest by acclamation, blowing kisses and throwing a bouquet into the crowd. Then the dancing resumed and we staggered out into Rue des Ecoles. It was three A.M. and the street remained packed, *mahu* mingling with French sailors, tourists, Tahitian couples. "No wonder we barely turned a head at Point Venus," Roger said. "In our stockings and wigs, we fit right in."

ON JUNE 3, 1769, from nine in the morning until half past three in the afternoon, the English peered through their telescopes at the transit of Venus across the face of the sun. Though the sky was clear, Cook noted a "dusky shade" blurring the planet's fringe. This caused him and his fellow observers to record differing times for the crucial moment of contact between the planet and star. Only later would astronomers learn that the entire exercise, carried out at Tahiti and seventy-six other points across the globe, had little value; the telescopes and astronomical knowledge of the day weren't precise enough to accomplish the complex task.

Banks, at least, had his customary good time, tagging along with a small observation party to a nearby isle: "3 hansome girls came off in a canoe to see us," he wrote, ignoring the celestial Venus. "They chatted with us very freely and with very little perswasion agreed to send away their carriage and sleep in the tent."

Returning to Matavai Bay, Banks promptly set off on another adventure. He and Cook boarded the pinnace (one of the ship's boats) "to make the Circuit of the Island," the navigator wrote, "in order to examine and draw a Sketch of the Coast and Harbours thereof." This is Cook in his element: surveying the contours of uncharted lands and setting down their coordinates on paper.

This is Banks in *his* element: "Many Canoes came off to meet us and in them some very hansome women who by their behaviour seemed to be sent out to entice us to come ashore, which we most readily did," he wrote, two days out from Matavai Bay. "I stuck close to the women hoping to get a snug lodging by that means as I had often done." Cook wrote of the same spot: "there are also harbours between this and the Isthmus proper and convenent for Shipping made by reefs of Corral rocks."

Midway down the island's eastern shore, Cook and Banks came to the place where Bougainville had landed the year before. Only later, though, would the English learn of a peculiar passenger who had been aboard Bougainville's vessel. The valet of the ship's naturalist was actually a woman disguised as a man. The French hadn't realized this until they arrived at Tahiti. Islanders, as familiar with gender-bending then as they are today, immediately recognized the valet's deception. She continued to serve the naturalist and disembarked with him later on the voyage; little more is known of her fate.

Continuing on, through heavily cultivated countryside, the English visited a *marae,* or open-air temple, which Banks described as "a most enormous pile, certainly the masterpeice of Indian architecture in this Island. Its size and workmanship almost exceeds beleif." Cook surveyed the structure's precise dimensions: a platform measuring 267 by 87 feet, with steps rising 44 feet in a pyramid shape. The English were astonished by the fineness of the masonry: vast stones squared and polished, without iron tools. Banks judged the construction so expert that it might have been done "by the best workman in Europe."

Just as awesome was the collection of bones on the site. First, the English studied wooden altars strewn with the remains of hogs and dogs, sacrificed at the temple. Then Banks and Cook walked along a road by the *marae.* "Every where under our feet were numberless human bones cheifly ribs and vertebrae," Banks wrote. The English also found fresh jawbones hung in houses, and learned that these were the spoils of a recent massacre, "carried away as trophies and used by the Indians here in exactly the same manner as the North Americans do scalps." Tahiti was emerging as something other than the Arcadia the botanist had at first imagined.

Returning to Matavai Bay, Cook prepared for the *Endeavour*'s departure, dismantling the fort for firewood. Two marines, on what was probably their final watch ashore, slipped out of the English camp and disappeared into the hills. "They had got each of them a Wife & would not return," Cook wrote. To recover the deserters, Cook seized prominent chiefs, holding them hostage until the Tahitians returned the two men. The tactic worked, though at the cost of whatever goodwill the English had engendered. "We are likly to leave these people in disgust with our behaviour towards them," Cook wrote, "owing wholly to the folly of two of our own people."

The spirit of desertion may have been more prevalent than Cook realized. At one point, the *Endeavour*'s master wrote of "Mutinous words spoke by some of our People." Twenty-one years later, following the mutiny on the *Bounty*, a former midshipman on the *Endeavour* confided in a letter to Banks that "most of the People" on Cook's ship had schemed to stay in Tahiti. The midshipman claimed he had forestalled this mass desertion with tales of "the Pox—the disease being there, their getting it certain & dying rotten most probable."

This account, if true, speaks to the "alurements of disipation" in Tahiti that Bligh later blamed for his own misfortune on the *Bounty*. It also reveals just how reckless and rootless were the young sailors Cook commanded, and how harsh life at sea must have seemed to them. Jumping ship in the eighteenth century, at the edge of the known world, meant severing ties to home and family in a way that is unimaginable today, even to FBI fugitives or Mafia informers in the witness-protection program. Yet some among Cook's crew were willing to risk all: for love (and lust), for a life of apparent ease, for escape from the horrors of maritime labor. Given what occurred during the rest of the *Endeavour*'s voyage, many of the men doubtless came to regret their decision to remain on board.

Cook, for all his severity, seemed to understand the temptations his men were subject to. He sentenced the two deserters to twenty-four lashes each, but quickly released them from confinement. In a curious postscript, one of the deserters, Samuel Gibson (described by the *Endeavour*'s master as "a wild young man"), joined Cook for both his second and third voyages, rising to the rank of sergeant and serving as a valued translator on Cook's return trips to Polynesia.

The *Endeavour*'s departure from Tahiti brought another surprise. A high priest named Tupaia, whom Cook described as a keenly intelligent man and very knowledgeable about the surrounding seas, wanted to sail on with the English. Cook was reluctant, apparently out of concern for Tupaia's welfare once he reached England. So Banks decided to take on the Tahitian as his own responsibility—and as his private pet. "Thank heaven I have a sufficiency," Banks wrote, referring to his personal fortune, "and I do not know why I may not keep him as a curiosity, as well as some of my neighbours do lions and tygers at a larger expence than he will probably ever put me to."

Tupaia brought along a servant boy named Taiata. The Tahitians' thoughts upon undertaking this astounding adventure—more daring, even, than that of Cook and his men—are lost to history. All we have is Banks's account of the *Endeavour*'s sail out of Matavai Bay, three months to the day after the ship first anchored at Tahiti. Banks and Tupaia climbed "to the topmost head where we stood a long time waving to the Canoes as they went off."

A FEW DAYS after our late-night bar tour, Roger and I climbed in the Panda to retrace Cook and Banks's circumnavigation of Tahiti. The trip was easier than in 1769: a seventy-mile, badly paved road circles the coast of Tahiti Nui, or Great Tahiti, the larger of the two land-masses that together form the hourglass-shaped island. Soon after we sprang free of Papeete's cement sprawl, buildings became scarce, except for churches, announced at regular intervals by signs saying *"Silence Culte."* The palm-fringed beaches were empty, as were the coconut groves rising up the steep green hills. It was beautiful but eerily abandoned, like so many rural areas the world over.

In Cook's day, Tahiti's bountiful landscape fed tens of thousands of people, as well as the hundred hungry sailors aboard the *Endeavour*. Now, the equation was reversed: a tiny fraction of Tahitians lived on the land, and roughly 85 percent of their foodstuffs were imported from Europe. Stopping to dip my toe in the surf, I found coconut shells intermingled with flip-flops, plastic containers of Nestle Lait Concen-traté Sucré, soap bottles, and Coke cans.

Driving on, we crossed a small bridge that bore an inconspicuous plaque noting that *"L. A. de Bougainville a Debarqué sur ce rivage le 6 Avril 1768."* A flaming bougainvillea, the blossoming vine named for the Frenchman, was the only other memorial to the explorer. We parked and gazed at the scene. Unlike Point Venus, this part of the island remained the "Nouveau Cythera" of which Bougainville wrote: azure sea, a lazy river winding into tropical green hills, two boys pulling fish from the stream with a simple line and hook, no reel or rod attached.

We wandered up the road to a store marked *"Boulangerie Alimen-*

tation" and chatted with the young Frenchman who ran it, Stéphane Petris. He had come to Tahiti as a sailor ten years before, married a Tahitian, and settled down. "I say, 'Why not? The sun, the sea, a beautiful woman, it is better than Toulouse.' " He rolled a cigarette. "But you can only have paradise for a month and then it is lost. You are bored, you need air, you need a plane to go away. I fly to New Zealand just to see snow. It is strange, no?"

I asked him what he thought about Bougainville's famous impression of the island. Stéphane pondered this for a minute, puffing on his cigarette. "What he saw, it is still true in a way. 'I need water, I drink.' That is how Tahitians think. Not like in France. We make so many complications. I need a glass, ice; I must decide, water with gas or without gas? Here it is very simple. They live for today. A little house, a little boat. That is all. Fish or go to the mountain for fruit."

Or to Stéphane's shop for *steak frites* and *chao-men*, the French-Tahitian rendition of Chinese food. He ran another business that delivered baguettes to the curious, tubular mailboxes we'd seen along the road, called *boîtes de pain*. "Every citizen of France must have his fresh bread, no?" Stéphane said, excusing himself so he could serve several customers who had patiently stood waiting while we talked.

At sunset we pulled in at a guest house by the water. The rooms, simple bungalows perched over a shallow lagoon, were open-air, like the Tahitian homes in which Banks and Cook often slept. We sipped rum as the moon rose over the water and felt, finally, as though we'd drifted into the Polynesia of lore. I lay on a mat on the floor, Roger climbed into the bungalow's loft. The air had grown sticky and hot. Then rain sheeted down. When it stopped, the air felt even heavier than before.

I kicked away my sweat-stained sheets and lay naked on the mat. Even the pillow became unbearable, like a hot water bottle at the wrong end of the bed. Then the insects arrived, silent and pitiless. We'd been warned about Tahitian *nono*s: microscopic bugs that don't so much sting as gnaw. But nothing had prepared me for the torment we now endured. I felt like one of Sydney Parkinson's canvases, my flesh standing in for paint.

"What *are* these fiends?" Roger gasped. "They're so bloated with my blood they don't even buzz. They're just whacking against my body and falling down. It's like Gallipoli up here." He turned on a light and fumbled in his pack for the "Safari Strength" repellent he'd bought in Sydney. Studying the fine print, he reported, "It kills elephants."

Unfortunately, it didn't kill *nono*s. No matter how much repellent we slathered on, the insects kept coming. "No wonder the English had so many things stolen," Roger said. "They were knackered by the heat and the bugs. Cook had his stockings nicked from under his head, for God's sake. He was in a coma."

The last thing I heard was Roger croaking, "Pass up the rum, if I'm going to die I don't want to do it sober." Then I somehow drifted off, to wake at dawn feeling deranged by blood loss, sweat loss, and lack of sleep. Roger sat on the balcony staring into his drawers. "I've still got black sand in my crotch from Point Venus. Jock rot can't be far behind. And I've probably got dengue fever from all those bugs." He lit a cigarette. "I won't forget this thatched sweatbox for the rest of my life, all five days of it remaining to me."

We fled to the Panda and continued our circumnavigation of the island. At midday, we pulled in at the Musée Gauguin, a tribute to the painter's life. Abandoning France and his family for Polynesia, the forty-three-year-old artist had hoped to live "in a primitive and savage state." Arriving in Papeete in 1891, he discovered instead "the Europe which I thought to shake off. . . . It was the Tahiti of former times which I loved. That of the present filled me with horror." Gauguin found some solace in the arms of a fourteen-year-old mistress whom he lived with and painted near the site of the present museum. But the art he produced didn't sell in Paris; he contracted venereal disease and died in Polynesia in 1903, a bitter and impoverished man.

Disillusion seemed to come with the territory in Tahiti, beginning with the *Dolphin*'s men aboard the *Endeavour*, who declared the island utterly changed from their visit just two years before. Cook, returning to Tahiti on his second and third voyages, lamented its descent into prostitution and greed. The writers and artists who flocked to Tahiti in the nineteenth century traced a similar parabola. "God's best—at least God's sweetest—works: Polynesians," Robert

Louis Stevenson exulted, only to later despair: "I don't much like Tahiti. It seems to me a sort of halfway house between savage life and civilization, with the drawbacks of both and the advantages of neither."

Tahiti was a victim of its extravagant hype, and of the Western ills this hype had produced. "It's always the same story, isn't it," Roger said, once we'd toured the Gauguin museum. "You try to escape, to find simplicity, and end up bringing all your baggage with you. So you end up turning paradise into the same hellhole you left." He bent himself into the Panda, scratching his *nono* bites. "Then again, you can't blame the West for black sand and bloodsucking bugs."

We drove on, toward the remains of the enormous *marae* Cook and Banks had described during their own circuit of the island. I'd picked up a booklet at the museum called "Sacred Stones and Rites" and read aloud to Roger as he sat grumpily behind the wheel. "It's a hundred and twenty degrees out," he moaned, "I've got one pint of blood left, and you want to go look at a pile of rocks!" As we neared the *marae*, Roger did an abrupt U-turn and pulled in at a roadside café called Beach Burger.

" 'The coastal *maraes* were formed in steps,' " I read on, as Roger drank beer, " 'generally three or four, but capable of reaching ten or so in number and 15 meters in height.' "

"I'm riveted," Roger replied. Desperate to stall the field trip, he tried out his French on a man drinking espresso at the next table. The man smiled and corrected Roger's grammar. "I teach English at the local school," he said, holding up the papers he sat marking. He seemed as delighted to be distracted from his task as Roger was to skirt ours. "It is very depressing," he said, showing us samples of his students' work on a multiple-choice test.

Question: "Is she going to invite the Garretts?"
Answer: "Sorry, I've only got some green ones."
Question: "Have you got any French cigarettes?"
Answer: "No, they're not warm enough."

The man smiled wanly and invited us to join him at his table. "It would be a pleasure to speak proper English for a while. May I offer you a warm cigarette?"

James Pouant resembled a storybook fox, intelligent and squinty-eyed, with thick spectacles and graying brown hair. Raised in a village in Bordeaux, he'd been teaching in French Polynesia since 1969 and planned to stay when he retired in a few years. "I came here as a young man, for adventure," he said. "Now I am becoming an old man, and all I want is to sit in the shade, drink my wine, look at the sea. That is what happens in Tahiti. You lose focus. Or maybe your focus changes."

He pointed at a young woman standing by the entrance to the café, staring into space. "That is one of my former students. She looks content, no? And see that one?" He gestured at a man by the road, leaning against a tree. "He was here when I arrived at noon. It is now two. He has not moved a muscle. He will be here another hour, probably."

James, who spoke fluent Tahitian, said islanders had a word for this state, one that didn't really translate into any other tongue: *fiu* (pronounced "phew"). On one level, *fiu* signified "fed up" or exhausted. "Someone will start to mow your lawn, do half, then never come back to finish or collect money because they are *fiu*," James said. "More often they will not show up in the first place because they are already *fiu*." In this sense, the word also connoted boredom, blankness, lack of motivation. "Gauguin painted it on the faces of his women. It is a sort of ennui, except drained even of ennui."

"A Zen state," Roger suggested.

James laughed. "For us, Zen means to empty our minds. For a Tahitian to have Zen, he would first have to fill it up."

This sounded harsh, but James didn't mean it that way. He showed us a few more test papers, some of them covered in bright drawings of rainbows and coconut palms, the questions left unanswered. "They feel they can do without all this learning, and live in the old way," he said. "Without electricity, cars—just fish and breadfruit, a simple life, like hippies in the 1960s."

In the years James had spent in Tahiti, this attitude had started to change. It was still true to a degree for families living in the country, as many of his students did. But the exodus to Papeete brought money and exposure to Western goods, and upset the traditional balance of power within families. Women tended to stay in school longer than men, found better jobs than their husbands, and felt more at ease in the wider, French-influenced world.

"The men have an inferiority complex, they're shy, their language is not so good, they keep their distance," James said. This helped explain the difficulty we'd had initiating conversations with Tahitian men; I'd tried a dozen times and rarely got beyond pleasantries, except with government officials. The women were another matter. "We're looking at them all the time, even when we do not realize it," James said. "Our eyes just drift to the women. And they know it. Their beauty and charm give them power."

I told him about our interest in Cook, and the strong impression that Tahitian women had made on the sailors. James smiled. He said that much of what Cook and Banks wrote still applied, particularly Tahitian frankness about what the English called "indecent" topics. "I have had Tahitian girlfriends," James said. "In the villages, they tell everyone the shape of your sex, what you are like in bed. And you are sure to be cheated on within a year. You must accept this. One girlfriend, when I was away, boys were jumping through the window to see her. We have a sense of guilt, we impose limits. They do what they feel like doing."

James glanced at his watch. He had to return to the school. "Why don't you come tomorrow and talk to my students?" he said. "It would be good for them to hear examples of English speakers."

"Can we ask them about Cook?" I asked.

James gathered his papers. "You can ask. Just do not be disappointed by the answers."

AT THE END of his Tahitian journal, Cook began a practice he would repeat throughout his voyages, appending a summary description of each land he explored. His "Description of King Georges Island"— Samuel Wallis's name remained—reads rather like a guidebook, filled with useful tips for travelers: the best anchorages and approaches, the finest watering spots, the scarcity of firewood. With a farm boy's eye, Cook also noted the quality of the soil and plant life and saw past the island's superficial splendor. "Notwithstanding nature hath been so very bountifull to it yet it doth not produce any one thing of intrinsick Value or that can be converted into an Article of trade," he wrote, "so that the value of the discovery consists wholly in the refreshments it will always afford to Shipping in their passage through those seas."

This analysis is vintage Cook: shrewd, mercantile, and modest, weighing the true value of what he'd seen rather than inflating it to impress his superiors. He was equally precise in describing the island's man-made resources, devoting pages to the making of *tapa*, or bark cloth, and the construction of canoes. "They manage them very dextrusly," he wrote of Tahitians' skill with the largest crafts, some of them seventy feet long and rigged with triangular sails. "I beleive [the Tahitians] perform long and distant Voyages in them, otherwise they could not have the knowlidge of the Islands in these seas they seem to have." Here, as so often in his judgments, Cook was correct, and far ahead of his time. Only in recent decades have scholars appreciated the astonishing voyages undertaken by Polynesians, centuries before Cook, without the assistance of compass or sextant.

Equally characteristic was Cook's habit of telling the reader what he did *not* know. "Religion," he wrote, "is a thing I have learnt so little of that I hardly dare touch upon it." Cook, unlike other observers, also avoided hyperbole in describing Tahitians. He studied people rather as he surveyed coasts and currents, calmly noting their shape, length, and tendencies. "They are a very cleanly people," he wrote, "always washing their hands and mouths immidiatly before and after their meals . . . their features are agreable and their gate gracefull, and their behavour to strangers and to each other is open affable and courtious." Except, of course, for their thieving, in which they displayed "such dexterity as would shame the most noted pickbocket in Europe."

But Cook strenuously avoided passing judgment, even on the delicate matter of sexual behavior. In noting young girls' performance of a "very indecent dance which they call Timorodee" (a rendering of the Tahitian phrase for intercourse, *ti moro-iti*), he nonetheless added, "in doing this they keep time to a great nicety." And he neither romanticized nor condemned the practice of free love. While Banks and others flattered themselves with their own seductive powers, Cook suspected that many, if not most, of the women who offered themselves to the English did so "merely for the lucre of gain." Expanding on this topic later, he cautioned against judging the whole population from the behavior of the few whom sailors met on the beach. "A stranger who visited England might with equal justice draw the Characters of the women there from those which he might meet on board the Ships in one of the Naval Ports or in the Purlieus of Covent Garden."

Banks compiled his own summary, titled "Manners & customs of S. Sea Islands." Reading his words alongside Cook's, it becomes obvious that the two men compared journals and in some cases plagiarized whole sections from each other, almost verbatim. In virtually all such instances, it appears that Cook copied Banks, adopting turns of phrase that are much more the botanist's than the navigator's. Banks, free of shipboard duties, had time to wander the island and closely observe customs such as tattooing in a way that Cook did not, and his linguistic skills—Banks recorded dozens of Tahitian words, even whole songs, with remarkable accuracy—gave the botanist insights the commander couldn't hope to match.

The affinity between their journals also speaks to the remarkable collaboration, even friendship, that had developed between the two men. The effects of this unlikely union would become much clearer in the course of the long voyage. Cook gradually opened up to matters well beyond his established talents as a navigator and surveyor, even writing at times like a natural philosopher. After Tahiti, he leaned much less on Banks when summarizing his own impressions.

Banks, in turn, matured under Cook's steady hand, discarding some of his "airy dreams" of entertaining the salons of London and gradually becoming an inspired scientist. Later in the voyage, it was he who often cribbed from Cook, relying on the navigator's precision in geography and other matters. To put it a way that Banks and Cook never would, the two men found themselves in the course of their vast discoveries.

JAMES POUANT'S HIGH school stood a few yards from the beach. A warm tropical breeze wafted across the water, and waves tumbled against a distant reef. We found James cleaning a blackboard between classes. Thirteen- and fourteen-year-olds filtered in, the girls with flowers in their hair, the boys wearing baggy shorts and baseball caps. James began by asking students to read dialogue from a dated English text, its content comically remote from tropical Tahiti.

" 'Good afternoon! I've come for the flat in Park Street. I read your ad in the *Evening Standard*. Can you tell me how much the rent is?' "

" 'It is eighty-five pounds a week.' "

" 'Do you often go to the ice rink?' "

" 'Yes, I love skating. What about you?' "

Then James handed the class over to us. Roger explained that he'd been born in England, puffed out his chest, and sang "God Save Our Gracious Queen." The students laughed, a trilling, high-pitched giggle. Roger asked if they knew any English songs. A few girls began singing, "Ob-la-di, ob-la-da, life goes on!" One of them came to the blackboard and wrote in careful block letters: "Les Beetles." Roger asked how old she was. "Thirty-three!" she exclaimed, writing her name, Vai Ana, which James translated as "Shining Water."

It was my turn. "I'm from America," I began. "What do you know about my country?"

A boy with two earrings and a necklace raised his hand. "I am surfer dude. Okay, man, hey brud." He turned his cap backward. "This is *la mode* skateboard. I drive boogie board also." His classmates collapsed in giggles. I told them that Roger and I had come to Tahiti to learn about James Cook. Roger assisted me by putting on the wig he'd worn at Point Venus.

"Is that him?" a boy asked.

"No. Cook is the man who is very dead," another said.

"Cook came from Australia."

"He was hungry. He wanted our food."

"He was the first *taero* here. A bad man."

James explained that *taero* was Tahitian for the pulp of a coconut. It was used as slang for white men, and also for smegma. Then he gave examples of Tahitian words influenced by English. Hammer was *hamara*. Nail was *naero*. And a common greeting, *yoana*, was believed to have derived from the English "your honor."

All island words ended in vowels, and certain English consonants had no precise equivalent in Tahitian. This explained why the English journals recorded that islanders called Cook "Toote" and Banks "Opane." Tahitian words, many of them impossibly crowded with vowels, gave Westerners just as much trouble. James asked us to try pronouncing a few for the amusement of his class, such as *faaaanoraa*, which means "widening," and *mauruuru*, meaning "thank you."

When the class ended, James told us another word, one that had relevance to Cook's visit: *horoa,* meaning "to give" or "to lend." Tahitians, James said, made little distinction between the two. "When someone uses *"horoa"* it means, 'I may return it to you, I may not. I'm not sure.' Behind that you see their sense of property. They will take my markers and books without asking, and never return them. It is the same if I leave clothes on the line at home. To us this is stealing, but to them, if you leave something out it is theirs to 'borrow.' "

James walked us around the school during the break before lunch. On one wall, an art class had painted a huge mural of a bare-breasted woman. Nearby, teenaged girls gathered round a boom box and performed a hip-thrusting dance much like the one we'd seen at the Captain Bligh nightclub. Then they ran to outdoor showers and soaked themselves, fully clothed, emerging like contestants in a wet T-shirt contest. "They are very casual about sex, even at this age," James said. He gave us another Tahitian word: *taurearea,* a period of adolescent license during which young people were permitted to indulge their desires. "We must constantly remind them that they are not allowed to kiss or hold hands in class."

Lunch was even more of a surprise, at least by American standards. James led us to an outdoor table set with silver, wineglasses, and a vase of hibiscus and bougainvillea. Six other teachers joined us, and two coquettish teenagers in short black dresses announced the menu: *salade verte,* followed by mussels, shrimp, veal, and assorted desserts—all of it prepared by a chef from France. "This is the best restaurant in Tahiti," James said, pouring us rosé. The waitresses, he explained, were students training for hotel jobs.

The teacher sitting to my right taught history. He said he devoted only a few hours each year to Bougainville, Cook, and other explorers. "You must remember, Cook fought the French in Canada, so he is not so popular for us," he said. "The winners write the history, no? In Canada, we lost, but in this place, we won." He took a sip of wine. "But really, Tahitians care very little about these old Europeans, it does not seem relevant to them."

He had much better success with ancient history. "They like Greece best, they see parallels to Tahiti. A land of many islands, tall mountains, great gods, and brave sailors. They also like Egypt and its sun god. This means much more to them than Cook or Louis Fourteenth."

He suspected that this fondness for myth and story had contributed, in the nineteenth century, to the success of Christian missionaries. "The great tales from the Old Testament, this would have had meaning to their life." Though the evangelical hold on islanders had loosened, he said many Tahitians still thought of their history as an evolution from pagan darkness to Christian light.

The literature teacher sitting on my left had also adapted her curriculum to suit island students. "They love romance and cry very easily, they like the sweet stuff," she said. *Romeo and Juliet* went over well, as did farces such as Molière's *Tartuffe*. "But they do not like Molière's miser, they cannot understand why someone would keep money to himself." Most of all, though, her students loved poetry and song. "The oral tradition is still very strong here, they prefer action and theater to reading."

After lunch, stupefied by food and wine, we walked to the Panda with James. I asked him for directions to the *marae* I'd planned to visit before we'd met him at the café the day before. "It is nothing now," he said. With the encouragement of missionaries, Tahitians had long ago torn up the temple's massive stones and used them to pave roads. "The Tahiti of Cook's day," James said, "it is entirely gone."

Chapter 3

TO BORA-BORA:

Sold a Pup

Where Do We Come From? What Are We? Where Are We Going? —TITLE OF A PAUL GAUGUIN MURAL OF POLYNESIA

Exploration generally springs from grand ambitions, however basely these dreams play out in practice: saving heathen souls, honoring nation and Crown, advancing scientific knowledge. It comes as a surprise, then, to read Cook's rationale for exploring an island cluster near Tahiti before proceeding in search of the Southern Continent.

"The Ships company," he wrote, "were in a worse state of hilth then they were on our first arrival, for by this time full half of them had got the Venereal disease." Judging his men "ill able to stand the cold weather we might expect to meet with to the southward," Cook "resolved to give them a little time to recover while we run down to and exploar'd the Islands." In other words, the famed isle of Bora-Bora and its neighbors would appear on English maps thanks to a raging case of the clap. Venereal disease was generally treated—if treated at all—with mercury, which often took care of the visible symptoms but caused side effects such as drooling and loss of balance.

With the high priest Tupaia acting as pilot and intermediary, the *Endeavour* sailed two days west of Tahiti to the small island of Huahine. Cook "set about surveying the Island" while Banks botanized. Neither man was impressed. Cook found few provisions, and Banks no plants or customs worth noting. "The people were almost exactly like our late friends, but rather more stupid and lazy," Banks wrote. "We should have gone much higher up the hills than we did if we could have perswauded them to accompany us, whose only excuse was the fear of being killd by the fatigue."

Invidious comparisons of this kind recur in English journals throughout Cook's voyages. From Polynesia to Australia to America, Tahiti became the standard by which all other places and people were judged—and invariably found wanting, most often in the beauty of their women. Tahiti lingered in the crewmen's minds like first love, a dreamy romance whose innocent intensity could never be replicated.

The *Endeavour*'s landings after Tahiti brought another new element: the solemn theater of "discovery." At Huahine, Cook presented a chief with coins, medals, and a plate inscribed "His Brittannick Maj. Ship Endeavour, Lieut Cook Commander 16th July 1769." Cook wrote: "This we thought would prove as lasting a Testimony of our having first discover'd this Island as any we could leave behind." A few days later, the *Endeavour* reached Raiatea, the largest and most central of the island group. Soon after landing, Cook "hoisted an English Jack and took possession of the Island & those adjacent for the Use of His Britk Majestys, calling them by the same names as the Natives do."

This small act, which Cook would repeat at countless shores, remains a subject of contention. The Admiralty instructed Cook that "With the Consent of the Natives [he should] take possession of Convenient Situations in the Country." The Royal Society's Lord Morton, in his "Hints" to Cook, added that natives were "the natural, and in the strictest sense of the word, the legal possessors" of their land. Europeans couldn't occupy that territory "without their voluntary consent."

Both the Admiralty's and the Society's advice begged the question of what "consent" meant, and how Cook might gain it, given the barriers of language and culture. How could natives accede to an act that must have mystified them, made in the name of a sovereign and country they couldn't possibly imagine? In any event, there is no record of Cook having gained consent before raising the flag at Raiatea, or at many of the other places he visited. Some modern scholars and critics have used this to indict him and his mission; ostensibly on a voyage of scientific discovery, Cook acted instead as the advance man of Empire. He also overstepped his own orders, making the act of "possession" invalid even by the standards of his imperialist masters.

With hindsight, the case is easy to make. Many of the lands Cook claimed for Britain became wretched colonial outposts. Dispossession, like disease, must be counted as one of Cook's legacies. From today's perspective, the notion of "discovery" also rings hollow; apart from a few empty islands, every place Cook landed had already been inhabited for centuries. In Polynesia, the true discoverers were pioneers who set off from Asia in sailing canoes several millennia before Cook, eventually settling the vast triangle of ocean bounded by Easter Island, New Zealand, and Hawaii.

But if Cook wasn't the uncomplicated hero of nineteenth century statuary—spreading "civilization and the blessing of Christian faith among pagan and savage tribes," in the words of one memorialist—neither was he a purposeful despoiler of natives and their culture. Cook's attempt to limit the spread of the "Venereal distemper" at Tahiti, and his regret at failing, gave early evidence of his regard for islanders.

In a small way, so too did his behavior upon raising the flag at Raiatea to mark his first claiming of inhabited islands untouched by Europeans. Rather than honor king or country, as European explorers typically did, he called the islands "by the same names as the Natives do"—however much these names might challenge English tongues. Raiatea, for instance, appears in the crew's journals as "Ulietea," "Uliatoah," "Olyatea," and "Yoolee-Eteah."

Cook displayed similar restraint in his naming of the archipelago to which Raiatea belonged: the Society Isles. Nineteenth-century historians assumed that Cook intended this name to honor his patron, the Royal Society—a myth that persists in Pacific history books to this day. Cook clearly states in his journal that he called the isles Society "as they lay contiguous to one a nother."

While Cook later honored his superiors with countless bays and bluffs, the signature he left on the map of the Pacific was, for the most part, as unvarnished as the man: Hen Island, Bald Hill, Beaver Inlet,

Celery Cove, Foggy Cape, Wet Jacket Arm. It wasn't Cook's style to christen a place New Cythera. Nor, for that matter, did he ever name a place after himself or any member of his family.

From Raiatea, Cook sailed to the small nearby island of Tahaa and then headed to Bora-Bora, distinguished by the dramatic, twin-peaked volcano at its center. The *Endeavour* reached "close under the Peek," Cook wrote, describing the mountain as "so perpendicular that it appears to be quite inaccessible." But contrary winds and a heavy swell kept the ship from threading a channel through the reef encircling the island. Having already provisioned his ship at the other Society Isles, and apparently having given his venereal men time to recover, Cook swung the *Endeavour* "to the Southward the way I now intend to steer."

ROGER SET THE helm on autopilot and slumped on the deck, lighting a cigarette. "You can smoke twice as much at sea," he said, "because the wind smokes half the tobacco for you. No sailor ever gets lung cancer."

"I'm reassured."

"Don't be. I've never sailed through a pass in a reef."

Huahine lay just ahead. Our French chart showed the island ringed by a ragged line marked *"Recif."* Sailing through the hazardous reef hadn't been my idea. A few days before, Roger had mutinied while I tried to doze through a rainy, *nono*-infested afternoon in a sweltering bungalow. "I can't face another night of this," he declared, disappearing into the rain and returning, a few hours later, having rented a forty-two-foot yacht for the rest of our island stay. "The boat's called *Courbet*, very classy, very French," he said.

And very much like the Fiat Panda Jolly. During our first day at sea, the lever on the vacuum toilet snapped, cleats dislodged, and the dinghy towing behind the yacht sprang a leak. "Every product that has proved an utter failure in metropolitan France has been shipped over here," Roger complained, tossing loose screws into the bilge that seeped through the hold and onto the deck.

Still, it was nice to be out on the water. I'd learned enough knots and maneuvers on the replica *Endeavour* to be of marginal use to

Roger. Anyway, he could pretty much sail the yacht without me. As we approached Huahine, I lay on the bow and read what the English had written about tropical reefs. "The Rock is every where full of small holes," an astronomer marveled, "which are larger underneath the surface & every one contains a Shell with a live fish in it." To the artist Parkinson, coral seemed a magnificent species of "sea mushroom," or "a grove of shrubs growing under water."

The print was small and hard to read in the rocking boat. After a few pages, my head began to feel heavy. When I closed my eyes, the weight shifted to my stomach. I got up to make a cup of instant coffee in the galley. It tasted like caffeinated fish broth. "They even send the bad coffee over here," I gasped.

Roger dipped a finger in my mug. "You filled the kettle from the saltwater tap," he said. The swell had increased, steady and inevitable. I moved to the rail. Roger sniffed at the saltwater coffee. "Smells a bit like that *fafaru* we tried last night." *Fafaru*, also known as "stinky fish," was a Tahitian delicacy made from fish heads and fish guts, soaked in seawater until they formed a pungent sludge. "Looks like the milk curdled, too," Roger added.

I retched over the side. Chunks of *poisson cru*, the raw fish in lime juice we'd eaten with the *fafaru*, floated in the water. What felt like a piece of spongy breadfruit clogged my nose. Roger handed me paper towels and bottled water. "You're pathetic," he said.

The reef loomed just ahead. Waves swirled against the coral, creating a brilliant, aquamarine froth, almost a mouthwash color, unlike any hue I'd seen in nature. The surf skipped along the reef rather than over it, rippling in a dead-straight line as if strafed from an airplane. Then the sea swept through a break in the coral, marking the channel we needed to enter.

Roger deftly steered the yacht through, and a moment later we glided across a lagoon as placid as the sea outside the reef was agitated. Coconuts floated in the jade water and the craggy hills of Huahine rose all around us. I felt instantly cured of seasickness, and of the lingering malaise that had afflicted me during much of our stay in French Polynesia.

We moored a short way offshore and motored the yacht's dinghy to the dock at Fare, the same harbor Cook had visited. Kids fished off the pier while a few people milled along a street of low shop fronts. We wandered over to an open-air café and settled in beside a young French couple, Guillaume and Isabelle. They were waiting for the ferry that ran several times a week between Tahiti and Huahine (an island administered, like its neighbors, by the colonial government in Papeete).

"When does it come?" I asked.

Isabelle shrugged and pointed at a notice by the café door: "The boats arrive when they are here. And leave when they are ready."

The couple had been bumming around the Pacific for months, recovering from a stint as aid workers in Rwanda. Like us, they'd found Tahiti a disappointment. "You see the posters on the Paris Métro, the Gauguin paintings at Musée d'Orsay," said Guillaume, a gaunt, goateed man with wire-rimmed glasses. "You expect the reality to be better than the pictures, but the pictures are the best of reality, almost a hyperreality. So you are let down."

Still, they'd enjoyed their two days in Huahine. I asked what they'd done. "Very little. Mostly sit and stare at the sea," Isabelle said. "*Comment se dit,* 'When in Rome . . . ' "

Roger smiled and ordered a beer. "My kind of place. People's heads stuffed with polystyrene balls." After a few rounds, he headed for a bench by the water and lay down. I was about to do the same when a woman bounced into the café and spoke to a patron in American-accented English. She was fiftyish, with olive skin and long black hair, turquoise earrings, silver bangles on each arm, and a long cotton dress. She wouldn't have looked out of place at an antiwar rally in Berkeley, circa 1969.

"Went to college in Santa Barbara, actually," she said, when I asked if she came from the Bay area. "But I'm sort of a mutt." Dorothy Levy's father, a Hollywood writer, had come to Tahiti during the production of the first *Mutiny on the Bounty,* in 1935, and married a French-Tahitian Jew. Dorothy had shuttled between California and Polynesia for most of her childhood, then settled in Huahine after college and married a local. "I went back to California for the first time a few years ago and felt like a Flintstones character," she said. "All those freeways and tense faces and right-wingers. It blew my mind. Like, what happened to America?"

Dorothy ran a café at Huahine's small airport, at the other end of the island, and had to go there in time for the arrival of the evening flight from Papeete. I asked if we could tag along. "That's groovy," she said. I collected Roger from his bench and we piled into Dorothy's Land Rover. A half-empty beer perched in the cup holder. "Want a hit?" she asked.

Unlike Tahiti, Huahine—only ten miles long and six miles across—was still largely agricultural, and more fruitful than I'd imagined from reading Cook's journals. We drove past farms of breadfruit and pineapple as Dorothy played tour guide. "*Hua* means 'genitals' and *hine* refers to female fertility," she said, "so the name of the island translates roughly as 'Pussy.' " A mountain thrusting up at one end of the island was known as Ite Ure Na Hiro, or Hiro's Dick, she added. "Penises are very important to the culture. When I learned to speak Tahitian I realized all the jokes and half the chat were about sex."

"Just like the dances," Roger said, perking up in the backseat.

Dorothy nodded. A few years before, she'd escorted a group of island dancers to a folklore festival in Seattle. The American emcee asked how he should explain to the audience what the dances were about. Dorothy told him, " 'What does it look like they're about? Making love and how good we are at it.' " She laughed. "I think he ended up saying something like, 'It's about the rhythms of the South Seas.' "

At the tiny airport terminal, Dorothy slipped Tahitian music into a tape deck while she made coffee and sandwiches. "In the sixties, I would have thought a job like this was very bourgeois. Now it suits me. I can work hard for a few hours a day and be free to do other things. Also, it's a good place to people-watch."

She pointed at two women sitting nearby, one with a toddler in her lap. "Typical *demis*," she said of the French-Tahitians. "Slim, long perfect hair, honey skin, gleaming teeth, not a nose hair out of place." The women were the most striking I'd seen in French Polynesia, or anywhere in the world. "At first I felt demoralized being surrounded by all these beauties," Dorothy went on. "I've gotten over it, but I'm still not sure the attitude here is healthy."

"What do you mean?"

"It's like a beauty cult, right from birth. They massage the babies with oil, put ribbons in their hair, dress them up in perfect clothes, just like that child." She pointed again at the women, and I tried not to stare. Dorothy laughed. "Stare at will—that's the whole point. It's probably been fifteen minutes since they looked in a mirror. They need another fix. The men are the same, they oil themselves and put flowers in their hair. It's very sensual. But at some point you wonder if there's more to life than looking good and making love."

"Is there?" Roger asked.

"Why don't you go and ask them?"

When we hesitated, Dorothy half-dragged us to the women's table. She spoke to them in Tahitian. They nodded and invited us to sit down. "I am Hinarii," one of the women said in English, holding out a perfectly manicured hand with scarlet fingernails. "This is my cousin Tania. Dorothy said you had a question for us."

Roger coughed. I didn't know what to say. "They want to know about Tahitians and sex," Dorothy said, getting up to tend the café.

"You are American, yes?" Tania said to me, without a hint of embarrassment. "I have been to Hawaii and L.A. If you want to have sex you must go to a nightclub and wait for a man to pick you up. They are very blunt, they drink too much and rub against you. No subtlety."

"Here it is not so direct," Hinarii added. "It starts with the eyes, with dancing, with seduction. Can you do the Tahitian waltz?"

I shook my head. "That is too bad," she said. "You will not have sex."

"That's okay, he's married," Roger said. "I'm single."

"This does not matter so much in Tahiti."

"What does?" I asked.

"You must not only behave a certain way, but look the way we like."

Using Roger as a prop, I asked what suited the women, and pointed first at his unshaven chin. *"Non!"* they cried in unison. "No beard."

I pointed at his rumpled shirt and shorts. "No way," Tania said. "He must be clean and neat, over his whole body."

I reached for Roger's hair. "Long or short?"

"Long, like his, but it must be shampooed and combed," Hinarii said, studying Roger's unruly curls with obvious disdain. "Perhaps you have a tattoo? It is part of our culture, to have them all over. Very sexy."

"No," Roger said. "Just a smallpox vaccination."

"Tant pis." The plane arrived. Tania applied lipstick to her four-year-old daughter, who wore flowers around her neck and a black pearl earring. Hinarii reached in her purse and handed me a lighter decorated with a picture of herself in a tight floral wrap. "Miss Tahiti, 1984," she explained. "I was young and beautiful then." She offered me a golden cheek to kiss, then the other, and held out a limp hand to Roger. *"Enchantée,"* she said, not very convincingly, and the three of them went to board the plane.

Roger's face crumpled. "I've just met Miss Global Crumpet 1984 and I'm quintessentially what she can't stand. A polecat. Mr. Fafaru. Did you see her shake my hand? She's probably soaking it in disinfectant as we speak."

"Can't blame her. Look at you."

"Look at *you*. I've been sailing, working with the outboard. A few hours ago you were puking *poisson cru*. She only liked you because you were taking notes. She's a total narcissist. They all are."

We walked over to help Dorothy clean up. "How'd you do?" she asked.

"Not as well as Cook's men," I said.

"I've wondered about that," Dorothy said. "Islanders didn't like the hippies who turned up here in the seventies: too funky. When you think about it, Cook's men must have looked the same. Unshaven, unwashed, ponytails, bandannas. The women probably took them to the beach and scrubbed them before they'd do anything." She paused. "Then again, I've heard women here say, 'A white man, that's something different. Why not try it just for fun?' I guess Cook's crew must have seemed exotic. Plus they had nails."

"We could pull the rest of the screws out of the yacht," Roger said. "They're going to fall out anyway."

Dorothy dropped us back at the pier in Fare. The outboard on the dinghy quickly flooded. We paddled the leaky boat to the yacht. Roger drank from a rum bottle, studying the Miss Tahiti lighter. "Our first 'artificial curiosity,' " he said, adopting the phrase Cook and his men used for the man-made relics they collected. "I'll treasure it for the rest of my life, leave it to the British Museum when I die."

THE NEXT DAY, we sailed across calm seas to Raiatea and found a mooring on the island's western edge, very close to where the *Endeavour* had anchored. Then the weather turned, bringing high winds, hard rain, and poor visibility. We'd planned to circumnavigate the island, as Cook had done, but after peeking from the cabin Roger retreated to his bunk. "Cook wouldn't sail in this slop and neither will I," he said, opening a Patrick O'Brian novel.

"We could explore on land," I suggested.

"And see what?"

"A famous *marae,* one of the most—"

"—boring piles of rock. That's a redundancy. Be my guest." He piloted the dinghy to shore and let me off. "I can't wait to hear all about it."

Like Tahiti, Raiatea had a coastal road ringing the island, which was fifteen miles long and nine across. After walking through the rain for a few minutes, I stuck out my thumb. A battered Citroën pulled over, driven by a barefoot Frenchwoman named Christine. She'd come to Raiatea for a visit twenty years before and never left. "No stress. No shoes. Easy life. Why leave? Maybe some day I find another island, farther away." We reached Uturoa, the only town on the island. I asked Christine what there was to do there on a wet afternoon. "To do? *Rien.* Same as in sunny weather. That is why I like it. What do you want to do?"

This was a good question. She let me out at the Quai des Pecheurs, though there were no fishermen in sight. I wandered past a London Missionary Society church, a gendarmerie, and a tin-roof Chinese-owned shop called Magasin Yee-Foo Alimentation Générale. Uturoa was the second largest town in French Polynesia, after Papeete. It took me ten minutes to walk from one end to the other.

I stuck out my thumb again and a pickup pulled over, the Tahitian driver pointing to the truck's open bed. Soon after I climbed in, the truck stopped again. A woman stood by the road, in the middle of nowhere, with two fish as big as she was, hooked to a tree. The driver paid a few francs and heaved one of the fish in the truck bed beside me. "Bonito," he said, climbing back in the cab. The road was windy, and the bed held several inches of rain. The gargantuan fish kept sloshing against me, its glassy eyes staring with evident reproach for all the *poisson cru* I'd consumed over the past ten days.

I distracted myself by gazing at the scenery, lush and jungly as a rain forest. The few buildings we passed appeared much poorer than those I'd seen in Tahiti or Huahine, mostly small wooden houses and sheds with trays of coconut meat. Once dried, the meat became copra, used to make coconut oil. Copra, along with the fish sold by the road, seemed to be all that remained of the island's rural economy.

When the driver reached a turnoff, I climbed out and took refuge from the rain beneath the broad, dripping fronds of a banana tree. The next ride I caught was in a Cutlass Supreme driven by a Chinese-Tahitian named Gilbert. He offered to take me to the *marae,* at the far end of the island, if I didn't mind a detour. His car needed fixing. Since automobile parts were scarce on Raiatea, he kept a junked Cutlass parked in the mountains and was headed there to cannibalize it. He'd found the old car first, which determined his choice of a new car. "I know I have the dead Cutlass to keep a new one alive," he said.

We turned onto an unpaved road covered in pale, gravelly shale that Gilbert called *soupe de corail,* or coral soup. He parked beside a tiny Catholic church. As he worked under the two hoods, transplanting spark plugs from one Cutlass to the other, Gilbert told me how his family had come to Raiatea. When the American Civil War curtailed cotton exports from the South, an enterprising Scotsman founded a plantation on Tahiti and imported Chinese laborers. The Tahitian cotton trade ended soon after the Civil War, but many Chinese stayed, fanning out across the islands, mostly as merchants.

"I am fourth generation here, but still we are different," Gilbert said. "We work to make a better life. The island man, he likes his life. He wants only to eat, sleep, drink, make love. If he gets this, he is very nice. If not, he becomes angry, *méchant.*"

Anti-French rioting in the 1990s had led to the looting and burning of Chinese-owned shops. Gilbert now feared that the islands might win their independence. "France is our protection," he said. "That is why many Chinese become Catholic, to fit in, seem more French, even if we are still Chinese inside."

His Cutlass repaired, Gilbert drove me to the end of the paved road at a sleepy village called Opoa, strung along the banks of a wide inlet. Beside it stood the vast *marae* of Taputapuatea, one of the most significant historic sites in the Pacific. The word "Polynesia," coined by a Frenchman in the eighteenth century, derives from the Greek *poly*, "many," and *nesos*, "islands." Tradition held that Taputapuatea was the starting point for great canoe voyages to far-flung outposts across the Pacific. It was also at Opoa that Cook had first raised the British flag, setting in motion the destruction of the culture and belief system this ground had once consecrated.

The site was dramatic and outward-looking, jutting from the jungly interior, with water lapping on three sides and waves roaring against the reef a half-mile offshore. Taputapuatea comprised a complex of temples centered on a vast courtyard cobbled with giant stones. A black slab, ten feet high and four feet across, rose from the terrace. A row of similar stones formed one wall of an altar by the sea.

Silent and empty, Taputapuatea seemed as abandoned and remote from the twenty-first century as Stonehenge—even though the temple had remained in active use until just 175 years before my visit. Adding to the eeriness was the mystery surrounding the rituals that took place at the *marae*. Traditional Polynesian belief was wreathed in secrecy and taboo, and passed on orally. Missionaries encouraged the abandonment of pre-Christian faith, and also the dismantling of once sacred sites. Epidemic disease, which took an especially heavy toll on the elderly, also helped extinguish memories and traditions. As a result, modern anthropologists know more about the practices of the ancient Sumerians than they do about the Polynesian priests who practiced their faith here only half a dozen generations ago.

Cook and his men were among the few Westerners even to glimpse the old religion. But the English couldn't penetrate much beyond the surface of what they saw. "The Misteries of most Religions are very dark and not easily understud even by those who profess them," Cook wrote. Later, on his second voyage, Cook had a revealing exchange with a Raiatean chief he'd befriended.

"He asked the name of my Marai," Cook wrote, "a strange quiston to ask a Seaman." Cook interpreted the query in its narrowest sense: the chief "wanted to know the name of the place where our bodies were to return to dust." He replied with the name of the parish his family occupied in London: Stepney. Cook's second in command, Tobias Furneaux, was asked the same question and answered: "No man who used the Sea could tell where he would be buried."

Neither man grasped that the chief may have sought something more than the name of a London churchyard. Cook's biographer J.C. Beaglehole, a New Zealander who also studied Polynesian culture, describes the *marae* as "an essential part of a man's social existence, and his relationship to the gods: the question was really, What place are you particularly identified with?" For a man as rootless and secular as Cook, there wasn't a ready answer to this question, even if he'd understood it.

Cook learned much more on a later trip to the islands, when he visited a *marae* on Tahiti to witness an "extraordinary and Barbarous custom": human sacrifice to the war god, Oro. Cook described "the unhappy sufferer" as a middle-aged man, killed by a stone blow to the head. He noted every detail of the long ceremony: incantations, drumbeats, and the plucking out of one eye, which was held to a chief's mouth for symbolic consumption. With typical precision, Cook also counted "forty nine Sculls" of earlier victims, set into the *marae*'s stonework, which led him to conclude, "These sacrifices are not very uncommon." A drawing of the scene by a ship's artist became one of the best-known illustrations from Cook's voyages. A lurid adaption of the original artwork also circulated in missionary pamphlets as evidence of Polynesian depravity—one example, among many, of the unintended consequences of Cook's travels.

Taputapuatea, dedicated to the war god, had likely been the scene of sacrifice, too. But scholars believe its primary purpose was as an "international *marae*," a gathering place for priests from across Polynesia, and the seat of spiritual power: a Pacific Mecca. The upright slab at the courtyard's center served as a backrest for leading chiefs. Nearby perched an eroded stone figure of a woman with a flattish face and hands crossed on her belly. This was a *ti'i*, or tiki, a symbolic representation of a guardian ancestor or god. Similar tiki survived, in different form, across Polynesia, including the enormous statues of Easter Island, believed to have been erected to honor illustrious forebears who watched over their descendants.

Wandering among the rocks, I found bits of graffiti, names scratched inside hearts, an asthma inhaler, and scraps of paper stuffed in cracks. I later learned these papers had been left by visiting New Agers, who believed that scribbling their sins and negative emotions and storing or burning these missives at the *marae* helped expel karma.

Walking back along the road toward the village of Opoa, I saw six teenagers on a pier, their legs dangling over the dock as they drank beer and rolled joints in banana fronds. They motioned me to join them, and asked in French where I came from. When I told them, one of the boys gave me a vigorous thumbs-up, exclaiming in English: "American wood—tops!"

Unsure how to respond—was he a carpenter?—I smiled and gave him a thumbs-up, too. He passed me a joint and asked, "Why you are here?"

I pointed at the *marae*, and asked if he ever went there. He shook his head. A girl ran a finger across her throat and said, "Before, much killing. Very bad place." The others nodded gravely. New Agers might romanticize the old ways, but young islanders evidently didn't. I asked if they knew about Captain Cook's visit to the bay.

"*Le premier voyageur.*"

"He stop the killing at *marae*."

"He think we are savages."

I wanted to learn more, but we quickly exhausted our common store of words. Their French was oddly accented and almost as halting as mine—they spoke it only in school, a girl said, and talked to each other in Tahitian. I had just as much trouble comprehending their broken English. The dope wasn't helping. I learned a few words of Tahitian by pointing—*te rai* (the sky), *te ua* (the rain), *te miti* (the sea)—and reciprocated with some American words they pantomimed, mostly to do with sports and music. But after a while we just lay on the dock, exchanging smiles and occasional gestures: a thumbs-up, or a bull's horns motion with raised pinkie and thumb, an all-purpose Polynesian greeting that translates roughly as "Hey."

Lolling on the narrow pier, surrounded by these mocha-colored youths, I became aware of my own pallid body in an unaccustomed way. "Like cats," George Biddle, an American painter, wrote of islanders in the 1920s, "they fall naturally into harmonious poses." Sprawled beside these languid felines, my sun-pink limbs poking from cutoff shorts and a sweaty T-shirt, I felt about as harmonious as a toad.

But the sensation wasn't altogether displeasing. For one of the first times on the islands, I caught an echo of the strangeness and wonder of Cook's travels. The scenery was little changed since Cook's visit to Opoa: a cerulean lagoon thrummed by rain, volcanic peaks robed in emerald flora, the massive black stones of Taputapuatea looming onshore. In their journals, the English often tried to express the wonder they felt when gazing at Pacific landscapes. "The whole exhibits a View which can only be discribed by the pencle of an able painter," Cook wrote in a typical passage. Despite their muskets and sextants and spyglasses, the English felt overawed by the strange majesty of the world into which they had sailed.

The islanders they encountered had no concept whatsoever of the West, unlike the TV-influenced teenagers on Opoa's dock. Still, as I fumbled to communicate with hand signs, exaggerated facial expressions, and mangled phrases, I also sensed some of the thrill and frustration the English must have felt as they mingled with Polynesian society.

As I got up to go, the boy I'd first spoken to coughed over his banana-leaf joint and repeated, "American wood—tops!"

Still mystified, I raised my thumb in reply before extending it, once again, beside the road running around the island.

WHILE I WAS away, Roger had done some exploring of his own. Our mooring lay near a marina run by Frenchmen, and Roger insisted I come meet some of the characters he'd encountered at the bar. "They're seriously damaged," he said. "Just shocking. Even compared to me."

I settled on a stool beside a hard-drinking, chain-smoking Frenchwoman of a certain age, named Sophie. She wore a flowing robe and a flowered tiara. "Flamboyant, bougainvillea, orchid," she said, ticking off the blossoms. A florist by trade, Sophie had lived for many years near the atoll of Mururoa, ground zero for the French nuclear tests that had taken place in Polynesia for decades. I asked if she'd worried about nuclear fallout. "Not at all," she said. "If the wind blew toward us, the authorities simply ordered us to run and hide in blockhouses."

At this, the club's owner, Jean-Pierre, reached under the bar and produced photographs of mushroom clouds. Under each one he'd written a sarcastic caption: "Good Place for a Honeymoon!" or "Hiroshima, Mon Amour." He grinned, pouring another round of drinks. "Do not worry for us," he said. "I drink twelve Pernods a day, and smoke five packs of Benson & Hedges." He pulled out a cigarette and groped the breast pocket of a barmaid for a lighter. The barmaid giggled; she was a he, a *mahu,* like the ones we'd seen at Papeete's Piano Bar. "Alcohol and tobacco, they will kill us long before radiation," Jean-Pierre said.

The adjoining restaurant was empty. Many of the hotels and restaurants we'd seen on the islands had also been vacant. When I asked Jean-Pierre about this, he explained the Byzantine workings of the local economy. Frenchmen who invested in the islands could bring their money home tax-free after five years. Businessmen enjoyed other perks: freedom from most taxes and deductible four-wheel-drives, needed for the islands' coral-paved roads. Also, many of the francs flowing through the economy were laundered, from drug sales in Marseilles or Mafia-like *syndicats* in Paris. Islanders facilitated this with crooked deals; one top official was known as "Mister Ten Percent" because of the cut he took of government contracts.

"The French here are gypsies," Jean-Pierre said. "Many have lived already in other colonies. New Caledonia, Martinique, Algeria in the old days. In a few years we will move on to take what we can from some other place." He poured another Pernod, lit another cigarette. "*La France!*" he said, raising his glass.

At midnight, Roger and I rowed the dinghy back to the yacht. "This whole place is built on exhaustion," Roger said. "Worn-out people, exhausted by their boring, terminal lives. By heat and booze and nuclear fallout. Anyone who can't make it in Europe ends up here—just like all the crappy products that wash up in Polynesia." He poured a nightcap. "It's good to know a place like this exists. I may end up here before too long."

ON THE NEXT afternoon, the sun finally emerged, and not a moment too soon. The *Courbet* had become a seaborne bachelor pad, its deck draped with sodden clothes, the sink filled with dishes (the faucet had stopped working), cigarette butts floating in the bilge, everything reeking of salt and sweat. "Nothing dries in this humidity," Roger said, wringing out his shorts. He tapped his wristwatch; it, too, had expired.

He bailed out the dinghy with a salad bowl and rowed ashore to take on supplies, as Cook had done, trading Jean-Pierre our spare briquettes for a bottle of gin. Then he unfurled a chart and plotted our course to Tahaa, and on to Bora-Bora. The former lay just a few miles from Raiatea, across a passage filled with barely submerged rocks. From there we'd have to exit through a break in the reef and sail across open ocean to the narrow passage through the reef circling Bora-Bora. Roger tapped his dead watch, then glanced at the sky. "Four hours of light," he guessed. "Should be just enough."

We cast off from the mooring and I hoisted the jib while Roger raised the mainsail. We glided along the coast, threading between *motu*, tiny satellite islands with straggles of palm trees. While Roger negotiated the channel markers, I alternately peered over the bow for shoals and consulted the color chart in Roger's sailing guide. If the water appeared midnight blue, it was very deep; if dark turquoise, we still had plenty of draft. Pale green signified only five or six feet of sea. Yellow meant the water was dangerously shallow.

This seemed an easy and entertaining way to navigate—except, as the sailing guide warned, the colors rarely became obvious until you were right on top of them. "Green, blue, green—yellow!" I called out. A rock poked just above the water in our wake. We skirted Tahaa, then sighted a break in the reef. Approaching it, we were lifted up and almost spat through the coral by a current flooding out to sea.

So far so good, except that it was later than we'd realized. We were sailing straight into the sun, which hung just a few degrees above the horizon. Long purple swells carried us out to sea, while a vanilla-scented breeze rolled off the mountains of Tahaa. The jagged peaks of Bora-Bora loomed in the distance. Maybe sailing wasn't so bad after all. "I'm intoxicated," I said.

"I'm nervous," Roger replied. He was studying his Pacific sailing guide. Of Bora-Bora's reef, it said: "A night entry would be inadvisable for a stranger." Inside the reef, there were shoals all around. "Night sailing is strictly FORBIDDEN in the lagoon," the guide went on. At the marina, Roger had also learned that the French Navy regarded boats entering Bora-Bora in the dark as probable drug smugglers. Nor was the *Courbet* insured for sailing at night.

"We could smash against the reef and be dead," Roger said, "or wish we were dead once the bill for the damage comes in."

"You're right. Turn back. We can go hang at the bar with Sophie and Jean-Pierre."

Roger groaned. "I'd rather drown." He plotted a course for Bora-Bora and cracked two beers. "Might as well enjoy the sunset."

We'd barely hoisted our drinks before the sun slipped beneath the sapphire horizon. The travelers' tales I'd read about the South Pacific often mentioned the speed of tropical sunsets. As I understood it, the sun angles down in temperate latitudes: near the equator it plunges. Gazing at the sun's descent was rather like my earlier task: watching the lagoon color change over the bow. The sky went pink, scarlet, and gray in quick succession. In the momentary twilight, the jagged peaks of the Society Islands were silhouetted all around us. Frigate birds swooped low across the sea, and the air turned soft and caressing, all trace of humidity draining from the sky as quickly as the light.

"The whole Polynesian cliché," Roger said, watching a full, tangerine moon rise behind us, casting a beam across the water bright enough to steer by. For a long while we sailed in silence, propelled by a fine breeze, the swell lapping gently against the hull. Then we heard another sound, a distant roar. As we sailed closer to it, the moonlight picked up the froth from waves crashing against Bora-Bora's reef.

Roger steered well away from the coral and hunched over charts, pencil and ruler in hand, consulting the boat's global positioning system, or GPS. "Okay, we'll go north of the island until we pass the break in the reef, cut back, and shoot the reef on a 113-degree course," Roger said, "then follow the harbor lights exactly a mile into the lagoon, then turn sharply left between the shoals and go due north for four hundred meters, then sharp right and due east for three hundred meters and we're in. At four knots, one mile takes fifteen minutes. Got that?"

"Aye, aye, Cap'n," I lied.

"Good. You check the GPS and keep track of our bearings while I steer."

Running parallel to the reef, we saw the red and green lights marking the pass through the coral. But it was hard to judge distance in the dark: at one moment the lights seemed right before us, the next moment they vanished behind ocean swell. Roger hit the instrument lights on the cockpit. They didn't work. He searched the cabin until he found a flashlight. It flickered for a moment and went dead.

"Miss Tahiti to the rescue," he said, reading the panels with the lighter we'd been given on Huahine. Then he handed it to me so I could check the GPS and scribble the latitude and longitude readings onto the chart.

As I chanted our position, Roger swung the wheel and guided us through the pass. Surf crashed against the reef a few yards to either side of us. We coasted into the lagoon, flat and gray in the moonlight. Roger navigated past a thumb of coral marked on the chart but invisible to us, then swung left, threading between shoals we also couldn't see. Then he turned right and straight toward the yellow buoys just visible on the gleaming skin of the lagoon. After blundering around in the dinghy with a broken boat hook, we snagged one of the buoys and tied up, secure and exhausted.

As tense as this was, we'd had it easy compared to Cook. Someone had already laid out the track we needed to follow; we had green and red lights, like giant traffic blinkers, guiding us in; and we steered a boat full of instruments, at least some of which worked. Even by day, Cook had sailed almost blind, creating his own chart as he went along.

"This is one of the great achievements of my sailing life," Roger said, reaching for the gin bottle, "and it doesn't hold a bloody candle to Cook. All he had were tired men with knotted ropes and lead lines bawling 'six knots' or 'sixty fathoms deep and fine hard sand.' Every day and every night. For three years. Here I am with a GPS, compass, depth sounder, charts, a radio, flare gun, life raft, and fifty-horsepower engine—and still I was about to crap myself."

Drums throbbed on the dark shore. I glanced at Roger, wondering for a moment if I'd hallucinated the noise. "Another restaurant dance show," he said, closing his eyes. "Been there, done that."

He was probably right. Still, it seemed eerily resonant of Cook's travels: a strange shore at night, drums sounding in the distance. I coaxed Roger into the dinghy and we rowed to a pebbly beach. Roger, scrambling ahead of me on a dirt path through the brush, turned and said, "Oh my God, it's real!"

I glimpsed what he'd just seen: a clearing in the woods, fringed by palm trees and lit by the moon, with fifty or so women dancing while shirtless men banged drums. The women were barefoot, wearing halter tops and wraparound skirts, which they hitched to their thighs as they shook their hips, side to side, front to back. It was the same dance we'd seen at the Captain Bligh nightclub. But out here in the moonlit woods, performed by women of all ages and sizes, sweat streaming down their faces, it was the most erotic thing I'd ever seen.

We crept forward into the clearing and found ourselves beside a middle-aged islander named Richard. I asked him what was going on. He said the women were practicing for an upcoming *heiva,* or festival, in which dance troupes from across Bora-Bora competed. They gathered three times a week in this clearing, which was set aside for the express purpose of dance. Richard was one of the *heiva* judges. I asked him what he looked for.

"To see if they move together, and how each one moves," he said. "And how well they tell the story." As he explained it, the dance we were watching told a Romeo-and-Juliet tale of a princess from Bora-Bora who falls in love with a Raiatean prince. The families, from enemy clans, oppose the courtship, but in the end the lovers elope. "Then, as you see, they make love," Richard said, as fifty women thrust their hips forward in unison, their eyes glazed, soft smiles forming on their lips. "It is the usual story."

Richard, whose day job was also as a judge, said that traditional dance had gradually reemerged in the 1900s, after a century of missionary suppression. At first, women performed only on holidays, in their cover-all Mother Hubbards. Then, in the 1950s, a schoolteacher researched the old dances and re-created the choreography as accurately as possible, from oral tradition and from the writings and drawings of early European visitors, including Cook.

"It is strange, no?" Richard said, as the drums died and the women collapsed in exhaustion. "The first Europeans, with them came disease and so many other things that destroyed our culture. But now we are using them to take it back. If I may speak as a judge, Cook and the others, they leave us the best evidence we have of our own lives before the white man came." He paused. "Still, they are guilty men."

COOK FINALLY LANDED at Bora-Bora on his third Pacific voyage, and then only briefly. He'd planned to anchor within the lagoon for a few days, "but the tide as well as the Wind being against us, after making two or three trips I found it could not be done." Instead, he took a boat ashore and traded with the natives before quickly returning to his ship. "The island which at a distance looks like a barren rock, seemd to be very fertile and to have a good deal of low land about it that was well covered with fruit trees & plantations."

That's about all Cook wrote of Bora-Bora. The islanders dwelled in relative obscurity until World War II, when thousands of American servicemen descended on the Pacific. Among them was James Michener, a reservist and naval historian who tapped out *Tales of the South Pacific* on a typewriter in Vanuatu. The book won a Pulitzer Prize and spawned the Rodgers and Hammerstein musical *South Pacific* and a hit movie of the same name. This helped ignite an American craze for everything Polynesian, from mai tais to hula hoops.

A myth also arose that Michener had modeled his fictional isle of Bali Ha'i on Bora-Bora, which he once called "the most beautiful island in the world." In fact, Michener wasn't posted to Bora-Bora until after he'd written his book; Bali Ha'i was a composite of islands he'd visited earlier. No matter. Cruise ships and airplanes swarmed the island, and travel writers churned out endless stories with "paradise" in the headline and openings so ripe they made Michener's prose seem minimalist:

"The peaceful Pacific kisses feet, its lagoon-snuggled surface warm as a lover's touch. Beneath toes stretched a blanket of sand that could have spilled from a celestial hourglass. . . ."

"Crooning 'Bora Bora,' the barefoot driver skimmed his outrigger canoe across milky aquamarine waters of beauty defying description. . . ."

"As I bathed in Pacific waters the color of Cameron Diaz's eyes . . ."

During our moonlit sail into Bora-Bora, I'd wondered if these stories, which I'd clipped and brought with us, might actually have credibility. By day, as we tied up at the island's main wharf at Vaitape, I quickly came to my senses. Vaitape was a tourist-clotted sprawl of "curio" shops stuffed with mass-produced junk: beads, wooden tikis made in Indonesia, loud Hawaiian shirts. Across from the wharf, we rented the only transport available: a three-wheeled, golf cart–like vehicle called a "fun car," equipped with a lawn mower engine and tooth-loosening suspension.

"I never thought I'd miss the Panda Jolly," Roger said, as we bounced south along the potholed road circling the main island, only six miles long and about the same across. In a few miles we came to Bloody Mary's bar and restaurant, named for one of Michener's characters. Outside, a board listed celebrity visitors, mostly Hollywood and TV stars. Inside, the bungalow décor included a sand floor and stools made of tree trunks. We joined a few expats at the polished lychee bar, and asked them about life on the island.

"It's great as long as you live in a five-star bungalow," quipped a ponytailed Californian who repaired visiting yachts. Bora-Bora, thickly settled with resorts—and a population of seven thousand on only twenty-three square miles of land—was on the brink of environmental collapse. With only one break in the encircling reef, the lagoon couldn't flush the sewage pumped into its once-crystalline water. If the wind and tide ran the wrong way, scum coated the surface. Overfishing had killed off much of the marine life. Fresh water was so scarce it had to be cut off each night from nine P.M. to five A.M.

But new hotels kept going up, even as others closed. Club Med had erected a sprawling new resort, leaving its old one, damaged by typhoons, to decay by the water like a ruined *marae*. Another abandoned complex was known as the Hyatt slums. A disconsolate beachcomber sitting beside me at the bar likened the island to Waikiki, Honolulu's overbuilt beach strip. "I'm headed for Mururoa next," he joked, Mururoa being the atoll that had been used for French nuclear tests. "I reckon no one's going to develop that."

We climbed back in the fun car and motored past elegant boutiques, black-pearl shops, and gated resorts. At one, we poked inside just long enough to watch bare-chested men paddling canoes filled with flowers and fruit to $700-a-night bungalows perched over the water. Puttering on, we reached Bora-Bora's eastern flank, a terrain as abject as the western shore was luxe. The one path we followed toward the water ended at a trash dump. Many of the homes were little more than shacks, lacking even windows. Their inhabitants, perched in doorframes, waiting for a breath of wind, stared sullenly out, and didn't bother to return our waves. Bumping past them in the fun car, dust and exhaust trailing behind us, I felt alien and voyeuristic: an intruder from Bora-Bora's tourist "paradise."

At the end of the day, our circumnavigation almost complete, we searched for something to eat in Faanui, site of the main World War II base on the island. American servicemen left behind Quonset huts, gun emplacements, and 130 half-caste children, many of whom perished, my guidebook said, when "forced to switch from their accustomed American baby formulas to island food." Now, even island food was scarce. Settling for Cokes and candy bars, we navigated an open drain in the street and wandered down to the water, accompanied by mangy dogs.

Roger lit a soggy cigarette with Miss Tahiti and gazed out at the trash-strewn beach. "The whole world's been sold a pup," he said.

"A what?"

"A raw prawn," Roger said, reaching for another bit of Australian slang. "Conned, gypped, sold a bill of goods. Polynesia's a swindle, probably always was."

The dogs scratched at our feet, hoping for a scrap of candy. "Think about it," Roger went on. "Those blokes on the *Dolphin*? They were scurvy-racked, sex-mad, fed on biscuits full of weevils. Anyplace off that ship would have looked like paradise."

He tossed a dog half his chocolate bar. "Then came Bougainville and his ship full of Frogs. They're sex-mad, too, only they write better than the Brits. So the myth takes off. Noble savages, New Cythera, the whole romantic rot. No mention of human sacrifice." He fed the dog the rest of his chocolate. "Cook, he's clear-eyed, but no one listens to a lowly Yorkshireman. So we get Gauguin, another French wanker, painting his fourteen-year-old crumpet. Fifty years later, Michener and the Yanks show up. Then come the travel hacks, who have to justify their fancy rooms and plane fare by telling us this shithole is paradise."

He stubbed out his cigarette. "Come to think of it, paradise probably *is* a shithole. The missionaries sold a pup with that one, too. At least I hope they did, because I'm certainly not headed there."

We motored back to our yacht mooring. In twenty-four hours we'd be flying off the island. As we walked out on the pier, our legs still vibrating from five hours in the fun car, I asked Roger if he planned to come with me to Cook's next landfall.

"To New Zealand? Good God, that's a pup even the Frogs couldn't sell me."

I told him that French explorers barely went to New Zealand, and the first who had gone there ended up being eaten by Maori.

Roger laughed. "Frog legs? Can't blame the Maori for that. Wait till you try New Zealand 'cuisine.' You'll be pining for *fafaru*." He slumped in the stern of the *Courbet,* idly flicking his lighter. "Me, I'll be like Cook's men, pining for Tahiti." He flicked again. "She loves me. She loves me . . . not."

Chapter 4

NEW ZEALAND:

Warriors, Still

Notwithstanding they are *Cannibals,* they are naturaly of a
good disposission and have not a little share of humanity.
— JOURNAL OF JAMES COOK

Cook left no record of when he opened the sealed packet of secret
orders he'd been given by the Admiralty. But on August 9, 1769, as he
left Bora-Bora and the other Society Isles behind, Cook put his instructions into action. "Made sail to the southward," he wrote, with customary brevity. Banks's entry had more sense of occasion: "We again
launched out into the Ocean in search of what chance and Tupia might
direct us to." The next day Banks managed only four words: "Myself
sick all day."

The *Endeavour*'s track wasn't quite so aimless as the botanist supposed. Cook's orders were to sail to 40 degrees south, well inside what
theorists believed was the boundary of the fabled southern continent.
If Cook failed to encounter land, he was to turn west and keep searching the same latitude until he reached a shore once glimpsed by the
Dutch and believed by many cartographers to be part of *terra australis
incognita.*

For almost two months after leaving the Society Isles, the *Endeavour* sailed out of sight of land. Life returned to its oceangoing routine: furling sails, swabbing decks, drinking to excess. In late August,

celebrating the first anniversary of the *Endeavour*'s departure from Plymouth, Banks and his retinue broke out Cheshire cheese and porter beer and "livd like English men." The People also indulged themselves. "Out of mere good nature," Cook wrote, the boatswain gave his young mate a bottle of rum, "which it is supposed he drank all at once." The next morning he was found in his cot, "speechless and past recovery." He died two hours later.

At 40 degrees south, the *Endeavour* encountered "very tempestuous" weather, but no sign of land. The ship had reached what has since become known as the Roaring Forties, a band of latitude where the wind blows around the southern hemisphere almost unimpeded by continental land. "The sea ran mountain-high and tossed the ship upon the waves," Sydney Parkinson wrote. "She rolled so much, that we could get no rest, or scarcely lie in bed, and almost every moveable on board was thrown down, and rolled about from place to place."

Cook swung west and held his course for a month, sighting little except seals and albatross. Then seaweed and barnacle-encrusted driftwood appeared, signs that land was near. Cook offered to name the approaching coast after the first man to sight it, and threw in a gallon of rum as well. Banks, who was convinced the southern continent—"our land of Promise"—lay just ahead, penned a self-conscious passage that gives a rare glimpse of life in the great cabin.

"Now do I wish that our freinds in England could by the assistance of some magical spying glass take a peep at our situation: Dr Solander [a Swedish naturalist] setts at the Cabbin table describing, myself at my Bureau Journalizing, between us hangs a large bunch of sea weed, upon the table lays the wood and barnacles . . . we were talking about what we should see upon the land which there is now no doubt we shall see very soon."

Four days later, a boy of about twelve, Nick Young, saw land from the masthead, and Cook duly named a coastal bluff Young Nick's Head. There is no record of what Nick did with the rum. The *Endeavour* had arrived at the east coast of today's North Island of New Zealand (a nation comprising two very large islands, separated by a strait, plus smaller outlying isles). In 1642, the Dutch explorer Abel Tasman had probed a bay at the northern tip of New Zealand's South

NEW ZEALAND

Pacific Ocean

Tasman Sea

35°

Auckland

Mercury Bay
4 Nov 1769

North Island

Tolaga
Bay

Gisborne
Poverty Bay

1 April 1770

8 Oct
1769

40°

*Golden Bay
(Murderers Bay)*

*Cannibal
Cove*
7 Feb 1770

Wellington

South Island

Christchurch
17 Feb 1770

17 March
1770

45°

9 March
1770

| 0 Miles | 100 | 200 | 300 |
| 0 Kilometers | | 300 | |

170°   175°   © 2002 Jeffrey L. Ward

Island. Men in canoes appeared, blowing shell trumpets. The Dutch sailors answered by playing horns. "These people apparently sought our friendship," Tasman wrote. The next day, when canoes returned, the Dutch waved white linen and other trinkets and sent out a boat. The natives paddled over and clubbed four sailors to death.

Tasman named the inlet Murderers Bay and sailed off without ever setting foot on land. Sketchy Dutch writings and charts (later naming the coastline for Zeeland, in Holland) were all that Cook possessed as he neared a bay three hundred miles from the one Tasman had so briefly visited 127 years before.

The natives watching the ship from shore knew even less of the approaching strangers than the English did of them. (Cook later visited Murderers Bay and found no surviving memory of the Dutch, even there.) In fact, it seems unlikely that *any* vessel had approached the North Island from open sea for six centuries or more. Most scholars believe that sailing canoes set off from the Society Isles, or the nearby Cook Islands, between A.D 800 and 1200, carrying pioneers as well as plants and animals. They landed on the unpopulated North Island and gradually spread out, making New Zealand the last major landmass on earth to be settled. Then, nothing—until Cook arrived, the first intruder on the North Island since roughly the time of the Crusades.

To me, this was the most extraordinary and enviable facet of Cook's travels: the moment of first contact between the "discoverer" and the "discovered." No matter how far a man traveled today, he couldn't hope to reach a land and society as untouched by the West as the North Island was in 1769. Cook, at least, anticipated first contact; finding new lands and peoples was part of his job description. For those he encountered, the moment of European arrival must have been so strange as to defy modern comprehension. The only experience that might resemble it today would be to find an alien spacecraft touching down in your backyard—except that Hollywood has prepared us even for that. Pacific islanders had no basis for so much as imagining a tall-masted ship, much less one from the other end of the globe carrying white men speaking an unfamiliar tongue.

According to stories told long after Cook's arrival in New Zealand, some natives thought the ship's billowing sails were the wings of a giant bird. Others saw three trees sprouting from the vessel's base and guessed it was a floating island. A much fuller account survives from Mercury Bay, up the coast from Cook's first landfall, where the *Endeavour* visited a month later. A boy about the same age as Young Nick, named Te Horeta, stood watching the ship's approach from shore and lived long enough to share his memory with colonists, several of whom recorded his words. Te Horeta's vivid and poetic detail, corroborated by the journals of Cook and his men, makes his story one of the most remarkable accounts in the annals of exploration.

"In the days long past," Te Horeta recalled, he went with his clan to gather oysters and cockles beside a calm bay known by the name Gentle as a Young Girl. One day, an apparition appeared on the water, a vessel much larger than any canoe Te Horeta had ever seen. Watching from the beach, the clan's elders wondered if the ship had come from the spirit world. Then pale creatures climbed from the vessel and paddled small craft toward shore, with their backs to the land. At this, the clan's aged men nodded and said, "Yes, it is so: these people are goblins; their eyes are at the back of their heads." Te Horeta fled into the forest with the other children, leaving the clan's warriors on the beach.

At first, the goblins did no harm. They gathered oysters and other food. One collected shells, flowers, and tree blossoms, and knocked on stones, putting them in bags. Curious, the children crept out of the woods. "We stroked their garments," Te Horeta recalled, "and we were pleased by the whiteness of their skin, and the blue eyes of some of them." The goblins offered food from their ship: hard, dry lumps that looked like pumice stones, and fatty meat so salty that even the warriors winced. Was it whale's flesh? A man's?

One goblin pointed his walking stick in the air. "Thunder was heard to crash and a flash of lightning was seen," Te Horeta said. Then a bird fell to the ground. "But what had killed it?" Later, a warrior offered to trade with the newcomers, then snatched a goblin's cloth and paddled away without surrendering his own dogskin cloak. A walking stick flashed and the warrior fell with a hole in his back. The clan buried him in the goblin's garment; because the warrior had caused his own death, there was no *utu*, no revenge. The site of his killing became known by the name A Warm Bad Day.

Trade gradually resumed, and one day the clan canoed out to visit the "home of the goblins." The children refused to walk around the ship. "We were afraid lest we should be bewitched," Te Horeta said. But he and the others let the strangers fondle their hair. "They made much gabbling noise in talking. As we could not understand them we laughed, and they laughed also."

From inside the ship appeared a tall man who spoke very little. He studied the warriors' weapons and patted the boys' heads. Then he marked the ship's floor with a piece of charcoal while pointing to shore. Te Horeta recalled: "One of our aged men said to our people, 'He is asking for a picture of this land.' " The elder took the charcoal and drew an outline of Aotearoa, the land of the long white cloud. He also sketched Te Reinga, the rocky headland near the top of the North Island from which spirits leapt into the next world. He illustrated this by lying on the deck as if dead. "But the goblins did not appear to understand anything about the world of the spirits," Te Horeta said. In parting, the tall figure gave the old man two handfuls of a lumpy plant. He also handed Te Horeta a small, sharp piece of metal. Then the goblins sailed away.

Te Horeta was an ancient and venerable chief when he told all this to pale men who appeared again in his bay, many decades later, in search of gold. "The days are numbered for my taking part in the things of life," he told the visitors. "But here I am, here I am, like the old stump, throwing out twigs again." By then, Te Horeta understood much that he had not in "the days long past," when he was but a boy. The strange plants left by the goblins had been seed potatoes, their salty meat was pork, and the pumice stone was ship's biscuit. Te Horeta had used the thunderous walking sticks in his own wars against enemy tribes.

He had also made use of the piece of metal he'd been given on the goblins' ship. Te Horeta wore it round his neck as a *hei-tiki*, a talisman or private god. He fitted it to the point of his spear, and used it to carve wood boxes and repair canoes. "I kept this nail till one day I was in a canoe and she capsized in the sea," he said. "I dived to recover it, but could not find it. My god was lost to me."

Te Horeta also remembered the tall man who had given it to him. He had heard that the man was a great captain named Kuku. This did not surprise him. On that day long ago, Te Horeta and his companions had been struck by the head goblin's kindness, and by his air of quiet command. In their own language they had a saying for this: *"E koro te tino tangata e ngaro i roto i te tokomaha."* A noble man cannot be lost in a crowd.

THE TWO-LANE HIGHWAY across the North Island wound through a green and pleasant land of sheep-covered hills, deep forest, and cozy cafés offering "Devon Tea," a pot of Earl Grey and scones filled with jam and clotted cream. The car radio droned cricket scores. On the plane a few hours earlier, I'd read that the square mileage of New Zealand was almost exactly that of the United Kingdom. New Zealand's two islands reached almost the same latitude in the south that the British Isles occupied in the north. The country's white settlers were overwhelmingly Anglo-Saxon, lured by Victorian boosters who had touted New Zealand's cool, wet climate, so similar to home. In Australia's blazing sun, one nineteenth-century writer declared, "man degenerates into an emasculated idler," while in New Zealand the Anglo-Saxon naturally thrives.

This was the stock image of New Zealand: the Britain of the southern hemisphere, more English than England, a woolly colonial throwback. During my first few hours in New Zealand, the stereotype seemed to fit. The map on the seat beside me bristled with imperial names: Nelson, Blenheim, Palmerston, Wellington. I lunched on fish and chips (or "fush and chups," as New Zealanders pronounce it), wrapped in a greasy tabloid with a headline that read: WE'RE DOWN TO LAST 45 MILLION SHEEP! This figure compared to a census of seventy million just two decades ago. Still, that left fifteen sheep for every human in New Zealand.

I saved the story for Roger, a connoisseur of ovine jokes. (What do you call a sheep tied up in a paddock in New Zealand? A leisure center.) Australians are close cousins to "Kiwis" in culture, accent, and political system. But they tend to regard New Zealand—only one sixth as populous as Australia—with mocking condescension, as a decent but dull little brother, much the way many Americans view Canada.

Bored with cricket, I twiddled the car radio dial and picked up a call-in show. The topic of the day was the Treaty of Waitangi, an 1840 compact between white settlers and Maori chiefs that was now regarded as modern New Zealand's founding document. Its signing date had become the country's national holiday. To me, the callers might as well have been speaking a foreign tongue. "They went to the *marae* and had a *hui* and sorted it out after a lot of argy-bargy," one said. "I think Willy Te Aho and Tu Wyloie were there. One of them was head of the Nooie Kewa, the Runanga, eh?"

This, I gathered, was a white speaker, or Pakeha, as he called himself, using the Maori term for Europeans. The radio host pronounced Maori names and places just as fluidly—a considerable challenge, judging from the road signs I passed. What was I to do with "Ngatea"? Or the unappetizing billboard announcing an agricultural town: "Stop and Taste Te Puke!" (I did stop, and learned that the town's name was pronounced "Tay Pookie," rhyming with "hey bookie.") It was hard to imagine white Americans designating a treaty-signing with Indians as the country's Fourth of July and debating the legal niceties of the pact on daytime commercial radio.

The show faded out as I crossed the mountains separating the interior of the North Island from its easternmost shore, where the *Endeavour* arrived in 1769. A few days after Nick Young sighted land, the *Endeavour* anchored near the mouth of a river. Cook took several boats ashore. While he explored on foot, four natives burst from the woods and frightened a coxswain guarding the boat. The sailor fired a warning shot over their heads; when the warriors didn't retreat, he shot and killed one of them.

The English returned the next day to find men performing a startling dance on the opposite bank of the river. "With a regular jump from Left to Right and the Reverse," wrote Lieutenant John Gore, "They brandish'd Their Weapons, distort'd their Mouths, Lolling out their Tongues and Turn'd up the Whites of their Eyes Accompanied with a strong hoarse song, Calculated in my opinion to Chear Each Other and Intimidate their Enemies."

This was the first European description of the Maori *haka*, an aggressive dance popularized in modern times by New Zealand's national rugby team, which performs the *haka* before each match. Cook ordered a party of marines to form a protective line behind him. Then he and a few of the gentlemen approached the river, joined by the Tahitian Tupaia, who called across to the warriors in his own language. "It was an agreeable surprise to us," Cook wrote, "that they perfectly understood him." Though the Maori had been isolated for hundreds of years, their speech still resembled the language spoken on the islands from which they'd originally sailed.

The English waved gifts and threw a nail that landed in the water. One of the warriors waded, unarmed, to a rock in the middle of the river. "I then laid down my Arms and went to him and gave him some presents," Cook wrote. The two men touched noses. Several other warriors came to the rock, carrying their weapons. When their comrades on the riverbank resumed their hostile dance, Cook "thought fit to retire."

Twenty or so armed warriors then came to the English side, and began snatching at muskets. "I got Tobia [Tupaia] to tell them that we was their friends and only come to get water and to trade with them," Cook wrote, "and that if they offer'd to insult us we could with ease kill them all." But the warriors persisted until one pried away an English sword. As he ran off, Cook ordered the thief fired at with "small shot," a pellet spray akin to birdshot. Though hit, the warrior defiantly turned and waved the stolen sword. Cook then ordered the ship's surgeon, William Monkhouse, to fire his gun, loaded with a musket ball, which mortally wounded the man.

This brief exchange typified Cook's style of command. He led from the front, laying down his arms as the warrior had done, and going to meet him in the river rather than putting one of his men at risk. Nor did he flinch when the warrior pressed noses in a *hongi,* the Maori equivalent of a handshake or kiss. But Cook wasn't reckless. When surrounded by armed men, he retreated. And when natives failed to reciprocate what he regarded as peacemaking, he didn't hesitate to threaten them, and to make good on his threats. Small shot, intended to wound and frighten, was his first recourse. If that failed, Cook shot to kill. Cook would hew to this carefully calibrated escalation during tense moments throughout his Pacific career, with considerable success, until he lost control of himself and his situation early one morning on a beach in Hawaii.

Also characteristic were Cook's actions once the fray ended. Unlike many other explorers, he didn't sail away, or engage in wholesale massacre. Instead, he respectfully draped the dead warrior with beads and nails, and decided to row elsewhere in the bay, to find fresh water, and, "if possible to surprise some of the natives and bring them on board and by good treatment endeavour to gain their friendship."

This plan also went awry. Firing over the heads of fishermen in a canoe, in hopes of scaring them into surrender, Cook instead provoked them. The seven men in the canoe threw rocks, lances, and paddles at an approaching English boat—even hurling fish once they ran out of other missiles. The English opened fire, killing several, an act Cook greatly regretted. "I can by no means justify my conduct in attacking and killing the people in this boat who had given me no just provication and was wholly igernorant of my design," he wrote. "But when we was once a long side of them we must either have stud to be knockd on the head or else retire and let them gone off in triumph and this last they would of Course have attributed to their own bravery and our timorousness."

The next day, when Cook returned to the riverbank, a well-armed crowd of about two hundred men again confronted the English. Cook decided to abandon the troublesome inlet, recording with disappointment, "We weigh'd and stood out of the Bay which I have named Poverty Bay because it afforded us no one thing we wanted."

I REACHED POVERTY Bay in the dark and found a motel by the water. Though Cook's unflattering name had stuck, a town of thirty thousand, called Gisborne, had grown up beside the bay. I'd timed my arrival for a small event that the town's tourist officer had told me about on the phone: a Sunday morning walking tour of Cook sites led by two women knowledgeable about local history.

"Good morning, I'm Sheila Robinson," said a lean fair woman who worked with the local museum and historical society.

"*Kia ora,* I'm Anne Iranui McGuire," said her fellow guide, a stout, brown woman who taught Maori studies at Gisborne's university. *Kia ora,* meaning "good health," was a common Maori greeting.

We'd gathered with a dozen other walkers at a park by the bay, beside a statue of Nick Young pointing at the headland bearing his name. Sheila began by telling us about Nick, a mysterious figure who wasn't listed on the *Endeavour*'s muster roll at the time of the ship's departure from England. No one knew for sure why he'd suddenly appeared on the roll in Tahiti, "in lieu of 7"—the number assigned Alexander Buchan, the deceased artist.

"Probably Banks's bum boy," whispered the walker beside me, an elderly, winking man.

As to the land Nick sighted from afar, Sheila said it was undoubtedly one of the mountains rising behind Gisborne rather than the low headland named after him. "Of course," she added, nodding at her fellow guide, "it's got a perfectly good Maori name."

"Te Kuri a Pawa," Anne said. "The Dog of Pawa." Pawa was an early Polynesian navigator who landed at the headland and then sailed off in search of wood to fix his canoe. "Our history says his dog died below the headland, waiting for Pawa to come back. If you look at the bluff closely, you can see it's shaped like a long skinny dog, on its haunches, looking out to sea for its master."

We walked along the river Cook had visited. A plaque on the wall of a food processing plant told of the first white settler in the area. "We stop here for European reasons," Sheila said, "so I'll tell you a bit and then Anne can add something if she wants." Our next stop was a park that occupied the site of a vanished Maori village. Originally named for Cook's ship, the park was now called Endeavour Heipipi Park, incorporating a Maori word for shellfish. At the center of the park rose a sculpture of a canoe prow. The inscription read: "Our Maori Seafaring Ancestors were sailing confidently around the Pacific Ocean centuries before European sailors dared to go further than the eye could see, fearing they would fall off the edge of the world."

This wasn't strictly true; Vikings sailed off the known map of the Atlantic at about the same time Polynesians ventured to New Zealand. "It's just a reminder that Cook wasn't the first one here," Anne said, "and that Maori were seafarers like the English. It's a connection between our two cultures."

This gentle, yin-yang presentation—thin, blond Sheila telling the European history; round, dark Anne relating the Maori version—continued as we crossed the river to the site of Cook's landing. Gisborne had become a busy industrial port, and this side of the river was crowded with old slaughterhouses, freezing works, and a vast "Debarking Facility" that produced a mountain of sawdust. Log trucks rumbled past, adding to the din from wood chippers and generators.

"The scenery's changed a wee bit since 1769," Sheila said, leading us behind one of the warehouses to a simple obelisk of rose-colored granite, erected in 1906 to commemorate Cook's landing. A recently added plaque, in Maori and English, explained that the first Polynesian voyagers had also landed here, centuries before Cook, in sailing canoes, or *waka*.

"It was their descendants who made the first contact with Captain Cook," the plaque said. "Close to this place, Maori and Pakeha began to learn about each other, exchanged gifts, and mourned the deaths which had occurred." "Pakeha" was believed to have derived from *Pakepakeha*, meaning "pale-skinned fairies," or imaginary beings. "Maori" was itself a postcontact word, roughly translating as "normal" or "usual" people, and adopted to distinguish native islanders from Europeans. Before Cook's arrival, the Maori hadn't had any concept of race, only of their tribal identities.

"This is a microcosm of New Zealand history right here," Anne said. "First the arrival of the *waka*. Then Cook. Then the commerce and change. It all happened within view of this spot."

"If it'd been whalers or traders who arrived first, ahead of Cook, we wouldn't have the observations and records that we do, of what life was like before European contact," Sheila added. "That's why this place is important to me. Cook first landed *here,* and as a result we are who we are today, both Maori and Pakeha. This is the real ground. I can't get that feeling at a museum."

Unfortunately, it was hard to get that feeling at the landing site, either. Landfill had extended the banks of the river and bay so that the monument lay far from any water. Warehouses, and a seawall of industrial rubble, obstructed all but a narrow glimpse of Poverty Bay.

The only way Cook could land here today would be by forklift or helicopter.

Still, preservationists had done their best to create a botanical reminder of the site's appearance in 1769. Sheila and Anne led us to a nearby plot labeled "Banks Garden." Imported plants had been pulled out and replaced with indigenous, thick-leafed shrubs and small gnarly trees like those Banks and his assistants found during their brief time on the riverbank. Plaques also explained the plants' native uses. The leaves of the pepper tree helped reduce swelling; a shrub called *ngaio* was a natural insect repellent; the bright orange fruit of the *karaka* plant had poisonous flesh but kernels inside that the Maori baked and ate at feasts.

"It's funny," said the elderly walker who had whispered to me about Nick Young. "When I was a boy, farmers regarded all these native plants as weeds."

"And the native people were worse," his wife chimed in. "In school, the Maori were presented as criminals and savages. No one told us Cook killed people when he landed."

At tour's end, as the walkers headed back to town, I lingered to chat with Anne and Sheila. Until recently, they'd been giving tours separately: Anne to Maori walkers, Sheila to Pakeha ones. Gisborne's population was evenly divided between the two groups. The two women also consulted about the wording for monuments and plaques, including the one beside the obelisk, identifying this as the site where Maori and Pakeha first "learned about each other" and "mourned the deaths which had occurred." I confessed that this struck me as a passive and sanitized way to describe a very violent encounter.

"It's squishy, that's true," Sheila said. "But before, the story was only told one way, and from one side, with 'God Save the Queen' and the Union Jack and all that."

"A lot of Maori don't want any part of the Cook history, they think it's just Pakeha propaganda," Anne added. "The only part of the story they like is the *haka,* the whole macho combat thing. We're trying to find a middle ground, a way to tell the story from a different perspective."

Anne had to go off to guide another tour. She and Sheila kissed and embraced. Watching them, and mulling their words, I was reminded of how meager the women's perspective was in the books I'd read about Cook, many of which were written by old-school scholars of a nautical bent. Native women rarely appeared in these histories except as objects of sailors' desires. Cook's wife, Elizabeth, remained a shadowy figure. To a degree, this simply reflected eighteenth-century reality; it would be anachronistic to inflate women's roles in events and societies that were so male-dominated. But watching Anne and Sheila, I wondered if the very maleness of Cook's story explained more than I'd realized about the way events unfolded, and how they were remembered.

We take it for granted that Cook's ships carried only men. But for natives, this was a source of confusion and curiosity. The English journals mention several instances in which islanders groped sailors' chests and groins, or asked them to undress, seeking proof that they were indeed men. At one stop in New Zealand, an Englishman bartered for sex. He was presented with a boy; when he complained, he was presented with another. The English related this incident with amusement, as a cruel joke. But the Maori may have supposed that homosexuality was the English norm. How else to account for the absence among them of women and children?

In 1769, New Zealand was a patchwork of warring tribes. The sudden appearance of a *waka* full of men, most of them young, quite reasonably aroused fears of bloodshed and plunder, even before the English opened fire. In Tahiti, "Queen" Purea held a prominent role; she and other women mediated first contact between sailors and islanders. In New Zealand, the English met only well-armed warriors, taunting and threatening them with the *haka*. Testosterone, on both sides, doubtless contributed to the violence that followed.

Now, on the same exact ground, a Pakeha and a Maori woman were trying to reach out in a way their forebears had failed to do 230 years before—a gesture many people today were still reluctant to undertake. It might be "squishy," as Sheila admitted, but it seemed better than the alternative.

When Anne left, Sheila offered to show me a Cook site that wasn't included on the morning tour. She led me up the steep hill behind the landing site. Its summit had once been a lookout from which Maori watched the *Endeavour*'s arrival. "We could plainly see a regular paling, pretty high, inclosing the top of the hill," Banks wrote. Unsure what to make of this palisade, Banks—perhaps homesick for his own estate—guessed it was a deer park or "a feild of oxen and sheep." In fact, New Zealand in 1769 had no land mammals, apart from dogs. The fenced enclosure was a fortified position, or *pa,* where Maori took refuge during attacks by enemy tribes.

No sign of the *pa* remained today. Instead, near the top of the hill, we reached "Cook's Plaza," an ugly wall and terrace made from brick the color of slightly off salmon. Facing the plaza, with its back to the sea, stood an unprepossessing bronze of a man in a Napoleon-style hat. His features were much softer and younger than those in portraits of Cook. Also odd was the triangle he clutched in one hand.

Sheila said the bronze had been cast from a nineteenth-century Italian statue purchased long ago by the owner of the Captain Cook brewery in Auckland. Believing it to be an image of Cook, the brewery had donated money for this replica, erected on the bicentenary of the *Endeavour*'s landing. "We call him the crook Cook," Sheila said. "Crook" was antipodean slang for "ill" or "counterfeit." She pointed at his hat. "Cook wore a tricorn, prow forward," she said, "nothing like this one." The statue's double-breasted uniform also didn't fit; lieutenants in Cook's day wore an open frock coat with lapels. As for the triangle in the statue's hand, Sheila said it didn't match any known nautical or astronomical instrument. "He looks as if he's about to rack up balls for a pool game."

"So who is it?" I asked her.

Sheila shrugged. "Some people think he's John Paul Jones. Or an Italian commander. Nobody knows."

The statue had also been subject to frequent vandalism. Someone with a truck and winch had once dragged it off its pedestal. Other vandals had knocked off the sword, covered the statue in graffiti, and spray-painted a pink bikini onto its breeches. "Cook's not very popular with Maori," Sheila said. "Even if he's crook."

Sheila and other Cook enthusiasts had waged a long campaign to erect a new, more accurate statue of the navigator. It was due to go up in a few weeks near the statue of Young Nick. "Why don't you stick around?" Sheila said.

AFTER LEAVING POVERTY Bay, Cook sailed briefly south, but, finding the coast barren, he turned north and continued counterclockwise around the island. Heavily manned canoes approached the ship, with warriors inside performing what Cook called their "strange contorsions" while shouting words that he later learned meant "Come here, come a shore with us and we will kill you with our patoo patoo's."

Banks described *patupatu* as bludgeons made of stone or hard wood, held onto the wrist by a strap, and "most admirably calculated for the cracking of sculls." Other weapons included fifteen-foot spears, "darts" with jagged points or stingray stingers attached, and "battle axes" made of heavy, bladed wood and notched to lift out pieces of fractured skull. "The mind of man, ever ingenious in inventing instruments of destruction, has not been Idle here," Banks concluded. Maori were also veritable Davids at throwing and slinging stones. "When they have pelted us with them on board the ship," Banks wrote, "I have seen our people attempt to throw them back and not be able to reach the Canoes, tho they had so manifest an advantage in the hight of their situation."

Full facial tattoos added to the warriors' ferocity. The artist, Parkinson, described the tattoos as "fine spiral directions like a volute," and his drawings show swirls and scrolls encircling eyes and mouths. He depicted the men's hair as tied in knots atop their heads in the manner of Sumo wrestlers. The Maori adorned the prows of their canoes in a similarly "wild and extravagant" fashion, the artist wrote, carving distorted human faces with lolling tongues and wide eyes made of mother-of-pearl that mimicked their own expressions as they performed their war dance. "Nothing is omittd which can render a human shape frightful and deformed," Banks wrote of the *haka,* which included the rhythmic beating of thighs, feet, and paddles, and a grunting chant that ended "with a loud and deep fetchd sigh."

As fearsome as this behavior seemed—and anyone who has seen the *haka,* even its rugby version, knows how intimidating it can be—the English quickly realized that it was ritualized bravado rather than genuine belligerence. The warriors taunted and threatened the English, but only rarely did they follow the *haka* with a sustained attack. Before long, the crewmen responded in kind. When a warrior waved his naked backside at the English, which William Monkhouse termed "the usual sign of contempt" among fishmongers in London, the surgeon decided to "retort the compliment" by baring his ass as well. This so enraged a warrior that he hurled a lance. The English replied with small shot, frightening the Maori—but only for a moment. "They felt the sting of our laughing at them," Monkhouse wrote, and resumed shouting and waving spears and paddles. Thus ended a fairly typical encounter, which reads today rather like a skirmish between soccer hooligans in Europe.

Maori behavior became so predictable that the English started describing warriors' elaborate performances in abridged form: they "began again their braging," or "became very saucy," or "sang the song of Defiance as usual which we took very little notice of." Even Cook's tone became droll. "Accompaned in here by several Canoes," he wrote of one bay, "and before they went away they were so generous as to tell us that they would come and attack us in the morning." Instead, the Maori returned and, "after Parading about the Ship near three hours," consented to trade and talk (or "chitchat," as Cook described a later such encounter).

In fact, for all their initial bellicosity, the Maori proved reliable trade partners and hosts. Once "they found that our Arms were so much Superior to theirs and that we took no advantage of that superiority," Cook wrote, they became "our very good friends and we never had an Instance of their attempting to surprize or cut off any of our people when they went ashore."

To paraphrase Margaret Thatcher's judgment of Mikhail Gorbachev, Cook found in the Maori a people he could do business with. Tahitians, for all their charms, had perplexed the hardheaded commander. They struck him as not only thieving but also mercurial. The Maori, by contrast, seemed refreshingly consistent and forthright, possessing a Samurai dignity that Cook admired. "They are a brave open warlike people and voide of treachery," he wrote. His description of the warriors' bearing—"strong raw boned well made Active"—could just as well be a description of himself.

A FEW DAYS after the walking tour, I stopped in to see Anne McGuire at her university office behind a Kentucky Fried Chicken in Gisborne. Her department taught Maori arts and language, both of which had nearly gone extinct in the latter half of the twentieth century. Government policies had encouraged the urbanization and assimilation of Maori, while cultural influences such as television and radio further eroded native identity. "When I was a child, the attitude, even among Maori, was that everything from our own culture was bad, and everything Pakeha was good," Anne said. "We'd play cowboys and Indians, and everyone wanted to be cowboys because they won and Indians were savages who scalped people."

Attitudes started to change in the early 1970s, when Anne went to university. "It grew out of the American Indian Movement," she said. "We thought, 'There's people who have a huge country, they lost so much more than us, and they're taking a stand.'"

The civil rights movement had also inspired Maori, who constitute roughly 15 percent of the New Zealand population, about the same as blacks in America. Maori and some Pakeha supporters began staging marches and sit-ins, and famously disrupted a tour by South Africa's rugby team by pouring onto sports fields and battling with police. Eventually, the government revived and amended the Treaty of Waitangi so that Maori could petition for financial compensation and the return of their land.

This political movement was accompanied by a Maori cultural renaissance. Canoe racing, dance, and traditional crafts now thrived; even facial tattooing, outlawed in 1906 as a sign of rebellion, was making a comeback among young people. Maori were also reconnecting to the land. Anne had grown up on a dairy farm in a seaside community called Tolaga Bay, then moved to Gisborne, attended university in Wellington, and lived in various cities before returning to the east coast. Now, she and her husband spent all their free time at Tolaga, where they kept a garden and "bach," New Zealand slang for a simple holiday cottage. She was headed up there after class and offered to take me along.

"Sorry about the mess in my *waka*," she said as we climbed into her cluttered sedan. *Waka* was the word Maori still used for all transport, from canoes to cars. A Maori-language commission had been set up to adapt native language to the modern world. *Rorohiko,* for instance, a new word for "computer," was a conjunction of *roro,* "brain," and *hiko,* "lightning."

As we drove north, on a two-lane highway between the sea and mountains, Anne also gave me a primer on Maori belief. The world began when the Sky Father, Ranginui, coupled with the Earth Mother, Papa-tu-a-nuku. They spawned children, but their embrace was so tight that the world remained dark. Finally, one of their boys managed to plant his feet against his father and his back against his mother and pry his parents apart. Thus came light. Cook, who had as much trouble divining Maori beliefs as he had Tahitian ones, offered an abridged version of this Freudian story. "There is one suprem god," he wrote, who "made the world and all that therein is—by Copolation."

Long after this mythical beginning came the great expeditions that brought Polynesian settlers to New Zealand. Maori today still identified themselves with reference to the sagas of these founding ancestors. "A true Maori can trace his or her family back fifty generations—and recite every one of them," Anne said. This elaborate, orally transmitted genealogy was known as *whakapapa* (pronounced "fuckapoppa").

Anne pulled over at a small settlement centered on a *marae,* a ceremonial space leading up to a meeting house (a variation on the Tahitian *marae*). The A-frame building was beautifully carved with sinuous designs similar to those Cook and his men had seen tattooed onto Maori faces and carved onto the prows of their canoes. Like the English, I admired the carvings' Escheresque artistry, but had no idea what to make of them.

"Think of the *marae* as a library, and each carving as a book, and each notch in the carving as a page in that book," Anne said. At the top of the A-frame was the figure of a man astride a giant fish; this was Paikea, a founding ancestor who came ashore on a whale. Wooden panels running down either side of the roof bore images of his descendants, some with monstrous faces and eyes made of abalone shell. One figure, shown with a forked tongue, was an ancestor remembered as a liar. In an era before literacy, these carvings, as well as songs and poems, served as the repository of Maori memory.

"On another side of my family I'm descended from Hauiti," Anne said. "That *whakapapa* is easier to recite because Hauiti's only seventeen generations back from me." Like almost all Maori, she also had Pakeha blood, which she'd traced to an English great-great-grandfather named Glover, Anne's maiden name. "I like to think that's another connection between Maori and Pakeha culture," she said. "A lot of English are obsessed with their genealogy, and so are we." She laughed. "Then again, I'd like to see an Englishman recite his family tree back ten centuries."

We drove on, past rolling fields and hills topped by *pa* sites: flattened summits ringed by moatlike ditches. Cook described these fortifications as dotting the entire coastline of New Zealand, like medieval castles strung along the Rhine. On closer inspection, he found picket fencing, platforms from which defenders hurled spears, and vast stores of fern root and dried fish in case of siege. "The best Engineer in Europe could not have choose'd a better [site] for a small number of men to defend themselves against a greater," Cook wrote of one *pa*. The Maori later adapted these forts for warfare against the British, turning the trenches into rifle pits and adding underground bomb shelters.

Tolaga Bay, which Cook visited in search of fresh water soon after leaving Poverty Bay, lay beneath a sacred mountain called Titirangi, or Sky Piercer. "When I'm at a meeting where formal introductions are required," Anne said, "I start by saying 'Titirangi is my mountain.' Then I name my river, my *marae*, my *iwi* or tribe, my *hapu*—that's my clan—and so on. It drives Pakeha crazy to sit through an hour of introductions before any business gets done."

THE SITE OF Cook's landing could only be reached by a rugged three-mile foot trail. Anne, an unenthusiastic hiker, left me at the trailhead and arranged to meet me in Tolaga Bay at the end of the day. I climbed a stile and walked through paddocks of sheep, feeling for a moment as though I were rambling in the Cotswolds. Then the trail plunged into a grove of massive ferns—or what I guessed were ferns—blocking out the sun. The ground became marshy and lush, blanketed with unfamiliar shrubs, spiky grass, purple thistles, and yellow flowers that looked a little like buttercups. Cook and his men had also struggled to describe flora they'd never seen, or even imagined. "Cloth'd with several sorts of trees," Cook remarked of the same countryside I hiked through.

After a mile or so, the trail opened onto a ridge overlooking Cook's Cove. The hills all around were now clothed in what looked like clumps of dirty snow. Sheep again. So many that I doubted the census figure I'd read in the paper. *Down to last 45 million?* There seemed to be thousands of sheep here alone, a creeping mass, like troops viewed from afar. "Nothin' but mutton, mate," an Aussie had told me when I'd asked about North Island scenery.

I gamboled along the rest of the trail and down to the cove. The *Endeavour* spent five days here, one of its longest stays on the North Island. Except for the very brief, unsatisfying stop at Poverty Bay, Cook and his men hadn't spent time ashore since leaving the Society Isles months before. Land—any land—must have seemed a relief after so much sea, and the crew's journals and artwork from Tolaga possess a leisurely air that is rare in the records of the *Endeavour*'s voyage.

"The country about the bay is agreeable beyond description," Sydney Parkinson wrote, "and, with proper cultivation, might be rendered a kind of second Paradise." In particular, the English were mesmerized by a rock outcropping beside the cove, pierced by an almost perfect circle that framed a view of sea and hills beyond. "It was certainly the most magnificent surprize I have ever met with," Banks wrote, adding that he'd "seen such places made by art"—namely, on the landscaped grounds of English country estates. Parkinson sketched the arch, which he judged "very romantic," and several amateur artists on the *Endeavour* drew it as well.

One anonymous watercolor from the *Endeavour* shows a Maori handing a crewman an enormous lobster in exchange for a piece of fabric. Scholars have recently concluded that this painting was done by Tupaia. According to Banks, the Tahitian "learned to draw" on board the ship and developed a "genius for Caricature." English journals also described the Tahitian priest displaying his tattooed hips to fascinated Maori and discoursing with them on religion.

On a slope by the cove, I found a historical marker. Set into it was a reproduction of a naïve sketch I'd often studied in books. It showed sailors in baggy knee-length britches, rolling water casks ashore while Maori looked on. The drawing intrigued me because it was the only one I'd seen from the voyage depicting common sailors. Also, while some books named the artist as Herman Spöring, a Swedish assistant to Banks, other sources—including this plaque—attributed it to Cook.

If this was Cook's work, it was a rare example of his drawing (not counting, of course, the hundreds of charts he made). I found a comfortable flat rock, which afforded a view of the cove exactly like that in the sketch, and tried to imagine Cook sitting here. During his stay at Tolaga he turned forty-one, the same age I was now. Perhaps he'd indulged himself just a little, with a few hours of quiet observation. The sketch's detail and firm, careful lines certainly suggested the surveyor's hand. So did the purposeful activity it depicted: one sailor pushing a barrel with his foot, a cooper raising his hammer, the Maori on shore tugging canoes and hoisting fish.

"I got as much Sellery and Scurvy grass as loaded the boat," Cook wrote on his birthday. "This day we completed our water to 70 Tons but have not got enough wood yet." Cook made no mention in his journal of the "romantic" rock arch that everyone else marveled at, nor did he include it in this sketch. But he did muster a few expressive words for the surrounding landscape. "I went upon some of the Hills in order to view the Country," he wrote, describing it as "luxuriously clothed with Woods, and Verdure and little Plantations of the Natives."

This was about as lyrical as Cook ever waxed about scenery. In the next sentence, he was back to business, noting the trees he cut down for firewood (one yielding a yellowish gum he thought "might prove useful in dying"), and the quality of the soil, which he judged "light and sandy and very proper for producing all kinds of Roots."

Banks also proved true to form, carefully studying native women and comparing all that he saw to his beloved Tahiti. While he admired the tidy gardens he visited near Tolaga and the sanitary layout of a village, which included a "necessary house," or outhouse, he judged the women much plainer than in Tahiti and felt that they "made themselves more so by painting their faces with red ocre and oil"—goo that transferred itself to the English each time they pressed noses.

Under rough-hewn, knee-length cloaks that "resemble not a little a thachd house," Banks wrote, women wore girdles of perfumed grass, to which they "fastned a small bunch of leaves of some fragrant plant which servd as the innermost veil of their modesty" (another journal keeper described this as a "stopper of dried grass"). One day, Banks "accidentaly" came upon several naked women diving for shellfish, but he was disappointed when they "shewd most evident signs of Confusion, veiling as well as they could their naked beauties with sea weed the only covering the situation afforded." This modesty extended to sexual behavior. Some women were "as great coquetts as any Europaeans could be," Banks wrote, but there was little of the frantic traffic in sex that had occurred at Tahiti.

Banks turned his attention instead to the natural wonders of "a countrey so totaly new." He marveled at a songbird that awakened him with "the most melodious musick I have ever heard, almost imitating small bells." Even the mollusks and barnacles thrilled him. "Here were also some fine whelks, one particularly with a long tooth, and infinite variety of *Lepades, Sertularias, Onisci* &c &c &c much greater variety than I have any where seen," he enthused.

By the end of the *Endeavour*'s tour of New Zealand, Banks and Solander had collected specimens of four hundred plant species unknown in the West, and &c &c &c of birds, fish, insects, shells, and stones. Fifteen years before the *Endeavour*'s departure, the great Swedish botanist Carl Linnaeus had estimated that the number of plant species in the world numbered no more than ten thousand, and he described only six thousand in his encyclopedic *Species Plantarum*. Banks and Solander recorded some fourteen hundred new species on the *Endeavour*'s voyage alone, helping to eventually explode the Linnaean orthodoxy. The world, as the *Endeavour*'s men were fast discovering, was a wondrously diverse place.

HIKING TO THE town of Tolaga, I met Anne in front of a tribal office on Cook Street. Though three-quarters of the town's four hundred residents were Maori, early English settlers had named all the streets after Cook's crew and ships. Anne wanted to consult with members of her *iwi* about the language Sheila Robinson had proposed for the new Cook monument in Gisborne. Inside, Anne greeted two women named Heeni and Ngahuia by pressing her nose against each of theirs. I followed her lead, expecting the nasal equivalent of a peck on the cheek. Instead, the women pressed hard, squashing my nose for several seconds with disarming intimacy, their dark eyes, coffee-colored skin, and high cheekbones swimming before me.

"Basically a *hongi* means, 'I want to share your breath,'" Anne said. "When the Pakeha first came, we thought their kissing was unhygienic. Now we wonder if pressing noses is worse."

Heeni, a tall, striking woman in a long skirt, unwrapped a newspaper filled with fish and chips. "Have a greasie," she said, slathering the mountain of fried potato with ketchup and salt. Anne took out the proposed text for the Cook monument and read aloud: "'James Cook was a fine seaman, a great captain and an honest man. After his three global voyages, the map of the world was substantially complete—'"

"This is shit!" Heeni cut in.

"'When misunderstood Maori challenges led to warriors being shot,'" Anne read on, "'the ship sailed without provisions—'"

"Bloody good thing, too. Otherwise he might have stayed!"

"'—and Poverty Bay was named.'"

"It wasn't poor to us! We just didn't want to give him our water and food."

"'From here, the *Endeavour* circumnavigated New Zealand—'"

"Enough!" Heeni cried, grabbing the paper out of Anne's hand. "This is too bloody long. Cook was a five-minute man, a fly-by-nighter, a storm trooper. He only stayed here long enough to shoot some Maori."

"So what should the inscription say?" Anne asked. "I'm supposed to give some input."

Heeni scribbled on the back of the paper and read: "'Here's where the first murderer stood. Sanctified by the queen. He died of syphilis.'"

"Sanctified by the *king*," the other woman, Ngahuia, corrected her.

"And by the Royal Society. I know, because I won a plate on the bicentennial of his landing for a project I did in school. I was ten. I didn't learn anything about my own culture, but I knew more about Cook than almost any kid in the country." She shook her head. "It's ridiculous, eh? I still have the plate. I eat off it."

"What do you eat?" Heeni asked. "Arms or legs?"

Ngahuia groaned. Of all the Western notions about Maori-dom, stories about long-ago cannibalism were the most despised. "If you want to get beat up," Heeni told me, "go to a Gisborne pub and call someone a cannibal." Among themselves, though, Maori still referred to the practice, in an insulting way, usually by calling someone a *pokokōhua,* or boiled head. "If you're arguing," Anne explained, "you might say, 'Carry on in that vein, mate, and you're going to end up in the pot, you *pokokōhua.*' " Maori believed the head was the repository of *mana,* one's spirit or authority. Threatening to devour it was the worst thing you could say.

"Of course," Ngahuia said, "Cook ended cannibalism and everything else bad. That's what we were taught. Cook was our savior. He gave us clothing and medicine. Then the missionaries came and gave us Christianity."

"And the rapists brought us Pakeha names," Heeni added.

Anne nodded. "When I was young and looking for apartments, I used to phone landlords in my poshest accent and say, 'This is Anne Glover. I'm ringing about your advertisement in the paper.' It wasn't until I turned up that they'd turn me down."

"I hated that I had this long unpronounceable name," Ngahuia added. "I wanted to be Mary or something. I named my daughter Sarah. Then when she grew up she took a Maori name. Now I'm proud of mine."

There was also talk of renaming some of the *Endeavour*-inspired streets in Tolaga. "Cook wasn't a five-minute man in Tolaga, he was a five-day man," Heeni said. "But the funny thing is, we hardly remember him. Maori have stories and songs about *everything*—this war, that feast, he lived up the road, she had a baby, there was a big fire. But Cook? Nothing. Like I said, a fly-by-nighter."

Ngahuia again corrected her. She said that Tupaia was remembered in local speeches and songs. A rock shelter in which he slept while on land was known as Tupaia's Cave, and a nearby watering place became Tupaia's Well. When Cook returned to New Zealand on his second voyage, he found that many Maori remembered the *Endeavour* as "Tupaia's ship."

"What about the beautiful rock arch?" I asked, referring to the holed stone at Cook's Cove that had so enraptured the English.

Ngahuia blushed. The Maori name for it was Te Kotore o te Whenua.

" 'Anus of the Land,' " Heeni translated. "No wonder the English loved it. Sodomy was their favorite sport."

When we finished the fish and greasies, Anne made one last attempt at querying the women about the wording for the Cook monument. "I'm on a historical and museum committee, I have to tell them *something*," she said. Heeni shrugged. "Tell them we won't be dragged into this, we don't want to be their rubber stamp. Let them write what they want. Some young blood will spray-paint over it anyway."

Anne and I climbed back in her *waka* for the drive through the dark to Gisborne. "You see what I'm up against, eh?" she said. "Maori are militants, just like in Cook's day. So if you talk about a conciliatory approach, you get pulled to pieces. At meetings sometimes I'm called a potato—brown on the outside, white on the inside. That hurts." The only thing worse was to be called a plastic Maori—someone who takes on the veneer of native tradition for the entertainment of tourists.

I asked Anne why she persisted. "You can't change the history," she said. "It happened. I'd rather have a say in how Cook's remembered, and remind Pakeha that we were here long before Cook—and that we're still here—rather than just let them have their way, and then complain about it." There was another issue. Anne doubted there was a Maori in all of New Zealand who didn't have Pakeha blood. "Our history is tied up in two peoples," she said. "It's silly to hate half of yourself."

Anne invited me home for dinner at the modest bungalow she shared with her husband, David, and her brother, Danny. We found the two men preparing a "boil-up" of *kumara*, or sweet potato, a zucchini-like vegetable called *kamokamo*, pork ribs, and watercress that Danny had collected the day before by the water at Tolaga Bay. I sampled the watercress and asked if it was related to the celery or "scurvy grass" Cook wrote of gathering at Tolaga and other spots, as protection against disease.

Danny shook his head and laughed. Maori knew scurvy grass by a different name: *tutaekoua,* or bird feces, because it made birds defecate. "I don't know if it worked against scurvy," he said, "but I bet it gave the English a helluva bellyache."

The indigestion went both ways. Cook and his men seemed omnivorous to the Maori, who therefore assumed that everything the English gave them was edible. According to one story, Maori prepared a big "nosh-up" after Cook left, tossing potatoes, shoes, and candles into a stew—everything but nails. Another tale told of Tolaga natives burying gunpowder they'd been given by the English, and which they thought were the seeds of a turniplike plant. Later, on New Zealand's South Island, several English journal keepers observed natives drinking oil from the ship's lamps—even consuming the wick.

Cook's ships carried something else the Maori weren't sure what to make of: pigs. Some of the pigs went feral and their descendants still roamed the woods, a long-nosed, stiff-haired breed rather like wild boars. New Zealanders call them Captain Cookers.

Danny announced that the boil-up was ready. We ate the entire pot, washed down with quart bottles of beer. At midnight, as I got up to go, David went to the freezer and brought out an enormous lobster, as big as the one in the watercolor made by an *Endeavour* artist at Tolaga. "Just in case you feel like a snack later on," David explained. Waddling back to my motel, clutching the lobster, I felt bloated but content, like the *Endeavour*'s Charles Clerke, who wrote of "The Happy taughtness of my Jacket" after gorging himself in New Zealand.

IF SEX HAD been the crew's principal obsession at Tahiti, in New Zealand it was food. After more than a year at sea, some of the *Endeavour*'s stores were running low. A week after leaving Tolaga, the *Endeavour* arrived at the bay where the young Te Horeta later told of a goblin killing birds with his thunder stick. The goblin was probably Banks, who wrote in his journal of shooting "shags" at the bay and quickly broiling them. "We find ourselves able to eat any kind of Birds," he observed. "Hunger is certainly most excellent sauce."

When the *Endeavour* later reached New Zealand's South Island, the English discovered that the native diet wasn't restricted to birds, fish, and vegetables. Cook and Banks found Maori cooking on the beach beside a basket containing a sinewy bone that appeared to be human. Cook, "in order to be fully satisfied," said to one of the Maori that this was surely the bone of a dog. "But he with great fervency," Cook wrote, "took hold of the flesh of his own arm with his teth and made shew of eating."

The place became known as Cannibal Cove, and crewmen penned lurid accounts of what took place there. One reported that Maori killed men for sport and dangled the thumbs of their victims from their own ears. Parkinson, evoking images of witches' covens, wrote that Maori consumed their own kind during "horrid midnight repasts." On a return to New Zealand during Cook's third voyage, a ship's surgeon even claimed that ravenous Maori spared nothing but their enemies' penises, which they somehow crafted into musical pipes.

Banks, amused by the *Endeavour*'s fanciful sailors, observed, "Eating people is now always the uppermost Idea in their heads." Human bones, he added, "become a kind of article of trade among our people who constantly ask for and purchase them for whatever trifles they have." Banks, ever the collector, joined in this grisly traffic, bartering a pair of linen drawers for a preserved head with its scalp and facial hair still attached. "The flesh and skin," he wrote with clinical admiration, "were soft but they were somehow preservd so as not to stink at all."

Cook also regarded cannibalism with startling matter-of-factness. "They eat their enimies Slane in Battell," he calmly noted. "This seems to come from custom and not from a Savage disposission." Cook's supposition was correct. Maori ate only their enemies, to degrade foes and ingest their spirit and power. Still, it is possible they took gustatory delight in so doing. Anthropologists have noted a craving for fat in traditional societies where lipids, and the calories they provide, are scarce. Maori, living on islands devoid of large mammals, may have been subject to this hunger for fat—a yen that would also explain their ravenous consumption of ships' candles and lamp oil.

Despite the tales of cannibalism the *Endeavour*'s crew carried home, some in England doubted their veracity. After all, no one had seen Maori in the act of eating another human. But any lingering doubt was dispelled during Cook's second voyage. An officer purchased a fresh head (for two nails) and brought it aboard, then asked a visiting Maori if he'd sample some of the flesh. "He very cheerfully gave his assent," wrote Charles Clerke, who duly broiled a bit and gave it to the man. He "devour'd it most ravenously, and suck'd his fingers ½ a dozen times over in raptures."

A few weeks after this episode, ten men from Cook's companion ship on the second voyage boated into a cove to gather greens. They never returned. A search party discovered, in the words of its lieutenant, the "most horrid & undeniable proofs" that the men had been killed and eaten. The evidence included baskets filled with roasted human flesh, the head of a black servant, and the tattooed hand of a sailor.

Even then, Cook defended the Maori against charges of barbarism. Later investigating the "Melancholy affair" himself, he concluded that the English had been killed after firing on natives for stealing food. If anything, Cook blamed crewmen for "too hastily" taking action. "I must," he wrote, "observe in favour of the New Zealanders that I have always found them of a Brave, Noble, Open and benevolent disposition, but that they are a people that will never put up with an insult if they have an opportunity to resent it."

MORE THAN TWO centuries later, the insult to Maori was Cook himself. I'd gotten a taste of this at the tribal office in Tolaga. Back in Gisborne, I learned that a visit by the replica *Endeavour,* four years before, had prompted death threats against the captain and warnings from tribal elders that they couldn't guarantee the ship's safety because of the "atrocities" committed by Cook and his men in 1769. "We see it as a menace floating around the Pacific," one activist said of the replica. Added another: "We wonder at those who would honour the scurvy, the pox, the filth, and the racism that Cook's arrival brought to this beautiful land."

The replica's visit went off without incident, but city officials were nervous about the possibility of Maori protests over the erection of the new Cook statue in Gisborne. I stopped by the office of Gisborne's tribal council to talk with the group's chief executive, Tracey Tangi-haere. She wore a black pants suit, black pumps, and small, rectilinear glasses of the sort that stylish professionals wear in America. This was the new, untattooed face of Maori leadership: young, smart, tough, and well armed with the language of empowerment. "We've survived colonial oppression by being proactive," Tracey said, "and by adapt-ing Western skills to our own ends."

To illustrate this, she showed me a three-hundred-page "working paper" for a land claim one local tribe had filed with the government. To prove such claims, tribes had to demonstrate a long-term pattern of use and settlement. "Cook's one of our best sources," Tracey said. With a surveyor's eye, Cook had carefully delineated the boundaries of villages, the location of shell mounds, the use of fishing nets. At one point, the *Endeavour*'s men saw fishing canoes more than twelve miles offshore—evidence the Maori now used to determine the extent of their traditional fishing ground.

At Tolaga Bay, Banks's assistant, Herman Spöring, had spotted what appeared to be a Maori kite. Some activists now wanted to use this and other evidence to seek "atmospheric rights," giving tribes a share of revenue from the radio and television spectrum, and perhaps even plane overflights. "It's come full circle, eh?" Tracey said. "Cook led to the destruction of our world, and now we're using him to put it back together again."

In 1960s America, Martin Luther King, Jr., cited Christianity and the words of America's founding fathers to craft a plea for civil rights that spoke to many whites. A generation later, at the far side of the world, Maori were using much the same tactic, seeking their own racial justice by deploying old treaties, English common law, and the journals of a man regarded by many Pakeha as New Zealand's found-ing father. When I suggested this analogy to Tracey, she smiled tightly.

"We admire King, and we're Christians, too. But we're not so keen as he was on turning the other cheek."

IT WASN'T JUST insults from Pakeha that Maori resented. All week in the local newspaper, I'd read about a trial involving the "Mongrel Mob," a Maori gang alleged to be active in the drug trade, drive-by shootings, and other crimes. The current case involved a rugby match that had been intended to reconcile the Mongrel Mob with a rival gang of Tongans (islanders from across the Pacific flocked to New Zealand in search of jobs). The Tongans had won the game. After the match, the two sides went to a popular Mob pub, a few insults were exchanged, and four Mob members stomped a Tongan man in the parking lot before slamming a car door on his head until they killed him. Upon their conviction, the defendants yelled *"Sieg heil!"* to their supporters on their way to jail.

I was curious to meet this twenty-first-century remnant of Poverty Bay's warrior cult. The pub where the killing occurred stood just across the street from Anne McGuire's house. But she didn't recommend I visit. "Have you seen the movie *Once Were Warriors?*" she asked. "It's like that. Big guys drinking too much and picking fights." However, she told me where to find the Mob by day, on a back street beneath Kaiti Hill, on which stood the "crook Cook" statue.

I waited until eleven A.M. on a Sunday, reckoning that would be a quiet, sober time to visit. As I navigated an alley alongside a dilapidated garage, following Anne's directions, a fully tattooed face poked out a side door and demanded, "Who the bloody hell are you?"

"I'm an American. A writer." I held my arms wide, clutching nothing but a notebook and pen, feeling oddly as though I was replaying Cook's meeting with a Maori warrior in the river a few hundred yards away.

The man gestured me inside. The garage was fitted out with tattered easy chairs, a bar, and pictures and carvings of bulldogs, the gang's symbol. Three men sat drinking beer and rolling cigarettes. They wore sleeveless black leather vests, black leather pants, heavy chains, and storm trooper–style boots. All had "Mongrel Mob," "MM," or bulldogs tattooed on their faces.

"We're mixed breeds, mongrels, mean dogs," one man said,

explaining the name and symbol. He opened his vest to reveal a Yale University T-shirt, adorned with the school's bulldog mascot.

"My grandfather went there," I said.

"Where?"

"Yale. It's a top university in America." As a child I'd worn bulldog pajamas that my grandfather bought at a reunion. I didn't mention this. "Very tough to get into Yale," I added.

The man nodded approvingly. He pointed at the garage's only window, adorned with a swastika and a picture of a bulldog in an SS helmet. This seemed an odd emblem for a mixed-race mob to adopt. "It's nothing to do with Nazis," he said "It's about our own supremacy. The swastika, it's like Satan. It's just saying, 'We're staunch. We're bad.'"

At this, his mates growled like bulldogs and wiggled their thumbs and pinkies in the same motion I'd seen teenagers demonstrate on the dock in Raiatea. In this context it seemed to mean "right on," or "amen." One of the men handed me a quart bottle of Steinlager beer and asked, "What you doing in Gizzy?"

"Researching a book about Captain Cook."

This brought more growls. "Cook and his mob, they put us in this position," one of the men said. "He put us down. We don't take shit like that anymore."

"Cook's a wanker. He can go to hell," another added.

One of the men disagreed. He had a scorpion tattoo on his neck, and wraparound sunglasses. "I wouldn't have hot water if it wasn't for Cook," he said. Of all the modern conveniences he might have mentioned, this seemed a curious choice. "Sooner or later someone else would have come here," he went on. "Could have been a lot worse than Cook."

"How so?" I asked.

"Like what if the Chinese had conquered us? Then what would we be eating? I don't like Chinese food." He paused. "You got to look at all angles."

The others shrugged and gazed into their beers. An older man came in. Heavyset, with a shaved head, he introduced himself as Bill Irwin, a gang spokesman. He told me there was a softer, gentler side to the

Mongrel Mob that the press never wrote about. "We're not a criminal gang, we're just outcasts who come together because we don't fit into the society," he said. "Ever since Cook, we did what the colonialists told us to, we opted for their way of life. It didn't work. We're unemployed, alienated, eh? So we make our own family."

Bill liked to paddle around Poverty Bay in a traditional war *waka*. "It gives me a feeling of *wairua*, a spiritual feeling of doing what my ancestors did." To him, the Mob's tattooing and toughness sprang from the same impulse. "Why does a Scotsman put on a kilt and blow bagpipes? Why do people still sail around in the *Endeavour*? That's their tradition. Ours is a warrior tradition, and there's nothing wrong with reclaiming it."

This seemed reasonable, if you overlooked the dead Tongan in the parking lot. A den full of hard-drinking Mongrels seemed like the wrong place to raise this. Instead, I asked Bill if the Mob objected to the new statue of Cook. He led me outside and pointed up at Kaiti Hill. "You've seen the crook Cook?" he asked. I nodded. "I feel sorry for Pakeha," he said. "We know all about our ancestors. We have many heroes. All they have is Cook and they hardly know the man. They can't even agree on what he looked like. It's kind of pitiful, eh?"

THE *ENDEAVOUR* STAYED almost six months in New Zealand waters but spent only a third of that time anchored near land. Most of the trip was devoted to charting the coastline of the country, some 2,400 miles in all, often in high seas and stormy weather. Cook accomplished this survey with such astounding accuracy that a French navigator who followed in his wake, Julien Crozet, declared with un-Gallic modesty: "I doubt much whether the charts of our own French coasts are laid down with greater precision." Several of Cook's charts—perfected on his two later voyages—remained in use until 1994, when the Royal New Zealand Navy finally updated his surveys with its own soundings and satellite readings.

Cook not only charted a country the size of the United Kingdom; he also dispelled the notion that it was a peninsula of the fabled southern continent. Several of his officers clung to this myth from the moment Nick Young first sighted land. The master's mate went so far as to label each new drawing of the coast "A Chart of Part of the So. Continent." Joseph Banks joined this giddy cadre of "Continent mongers," as he called them, and refused to abandon his faith until the March day when a fresh wind finally carried the *Endeavour* around the southern-most point of New Zealand, "to the total demolition of our aerial fab-rick calld continent."

Cook expressed no such disappointment. While most explorers might dream of the glory attending discovery of a new continent, Cook reveled in the opposite. A born skeptic, he prized fact over fantasy throughout his career, becoming a master of what the historian Daniel Boorstin terms "negative discovery"—the uncovering of what's *not* there. Less admirable, perhaps, was Cook's obvious delight in being proved right. On the day the *Endeavour* finally circled the bottom of the South Island, he wrote: "I then called the officers upon deck and asked them if they were now satisfied that this land was an Island to which they answer'd in the affirmative."

Cook's summary remarks on New Zealand reveal how much his horizons had broadened during the year and a half he'd spent at sea. He ventured opinions on a wide range of subjects, including linguistics and ethnography. Observing that the scattered tribes of the North and South Islands spoke a very similar dialect, and that this language closely resembled Tahitian, he speculated that South Sea islanders and New Zealanders "have had one Origin or Source."

As to where this original homeland lay, Cook couldn't say, but he ruled out the possibility of Pacific islanders having come from the south, and doubted they'd arrived from the vast empty ocean to the east, either. Cook's thinking was far ahead of his time. Despite the claims of Thor Heyerdahl, who wrote in the 1950s that Pacific islanders arrived from South America, contemporary scholars are almost unanimous in believing that the first Polynesians migrated in canoe voyages from Southeast Asia.

Cook also ventured into what today would be called political sci-ence. "It doth not appear to me to be attall difficult for Strangers to form a settlement in this Country," he wrote. "They seem to be too much divided among themselves to unite in opposing, by which means and kind and gentle usuage the Colonists would be able to form strong parties among them." In other words, divide and conquer—a prescription for what the British eventually did in New Zealand, and what settlers did to Indian tribes in America.

Cook wrote as a shrewd mercantilist, too, carefully calculating the value of New Zealand's natural resources. "I judged that there was 356 solid feet of timber in this tree," he wrote of an astonishingly tall, straight pine that soared eighty-nine feet before its first branch. Of New Zealand's hemplike flax, he wrote that it would make "the very best of Cordage, Canvas &ca." His walks on the beach also revealed "great quantities of Iron sand," which suggested ore deposits. And in the gardens where Maori planted sweet potato, Cook conjured fields of European grain and flocks of sheep and cattle. "In short," he concluded, "was this country settled by an Industrus people they would very soon be supply'd not only with the necessarys but many of the luxuries of life."

Cook, once again, proved remarkably prescient. Within two centuries of his visit, resource-rich New Zealand would enjoy the highest per capita income on earth. But Cook's remarks were also unsettling. They presaged the fate of New Zealand's natives and their environment, just as Lewis and Clark's journals foretold the ravaging of the American West. With hindsight, the line between exploration and exploitation, between investigation and imperialism, seems perilously thin.

Cook couldn't really be blamed for this. His orders were to "observe the Nature of the Soil . . . the Beasts and Fowls . . . Minerals or valuable stones . . . the Genius, Temper, Disposition and Number of the Natives." Also, as Cook noted on a return trip to New Zealand: "We can by no means [tell] what use future ages may make of the discoveries made in the present."

But if Cook couldn't know that the stately pines he extolled would be quickly logged out, or that muskets traded to one Maori tribe would lead to the near extermination of neighboring clans, he lived long enough to lament some of the consequences of his own discoveries. Returning to New Zealand in 1773, and again in 1777, Cook found the Maori prone to thievery, deploying Western hatchets as weapons rather than tools, afflicted with venereal disease, and eager to prostitute their wives and daughters in exchange for spike nails.

"Such are the concequences of a commerce with Europeans," Cook wrote, in one of the most despairing passages he ever penned. "We debauch their Morals already too prone to vice and we interduce among them wants and perhaps diseases which they never before knew and which serves only to disturb that happy tranquility they and their fore Fathers had injoy'd. If any one denies the truth of this assertion let him tell me what the Natives of the whole extent of America have gained by the commerce they have had with Europeans."

ON MY LAST day in Gisborne, I went to the shore of Poverty Bay and joined Sheila Robinson, my first-day tour guide, as she watched workmen lay concrete for the new Cook statue. The bronze navigator lay on the ground, facedown, bound and gagged by yellow straps, with a noose around his neck tagged "10 Hints for Safe Lifting." His cutlass poked behind him, like a tail. "It's a bit sacrilegious," Sheila said, "but they couldn't put him on his back because that might break his sword."

For the workmen, the statue's pose made for light relief while they shoveled concrete.

"He flogged his share. Now he's having a wee rest."

"Cook's looking a bit overdone lying there in the sun."

"He's keeping his ear to the ground. Or his eyes. Maybe he's trying to look all the way through the globe to see what his wife's up to back in England."

For Sheila, this day was the culmination of years of lobbying, fundraising, and mediation. She'd brought a "chilly-bin," or cooler, filled with sandwiches and sodas so she could spend the day watching the monument go up. I settled beside her in the shade of a pohutukawa tree and asked what had drawn her to Cook.

"He was a self-made man, he got where he was through sheer competence at his job," she said. "He's the sort of person New Zealanders admire. We don't have a lot of time for people born to greatness. Most of the Pakeha who first came here were lower middle class, working people who labored hard and had had a miserable time in Britain. They can identify with Cook."

Sheila was the daughter of a Presbyterian parson and had grown up on the South Island, where Scottish influence remained very strong and Maori were relatively scarce. In her thirties, Sheila had gone with her husband to teach at schools in Borneo and Samoa. "I came home much more aware of other cultures," she said, and began learning about Maori ways while teaching in Gisborne. Among other things, she'd come to envy the Maori sense of belonging. "They're part of a land where I feel I belong, but never quite do. Maori have their *turangawaewae*, a 'standing place' by their *marae*. I have none."

When she later became a curator at the local museum, Sheila also realized how blinkered Pakeha could be about the past. In their attitude to history, some New Zealanders resembled die-hard white Southerners in America, who enshrined Confederate leaders and symbols without acknowledging the offense this might cause to others.

Sheila had tried to change this by gathering more Maori content for the museum's archives, and urging local leaders to put the new Cook statue in this park, close to where the captain encountered Maori, rather than in the middle of town. At the same time she'd reached out to Maori. This wasn't always easy. Political differences were one obstacle; personality was another. Scots had a reputation for being dour, austere, buttoned-up. Maori, as I'd seen, tended to be demonstrative and outspoken. Also, to Presbyterian Pakeha, pride was a deadly sin. Sheila admired the fierce pride of many Maori. "That's part of what makes them so strong," she said. "But it can clash with some Pakeha, who think it's a virtue to be self-effacing."

Sheila had learned to enjoy the cultural difference, even the endless nose-pressing, speeches of welcome, and exchanging of gifts that began Maori meetings. "It's made me realize how little ritual Europeans have anymore," she said. "By the end I always leave feeling warmer-hearted than when I arrived." She'd also become more relaxed about physical contact. "I think Pakeha kiss and hug more than they did a generation ago; they've picked that up from Maori."

She paused as workmen yanked the statue's plinth into place. "My family has its own piece of granite in Samoa," she said quietly. While Sheila and her husband were teaching on the island, their seven-year-old son contracted meningitis and died. "We had three other children and no wider family with us, and just felt we had to carry on, or pretend to. We never really talked to the kids about it." Thirty-five years later, she wondered if that had been the best approach.

"I now find the old Pakeha attitude to death very cold," she said. "We had closed coffins, sang a few hymns, talked a lot about God but hardly at all about the dead." Maori, by contrast, held open-coffin funerals with lamentation and long speeches and songs about the deceased, followed by a party. This was a way of staying with the dead as long as possible, helping them back to their mountain, and celebrating their life. Some of this had rubbed off on Pakeha, too. "Stoicism's a virtue," Sheila said. "Where would Cook have been without it? But I've come to realize the price you pay for that."

We sat quietly until the workmen were ready to raise the statue. "Okay, time to stand Jimmy up," the foreman shouted. A truck with a crane lifted the statue onto its perch: a short column set atop a half-globe that was etched with the path of Cook's voyages. The statue had been carefully crafted to satisfy all constituencies. Legs spread wide, hands on hips, Cook looked properly commanding, as if at the prow of a ship plowing across the map. But the sculptor had chopped the globe in half so Cook wasn't standing imperially on top of the whole world. The statue had also been sprayed with a special anti-graffiti wax.

The foreman grabbed a glue gun and squirted around the statue's feet, megapoxying Cook for eternity. Sheila stood back and gazed at the statue approvingly. "He's human-sized, not too far off the ground. I think Cook would be comfortable with that."

The new statue, though, created a slight problem: what to do with the crook Cook atop Kaiti Hill. Some Maori had publicly suggested blowing the statue up, or melting it down, and putting up a memorial to Polynesian navigators instead. Others felt the crook Cook was such a fixture of the local landscape—appearing on postcards and tourist brochures for the city—that he should stay where he was. One local wag thought the statue should replaced with a monument to surfing.

Sheila had an impish solution of her own. In 1919, Gisborne had acquired a cannon believed to have come from the *Endeavour*. This had turned out to be a counterfeit, too. The gun now resided in the town's museum, beside a plaque labeling it "Not Captain Cook's Cannon." Sheila felt the statue should be moved to the museum and put beside the cannon. "It could have its own plaque," she said. " 'Not Captain Cook.' "

Chapter 5

BOTANY BAY:
In the Pure State of Nature

Australian history is almost always picturesque. . . . It
does not read like history, but like the most beautiful lies.
— MARK TWAIN, *MORE TRAMPS ABROAD* (1897)

In late February 1770, after eighteen months and roughly twenty
thousand miles of sailing, Joseph Banks confided in his journal that the
Endeavour's crew had split into two camps. The first, comprising the
botanist and a very few others, still dreamed of finding a southern continent. "The rest," he observed, "begin to sigh for roast beef."

A month later, after completing his circumnavigation of New
Zealand, Cook also cast his gaze toward England. "Now resolved to
quit this country," he wrote, "and to bend my thoughts towards
returning home by such a rout as might conduce most to the advantage
of the service I am upon." Cook's first choice was to return via Cape
Horn, at the highest possible latitude, "to prove the existence or non
existence of a Southern Continent." But the *Endeavour*'s worn state,
and the approaching winter, made this impractical. He also dismissed
the most direct path home: sailing straight toward Africa's Cape of
Good Hope. "No discovery of any moment could be hoped for in that
rout."

So Cook chose a third, more circuitous route. He would steer west
until he fell in with another vaguely known land, this one also discovered by the Dutch, and follow its coast to its "northern extremity"

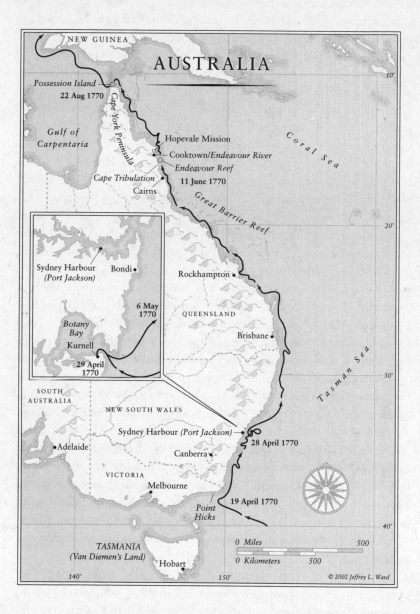

NEW GUINEA

AUSTRALIA

10°

Possession Island
22 Aug 1770

Cape York Peninsula

Gulf of
Carpentaria

Coral Sea

Hopevale Mission
Cooktown/*Endeavour River*
Endeavour Reef
11 June 1770

Cape Tribulation
Cairns

Great Barrier Reef

20°

Sydney Harbour
(*Port Jackson*)   Bondi

Rockhampton

6 May
1770

QUEENSLAND

Botany
Bay
Kurnell

Brisbane

29 April
1770

30°

SOUTH
AUSTRALIA

NEW SOUTH WALES

Sydney Harbour (*Port Jackson*)

Adelaide

Canberra

28 April 1770

VICTORIA

Melbourne

Tasman Sea

19 April 1770

Point
Hicks

40°

TASMANIA
(*Van Diemen's Land*)

Hobart

0 Miles   500
0 Kilometers   500

140°   150°   © 2002 Jeffrey L. Ward before heading home via the Indies. Cook's calm declaration of this verdict, occupying one line in his journal, makes his choice seem straightforward, almost tame. In reality, Cook had bent his thoughts toward an uncharted course that would eventually carry the *Endeavour* closer to disaster than at any point during its long voyage.

The going turned rough as soon as the *Endeavour* reached open sea west of New Zealand. First, the ship met "flying showers of rain and a large hollow sea." Then sultry doldrums. Then a hard gale with heavy squalls. "We had a broken sea that caused the ship to pitch and roll very much," wrote Sydney Parkinson. "At the same time we shipped a sea fore and after, which deluged the decks, and had like to have washed several of us overboard." Having endured the replica *Endeavour*'s stomach-churning roll in even mild winds, I felt armchair seasickness just reading this passage.

It no doubt came as a relief when Lieutenant Zachary Hicks "saw the land making high" at daybreak on April 19. Point Hicks, as Cook named it, lay east of the present-day city of Melbourne. Though this was the edge of the vast continent that would later become known as Australia, it was not the bountiful *terra australis*, surrounding the South Pole, that Cook had been dispatched to find. Rather, it was New Holland, so called because Dutch ships had briefly touched its northern, western, and southern flanks in the seventeenth century.

The *Endeavour* was the first European ship known to have reached the continent's two-thousand-mile eastern coast. As in New Zealand, Cook and his men were also the first visitors to describe the land and its people in detail, and to have a lasting impact. The Dutch had coasted the continent in search of fortune and fresh trade routes, but finding nothing of commercial value, they'd quickly lost interest and initiative. Apart from marking their arrival by nailing pewter plates to trees, and tormenting generations of Australian schoolchildren with hard-to-spell place names—Van Diemen's Land, the Houtman Abrolhos, Capes Keerweer and Leeuwin—the Dutch left no real imprint on the continent.

Nor were their sketchy reports of New Holland encouraging. "We could not find one fruitful tree nor anything that could be of use to mankind," the explorer Jan Carstensz wrote of his 1623 stop in northern Australia, which he termed "the driest, poorest area to be found in the world." The inhabitants were worse. "Naked beach-roving wretches," Abel Tasman called them. Most scathing of all was William Dampier, an English privateer who visited Australia's northwest coast in 1688 and again in 1699. "The Inhabitants of this Country are the miserablest People in the World," he claimed in a best-seller about his adventures. "Their Eye-lids are always half closed, to keep the Flies out of their Eyes."

Dampier's popular travelogue remained so influential—no European had touched any part of the continent in the seventy years since his visit—that it was part of the *Endeavour*'s library, along with books on natural history and volumes by Homer, Chaucer, Shakespeare, and Dryden. Joseph Banks, peering through his spyglass at his first sight of distant New Hollanders, judged them "enormously black," but wryly added: "So far did the prejudices which we had built on Dampiers account influence us that we fancied we could see their Colour when we could scarce distinguish whether or not they were men." At first glance, the landscape also looked as arid and unpromising to Banks as it had to Dampier and the Dutch. The botanist likened it to the back of a lean cow, "where her scraggy hip bones have stuck out farther than they ought."

Deterred from landing by violent surf and contrary winds, the *Endeavour* coasted up Australia's east coast for ten days before reaching a calm, wide harbor. Here, the English found timber, teeming fish, and so many unfamiliar plant species that the naturalists quickly stopped collecting so they could preserve and sketch their specimens before they spoiled. "The great quantity of New Plants &c Mr. Banks and Dr. Solander collected," Cook wrote of the inlet, "occasioned my giving it the name of Botany Bay."

The *Endeavour* stayed at the bay for nine days. Continuing north, Cook made passing mention of a nearby "Harbour wherein there apperd to be safe anchorage." He named it Port Jackson, after the second secretary of the Admiralty, but didn't bother to explore the harbor and sailed blithely on.

Nine years later, Britain's Parliament began canvassing sites for a convict settlement to replace the rebellious American colonies, which had long provided a dumping ground for prisoners sentenced to "transportation." Parliament sought a "distant part of the Globe, from whence [convicts'] Escape might be difficult," and where they would be able to "maintain themselves . . . with little or no aid from the Mother Country." Joseph Banks recommended Botany Bay, which he said enjoyed a gentle Mediterranean climate and could support "a very large Number of People." A former midshipman on the *Endeavour*, James Magra (a man Cook called "good for nothing"), fancifully touted Botany Bay's advantages as a strategic and commercial outpost. And Cook himself, by then dead, had written glowingly of Botany Bay's "deep black Soil which we thought was capable of produceing any kind of grain."

So, in 1787, Britain dispatched a fleet of eleven ships, transporting 736 convicts to the remote bay that the *Endeavour* had briefly visited seventeen years before. Arriving after an eight-month passage, the pioneers discovered that Cook and his men, for once, were unreliable reporters. The *Endeavour* had landed at Botany Bay in mild autumn, after what seems to have been an extremely wet season. The "First Fleet," landing in high summer, found a broiling, parched land that "did not afford a spot large enough for a cabbage garden," its captain wrote. Botany Bay also proved too shallow and exposed for a colonial port.

So the convict ships quickly decamped to the nearby inlet that Cook hadn't bothered to explore, Port Jackson, which the fleet's surgeon declared "the finest and most extensive harbour in the universe." A settlement arose, and some 160,000 convicts eventually followed, creating the world's largest jail and, ultimately, the only nation to span an entire continent. In time, Port Jackson would become known as Sydney Harbour, the most celebrated body of water in the southern hemisphere.

As for Cook's Botany Bay, it would languish into an historical footnote, and a septic field for the nearby metropolis. Even a late-twentieth-century mayor of the Botany Bay district found it hard to praise his domain. "The anus of Sydney," he called it.

THE ONLY WAY to understand Cook's mistake, if you could call it that, was to view both Botany Bay and Sydney Harbour from sea. I had my first chance to do this on Australia Day, which commemorates the First Fleet's arrival at Port Jackson on January 26, 1788. The ships' landing launched white settlement on the continent, and therefore marked the birth of modern Australia. But few present-day Australians regard the holiday with patriotic fervor. It's hard, first of all, to celebrate the founding of a penitentiary—except, perhaps, to appreciate the long-term irony; thanks to the First Fleet, today's Sydneysiders occupy a semitropical paradise instead of wet, chill England.

Also, Aborigines condemn the anniversary as Invasion Day, the start of their dispossession. So while city officials stage speeches and fireworks, and Aborigines hold a protest concert, most Sydney residents head to the pub or beach to enjoy the traditional end of summer vacation.

For Roger, my travel companion in Tahiti, Australia Day heralds an annual yacht race from Sydney Harbour to Botany Bay. I asked to come along so I could see the coast from Cook's perspective. "We'll finish dead last," Roger assured me, motoring his thirty-foot boat, *Aquadisiac,* toward a yacht club where his fellow sailors waited. "I only get the dregs as crew. Guttersnipes and barflies, mostly. Not to mention you." He ducked below to check the weather report on the radio. "Winds north to northeast, strengthening to thirty knots, with a three-meter swell and two-meter chop," he reported. "Sounds disgusting."

We stopped to give a ride to a crewman from another boat, a stout man Roger introduced as Pugsy. Australians are ruthless with nicknames—and toward their national symbols. Roger and Pugsy jeered at a replica of the First Fleet as it sailed beneath the Harbour Bridge. As we passed several gray warships moored at the naval station in Woolloomooloo, Pugsy put a hand over his heart. "The Australian Navy, all three of it. Makes you proud."

The Navy gave me an excuse to ask Pugsy the same question I'd posed to Roger months before. What came to his mind when I said "Captain Cook"?

"Cook? Did him in school," Pugsy replied. "Don't remember much. Ugly man. Face like a dropped pie."

At the yacht club, Pugsy departed and three women climbed aboard. They introduced themselves as Karen, Susie, and Susie, though the younger of the Susies said everyone called her Spider. I assumed this referred to her long, slim legs, poking from the short shorts she wore. Then I noticed a hideous scar on her shin. "Bitten by a white-tailed spider," she gaily explained. "You should have seen me a month ago. The bite caused necrosis, and I had an ulcer so deep you could put your thumb in it." With that, Spider skipped ashore to pick up a "slab of VB"—a case of Victoria Bitter beer—and a dozen bacon-and-egg rolls. "The grease settles your stomach," she said, handing me a sandwich. "You'll need it out there."

As we motored to the starting line, I studied the competition, mostly large yachts with sails touting corporate sponsors: Nokia, Hewlett-Packard, Bloomberg. But even the largest boats bore raffish, self-deprecating names, befitting the Australian temper: *Ragamuffin, Rapscallion, Occasional Coarse Language.* Roger said the yachts belonged to three racing divisions, depending on the vessels' size: maxi, medium, and "the rabble—shitbox boats like ours."

A gun sounded, and we quickly pulled ahead; Roger had timed the start perfectly. "We've got them caned!" he shouted. For all his jocular put-downs, of himself and his crew, Roger was a skilled and cutthroat competitor. It was part of the Australian sports mask—of the Australian personality, really—to never seem to care too much or try too hard.

It also became obvious that I hadn't tagged along on a sight-seeing cruise. I quickly found myself grinding a winch and barking my shins as I tried to interpret Roger's shouted commands. "Fire the halyard! Ease the main sheet—fast! Hike out, damn it. Hike out!" Then, as we left the harbor and hoisted the spinnaker for the long run south to Botany Bay, Roger issued an order I could understand: "Go below and put the beer on ice!"

Glancing back, it was easy to see how Cook had failed to appreciate Port Jackson. Just beyond the golden sandstone headlands flanking its mouth, the harbor doglegged, obscuring what lay beyond: a drowned river valley that wended its way inland for miles. Even today, Sydney's majesty—the scalloped Opera House, the soaring arch of the Harbour Bridge, the city's lush foreshore of fig trees and fruit bats—doesn't unfold until you've sailed well inside the headlands.

The harbor entrance slipped out of view and we glided parallel to

the coast, with the rolling Pacific to port and the crowded beach suburb of Bondi to starboard. "Just think," Roger said, gazing at the
beach, "the *Endeavour* sailed past this same exact landscape. White
sand, red tile roofs, string bikinis."

I sensed the crew-women were rolling their eyes, though it was
hard to tell. Their faces were obscured by sunglasses and visored caps.
The few bits of tanned cheek or chin I could glimpse were streaked
white with sunblock, like the clay-painted faces of Aborigines. I turned
to a woman I guessed was Susie and asked what had drawn her to sail
racing.

"I started after my husband died," she said.

"Oh, I'm sorry."

"Don't be. It was a long time ago. He was sailing a boat to Adelaide
and a freak wave washed him overboard. His body was never found."
She paused. "I hadn't done any sailing to that point, but ever since I've
been keen as mustard."

She ducked below to get a beer, leaving me to ponder her story. Roger
whispered: "They'd been married ten years, so it may have been expedi-
ent and a blessing. Any earlier and you'd have to regard it as a tragedy."

When Susie returned, I changed the subject and asked how Roger
compared to other captains.

"He's fine so long as the wind blows to buggery, like today," she
said. "Roger's much worse when the wind's light. Then he gets bored
and hits the turps."

"I drink to keep my hand steady," Roger insisted. "Steering's the
most important job."

"All captains say that," Spider chimed in. "It keeps their egos up."

"Among other things," Karen added.

Roger groaned. "Cook didn't have to endure this. No women on
board. No democracy. And no limits on his grog."

At the mention of Cook, I repeated the question I'd posed to Pugsy.
What did the captain mean to Australians?

"Mean?" Susie said. "He doesn't mean a bloody thing."

"He's boring," Karen added. "Australians can't stand boring."

I looked at Spider. She shrugged. "Captain Cook, Captain Hook, I
can never keep them straight."

I cracked a VB and vowed never to ask the question again. After living in Sydney—and being married to a native for fifteen years—I should have known better. Australians mock almost everything, authority in particular and British authority most of all. They have no national heroes in the American sense, only lawbreaking folk heroes, like the horse thief and bank robber Ned Kelly, an Irish convict's son who donned homemade body armor before battling police. Or the drunken gold prospectors who erected a stockade called Eureka rather than pay mining taxes. The nation's best-known song, "Waltzing Matilda," eulogized a sheep rustler.

Kelly eventually hanged, the Eureka Stockade fell after a fifteen-minute battle, and the "jolly swagman" drowned himself. But Australians love losers, so long as they lose with panache against overwhelming odds, or as martyrs to British authority (the Poms, Aussies derisively call Brits). The true national holiday wasn't Australia Day; it was Anzac Day, commemorating the doomed, British-ordered assault by Australian troops at Gallipoli in 1915. James Cook—a winner, a faithful servant of His Majesty, a wigged Pom without much flair or humor—had little hope of entering Australia's pantheon of antiheroes.

I was mulling all this somewhere between Bondi and Botany Bay when I realized I felt sick. "Sea's getting lumpy out here, isn't it?" Roger said. Lofty seemed more like it. Alpine, even. Huge swells formed behind us, pushing *Aquadisiac* to watery summits and plunging it into cavernous troughs. The beer sloshed in my stomach, mingling with the bacon-and-egg rolls, which hadn't produced their intended effect.

Spider glanced at me with concern or curiosity, I couldn't tell which. "Are you about to spew?" she asked.

"Chunder from Down Under?" Susie added.

"Hurl?" Karen offered. "Heave-ho?"

I sprawled flat with my face against the deck. This seemed to help, so long as I hugged the mast and kept my eyes firmly shut. Eventually I felt not so much sick as listless and profoundly apathetic, like a polar explorer who announces, "I'll just lie down in the snow for a while." Or like the pitiable few in Bligh's longboat who, after being set adrift from the *Bounty,* became so thirsty and despairing that they drank seawater and died. It was depressing to realize that I was the type who wouldn't have made it.

Roger stuck a foot in my ribs as we approached Botany Bay. "Get up, you pathetic worm, and pay your respects to the cradle of white Australia." I opened one eye and saw a rock shelf with waves crashing against it, beautiful and forbidding. As we tacked into the bay, I forced myself upright for a full frontal view. The mile-wide entrance opened on to the "safe and commodious" harbor that Cook had described. Except that an oil refinery and mushroom-shaped fuel tank now loomed on one bank. Sydney's airport crowded the other shore with a runway extending over the water. And dead ahead lay a vast shipping container terminal, piled with metal boxes.

There wasn't time to take in more. We were too busy maneuvering toward a red channel buoy, the midpoint of the race. As we tacked around it, Roger steering close to shave seconds off our time, I noticed a metal plate affixed to the float. It was the "Captain Cook Buoy," marking the site where the *Endeavour* dropped anchor 230 years ago.

"Look at that!" I shouted. "We're at the exact spot Cook was!"

Roger barely glanced away from the luffing sails. "Bugger Cook. We're still caning the rabble!"

On the return leg to Sydney, the sky and sea turned threatening, with squalls and whitecaps and wildly shifting winds. Susie and Roger began bickering about his beer intake. Spider became tangled in a line while Karen lost control of the spinnaker. I resumed my former posture: prone, with my eyes closed, absorbing little except Roger's despairing reports. "We've fallen in a hole, we're getting headed to buggery. . . . This is awful, it's ugly to watch. . . . The whole thing has gone to pieces."

We crossed the finish line at sunset, so late we'd been disqualified. "A dismayed crew, a disgusted captain," Roger said. "We did our best and it wasn't great."

The water was calm now, and I opened my eyes. The Opera House lay just ahead, ringed by a motley fleet of tall ships, ferries festooned with flags, and party boats pulsating with strobe lights and disco music. Fireworks exploded overhead. It was Sydney at its hedonistic best. "Oh, Australia Day," Susie said, yawning. "I forgot."

Roger smiled wearily. "Makes you proud," he said.

AS SOON AS Cook anchored in Botany Bay, on April 29, 1770, his attention turned to "the natives and a few hutts" he'd glimpsed on shore. "I went in the boats in hopes of speaking with them," he wrote. Having earlier sailed for two months from the Society Isles to New Zealand, Cook had found people whose language closely resembled Tahitian. So he had reason to hope that, with Tupaia's assistance, he'd also be able to communicate with the New Hollanders, separated from New Zealand by just a few weeks' sail.

Cook had no way of knowing that the *Endeavour*'s pinnace and yawl were about to pierce a community that had remained cocooned from the rest of humanity for millennia. "Aborigine" is Latin for "from the beginning"—an apt name for a people whose culture is probably the oldest surviving on earth. Most scholars believe that the first Australians island-hopped from Southeast Asia in small craft before 40,000 B.C., roughly the time that Cro-Magnons supplanted Neanderthals in Europe. As the Australian pioneers spread across the continent, rising sea levels cut them off from their neighbors. Apart from a few tribes along Australia's northern rim, who had intermittent contact with Asian fishermen, Aborigines, scattered in clans across an island the size of the continental United States, were completely isolated from every other people on the planet. Those living around Botany Bay in 1770 are believed to have dwelled there, undisturbed, for eight thousand years.

In his sweeping survey of human history, *Guns, Germs, and Steel,* Jared Diamond posits two keys to the development of agriculture and technology: exposure to the ideas and tools of other societies, and easy access to resources such as timber, iron, fertile soil, and large animals to domesticate. Aborigines, sequestered on a predominantly arid and intractable continent, lacked all these advantages. The most isolated tribes, in Tasmania, subsisted without nets, bone tools, wheels, or the ability to make fire. As a result, Diamond writes, their material culture at the time of Western contact was "simpler than that prevalent in parts of Upper Paleolithic Europe tens of thousands of years earlier."

Aboriginal belief was as intricate as the material culture was simple, weaving together ancestors, animals, and the land in a rich body of lore and law that today is called the Dreaming or Dreamtime. Wreathed in secrecy and taboo, and profoundly non-Western in character, traditional Aboriginal culture remains baffling to modern-day outsiders. For Cook and his men, there was almost no hope of comprehending the natives they met at Botany Bay.

Even before Cook's boats landed, it became clear to the English that the shore dwellers were very different from those they'd previously encountered. Banks observed that a fishing party "scarce lifted their eyes from their employment," while an old woman on shore "lookd at the ship but expressed neither surprise nor concern." Others began preparing fish to eat, "to all appearance totally unmoved at us." This indifference startled the English. Where was the well-organized belligerence of the New Zealanders, or the urgent curiosity of the Tahitians?

The "Indians," as the English called them, also looked different from Polynesians, who were generally tall, tawny, and powerfully built. "The Natives of this Country are of a middle Stature straight bodied and slender limbd," Cook wrote, "their skins the Colour of Wood soot or of a dark Chocolate." The men had thick black hair and bushy beards and went naked except for "White paist or Pigment," which they daubed on their foreheads and in broad bands around their legs and shoulders. Banks, as ever, studied the women, who "did not copy our mother Eve even in the fig leaf."

Most of the natives fled as the English boats came close to land. But two men stood their ground. "They calld to us very loud in a harsh sounding Language of which neither us or Tupaia understood a word," Banks wrote. Parkinson recorded their words as *Warra warra wai.* Cook, meanwhile, attempted his usual peacemaking, throwing "nails beeds &c a shore." The two Aborigines responded by throwing stones and pronged fishing gigs, one of which landed between Parkinson's feet. Cook fired small shot, striking one man in the legs. The warrior hoisted a bark shield with two eyeholes cut into it, and hurled a "dart." Only after three rounds of musket fire did the natives finally retreat, though with a defiant lack of haste.

Exploring the shore, Cook found a few bark canoes, which he judged "the worst I think I ever saw." For shelter the natives had only "mean small hovels not much bigger than an oven." On the floor of one, the English scattered nails, beads, ribbons &c. When they returned the next day, the trinkets remained, untouched. A landing on the other side of the bay followed the same pattern, with hostile gestures and then retreat, the natives leaving the sailors and their gifts alone on the beach.

"Neither words nor actions [could] prevail upon them to come near us," Cook wrote. At one point, "alone and unarm'd," he went so far as to follow ten armed men "some distance along the shore." Even this bold and pacific gesture aroused nothing but stony indifference. "All they seem'd to want," Cook concluded, "was for us to be gone."

Englishmen aboard the First Fleet would later learn that the phrase Parkinson had recorded, *warra warra wai,* meant "Go away."

A MONTH AFTER my sail with Roger, I returned to Botany Bay, this time by land. The drive south from Sydney took me along a bitumen scar of discount centers and car-repair lots with names like Jap World Spares. Then I crossed the Captain Cook Bridge and rode along the looping southern shore of Botany Bay, known as the Kurnell Peninsula. As the kookaburra flies, Kurnell lies just fifteen miles from downtown Sydney. But it felt like another country, an exurban netherworld of scrub, sand, and high-voltage electricity pylons. I passed a turnoff named Joseph Banks Drive and a sign saying "Road Tanker Entrance," leading into a landscape the botanist would not have recognized: a vast oil refinery burning off gas in plumes of flame from its forest of smokestacks.

Just beyond the refinery lay the community of Kurnell, comprising a dozen residential streets, most of them named for Cook's crew. I spotted a mob of scabby-kneed boys in gray shorts and girls in maroon tunics, all wearing broad-brimmed hats bearing the motto "We Endeavour." These were eight- and nine-year-olds from Kurnell's primary school. I'd arranged with their teacher, Leanne Noon, to tag along when her Year Three students made their annual trip to the national park enclosing Cook's landing site.

"For most of the term we've been talking about the Dreamtime and the culture that was here for thousands of years before Europeans arrived," Leanne said when I fell in beside her. A dark-haired woman in her thirties, with striking hazel eyes, Leanne had grown up just across the bay. "When I was a kid, we learned that Australia began with Cook, but that's all changed. We only spend a day or two on him now."

The school group was met at the park entrance by John Atkins, a trim ranger in olive pants and a shirt adorned with a logo of a banksia, a gnarly, nectar-sweet plant named for the *Endeavour*'s botanist. "We're going to concentrate today on Cook," he told the schoolchildren, who sat cross-legged before him. "But there were people living here when he arrived. Do you know who they were?"

Twenty hands shot in the air. "Aborigines!"

"That's right. But they didn't call themselves that. The ones who lived here were the Gwyeagal or Gwygal people. Do you know why we pronounce it both ways?"

"Because it's hard to say?"

"Because they spelled it different ways?"

John shook his head. "No. I say both 'Gwyeagal' and 'Gwygal' because we don't know how they said their name. They aren't here to tell us anymore." Kurnell, I later learned, was an English corruption of the name of the last full-blooded Aboriginal elder born on the peninsula, Cundlemong, who died in 1846. By then, disease, displacement, and attacks by settlers had killed or driven off virtually all the Gwyeagal.

John led us to the park's small museum and paused next to a model of the *Endeavour*. "How many of you would want to ride in this across the world?" he asked. Almost every hand shot up. "But you'd be away three years," he said. "You'd be in Year Six by the time you came back."

"Cool!"

"Or you might not come back at all," John added. "Do you know why?"

"Pirates?"

"Sharks?"

"How about health?" John asked. "Sailors couldn't just pull fruit and veggies from the fridge. So sometimes they got sick with a terrible disease called scurvy."

"That's not as bad as what I have," a boy called out.

"What's that?"

"A.D.D."

John swiftly moved on to another exhibit, "The Owners and the Invaders." "Owners," or "traditional owners," was the term that polite Australians now used when referring to the country's indigenous population. The exhibit quoted Lord Morton's words to Cook about acquiring the consent of the natives before taking possession of any land. "Cook disregarded these orders or at best misinterpreted them," the exhibit said, noting that Cook raised the flag at Botany Bay without native consent.

John took the class outside to a sloping lawn leading down to the bay. He pointed to a reconstructed building and said this was the site of the first white homestead in Kurnell, an 1817 land grant called Alpha Farm. A semiliterate clerk rendered this classical name as "Half-a-Farm," and the puzzling designation remained on maps and in official documents. A nearby stream, referred to in the *Endeavour* journals as the "watering place," was now a brackish, weed-choked trickle.

John continued on toward the site of the first English landing, a puckered rock shelf with a small plaque to Cook that was unreachable at high tide. A refinery wharf loomed in the background and jets roared overhead. John reached into a prop bag and said, "Okay, now we're going to act out Cook's landing. You two there, you're Aborigines," he said, handing spears to a boy and girl. Then he gave a red jacket to a "marine," a wig to "Banks," and a tricorn and blue jacket to "Cook," a little girl with pigtails.

"Aborigines," John said, "these blokes are rowing towards you. Do you like the look of them or not?"

They shook their heads. "They're white," the girl said. "They have silly clothes and funny hats." She brandished her spear and shouted, "Go away!"

DURING THE LUNCH break, I chatted with John as he microwaved spaghetti in the rangers' office. A former history teacher, he'd been guiding school groups through the park for several decades. "I try to walk a line between admiring Cook and recognizing the damage done in his wake," he said. "But I'm dealing with nine-year-olds. I may go on all day about Cook, and what impresses them most is a lizard running across the road."

He found it easier to talk about the environmental change since Cook's day. The owner of Alpha Farm was declared "lunatick" in 1828; the settlers who followed him were demonstrably so. If cool, damp New Zealand seemed a mirror of Britain, much of Australia—thirty times the size of the U.K.—represented its opposite: dry and harsh, with only 6 percent of its land arable. Yet colonists at Botany Bay, and across Australia, imported English notions of land management to terrain that was horribly ill suited to European husbandry and agriculture.

Kurnell's settlers introduced 13,000 sheep, most of which quickly died of foot rot. Cattle followed, overgrazing the peninsula's scrub. Loggers felled the fine stands of timber that Cook had admired. Stripped of vegetation, Kurnell became a waste of shifting sands, so duny and desolate that it would later serve as a set for movies about desert warfare, as well as the postnuclear fantasy *Mad Max—Beyond Thunderdome*.

In the late nineteenth century, the ravaged peninsula was also designated a zone for "noxious trades" needed by the nearby city: tanneries, wool-scouring mills, sewerage works. In the twentieth century, when Sydney Harbour acquired its famed bridge and Opera House, Botany Bay got an airport, chemical plants, and oil refineries. "On cloudy, humid days, it feels like you're sitting behind a diesel bus," John said of the fumes.

The refineries and sewage works dumped waste straight into the bay and ocean, making Kurnell's beach the most polluted in greater Sydney. As a final insult, sand-mining companies carted off dunes wholesale and dug below sea level, extracting sand for construction sites and filling the holes with demolition waste. "People have tried everything they can on the peninsula," John said, "so it's gotten to the point where they're just digging it up and hauling it away."

In 1770, Cook wrote of Australia: "We see this Country in the pure state of Nature, the Industry of Man has had nothing to do with any part of it." Two hundred and thirty years later, Botany Bay—a name Cook intended as a bucolic tribute to Banks and Solander—had become a cruel historic joke, like the toxic "Meadowlands" in the "Garden State" of New Jersey, now sown with industrial plants.

As John cleaned up his lunch, he said that Botany Bay represented a "type locality" for dozens of native species, meaning this was the place where they'd first been "discovered" and described. The woods once abounded with wattle, scribbly gums, lillypilly trees, and a palm called burrawang. Koalas were once so common in Kurnell that they were hunted for sport. Now, John said, the koala, as well as the bandicoot, the ring-tailed possum, and many other species were what naturalists term "locally extinct."

SO, TOO, IN a way, was memory of Cook. Later in the week, I returned to Kurnell to sit in on Leanne Noon's classroom discussion of the field trip. She began by reading to her students from a book called *Too Many Captain Cooks*. Its cover showed a cartoonish image of Australia, with the modern-day Aboriginal flag at the center and warriors brandishing spears at European ships that invaded from all directions. Skulls decorated the ships' sterns and tricorn-clad captains stood on the vessels' decks waving pistols and rapiers.

While Leanne's students sketched maps of Cook's route, she showed me the new, state-mandated curriculum for the course she was teaching. Cook appeared in a section about the British "invasion" and "occupation" of Australia. The man himself merited two brief mentions in the eight-page document: students were to learn about "the voyages of James Cook in relation to colonisation" and also about his role in dispossessing Aborigines by claiming the continent for Britain. This was all students learned of Cook. When they resumed Australian history in secondary school, the course started off with the country's federation in 1901.

"Because we're just a few hundred yards from his landing site, we do a lot more on Cook than most schools," Leanne said. After class, she took me to the school assembly in a nearby auditorium. The students arranged themselves in color-coded groups named Cook, Solander, Banks, and Phillip (Arthur Phillip was the captain of the First Fleet). Then they sang the school song, the lyrics of which obviously predated the new curriculum: "Kurnell, birthplace of our nation, our home and our symbol, of our land Australia, our land of hope and freedom!"

The principal appeared onstage, toting a stuffed doll wearing a blue jacket and buckle shoes. Leanne nudged me and said, "That's Captain Cookie." The doll, placed on a little red throne called "Cookie's Chair," was awarded each week to the class that behaved best, and he occupied that classroom until the following week's assembly. The tradition had begun decades ago when a sewing teacher at the school decided to craft the doll.

"Parents take Captain Cookie home and mend him," Leanne whispered. "He's killed with kindness."

IN THE AFTERNOON, I returned to the landing site park. The booth at the entrance was unmanned. There were no school groups visiting—there were no visitors at all, in fact—and the only person in sight was the park manager, Gary Dunnett. He said the park's shop, café, and information center had all closed in recent years for lack of patronage. In earlier decades, British dignitaries often visited, leaving the silver spades and trowels they used to plant trees by the park's monuments. Now, even that steady trickle had dried up.

"I'm not sure how you curate a shovel," Gary said, pointing to a storeroom cluttered with the ceremonial spades, as well as with dusty photographs, a replica of Cook's sword, and other relics the museum had once displayed. These items now lay forgotten and uncatalogued for lack of money and interest. "No one seems to give a stuff about any of this," Gary said.

In an attempt to attract more visitors, officials were gradually recasting the park to reflect modern sensibilities. Gary handed me a dense "Draft Plan for Management." Originally called the Captain Cook Landing Place Reserve, the 250-acre site would now become the "Kamay–Botany Bay National Park"; "Kamay" was believed to have been the Aboriginal name for the bay, though no one knew for sure. "Open air multicultural events" and Aboriginal "story telling and celebrations will be encouraged," the document said. New signs and educational programs would also be designed to "reflect the meeting of cultures rather than the domination of one culture by another."

"We're not denying either side," Gary said. "You can choose which side of the meeting to emphasize, but respect the other. If there's any space in which we should ask questions about cultural exchange, it should be here."

As Gary closed up the museum for the day, I wandered outside and read the rest of the document beneath a monument to Solander. Apart from the draft plan's soulless language, the new agenda seemed well-meaning. But I couldn't help feeling the same unease I'd experienced when scanning the school curriculum, and while visiting Cook's landing site in New Zealand, where the plaques spoke of how the English and Maori "learned about each other."

Reinterpreting history was one thing, rewriting it quite another. At Botany Bay, the English and Aborigines didn't even speak, at least not in words the other party could understand. As for "cultural exchange," as Gary Dunnett put it, this had consisted of musket fire and spears. The two societies didn't "meet" on the beach of Botany Bay. They collided.

But conflict was unfashionable. Better to skirt the whole issue of "the domination of one culture by another." Better, still, to omit Cook altogether. In late April, on the anniversary of the *Endeavour*'s landing, I returned to Kurnell for the annual commemoration hosted by local and park officials. In years past, it had been a rather traditional affair, featuring speeches about Cook, gun salutes, and reenactments. Now it was somberly dubbed "The Meeting of Two Cultures Ceremony," and included an "expression of our cultural differences in verse and song," as well as a moment of silence to remember "those who lost their lives when our two cultures first met"—even though no one died during Cook's stay at Botany Bay, except for a consumptive sailor named Forby Sutherland.

The ceremony ended with the singing of "Advance Australia Fair." Cook had been written out of this, too. The nineteenth-century song had recently become the national anthem, replacing "God Save the Queen"—though not before officials deleted an offending verse, which began: "When gallant Cook from Albion sail'd, / To trace wide oceans o'er, / True British courage bore him on, / Till he landed on our shore." This cleansing occurred, appropriately, in 1984.

I drove back to Sydney in a state of bewilderment. Small wonder that so few Australians gave a stuff about Cook, or bothered to visit his landing site. Bureaucrats had turned the great adventurer into one of their own: a dull, bloodless figure who attended lots of meetings. Worse than bloodless: invisible. Cook had been curated out of sight, like all those royal shovels.

"MATE, YOU'VE BEEN away too long," Roger said, inviting himself over for a drink or three after work, as he often did. He listened politely to my report on Kurnell, then pulled a dictionary from the shelf and read aloud, with some revision: "Captain Cook. On the ritual Day of Atonement, that goat chosen by lot to be sent alive into the wilderness, the sins of the people having been symbolically laid upon it." He closed the dictionary and topped up his drink. "As you know, I'm not much for atonement. Also, I'm a Pom—at least when it's convenient to be one. We have enough 'fuzzy-wuzzies' to feel guilty about. I'll leave it to the colonials to say sorry to theirs."

Roger was right, at least about my having been away too long. When I'd worked as a newspaper reporter in Sydney in the mid-1980s, racial issues rarely blipped across the radar screen of white Australian consciousness. Aborigines, only 2 percent of the nation's population, were all but invisible in the coastal cities where 85 percent of Australians lived. Few urban Australians ventured into the country's forbidding interior. Why bother when you could fly for less to Bali?

I'd made a point of visiting the outback whenever I could, on reporting assignments that few other journalists wanted. What I found out there felt like a foreign land, populated, if populated at all—Australia trails only Mongolia and Namibia as the most thinly settled country on earth—by beer-swilling roughnecks, farmers who tended vast sheep and cattle "stations" with helicopters, and Aborigines whose camps reminded me of the most wretched Indian reservations I'd visited in America. Like modern-day Sioux, Aborigines seemed caught between two worlds, unable to reclaim their traditional life but ill equipped, or disinclined, to enter mainstream society. The result, as often as not, was dependence on drink, drugs, and welfare, all of which deepened the racism of rural whites.

But each time I flew home from the outback to Sydney, Aborigines and their problems fell away as abruptly as the dust- and fly-choked landscape I'd left behind. I found myself back in the voluptuous Lotus Land that D. H. Lawrence captured so well when he wrote about "the indifference—the fern-dark indifference of this remote, golden Australia. Not to care—from the bottom of one's soul, not to care."

Returning to live in Sydney fifteen years later, I found that everyone now seemed to care. Dinner tables, talk radio, and parliament all brimmed with debate over whether the prime minister should apologize to Aborigines for past wrongs. Soon after my visit to Kurnell, 200,000 people marched across Sydney's Harbour Bridge as skywriters trailed "SORRY" in the glittering cobalt air overhead. Similar marches followed in every other Australian city, the largest demonstrations in the nation's history.

For a history-obsessed interloper, what was most striking about this ferment was the way it focused on the past as much as on the present. White Australians, many of them for the first time, were confronting the dark side of their nation's history. After visiting Kurnell, I decided to do the same.

Once I plunged into the archives, it didn't take me long to encounter bloody stories of early contact between Aborigines and Europeans. Just two years after Cook's departure from Botany Bay, a French ship arrived in Tasmania under the command of a Rousseau-loving captain named Marion du Fresne. He ordered his sailors to strip before wading ashore so they could climb from the sea as "natural men" to greet their brothers, the naked Aborigines. Marion du Fresne even hoped that the two parties might compare notes on life in the state of nature.

Instead, this nudist confab collapsed in confusion and conflict. The French quickly opened fire, killing and wounding several Aborigines. The quixotic Marion du Fresne sailed on to meet the noble Maori of New Zealand, who killed and ate him, prompting a retaliatory massacre by the French. "They treated us," a French lieutenant wrote of the Maori, "with every show of friendship for thirty-three days, with the intention of eating us on the thirty-fourth." *Sic transit* noble savage.

Tasmania's first English settlers picked up where the French had left off. They not only slaughtered natives, but also salted down their remains and sent them to Sydney as anthropological curiosities. Later, when Aborigines speared colonists and their stock, Tasmania's lieutenant governor ordered 2,200 settlers and convicts to form a human dragnet and march across the island with muskets, dogs, bayonets, and bugles, flushing Aborigines from the bush like so many grouse.

This so-called Black Line failed—Aborigines simply slipped through it—but disease, displacement, and ad hoc shootings eventually succeeded. An estimated four thousand Aborigines lived in Tasmania when Cook visited the island on his third Pacific voyage, in 1777. Seventy years later, Tasmanian Aborigines numbered fewer than fifty. When a woman named Truganini died in 1876, she was declared the island's last full-blooded native. Her skeleton was exhumed and put in the Tasmanian Museum as a relic of an extinct race; it remained on display until 1947.

I made my own visit to Tasmania and searched for a monument to Truganini, which read: "They roam no more upon this isle so stay and meditate awhile." I never found it: the memorial, I later learned, had been repeatedly vandalized, and the inscription no longer existed.

Tasmania represented the starkest instance of ethnic cleansing in Australia, but the island's history differed in degree rather than in kind from what happened elsewhere in the country. Estimates of the Aboriginal population of Australia in 1770 range from 300,000 to a million. In 1901, when Australian states federated to form today's nation, Aborigines numbered 94,000. That year's census marked the last official count for decades. Australia's new constitution didn't regard Aborigines as citizens; they were denied the vote and other rights, and excluded from the census. Australia also celebrated its nationhood by instituting the "white Australia policy," to keep out Asian and dark-skinned immigrants.

Massacres of Aborigines continued on the frontier until 1928. In the following four decades, state and church officials routinely took light-skinned Aboriginal children from their families and placed them in orphanages, or with childless white families, in an attempt to assimilate Aborigines and "breed out" black blood. Aboriginal mothers were so fearful of losing pale offspring that they smeared ash or bootblacking on their children to make them appear darker. In 1966 the government finally scrapped the white-Australia policy, and the next year a referendum granted Aborigines full citizenship.

In many respects, this history mirrored the United States' hideous treatment of its own natives, as well as its oppression of imported slaves and their descendants. But there were crucial differences. The United States, like Canada and New Zealand, often paid for native land, as well as signing—and quickly breaking—countless treaties. These flawed pacts at least acknowledged native society and sovereignty, creating a basis for modern claims to land and rights.

In Australia, there was no such legacy; the colony was the only British possession where no government pacts were ever signed with natives. Instead, settlers pronounced their continent *terra nullius,* "land belonging to no one," thereby justifying the seizure of Aboriginal land without even the fig leaf of a treaty.

But the most profound difference between the United States and Australia was the way in which the two countries regarded natives themselves. Americans often romanticized Indians, even as the natives were being slaughtered and dispossessed. By the mid-nineteenth century, there were calls to preserve both the American wilderness and its inhabitants before plows and guns extinguished them. Writers and artists sentimentalized Apaches and Mohicans; baseball teams adopted names such as "Braves"; the government emblazoned Indian heads on pennies and created the national holiday of Thanksgiving to commemorate a friendly encounter between Indians and settlers.

Nineteenth-century Australians, by contrast, typecast Aborigines as Stone Age savages, a people of little interest except as human fossils: a Darwinian link between modern man and his primitive ancestors. Physical anthropologists likened Aboriginal skulls to those of chimps and gorillas. The race, they believed, was doomed to disappear due to natural selection.

While Americans tried to justify and glorify their Indian-killers, George Armstrong Custer in particular, Australians simply wrote blacks, and the slaughter of them, out of the nation's history. Until about 1970, history books and school texts hardly mentioned Aborigines at all. "The great Australian silence," the anthropologist W.E.H. Stanner termed this amnesia in 1968. "A cult of forgetfulness practiced on a national scale."

THREE DECADES LATER, prompted in part by a new generation of Aboriginal activists, white Australia was waking to its unremembered past. The pendulum had swung from one extreme to the other. Aborigines, reviled for more than two centuries, were celebrated at every turn. In the few months after my visit to Kurnell, Aboriginal dancers performed at the Opera House, Aboriginal writers garnered major literary awards, the sprinter Cathy Freeman lit the Olympic torch, and the works of destitute desert artists sold at Sotheby's for half a million dollars.

This belated embrace was exhilarating to watch, even though many white Australians resisted practical steps to recompense Aborigines, or to help them repair their shattered lives. By every statistical measure, Australia's indigenous population, at the turn of the millennium, remained the most disadvantaged in the First World. The life span of native Americans trailed others in the United States by three to four years; Maori lagged Pakeha by five. Aborigines' life expectancy was twenty years less than that of other Australians, putting them on a par with inhabitants of the Sudan. Aboriginal unemployment ran four times the national average, the poverty rate three times as high. And the government was trying to reverse court orders for the return of mining and grazing lands, or stalling in the orders' execution.

It was much easier for officials to take symbolic steps—not just toward the victims, but also toward the alleged perpetrators. Which brought Cook back into the picture: or rather, screened him out of it. Already half forgotten, the captain now had to be completely expunged for the original sin of raising the British flag. Even the south Sydney district encompassing Cook's landing site had joined in the purge. Councilors suggested removing the captain from the shire's logo, which they declared "outdated" and a "symbol of the invasion of our country." The proposed new emblem, a dancing dolphin, would, in the words of one councilor, give the district a fresh image as "friendly, approachable, progressive and environmentally sensitive."

This gesture, like the rewriting of the national anthem, was a minor masterpiece of Orwellian doublethink. A metropolis that had virtually exterminated or expelled its original population, and polluted a place

Cook described as a botanical paradise, could now proclaim itself a champion of Aborigines and the environment. The council had also fingered a culprit for its wrongs: Cook, the invader, yesterday's man, to be airbrushed from public record like a disgraced Soviet commissar.

The final irony in all this lay in Cook's own journal. After leaving Botany Bay and following the continent's coast north, he finally had a chance to meet Aborigines, and to understand a little about their culture. The words Cook wrote while off the Great Barrier Reef, my next stop in the *Endeavour*'s wake, would prove far more sensitive and friendly to Aborigines than anything that white Australians had conceived in the two centuries following the captain's now reviled visit.

Chapter 6

THE GREAT BARRIER REEF:
Wrecked

A seaman in general would as soon part with his life, as
his Grog. —JOHN WILLIAMSON, LIEUTENANT TO COOK

Cook originally intended a different name for Botany Bay. He
planned to call it Stingray Harbour, due to "the great quantity of these
sort of fish found in this place." During the two days before leaving the
bay, crewmen pulled aboard half a ton of stingray. "AM: Served 5 lb of
fish to all hands," Lieutenant Charles Clerke wrote on May 5. "PM:
Served 6 lb of fish per man." The next day, yet another dose of stingray
prompted a crewman to complain: "It was very strong and made a
great many of the Ships Company sick which eat of it."

This in itself might be enough to make an Englishman "sigh for
roast beef," as Banks had put it. Sugar, salt, tea, and tobacco were also
running low. Even Cook seemed impatient to reach home. Propelled by
a brisk wind, he sailed north from Botany Bay for several weeks, barely
pausing to explore the coast. When he did, the English stayed just long
enough for Banks to catalogue the notorious miseries of the Australian
bush: stifling heat, stinging grass, a "wrathful militia" of prickly cater-
pillars, ants "biting sharper than any I have felt in Europe," and
"Musketos" so dense they "made walking almost intolerable."

Back at sea, the crew also grew nettlesome. One night, several men
assaulted Cook's clerk as he lay drunk in his bed, cutting off his clothes

and severing parts of both ears. Cook regarded this "very extraordinary affair" as "the greatest insult that could be offer'd to my authority." He promised a rich reward of fifteen guineas and fifteen gallons of arrack to any crewman who exposed the perpetrators. No one did, though a midshipman suspected of the crime later indicted himself by jumping ship in the East Indies.

Cook's talent for geographical names also seemed to desert him as the *Endeavour* made its way north. Instead of evocative place-names such as the Society Isles or New Zealand's Dusky Bay, the reader plods past bluffs and harbors named for a roll call of earls, admirals, dukes, and second viscounts, as if Cook were cribbing from Royal Navy lists or a copy of *Burke's Peerage*. Nor were all these namesakes deserving of honor. Cook's biographer, J. C. Beaglehole, notes that one was a "disastrous First Lord," known for his ugly face, while another was "a man so foolish that even George III deplored his lack of judgment."

This pattern reversed abruptly a month out from Botany Bay, when the *Endeavour* rounded a point that Cook named Cape Tribulation, "because here begun all our troubles." At sunset on June 11, shoals appeared off the ship's port bow. Cook steered away, toward what he thought was the safety of open sea, "having the advantage of a fine breeze of wind and a clear moonlight night."

Leadsmen hurled heavily weighted lines to determine how much water lay beneath the ship. "All at once," Cook wrote, "we fell into 12, 10 and 8 fathoms." Then the water abruptly deepened; just before eleven o'clock, a leadsman called out a comfortable seventeen fathoms (102 feet). "Before the Man at the lead could heave another cast," Cook wrote, "the Ship Struck and stuck fast."

Running aground was an occupational hazard that eighteenth-century sailors feared but felt confident of surviving. The *Endeavour*, however, hadn't run aground on coastal sand or rocks. It had pinned itself, thirteen miles offshore, on an outcrop of the world's largest coral shelf, the Great Barrier Reef. Banks, shaken from his bed, described an alarming sound "very plainly to be heard": the grate of wood against coral, its "sharp points and grinding quality which cut through a ship's bottom almost immediately." Surf pounded the ship against the reef, rocking the *Endeavour* so violently that "we could hardly keep our legs upon the Quarter deck." The men working aloft, quickly reefing sails in the dark, must have felt as though someone were trying to shake them from a treetop.

Cook seems to have retired just before impact, because Banks later described the commander as managing the crisis in his drawers. First, Cook hoisted out boats to sound for deep water. Then he tried to wrench the ship off the coral by dropping anchors from the boats and winding them up with the capstan and windlass. Despite this "very great strean," the ship didn't budge. Cook took a more desperate measure: lightening the ship in hopes it would lift off the coral. All night, men hauled massive weights up and over the rail and into the sea: six cannons, fifty-six-pound pigs of iron ballast, firewood, even water casks and food stores—fifty tons in all. Still the ship stuck fast.

In the morning, the *Endeavour* began to leak. Every man, including Banks, labored at suction pumps made of bored elm trees, relieving one another at fifteen-minute intervals. As night fell again, water in the hold rose to almost four feet. A third pump was deployed, but the fourth and last failed to work. "The leak gained upon the Pumps considerably," Cook wrote. "This was an alarming and I may say terrible Circumstance and threatened immidiate destruction to us as soon as the Ship was afloat."

This was unusually strong language for Cook. High tide approached, his best chance for heaving the ship off the coral. If he tried to do this, water might flood through the ship's gashed bottom. But he couldn't stay, either. "I resolved to resk all," he wrote. Men toiled at the capstan and windlass, tugging cables and anchor lines until the ship finally sprang free. Cook's worst fear instantly materialized. Water poured into the hold—or so the man measuring it reported. This news, Cook wrote, "for the first time caused fear to operate upon every man in the Ship."

It seems hard to believe that every man wasn't already terrified. But up to that point, Banks wrote, the crew had worked nonstop, for twenty-four hours, with "inimitable" calm and "surprising chearfullness and alacrity; no grumbling or growling was to be heard throughout the ship." Banks credited this to Cook's "wonted coolness and precision," and to that of his officers. Perhaps, too, exertion and exhaustion kept the crewmen from fully apprehending the peril they were in.

But there was no denying the danger once water flooded into the ship. "Fear of death now stard us in the face," Banks wrote. "I intirely gave up the ship and packing up what I thought I might save prepard myself for the worst." Ships' boats in the eighteenth century were small craft designed for labor, not lifesaving. "We well knew," Banks wrote, "that some, probably the most of us, must be drownd: a better fate maybe than those who should get ashore without arms to defend themselves from the Indians or provide themselves with food, on a countrey where we had not the least reason to hope for subsistance."

Nor was there any reasonable hope of rescue. In fact, no European ship would visit this shore again for fifty years. Even Cook abandoned his customary calm, later confiding in his journal that his "utmost wish" at this moment had been to somehow beach his wrecked ship and salvage enough timber to "build a vessel to carry us to the East Indies."

Then, just as suddenly, deliverance arrived. The crewman who had earlier reported a frightening rise in water was found to have measured incorrectly. "This mistake was no sooner clear'd up than it acted upon every man like a charm," Cook wrote. "They redoubled their Vigour" at the pumps. Cook also took counsel from a midshipman, Jonathan Monkhouse, who had once helped save a sinking ship with a technique known as fothering. As Cook described it, men covered a sail with a sticky mix of oakum, wool, and "sheeps dung or other filth." Then they maneuvered the sail under the ship with ropes until water pressed the gluey canvas into the largest gash. Monkhouse, who directed this operation, "exicuted it very much to my satisfaction," Cook wrote, bestowing one of the highest plaudits in his vocabulary. The rest of the crew also came in for rare praise. "No men ever behaved better than they have done on this occasion."

But the *Endeavour* wasn't out of danger. The Barrier Reef angles toward shore and is farthest from land at its southern edge, which the ship had passed two weeks before. In other words, the *Endeavour* had sailed into a virtual cul-de-sac. And the leaking ship had to somehow maneuver through coral-studded seas with "nothing but a lock of Wool between us and destruction," Banks wrote.

Cook set his sights on two barren sandbars, naming them Hope "because we were always in hopes of being able to reach these

Islands." Unable to do so, he pinned his hopes instead on a harbor he named Weary Bay. But the bay was too shallow. At sunset, men in the pinnace found a river mouth deep enough to bring the ship in. But as the *Endeavour* approached, the weather turned so wet and blowy that the badly damaged ship "would not work," Cook wrote. For two days the vessel lingered offshore, "intangled among shoals." Finally, on June 18, a full week after striking the reef, Cook sailed into the narrow river, twice running aground before finally mooring beside a steep bank.

Whatever relief the English must have felt wasn't recorded in their journals. Perhaps they were too exhausted, or alarmed by their situation. When Cook finally had a chance to examine the ship's bottom, he found the damage "hardly credable." The reef had shorn off much of the keel and sheathing, and torn planks so cleanly that "the whole was cut away as if it had been done by the hands of a man with a blunt edge tool." Most astonishing of all was "a large piece of Coral rock that was sticking in one hole." The coral had snapped off and plugged the gap it had created. This was literally a lucky break. Without it the ship might well have sunk.

The repairs would obviously take weeks. Cook climbed a hill by the river to survey the countryside. He found a "very indifferent prospect" of mangrove swamps skirted by "barren and stoney" ground. A fierce wind blew constantly. This unpromising venue was to be the crew's home for almost two months, its longest stay on land since the ship's departure from Matavai Bay a year before.

ONE OF THE small ironies of Cook's voyages is that a man who charted and named more of the world than any navigator in history has few places of consequence called after him. Magellan and Bering were honored with famous straits and seas; Hudson merited a major river and bay. Columbus garnered ten American cities, including the U.S. capital ("Columbia" is a feminized version of "Columbus"), as well as a national holiday. Cook came away with two glaciers, several remote passages, inlets, and peaks, a tiny island group he barely visited, and a crater on the moon.

One reason for this slight is that Cook narrowly missed several harbors that later became major cities: not just Sydney, but also Auckland,

Wellington, Vancouver, and Honolulu. Still, Cook seems ill rewarded, particularly on the map of Australia. Tasman never set foot on the island state that bears his name, nor did Darwin visit the modern capital of Australia's Northern Territory. Yet Cook, who traced the continent's entire east coast, has little to show for it except a south Sydney electoral district and a weird town in far north Queensland, beside the river where the *Endeavour* found refuge after hitting the reef.

Cooktown has seventeen hundred inhabitants and a reputation in the rest of Australia as a beer-swilling, cyclone-racked, crocodile-infested outpost—in other words, a fairly typical bush settlement. Cooktown also hosts a "Discovery Festival" each year to mark the anniversary of the *Endeavour*'s landing. Judging from a festival brochure I received from Cooktown's tourist office, this event wasn't quite so earnest as the one I'd attended at Kurnell. The three-day bash included a wet T-shirt contest, a race down the main street by revelers pulling beer coolers mounted on wheels, and a reenactment of Cook's landing by "local residents in authentic costumes."

"It'll be a shocking piss-up," Roger predicted a week before the festival. "We better start drinking now to lay down a foundation so we don't disgrace ourselves." Instead, I headed to Cooktown for a few days of sober reconnaissance before Roger joined me at the weekend. Just getting to Cooktown, which is closer to New Guinea than to the Queensland capital of Brisbane, presents a challenge. The sea approach remains almost as treacherous as in Cook's day; large ships traveling the north Queensland coast carry specially trained "reef pilots" to navigate the shoals. The schedules of the small planes flying into town are subject to frequent disruption by high winds and other hazards. Driving to Cooktown from Cairns, the nearest town of any size, isn't easy, either. The coastal road through the Daintree rain forest is impassable during the six-month-long wet season; during dry months, it is a slippery, spine-shuddering track, so filled with craters and fallen trees that traveling it resembles a land version of navigating the nearby reef.

Having endured many such drives during my earlier travels in Australia—including one that left me bleeding in a ditch after I triple-flipped my car off a road near Alice Springs—I opted for the much longer inland road from Cairns to Cooktown. This route, at least, offered the luxury of occasional paved stretches and a reasonable hope of rescue if I broke an axle or my tires became bogged. "In an hour or so you'll want to go into high-four and lock down the wheel hubs," the car rental agent at Cairns informed me, handing over a Land Cruiser with a shorn-off aerial, gravel-dug acne, and an inch-deep skin of dust and mud from its last trip to Cooktown. "Otherwise," he added dryly, "you'll run into a bit of drama."

Drama of any kind might have proved a relief during the daylong drive. Australians have a colorful vocabulary to describe their country's vast interior: outback, bush, scrub, woop-woop, never-never, back of beyond. Whatever the term, the view remains much the same: mile upon mile of desiccated soil and stunted shrubs. At times, even this ground cover vanishes. One early explorer of Australia's central desert called it the Ghastly Blank.

Since most of the continent's exotic fauna is sensibly nocturnal, there's little to look at, except signs warning of the many ways that a motorist can come to grief on outback roads. First, kangaroos, bounding out of the scrub at dawn and dusk (my Land Cruiser, like all outback vehicles, came equipped with a massive "roo bar" to repel marsupials). Then, unfenced cattle roaming all along the route, a danger advertised with pictograms of cars crushed against cows. And finally, extreme weather patterns, prompting the curiously unhelpful sign: "Drive According to Prevailing Conditions." If the prevailing condition was a dust storm or flash flood, how should one drive? Should one drive at all?

Compounding these hazards is the Australian institution misleadingly named a roadhouse. To American ears, this conjures a diner or truck stop offering bottomless cups of coffee. In the outback, it usually signifies a single gas pump and a corrugated-metal shed in which drivers wash away dust and boredom with staggering amounts of beer.

The Lion's Den, an hour short of Cooktown, typified this outback vernacular. "Keep your Dog Outa the Bar and I'll Keep My Bullets Outa Your Dog," announced a sign in front of the lean-to, which was unadorned except for the "XXXX" painted on its side—the label of Queensland's favorite beer—and a notice saying, "Current Opening

Time 10 A.M." The bar had been open since eight A.M., and several flea-bitten mutts lounged on the plank floor, offering confirmation that dogs resemble their owners: in this case, unshaven men with stringy beards and work clothes worn to an even dun color.

I ordered a "pot" of XXXX and studied the pub's décor, which included a display of pickled spiders and snakes, crocodile skins, and a calendar titled "Roadkill Collection." January featured a photo of a squashed bird named "Sleeping Beauty," February "The Battered Bat," March "The Flatted Calf," April "Roll over Rover," and so on through the year and the animal kingdom. Each month's pinup also bore a caption announcing where and when the creature had expired.

Equally eye-catching was a small sign advertising "Safe Riverside Camping" behind the pub. Safe from what, I wondered?

"Crocs," the barmaid said. "Usually."

Crocodiles are rife in estuaries and streams like the one running behind the pub. "How can you be sure it's safe?" I asked.

The barmaid shrugged. "No one's ever been taken there," she said, "at least not that anyone can remember." Being "taken" was characteristic Aussie understatement. Crocodile attacks typically result in sheared limbs, massive hemorrhaging, and, if the croc takes its prey into a "death roll," drowning.

Driving on, past Boggy Creek, Scrubby Creek, and Forgotten Road, I reached the outskirts of Cooktown, announced by a bullet-riddled sign that read: "Check Your Pulse." I crossed a muddy stream and reached Cooktown's main drag: a wide avenue lined with wooden buildings, their verandahs overhanging the sidewalk. At first glance, the town looked quaint and deserted, like a Wild West set just before the climactic shoot-out.

Stepping from the Land Cruiser, I realized why there were so few people about. The street was a wind tunnel. Struggling to stay on my feet, I walked bowlegged past secondhand stores and a souvenir joint named the Croc Shop before taking refuge in a pub called the Cooktown Hotel. A rugby league match blared on the television. Though I've resided for a decade in rugby-playing countries, the sport, to me, remains a bewildering cross between American football and the combat scenes from *Braveheart*. A mirror image of the game was under way in the pub. Dangerous-looking men in sweat-stained singlets and shorts formed a scrum beneath the TV, sloshing beer on one another as they jeered at the screen.

"Ya wankers!"

"Fuckwits!"

"Mongrels!"

I took a XXXX to a vacant tree stump at the far end of the bar and settled beside a barefoot, ponytailed man about my own age. Shouting over the TV and the imprecations, I tried to make conversation about the weather. "Is the wind always like this in Cooktown?"

"No, mate," he replied. "Come July and August it'll blow to buggery."

"Is it always, uh, this rowdy in here?"

"Bloody oath. This is nothing. Usually it's a drunken riot."

Laurie Downs told me that he worked at the bar. This was his day off, so he was drinking beer instead of serving it. "They say Cooktown's the largest unfenced asylum in Australia," he said.

"Is it?"

"Not really. I reckon it's the largest unfenced asylum in the world."

The way Laurie described it, the asylum had four wings. The crowd at the other end of the bar represented a sort of middle class, "your basic upstanding Cooktowners: laborers, drunks, blokes on the run from the law or their wives in the lower states." Aborigines, many of them poor and jobless, gathered at a pub down the street called the West Coast. The town's third tavern, the Sovereign, attracted the "snobs," mostly newcomers who ran businesses or held professional jobs. Finally, there were "ferals," a fringe-dwelling population of hippies and desperadoes who worked, if they worked at all, in the "horticulture industry"—i.e., growing dope.

"You'll see ferals come in here who haven't had a bath or shower or been near water for six months," Laurie said. "One bloke ordered a beer and I handed him a bar of soap instead."

Laurie studied my dusty khakis, stubbly cheeks, and relatively clean T-shirt. "Not a snob, are ya?" he asked.

"Hope not. Just passing through." I told him about my travels and asked if I could hire someone to take me out to the reef where the *Endeavour* came to grief.

"There's your fleet, mate," he said, pointing at three grizzled men hunched at the bar. One, a florid fisherman with flaming red hair, went by the name of Blue. Laurie identified the other two as "real nutcases. They'll die at sea if they don't die here first."

This wasn't too encouraging. Nor was Blue's response when I asked if I could hire a boat to see the reef. He said no one risked going out that far until the wind died down in September. Blue also warned against touring the inland waterways. A few days before, the Coast Guard had been called out to rescue a seaplane attacked in the night. "A croc tried to root the plane, then decided to bite it instead and do the death roll thing." Blue laughed. "I'd like to see the insurance claim on that one."

I returned to my tree stump and shared this tale with Laurie. "You've got some real Crocodile Dundees in here," I said. "Great bull-shit artists." Laurie responded by going behind the bar and bringing back a beer-stained local newspaper. Under the headline "Love at First Bite," I read a news item corroborating Blue's story in every particular. Other police news, which consumed half the paper, told of a woman whose ear had been bitten off by her husband, a man who paid for groceries with "a very badly photocopied fake $100 bill," a pub brawl, a window smashed with a beer bottle, several drug busts, and innumerable arrests for drunk and disorderly conduct.

"Quiet week," Laurie said. "Most people are lying low till the Cook festival." Laurie, it turned out, was responsible for buying the Cooktown Hotel's supplies for the weekend: one hundred cartons each of Jim Beam whiskey and Bundaberg rum, a thousand cartons of beer, plus smaller quantities of vodka, gin, and wine. Seventy thousand dollars of alcohol in all.

"I know, it doesn't sound like much," Laurie said. "But we had a lot in stock already." He drained his beer and went to the bar for another. "Stop back this weekend. There may be a bit of drama."

TO MEND THE *Endeavour,* Cook had to unload the ship, float it ashore with the tide, then raise the vessel on its side so carpenters and caulkers could patch the bottom. "The rest of the people I gave leave to go in the country," Cook wrote. Elsewhere, this would likely have meant searching for women, or bartering for "artificial curiosities." But the natives in north Queensland were as shy as those the English had encountered farther south. So the men's interest turned instead to tracking a strange and elusive creature they'd glimpsed at Botany Bay.

The first sightings in Queensland, Banks wrote, were of "an animal as large as a grey hound, of a mouse colour and very swift." A few days later, the botanist glimpsed one himself. While resembling a greyhound in size, it had a very long tail and jumped not on four legs but on two, "making vast bounds" like those of an African rodent called the jerboa. But this didn't quite capture the creature, either. "What to liken him to I could not tell," Banks wrote, "nothing certainly that I have seen at all resembles him." Bereft of analogies, the English began referring to the creature as "the wild animal" or "the beast so much talkd of."

Nor was this the only strange wildlife. One sailor told Banks that he'd been frightened by a creature the size of a small beer keg; it was "as black as the Devil and had 2 horns on its head." This was probably a flying fox or fruit bat, its ears mistaken for horns. The men also saw wild dogs, or dingoes, which they took for wolves, and seven-foot-long "alligators," actually crocodiles. Banks, meanwhile, marveled at man-high termite hills, and debated with Solander whether they more closely resembled "English Druidical monuments" or "Rune Stones on the Plains of Upsal in Sweden." Less exotic were the "musquetos," so rife that at night "they followd us into the very smoak, nay almost into the fire, which hot as the Climate was we could better bear the heat than their intolerable stings."

Finally, a month after the *Endeavour*'s arrival, the sharpshooting American, Lieutenant John Gore, bagged "one of the Animals before spoke of." It weighed thirty-eight pounds, and had disproportionately tiny forelegs and shoulders and short, ash-colored fur. "Excepting the head and ears which I thought was something like a Hare's," Cook wrote, "it bears no sort of resemblance to any European Animal I ever saw." This didn't deter the English from sampling its meat, which Cook termed "excellent food" and Parkinson likened to rabbit. Gore later shot what he called "another of them beasts," this one weighing eighty-four pounds. Parkinson sketched one of the animals mid-hop, with remarkable accuracy, and Banks kept a skin and skull. The English drawings, descriptions, and specimens would give Europe its first detailed image of the Australian marsupial. Banks, still struggling to classify it, later referred to the creature as an eighty-pound "mouse."

Eventually, the English also made contact with Aborigines, who had been as tantalizing and elusive as the still-unnamed beasts. One day, four native men appeared on the opposite bank of the river and called across to the crew. Cook decided it was the English who should play hard to get, and instructed his men to ignore the visitors. This stratagem worked. Eventually, the men paddled alongside the ship. The crew gave them cloth, nails, and paper, but they showed as little interest in trinkets as had the inhabitants of Botany Bay.

"At last a small fish was by accident thrown to them," Banks wrote, "on which they expressd the greatest joy imaginable." Tupaia prevailed upon the visitors to lay down their weapons and come sit on shore. They stayed only briefly, but returned the next day with more men, all of them naked except for the ocher smeared on their skin and the long fish bones stuck through their septums. They were short, and so lean and small-boned that Parkinson found he could wrap his hand around their ankles and upper arms. The artist also recorded more than 150 words of the native tongue, including *kangooroo*, the local term for the "leaping quadruped" that so intrigued the English.

But communication remained very tentative and prone to sudden breakdown. Curiously, the Aborigines seemed disturbed by the sight of caged birds on deck and attempted to throw them overboard. They also asked for some of the enormous turtles the English had caught near the river. When the crewmen refused (turtle had replaced stingray as their dietary mainstay), the Aborigines tried to drag two of the creatures off the ship.

"Being disapointed in this they grew a little troublesome and were for throwing every thing over board," Cook wrote. The Aborigines then lit some dried grass and encircled the shore camp in flames. As they attempted to also ignite English nets and clothes, laid out to dry, Cook fired small shot, slightly injuring one of the men. The Aborigines fled, but returned soon after and resumed relations "in a very friendly manner."

This confusing courtship continued for the rest of the English stay. One day while botanizing, Banks found the many clothes the crew had given the Aborigines, "left all in a heap together, doubtless as lumber not worth carriage." He suspected that other trinkets the English had given them had been discarded, too. "These people seemd to have no

Idea of traffick nor could we teach them." Banks was also frustrated in his attempts to make contact with women, once going so far as to follow several Aborigines into the bush in hopes of glimpsing females.

Thwarted, and tormented by mosquitoes, Banks found little to recommend northern Queensland. As for Aborigines, he viewed them as "but one degree removd from Brutes." Like kangaroos, they seemed to Banks almost unclassifiable creatures. "What their absolute colour is is difficult to say, they were so completely covered with dirt, which seemed to have stuck to their hides from the day of their birth," he wrote. "I tryd indeed by spitting upon my finger and rubbing but alterd the colour very little." The large fish bones in their noses struck Banks as "ludicrous," their voices as "shrill and effeminate" or, because of the nose bone, "scarce intelligible." As for their shy nature, he thought it "pusillanimous," even calling Aborigines "rank cowards."

Banks's unkind assessment may have reflected the influence of Tupaia. The Tahitian priest, like Banks, hailed from the upper tier of a hierarchical society and shared the botanist's preference for well-bred, mannerly people. Tupaia had regarded the Maori as degenerate cousins to Tahitians, and Aborigines struck him as even worse: what he called *ta'ata 'ino,* degraded people who in his homeland would be doomed to human sacrifice.

By contrast, Cook's own summary remarks on "New Hollanders" are strikingly sympathetic. "Their features are far from being disagreeable and their Voices are soft and tunable," he wrote. "I think them a timorous and inoffensive race." Like Banks, he was struck by their lack of agriculture, iron, or tools more sophisticated than fish gigs. But he seemed intent on dispelling William Dampier's dismal image of New Holland and its "miserablest" inhabitants. Cook's concluding passage on Aborigines is among the most extraordinary he ever penned:

They may appear to some to be the most wretched people upon Earth, but in reality they are far more happier than we Europeans: being wholy unacquainted not only with the superfluous but the necessary Conveniences so much sought after in Europe, they are happy in not knowing the use of them. They live in a Tranquility which is not disturb'd by the Inequality of Condition: The Earth and sea of their own accord furnishes them with all things necessary for life. . . . They seem'd to set no Value upon any thing we gave them, nor would they ever part with any thing of their own for any one article we could offer them; this in my opinion argues that they think themselves provided with all the necessarys of Life.

Many scholars regard this passage as some sort of momentary lapse, inspired by an excess of brandy or by a Banks soliloquy on noble savages. Even the admiring Beaglehole dismisses this "panegyric" as "nonsense," and expresses relief when Cook's journal quickly returns to "the clear head, the hydrographer, with 'a few observations on the Currents and Tides upon the Coast.'"

Cook's words do partly echo those of Banks, who contrasted Aborigines, "content with little nay almost nothing," to insatiable Europeans, for whom "Luxuries degenerate into necessaries." But the rest of Banks's journal makes it obvious how little the botanist admired or envied Aborigines. Banks was a man of large appetites, accustomed to opulence, who would never live rough again. When his grand tour was complete, he became a corpulent and gout-ridden socialite for whom luxury was very much a necessity.

Cook was a man of much simpler tastes. As one of his midshipmen memorably observed, Cook's palate "was, surely, the coarsest that ever mortal was endued with." Kangaroo, dog, penguin, albatross, walrus, monkey—all to him were "most excellent food," as fine as English lamb. (Banks, who followed Cook's lead, though not always with equal relish, later observed: "I believe I have eaten my way into the Animal Kingdom farther than any other man.") Cook displayed the same intrepidness toward the vegetables he so obsessively gathered. "The tops we found made good greens and eat exceedingly well when boiled," he wrote in a typical passage, on Queensland yams. "The roots were so Acrid that few besides myself could eat them."

This culinary stoicism wasn't simply a reflection of an undiscriminating tongue, bred on Yorkshire farm food and the sailor's diet of salt pork and biscuits. Cook, when extolling found foods, invariably observed that others would concur in his opinion if only they trusted their taste buds rather than their prejudice. "Few men have introduced more novelties in the way of victuals and drink than I have done," he later wrote, complaining, "every innovation . . . is sure to meet with the highest disapprobation from Seamen."

This stubborn Enlightenment faith in firsthand observation, rather than in received opinion, extended to everything Cook did. As a navigator, he remained unswayed by "expert" theories about the existence of a southern continent. So, too, as an observer of strange lands, he suspended judgment about cannibalistic Maori or naked Aborigines whom men of superior education and social standing regarded as "brutes." Also, having experienced class prejudice, Cook may have seen value in a life undisturbed "by the Inequality of Condition" in a way that Banks could not.

"They sleep as sound in a small hovel or even in the open as the King in His Pallace on a Bed of down," Cook later wrote of Aborigines in a letter to a Yorkshire friend. To a degree, these words also described Cook, a man who uncomplainingly endured—even enjoyed—whatever sustenance and shelter the world afforded him.

Courage, Winston Churchill once observed, is "the greatest of all human virtues because it makes all the other ones possible." Cook's uncommon bravery amid spears, reefs, and icebergs has been amply documented. Less recognized is the rare courage he showed in his own convictions, a trust that made possible so much of what he did.

WHEN THE WIND died down, from gale force to intermittent gusts, I ventured beyond Cooktown's pubs to tour the rest of the settlement. I found the *Endeavour*'s landing site along a muddy, mangrove-tentacled stretch of riverbank, beside a red sign warning: "Estuarine crocodiles inhabit this river system." In a nearby park stood a late-nineteenth-century monument to Cook and his men, inscribed *"Post Cineres Gloria Venit"* (After ashes, glory comes). Town fathers had originally planned to flank the monument with the cannons Cook dumped on the reef. But a large reward and a weeklong search failed to uncover any of the guns (which weren't retrieved until 1969, by an archaeological team from America). Instead, a single weapon now stood by the monument with a plaque that read: "On April 10th, 1885, the Cooktown Council carried the following motion, 'a wire be sent to the premier in Brisbane requesting him to supply arms and ammunition & a competent officer to take charge of same, as the town is entirely unprotected against the threat of Russian invasion.'"

Queensland authorities didn't take the threat too seriously. They sent the 1803 smoothbore cannon that now stood beside the Cook column, as well as two rifles, three cannonballs, and an officer. A sign beside a nearby stone well reported: "In the 1940s the well was cleaned. At the bottom, three cannon balls and a skull were found."

The rest of the town's history was equally curious. For a full century after Cook's visit, not a single European settled along the river that the navigator had named after his ship. Then, in 1872, gold was discovered a short way inland. Almost overnight, a town named for Cook sprang up. By 1874, the settlement had forty-seven licensed pubs, plus countless illegal "grog shops." The gold rush also drew three thousand Chinese, who ran their own newspaper and shipyard. Before long, Cooktown boasted a botanical garden, cricket pitch, and roller-skating rink.

Then, just as abruptly, the boomtown went bust. A planned rail line was never completed, the gold played out, and cyclones, floods, and fire almost finished off the town. Within a few decades of the gold rush, the population dwindled from more than thirty thousand to four hundred. Cooktown had staged a modest recovery in the latter half of the twentieth century, thanks to tourism and the "horticulture industry" Laurie Downs had told me about at the pub. But little evidence of the town's onetime glory remained, apart from the elegant granite curbing on the main street. The overgrown botanical gardens had historic plaques bearing Victorian photographs of men in straw boaters and women in linen dresses, gathered by the cricket oval for "dignified recreation." Given the contemporary scene at Cooktown's pubs, this image seemed almost surreal.

The town's former convent—another hard-to-imagine institution—had become the James Cook Historical Museum. Despite its name, the museum contained little Cookiana, apart from one of the *Endeavour*'s anchors and a dusty diorama of a kangaroo and wallaby, intended to illustrate the ongoing debate over precisely which marsupial the English had seen (*Macropus giganteus*, or the great gray kangaroo, seems the likeliest candidate).

In another room I found a giant cauldron fitted with oars. This was a reproduction of the crude vessel in which a settler named Mary Watson had fled to sea in 1881 after Aborigines attacked a camp of sea-slug hunters on Lizard Island, near Cooktown. Rowing the pot, which also carried her infant son and a wounded Chinese workman, Mary beached it on a desert isle. Their decayed bodies were later found on the island, alongside a copy of Mary's journal. "Nearly dead of thirst," the last entry read. She was honored with a grand public funeral and a monument on the main street describing her as "the Heroine of Lizard Island."

There was no presentation of the Aboriginal side of this story. The museum's entire Aboriginal content consisted of a few spears, boomerangs, and chisels, piled on the floor beside handwritten cards. The racial sensitivity so obvious in Sydney had evidently failed to migrate this far north. And local Aborigines, whom Cook regarded as healthy and happy, now appeared neither. Most of those I'd seen in Cooktown were disheveled, rheumy-eyed men, rolling cigarettes in front of the West Coast Hotel.

AT THE TOWN'S library, I learned that the Aborigines Cook encountered belonged to a tribe called the Guugu Yimidhirr. In 1873, at the start of the gold rush, they numbered about a thousand and lived much as they had when Cook arrived. Soon after the gold prospectors came, a newspaper correspondent wrote: "Cooktown is a wonderful place. Barely six months ago it was a camp for black-fellows. Presto! All is changed. A large town exists and not much is heard of the blacks."

Most of the Aborigines had simply been driven from their land. Others resisted, though spears proved no match for breech-loading rifles. In late 1873, several hundred warriors faced off against government troopers at a site near Cooktown known as Battle Camp. The name was a grisly misnomer: most of the warriors were instantly slaughtered. Those who survived, reported a correspondent for the *Cooktown Herald,* "ran into large water holes for shelter, where they were shot." There were no recorded white casualties.

When guerrilla attacks on prospectors continued, the *Herald* advocated "the complete repression of these pests" and "extermination if the poor blacks will not recognize the paramount influence of the law." Guns weren't the settlers' only weapons. Aborigines had little resistance to Western disease, or to alcohol. Chinese immigrants introduced opium, which Aborigines consumed by mixing the drug's ash with water and drinking it. The Guugu Yimidhirr, like many Aboriginal clans, appeared headed for extinction—a fate little mourned by white Australians. "The law of evolution says that the nigger shall disappear in the onward march of the white man," a Queensland representative told the federal Australian parliament in 1901.

In the case of the Guugu Yimidhirr, it was Cook who proved their salvation, albeit indirectly. A German translation of Cook's voyages inspired a young Bavarian, Johann Flierl, to set off in the 1880s "as a missionary to the most distant heathen land with its still quite untouched peoples." He created a Lutheran mission near Cooktown that became a refuge for Aborigines. Flierl named the mission Elim, after an oasis the Israelites found during their exodus from Egypt. As oases went, Queensland's Elim wasn't much: a sandy, infertile patch north of Cooktown. But it grew into a stable community, and its school educated scores of Aborigines, some of whom became nationally prominent.

One such success story was Eric Deeral, who served in the 1970s as the first Aboriginal representative in Queensland's parliament. I tracked him down late one afternoon at his daughter's modest bungalow a few blocks from Cooktown's main street. A small, very dark-skinned man, he met my knock at the door with a wary expression and a curt "May I help you?" When I burbled about my travels, his face widened into a welcoming smile. "Come in, come in, I love talking about Cook!" After several days of conversing about little except "ferals," rooting crocodiles, and rugby league, it was a relief to find someone who shared my passion for the navigator.

Eric showed me into a small office he kept at the front of the bungalow. The bookshelf included several volumes about Cook. Like Johann Flierl, Eric had been fascinated since childhood by the image of first contact between Europeans and native peoples untouched by the West. He'd quizzed Aboriginal elders about stories they'd heard of Cook and his men. "At first, our people thought they were overgrown babies," he said. Aboriginal newborns, Eric explained, are often much paler than adults. But once the Guugu Yimidhirr saw the newcomers' power, particularly the noise and smoke from their guns, they came to believe the strangers were white spirits, or ghosts of deceased Aborigines. "Lucky for Cook, white spirits are viewed as benign," Eric said. "If they'd been seen as dark spirits, my ancestors probably would have speared them."

Eric flipped through Cook's journal to the strange incident in which native men took umbrage at the sight of captive birds and turtles. "It's no longer true that Aborigines live at one with the land, but in those days it was so," Eric said. "The belief was that all creatures deserve life, each have a place in the world. If a bird or kangaroo got away when you were hunting, the attitude was 'Good on him, he's got his rights too.' Also, you only hunted what you needed for that day; you didn't take more than you needed."

This probably explained why Aborigines had tried to free the birds on deck. As for the turtles, the creatures were highly prized by the Guugu Yimidhirr; only designated men could hunt them, and only at certain times and places. "In today's terms, it was if the English had gone into a supermarket and pinched food from the shelves," Eric said. He suspected that the men who set fire to the English camp were the tribe's sanctioned turtle hunters, angered by what they saw as a violation of their laws. The same impulse probably prompted the attack, a century later, on Mary Watson's camp at Lizard Island, both a sacred site and traditional hunting ground.

I asked Eric about another action that had puzzled the English. After the turtle incident, as the two sides restored peace, Banks wrote that a warrior "employd himself in collecting the moisture from under his arm pit with his finger which he every time drew through his mouth." Eric laughed. "Even Blind Freddy knows what *that* means," he said, deploying Australian slang. The armpit motion was a traditional gesture intended to calm warriors and protect them against harm and evil spirits.

Listening to Eric, I felt the giddy thrill of unlocking small mysteries that had been sealed inside the English journals for more than two centuries. Blind Freddy might know the answers, but no books I'd read had provided them. Eric ran his finger down the list of native words Parkinson had collected. "If you read closely, you can almost see these men, groping to understand each other," he said. *Yowall,* for instance, meant beach, not sand, as Parkinson had written. "One of our men probably pointed across the river at the sandy shore on the other side," Eric said. Similarly, *wageegee* meant scar, not head—perhaps the man who had told it to the English was pointing to a cut brow when he said the word.

As for *kangooroo,* this was a fair approximation of the Guugu Yimidhirr word, which Eric rendered *gangurru.* But Aborigines, unlike Maori and Tahitians, didn't have a shared language; living in small, widely scattered groups, they spoke scores of different tongues. The English failed to recognize this. The result was a comically circular instance of linguistic transmission. Officers of the First Fleet, familiar with the *Endeavour*'s journals, used the words Cook and his men had collected in Queensland to try and communicate with Botany Bay Aborigines eighteen years later.

"Whatever animal is shown them," a frustrated officer on the Fleet reported, "they call *kangaroo.*" Even the sight of English sheep and cattle prompted the Gwyeagal to cheerfully cry out "Kangaroo, kangaroo!" In fact, the Gwyeagal had no such word in their vocabulary (they called the marsupial *patagorang*). Rather, they'd picked up "kangaroo" from the English and guessed that it referred to all large beasts. So a word that originated with an encounter between Cook and a small clan in north Queensland traveled to England with the *Endeavour,* then back to Botany Bay with the First Fleet, and eventually became the universal name for Australia's symbol. There was an added twist. The Guugu Yimidhirr had ten different words for the marsupials, depending on their size and color. "*Gangurru* means a large gray or black kangaroo," Eric said. "If Cook had asked about a small red one, the whole world would be saying *nharrgali* today."

At sunset, Eric took me to the top of Grassy Hill, the 530-foot knoll from which Cook had surveyed the surrounding countryside. The sweeping view of estuary and plain appeared unchanged—except for the matter of perspective. Cook, eager for provisions, found it an "indifferent prospect." To me, the "barren and stoney" hills he described seemed wonderfully scenic and empty, and the lowland "over run with mangroves" was a lovely river valley carpeted in green shag. Cook later returned to this summit to plot the ship's eventual return to sea. "I saw what gave me no small uneasiness," he wrote of the coral shoals extending as far as his spyglass could see. The "Grand Reef," as Banks called it, was dread-inspiring to the English—and now a magnet for tourists in scuba gear and glass-bottomed boats.

Through Eric's eyes, the view took on an entirely different aspect. Every feature told a Dreamtime saga about the creatures that had formed this landscape. For instance, when a black bird called Dyirimadhi threw a rock at the scrub python, Mungurru, the snake, wound down the hills to the sea, creating the serpentine path of the Endeavour River. The landscape also told a much grimmer, man-made story. Eric pointed to a small branch of the river, Poison Creek, so called because a white storekeeper put strychnine in flour, killing sixty Guugu Yimidhirr. Near it ran Leprosy Creek, the site of a quarantine station. "Over there," he added, pointing at a bluff, "some of our people speared two Europeans who took cedar logs we used to make canoes. The town sent troopers, who shot all but four of the clan, twenty-six people in all."

Eric told me about these incidents without apparent rancor. This was characteristic of most Aborigines I'd met, apart from a few urban activists. While Maori held to a powerful sense of grievance, and never hesitated to express it, Aborigines tended to be private and undemonstrative about their pain. When I mentioned this to Eric, he smiled and said, "Our man Cook wrote about that, too. The Maori were fierce people—still are. I think Cook's word for us was 'inoffensive.'" He paused, kicking at the grass. "Maybe if we'd been more like the Maori we'd be better off today."

We walked down the hill in the dark. Eric gave me the name of a cousin who still lived near the site of the Lutheran mission of Elim, a community now known as Hopevale. "Have you got a good sturdy car?" he asked. I nodded. "You'll probably make it, then." He smiled. "If you don't, stay clear of the water. There's been a few folks taken this year."

THE NEXT NIGHT, I attended a reception for local officials and festival organizers at the Sovereign, the pub I'd been told was the "snob" hangout. Curious to glimpse the upper crust of Cooktown society, I donned a coat and tie and arrived just in time to hear a short speech by the Honourable Warren Entsch, who represented north Queensland in the Australian parliament. Clad in casual slacks and an open shirt, he tossed back a drink while giving his own version of the *Endeavour*'s visit.

"Jimmy Cook wasn't interested in Sydney. He took a leak over the side and sailed on. But when he got here and saw the good-looking sheilas and friendly blokes, he tied up for two months and blew his credit giving away beads and having a good time. He had to explain to the queen why he'd spent all his money, so he cooked up the story about running on the reef. It was all a pack of lies."

The crowd roared with applause. After the speech, I joined Warren as he refilled his drink, and gently noted that the British sovereign at the time was a king. He shrugged. "Even if he was a king he was probably a queen, if you know what I mean. He was English, after all."

Warren's parliamentary district encompassed roughly 100,000 square miles, an area almost twice the size of England. He was a good match for his frontier constituency: a crocodile farmer and cattle grazer who combined conservative views with a diamond stud earring, lewd tattoos, and a disdain for the "pack of hyenas" and "bloody sewer rats" who served with him in Canberra. "You've got to be one of the people up here, you can't be a stuffie," he said. "If anyone tries to talk to me about politics, I tell them to piss off."

Warren said he'd last visited Cooktown during the run-up to the 2000 Olympic Games in Sydney, when organizers of the torch relay across Australia decided to skirt the far north of Queensland because it was too remote. This so enraged Warren that he'd sponsored an alternative Olympics in Cooktown, called the Complete Relaxation Games. Events included chair sleeping, wave watching, and synchronized drinking. The Cooktown Games even had an Olympic-style scandal. "We had to disqualify some participants in the armchair-sleeping competition because they'd been on the grog," Warren said. "In that event, alcohol's a performance-enhancing drug."

Warren turned to greet another man: Rob Buck, who played Cook during the annual reenactment of the *Endeavour*'s landing. Standing about five foot nine, with red-rimmed eyes and the beginning of a beer belly, Rob didn't much resemble the captain. "Cook probably wore platform shoes," he said of the height difference. "It was the seventies, after all."

"You mean the 1770s," I said.

"Whatever."

The reenactment, in its thirty-seventh year, remained an improvised affair. "There's a script, but I usually forget my lines," Rob said. The previous year, he'd gone blank at the moment when he was supposed to tell his men to gather water and firewood. "So I ended up saying, 'Lieutenant Hicks, get your men to do some stuff.'" He shrugged. "Most of the crowd was too far gone to notice."

The reenactment also had a shifting cast. A mainstay of the troupe once failed to show up because "he was on holiday at the Queen's request," Rob said; in other words, in prison, for possession of drugs. Another lost his part due to "lead poisoning," meaning he'd shot himself. Also, since the reenactment came on the last day of the festival, it inevitably suffered from AWOL sailors: men too hung over to show up. This gave me an idea. I asked Rob if Roger and I might serve as fill-ins.

Rob smiled. "See how you feel come Sunday morning." Then he told me where to meet the reenactors: at eight-thirty A.M. in a garage behind the police station. "We may have to spring a few blokes to fill out the crew."

ERIC DEERAL HADN'T exaggerated when warning me about the drive to the Aboriginal settlement at Hopevale. Several miles from Cooktown, the highway dwindled to an unpaved track winding into the wilds of the Cape York Peninsula. The few vehicles coming the other way looked like lunar landing craft, emerging from dust clouds with spare tires, jerry cans of petrol and water, and other life-support systems strapped to the roof. They had their headlights switched on to navigate the murk, and snorkel-like tubes extruding from the hood so the engine could suck in air if the rest of the car was submerged. The only other signs of life during the hour-long drive were the towering termite hills that Banks and Solander described. To me they looked less druidical than dunglike, as if deposited by a dyspeptic elephant.

Hopevale, which lay well off this "road," seemed at first an outback mirage. It looked like a modest outer suburb of Sydney: traffic round-abouts, tidy rows of corrugated-roof bungalows, and gardens splashed with bougainvillea and frangipani, as well as Hills Hoists, the rotating clotheslines that are as ubiquitous in Australian backyards as barbe-cues. A small shopping mall anchored one side of the settlement, a Lutheran church the other.

On closer inspection, Hopevale had the air of a rural encampment. Between the clusters of houses lay large patches of open ground filled with horse droppings and fleabitten dogs. People gathered around small, open fires. I found Eric's cousin, George Rosedale, sitting on a rickety chair in front of his sister's house. White-haired, with thick glasses, he had the distinctive physique of many Aborigines I'd met: long, thin legs that seemed birdlike when paired with his barrel chest and large, square head. A black dog curled beside his bare feet.

George greeted me with a cheerful "G'day, mate." But beneath the Aussie slang I caught a discernible German accent. Missionaries only recently arrived from Europe had educated George, a few years older than his cousin, and he'd later become a Lutheran pastor.

In other places I'd visited, Tahiti in particular, Christianity had proved a mixed blessing at best, displacing and in some cases destroy-ing native belief and culture. But when I asked George about this, he said the Aboriginal experience was different. Elsewhere in the Pacific, Christianity preceded colonialism. "By the time the missionaries arrived here," George said, "much worse damage had already been done."

Even so, Aborigines hadn't taken easily to Lutheran ways. George said the Guugu Yimidhirr resented the Germans' regimented work schedule, preferring to fish and hunt when they felt like it. The mis-sionaries also spoke poor English and little of the native tongue, mak-ing it hard to convey the finer points of Lutheran theology. (For instance, there is no word in Guugu Yimidhirr for love, so "Jesus loves me" had to be translated as "Jesus is my best friend.") It took a decade for the missionaries to conduct their first baptism and many more years before Aborigines agreed to Christian marriage rather than informal, often polygamous unions.

The mission's German flavor also caused problems during the Sec-ond World War. As combat raged offshore and in nearby New Guinea, the government interned the missionaries and evacuated the Aborigines, fearing they might somehow collaborate with the Japanese—possibly by sending smoke signals. George, then twelve, was loaded into a truck with the others and sent twelve hundred miles south to Queensland's much drier and cooler interior. A quarter of the Guugu Yimidhirr quickly died from flu and dengue fever. "We were treated like little black Germans, almost prisoners of war," George said. "Kids at school called us names and threw stones at us." Not until 1949 were they allowed to return to Elim, which was moved to its present location from the now-abandoned mission site.

Hopevale had since become one of the first Aboriginal settlements in Australia to win title to its own land. Aborigines, like Maori, had also revived many of their crafts; young people in Hopevale learned traditional arts such as bark painting. "It's strange to think that when I was in school, we'd get in trouble if we spoke our own language or drew pictures of the Rainbow Serpent," George said. "Now, even white schoolchildren learn about the Dreamtime, and their parents pay thousands of dollars for our artwork."

But acceptance and assimilation came at a price. Like his cousin, George had been struck by Cook's writing about Aborigines and their lack of interest in material goods. "To my grandparents, life was important, the land was sacred, but not things and not surplus," he said. "If we went fishing and hunting and got more than we needed, we gave it away." As Aborigines became integrated into the cash economy, taking farm and mining jobs, or government subsidies, the old attitude changed. "Now people want more of everything, they destroy too much. Instead of one turtle they'll kill two or three, and they want the meat only for themselves. They're never satisfied."

George still lived simply, without a telephone or other conveniences. "But I am retired now, in the long paddock," he said. "When my generation goes, there will be no living connection to the old ways."

I asked him if he ever went to the annual Cook festival. George winced. Hopevale remained a church-centered community and prohibited the sale of liquor, thus sparing itself the rampant alcoholism that afflicted many Aboriginal settlements. Cooktown, by contrast, was a veritable Gomorrah, particularly during the upcoming weekend. But people in Hopevale joked about one day printing up a T-shirt for sale at the festival. It would picture an Aborigine on the front and Cook's famous quote on the back: "In reality they are far happier than we Europeans." George smiled. "That'd give whitefellas something to think about."

Perhaps it was his talk of the Dreamtime, but as I bumped back to Cooktown I was struck by the mythic overtones of the *Endeavour*'s voyage along the coast of Australia. After the crew's brief and mystifying encounter with Botany Bay's Aborigines, who reject Western trinkets, Cook sails for home—and is trapped in the unseen labyrinth of the Great Barrier Reef. The only escape lies in literally throwing away his weightiest possessions: weapons, casks, ballast, food stores. Only after being relieved of these wordly goods is he delivered from the reef and driven back to shore—and to a much deeper encounter with the nonmaterialist Aborigines.

It seems doubtful that Cook read the copy of Homer on board the *Endeavour,* or spent much time perusing the Bible, except when he was obliged to conduct divine service. But in his journal and letters he frequently referred to "Fate." Perhaps that's why Aborigines, content with so little, struck a powerful chord in Cook: a sense that his trials off the reef were a cautionary commentary on his own ceaseless striving.

LATE ON FRIDAY, I collected Roger at Cooktown's tiny airport. He stepped from the single-engine plane looking green from the short but bumpy flight from Cairns. "I need a drink," he said. "Any decent pubs up here?"

"Depends what you call decent."

"Cold beer. No class. Some colorful louts."

"I think we can arrange that."

The town had filled up in the course of the week and we had to elbow our way to the bar of the Cooktown Hotel. I told Roger about "ferals," but couldn't find an example to point out. He studied the ragged, shouting crowd. "You mean there's people more feral than this? Even the barmaid's got mad wolf eyes." I spotted Rob Buck, a.k.a. Captain Cook, and took Roger over to introduce him. Rob was studying the final schedule for the weekend, which had been printed only hours before.

"The snobs are trying to clean it right up, turn it into a family occasion," he griped. Gone was an annual sculling contest, in which competitors swilled beer from chamber pots. Also canceled was a lawn mower race. The previous year, Rob said, a drunken contestant had mowed down a spectator. In the place of these events were activities such as a mock bank robbery and a children's fun run. Rob doubted all this would change the tone of the festival. "They can try and make it tasteful," he said, "but they can't take Cooktown out of it."

After a few rounds, Roger and I wandered over to the West Coast Hotel, the Aboriginal hangout. A sign near the entrance said, "This is a Bloody Pub. Not a Bloody Bank. Or a Bloody Finance Company." We crowded onto stools by the L-shaped bar, the only furniture in the place. Roger was impressed. "It's barely a building, just a bar. A place to vend alcohol."

A reggae-style band began playing in an adjoining room. We carried our beers to the edge of the dance floor. Before I could take another sip, a young man with a very firm grip relieved me of my can and emptied it in one guzzle. Roger, who had an Australian's instinct for clinging to beer cans, managed to fight off another patron attempting to do the same. But an enormous woman dragged him onto the floor for a sloppy slow dance as the band played "I Shot the Sheriff." He emerged from the throng a few dances later looking rumpled and dazed.

"How was it?" I asked him.

"Remember the Tahitian waltz? Like that, without the waltz. Or the Tahitian."

Suddenly the lights came on and the barmaid shouted, "Last call!" It was only ten-thirty, doubtless a record early closing for a Cooktown pub. We asked a security guard by the door what was up. "Publican woke a guy sleeping at the bar," he said. "Bloke sat up and gave him a black eye. So the barkeep reckoned he'd pack it in for the night."

We decided to do the same and save our strength for the rest of the weekend. The next morning, drinking coffee in front of our motel room, we watched as guests emerged on either side of us and opened beers. "Starting early, eh?" Roger said jovially to the couple beside us, as they drained their breakfast. The man looked at Roger strangely. Then, glancing at his watch, he said, "Mate, it's already nine o'clock."

We wandered up the main street to watch the parade kicking off the festival. Several thousand people crowded the avenue, many of them toting beer coolers, or "eskies" as they're called in Australia, short for "Eskimos." Many of the coolers had been mounted on wheels, hooked to strollers, piled into supermarket trolleys, or rigged atop tricycles and lawn mowers. Some of these homemade beer wagons came equipped with foot brakes, license plates, and umbrellas for shade. One had a picture painted on its side of Cook clutching a can of XXXX. I was also struck by the array of exclamatory T-shirts. "Happier Than a Two Peckered Puppy at the Cooktown Festival!" "Losing Is Nature's Way of Saying You Suck!" "The Liver Is Evil and Must Be Punished."

The parade began an hour late, led by men clad as escaped eighteenth-century convicts. They dragged balls and chains while one lashed the others with what looked like a skipping rope. Near the back of the parade came the local police, waving from a pickup truck. They were greeted with a hail of curses, water balloons, and crushed beer cans. The police turned a water hose on the crowd. In the midst of this melee, a policeman tumbled from the truck and lay in the road, where he was assailed with still more water balloons.

"Good God, this looks like the West Bank," Roger said. "Casualties already."

"Naah," said a woman standing beside us. "He's dead drunk, that's all. The coppers always get on the piss." A few of the officer's colleagues dragged him back into the truck and motored off. "Our last police chief got done for having sex in a cell with his secretary," the woman went on. "His wife caught him in the act."

The parade was followed by a truck-pull contest, the vehicle, of course, being a beer truck. There was also a soapbox derby, in which the go-carts included a coffin borrowed from a funeral parlor. "It's a real deathtrap," the driver declared, climbing inside and closing the lid. After this came the "Great Esky Race," though it was less a race than a riot. Lining up at one end of the main street, contestants took off, pulling or riding their coolers until they collapsed twenty yards from the starting line in a pileup of crushed vehicles, skinned knees, and broken bottles. "We've lost wheels, we've lost people!" the emcee shouted. "And, tragically, we've lost beer!"

Rob Buck's concern that the weekend might shape up as a tame family affair was rapidly dissipating. And that was before the wet T-shirt contest. Late in the afternoon, the crowd surged up the main street to a scrubby vacant lot adjoining the West Coast Hotel—a paddock, I'd noticed the night before, that served as a latrine for those too drunk to find a toilet. At the back of the lot stood a dusty tractor-trailer, opened on one side to form a makeshift stage.

The crowd stretched all the way across the main street to the curb in front of Cooktown's preschool. A bearded, ponytailed man climbed on the truck trailer and tested the microphone. This was the emcee, who went by the name of Dirty Pierre. "Can you hear me back there at the kindergarten?" he called out. Then, spotting a teacher in front of the school, he added, "Hey, she's got a good set."

"Pierre, you're a sick puppy!" bellowed a man standing beside me.

"Bring on the tits!" yelled another.

"Okay," Pierre said, glancing at his watch, "since it looks like everyone in town is already here, we'll get away on time." This was the first and only event of the entire weekend to start on schedule. "There's a bar over there," he said, pointing at the West Coast, "so you don't have to die of thirst."

Then he explained the rules, such as they were. A rubbish bin filled with ice water would be poured over each woman, with the crowd electing the winner by the volume of its cheers. "Now, does anyone have a girl to nominate?" Pierre asked. "I see a young lady right over there, in the blue tank top. Come on up!" She did, and six others quickly followed. Pierre handed each of the women a beer and asked their hometowns. One of the contestants was a British tourist. "She's a little English rose, so she needs encouragement," Pierre told the crowd. This wasn't strictly true. As soon as cold water was poured over her, she put her hands beneath her breasts and shook from side to side.

"Take it all off!" the crowd chanted. "Off off off!"

This went on for twenty minutes, until the women had been

drenched several times and prodded around the truck like cattle on auction. The English rose won, although she refused the crowd's and Pierre's pleas that she remove her T-shirt.

"Don't give her the trophy!"

"Bring on the dog!"

The dog? When the show concluded, I asked Pierre what this meant. Three years before, he said, someone had entered a bull terrier bitch in the contest. She had recently had a litter, and she won. "She had eight tits," Pierre said. "The general feeling was that quantity was better than quality."

I found this year's winner cradling a trophy while tossing back a beer with her boyfriend. It turned out that she came from a small town in North Yorkshire, near Cook's childhood home. I asked her what she thought the navigator might have made of this event.

"He'd think I was a complete lunatic," she said. "Women in his day covered up."

"His loss," her boyfriend said proudly. "If Cook had seen a pair like this, he never would have left England."

Pondering this version of what-if history, I tried to imagine what Cooktown might be like if the *Endeavour* hadn't come: a French colony, perhaps, or still a mangrove wilderness. Reflecting on this, I realized I was drunk. Though not nearly so drunk as the crowd flooding from the paddock and down the street to watch a tug-of-war contest. I found a place on the curb beside an older woman who seemed one of the few sober people in Cooktown. A man in a "Legless as a Blind Chook on Crutches" T-shirt staggered in front of us, clutching a beer in one hand and a rum bottle in the other.

"They don't know when to stop, do they," the woman said.

"Guess not," I replied, hoping she couldn't smell the beer on my breath. Then I realized she was gazing, not at Legless and his mates, but at a small party of Aborigines, quietly drinking amid the white revelers.

"It's sad how they're always drunk," she said.

A howl went up as the tug-of-war began between two women's teams. "Fuckin' dykes!" Legless shouted.

"When they're not drinking," the woman went on, "Aborigines are very docile. But as soon as they're on the grog they're barely human."

"If you sheilas can't pull, then suck!" Legless shrieked, cracking a fresh beer and covering himself in foam.

"It's supposed to be their country. But do you see them participating in all the fun here? Not bloody likely. Too lazy and drunk."

I resisted the urge to argue and went in search of Roger, whom I'd lost in the crowd several hours before. I found him sipping beer in front of the West Coast and watching police wrestle two brawling drunks into a paddy wagon. Prone, dusty figures lay splayed in the street, beside overturned eskies spilling empty beer cans. "I'm outgunned," Roger said, shaking his head. "It almost makes me want to be sober."

THE NEXT THING I recall clearly is waking Sunday morning on the couch in our motel room, a few minutes before the reenactors were scheduled to muster behind the police station. I rousted Roger and we ran down the main street. No one was there. Inside the station, I asked the constable on duty how the weekend was going.

"It's dead, thankfully," he said. Four years before, there had been ninety-seven arrests. So far this year, there had been only six. "Don't know why, but people aren't drinking as much."

Forty-five minutes after the scheduled assembly time of eight-thirty, a few reenactors arrived, led by Rob Buck. "Sir," one of the crew said to him, "we refuse to get dressed until we've been issued our rations." Rob glanced at his watch. "You're correct, sailor. It's beer o'clock." Two men went to a truck and brought back a faux sea chest filled with cold XXXX.

"Haven't had one since three," a sailor said, quickly downing one.

"That's six hours on the wagon."

"Best all year."

"We're being historically accurate, of course," Rob said, reaching for a second beer. "Why do you think Cook ran up on the reef? He was on the piss."

We drank for another half hour until the rest of the crew arrived and slowly began donning their costumes. A man playing the ship's one-handed cook put on a chef's hat and placed a hook in his sleeve. The pale teenager acting the part of Tupaia smeared dirt on his face.

The surgeon, Monkhouse, carried a tattered briefcase, meant to represent a medical bag. "I've got a crook back, a hernia, and bad kidneys, so I know plenty about doctors," he said. He held his head. "I could use some laudanum right now."

Rob pulled on a blue jacket, tights, and an ill-fitting wig. He retired to a back room to study his lines, calling out, "Lieutenant Hicks, bring a beer and the drummer boy to my cabin."

"Sir, you said last night to bring the goat."

"So I did."

The People glanced at cue cards, then begged the captain to distribute more rations. Six women showed up wearing hoop skirts, mobcaps, and low-cut bodices. "Wenches here—where's our drinks?" they shouted in unison. Then a few Aborigines appeared in body paint and skirts made of torn burlap. I asked a man named Lindsay if he had any qualms about participating in a celebration of Cook's landing. He shrugged. "His ship was crippled, he didn't invade. The bad stuff happened later."

"Of all-time white people," added another man, "Cook would be near the top of my list. Maybe that's not saying much. My list wouldn't be too long."

Lindsay said that Aborigines had boycotted the event in 1988 as part of a nationwide protest against the bicentennial celebration of the First Fleet's arrival. "Some whitefellas put on skirts and blackened their faces and played our part," he said. "They looked so bad we decided to come back the next year."

Rob emerged from his "cabin" and did a quick head count. Then he pointed at Roger and me and said, "Mr. Hicks, press-gang these men." We slipped into the remaining sailors' uniforms: gray shorts, white tunics, blue neckerchiefs, and wool caps. Roger, broad-shouldered and English-featured, almost looked convincing, and I told him so. "That makes one of us," he replied.

We staggered to the river and climbed into wooden boats. The wind was blowing hard and several men fell as they stumbled aboard. I was ordered into Cook's pinnace to man an oar while Roger boarded a separate vessel carrying the marines. Our destination, a hundred or so yards upriver, was a park near Cook's landing site.

"Stroke!" called out the man at the tiller.

"I prefer a soft rubbing motion," the oarsman beside me replied.

We began rowing, badly out of sync, and made poor headway against the breeze and current. "Bloody oath, we're going backwards!" the tiller man shouted. We finally coordinated our rowing long enough to reach the beach, ten minutes after the marines. A thousand or so spectators looked on as we pulled the boat ashore.

"The sailors are happy at being on land after many perilous days at sea," announced an emcee. "Look at them work! Men were made of sterner stuff in those days." I cut my bare feet on a rock and fell into some brambles. Another man refused to carry the officers over the muddy water because he was scared of crocodiles. "You're expendable," Rob said, shoving him over the rail.

We straggled onto the grass as the emcee continued to narrate the *Endeavour*'s story. "One of the blokes with Cook was a Swede named Solander," he told the crowd. "He was born in Sweden, I think, and went to England nine years earlier."

Nine years before his birth? "Who is this clown?" one of the sailors asked Rob.

"Town historian. He's drunker than us."

"Tupaia was a Tahitian boy that Cook liked," the emcee went on. "The crew took him back to England, I'm not sure what happened to him after that." In fact, Tupaia was about forty and never reached England. But the dirty-faced teenager playing the Tahitian looked in Rob's direction and slapped his rear, much to the crowd's delight.

We set up tables for the artist and surgeon and milled around, waiting for cues from the emcee, who had lost his place in the script. "Lieutenant Cook scans the surroundings with a telescope," he finally announced. Rob dutifully peered through his spyglass. His lines, scribbled on a piece of paper stuffed up his sleeve, fell to the ground. "Lieutenant, have your men be on the alert!" he commanded. Then he whispered to Hicks, "Fuck, what's next?" Hicks shrugged. Rob went on, "I hereby name this stream the Endeavour River."

The emcee drew the crowd's attention to the marines' boat, now lying offshore. Roger and two other men stood flailing away at something in the bottom of the craft. "Those boys have caught some tucker!" the emcee cried as one of the men held up a battered fish. Then they rowed ashore and presented the catch to the cook. Roger was covered in fish guts. I asked him what they'd caught. "Two fish and two crabs a marine brought down in an esky," he said. "Pre-deceased and very frozen."

We milled around some more as the cook pretended to cook, the surgeon rummaged through his briefcase for laudanum, and Banks and Solander kneeled to study grass, cigarette butts, beer tabs. Then the Aborigines burst from the mangroves, brandishing spears. "These local boys look a bit vicious!" the emcee exclaimed.

The marines raised their muskets. "Hold men, there will be no vio-lence here!" Rob shouted. He flung some plastic beads on the grass. One of the Aborigines grabbed a fish instead and ran off with the oth-ers. We raised a flagpole, rather unsteadily, as the marines fired a vol-ley of wadded paper. The Union Jack had a patch where a marine had accidentally blown a hole in it the previous year.

"What a lovely erection!" the emcee shouted. Then Rob read a proclamation claiming the land for His Majesty, signaling the end of the reenactment. "Three cheers for these local boys who have trained all year for this!" the emcee concluded. The crowd gave us a lackluster round of applause and hurried from the park for a second round of the Great Esky Race. The cook took off his hook. "I've done thirty-six of these," he said, "and this was the best yet."

We returned to the garage behind the police station to empty the rest of the sea chest. At some point it dawned on me that I'd consumed little except beer for the better part of forty-eight hours. Even Roger looked wrecked. He leaned against a tree, staring numbly at his watch. "It's stained with vomit not my own." He wiped the face with his gut-smeared smock. "Three P.M. I've never retired from the field this early."

"We started early. Beer o'clock."

"That's true. I haven't completely disgraced myself."

Several "officers" and "wenches" lay unconscious on the grass all around us. Raucous cries erupted from down the street; the wet T-shirt contest was under way again. Roger closed his eyes. "I'm glad Cook didn't live to see this," he said.

Chapter 7

HOMEWARD BOUND:

The Hospital Ship

Fear of Death is Bitter.　　—JOURNAL OF JOSEPH BANKS
(AUGUST 16, 1770)

On August 4, 1770, Cook hauled his ship out of the Endeavour River and back into the treacherous waters he'd survived in June. If anything, his situation appeared even more daunting than before. His patched ship was barely seaworthy, stores ran dangerously low, and the sea afforded no obvious escape route. If Cook retraced his path south, he'd have to beat straight into the prevailing wind. But the waters to the north and east appeared barricaded by shoals and reef. "I was quite at a loss which way to steer," Cook confessed.

He sailed east, then north, then east again, taking constant soundings and dodging shoals so tortuous that Cook wrote "LABYRINTH" in capital letters across his chart. (Few ships have since risked these waters; some areas are still labeled "Unexamined" or "Numerous Coral Patches Reported.") Going ashore on a small island, Cook climbed a hill and glimpsed distant sea breaking high against the outermost wall of the reef. He also saw several channels through the barrier, and soon after managed to thread one of them.

"In a short time got safe out," he wrote, after escaping into open sea for the first time in months. Banks, as usual, wrote more fulsomely. "That very ocean that had formerly been looked upon with terror by (maybe) all of us was now the Asylum we had long wished for and at last found," he observed. "Satisfaction was clearly painted in every mans face."

This satisfaction lasted one day. The wind, blowing hard from the east, pushed the damaged ship back toward the reef it had just escaped. Then the wind died, leaving the ship unable to maneuver through mountainous waves that washed it ever closer to the coral. "Now our case was truly desperate," Banks wrote. "A speedy death was all we had to hope for." This wasn't hyperbolic. When the ship had run aground in June, it did so in relatively calm water, against a coral outcrop detached from the main reef. Two months later, the ship lay in rough seas much too deep for dropping anchor, and it was rapidly approaching a semi-submerged cliff.

"A Reef such as is here spoke of is scarcely known in Europe, it is a wall of Coral Rock rising almost perpendicular out of the unfathomable ocean," Cook wrote. "All the dangers we had escaped were little in comparison of being thrown upon this Reef where the Ship must be dashed to peices in a Moment."

The surf brought the ship within forty yards of the reef, "so that between us and distruction was only a dismal Vally the breadth of one wave," Cook added. A puff of wind enabled the ship to veer away from the reef, though only for a few minutes. Men in boats tried to tow the *Endeavour* through the heavy surf while sailors desperately tossed paper over the side to judge whether the becalmed ship was moving forward at all. It wasn't. But another breath of air—"our friendly breeze," Cook called it—carried the ship within reach of a narrow break in the reef.

Cook determined to shoot through it. He failed, but "the Tide of Ebb gushing out like a Mill stream" pushed the ship several hundred yards from the coral. Cook spotted another slim passage. When the tide shifted, he used it to flood through the gap, sweeping instantly from the raging sea to the calm though shoal-strewn waters enclosed by the reef.

"This is the narrowest Escape we ever had," wrote the master's mate, Richard Pickersgill. "Thir would have been no hopes of saveing one Single Life in so Great a Surf." Even Cook's nerves had been frayed by the eighteen-hour ordeal. With a rare glance heavenward, he named the passage through the reef Providential Channel. He also penned an unusually personal entry that exposes the extraordinary pressure he labored under.

"Was it not for the pleasure which naturly results to a Man from being the first discoverer, even was it nothing more than sand and Shoals, this service would be insuportable," he wrote, "especialy in far distant parts, like this, short of Provisions and almost every other necessary." Danger and deprivation weren't the only source of strain; there was also the weight of expectation riding on an explorer's shoulders.

"The world will hardly admit of an excuse for a man leaving a Coast unexplored," Cook went on. "If dangers are his excuse he is than charged with *Timorousness* and want of Perseverance and at once pronounced the unfitest man in the world to be employ'd as a discoverer; if on the other hand he boldly incounters all the dangers and obstacles he meets and is unfortunate enough not to succeed he is than charged with Temerity and want of conduct."

If this was the only such passage in Cook's journals, it wouldn't merit much analysis. Exhausted by two years of sailing, several months of exceptional stress, and one day of sheer terror, Cook succumbed to a moment of doubt and self-pity. But there would be other entries that echoed this one, usually written when things went wrong. Taken together, they hint at a brittle and unhappy side to Cook's personality.

Throughout his troubles on the reef, he'd displayed cool nerves, keen nautical judgment, and absolute command over men he'd trained expertly. Yet his principal thought on saving his ship—for a second time—was that his narrow escape might loom as evidence "the world" could use to judge him "unfit." Cook wasn't paranoid. Most Pacific explorers before him had failed in their assigned missions, and none in the eighteenth century was given a second chance to prove his mettle. Still, that such a consummate overachiever could imagine he might be viewed as an underachiever suggests how hard the man was on himself.

Cook's angst off the reef also carried echoes of his fury over Tahitian thievery and the attack on his drunken clerk—incidents that struck him as personal insults against his authority. At these and other moments, Cook's extraordinary drive and self-reliance can seem corrosive: the marks of a compulsively driven loner, obsessed with control and prone to gnawing fears of persecution.

Cook's background could explain some of this. Having navigated his way from the bottom of English society, he may have seen the world as one vast reef arrayed against him. Perhaps, too, Cook's extreme independence and ambition were prerequisites for great exploration. Few "normal" men, particularly family men in their forties, would endure the risks and wretchedness that Cook abided in the Pacific—not once, but three times. After the *Endeavour*'s voyage, Banks would spend the rest of his long life reaping the rewards of his youthful adventures, and dining out on them. Cook, lacking Banks's fortune and status, had more to prove. Even after his second voyage, which sealed his fame and brought him the offer of a comfortable retirement, Cook chose to set off again, ultimately at the cost of his life.

As for the "pleasure" of discovery that Cook mentioned off the reef, he never alluded to it again in his journals. The farther he went, the less pleasure exploration seemed to give him. Toward the end, he would rail against everything: his indefatigable sailors, his superiors, even the wind.

COOK'S ESCAPE THROUGH the Providential Channel saved his ship from destruction, but he still had to wend his way north between shoals, sandbars, and tiny islands. Eighteen days from the Endeavour River, Cook finally ran out of coastline and reef to follow. He went ashore at a small island and climbed a hill to confirm that he'd reached the end of the continent. "Confident" that the eastern coast he'd surveyed over the prior four months "was never seen or visitd by any European before," he hoisted a flag and took possession of the entire shore in the name of King George III. He also claimed "all the Bays, Harbours Rivers and Islands situate upon the said coast." Three times, the men fired their guns and cheered—more out of relief, one suspects, than reverence for His Majesty.

This would prove the most consequential of all Cook's acts of possession, effectively laying the foundation for white settlement in the Pacific. But it was also the most confusing of Cook's many land claims. He obviously hadn't acquired the consent of the natives, as he'd been instructed to do; the few Aborigines whom Cook encountered on this northernmost bit of land, which he named Possession Island, appeared intent on opposing the English before suddenly retreating. Cook's claim was also oddly imprecise: "a vague assertion of authority over a quite vague area," Beaglehole writes. How far inland, for instance, did his claim to the coast extend? Cook didn't help matters by naming this nebulous possession New South Wales. No one knows why. The east coast of Australia doesn't bear any discernible resemblance to the Welsh shore. And why *South* Wales? Also, Cook's cumbersome name already existed on the world's map, attached to a bit of land in northern Ontario.

It was left to the explorer Matthew Flinders, who circumnavigated the continent thirty years after Cook, to popularize the name "Australia" (which had been used previously, in a loose way, for various parts of the southern hemisphere). This gradually supplanted New South Wales—providing irreverent Aussies with yet another opportunity for mockery. Their country's name, poets and songwriters often complain, rhymes with little except "failure" and "genitalia." "New South Wales," meanwhile, survives as the unsuitable tag for a state encompassing vast stretches of outback that receive less rain in a year than south Wales does in a week.

Cook, in any event, was almost done with naming. Having established that open sea separated New Holland from New Guinea, a subject that had been much debated by mapmakers, he was ready to sail home through previously charted waters—a circumstance that delighted his exhausted men. The People, Banks wrote, "were now pretty far gone with the longing for home which the Physicians have gone so far as to esteem a disease under the name of Nostalgia; indeed I can find hardly any body in the ship clear of its effects but the Captn Dr Solander & myself, indeed we three have pretty constant employment for our minds which I beleive to be the best if not the only remedy for it."

Desperate for provisions and repairs, Cook stopped only briefly at New Guinea and the island of Savu before heading to Batavia, the principal port of the Dutch East Indies and site of today's Indonesian capital, Jakarta. The *Endeavour* arrived on October 5, 1770, in horrid shape, unable, having jettisoned its large guns off the reef, to provide the customary cannon salute upon entering harbor. Once in Batavia's dock, the *Endeavour*'s carpenter gave a report to Cook that made the vessel sound like the survivor of a great sea battle: "The Ship very

Leakey . . . Main Keel being wounded in many places . . . The False Keel gone beyond the Midships . . . Wounded on her Larboard side . . . One Pump on the Larboard side useless the others decay'd." After surveying the ship's shattered, worm-eaten underside, Cook wrote, "it was a Matter of Surprise to every one who saw her bottom how we had kept her above water." He had no choice but to settle in for a long stay to make the ship seaworthy for its onward passage.

Cook's men, on the other hand, were as fit as the ship was foul. On the *Endeavour*'s approach to Batavia, a Dutch officer and several crewmen came out from shore. "Both himself & his people were almost as Spectres, no good omen of the healthyness [of the port] we were arrived at," Banks observed. "Our people however who truly might be called rosy & plump, for we had not a sick man among us, Jeerd & flouted much at their brother sea mens white faces."

Cook couldn't resist gloating, either. In a letter he quickly dispatched to the Admiralty by a Europe-bound Dutch ship, he wrote, "I have the satisfaction to say that I have not lost one man by sickness during the whole Voyage." By "sickness" Cook evidently meant scurvy, as one man had died of tuberculosis and one of epilepsy, diseases they'd carried with them from England. Cook had ample reason to crow; it was unprecedented for a ship to survive such a long ocean passage without losing anyone to scurvy. All told, eight of the ship's original complement of ninety-four men had died from disease and accidents, a remarkable record given the hazards the *Endeavour* had encountered.

The high spirits of Cook and his crew weren't due solely to their comparative good health. After more than two years at sea, much of it in waters and on shores unvisited by Westerners, the English now found themselves in a "civilized" outpost peopled by a rich curry of Dutchmen and other Europeans, as well as by Indians, Chinese, Malays, native Javanese, and slaves from Bali and Sumatra. Batavia, principally a dockyard and trading post, also bore the grand stamp of its Dutch engineers: broad paved streets, tree-lined canals, and fortified bastions named Diamond, Ruby, Pearl and Sapphire. Merchants, exchanging a babel of tongues and currencies, trafficked in ducks, geese, pineapples, tamarinds, incense, opium, nutmeg, and flowers.

The English even found months-old London newspapers, which informed them, among other things, that the American colonists were on the verge of revolt over taxes.

None among the *Endeavour*'s company were more exhilarated by Batavia than the Tahitians. Tupaia's young servant, Taiata, "was all-most ready to run mad," Banks wrote. "Houses, Carriages, streets, in short every thing were to him sights which he had often heard described but never well understood, so he lookd upon them all with more than wonder." While Taiata "danc'd about the streets," Tupaia admired the fine and varied dress of the Batavians, which included silk, velvet, and taffeta. "On his being told that every different nation wore their own countrey dress," Banks wrote, Tupaia decided to promenade around town in his "South Sea cloth."

Banks found lodging for his party at an inn where the amenities included fifteen-course dinners, as well as "Tea, Coffee, Punch and Pipes and tobacco as much as we could destroy." He also hired two carriages, "drove by a man setting on a Coachbox," and a servant he described as "a mongrel between a Dutch man and a Javan woman." While Cook busied himself at the dockyard, Banks visited country houses "built upon the Plan of Blenheim," and admired the "inexpressibly elegant" women with jasmine-wreathed hair piled high atop their heads.

This idyll came to an abrupt halt just two weeks after the *Endeavour*'s arrival. The Tahitians fell ill, and so did many of the rosy, plump sailors. Before long, Cook wrote that he and every other man had become sick, "except the Sail Maker an old Man about 70 or 80 Years of age, and what was still more extraordinary in this man [is] his being generally more or less drunk every day." The others had apparently contracted malaria or an ailment they called "putrid dysentery," probably typhoid fever or cholera. Cook, who had initially admired the Dutch port and the skill of its shipwrights, now damned the "unwholsome air of Batavia which I firmly believe is the death of more Europeans than any other place upon the Globe."

He wasn't far wrong. Batavia's ubiquitous canals, which doubled as sewers and dumping grounds for dead animals, formed stagnant breeding grounds for mosquitoes and disease. Ships arriving from all over the world brought illnesses of their own. Beaglehole estimates that eighteenth-century Batavia had an annual mortality of fifty thousand. When Cook lamented to other visiting captains that the *Endeavour* had become a "Hospital Ship," they told him "we had been very lucky and wondered that we had not lost half our people."

On November 5, a month after the *Endeavour*'s arrival, the ship's surgeon died. He was an able man, though medicine of the day could offer little to combat the illnesses afflicting the crew. Eighteenth-century medicine still hewed to the ancient notion of balancing the body's four "humours"—yellow and black bile, blood, and phlegm—with drastic measures such as bloodletting and purgation to induce vomiting and diarrhea. When Daniel Solander became gravely ill, Banks wrote that a Dutch physician put mustard plasters on his feet and blistering agents on his legs, to draw out bad humors. Banks, so sick he was "scarcely able to crawl," submitted to bleedings and purges, but had the good fortune to dose himself with quinine-bearing bark. He also retreated with several others to a country house, accompanied by a number of "Slaves," including female nurses, "hoping that the tenderness of the sex would prevail even here."

Tupaia, however, grew sicker and asked to be moved to a tent by the water where he could feel the sea breeze. On December 17, his servant, Taiata, announced, *"Tyau mate oee,"* "My friends, I am dying," and soon after perished. Tupaia became inconsolable, refused all medicine, "and gave himself up to grief," Parkinson wrote, "regretting, in the highest degree, that he had left his own country." He died three days later. One can only imagine what Tupaia, a skilled linguist and keenly intelligent man, might have one day told of his adventures, and contributed to Cook's later voyages.

With so many of his men sick, Cook could do little to hasten the repairs to his ship and the provisioning needed for the voyage's next leg, across the Indian Ocean to Cape Town. The *Endeavour* finally left Batavia on the day after Christmas, carrying the fevers and dysentery, or "bloody flux," with it. During ten weeks in port, seven men had died and another had deserted—a loss equal to that suffered during the prior twenty-seven months of sailing.

A week out to sea, the dying resumed in earnest. Cook's and Banks's journals became little more than obituary pages. The botanist, afflicted with dysentery that caused "the pains of the Damnd almost," barely wrote at all. On one day, his entire journal entry reads: "Self still Bad: three more of the people died this day." On another day he managed six words: "One more of the people died." Followed the next day by "Another died," and then, "Lost another man."

The losses included the one-handed cook, John Thompson, the astronomer Charles Green, the naturalist Herman Spöring, and the twenty-five-year-old Sydney Parkinson, who had done almost a thousand drawings. The aged, drunken sailmaker, who had remained miraculously healthy in Batavia, also died. On January 31, four men perished, and in February, a hot and sultry month, sailors died almost daily, including Jonathan Monkhouse, the midshipman who had helped save the ship by fothering its bottom off the Great Barrier Reef.

On February 7, the carpenter, without whose skill the ship might never have left the Endeavour River, dictated his will in the presence of Cook and two other shipmates. "My Body I commit to the Earth or Sea as it shall please God to Order," the document began. Five days later, Cook wrote in his journal: "At 7 in the AM died of the flux after a long and painfull illness Mr. John Satterly, Carpenter, a man much Esteem'd by me and every Gentleman on board." It is excruciating to imagine how painful and wretched it was to perish of dysentery, on a ship full of sick men, with the surgeon already gone and only the "seats of ease" for relief.

The survivors, most of whom were ill themselves, had to cope not only with the dying all around them, but also with sailing the undermanned ship. Before long, an anarchic despair took hold among the crew. Cook wrote of punishing the marine drummer with twelve lashes "for getting Drunk, grossly Asaulting the Officer of the Watch and beating some of the Sick." Another man felt the first stirrings of dysentery and started shrieking, "I have got the Gripes, I have got the Gripes, I shall die, I shall die!" He soon recovered.

However dire Cook's situation had been off the Barrier Reef, he'd at least been able to bring his nautical expertise to bear on the crisis. Now, he could do little except witness wills and try to keep his ship afloat with a diminished and sickly crew. In one twenty-four-hour period, four men died while a squall battered the ship. "Melancholy proff of the Calamitous Situation we are at present in," Cook wrote, "having hardly well men enough to tend the Sails and look after the Sick."

When mountaineering expeditions go bad, surviving climbers often believe that those dying beside them have made mistakes, as if to say, "It won't happen to me," or "It's not my fault." War correspondents resort to the same defense mechanism. Cook, struggling to make sense of his ship's epidemic death rate, cast blame on the "extravecancy and intemperance" of some of the deceased. Upon the death of the astronomer Green, on whose skills he had so often relied, Cook wrote that he "lived in such a manner as greatly promoted the disorders he had had long upon him, this brought on the Flux which put a period to his life."

In his despair, Cook's tone also became wallowing, as it had off the reef. He obviously feared not only for the health of his crew but also for his own reputation, doubtless regretting the letter he'd sent to the Admiralty from Batavia boasting of his crew's exceptional health. Reaching Cape Town, having lost twenty-four men since leaving Batavia eleven weeks before, Cook encountered several other ships that had lost even more men, in a shorter time, and observed: "Their sufferings will hardly if atall be mentioned or known in England when on the other hand those of the Endeavour, because the Voyage is uncommon, will very probable be mentioned in every News paper."

Cape Town proved a much healthier port than Batavia. Only a few men died between there and England, including two valued young officers: the ship's master, Robert Molyneux, and Lieutenant Zachary Hicks, who had first sighted the east coast of Australia. "He died of a Consumption which he was not free from when we sailed from England," Cook wrote of Hicks, "so that it may be truly said that he hath been dieing ever sence." Ultimately, thirty-eight of the Endeavour's original company of ninety-four failed to make it home (including the deserter, and a man who died as soon as the ship reached England). Eight others who had joined the ship in the course of the voyage also perished.

Still, this was better than many in London had anticipated. In late 1770, a fanciful dispatch appeared in an English gazette claiming that the Endeavour had sunk with all hands. Previous Pacific journeys had generally taken two years, and the Endeavour stayed away for almost three. "Wagers were held that we were lost," Cook learned from a passing vessel as he approached England. Cook, characteristically, resisted the urge to dramatize. A week later, on July 13, 1771, after more than a thousand days and forty thousand miles at sea, he wrote a one-line entry: "At 3 oClock in the PM Anchor'd in the Downs, & soon after I landed in order to repair to London." So ends the journal of one of the most extraordinary expeditions in history.

THE RESPONSE ONSHORE was rather more ecstatic, though it was Banks rather than Cook who garnered most of the public attention. The dashing young gentleman had lofty connections and an ego to match. Early press reports, based on anonymous letters from "ingenious gentlemen" who sailed on the *Endeavour*, failed even to mention Cook, dwelling instead on the triumphs of "the immortal Banks" and his assistants, who "have made more curious discoveries in the way of Astronomy, and Natural History, than at any one Time have been presented to the learned World."

Once in London, Cook busied himself writing dry dispatches to the Admiralty. Banks swanned around town: "frequently waiting on his Majesty," regaling aristocratic dinner parties with tales of his adventures, and paying £5,000 to extract himself from an engagement, made before the voyage, to a young woman named Harriet Blosset. He also displayed and distributed the many "curiosities" he'd gathered. The kangaroo skin Banks brought from the Endeavour River was inflated and stuffed to serve as a model for a famous oil painting by George Stubbs. The image proved so popular that it was reproduced in engravings and on Staffordshire drinking mugs. But several decades passed before naturalists agreed on how to classify the anomalous creature. One suggestion was that it be named for the *Endeavour*'s botanist: *Yerbua banksii gigantea*.

If Cook felt slighted by the hero's welcome accorded Banks, he left no record of it. Ever deferential and diplomatic toward his social betters, Cook modestly accepted his own share of laurels, including a captain's commission and an audience with the king (eleven days after Banks's first visit to the palace). Others aboard the *Endeavour* enjoyed modest fame, too—even the ship's goat, which had survived its second circumnavigation. Samuel Johnson composed a bit of Latin doggerel for the animal to wear on its silver collar. The verse translates as "The globe twice encircled, this the Goat, the second to the nurse of Jove, is thus rewarded for her never-failing milk." The hardy goat was also given the privileges of a naval pensioner at the Greenwich Hospital and retired to a field near London, where she perished a month after Johnson bestowed his poetry on her.

Cook, meanwhile, returned to his home in Mile End, a middle-class neighborhood at London's eastern edge where he'd moved a few years after marrying Elizabeth Batts in December 1762. On their marriage license, Cook, then thirty-four, is listed as "Mariner and John Doe," while Elizabeth appears as a "Spinster" of twenty-one. She was the daughter of a pub owner at Execution Dock in Wapping, the waterside district that was the hub of London shipping. Not much is known of the Cooks' life together—in part because they had so little of it. Cook was almost constantly at sea from the time of their marriage, sailing on surveying trips to Newfoundland four times before setting off on the *Endeavour*.

During his brief pauses between sails, however, he'd fathered four children by Elizabeth, three of them born while he was at sea. Cook had listed his two young boys, James and Nathaniel, as a servant and a sailor aboard the *Endeavour*, though they were aged only five and four at the time. This was a sanctioned fiction that earned the boys several years' time toward taking an officer's exam, should they one day join the Navy.

The two other children had died while Cook was circling the globe: a four-year-old daughter and a three-week-old son, born a day after the ship's departure. Upon Cook's return, Elizabeth quickly became pregnant again and accompanied her husband on a long winter road trip to visit his family and friends in northern England. We know nothing else of Elizabeth during this time, except for a brief mention in a letter Cook wrote to a friend, apologizing that he was unable to visit Hull as planned: "Mrs Cook being but a bad traveler I was prevailed upon to lay that rout aside on account of the reported badness of the roads." The son Elizabeth was carrying arrived in July 1772, as Cook set off on his second voyage, and died just four months later.

Cook had begun mulling a return trip to the Pacific during the

Endeavour's long sail home and composed an addendum to his journal, which he submitted on his arrival in London. "I hope it will not be taken a Miss if I give as my opinion," he wrote, "the most feasible Method of making further discoveries in the South Seas." The fundamental question of the first voyage remained: Was there a southern continent? Cook had narrowed the continent's parameters (if it existed) and located bases in New Zealand and Tahiti from which to probe the southernmost latitudes. In winter, when it was too cold to search for *terra australis*, he could explore vast stretches of the Pacific that remained unknown or vaguely charted. "Thus the discoveries in the South Sea would be compleat," he wrote at the end of his postscript.

This bold scheme found a willing audience at the Admiralty. Within two months of Cook's landing in London, plans were under way for a return trip along the lines he'd laid out. There would be notable differences from the first voyage. Cook would reach the Pacific by sailing around Africa rather than South America, to take advantage of the westerly winds prevailing in high southern latitudes. He would also have a consort vessel, as defense against the near-stranding he'd endured off the Barrier Reef.

The Admiralty purchased two new colliers from Whitby "for service in remote parts." (The *Endeavour* was put out to pasture as a transport ship to the Falklands.) Cook became commander of the lead ship, the *Resolution* (at 462 tons, a quarter larger than the *Endeavour*), while a veteran of Samuel Wallis's Pacific voyage, Tobias Furneaux, took charge of the smaller *Adventure*. Seventeen men from the *Endeavour*, including Charles Clerke, promoted to second lieutenant, signed on for the second voyage. So did several urbane and well-connected young men, a testament to Cook's growing fame. "It would be quite a great feather in a young man's Cap," wrote a midshipman, John Elliott, "to go with Captn Cook, and it required much Intrest to get out with him."

Banks, meanwhile, had begun approaching some of the best scientific minds of the day, including the chemist Joseph Priestley, to accompany him on the *Resolution*. "O! How glorious to set my heel upon the Pole!" the botanist exclaimed in a letter to a French count. "And turn myself round three hundred and sixty degrees in a second." Banks also asked the Admiralty to modify the *Resolution* to accommodate an entourage of seventeen, including six servants and two horn players. Cook at first consented, even ceding Banks the captain's quarters. But refitting the *Resolution* to meet Banks's demands made the ship so "crank," or prone to capsize, that it flunked a trial sail. "By God I'll go to Sea in a Grog tub if desir'd," Charles Clerke wrote to Banks, "but must say, I do think her by far the most unsafe Ship, I ever saw or heard of."

When the *Resolution* returned to dock to have the renovations torn out, Banks "swore and stamp'd upon the Warfe, like a Mad Man," one midshipman wrote, "and instantly order'd his servants, and all his things out of the Ship." Banks's appeals to the Admiralty for a larger ship failed, and in a fit of pique he withdrew from the expedition, later taking his party (as well as a French cook) on a consolation voyage to Iceland. The *Resolution* was made right and readied for its departure.

Left stranded by Banks's withdrawal was a would-be passenger named Burnett, who had planned to board the *Resolution* in Madeira. Burnett claimed to be a botanist, one of Banks's retinue, but left Madeira just before the *Resolution*'s arrival, apparently having learned that Banks wasn't on board. Islanders who had met this mysterious person informed Cook that "every part of Mr. Burnetts behavior and every action tended to prove that he was a Woman." No more was ever heard of Banks's mistress.

The dispute over the *Resolution*'s refit temporarily strained the friendship between Banks and Cook, and deprived the captain—and history—of the botanist's supple intellect and social deftness, which had served Cook so well on his first voyage. Banks's last-second replacement on the *Resolution,* a prickly, Prussian-born naturalist named Johann Reinhold Forster, would prove an irritant to Cook and almost everyone else aboard. "He was an incubus," writes Beaglehole. "Dogmatic, humourless, suspicious, pretentious, contentious, censorious, demanding, rheumatic." On a more positive note, the proto-Marxist views of Forster and his son George, who accompanied him, provide an illuminating counterpoint to the journals of the mercantile English.

Cook also carried new cargo, including a carrot marmalade concocted by a Berliner named Baron von Storsch and believed to have value as an antiscorbutic. But the most significant freight for maritime history was a newfangled timepiece. As Dava Sobel relates in her book *Longitude,* an inventor named John Harrison had spent four decades perfecting a "clock machine" that promised to keep accurate time at sea, freeing sailors from the painstaking and often faulty astronomical calculations used to determine a ship's position. But the obstinacy and elitism of the scientific establishment had denied the inventor his due. In Cook, Harrison—like the captain, a Yorkshire-born man of humble background—finally found the fair, fine judge he deserved. Cook's later endorsement of Harrison's clocks (four copies of which the *Resolution* and *Adventure* carried) proved crucial to the invention's eventual adoption by the Royal Navy.

On July 13, 1772, a year to the day after Cook's return from his first voyage, he sailed from Plymouth again, making no more note of the occasion in his journal than to mention the direction of the wind.

Chapter 8

SAVAGE ISLAND:
The Hunt for Red Banana

The Pacific is a strange place.
—ROBERT LOUIS STEVENSON

Cook spent a year sailing home from the Great Barrier Reef, and another year preparing for his second voyage. It took me a day to travel from Cooktown to Sydney, and by the next I was plotting my onward journey.

The sandstone cottage where I worked had become an ersatz Admiralty office. A standing globe filled one corner, an atlas compressed my desk, antique charts carpeted the floor. The plywood bookshelf sagged beneath almanacs, nautical tomes, and the ballast weight of Beaglehole's blue-bound edition of Cook's journals. I hoisted Volume I, *Remarkable Occurences on Board His Majestys Bark Endeavour,* back onto the shelf, and brought down Volume II, *Journal on Board His Majesty's Bark Resolution.* Opening it, I paced from globe to atlas to chart, cross-checking Cook's coordinates like a pilot scanning instruments on the bridge of a ship.

Even so, I found myself completely fogged in as soon as I embarked on the *Resolution*'s voyage. Tracking the *Endeavour*'s route had proved relatively easy. The ship rarely strayed from its westerly course and lingered at only three Pacific ports: French Polynesia, New Zealand, Australia. The path of Cook's second voyage, by contrast,

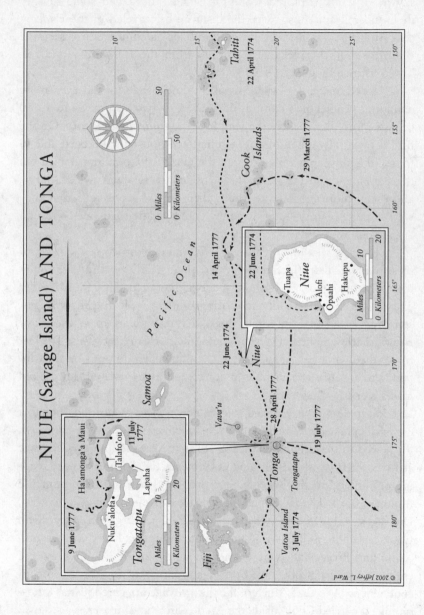

NIUE (Savage Island) AND TONGA

Pacific Ocean

Tahiti
22 April 1774

Cook Islands
29 March 1777

14 April 1777

22 June 1774

Niue
22 June 1774

Niue
Tuapa
Alofi
Opaahi
Hakupu

0 Miles 10 20
0 Kilometers

Samoa

Vava'u

28 April 1777

Tonga
Tongatapu
19 July 1777

Vatoa Island
3 July 1774

Fiji

Tongatapu
Ha'amonga'a Maui
Talafo'ou
11 July 1777
Lapaha
Nuku'alofa
9 June 1777

0 Miles 10 20
0 Kilometers

0 Miles 50
0 Kilometers 50

10°
15°
20°
25°
150°
155°
160°
165°
170°
175°
180°

© 2002 Jeffrey L. Ward

looped and backtracked across the map like the doodles of a drunken skywriter. Cook explored scores of islands and sailed some seventy thousand miles, almost twice the distance he traveled in the *Endeavour*. And that was just the *Resolution*; Cook's companion vessel, the *Adventure,* quickly became separated from the *Resolution* and followed its own tangled trail across the Pacific.

I glanced at the bookshelf; Cook's third voyage looked even more daunting. Beaglehole's edition of *that* ran to two volumes and 1,650 pages—more than double the length of the *Endeavour*'s story. On the first voyage, only a handful of men had kept journals; I'd been able to follow the journey mainly through the words of Cook and Banks. On the second and third voyages, the cast of characters was twice as large, and many more men wrote about their travels, conscious that they were making history—and that they could peddle their tales of South Sea adventure.

At the archives in downtown Sydney, I'd photocopied dozens of these manuscripts, which now formed an unsteady ziggurat in another corner of my office. Beaglehole spent the better part of four decades unearthing and sifting all the writings about Cook and his voyages: smudged letters, badly copied logs, dry dispatches from the Navy Board, diaries penned in German decades after Cook's travels. The historian died while revising Chapter 19 of his magnum opus on the captain. It was left to Beaglehole junior to complete and publish the old man's work.

I doubted my four-year-old son would do the same for me, though a quick calculation revealed that he'd be in college by the time I finished, if I hewed to my original plan: following the second and third voyage as I had the first, island-hopping in Cook's wake. Several days of reading put an end to this scheme. The problem wasn't just the immense distances Cook covered; it was also the bleak-sounding places he went. On the second voyage, when not dodging icebergs off Antarctica, Cook busied himself charting uninhabited outposts like Cape Circumcision and Freezeland. One of the old maps on my floor labeled the entire region that Cook sailed through while searching for a southern continent as "Frigida." Much of the third voyage appeared just as inhospitable; it carried Cook inside the Arctic Circle until frozen sea stopped him between Alaska's "Icy Cape" and the far northeast coast of Siberia.

Some people thrill to visions of pack ice and sled dogs. I'm not one of them. It wasn't just the polar climate that left me cold. I like adventures where I encounter people, not penguins. There seemed little chance of that in Antarctica, unless I hitched a ride on an icebreaker, or traveled to a science station in Frigida. Anyway, it was winter in the southern hemisphere. Even Cook acknowledged that this was "a Season by no means favourable for discoveries" in the southernmost latitudes.

Stuffing logs in the cottage's potbelly stove, I turned instead to the territory Cook traversed between his summertime probes of Antarctica. He spent many months repairing and resupplying the *Resolution* in New Zealand and Tahiti, or struggling to rendezvous with the *Adventure,* at one point even leaving a bottled message for the ship's captain, Tobias Furneaux, buried at the foot of a tree on which was carved "Look underneath." Furneaux found it but was too late to catch up with the *Resolution* at Cook's next proposed meeting point.

Cook also sailed across a vast swath of the South Pacific he hadn't toured on his first voyage, stretching from Easter Island to the New Hebrides, with dozens of isles and atolls between. Somewhere in this vastness, I decided, lay unknown territory for me to explore. I'd save the cold travel for Cook's third voyage, which at least brought the captain into contact with Aleuts and offered the added consolation—for me, at least—of ending in Hawaii.

As for Antarctica and the other places I skipped over, well, I would read everything I could about them. Settling in by the stove, I opened Volume II and rejoined Cook as he left Cape Town in November 1772 and dipped south in search, once again, of *terra australis.*

THE *RESOLUTION*'S FIRST southern sweep carried Cook and his men out of sight of land for 117 days. Clad in the thick woollen fabric called fearnought, and warmed by an extra shot of brandy at breakfast, the crew climbed "Rigging and Sails hung with Icikles," Cook wrote. Snow and sleet fell ceaselessly, men suffered from "froze bit," and in the fog the *Resolution* lost contact with the *Adventure.* Cook also maneuvered between enormous bergs, or "ice islands," some twice the height of the mainmast. To the naturalist George Forster, "The whole scene looked like the wrecks of a shattered world."

With little experience of sailing through ice, and charts that were more hindrance than help, Cook plunged on through the "pinching cold," becoming the first navigator to cross the Antarctic Circle. Pack ice finally forced him back, just seventy-five miles from the Antarctic continent. The only diversions during these chill four months were Christmas Day, celebrated with drunkenness and boxing, and the periodic amusement provided by penguins. The creatures' "very Whimsical appearance" put Lieutenant Richard Pickersgill in mind of soldiers on drill: "They Seemd to perform their Evolutions so well that they only wanted the use of Arms to cut a figure on Whimbleton Common."

Cook resumed his polar probe during the next southern summer, after wintering in Polynesia. The second approach to Antarctica proved even more wretched than the first. Livestock perished, tropical provisions ran out, and the men—eating little except weevil-ridden biscuits and salt rations—began to show signs of scurvy and depression.

"Salt Beef & pork, without vegetables for 14 weeks running, would probably cure a Glutton, even in England," wrote William Wales, the ship's astronomer. According to George Forster, even the resilient Cook became "pale and lean, entirely lost his appetite, and laboured under a perpetual costiveness [constipation]."

Undaunted, Cook pushed deep inside the Antarctic Circle, crossing the 71st Parallel before he stalled in pack ice. "We could not," he realized, "proceed one Inch farther South." Cook, once again, had narrowly missed his mark. Although he'd probed far enough south to sight land several times, he'd repeatedly done so at the wrong spots. Instead of hitting one of Antarctica's peninsulas, Cook kept sailing into the continent's recesses.

Cook's breaching of the 71st Parallel nonetheless marked an astonishing moment in the history of exploration. Sailing blind, in a lone wooden ship, Cook had added ten degrees of latitude to the map. Almost fifty years passed before another vessel so much as crossed the Antarctic Circle. In 1821, American sealers finally stepped ashore on one of the continent's peninsulas—7 degrees north of Cook's 71st Parallel. Of the *Resolution*'s path, Beaglehole observes: "No ship in or near that longitude would ever sail so far south again."

Yet Cook felt it necessary to apologize for turning back. He carefully described the prospect that lay before him at 71 degrees south: an "immence Ice field" rising to "Ninety Seven Ice Hills or Mountains." Lest anyone suppose he lacked fortitude, Cook added what would become the most famous line in his journals: "Ambition leads me not only farther than any other man has been before me, but as far as I think it possible for man to go."

Three weeks later, Cook collapsed. He doesn't reveal much about this in his journal, except to note that he was confined to his cot for a week because of a gastric affliction he called "Billious colick." George Forster makes it clear that the captain's condition was much graver than Cook suggests. The captain suffered from "violent pains" and "violent vomiting," Forster wrote. "His life was entirely despaired of."

The treatment given Cook—opiates, clysters (suppositories), plasters on his stomach, "purges" and emetics to induce vomiting—probably didn't help. When Cook finally recovered, his first meal in a week was the only fresh meat on the ship: the Forsters' dog. "Thus I received nourishment and strength from food which would have made most people in Europe sick," Cook wrote.

The captain's catholic tastes made him desperately ill again, six months later, when he and several others dined on a tropical fish "with a large ugly head" off the coast of New Caledonia. "We were siezed with an extraordinary weakness in all our limbs attended with a numness or Sensation like that caused by exposeing ones hands or feet to a fire after having been pinched much by frost," Cook later wrote. "Nor could I distinguish between light and heavy bodies, a quart pot full of Water and a feather was the same in my hand." After "each of us took a Vomet," he added, the men recovered, though a pig that dined on the fish died. Scholars have since concluded that Cook ate a poisonous toadfish filled with neurotoxins.

Soon after, as summer approached, Cook embarked on his third "Southern Cruse" in search of *terra australis,* completing his tour of the Pacific's highest latitudes and then sailing the entirety of the far south Atlantic. With stores running low, the men consumed sea lions and cubs, "sea bear" (a South Atlantic fur seal), albatross, and penguins, of which even Cook admitted, "I cannot say they are good eating." This diet also seems to have deranged his crewmen, three of whom were confined in irons after "going into the Galley with drawn knives and threatening to stab the Cook."

By the late southern summer of 1775, even the captain had reached the limit of his endurance. "I was now tired of these high Southern Latitudes," Cook confessed, on a day so foggy that "we could not see a Ships length." With his provisions so meager that they were "just enough to keep life and Soul together," Cook finally turned north and headed home, having covered twenty thousand leagues, or three times the circumference of the globe—"a distance I will be bold to say, was never sailed by any Ship in the same space of time before."

Cook devoted the final line of his journal to another point of pride: "Been absent from England Three Years and Eighteen Days," he wrote on July 29, 1775, when the *Resolution* reached Plymouth, "in which time I lost but four men and one only of them by sickness." (The ill man had tuberculosis; two others drowned and one suffered a fatal fall down a hatchway.) By contrast, the *Adventure,* which carried forty fewer men and returned home a year ahead of the *Resolution,* lost thirteen out of eighty-three crew (including ten killed and eaten by Maori). At one point, a third of Furneaux's passengers suffered from scurvy. A paper that Cook wrote soon after his return to London, about the measures he took to keep seamen healthy, earned him the Royal Society's highest prize, the Copley Medal, an honor bestowed in other years on luminaries such as Benjamin Franklin and Albert Einstein.

While Cook had failed to find the fabled southern continent, his circling of the globe, near its southernmost latitude, demolished forever the fantasy that a land of plenty girdled the bottom of the world. If a southern continent existed, Cook wrote, with his usual acuity, it was "a Country doomed by Nature never once to feel the warmth of the Suns rays, but to lie for ever buried under everlasting snow and ice."

SYDNEY IN WINTER was a joke by comparison, about as rugged as Los Angeles in January. The only thing that made it uncomfortable was that houses were drafty and uninsulated, designed for Australia's long summers rather than the fleeting cool months. Still, reading Cook's account of his Antarctic probes was the literary equivalent of chewing on ice cubes. So it came as a relief when I turned to his writings about the Pacific islands he visited between his frigid southern sweeps.

I'd always wanted to see Easter Island, having marveled as a child at one of its astonishing stone figures in the Smithsonian Museum. But Cook was so sick during his brief stay at Easter Island that he barely went ashore, leaving it to his men to measure "those Colossean Statues" and to wonder how they'd been erected. Cook also made the island sound almost as bleak as the Antarctic seas he'd just departed. "No Nation will ever contend for the honour of the discovery of Easter Island as there is hardly an Island in this sea which affords less refreshments and conveniences."

Idly tracing the *Resolution*'s path westward across the Pacific on an old chart, my finger brushed against a flyspeck labeled "Savage Island." I checked the index of Cook's journal. A brief entry from June 1774 explained the atoll's intriguing name. When the English attempted to land, islanders burst from dense woods "with the ferocity of wild Boars," Cook wrote, hurling rocks and spears. Cook and his men fired at their attackers, "stout well made men and naked except their Natural parts." A footnote said that the warriors' mouths were smeared red, as if with blood. "Seeing no good was to be got of these people," Cook wrote, he withdrew to the boats, gave the island its unflattering name, and sailed off.

I consulted my atlas. No mention of Savage Island. Nothing on my globe, either. Beaglehole, as so often, came to my rescue. He identified the island as present-day Niue. An almanac on my shelf described Niue as "the world's smallest self-governing state." A country I'd never heard of!

Then again, a lot of Pacific islets hadn't crossed my radar before I'd begun tracking Cook's voyages. I rang Roger on his cell phone. He was on a business trip, peddling books to librarians in Canberra, a much colder city than Sydney. "I'm driving through a bloody snowstorm," he said.

"Have you ever heard of Niue?"

"What?"

"Knee-ooo," I repeated, guessing at the pronunciation. "N-I-U-E."

"Is that a disease? In Africa? Or is it something *I've* got?"

"It's a country. Cook went there. He called it Savage Island. The natives had red teeth."

"Is it warm?" Roger asked.

"Must be. It's in the middle of the South Pacific."

"Let's go, then. Right now. I'm freezing here." The line crackled and dropped out.

The notion of just setting off appealed to me. Following in the *Endeavour*'s wake had filled me with a certain wistfulness. I'd gone where Cook went, but I couldn't share his experience. The problem wasn't simply that I traveled by jet, rather than by wooden ship, to lands that had changed utterly since Cook's day. It was also that I carried an image of every place I went before I got there. This was the curse of modern travel: it was like reading a book after you've already seen the movie adaptation.

Niue seemed different. All I knew was its name and vague coordinates, plus the few paragraphs I'd scanned in Cook's journal. I decided to keep it that way. Traveling virtually blind to a land I hadn't known existed, and whose name I couldn't even pronounce, seemed as close as I could get to the freshness of discovery I so envied in Cook's voyages.

Still, I had to get there. I called a travel agent. She hadn't heard of Niue, couldn't even find it in her computer. I rang Qantas, Air New Zealand, Polynesian Airlines. No Niue. But a saleswoman suggested I try Royal Tongan.

"You mean NEW-ay," a reservation agent said, correcting my pronunciation. Royal Tongan Airlines flew there once a week, from New Zealand. "But we don't fly back," she said.

"You mean I'm there forever?"

"Not exactly. If you stay a week, there's a flight from Niue to Tonga. You can come back from there."

That was fine. I wanted to see Tonga, too. Cook spent several months touring Tonga's many islands and liked the place so much he named it the Friendly Archipelago. Still, a week in Niue sounded like a lot. Given the paucity of flights, there probably wasn't much to do on the island, perhaps not even a place to stay. I called Roger again to make sure he wanted to blow off his job for a few weeks to see both Tonga and Niue. He was staring out his hotel window at the swimming pool.

"It looks like an iceberg," he said, "or an 'ice island,' as Cook would call it. Count me in."

"What will we do in Niue for a week?"

"Drink."

"What if there's no booze?"

"We'll chew betel nuts. That's probably what turned their teeth red. Either that or they were cannibals." He laughed. "Maybe they still are. There's probably not much food. We'll be scratching around in the sand and drinking from coconuts." We made a pact to learn nothing more about Niue, and booked tickets on the next available flight.

IT WAS ODDLY relaxing to set off on a trip for which you couldn't prepare. What *do* you take to a desert island? Cook carried nails and beads; I packed lots of cash, in several different currencies. During our stopover at the Auckland airport, Roger added bottles of gin, rum, and chardonnay. "That's a fraction of what Cook carried," he said defensively. "He had barrels of Madeira, and we're not taking a drop of that." Then, at the departure gate, Roger spied a man toting aboard a case of lager. "Oh no, maybe they don't sell beer in Niue."

I was struck by something else: the size of our fellow passengers. Some were so big they could barely squeeze down the aisle of the small jet. The man seated next to me oozed over the armrest and almost into my lap before falling asleep.

Midway through the flight, a steward handed out customs forms for Niue. The list of prohibited goods included "handguns, flick knives, swordsticks, etc." *Swordsticks?* Also banned were "indecent goods," such as adult videotapes and magazines. Roger groaned. "You can be sure they'll be mad Christians, every crackpot cult." Making matters worse, our flight left early on a Monday morning and crossed the international dateline. "So we'll have to do Sunday all over again," Roger said. "Our Sunday and their Sunday. Not my favorite day and I get two on the trot."

For hours we saw nothing out the window except cloud and ocean. Then, as the plane descended, I spotted a fleck of green floating on the water like a strand of seaweed. "Ladies and gentlemen," the pilot announced, "we are approaching Niue International Airport." We touched down on a narrow strip cut into the jungly foliage and taxied to an open-air terminal the size of a golf clubhouse. If the airport's name seemed grandiose, Niue's immigration form was even odder; it asked what plane we'd arrived on. There was only one flight: ours. If you didn't take it, you had to come by cargo ship.

We stepped from the terminal into a blazing tropical afternoon. Several hundred people in brightly colored dresses and shirts stood holding umbrellas against the sun. Their copper-colored faces were wide and handsome, a shade darker and more Asiatic than those of Tahitians or Maori. A few people came up to greet arriving passengers, but most simply watched until everyone had disembarked, then wandered off.

"Are you going to the hotel?" a young man asked us in English.

"Hotel? Sure. That sounds great." He tossed our bags in the back of a pickup. I asked him about the crowd. "It is plane day," he said. "People want to see who is coming. There is not much else to do on Sunday, except church."

We drove through low, thick scrub and arrived at a modest building fringed with palms. At the reception desk, a woman handed us coconuts with straws and led us to a motel-style room. There was a TV, phone, and fridge. Outside lay a kidney-shaped swimming pool. I felt vaguely disappointed. Not Roger. "Told you we'd be drinking from coconuts," he said, splashing a bit of rum into his. "Beats the hell out of Canberra."

"What now?"

"We'll wait for sunset," Roger said. "We can watch the last of this day in the entire world—the end of yesterday. We've already seen the first of tomorrow. We'll have seen the future and the past in one day. We'll be time travelers."

I struggled to unravel this. The international dateline, like longitude and the transit of Venus, still bewildered me. Bells tolled in the distance. "Let's go to church," I said.

Roger laughed. "Pray for me," he said, slumping into a deck chair.

I walked up the road to a small church marked "London Missionary Society." Inside, fifty or so people sat in pews and chairs, wearing stiff straw hats and cooling themselves with leaf fans. Most of the children were barefoot. At an unadorned altar, the minister droned in a language unfamiliar to me, apart from the word "Amen." It began to rain, a heavy tropical downpour; then the sun reemerged and the palm trees through the open window looked washed and electric green against the cobalt sky. I couldn't see the nearby ocean, but the surf thundered so loudly that the minister had to raise his voice. Polynesian Christianity seemed incongruous this way: the austere creed of starched English missionaries, transplanted, like some moorland thistle, to the extravagant tropics.

Returning to the hotel, I asked the woman at the desk where I might go for a swim in the ocean. She said swimming was forbidden on Sunday, and fishing, too. I told her I'd just visited the church. "Oh," she said, smiling. "There's another service this evening. Wednesdays, too."

Roger sat where I'd left him, working on his second coconut. "Lest you think I've been bone idle," he said, "I've arranged for us to rent a car." A few minutes later, an elderly New Zealander named Mary picked us up and drove to a lot strewn with old Japanese sedans. She handed me the keys to one, and said to return the car when we left the island.

"Don't you want money?" I asked. "A driver's license?"

She shrugged. "You can pay when you come back. It's not as if you can run off anywhere." As for the license, we were required to pick up a Niue permit at the police station, which was closed on Sundays. We could drive without a license until the station opened, she cheerfully explained.

I asked Mary how she'd ended up in Niue. "My husband saw an ad in a New Zealand newspaper five years ago. 'Own Your Own Business in Paradise.'" The car rental agency came with a yacht club, though there were no yachts on Niue. "I'd put it in the category of 'sounded good at the time,'" she said.

Mary gave us a map and warned against inland roads, which she described as rutted tracks strewn with rocks. That left little to explore, except for a coastal road circling the island. Niue was only seventeen miles long and eleven miles wide. "It'll take you about two hours if you drive very, very slowly," Mary said.

On the way back to the hotel we passed church traffic, the drivers smiling and waving at us as they went by. Savage Island was beginning to seem like a disarmingly safe and pleasant place. We watched the sunset from the hotel deck with the few other guests, mostly delegates from the New Zealand government. They explained that New Zealand had inherited Niue from the British empire a century ago: hence the

English spoken by most islanders. While Niue had been self-governing since 1974, New Zealand still looked after the island's external affairs and provided a great deal of financial aid. Also, thirteen thousand Niueans worked in New Zealand, almost ten times as many as still lived on the island.

"There's no real economy here," one of the diplomats said. Some Niueans eked out a subsistence from fishing and farming, but 90 percent of employable adults worked for the heavily subsidized public sector. Islanders' attempts at diversifying their economy had led down "some very crook paths," he added. I pressed him for details. "Just drive around the island," he said, diplomatically, "and keep your eyes open. You'll see."

IN THE MORNING we paid two New Zealand dollars for our drivers' licenses: stamp-sized slips of paper with "Niue" misspelled. The police station and its seven-cell jail stood in Alofi, the island's main settlement, which was anchored at one end by the corrugated-roof headquarters of the London Missionary Society. A meeting was going on inside, but when we peered in the door, two men came out to chat. "Greetings in the name of Jesus Christ," said a young pastor in a well-starched white shirt. He introduced himself as Matagi. The other man, Hafe, was his grandfather and also a minister. "May we help you?" he asked.

I told him about our travels and asked if Cook's brief visit to the island was remembered today. "Oh yes," Matagi said. "Traditionally, our foes came from the sea. So anyone landing here was seen as an enemy. Cook's men fired at our people, we retaliated with rocks and spears, and Cook ran away." He said the musket fire reminded the Niueans of thunder, so they called the sailors *palagi*, or sky burst, and still used the term today when speaking of foreigners. (The same word appears, in different form, across Polynesia; some scholars believe it refers not to gunfire, but to the belief that the strange ships had "burst from the sky.")

"What about the red teeth?" I asked. Matagi looked at his shoes. His grandfather lit a Rothmans. "You must understand, we are not cannibals," Hafe said. "People wanted to defend their property, that is all. We had a tradition: when enemies came we did a war dance like the Maori. Warriors painted their lips and teeth with the juice of the *hulahula*, the red banana, to frighten people off."

"Does anyone still call this Savage Island?"

Hafe's face reddened. "Cook called Tonga the Friendly Isles, probably because he had so many girls there. Tahiti he called the Society Islands, same reason. The Cook Islands were named after him. Nice names. But because we throw a few stones and spears, we're savages." He stubbed out his cigarette. "No one likes Cook much in Niue." The two men returned inside.

"Good one, mate," Roger said. "You with your crass, bull-nosing American technique, exposing a raw nerve and then poking at it."

"But we learned something. Cook got scared off by red bananas!"

"Too bad. I was looking forward to chewing betel nut. The rare vice I've never tried."

Roger headed off in search of cigarettes while I toured a cluster of buildings at the center of Alofi. The post office had a philatelic annex for collectors; Niue, like other tiny states, trafficked profitably in stamps. A small grocery had a notice in the window that said: "For Sale $200, 1 Female Pig Half Niuean Half Palagi." A few doors down I found an office displaying a Panamanian flag. Curious, I poked my head inside and was greeted by a lithe, sharply dressed woman who wouldn't have looked out of place at a Manhattan law firm.

"Are you interested in registering a company?" she asked. Caught off guard, I smiled noncommittally. She handed me a folder detailing Niue's banking and corporate laws. Offshore firms weren't required to pay tax or file financial statements and they enjoyed "complete business privacy and confidentiality." It cost only $385 U.S. a year to register a company in Niue. "Much cheaper than in the Caymans or Bahamas," the woman said. When I asked about the flag in the window, she said the office belonged to a Panamanian law firm, hired by the government to handle offshore licenses.

The relationship appeared cozy: the law firm shared space with the office of Niue's attorney general. But if tax evasion was encouraged in Niue—at least for foreigners—other transgressions were not. A sign in the attorney general's office listed fines for "Scandalous Conduct," including "profane, indecent, or obscene language," adultery, and "persons of the opposite sex who, without being married to each other, live together as husband and wife to the annoyance of the public."

The next office along the mall was also intriguing: Niue Telecom. I was greeted by a handsome young manager named Richard Hipa, who regaled me with fun facts: Niue had the world's smallest phone company but the highest "penetration" on the globe, with almost every one of the island's eight hundred households hooked up. Niue also had thousands of excess lines. It leased this surplus to Asia Pacific Telecom, which used the lines for the sort of 900 calls advertised in tabloid magazines and on late-night television. Niue Telecom was now the island's largest generator of revenue.

There was one hitch. Most of the 900 numbers switching through Niue Telecom's tiny office were used for sex-chat services. If a caller misdialed, he often reached a Niuean instead of his intended partner at a foreign phone bank. "People here began getting heavy-breathing calls in the middle of the night from someone wanting to speak to Wanda," Richard said. This didn't go over well in Christian Niue. "I was labeled 'Mr. Sex' and had to go to meetings in every village to apologize and explain."

The scandal eventually blew over. Locals were mollified when they realized their government salaries were subsidized by the phone scheme. "It's other people's morals, not ours, that are being corrupted by these calls," Richard said.

Entrepreneurs on the island had also peddled Niue's Internet domain, .nu, which appealed to adult-site purveyors in French-speaking countries, where *nu* means naked. The ISP for Niue was sin.net.nu, a double entendre, as "sin" was short for "Savage Island Network." "It's unique, it's catchy," Richard said. "We don't have many assets, so why not use the few we've got?" He smiled. "Of course, not everyone here likes us using that name."

I found Roger smoking beside a clump of graves by the water. He listened patiently while I burbled about the sex lines and offshore licenses. Then he smiled and said, "Now let me tell you what *I* saw." Meandering down the road, he'd noticed a sign saying BAR OPEN, and beside it a sign for Lord Liverpool University George Washington School of Medicine.

"I've always wanted to visit a medical school with a bar attached,"

Roger said. Inside, he found a Canadian in hospital scrubs, and learned that the bar belonged to a defunct hotel that had been turned into a medical school for foreign students. Except there were no foreign students, almost no medical equipment, and no staff apart from the Canadian and two other men. "It was fabulously silly," Roger said. "If that's a genuine medical school, then I'm Albert Schweitzer."

We climbed in the car and drove slowly along the coastal road. The dense growth on either side made it hard to see much apart from graves set at regular intervals, like mileage markers. Most of the graves were well-tended and extravagantly decorated with shell necklaces or other baubles. One stone had a walking stick perched beside it, another a motorcycle.

Reaching the top of the island, we spotted several New Zealanders we recognized from our hotel. They were studying a monument to the first missionaries on the island, Niuean men named Toimata and Peniamina who had been taken aboard a missionary ship to Samoa, converted to Christianity, and returned to their native island in 1846. Toimata, the first ashore, "was greeted with a painful reception," the monument said. "His body was seriously bruised from the beating." Eventually, he persuaded islanders to allow Peniamina ashore "to teach the good news of the Kingdom of God." The memorial's praise of Toimata concluded: "Your courageous effort made Penis landing possible. Thank you. Thank you, Toimata, your name shall always be remembered."

As we puzzled over "Penis," the New Zealanders' guide, a Niuean named Misa, explained that Peniamina had been known as Peni for short. The inscription should therefore have read "Peni's landing," but someone had left out the apostrophe.

I asked Misa about Cook and the red banana. "The *hulahula*? It is like a red Popsicle in what it does to your face when you eat it," he said. "Very colorful, as if you've eaten a human being. Cook saw this, and the warriors' fierce faces and long hair and beards, and assumed we were savages." Misa said the traditional Niuean word for "savage" was the same as that for "cannibal," making Cook's name for the island particularly offensive.

I asked Misa where we could find a *hulahula*. "Not many people grow it anymore," he replied, before driving off with the others.

BACK AT THE hotel, we joined other guests for an evening of food and entertainment hosted by the villagers of Hakupu, the second-largest settlement on the island. The fête began with a tour by a schoolteacher named Tiva. At the village green, she showed us a wooden drum, thumped with a log to summon villagers for public occasions. Until recently, it had also been used to announce the arrival of mail. Now, letters were delivered to boxes before each house. Television was another new service, though programming was limited to evening hours and a small menu of news and taped shows from New Zealand and the United States.

The homes themselves were mostly low-slung concrete "hurricane houses," built after a 1959 cyclone; before, many houses were traditional structures of limestone and thatch. Most of the hurricane houses now stood empty. Their occupants had left for New Zealand, Tiva said, where Niueans usually found blue-collar jobs. Since the opening of the island's airport in 1977, the population had fallen by two-thirds, forcing sports teams to fold and schools to consolidate.

"We hope that some of you will enjoy your stay so much that you'll want to settle here and raise a family," Tiva concluded. In its attempts to repopulate, Niue had begun taking refugees from Tuvalu, an atoll cluster to the north that was threatened by rising sea levels.

Tiva led us to Hakupu's closed schoolhouse, which now served as a community hall. Inside, we found large women laying out our dinner, which they'd steamed on hot rocks in an underground oven, called an *umu*. The meal was vast, even by Polynesian standards. At the center of the buffet sat a suckling pig, its sharp teeth exposed in a posthumous snarl. Around the pig lay dozens of dishes mummified in foil and banana leaf. Tiva unwrapped each in turn and identified the contents: coconut crab, tapioca-root bread, a shellfish called cat's eye, bird's-nest fern, yams, whole wahoo, raw fish, and taro cooked every which way (with coconut, spinach, banana, butter, pawpaw). "Usually we have pigeon, too, and bat," Tiva said. "I'm so sorry, not tonight. I hope there's enough for everyone."

Roger reached for a piece of taro and had just taken a bite when the women joined hands and began saying grace. "Oh God," he muttered, compounding his sin. The moment the prayer ended, our hosts dug in with their hands, eating much of the food while still in line. We followed their example as best we could.

"It's impossible to eat this with any decorum," Roger said, paws filled with fish. I tried to sample every dish, but quickly lost track of which was which. At the end of the table lay several types of banana. I asked Tiva if any of them was a *hulahula*. She blushed and shook her head. "Oh no, we wouldn't serve that. Anyway, you don't find it anymore."

The women pushed aside the tables and began strumming guitars and ukuleles. Young girls in coconut-leaf skirts swayed their hips, making feathery motions with their upraised fingers. It was Tahiti without the bump and grind, or the glazed-eyed boredom of professional dancers. The women and kids were obviously enjoying themselves, and so were we. "Now," Tiva said, when the music ended, "who needs more food?"

After the show, the women showed us baskets they'd woven from coconut and pandanus leaves, intricate and boldly colored, the most beautiful craftwork I'd seen in the Pacific. The children formed a circle so we could shake their hands before leaving. For one evening, at least, I felt as though we'd glimpsed a bit of Polynesia not yet ravaged by mass tourism.

Even Roger let go of his customary cynicism. "It's wonderfully innocent here—none of the deep corruption of Tahiti," he said, as we drove back to the hotel, past kids playing soccer in the twilight. We stopped to watch girls hunting coconut crabs with flashlights. They deftly grabbed the skittering, bluish-black crustaceans behind the creatures' heads and tossed them into burlap bags. Then they offered several crabs to us. Roger waved his hand as if warding off demons. "If I eat one more of those I'll grow claws."

I WOKE THE next morning from a disturbing dream in which I'd killed Beaglehole with a cannonball. My stomach was churning, and so was Roger's. "I feel like I've smoked bad dope," he said. "The food here doesn't just make you fat, it makes you mad."

He flopped on his side and lit a cigarette. "Maybe they're poisoning us so we won't find a *hulahula*." He puffed meditatively. "I've been thinking about it. There's a conspiracy here to hide the red banana because of people's shame over the name Savage Island. Everyone says they used to have these red bananas, but not anymore. Very suspicious."

"You're paranoid."

"No I'm not. We've gone straight to their greatest national sensitivity in a blunt, brutal way—as usual. We're reminding these pious people of their violent past and their attacks on innocent people." He paused. "If you don't write about it, I will. *The Hunt for Red Banana: A Fruit Thriller.* Tom Clancy fans will love it. You could have a terrorist cell called the Red Banana Faction."

Rain pelted down outside. A bad day for banana fishing. Roger lolled in bed reading Beaglehole. "We've got six more days here and we've already seen most of the island," he said when I tried to dislodge him. "Our productivity is way too high. We have to stop this manic dashing around."

I drove without him to Alofi, searching for some indoor distraction. A sign caught my eye: "Niue National Library and Archives." This led me to a one-room building with dusty, half-empty shelves. I read everything on Niue, which amounted to a few slim books and monographs. Among other things, I learned that the island was basically one big volcanic rock with a bit of vegetation pasted on top. It had no beaches and no harbors; waves crashed right into the high cliffs circling the entire island. Niue had originally been populated by voyagers from Samoa and Tonga, and its name meant "Behold the Coconut," apparently an expression of relief by early settlers upon finding something to eat on the inhospitable islet.

I also learned that Niue had always been more egalitarian than other Polynesian societies. Islanders eschewed hereditary kings and chiefs, elevating leaders on the basis of merit—and deposing or killing them when famine, drought, or other disaster struck. Niueans' fierce defense of their shore was due, in part, to a fear of imported diseases, which had ravaged the island at several points in its history. This dread of epidemic may have explained the hostile reception accorded Cook.

The captain's unfavorable report on the island deterred other visitors; in the half century after Cook, while missionaries, traders, and whalers swept across the Pacific, Westerners steered clear of Savage Island. When passing ships did anchor offshore, Niueans sent men aboard, one book said, "with their faces blackened, their bodies smeared with ash, their hair tangled and matted, shouting, and gesticulating wildly. This strategy brought about the speedy departure of many ships." Fear of disease wasn't the only source of native enmity. Nineteenth-century visitors included slavers, or "blackbirders," who kidnapped Niueans to labor in guano mines on other islands.

At a small museum across from the library, I learned of another sad chapter in the history of Niuean/Palagi contact. In October 1915, without prior warning, a New Zealand transport steamed into Niue and carried off 150 men for service in World War I. The recruitment was more political than practical: an effort to bolster morale by demonstrating to white New Zealanders that even their "dusky" brethren (including Maori and Cook Islanders) were doing their bit for king and empire.

During their training in New Zealand, however, many Niueans quickly fell sick. "It has been found that they are very susceptible to cold," an official confided in a cipher telegram to his superiors in Britain. "Should they be found unsuitable for the climactic conditions of Europe it is suggested that their services be utilized in Egypt or Aden."

This warning was ignored. By the time the Niueans reached France in April 1916, their ranks had dwindled by a third. Within weeks, almost the entire unit fell ill with pneumonia, trench foot, and other ailments. One died in combat, several more from disease, and the survivors were evacuated to a hospital in England. More died there, and during the long ride back to the South Pacific.

"They return to their homes proud no doubt of the valuable service they have rendered in assisting to consolidate the Empire," read an official letter of appreciation sent by New Zealand to the people of Niue. It was accompanied by engravings of the king, the queen, and Lord Kitchener for display in island schoolrooms. Not until long after the war did a New Zealand official acknowledge: "There is a sadness of lonely Niuean graves in countries the names of which were hardly known hitherto to the Natives."

When I asked a woman at the museum about Niue's history since World War I, she recommended I visit an elderly doctor who lived nearby. I found Harry Nemaia, a slim barefoot man, on the back porch of his home, fixing a fishing rod. His wife sat weaving a stiff black-and-white "church hat" of coconut leaf. "No plan," she said, when I asked her about the beautiful design. "Just did it." As soon as she was finished, she started sewing.

I commented to the doctor that Niueans struck me as unusually versatile and industrious people. He smiled and said, "We have to be. There are so few of us here that everyone must do several jobs." His career bore this out. Though trained as a dentist, he'd served for many years as the only doctor in Niue: setting fractures, performing appendectomies, delivering babies by kerosene light. "I wasn't very expert at any one thing," he said, "but I could get by at everything." He was even called on to treat mental illness. "I had no training for this, so I relied on common sense."

Harry had made his rounds twice a week, circling the island on bicycle and later by truck. The sick in each village would gather in one building, or, if they were too ill to leave home, put a red flag in the window. Conditions were much better today; Niue had a small, well-equipped hospital, and planes flew in from New Zealand to evacuate emergency cases. Many once-fatal conditions could now be treated safely.

But Harry feared that Niue itself was a dying community. "In New Zealand, the money is big, people get used to the bright lights, the sports, the pubs. It is difficult for them to come home." In the "old days," meaning before about 1960, life on the island had been simpler but more secure. "If you had no money you didn't care. There was coconut and fish to live from, you had a house and some land."

Niueans also had a long tradition of rugged self-reliance. This individualism explained, among other things, the roadside graves I'd seen all over the island. Most people buried family members on their own land rather than in cemeteries, and they personalized the graves with possessions of the dead (including, in the case of some deceased women, their sewing machines).

Christianity was the one powerful communal force on Niue. In

Harry's childhood, the church was so strict that food couldn't be cooked on Sundays (it was prepared before dawn and then reheated). People apprehended making "bush beer" were jailed for six months, and sexual "crimes" were also harshly punished. Even today, Niueans rarely displayed affection in public; husbands and wives didn't so much as hold hands.

"We are restrained people, except when eating," he said. As a doctor, Harry didn't approve of islanders' fondness for feasts like the one Roger and I had attended the night before. "When I was young, we walked or biked to the fields and labored from dawn to dusk. People don't live like that now, but they still eat as if they do. No wonder so many are fat."

One starch, however, had disappeared from islanders' diet: the red banana. "*Hulahula* is not a good eating banana," he explained. There was also its connection to Cook. Harry brought a doctor's perspective to stories about the English landing. While red teeth may have scared the English, Niueans had probably found the foreigners just as frightening. "They must have looked very abnormal to our people. Perhaps their pale skin made us think they were sick and would bring disease."

Harry glanced at his watch. Though he was seventy-eight, he still performed eye checks at his home and had several patients to see. He did this on a voluntary basis, as a service to the community, and to himself. Niueans liked to stay useful and self-reliant, even in old age.

"Going fishing later?" I asked, pointing at the rod he'd been working on.

The doctor shook his head. "I used to go very often," he said. "But no longer. I cannot carry my own canoe anymore."

WHILE I'D BEEN out, Roger had done some research of his own. "I found out there's a Palagi joint on the island that serves Australian beer," he said. "I need a break from rum and coconut."

We discovered the Wicked Wahoo Bar at the far end of the island. It was a pleasant open-air establishment overlooking the sea. A half-dozen patrons perched on stools with their backs to the water, facing a bar fridge adorned with bumper stickers: "You're Ugly and Your

Mother Dresses You Funny" and "The Problem with Political Jokes Is They Get Elected."

I ordered a glass of wine. "Château de Cardboard all right?" the bartender asked, reaching for a cask. The man beside me started telling jokes about his hometown in outback Australia. "The local prostitute is still a virgin," he said. "That's how small and poor it is." The others smiled wearily and stared into their beers. The place had the stale, disaffected air of expat bars the world over.

Then I noticed a periodical on the counter headlined *Niue Economic Review*. Given what we'd seen of the island's economy, I assumed this was another feeble bar joke. Flipping through it, though, I found lengthy, well-written stories about the latest doings on "the Rock," as Niue's handful of expats called the coral island.

"Where can I find Stafford Guest?" I asked, reading the editor's name from the back of the review. The others laughed. "You're looking at him," said the balding, mustachioed barman. Stafford turned out to be a journalist from New Zealand who had married a Niuean and lived here for decades, running the bar and an adjoining guest house as well as publishing his journal.

He deposited two years of back issues on the bar. They were filled with muckraking stories on astonishing scams. A small airline had secured a loan from the Niue government and vanished without ever providing service to the island. A man wanted for fraud in three countries had convinced the government to give him land for a fanciful "Cyber-City" on the island, which was never built.

There were also stories on the curious enterprises we'd glimpsed in Alofi. The offshore company registry had earned Niue a place on regulatory blacklists, as one of fifteen countries accused of international money laundering. The grandiosely named Lord Liverpool University George Washington School of Medicine didn't actually qualify anyone to practice medicine. The Canadian Roger had met at the bar was the school's dean of medicine; though he was a chiropractor, not an M.D., he wore surgical scrubs to impress government ministers, who had showered the school with subsidies.

"You have these carpetbaggers flying all over the Pacific peddling get-rich-quick schemes," Stafford explained. "They come with a smile and a tie and an alligator briefcase and the government gives them everything—laws, land, loans. If these con men don't succeed at one island, they just fly on to the next."

Given all this, I was curious why Stafford chose to stay in Niue. It couldn't be easy to live in such a small place while exposing his neighbors' dubious dealings. But Stafford said he'd lived on other Pacific islands and disliked their pervasive emphasis on clan and hierarchy. "Here, the attitude is, 'I come first, my family second, my village third, Niue last.' People say, 'Don't tell me what to do, I'm free to do what I want.'"

Niue had another advantage: its laws were modeled on New Zealand's, making it comparatively open and democratic, with a Westminster-style parliament and elections by secret ballot. "On a lot of islands they'd have shot me by now." He laughed, gathering up the pile of reviews. "Anyway, where else in the world would I find so much weirdness to write about?"

STAFFORD STIRRED MY journalistic juices. I resolved to crack the red-banana story before leaving the island. If nothing else, this mission would give Roger and me something to do other than going to church or expiring at the Wicked Wahoo Bar. So the next day we headed off to tour Niue again, searching the roadside foliage for red bananas.

It's hard to find a plant you've never seen. Nor were there many people to guide us, only the occasional rooster or dog or coconut crab skittering across the road. "Another ribbon of tar, another coconut tree," Roger said, as we completed our second circumnavigation of the island. The only breaks in the monotony were the ubiquitous graves, many of them curiously inscribed; one memorialized a woman "who fell on sleep May 30th 1917."

Then, as we were preparing to retreat to the hotel, we passed a small house with a sign in the yard:

NIUE CONSULTING AGENCY

GENERAL CONSULTING SERVICE

LAND MATTERS

SHELL COLLECTION

Even by Niuean standards, this seemed strange. We knocked on the door and were met by a madly barking dog and a small, muscular man in shorts and a cut-off T-shirt. "Sorry about Sweetie," he said, holding back the hound. "He loves Palagi blood." The man thrust out his hand. "Herman Tagaloailuga. How can I help you?"

"We were curious about your sign," I said. "What exactly do you do?"

"I'm private sector. Accountant. Economist. Legal consultant. Also a conchologist."

"A what?"

"Conchologist. Student of shells." He wrestled Sweetie aside and welcomed us into a small living room with a bare bulb dangling from the ceiling. At one end stood a low table covered with legal papers and tomes titled *Niue Fish Protection* and *Concise Law Dictionary*. Against another wall perched a shelf filled with books such as *Mollusca* and *Cowrie Shells of the Pacific*. Tourist pamphlets lay scattered on a side table. "I am also in the travel trade," Herman said, handing us a brochure.

I asked if we could see his shell collection. "Museum," he corrected me. "Five dollars each."

Roger handed him ten New Zealand dollars. I expected to be shown into another room. Instead, Herman went to his law desk and threw back a tablecloth to reveal a glass case beneath. Inside were several dozen shells: gold, pink, speckled. "This one is very rare," Herman said, showing us a golden cowrie. Roger asked how much it was worth. "Price on request," Herman replied. He let the tablecloth down. "Do you need any consulting services?"

"Actually, yes. We're interested in Captain Cook and the red banana."

Herman frowned. "I wish the world would forget all that." Herman had attended a boarding school in Samoa, and once performed a war dance with other Niuean students as part of an "island night" show. "We painted our teeth red and danced with sticks, singing 'We are savage people!' We didn't know any better."

Like other Niueans, Herman hated Cook's name for the island, which had survived on maps and in some books well into the twentieth century. "We're actually much cleaner and better educated than other islanders," Herman said. "In Tonga they still have pigs running down the roads. In Fiji the villages are very poor. Tahiti is full of whores. But *we're* the red-teethed savages. Anyone who tours the island will see that's not so."

"We've toured it, but didn't know what to look for," I said. "Will you show us around?"

"I'm a professional guide," Herman replied. "Price on request."

"Okay, how much?"

"Depends what you want to see."

"Cook-related sites. And a *hulahula*."

Herman shook his head. "This is hard. It will take some research." He paused. "Fifteen dollars an hour, and you drive. I don't have a car."

"Fine. When can we go?"

Herman went to his desk to consult a calendar. "I could probably fit you in a week from Friday." I told him we were in Niue for only a few more days. "Tomorrow morning, then," he said, showing us to the door.

As we drove off, I read to Roger from the tourist brochure Herman had given us. The listed attractions included "Village Visit with Enthusiastic Resident."

"Only one?" Roger said. "The others fucked off?" We passed a row of roadside graves. "Either that or they 'fell on sleep.' The headstones outnumber the living here, it's depressing. They should call this island Gravesend." We entered a village seemingly devoid of inhabitants. "Where's Enthusiastic Resident?" Roger quipped. Then he saw an old lady snoozing on her front porch. "Oh, there's one. She'll be lying by the road before long, too."

At the end of the day we stopped at the Lord Liverpool University George Washington School of Medicine. It was just as Roger had described. The only items of medical equipment we could find were an elastic bandage and a blood pressure machine. The library had a few medical texts wedged between self-help books such as *The Keys to Growing in Love* and *The Inspirational Writings of Pat Robertson*. There were no students or instructors in sight.

But the bar was crowded with large men in coats and ties. This turned out to be the bulk of Niue's government, including the premier and several of his ministers. The premier handed me his business card, which listed his portfolios: finance, economic planning, customs and revenue, offshore banking, external affairs, civil aviation, shipping and trade, tourism, philatelic and numismatic coins. I'd never visited a place where so few people held so many jobs.

Like everyone else we'd met, the ministers were open and friendly—until we asked about the medical school, the sex lines, and other island business. Roger didn't help matters by regaling the ministers with loud and rather lewd praise of two Niuean beauties he'd met at the Panamanian law firm and offshore business registry.

"One's my daughter, the other's my niece," the police minister, Robert Rex, observed rather coolly. Roger changed the subject. "Can you tell us where to find a *hulahula*?" he asked.

It was dark when we wobbled outside. Roger fumbled in his pocket for the car key, then saw that he'd left it in the ignition, as was the custom on this small, safe island. "Why do they have a police minister, anyway?" he wondered. "Unless it's to arrest oafs like me for ogling the local crumpet."

We were awakened the next morning by a gentle tap at the door. "Sorry to bother you," said a teenager from the hotel staff, "but did you take the police minister's car when you left the bar last night?"

We went outside. A white sedan just like ours was parked where we'd left it, except that it had a different license plate and none of our clutter in back. The teenager smiled and said Rex had left the bar soon after us, only to find his car missing. He called one of his officers, who reported that his car had been seen at the hotel. The police were nice enough to leave the matter until morning. After all, where could we go?

"It's no problem, really," the teenager said. "I'll go switch them."

As he drove off, Roger slunk back to bed. "This is a new low, even for me. Stealing the police minister's car. Thank God I haven't met his wife yet. I'd probably have leered at her, too."

WHEN OUR OWN car was returned, we went to collect Herman for our tour of Niue. He greeted us with a wide grin. "You're the big news on the island," he reported. "First car theft in years. I'm the public defender on Niue, you know." He reached for a law book. "Let's see, grand larceny. Are you a first offender? I could probably get you only a short sentence. Mitigating circumstances?"

"Stupidity," Roger said, "and five beers."

Herman laughed. "Don't worry, I'm sure Rex is delighted to have an actual crime statistic to report. Parliament will increase his budget."

We climbed in the car and headed off in search of Cook and the *hulahula*. Herman stopped first at the home of a neighbor, in hopes she might know where to find the banana. When he introduced us, the woman giggled and spoke in Niuean; the only words I caught were "Palagi" and "Rex." As to the *hulahula*, she was no more help than anyone else. "She says it only grows in the middle of the island," Herman translated. "Very hard to find."

We drove on to the village of Tuapa, close to where Cook had first landed. Herman led us to a steep path winding down a cleft in the coastal cliff. We walked out on the reef, pink and yellow coral bursting flowerlike beneath the brilliant, Curaçao-colored water. Black and orange parrotfish swam all around us, and frigate birds skimmed the surface. With no rivers or streams, and almost no pollution, Niue was free from silt or other runoff; its waters were among the clearest in the world.

At the Niue archives, I'd photocopied a monograph by a New Zealand anthropologist who had gathered natives' accounts of the English landing. From this, and the journals of Cook and his men, it was possible to reconstruct the *Resolution*'s brief visit. Cook had come ashore near where we now stood, accompanied by a few sailors, the naturalists Johann and George Forster, and the Forster's Swedish assistant, Anders Sparrman.

While the botanists gathered plants, sailors raised the Union Jack ("the idle ceremony of taking possession," George Forster mockingly called it). Then, as the landing party ventured up the chasm we'd just hiked down, several natives appeared above them. Cook's men waved white cloth and green branches and called out friendly greetings "in those South Sea dialects which we were acquainted with," George Forster wrote. Sparrman added that the natives "were painted coal-black, red, and white, in all sorts of horrible stripes," and made hideous "grimaces" that reminded him of devils "in theaters and on the walls of old country churches."

One of the Niueans hurled a chunk of coral, hitting Sparrman's arm. He and Johann Forster replied with musket fire, chasing away the natives but annoying Cook, who felt patience might have allowed for "some reconciliation." The party returned to the boats and headed down the coast, looking for another place to land.

We followed their course by road, stopping first at the site of a vanished village near Tuapa. Curiously, Niuean accounts claimed that Cook had come up here, exchanged gifts with islanders, and cooked a meal in an underground oven. "One person missed out and became angry, so he painted his teeth red, did a war dance, and scared the English away," Herman said. This incident may actually have occurred—fifty-five years after Cook, when an English missionary came to Niue. Such errors were common across the Pacific; Cook's landings often blurred, in local memory, with the arrival of later visitors.

We continued down the coast to a reef called Opaahi where Cook had tried to land again. Canoes lay by the water, covered in coconut fronds to keep them from drying and cracking in the sun. Cook had found canoes here, too, and filled them with "some trifles (Medals, Nails &c) to induce the Natives to believe we intended them no harm." Instead, men armed with spears charged down the chasm above the reef, Cook wrote, "with the ferocity of wild Boars and threw their darts." One spear flew close by the captain's shoulder. The English unleashed their own weapons, though Cook's musket misfired. "I was not five paces from him when he threw his spear and had resolved to shoot him to save my self," he wrote, "but I was glad afterwards that it happened otherwise."

Cook withdrew his men to the boats. "The Conduct and aspect of these Islanders occasioned my nameing it Savage Island," he wrote. George Forster was a tad more charitable: "The nature of their country, which is almost inaccessible, seems to have contributed to make their tempers so unsociable."

Opaahi still looked just as Cook described it: a stony beach with "a perpindicular rocky cleft" topped by dense foliage. It was easy to see how a few determined warriors had managed to chase off the well-armed English. The crevasse was not only steep, but also littered with rocks perfectly shaped for throwing. "Even I could pick off a Pom," Roger said, hurling a chunk of coral down into the sea.

Cook had also chosen an inauspicious spot to come ashore. Herman said Opaahi lay close to a famed site called Cave of the Tongans. A few centuries before Cook's landing, invading Tongans were lured to a shaft that Niueans had covered in brush. When the Tongans fell in, the Niueans buried them alive. "Cook was probably lucky he didn't get any further than he did," Herman said, "or he might be lying with the Tongans to this day."

From Opaahi, we headed inland on a narrow road fringed with moss, coconut groves, and grenade-shaped young papayas. Herman asked Roger to stop a few times so he could poke around in search of *hulahula*. I asked him what the plant looked like. "Very straight, thick stalk, broad leaves. The fruit doesn't droop, it goes straight up." Then, in a slash of open field, we saw an old man digging taro with a machete. When Herman asked him about the *hulahula,* the man responded with a toothless laugh and a few words of Niuean. "He says you asked the wrong question," Herman translated.

The farmer, a lean eighty-year-old named Kahika, said the *hulahula* had been common in his childhood. During weddings, or the installation of a chief, people smeared their faces with the fruit and performed a war dance. But island pastors disapproved, and gradually the custom died out. "We don't have the old ceremonies anymore so we don't need the *hulahula,*" Herman explained. "It isn't nearly so sweet as other bananas. You could say the *hulahula* is cosmetic rather than culinary."

We asked Kahika how he felt about Cook's name for the island. He shrugged and told Herman, "It is tradition, and sometimes tradition doesn't work in your favor. But I am proud we fought them off. If we hadn't, the Palagi would have taken this place much sooner than they did." Then he returned to his digging.

Herman had one last idea. A former legal client of his was an equipment driver who knew every inch of the island. His wife kept a bush garden. Perhaps they could point us to a *hulahula*. We went and knocked on the door of their ramshackle house, but no one answered. Herman raised his palms. "Maybe we could find a picture of a *hulahula* at the archives," he said.

I shook my head, and asked how much we owed him. "I have used all my skills, legal and investigative," Herman said, studying his watch. When I paid him, he smiled and turned to Roger. "Remember to call me if you need legal counsel. Price on request."

BY THE END of the week, we'd exhausted every lead, as well as islanders' patience. Stopping again at the medical school, Roger and I were greeted not simply with a cold shoulder but by a wall of them: the broad backs of government ministers, hunched over their beers in a scrum blocking our path to the bar. Other Niueans seemed weary of our ceaseless queries about Cook and the red banana. Even the New Zealand diplomats steered clear of us. "We haven't just worn out our welcome," Roger said, "we've extinguished it."

Retreating to the hotel one evening, we learned that a special event was about to commence: the first round of a Miss Niue pageant. Roger found us seats next to a young woman named Amanda, who turned out to be a former Miss Teen Niue. I asked her what it was like competing in a beauty contest on this modest, church-oriented island. "You have to think sexy, because you can't look it," she said. "No skin and no wiggling." Even when swimming, Niuean women wore sarongs over their bathing suits.

These strictures didn't bother Amanda. "Westerners are very hypocritical about Polynesia," she said. "First the Palagi sailors came to our islands and went, 'Ooh, bare breasts!' Then the missionaries came and said, 'Cover up!' Now tourists in bikinis look at us and say, 'Why are you hiding under sarongs?' "

The pageant began with a question-and-answer session for teen contestants clad in long gowns. By far the biggest crowd-pleaser was a girl who said she planned to stay on Niue and raise a family, "to keep the population up." Each of the girls also performed a chaste walk and turn, accompanied by a male chaperone.

The older contestants were almost as demure. "Greetings to you all in the name of Jesus Christ," one began, before twirling her hips just a bit. Despite the show's primness, Amanda said the contest had become much more Western in the five years since she'd competed. "Thin didn't use to be in," she whispered. "Now look how slim the girls are!"

It seemed unlikely they would remain so for long. When the show ended, the audience swarmed around a buffet even more staggering than the one we'd helped devour earlier in the week. Roger, who sat out the initial rush, returned with his plate empty. "It's been stripped," he said. I noticed that several diners had wrapped food in foil and taken it back to their seats. Amanda said this was customary in Niue; guests were expected to take extra portions home to eat later.

Roger shrugged, content to drink instead. After a week of Niuean cuisine, we'd both let out our belts a notch. "If we stayed here much longer I'd blow out to fantastic proportions," he said. "They'd have to dismantle the doors to let me through."

On our last full day in Niue, I proposed one more drive around the island. Roger refused. "I'm starting to recognize every palm tree and vanilla pod," he said. "Whenever we get in the car I feel like Bill Murray in *Groundhog Day*." So I headed off without him, idly steering past all the places we'd seen. A truck stood parked beside the house of the equipment driver Herman had taken us to visit, in hopes of locating a *hulahula*. Cook never turned back from the chance of discovery, however slight. I stopped and knocked on the door.

A woman in a nightgown appeared, carrying a cleaver. She blushed, no doubt unaccustomed to greeting a Palagi stranger while barely dressed. I could smell something cooking. "Sorry," I said, feeling intrusive and suddenly hesitant about my frivolous mission. "I was here the other day with Herman Taga—Herman the lawyer."

"Herman Tagaloailuga," she said. "I am Carol."

"We were looking for your husband."

She appeared a bit alarmed. "He's not home." I'd forgotten that Herman had helped her husband with legal troubles. "Actually we were just looking for a *hulahula*," I blurted. "Herman thought you or your husband might know where to find one."

Carol went inside for a moment and returned in a housedress, still carrying the heavy knife. She led me to a side yard and pointed to a thick, straight plant beside the water tank. "I bring it from the bush to save it so it won't disappear," she said.

"That's a *hulahula*?"

She nodded. "No fruit now. In a few months. The bananas turn red, with spots, then black, then they fall down. No one eats them anymore. I use leaves for the *umu* and cook the stalk to weave things. But mostly just to look at."

"Why?"

Carol shrugged. "I like it, it is from our history. When I was young,

I hear the story about our men scaring the Palagi with the color of that banana. I really enjoy that story. So I went to the bush and got the seeds so I can remember how Niue scared Captain Cook with red teeth." She studied the plant proudly. "I may be the only person on Niue with a *hulahula*. I don't give the seeds to anyone else. Just for me."

We stood and gazed at the plant, an appreciation society of two. We fondled the stalk and studied the broad leaves. I took Carol's picture in front of the tree. One thing puzzled me. Cook had come here in winter, as I had. But the bananas didn't ripen at this time of year. How had the warriors painted their teeth red?

Carol took her cleaver and whacked off a piece of stalk. Purply juice seeped out. "The weather has been cold, so it is late this year," she said. "Soon the juice will turn very red, like blood." I asked for some stalk, thanked Carol, and rushed back to the hotel. At the door to our room, I smeared the stalk against my lips and teeth before bursting inside.

"You bastard!" Roger cried, bolting up from his chair. "I wanted to be there on Everest!"

I performed a half-baked war dance and snarled until the astringent juice made me gag. "Of course it's totally unconvincing, at least on you," Roger said. "But the stain is there. They can't deny it anymore. Red-teethed savages!"

ON SUNDAY, WE headed to the airport along with almost everyone else on Niue. The handwritten passengers' list rendered my surname as "Hatzsky." Roger's didn't appear at all. No one seemed to care. Officials stamped our passports and performed the other formalities of international disembarkation, then welcomed us back into the country. "The plane is late, it won't be in for another hour or so," an official said. "You can go back to the hotel if you want."

Instead, we lolled in the sun outside the terminal, beside the crowd of onlookers. By now we recognized many of them, and all of them recognized us. A few nodded and smiled, but most looked away. "They're here to make sure we actually leave," Roger said. When the Royal Tongan plane finally swooped onto the runway, the crowd broke into applause. My spirits lifted, too. Niue was one of the nicest, least spoiled places I'd ever visited. But I'd begun to feel restless and confined, a sensation that expats on the island called Rock fever. Like Cook, I was ready for new territory.

"Hatzsky and No-Name," Roger said, handing our boarding passes to a steward. He looked at us blankly and pointed to seats beside an immense, stony-faced Tongan whose expression put me in mind of the statues at Easter Island. The pilot announced that our short flight would take us back across the international dateline.

"It's only two o'clock and we're done with Sunday," Roger said, perking up. "Thank God for that."

Chapter 9

TONGA:
Where Time Begins, and Goes Back

Such resks as thise are the unavoidable Companions of
the Man who goes on Discoveries.
— CAPTAIN COOK, AFTER NEARLY RUNNING
AGROUND OFF TONGA

Explorers live or die by first impressions. Is the approaching inlet a
shelter or a shoal-strewn trap? The figures beckoning from the beach—
are they friends or foes? Act too cautiously, and you will discover
nothing. Too recklessly, and you may end up dashed against rocks, or,
like Magellan, lying on the sand with a spear through your gut.

Cook was adroit at this balancing act. By the midpoint of his second voyage, he also had considerable experience on which to base his
impressions. Few shores struck him more favorably than the archipelago he reached in October 1773, after his first Antarctic probe. "Without the least hesitation," he observed, natives canoed out to the
Resolution and came aboard. "This mark of confidence gave me a
good opinion of these Islanders."

So did his reception on the beach. "We were welcomed a shore by
acclamations from an immence crowd of Men and Women not one of
which had so much as a stick in their hands." Cook ordered his men to
play bagpipes. Young island women replied with a "musical and harmonious tune." Then a chief conducted the English to a feast of
bananas, coconuts, and kava, a mildly intoxicating drink made of pepper root.

Servants prepared the kava by chewing the plant into pulp before spitting it into bowls and adding water. Ever the diplomat and gastronomic adventurer, Cook—alone among his men—sampled the beverage. "The manner of brewing," he dryly observed, "had quenished the thirst of every one else." Cook described kava's flavor as "rather flat and insipid," but he appreciated the gesture. "Can we make a friend more welcome than by seting before him the best liquor in our possession?"

Unarmed and hospitable, the natives also traded on very favorable terms—even hurling provisions into English boats without asking for anything in exchange. But it was island agriculture that impressed Cook most. "I thought I was transported into one of the most fertile plains in Europe," he wrote. Every acre "was laid out in Plantations" and enclosed by "neat fences made of reeds." Wide public roads, "as even as a Bowling Green," cut through the countryside. Completing this air of pastoral gentility were fruit trees planted "in great taste and elegancy" beside the roads and around chiefly houses. "The air was perfumed by their fragrancy."

Cook was so enchanted by his "delightfull Walks" that he wrote with rare humor, even about subjects that usually irritated him. He noted with amusement that William Wales had to stumble around without shoes or stockings because natives had stolen the astronomer's garments as he waded in the water. Cook also wrote that crewmen bartered so profligately for island curiosities that "one waggish Boy took a piece of human excrement on the end of a stick and hild it out to every one of our people."

Cook poked fun at himself, too. When he came ashore at one beach, an elderly woman presented the captain with a comely young "Miss." Cook declined, apologizing that he had nothing to give her. "[I] thought by that means to have come off with flying Colours," Cook wrote, "but I was misstaken, for I was made to understand I might retire with her on credit." When he again declined, the elderly woman berated him, "Sneering in my face and saying, what sort of man are you thus to refuse the embraces of so fine a young Woman, for the girl certainly did not want beauty which I could however withstand, but the abuse of the old Woman I could not and therefore hastn'd into the Boat."

Other Englishmen weren't so insistent in resisting native charms. "The Women are in general handsome and to the last degree obliging," wrote Charles Clerke. Another crewman, William Bayly, judged the women "fat & Jolly," and wrote that they often swam to the ship, exchanging their favors for a nail. "Virtue is held in little esteem here." This judgment echoed that of a Dutch surgeon who briefly visited the islands with Abel Tasman 130 years earlier. "Two frightful giantesses grasped me," he wrote. "Other women felt the sailors shamelessly in the trouser-front, and indicated clearly that they wanted to have intercourse. South-landers what people."

Cook stayed on the islands only a few days in 1773, and returned for another brief tour the following year, immediately after visiting Niue. His concluding remarks on the isles couldn't have differed more from those he'd just penned about Savage Island. "Joy and Contentment is painted in every face and their whole behaviour to us was mild and benevolent," he wrote. "This groupe I have named the Friendly Archipelago as a lasting friendship seems to subsist among the Inhabitants and their Courtesy to Strangers intitles them to that Name."

COOK'S JOURNAL MADE for pleasant reading during the short flight from Niue. But it proved a poor primer for our own arrival at Tongatapu, the principal island of the Royal Kingdom of Tonga. (*Tonga,* a native word meaning "south"—the main island's position in relation to the rest of the archipelago—supplanted Cook's name in the nineteenth century.) We were greeted, not by "acclamations from an immence crowd," but by sullen officials who stamped passports and inspected bags without so much as looking up. Outside the terminal, a woman from the International Dateline Hotel pointed us to a bus. "Why was your plane late?" she demanded. During the half-hour drive to the hotel, she stared blankly ahead, ignoring our questions.

My first impression of Tonga's landscape, viewed through the bus's smudged windows, was as dismal as Cook's had been admiring. Pigs snuffled in the garbage that littered roadside fields. We passed graffiti-covered billboards for cigarettes, a vegetable stall named Prison Market, and a battered sign arcing over the road, emblazoned with the words "Long Live Your Majesty." Sweeping under this arch, we entered downtown Nuku'alofa, the Tongan capital, which seemed at first glance a dreary expanse of ferroconcrete boxes.

The International Dateline Hotel rose beside the waterfront, facing its namesake, 180 miles to the east. Tonga claimed to be the first landfall on earth struck by the dawn sun; "Where Time Begins," said the inscription on a clock face by the hotel entrance. Erected in 1967 to accommodate guests at the king's coronation, the state-owned Dateline also billed itself as Tonga's leading hotel. Since Roger and I had anticipated sleeping rough in Niue, we'd splurged when making reservations in Tonga.

Stuffed birds stared forlornly from a glass case in the Dateline's cavernous lobby. Porters loitered in the shadows, ignoring a crowd of newly arrived guests, who toted their bags past a broken elevator and up a peeling stairwell. Our "deluxe" room featured a naked bulb dangling from the ceiling, torn window screens, and a soggy carpet pocked with cigarette burns. "The furniture looks like it was stolen from a suburban house in Melbourne thirty years ago," Roger said, settling into a mildewed chair. He reached for an ashtray, already full of butts. A can of peanuts, open and half empty, sat atop the fridge.

We fled outside for a walk through the stifling heat. A few blocks from the hotel, we entered a residential neighborhood of dirt and gravel lanes. Many of the homes appeared unfinished: jumbles of corrugated iron, cinder block, and scrap lumber. Pigs, ducks, and roosters wandered in the alleys. On the main streets, road signs hung askew and power poles teetered. Even a park enclosing the tombs of Tongan royalty appeared vandalized; chickens and dogs slipped through the torn fence to defecate around the imperial graves.

I like untidy places. As a traveler, nothing bores me more than bland tourist traps. But Nuku'alofa's squalor surprised me. In Niue, I'd had ample time to read about Tonga. Among other things, I'd learned that the kingdom—which encompasses 171 far-flung islands, many of them uninhabited—ranks among the wealthiest nations in the South Pacific. Tonga's royal family owns multiple palaces, as well as properties all over the world, and the king's personal wealth has been reported at $350 million U.S. Most of the travelers' accounts I'd read depicted Nuku'alofa as quaintly picturesque. To me, the place seemed old-fashioned in a charmless way, neglected rather than nostalgic.

The only sign of public improvement was a curious plaque near the water, commemorating "the inauguration of this extension of the Vuna Road streetlighting by HRH Crown Prince Tupouto'a at 7:00 P.M. on Thursday 30 June, 1988, to mark the 70th Birthday of His Majesty." Roger shook his head. "It's weird, almost Marie Antoinette. Let them have light!"

The people we passed on the streets also surprised me. Big, I expected. Tongans rank among the largest people on the planet, beginning with their king, who was once cited by the Guinness Book of Records as the world's weightiest monarch, at 444 pounds. I also recognized Tongans' features from the journals and artwork of Cook and his men: soft and handsome faces, dark copper skin, black hair. Tonga was the only South Pacific nation never to have been colonized. It also had a long history of barring immigrants. ("Tonga for the Tongans," a nineteenth-century monarch declared.) As a result, the hundred thousand islanders were so ethnically "pure" that biotechnology firms sought Tongan DNA to study genetic links to disease, which are easiest to isolate in homogenous populations.

But if Tongans' bloodlines appeared little changed since Cook's day, the same didn't seem true of their temperament, at least in the presence of foreigners. The captain described islanders as not only exceptionally hospitable, but also as "a people of a good deal of levity." The women, he added, were "the merriest creatures I ever met with and will keep chattering by ones side without the least invitation."

Levity and chitchat weren't much in evidence now, as we'd already seen at the hotel and airport. During our three-hour walk, we occasionally sought refuge in fan-cooled stores. Most shopkeepers ignored us. On the streets, cars didn't give way to pedestrians, and neither did pedestrians. We were almost knocked off the sidewalk several times by men barging the other way as if we were invisible, or of no more consequence than gnats. At the waterfront, I paused to snap a picture. A pack of young men on bicycles rode into the frame. "What the *fuck* you doing!" one shouted at me. "No fucking pictures!"

The women weren't hostile, but nor were they the gay, flesh-baring "Lasses" described by Charles Clerke and other crewmen. Most of those we passed wore a traditional woven girdle called the *ta'ovala*. Stiff and dun-colored, the *ta'ovala* looked like a floor mat that had been picked up and tied, apron-style, over the women's other clothes, covering them from the knee to the solar plexus. The garment appeared hot and uncomfortable, and served to emphasize the women's girth.

Many of the women held hands, and some men locked fingers with other men. But there was no such contact between the sexes—a restraint absent in Cook's day, when the English observed Tongans making love in public. While the Tongans had escaped colonialism, they had fervently embraced Western missionaries, Methodists and Mormons in particular.

Before leaving Sydney, Roger and I had lunched with a diplomat who often visited Tonga. Inevitably, Roger asked about island women. "They are not only very large, but very very Christian," the diplomat told us. Glancing downward, he added, "In Tonga, Percy sleeps quietly at night."

At sundown, larded with sweat and vaguely depressed, we retreated to an open-air pub by the waterfront. The walls were covered with recruitment posters for the U.S. Marines ("Tough and Proud of It"). Ten or so men, broad-shouldered and bull-necked, stood guzzling Royal Beer and gazing at us with what seemed a certain menace. "I feel like I'm at a Mike Tyson convention," Roger said. At six feet, three inches, and over two hundred pounds, he wasn't accustomed to feeling physically intimidated.

We were about to leave when the barman asked, in American-accented English, where we came from. He'd lived in California for many years, become a U.S. citizen, and served in the military: hence the posters. "Tongans are trained from birth to be tough," he said, "and we respect authority. So we make good soldiers." Most of his patrons had worked overseas, too, usually in Australia or New Zealand. "Tongans also make good bar bouncers," he said. Then he asked what brought us to Nuku'alofa.

"We're going to all the places Captain Cook went," Roger said.

"Oh yeah, Cook," the barman replied. "His great-great-granddaughter lives out back. She works at the bar."

This was news. I asked if we could speak to her. The barman headed through a yard behind the pub and returned with an attractive, fair-skinned woman of about twenty, named Macy Cook. She had reddish-brown hair, tattoos on her upper arms, and a nose ring. Her skirt and halter top exposed much more skin than was customary in Tonga. "My father's dad was Captain Cook's grandson," she said. "I forget all the history." She smiled suggestively. "There are plenty of Tongans related to Cook. He liked the girls."

Macy didn't know any more about her lineage. But she told us to return in a few days when she went each week to visit her mother. "She has a book on family history," Macy said. "It's got a picture of Cook that looks a lot like my father."

READING COOK'S JOURNALS is a constant reminder of how specialized our skills have become in the modern era. On one page, Cook discusses astronomy, geology, meteorology, and animal husbandry. On the next, he offers insight into management, commerce, and diplomacy. Then he veers into lengthy speculation about ocean currents and the formation of islands. Few people today would even dream of dabbling in so many disciplines, much less mastering them.

Cook didn't excel at everything. He was a merely competent linguist who leaned heavily on other crewmen when assembling native vocabularies. Cook also freely acknowledged that religion remained a mystery to him. Nonetheless, he seems such a polymath that his occasional blind spots come as a shock. One such limitation was his shaky grasp of Polynesian politics. In his approach to almost every other realm of Pacific life—including sexual mores and cannibalism—Cook displayed a steady shrewdness and lack of bias. But when it came to navigating island governance, Cook often tried to squeeze very foreign customs into an inelastic British box.

Nowhere was this more obvious than in Tonga, to which Cook returned in 1777, on his third Pacific voyage. He toured the archipelago for more than two months, one of his longest visits anywhere. Eager to secure a steady flow of provisions, and to make sense of Tonga, Cook spent much of his time seeking out island rulers. "It was my intrest as well as my inclination to pay my Court to all these great men," he wrote with characteristic deference. Also very English was Cook's presumption that Tonga had an absolute sovereign akin to

George III. He referred to this figure as "the king," and became obsessed with finding him.

Tonga's hierarchy, however, didn't conform to British norms. Power and rank flowed through an intricate lacework of chiefs, plenipotentiaries, and taboo-wreathed relatives of the Tu'i Tonga, a hereditary leader who came closest to Cook's notion of king. Complicating matters still more, several female kin of the Tu'i Tonga had a status superior to any man's. Island leaders also jostled for power, and saw the English and their ships as potentially useful in this struggle. As a result, the English became enmeshed in an extended game of "take me to your leader" that almost cost Cook and his crew their lives.

On his first Pacific voyage, Cook had been able to rely on Banks's charms and aristocratic instincts, as well as on Tupaia's interpretive skills, when trying to divine Polynesian politics. The captain wasn't similarly blessed on his later voyages. At times, he also showed signs of becoming a little too confident in his own judgment. In labyrinthine Tonga, this inevitably led to misunderstandings, some of them quite comic.

Early in his wild-goose chase after Tonga's "principal man," Cook was led to a young person whom islanders treated with exceptional awe. "I found him seated with so much sullen and stupid gravity that I realy took him for an ideot," Cook wrote. His vain attempts at communicating with this "Post stuck in the ground" confirmed the captain's low opinion. Cook was about to depart when a Tongan insisted that the immobile figure was, in fact, "the principal man on the Island." So Cook rather grudgingly showered trinkets on the "little brat," as the captain called him. This taciturn youth, it turned out, was Tonga's *tahama*, or sacred child, so revered that even the Tu'i Tonga couldn't eat in his presence.

Much more serious was Cook's confusion over a charismatic young chief named Finau, who led the English to believe that *he* was ruler of Tonga. Tall and handsome, and possessing what a lieutenant called "much fire and vivacity," Finau ostentatiously displayed his own power, inviting Cook to watch as subjects paid homage to the chief by delivering immense piles of yams, pigs, turtles, and other food. Finau also flattered the English with his extravagant hospitality. One gift of provisions was so massive that Cook wrote: "There was as much as loaded four boats and far exceeded any present I had ever before received from an Indian Prince."

Finau also engaged Cook in a curiously competitive round of entertainment. The Tongans staged boxing and wrestling matches, inviting sailors into the ring and promptly knocking them down. ("A couple of lusty wenches" also boxed, Cook wrote, "with as much art as the men.") Cook reciprocated by showing off his marines and musicians. The Tongans then performed a war dance, a "harlequin" show, and a torch-lit concert that, Cook wrote, "whould have met with universal applause on a European Theatre and so far exceeded any thing we had done to amuse them that they seemed to pique themselves in the superiority they had over us."

Not to be outdone, Cook concluded the revelry by firing off "sky and Water Rockets which astonished and pleased them beyond measure and intirely turned the scale in our favour." William Anderson, a surgeon, wrote that Tongans "compar'd the sparkles which fell from the sky rockets to falling stars," and supposed that the smoke "remained and became a cloud."

The Tongans' day-and-night-long "deversions," as Cook called them, were intended as exactly that. Years later, an Englishman living among the Tongans learned that Finau had staged the extravaganza to deflect his visitors' attention so that he and his accomplices could massacre the English and seize their booty-laden ships. At the last moment, a tactical dispute among the Tongan chiefs led to the scheme's abandonment. But Cook fell prey to another of Finau's deceptions. When the captain asked to accompany Finau to his home island of Vava'u, "he seemed not to approve of this and by way of deverting us from it, told me there was neither harbour nor anchorage." Vava'u, in fact, offered the best harbor in all of Tonga. Finau apparently feared that the English, if they found it, would take over his island.

Sailing south instead, Cook discovered that Finau was "not the King," though he evidently wished to command all the isles. Rather, the most kinglike figure in Tonga was a man whose family name Cook rendered as Fattafee—appropriate, given that "he was the most corperate plump fellow we had met with." Fattafee—more accurately, Fatafehi—was the Tu'i Tonga, number thirty-six in a line of hereditary rulers. The surgeon, Anderson, recognized that size amplified the "rank and power" of Polynesian leaders. He described Fatafehi as a man "of a monstrous size with fat which render'd him very unwieldy and almost shapeless."

This imperial blob studied everything aboard the *Resolution* with keen curiosity. However, when Cook invited him below, "his attendants objected to this, saying if we went there people would walk over his head." The king's head was so sacred that no one else's could ever rise above it. When subjects approached, they bowed their heads between their knees and reverently tapped the soles of the king's feet. Attendants also carried the king ashore in what Cook described as a "hand barrow." They fanned flies from his face, and when he lay down, women beat him gently with their fists, a sleep-inducing massage that continued through the night.

"I was quite charmed with the decorum that was observed," Cook wrote of the fawning treatment accorded Fatafehi. "I had no where seen the like, no not even amongst more civilized nations."

The king escorted the English to Tongatapu and entertained them almost daily with feasts and kava ceremonies. The captain reciprocated on board the *Resolution*. This endless round of eating and drinking consumed the rest of Cook's stay in Tonga. His journal starts to read a bit like Banks's in Tahiti: the jaded account of an inveterate socialite, detailing who sat where, in what order they drank kava, how much food they consumed, what dances they performed. His men also made themselves at home, learning to shave with shells, timing canoe races, and enjoying the favors of island women, who, Charles Clerke wrote, "render'd our Bill of Fare compleat."

The English didn't entirely approve of their hosts' "feudal" ways, as Cook put it. He noted that a chief, angry with his subjects, "beat them most unmercifully" with a club until one man fell bleeding and went into convulsions. "On his being told he had killed the man he only laughed," Cook wrote of the chief. Later, Cook saw a royal canoe run over two small boats, "with as little concern as if they had been bits of wood." He also watched as the king plundered canoes "and took from them every fish and shell they had got."

But overall, Cook considered Tonga a "Humane and peacable Nation," one with which he obviously identified. Hereditary rule gave

the government a "solid basis," he wrote. Cook also sought to anglicize the subtropical landscape, sowing turnip seeds from England and
presenting his hosts with a veritable menagerie: a bull and cow, ram
and ewes, a boar and sows, a buck and doe, goats, and rabbits. He
concluded, rather grandly, by telling islanders: "They and their Children were to remember that they had them from the Men of Britane."
Later, climbing a hill, he mused: "I could not help flattering myself
with the idea that some future Navigator may from the very same station behould these Medows stocked with Cattle the English have
planted at these islands."

WE AWAKENED OUR first morning in Tonga to find that time did
indeed begin at the International Dateline Hotel. The dawn sun poured
through our unshaded east-facing window, making us among the first
people awake on the planet.

"You're on the wrong track with this Cook family thing," Roger
said from his bed.

"Huh?"

"That gum-chewing sheila at the bar last night. Macy Cook. She's
leading you down a blind alley. Cook wasn't a root rat."

"Nine years in the Pacific? With all his men going at it like mad,
and chiefs throwing naked women at him? Not one moment of weakness?"

"Not Cook. He kept Percy in his pants."

I pondered this for a moment. "What about Jefferson and his slave
Sally Hemings? Historians insisted he never touched her. Then they did
a DNA test."

"That's your filthy American. Cook was a Yorkshireman. Self-
disciplined. I won't have it."

We agreed to leave the topic alone until meeting with Macy later in
the week. In the meantime, I had another bloodline to follow. The current monarch, His Majesty King Taufa'ahau Tupou IV, was descended
from the Tu'i Tonga Cook had met. It seemed appropriate that I seek a
royal audience, too. The king certainly sounded like a colorful character. His passions included numerology, American televangelists, and
controversial business schemes such as selling Tongan citizenship and

passports to wealthy Asians, including Imelda Marcos and other fugitives. Though exceptionally large, the king was also a keen athlete; he still visited the gym, in his eighties, and promoted sports. "It is good for girls," he once declared of field hockey. "It will keep them busy with their training, and going to bed early instead of going out to night clubs and pursuing a lustful lifestyle."

The etiquette surrounding the king also intrigued me. I'd read that his subjects still approached him as they had the Tu'i Tonga in Cook's day, by scuttling forward on their hands and knees and kissing the monarch's fingers or feet. When departing, they crab-walked backward, to avoid showing the king their rear.

"You groveling Americans will crawl at the hint of any royalty, no matter how ridiculous," Roger said, when I confessed my desire for an audience. "I've got a queen already, and that's one monarch too many." He opted to lounge by the hotel pool while I headed off in pursuit of an interview.

The king's principal palace—one of seven royal residences—stood by the water a half mile from the Dateline. As palaces go, it was unpretentious: a rambling Victorian weatherboard, prefabricated in New Zealand, with gables, a turret, a rust-red roof, and a wraparound porch. It looked like a gingerbread guest house on Cape Cod. A broad lawn swept down to the sea, and ducks squawked in a yard behind the palace. The security consisted of a guard in an olive uniform and black beret, snoozing in a sentry box.

Before leaving Sydney, I'd tried without success to contact the king's private secretary, 'Eleni 'Aho, by phone, fax, e-mail, and courier-delivered letter. Now that I was here, I decided to press my case in person. I found the secretary in a small wooden building across from the palace. A handsome, middle-aged woman, seated beneath a portrait of the king, 'Eleni 'Aho seemed less than delighted to see me.

"Did you receive my request for an interview with the king?" I asked.

Her eyes darted away, then settled on her cluttered desk. "I might have," she said. "How long are you staying?"

"Until Monday morning."

"I am so sorry. We might have fit you in later next week."

"Next week is okay. I can stay."

She sighed, flipping through a desk calendar. "I will have to speak to His Majesty, of course." I gave her another copy of the obsequious letter I'd sent, including a list of sample questions about Cook and Tongan history. Then I tried to make small talk. The secretary regarded me coldly. So I asked whom else I might speak to while waiting to hear from the king.

"Have you been to the tourist office?" she asked.

I'd stopped there on my way to the palace and collected faded, dispiriting pamphlets, including one filled with useful phrases for tourists: "May I have a mosquito net?" "Is it ripe?" "Is it safe to swim here?" I asked 'Eleni if she might recommend anything else. We engaged in a brief staring contest. Finally, she gave me the name of the Tongan government's official spokeswoman. "Good luck," she said, with a tone that suggested I'd need it.

Wandering the streets around the palace, I saw a more picturesque side to Nuku'alofa than I had the previous day. Across from the palace stood the members-only Nuku'alofa Club, a weatherboard antique shaded by an enormous bougainvillea. Peering through the window, I saw dartboards, billiards tables, and pictures of British and Tongan royalty. The nearby headquarters of the Free Wesleyan Church had jigsaw curlicues and a widow's walk. Even more reminiscent of New England was the parliament building, a white clapboard box with high windows and a peaked red roof. It looked like a whalers' church in New Bedford or Nantucket.

I found the government spokeswoman, 'Eseta Fusitu'a, in a modern office block beside the parliament. Like the king's secretary, she seemed very put upon by my presence. As head of the Government Information Unit, and the person recommended to me by the king's secretary, she couldn't ignore my request for information. However, she made it clear she didn't suffer fools, cutting me off as soon as I asked about Cook by reciting her graduate degrees in Pacific history.

"I think Cook liked and respected Tonga because he saw in it a mirror of England," she said. "Order, hierarchy, tidiness—it was like the world he came from, and much better than the primitive societies he'd visited elsewhere." Tongans, in turn, admired Cook and his men, and gradually adopted British customs: titled nobility, a coat of arms, a parliament with lords and commoners, and a monarch who took the name of the reigning British king, George. "You could say Britain is just a Western form of the Tongan system," 'Eseta said.

If anything, she felt Tonga's system was far superior to Britain's because it had stayed true to its origins. The king and thirty-three noblemen (including 'Eseta's husband) still controlled almost all the land and power. The church remained potent. And islanders clung to their fierce sense of autonomy and distinctiveness, rather like British Tories who resisted the European Union. "The world does one thing and we go on our merry way," she said.

From what I'd read about Tonga, this was certainly true. The tiny island nation had earned some $30 million U.S. by selling citizenship and passports, despite international condemnation. Tonga also ignored censure by Amnesty International and the U.S. State Department for its imprisonment and intimidation of journalists and political dissidents. Nor did Tonga have much regard for the conventions of the United Nations, which it had recently joined. "The U.N. is a joke," 'Eseta said, waving her hand in the air. "It must restructure itself and its attitudes and stop telling countries how to run their affairs."

She had even less time for Tonga's neighbors. "We're more independent and have greater confidence than other Pacific nations. That's very much part of our psyche." She shrugged. "They think we're arrogant. So what? We tend to know our minds and are unconcerned about what others think of us."

This indifference extended to me. 'Eseta studied the clock throughout our brief chat, yawned histrionically each time I opened my mouth, then asked, "Where are you parked?" I tried one last question: Where could I find a copy of Tonga's constitution? "At a public library," she said.

I'd asked about a library at the tourist office and been told that Tonga didn't have one. When I mentioned this to 'Eseta, she yelled to a secretary to make me a copy of the constitution. Then she held out a limp hand and vanished down the hall.

Interviews with disobliging officials are a staple of foreign reporting. I'd spent the better part of a decade being lied to or thwarted by Middle Eastern gatekeepers. Tonga was starting to remind me of Saudi Arabia, another haughty kingdom that regards the rest of the world as rabble. Saudis, however, can afford to be arrogant: they're guardians of Islam's holiest places—and of a quarter of the world's oil reserves. Also, even the most unhelpful Saudi official will ply you with pleasant chat and endless cups of tea. In tiny Tonga, I was barely managing eye contact.

ROGER HAD ATTRACTED much more solicitude simply by lounging beside the hotel pool. As soon as I joined him, an enormous man appeared. "Your friend insists he is not yet ready for his massage," the man said, rubbing meaty hands. "How about you?" I shook my head. The man smiled at Roger. "Any time, my friend, I wait for you. My bed and oil are just over there."

This freelance masseur had been pestering Roger all morning. "I can't pull crumpet to save my life," he said, nodding at two bikini-clad tourists on the recliners beside him. "But this Sumo wants to wrestle me onto his mattress and slather me with coconut oil."

When not fending off rubdowns, Roger had been reading about Tonga. He'd learned that a tortoise Cook gave the Tongans in 1777 had survived until 1966. It had roamed the palace grounds, been given a noble name, Tu'i Malila ("King of the Residence"), and even accorded a place in royal kava circles. The tortoise's remains now resided at a museum called the Tongan National Center. "Let's go pay our respects," Roger suggested.

Like the rest of Nuku'alofa, the Tongan National Center was expiring from neglect. The museum had dead lightbulbs, and dead flies littering the floor. An unconscious caretaker rested his head on the front desk. We found Tu'i Malila's stuffed remains in a large, dusty case. The tortoise's shell looked discolored and dented, slightly charred. A sign explained why. During its long life, Tu'i Malila went blind and "endured being kicked by a horse, struck by wheels of a carriage, and being caught in a grass fire in the royal gardens." Oddly, its sex remained in doubt: "Although scientists believe it's a female, Tongans believe it was male."

There wasn't much else to see in the museum, apart from the outfit worn by the current monarch's mother, Queen Salote, at the 1953 coronation of Elizabeth II in London. Salote had charmed the British public by riding through heavy rain in an uncovered carriage, as a gesture of respect for Elizabeth. The London press dubbed her "the largest queen of the smallest kingdom." Salote's enormous red gown looked as though it would be baggy on Roger, and her leather sandals were twice the size of mine. *Sino molu,* "soft body," was a quality much admired by Tongans. As in Cook's day, Tongans expected their rulers to be especially large.

We stayed to watch an evening dance show in a building adjoining the museum. The women, clad in knee-length grass skirts and strapless tops made of tapa, swayed with the easy grace that Cook noted in describing island dance, but with none of the "indecent actions" he alluded to. However, a master of ceremonies urged us to come up and stick paper money to the dancers' well-oiled skin. "Somehow I don't imagine Cook doing this," Roger said, pasting a banknote on a woman's gyrating shoulder.

The kava ceremony that followed was also modified for modern consumption. Women mashed the root and strained the juice rather than masticating it. Served in coconut shells, the kava had the grayish-brown tint of old dishwater, and a flavor that was faintly bitter and peppery. I emptied three shells, hoping to experience the opiumlike "stupefaction" described by Cook's surgeon, but felt no more effect than a slight numbing of my tongue.

Back at the hotel, we drank rum instead and watched TV, which had come to the kingdom only a few years ago. The two state-owned stations offered sycophantic reports on the king, a Billy Graham special, and strange documentaries. One, about Chinese calligraphy, was broadcast in Chinese, with Chinese subtitles. Another told of a Berber bride fair in North Africa where women accepted proposals of marriage by saying, "You have captured my liver."

Roger chortled over his rum. "They'd never capture mine. They'd never find it."

I FELL ASLEEP to a program even more peculiar in these surroundings—a curling match between Canada and Sweden—and woke to yet another blinding dawn. The bathroom door fell off and splintered as I stumbled into the shower. Roger opted for a swim instead and found his friend, the masseur, waiting for him. In the ill-lit restaurant, an elderly couple stared glumly into space, waiting for signs of breakfast, which failed to appear. Expatriates, we later learned, referred to the Dateline as the Dead Line.

"Let's get out of town," Roger said.

"Fine. Where to?"

"Anywhere but here."

We hailed a taxi and asked the driver, a man named Sione, if he'd show us around the island, which was only about twenty miles across and a few miles wide (all of Tonga's scattered landmass covers just several hundred square miles). Luckily, Sione spoke English and was by far the friendliest Tongan we'd met. Less fortunate was his flatulence. Big, even by Tongan standards, he lifted one buttock every few minutes and unleashed a thundering fart. Roger, seated up front, struggled with the broken passenger-side window, which refused to go down. He lit a cigarette instead, and Sione joined him. The airless taxi quickly filled with a foul-smelling fug.

As we passed the palace, I mentioned my visit there the previous day. "We love our king!" Sione exclaimed.

"Why?"

"Because he is fat. Too fat!" Sione meant this as a compliment. "A little man cannot have big power. And a big man needs a big woman. So everyone is fat!" He laughed, raising one buttock again.

We asked Sione to drive us to the far end of Nuku'alofa's waterfront, close to where Cook had anchored on his third voyage. The paved coastal road ended at a rubbish dump, and just beyond it sprawled a shantytown of houses that were little more than animal pens, with outdoor privies and pigs taking cover from the sun in rusted cars. Some of the shacks teetered on concrete stilts above pools of fetid water. Sione said the people who lived here were poor migrants from other islands who flocked to the capital in search of work, swelling Nuku'alofa's population to thirty thousand. Many ended up in flood-prone lowlands like this.

He seemed embarrassed by the squalor and steered us around the coast to a lagoonside neighborhood of grand, villa-style houses. Many had high-security gates, tennis courts, and Mercedeses and BMWs parked in the drive. "The nobles," Sione said. A few minutes later we passed a vast estate that appeared to be modeled on a Southern plantation, perched on a hill well back from the road. This was the home of the crown prince, a globe-trotting businessman who drove around Tonga in a black London cab. His sister, the princess, lived across the road; two enormous stone tigers guarded the entrance to her drive.

A short way on, we sprang into open countryside. Fields of tomato, banana, and yam spread on either side of the road, fertile and orderly, much as Cook had described them. Sione pulled over beside a plaque that said: "Here stood formerly the Great Banyan or Captain Cook's Tree under the branch of which the celebrated navigator came ashore."

The spot was peaceful, skirted by mangroves and facing a lagoon. At the time of Cook's visit here in 1777, he found "a Villige most delightfully situated on the bank of the inlet where all the great men in the island resided." Cook also admired the well-fenced estates, which included ornamental plants.

The "great men" had since decamped to Nuku'alofa, leaving no sign of humanity apart from a graveyard. Tongans, like Niueans, lavished great care on the dead, though their style was much gaudier. The graves were decorated with plastic flowers, porcelain cupids, teddy bears, and Madonna figurines. Brilliant quilts, hoisted on posts, rose behind many of the graves. It seemed as though all the effusion lacking in the Tongan personality found expression in funereal exuberance. When I queried Sione about this, he shrugged and said, "Life is short. Death very long. Too long!"

We continued along the coast to a village called Talafo'ou. According to my guidebook, the village was famed for its "smart pigs." Sione pointed across a tidal flat at a dozen or so porkers snuffling in the sand and mud. "Look, pigs go fishing!" We walked out for a closer view and saw that the pigs were rooting for crabs, even wading into the snout-deep water. Sione said the pigs were not only smart but also exceptionally tasty. "Tongans love to eat pig," he said. "Also ducks, chickens, dogs. Cats, cars, houses. Everything!"

Our next stop was Tongatapu's premier tourist attraction: Ha'a-monga'a Maui, a massive stone arch that resembled one of the trilithons at Stonehenge. The three stones weighed some forty tons each, with the lintel fitted into notches atop seventeen-foot-high uprights. Simply moving the stones would be a major engineering feat today, and much more so in the thirteenth century, when Tongans had erected them. No one knew for sure how this had been done, or what purpose the structure served. The current king, who took an interest in such things, hypothesized that the trilithon acted as a seasonal clock, and tests conducted during the solstices lent support to this theory.

Nearby stood another impressive stone, labeled "Sitting Mound and Stone Backrest." A sign explained that Tu'itatui, the ruler who oversaw construction of the trilithon, was so fearful of assassination that he shaped his coral throne as a gargantuan backrest, to protect against attacks from behind. He also used a stick to ward off anyone who came too close while serving kava: hence his name, which translated as "King-Strike-the-Knee." Tu'itatui was a huge man, the sign said, with "an exceptionally large (big long) head." I wasn't sure what this meant. But when Sione leaned against the stone, even he seemed puny against its coral bulk.

I was curious to learn more, but the historic park enclosing the site had the same air of abandonment as every other such place we'd seen. The strangely worded sign sat on rusted poles and had been made almost illegible by age and grime. The grass was uncut, and the souvenir stalls by the park entrance were unattended.

Sione drove a different route back to Nuku'alofa, taking us first through thinly inhabited countryside. We saw a few traditional houses similar to those Cook and his men observed, oval-shaped and thatch-roofed, with sidings made of reed. We also passed women making *tapa* much as they had in Cook's day, beating the bark on a log with heavy sticks and then laying it out on the grass to dry.

The other side of the island appeared much more modern and prosperous. Sione drove us past brick ranch houses and Spanish-style villas that looked as though they'd been transplanted from southern California. He said most of these belonged to people who had worked abroad, or to noblemen and their families. But none of the houses could compete with the churches, some as grand as cathedrals and ringed by acres of manicured grounds. As we passed a flying fox sanctuary where royals, and only royals, were permitted to hunt the immense bats, I thought back to my conversation with the government spokes-woman. She'd been right. Tonga *was* England in aspic—England, that is, circa 1400.

In the wake of Cook's voyages, Europeans looked to the Pacific to understand their own "primitive" past, as noble savages or barbarous heathens, depending on the writer's perspective. Tonga in the twenty-first century offered something else: a portal into premodern Europe, with its absolute monarchy, its barons and serfs, its union of church and state. Tonga wasn't the land where time began. It was the place where time had gone back.

THAT NIGHT, WHILE Roger watched weird documentaries, I read the Tongan constitution. Drafted in 1875 by an English reverend who had served as the king's adviser and later as prime minister, the constitution included lines such as "The person of the King is sacred" and "All the land is the property of the King." No prospective heir to the throne could marry without the king's consent. One of the current princes had done so, and forfeited his right to succession. The king also handed out hereditary estates as he saw fit. There was a legislative assembly, but the king could "dissolve it at his pleasure." Not that he needed to bother; nine noblemen, and eleven ministers appointed by the king for life, held an unassailable majority over nine representatives elected by commoners. "My inheritance consists of God and Tonga," read the motto on the royal seal.

The next day, I made the rounds of Nuku'alofa's foreign consulates and learned that Tonga was even more feudal than I'd supposed. Diplomats said that it was still almost impossible for commoners to own land; most Tongans lived as tenants of the nobility. The nobles also asked for periodic "contributions" from their vassals, such as food for a daughter's wedding. Churches made even greater demands, exacting donations that often totaled a fifth of a household's income, and publicly announcing each family's giving. The annual budget of the Mormon Church alone was half that of the Tongan government's.

While most Tongans accepted this system, the diplomats said, there was growing discontent over the islands' collapsing economy. As in

Niue, emigration had long served as a safety valve, providing jobs to young people and remittance money for their families in Tonga. But young Tongan men were renowned for overstaying their visas and joining gangs. As a result, Western countries were now deporting them in large numbers. These youths returned home, angry and unemployed, to a country where jobs were scarce and ill-paid, labor unions banned, and social customs much less libertine than in the West.

This partly explained the surliness of some Tongans we'd met, and it had also contributed to a rash of attacks on foreigners. The government's passport-selling scheme, and the king's recent embrace of Beijing (which had helped Tonga enter the U.N.), had brought an influx of Chinese, some of whom took over small retail shops once run by Tongans. A number of the stores had been looted and burned, and their owners beaten. Tongans' ingrained xenophobia also undercut tourism, on which Tonga claimed to stake its economic future. "They want tourism," one envoy said, "but they're not sure if they want tourists."

A small but vocal democracy movement was also stepping up its dissent, charging the regime with corruption and demanding to know why royals and nobles lived grandly while so much of the country lay in shambles. The heir to the throne, whose vast mansion we'd passed, was a playboy who spent much of his time on the Riviera. He was famed for making disparaging comments about ordinary Tongans; "left to their own devices," he once declared, they would "urinate in elevators." His sister had made a fortune as head of a company that leased Tonga's satellite space above Asia.

Their father, meanwhile, was becoming ever more eccentric with age. He'd issued a royal decree naming as "court jester" an American Buddhist who was also entrusted with managing the country's trust fund. The jester gambled most of the fund on America's unregulated "viatical industry"—buying the insurance policies of elderly or terminally ill patients, in hopes they'd die while the policy was still worth more than its cost—and promptly lost $20 million U.S., or more than half the annual budget of Tonga's government.

Despite such scandals, the royal family showed little sign of acceding to demands for accountability and democracy. "Power is delightful," one diplomat concluded, "and absolute power is absolutely delightful."

WHILE I WAS out, Roger had received a call in our room from the king's secretary. My interview request had been granted—for the next morning! I was to appear at 'Eleni 'Aho's office at 9:30 sharp, and the dress code was specific: coat, tie, and a shirt with a collar. "Guess that means I can't come along," Roger joked. "I've only got T-shirts, and my shorts need pressing." In fact, he had to fly back to Sydney the next day to go back to work.

My wardrobe wasn't in much better shape than Roger's. The coat and tie I'd packed in hopes of meeting the king lay rumpled at the bottom of my bag. The one decent shirt I'd brought was on my back: a sweat-stained rag. It was six in the evening. There was no iron in the room, and I didn't relish trying to wash and dry my shirt in the mildewed bathroom.

I went to the hotel desk and shamelessly pulled the only string I had. "I'm seeing the king first thing tomorrow." The receptionist reluctantly allowed as how the hotel laundry might iron my jacket and tie by breakfast, but that was all. So I sprinted several blocks to a clothing store and managed, as the shopkeeper pulled down his shutter, to purchase a white shirt, tightly packaged in plastic and labeled "medium."

When I unwrapped it the next morning, I discovered that "medium" meant something very different in Tonga than elsewhere. The arm and neck holes could easily accommodate two of each. The fabric, if you could call it that, felt like cardboard and caused me to sweat the moment I put it on.

"One hundred percent man-made fiber," Roger said, checking the label. "The collar makes you look like a starved chicken." Meanwhile, the hotel had returned my jacket and tie with shiny scorch marks, stiff and glossy. "They go nicely with the shirt," Roger said.

He charitably agreed to carry my jacket as far as the palace before catching a cab to the airport. On the way, we stopped for coffee and chatted with a New Zealand businessman at the next table. When I told him I was headed to the palace, he shook his head sympathetically. Royal audiences, of which he'd had several, ranged from good to shocking. "During the shocking ones, the king sits there and says nothing."

By the time we'd shuffled the last humid blocks to the palace, my oversized shirt was stuck in damp clumps to my torso. My tie had turned rigor-mortal, curling from the bottom and tonguing straight out. Roger couldn't glance at me without cracking up. "You look more ridiculous than I've ever seen you, which is saying a lot." He helped me into my oven-fried jacket, then convulsed with laughter again. "Maybe you can apply for a job as the new court jester."

He left me at the private secretary's office. The door was locked, and no one answered my repeated knocks. I went outside and looked through the window. 'Eleni 'Aho sat at her desk, ignoring my waves and taps on the glass. I went back inside and waited as patiently as I could in the hall by her office. The only furniture was a swivel chair with a wheel missing; as soon as I sat down I was dumped on the floor. I knocked again. Still no answer. Was the interview off? Had the secretary caught sight of my clothes and decided to cancel?

I saw a woman down the hall and almost tackled her, babbling about my nine-thirty appointment. It was now almost ten. She shrugged and showed me into a room with royal portraits, most of them askew. Ten minutes later, a man in an olive military uniform appeared and asked for my passport. This was a member of Tonga's two-hundred-man army. "How do I pronounce your name for the king?" he asked.

"Horwitz. Whore-wits."

"Howid?"

"That's fine."

The soldier led me outside, past a stretch Cadillac with a crown on the license plate, and through a side gate to the palace grounds. I asked him how I should address the king. " 'Your Majesty' and a handshake is fine," he said. Only Tongan subjects had to crawl in his presence. Another guard escorted me across the lawn to an airy room of the palace, just off the porch. It was furnished with a long table and a massive chair of heavy oak, etched with a coat of arms. The décor included a book titled *Songs of Worship*, a satellite photograph showing "oil seepage" on Tonga (another of the king's obsessions, though no consequential oil deposits had ever been found), and a topographical map of the islands signed by Ronald Reagan.

I heard heavy breathing in the hall and a moment later the king appeared, a cane in each hand. He wore a lemon Nehru jacket over an ankle-length robe from under which poked heavy sandals. Very stooped, he looked much less formidable than in his portraits. Exercise, as well as illness, had diminished his stature from his Guinness World Records days. Still, at six foot three and three hundred pounds, he was very large, particularly for a man of eighty-two. As he slowly settled his bulk into the high-backed oak throne and gazed in my direction with hooded eyes, I felt as though I were seated before a Buddha.

"Mr. Howid," he said, extending his hand and enfolding mine, as if with a boxing glove.

"Your Majesty." I waited for him to speak again, but the onus was evidently on me. I'd been told that it was customary to bring the king a small gift. Unable to think of anything I could buy in Tonga that the ruler of the land didn't already possess, I'd taken a cue from other writers and brought a copy of a book I'd written about the American Civil War.

Passing the book across to the king, I told him about my reason for coming to Tonga and recited the first of my prepared questions: How was Cook's visit remembered? My query hung in the air. The king remained absolutely silent and still, eyes trained on the table. He wore gold watches on both wrists and I watched them tick, and tick, for three minutes. I thought of the businessman I'd just met at the coffee shop: the word "shocking" echoed in my head.

Then the king mumbled something. I'd been warned of this too: not a speech impediment, exactly, but a tendency to slur his words.

"Pardon?"

"They built the first submarine," he repeated, slushing the "s."

Submarine? Perhaps he'd misunderstood my question. I was pondering a polite way to rephrase it when the king pointed a hot-dog-sized finger at the book I'd given him. The cover showed a man in Confederate uniform.

"The submarine was hand-cranked," he said. "It sank on its first trip after destroying a Union vessel. The men inside just breathed the air they took down with them and quickly ran short of oxygen."

He was referring to the *Hunley,* a Confederate submarine that sank in Charleston Harbor in 1864. This was an arcane bit of naval history known to few except Civil War buffs.

"It was a pioneering effort, a productive failure," the king continued. "In World War One, the Allies had such a failure during the invasion of Gallipoli. They didn't know how to land troops on beaches. But they learned from that, and the success of the Normandy invasion came in a way from the failure at Gallipoli. It was the same with the Confederate submarine."

I was relieved, and, at the same time, alarmed. The man was obviously clear-headed, he knew his history, and he seemed in a voluble mood. Then again, I had only an hour, and I sensed that the king could easily fill it with musings about the Confederacy. I steered us back to Cook and asked the king what he'd learned as a child about the captain.

"I knew that he'd visited three times, and that he was an admirable man, very interested in the health and welfare of his crew. This was not typical of the day. Many sea captains were only interested in controlling their men." I listened politely to a discourse on naval discipline. When he paused for breath, I broke in with a question about the tortoise Cook had given the Tongans.

"I believe it was from Madagascar, not the Galápagos as many people think," he said. "Galápagos tortoises are much bigger, and not so long-lived." As a boy, the king had ridden around the palace grounds on the tortoise's back, and he recalled that Tu'i Malila sometimes strayed as far as a mile away. "Cook also left some red cloth used for making marine uniforms. It was displayed for many years." He laughed, his dark eyes becoming suddenly merry and warm. "Did you know Americans called British marines lobsterbacks because of their red uniforms?"

A servant entered with a silver tray on which sat two crystal glasses of orange juice. Kava was no longer the royal drink of choice. "I go through the gesture and pretend to drink it at ceremonies," the king said. "I don't think it's very clean." He also avoided alcohol and tobacco and kept to a rigorous exercise schedule, visiting the gym three times a week and walking around the palace grounds. This had helped him shed 150 pounds since his peak.

"When I was fourteen I pole-vaulted about ten feet," he said. "No fourteen-year-old has leaped higher yet in Tonga." It was hard to imagine a man of his size having performed this feat, and harder still to imagine that any Tongan teenager would try to break the monarch's record.

The king sipped juice, fingering my book again. "I was born on the Fourth of July, so I've always had an interest in America. Europe, too. I just read a biography of Napoleon and am very interested in Bismarck." This led to a discourse on battle tactics and Bismarck's sound judgment on and off the battlefield. "I am very interested in history of all kinds," he concluded.

All history, that is, except Cook's. I tried to broach the topic one more time, pointing to drawings of Tonga on the room's wall, made by an artist aboard an early French expedition. Did the journals and art of European explorers have value to Tongans today?

"Yes, it is strange in a way. We must look to what the Europeans saw two hundred years ago to teach ourselves about Tonga as it was. We just built a hundred-foot double pirogue. We learned what it was like from European sketches." He paused. "When William the Conqueror came to England, Normandy was a territory settled by Vikings, and the ships William built were still Scandinavian in style."

I gave up on Cook and asked about politics instead. The king had brought the Tongan monarchy into the twenty-first century. Would it still be here in the twenty-second?

"I think so, yes. Without such an institution, the islands would fall apart and go their own way. Look at the Philippines, at Fiji. You need a sense of unity." He went silent for a moment. "Monarchy is a very old view of society, it started off, really, as war leaders. The Vikings, each of their early ships had a leader. It grew from that."

As he went on, about Norsemen and ship design, my attention began to drift. But it was hard to take my gaze off the king. He filled most of my field of vision. Studying his face, I noticed that the lower half was much larger than the upper, and that his head seemed too small for his titanic body. He looked a bit like the wrinkled tortoise he'd ridden as a child.

"In America, the constitution was made for a republic but it is not one really," he said, following the Norsemen across the Atlantic. "The president appoints his ministers, the same as here. So it is not really so different." This put him in mind of the new U.S. president, whose father he'd met. He was pleased that a second Bush was in the White House, though his preference was dynastic rather than political. "It is a good family," he said.

He felt even closer to the Chinese, who now gave Tonga considerable aid. The king, a fundamentalist Christian and formerly a fierce anticommunist who had kept close ties to Taiwan, seemed an unlikely ally of Beijing. But he felt there was a strong kinship between Tongans and Chinese. "They belong to the Mongoloid race and so do we. All Mongoloid people have blue spots on their spines when they are born."

I learned later that this unlikely sounding birthmark did exist. Still, it seemed an odd basis for international alignment. Even stranger was the king's belief that his tiny Christian nation might have spiritual influence over China's billion-plus people, and that Tongan missionaries would be allowed to proselytize on the mainland. "Religion comes very late in a society's development," he said. "Christianity changed Tonga from top to bottom. Perhaps China will change, too."

The king appeared tired. I could see from his two watches that we'd been talking for an hour and a quarter, longer than scheduled. I asked to take his photograph. He assumed a solemn pose and then pointed to the palace lawn. "You should take a picture of my statue, too. It was a gift from the Chinese." He saw me to the door. "There used to be tall Norfolk pines on the grounds, but they were chopped down so the trees would not fall on my statue."

A guard escorted me across the grass to the towering bronze. The statue made the king appear strikingly Mao-like, with Asiatic eyes, a martial uniform, and a military cap tucked under his arm. I could see why the statue pleased the king. He looked like a wise and imposing commander, an oriental Bismarck.

Once outside the palace gate, I stripped off my coat and tie and found a shade tree to slump under. I flipped through my notes, trying to make sense of my audience. The king seemed a gentler, more modern figure than I'd expected from the medieval cast of his domain. Also, despite all the trappings, he wasn't particularly regal. If anything, he appeared miscast for monarchy: a man who would probably have been happier teaching at a war college in the West. He'd answered my questions about affairs of state with detachment, becoming much more animated each time we talked about something other than Tonga.

Perhaps this explained the neglected state of his kingdom, and also why he'd agreed to see me, an American writing about naval history (or so I'd described myself in my letter to his secretary). I felt a little bad that I'd asked him about other things, rather than spending a pleasant hour chatting about Confederate submarines.

LATER IN THE week, I went to see one of the few outspoken mavericks in Tonga. Futa Helu ran a high school and university called 'Atenesi (Tongan for Athens), and had modeled its curriculum on Oxford's. Not that 'Atenesi's campus bore any resemblance to its English counterpart. A taxi deposited me at the end of a dirt road in what seemed another of Nuku'alofa's flooded shantytowns. The school's main building was an ugly concrete edifice with broken windows. Futa Helu kept office at home, a ramshackle wood house with pigs rooting in puddles outside.

"Welcome to Athens, the capital of critical thought," he said with a faint smile, showing me into the simple but immaculate interior. Futa was a man of about sixty, with flyaway Einstein hair. He wore a matted Tongan skirt. On Fridays, Futa explained, faculty and students donned traditional garb. On other days they wore Western dress. Classes were conducted in English and emphasized liberal arts.

"Western Europe had the seed of the Greeks," he said, "while in Polynesia criticism has never been encouraged. We are trying to change that. There are enough automatons already in Tonga." Futa clearly wasn't one of them. "We are what anthropologists call a shame culture. People spend their time polishing their personal and family image, they don't want to lose face or security. The church and nobility exploit this."

Futa had started 'Atenesi in 1966 as an alternative to other schools in Tonga, over 80 percent of which were church run. A school emphasizing Western classics might seem old-fashioned, even reactionary, elsewhere in the Pacific, where the emphasis was on reclaiming indigenous culture and language. Tonga was different. "We don't have the mentality of former colonial places," Futa said. "We believe Europeans are clever and rich, but we never had the deep inferiority complex you see in some countries." He laughed. "If anything, we look down on other people, we're proud and assertive, which is why many Polynesians hate us."

At the same time, Tongans had been spared the deep resentment of the West common in many colonized societies. "So we are open to learn from European sources," he said. This included Cook. The captain's journals were a primary source for classes on Tongan history and culture at 'Atenesi. Futa felt that Cook's journals cast light not only on Tonga's culture but also on its character. "He wrote that commoners built towers of yams for the chiefs. We still see that today: the size of an offering is a mirror of your heart, how much you value a person. People express loyalty to nobles and the church by giving more than they can afford. Otherwise, they will feel shamed." This deference was built into the language, too. Futa said there were different ways to ask "How are you?" depending on whether a Tongan was speaking to a commoner, a nobleman, or the king. "All three phrases mean the same thing," he said, "but it's a linguistic way of acknowledging class and rank."

Cook's description of island plenty also offered insight into Tonga's current economic plight. A surgeon aboard the *Resolution* wrote that islanders led "a very easy and indolent Kind of Life," a judgment Futa concurred with. "Tonga enjoyed a kind of Stone Age affluence," he said. "Now we have a cash economy but the old habits remain. Tongans are still laid-back and lazy, they don't have staying power. So everything becomes run-down, neglected."

Futa was an excellent teacher; in an hour, he managed to explain much of what I'd seen in Tonga. I asked if I could sit in on the university class he was about to teach, on political philosophy. "Absolutely!" he said, gathering up a few books. Then he led me to his classroom: a wooden building perched on concrete stilts above a flooded field. Inside, a dozen students sat on benches. There were holes in the floor, and Futa left the doors open to offer some relief from the stifling humidity. Standing at the front, with a dog curled at his feet, Futa began, "I was talking in our last class about Hegel. Today I will cover Marx and dialectical materialism."

The lecture that followed resembled many I'd heard in college, except that Futa illustrated each point with reference to Tonga. "Marx believed in the inevitability of class conflict, but in Tonga it hasn't happened that way. Here, the landed nobility has moved into business, they have become the owners of capital. It is a depressing thought, really. We'd like to see the aristocracy to be weakened, but instead it is strengthening."

Futa returned to Marx, to class conflict, but only for a moment. "We have been conditioned to fawn. Parents beat their kids to bow down in the presence of their social superiors. Perhaps market forces will erode these traditional honors and work for a kind of egalitarianism. But only if we think critically, for ourselves."

The students took copious notes, asked a few questions, and after an hour they rose to attend the next class. 'Atenesi had no bells. "I urge you to read *Das Kapital*, it is in the library," Futa concluded. "Also the *Communist Manifesto*. Next week we'll talk about American legal theory."

I spoke with Futa for a few more minutes outside the classroom. In the Tongan context, his lecture seemed frankly subversive and I wondered if the authorities took notice. "At the beginning the government was pretty hostile," he said. "But they've learned to live with us. And many people secretly believe this is the only way to move forward, by educating the young like this."

I asked him if he thought his efforts would change Tonga. He smiled wearily. "Not in my lifetime, perhaps. But it is a bit of leaven that will work slowly through the flour." Followed by his dog, Futa hiked up his skirt and headed through the mud to teach his next class.

THE CHRISTIAN SABBATH in Tonga was so sacrosanct that it began on Saturday. At Nuku'alofa's central market, men in shirts and ties shouted through loudspeakers, urging people to attend church the next day. Most businesses closed at noon. By Sunday morning, the capital was so quiet you could hear a coconut drop. Movie houses and bars closed for the day, fishing and swimming were prohibited, planes didn't fly, and any contract signed on the Sabbath was considered void. "I never looked forward to Monday until I came here," a Fijian doctor told me, settling in for a long day at the hotel snack bar, about the only place in town serving food and drink.

At ten A.M., bells started pealing and the streets filled with families headed for church. (Most congregations held three services on Sunday.) In hopes of glimpsing the monarch in public, I decided to visit a Methodist church he often attended, a huge concrete edifice near the palace that was big enough to seat several thousand people. Its interior was utterly plain, except for the king's box: a high-backed chair with a coat-of-arms, a plush red pillow, and a fan perched on the rail.

The king didn't show, but I lingered by an open door listening to the choir. Everyone seemed to glow. As people came into the church they made eye contact with me and smiled broadly. I thought back to Futa's lecture on Marx. Religion might be the opiate of the masses, but in dour Tonga it seemed a welcome drug.

One man paused to chat before going in. He'd just visited America, and we talked for several minutes: about baseball, about fast food, about the weather in California. It was the first small talk I'd made during my entire stay in Tonga—the first idle chat of any kind with a complete stranger. I asked his name.

"Vaea," he said.

"*Baron* Vaea?" I'd heard this name many times over the past week. In hierarchical Tonga, he ranked very close to the top.

"Yes, that's me." He shook my hand and went inside. I'd just met the only baron in the realm and he seemed a regular, unassuming guy. Not for the first time, I realized that Tonga confused me as much as it had Cook.

One mystery in particular still lingered. Several times during the week, I'd gone back to the bar where Roger and I had met Macy Cook, the captain's alleged descendant. We'd failed to find her, much to Roger's satisfaction. Now it was Sunday, the bar was closed, and my flight to Sydney left the next morning. But there wasn't much to do, except lie by the hotel pool. So I went in search of Macy's house, which the barman had said lay somewhere behind the pub. I found her washing clothes in a tub before a shack not much bigger than a chicken coop.

Macy said her mother hadn't been able to find the family history she'd mentioned to us. But Macy had an uncle, Albert Cook, who lived on the outskirts of Nuku'alofa. Maybe he could help me. Macy declined my invitation to come along, but gave me vague directions. I hailed one of the few taxis operating on Sunday and spent an hour circling through the rural fringe of Nuku'alofa, the driver pausing every few minutes to ask passersby if they knew where we could find "Albert Cookie."

At sunset, when we were about to give up, a man directed us to a field where four women sat on the ground, peeling and bundling long brown leaves for weaving. One of them was Albert Cook's wife. She said Albert had gone to dig taro for dinner, but she invited us to their home across the road, a modest, four-room structure that housed eight family members. Following her lead, I took off my shoes and sat cross-legged on a black-and-white tapa mat. A few minutes later, Albert appeared at the door carrying a pitchfork. A gray-haired, barefoot man of about sixty, he spoke little English, but the taxi driver interpreted my questions.

"Captain Cook had a wife in New Zealand," Albert said. "Their child came here as a whaler and married a Tongan, and their son was my grandfather." The plot had thickened. Unfortunately, Albert didn't know any more of it. He recommended I go see his cousin, Tom Cook, who lived in Nuku'alofa. "He speaks much better English than me and is very interested in history."

This sounded promising. Except that it was dark out and Albert's directions were even vaguer than Macy's had been. It was nine o'clock before the driver finally found Tom Cook's house, a wooden bungalow just a few blocks from the Dateline. I'd stopped by the hotel to pick up the last of Roger's liquor supply, a bottle of Australian wine, to bring as a gift. As soon as Tom invited me inside, I sensed the wine was a mistake. The living room was dominated by an enormous, 1950s radio blaring a religious program. "I am a Mormon," Tom said, when I handed him the bottle.

A big man with a coronal of white hair, Tom wore a striped business shirt over his Tongan skirt. As Albert had promised, he spoke perfect English, and his face lit up when I said I was interested in Tongan history. Like the king, Tom was particularly intrigued by the Stonehenge-like trilithon I'd visited, and the massive backrest beside it. Tom said a skeleton had been found at the site that was believed to be that of the King-Strikes-the-Knee. "His skeleton measured ten feet two inches, and that was just the bones," Tom said. "So you see, Tongans are not eating as well as we used to."

This was an arresting thought: Tongans could be bigger. "When I was a child," Tom went on, "we cooked outside in an *umu*, on hot stones. Now everyone goes to the store and buys fatty mutton flaps or food filled with sugar. People used to die with their own teeth. Not now." He also believed that the size of the thirteenth-century king explained how the trilithon had been built. "If people were ten feet tall, enough of them together could have lifted the stones."

I nodded politely and asked Tom if he'd also studied Captain Cook. His face brightened again and he gave me an excellent summary of Cook's voyages, with details and exact dates for each of the captain's visits to Tonga. This was encouraging. So was Tom's precise knowledge of his own family's history. Tongans, like Maori, are renowned for being able to recite their genealogy going back thirty or more generations.

"That is how I know I am related to Captain Cook," Tom said, working his way back through the generations, very slowly. "Albert Edward Cook, my grandfather, ran away from a prison in New Zealand on April 25, 1863, and stowed away on a ship to Tonga. He'd been put in prison for drunkenness. My grandmother was his fourth wife. They married on May 10, 1911."

Tom said he'd used this information to apply for permanent residency in New Zealand. The request had been granted, another encouraging sign. Tom continued back through the generations. His grandfather's father, George Cook, was one of twelve children born to an English father and a Maori mother. Tom told me about each of George's siblings, again with precise dates. It had taken us two hours to reach the early nineteenth century.

"And before that?" I asked.

"Captain Cook," Tom said. "He was George's father."

"You're sure?"

"Absolutely. There is a book in New Zealand showing the lines of descent."

"So Captain Cook had a Maori wife?"

"Yes. A princess named Tiraha. As I said, they had twelve children."

I studied the tangle of names and dates Tom had given me, and sketched a family tree, with James Cook and Tiraha at the top. "Have I got it right?" I asked, passing the tree to Tom.

He corrected the spelling of a few names, then scratched out "Captain James Cook" and wrote in "Captain William Cook" instead.

"Who's he?"

"James Cook's son, William," Tom said. "He came to New Zealand in 1780 and became a sea captain. He's the one who married Tiraha."

"I see. And what about James Cook? Didn't he have a Maori wife?"

"Oh no. He was a very faithful man, we know that from the history. A Christian man, like me. He had six children by his wife, Elizabeth."

This was true. Unfortunately, none was named William. Nor had any visited New Zealand. A rare onset of tact forbore me from mentioning this to Tom.

"It makes me so proud to be related to Captain Cook," he said. "As Cooks, the sea is in our blood. All my family has been fishermen or boatbuilders. I have a boat in Auckland. And my uncle's grandson has a degree in fishing and sailed a boat here from Tasmania." He smiled proudly. "Cook sailed with a hundred men, but that boy sailed alone. So you see, the blood is getting better."

It was almost midnight. I thanked Tom for his time, sprinted back to the Dateline, and phoned Roger in Sydney. I told him I'd tracked down Cook's descendants.

"You did not."

"Did so. A man named Tom Cook told me the whole story, with exact dates. Captain Cook had twelve children by a Maori princess."

Roger went uncharacteristically silent. "Oh, God. Give me the bloody details." Which I did, saving Captain William Cook for last.

Roger sighed audibly with relief. "For a minute there I thought you'd nailed Cook—a root rat, like me," he said. "Now we know. Percy slept quietly at night."

Chapter 10

NORTH YORKSHIRE:
A Plain, Zealous Man

We know all about Cook and we know nothing about him.
—ALISTAIR MACLEAN, *CAPTAIN COOK*

The autumn sky lowered so gloomily that it hardly qualified as daylight. After a year in the radiant Pacific, I'd lost the vocabulary to describe this flat an atmosphere.

"Leaden," Roger said. "That's the only word for it."

"Pewter?"

"Too poetic. Anyway, pewter's made of lead." He switched on the headlights. "You can't even say it's 'pregnant with rain.' Just leaden. Like the lid of a lead coffin."

The scenery had also lost its luster since we'd left the walled city of York an hour before. At first, we'd driven through meadows filled with sheep and piled with turnips for winter forage. We passed Castle Howard, the setting for *Brideshead Revisited*. A hare sprang from a hedgerow, followed by a fox. I waited for a hunting party to appear, in pinks and blowing trumpets.

Instead, a short way on, the fall foliage and stone farmsteads and cozy pubs suddenly vanished. We'd reached the North Yorkshire moors, barren except for a veil of heather and bracken. Purple in high summer, the moors now looked coarse and khaki, as drab as the leaden sky. The only landmark for miles was a brutalist military pyra-

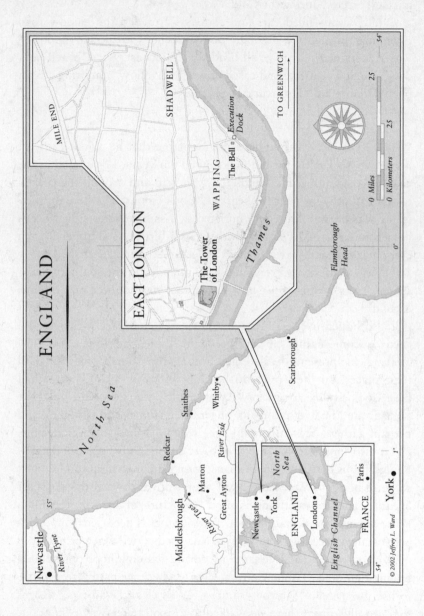

ENGLAND

EAST LONDON

MILE END

SHADWELL

WAPPING

The Bell ▪ Execution Dock

The Tower of London

Thames

TO GREENWICH

Flamborough Head

North Sea

Newcastle

River Tyne

Middlesbrough

River Tees

Marton

Great Ayton

River Esk

Redcar

Staithes

Whitby

Scarborough

Newcastle
York

ENGLAND

London

North Sea

English Channel

FRANCE

Paris

York

© 2002 Jeffrey L. Ward

0 Miles   25

0 Kilometers   25

mid; Roger said it was Fylindales, an early-warning station for ballistic missiles, erected during the Cold War.

Oddly, family-filled cars and caravans crowded the narrow road ribboning through the desolate moors. "School break starts today," Roger explained. "They're all headed to the coast. For a beach holiday!" He lit a cigarette and eased down the window, admitting a blast of cold, damp air. "It's great to be home."

WHEN ROGER HAD told me a month before that he planned to visit his native Yorkshire, for the first time in ten years, I'd jumped at the chance to tag along. His childhood haunts in and around the coastal town of Whitby lay near the heart of "Cook Country," where the navigator was born, reared, and initiated as a sailor. Better still, Roger's homecoming would coincide with Cook's birthday, October 27, an event marked each year by a week of local festivities. After the strange and ambivalent Cook ceremonies we'd attended in the southern hemisphere, I was curious to see how the captain was honored on his home ground.

I also hoped to get a better fix on Cook's character. Whenever I'd tried to conjure him on the beach in Tahiti, or Tonga, or New Zealand, his presence had seemed fleeting and faint. Cook visited all these places, but he wasn't *of* them. Yorkshire was different; it had been Cook's home for twenty-six of his fifty years. I could tread the same ground he had as a child, linger in his homes and churches, and perhaps gather a few clues to his personality that had so far eluded me.

I'd also have a chance to see Roger in his native surroundings— though in his case, the "inner man" wasn't quite so inscrutable. "Just so you know," he warned, as we wound down toward the sea, past Sneaton Thorpe and Ugglebarnby, "the crumpet here is appalling. Percy doesn't just sleep quietly in Yorkshire. He's deceased."

Nostalgia breeds strange rituals. Roger's dictated that our first stop in Whitby should be the same as during his childhood visits: at a building marked "Public Conveniences," where we paid fifteen pence to use the urinal. "Whitby's famous for its clean lavatories," Roger said proudly. From there we walked to a small take-away restaurant, or "caf," so Roger could revel in his native cuisine. As we stood in line, listening to the strongly accented chat, I felt as though I needed subtitles.

"Cheese and tom in a bap."

"There you go, loov."

"Mug of Oxo and a chip buttie, ta."

"Tom" was tomato, "bap" a roll, Oxo a brand of beef bouillon. "Chip buttie" was a heavily buttered bap stuffed with french fries. Roger ordered a cold pork pie and "scratchings," local slang for crackling. "Ahh, the taste and smell of fried pig fat," he sighed, gobbling the greasy snack. I dreaded to think what ritual came next.

"We have to walk to the end of the pier and gaze out to sea," Roger said.

"You sure? That sounds too normal and nice."

"Not in Whitby it's not."

We descended a steep street to the River Esk, which ran through the middle of Whitby. ("'Esk. North Sea feeder,'" my wife, Geraldine, had told me. "Very popular in crosswords.") As soon as we stepped from the shelter of a riverside building, the wind hit me so hard that I thought Roger had clapped my back. Vacationing families, clad in hooded anoraks, stumbled around us like drunks. A girl, weepy from the wind, or from fright, clutched her father with one hand and a stick of cotton candy with the other. The pink floss flew from the stick like seeds from a dandelion.

Hunched over almost double, we struggled as far as a wind-chewed sandstone lighthouse. "You go ahead without me!" I shouted, feeling like a climber at Hillary's Step on Everest. Roger persevered to the end of the pier, clutching lampposts bent by the wind and crashing surf. Herring boats bobbed in the North Sea whitecaps, the waves washing over their sides. Roger returned, red-faced and runny-nosed, and slumped beside me in the lee of the lighthouse.

"Cook's first sail was in that," he yelled, nodding at the mountainous waves. "No wonder he was never fazed at sea, even off Antarctica." Then Roger pointed at children frolicking beneath a cliff at the water's edge, their pants rolled above their knees as they raced the frigid surf. "Cook insight number two. Yorkshire makes for tough people. Farming the moors is tough. The fishermen are very tough. Even the kids are tough. It makes sense that Cook started here."

COOK HADN'T STARTED exactly *here*; he was in his late teens by the time he reached Whitby. I wanted, as much as possible, to retrace his early life in chronological order. So after warming ourselves over a mug of Oxo, Roger and I left the rest of Whitby for later, and drove toward Cook's birthplace. The village of Marton lay only twenty-five miles away, over the Cleveland Hills west of Whitby. But getting there required some navigation. One of our maps didn't show Marton at all. The other marked it in microscopic print that was almost obscured by a highway cloverleaf and large block letters: MIDDLESBROUGH.

Middlesbrough was a map-eating sprawl that hadn't existed in Cook's day. The city arose during the Industrial Revolution, becoming one of the largest iron and steel centers in the world, and gradually smelting the once rural villages around it. Middlesbrough, in turn, belonged to an industrial expanse called Teesside, after the River Tees, the banks of which teemed with refineries, a nuclear power station, blast furnaces, and chemical plants.

Approaching from the coast, we saw steam and smoke billowing above the green Cleveland Hills before we could see actual industry. It was eerie, like driving toward a distant battlefield. Then, cresting a sheep-studded rise, we descended into a plain of smokestacks, stump-like cooling towers, cranes, and high-rise public housing. The sky, mingling noxious fumes with the natural gloom, was now truly leaden. Teesside harbored three of the ten most toxic factories in Britain; asthma and cancer rates were four times the national average, and a smog alert shortly before our visit had forced residents with respiratory problems to stay indoors.

Lost in a maze of roundabouts, we finally spotted a sign adorned with a sailing ship, pointing the way to Cook's birthplace. This led us to a park sealed off from its congested surroundings by a perimeter of trees. As we got out of the car, gulping the relatively fresh air, I reflected on one of Cook's minor legacies. Here, as at Gisborne and Botany Bay, memory of the navigator provided an excuse for a green and tranquil refuge, however small.

Musket fire crackled from inside the park. Cook's weeklong birthday party was already under way. Hiking toward the noise, we met a periwigged man with a painted-on mustache and asked him what was going on. "Plains of Abraham," he replied, pointing at a five-foot-high wall of plywood, topped with castlelike crenellations. "That's Quebec City." He rushed off to join the fray.

In 1759, as a young officer, Cook charted and buoyed the St. Lawrence River, helping British forces land troops near Quebec and defeat their French and Indian foes on the Plains of Abraham. I didn't know many details from this period of Cook's career. Unfortunately, I wasn't about to learn much more.

"Bloody Frogs!" shouted a Highlander in a kilt, his legs blue from the cold as he charged the walls of "Quebec." Our mustachioed friend popped up from behind the plywood fortress and shouted back, *"Cochons d'Angleterre!"* English pigs! A few "Indians" burst from the woods, wielding wood tomahawks. After some clumsy wrestling with the British, the Indians held aloft mock scalps and whooped at the small crowd that had gathered to watch.

"This is almost as lamentable as Cooktown," Roger said, "and without a drop of grog in sight." We spotted a commander in a tricorn and tight naval uniform that resembled Cook's. "Do you notice how breeches always draw attention to the gonads?" Roger observed, as we walked over to meet him. "It's hard to look these people in the face."

The officer turned out to be Ian Stubbs, a curator at the Captain Cook Birthplace Museum, which lay at the center of the park. "I'm about six inches too short to play Cook," he confessed, pronouncing the captain's name with a strong Yorkshire accent, as "Koook." It dawned on me that this was probably how Cook said his name. This might explain why Tahitians, who had no hard "C" or "K" sound in their vocabulary, and ended all words in vowels, had rendered his name as "Toote" or "Tute."

When the battle ended, Ian invited us to join a tour of the park, beginning at Cook's birth site, in what was now a soggy field. Cook's father, James, was born in Scotland, the son of a tailor, and had migrated across the border to northern England, where he married Grace Pace. Their mud-and-thatch biggin in Marton had been torn down in 1786, to make room for a stable yard behind a newly built mansion. But the owner of the estate marked the outline of the Cooks' cottage with a quadrangle of flint. Then, in the mid-nineteenth century, a prosperous German-born ironmaster named Henry Bolckow bought the estate. In his eagerness to anglicize, Bolckow built a grand hall and erected a plinth topped by a pink granite urn to mark the site of the cottage.

Ian said that the name Marton, a settlement first mentioned in the eleventh-century Domesday Book, was probably short for "Marsh Town." I gazed at the urn and tried to conjure the site as it might have appeared in October 1728. The ground felt spongy, the chill air moist and penetrating. Traffic roared in the distance. An Indian reenactor wandered past in buckskins, gnawing on a candy bar.

Ian led us through a garden Bolckow had planted with exotic species from lands Cook visited, and across a busy road to St. Cuthbert's, the twelfth-century church where Cook had been baptized. St. Cuthbert's was low and dun-colored and ringed by crooked headstones so ancient that the inscriptions had worn away. The interior was even more evocative: cold stone floor, timber ceiling, columns carved with leering griffins. "We think this grave belongs to a Crusader, possibly a Knight Templar," Ian said, casually peeling away a carpet to expose a rectangle etched with a cross and sword.

Then he showed us the church register, listing centuries of births, deaths, and marriages. The yellowed page for November 3, 1728, contained the first recorded mention of the Great Navigator: "James ye son of James Cook day labourer baptised." Fifteen years after Cook's baptism, news of Joseph Banks's birth appeared in *The Gentleman's Magazine,* alongside notices for the arrival of other newborns of exalted parentage. Cook's merited only the terse entry in St. Cuthbert's registry, his status etched beside his name, like that of neighboring infants: a bricklayer's son, a mariner's daughter.

Studying the page, I felt the cold draft of eighteenth-century class, and was reminded, yet again, of the extraordinariness of Cook's rise. It was a feat that still resonated today. As we strolled back to the birthplace park, I asked Ian what had drawn him to Cook. "He had nothing at all to start with, yet through hard work and a few coincidences, he became a great man," he said. "I guess you could say he gives hope to others."

"Oh, aye," said an old woman walking beside us. "Cook wasn't to the manor born, was 'e?" She paused, staring at her stout shoes. "But what I like most is his grit and stickability and stubbornness. That's very Yorkshire."

The leaden sky opened up, pelting us with cold rain. This was very Yorkshire, too. We fled inside the Captain Cook Birthplace Museum, which offered a lively and informative tour of Cook's life and voyages. But it contained little on his boyhood in Marton, for the simple reason that almost no hard information existed, apart from the church registry.

"Did you feel his presence?" Roger asked, as we hiked through the rain to the car.

"I felt cold and damp. That's about it. And you?"

"No. Nothing. Just an urn. The church made me panicky and depressed, the way I always feel in church." He slipped in the mud. "I need a drink."

Just across from the park stood an ugly brick pub called the Ladle. Inside, the smoke was so thick that we could barely see our way to the bar. Most of the patrons had hand-rolled cigarettes hanging from their lips, like extras in an Andy Capp cartoon. "Good God," Roger whispered, "the entire tobacco industry of Great Britain is supported out of this single pub."

The bar menu listed two items: "turkey curry" and "mince and dumpling." I opted for the turkey. The substance that appeared some minutes later was a color I'd never seen on a plate, a radioactive yellow-orange. Poking from this vivid curry sauce was a mound of gray and stringy turkey. Roger looked at it in horror. "They wouldn't even serve that in the Army."

We fled, coughing, into the rain, and headed for another Cook site in Middlesbrough: a striking metal sculpture by Claes Oldenburg titled *Bottle of Notes*. The late-twentieth-century work was a tribute to Cook, with the steel cut into ribbons of script and molded in the shape of a tilted jug. "It's meant to suggest a message in a bottle," I said, reading from a tourist brochure, "left on the sand by a receding wave."

We studied the steel script to see what the message said. It was indecipherable, except for the sentiment spray-painted onto the sculpture:

ALL POLICE ARE DICKS. The rest of downtown Middlesbrough was also dispiriting. On the main shopping street, we passed tanning parlors, heavily pierced youths in enormous black boots, and a newsstand displaying a poster of the day's local headline: MORE JOBS MISERY.

Stopping at a coffee shop, I asked the young man behind the counter if locals took pride in their most famous native son.

"Cook? Learned about him in school. Didn't learn much." He paused. "But I admire the man a lot."

"Why's that?"

"He got out of this place, didn't he? I plan to do the same as soon as I can."

IN 1736, WHEN Cook was eight, his day-laboring father moved up a notch. He became a "hind," or overseer, on a farm owned by the lord of the manor in the village of Great Ayton, and moved there with his family. Ayton lay just five miles from Marton, but it felt like a different universe. While the surrounds of Marton had become a William Blake nightmare of "dark Satanic mills," Ayton represented the poet's opposing dream, of "England's green and pleasant land." We drove through verdant pastures arranged beneath a peak called Roseberry Topping, and entered a village of rose-covered cottages lining a duck-filled stream.

In the village green stood a statue of Cook as a shoeless and bare-chested lad, a shirt slung over his shoulder. "Must have been a mild day," Roger quipped, standing in the chill rain. "At least forty degrees." More realistic was a bas-relief on the wall of an old stone building. It depicted Cook as a teenager, clutching his hat and holding a staff, the trees around him bent by the wind. "In this building," stated a plaque on another wall of the same structure, "James Cook, the son of a day labourer, attended school."

The building now housed the Captain Cook Schoolroom Museum, which offered an excellent précis of education in eighteenth-century England. Public education in the modern sense didn't yet exist. The gentry generally hired tutors for their children, while middle-class parents sent their offspring to private grammar schools. Children of low status received no formal schooling. Roughly half of Britain's populace remained illiterate, including, most likely, Cook's parents.

But young James was gifted—and lucky. Thomas Scottowe, the lord of the manor who employed Cook's father, was the first in a long line of Cook's "social betters" to recognize the future navigator's potential. Scottowe paid for the boy to attend Ayton's charity school. This institution was a new phenomenon in Cook's day, and one that not everyone approved of. "The more a shepherd or ploughman know of the world, the less fitted he'll be to go through the fatigue and hardship of it with cheerfulness and equanimity," the writer Bernard Mandeville observed, five years before Cook's birth.

The school museum included a reconstruction of Cook's classroom: hard benches, muddy boots set in one corner, a weekly "Table of Faults" that listed misdemeanors such as lying, swearing, and "playing at church." Corporal punishment was the norm. As for the education Cook received, it was rudimentary and rote: basically, the three Rs and the catechism.

A display on penmanship revealed how meager life had been for charity-school youths. "Children had to be taught how to hold a pen because unlike modern children, they had never played or drawn with crayons or pencils." Also, quill pens made from goose feathers were delicate and easily broken. Ink was manufactured by the teacher in a laborious, twelve-hour process involving galls, gum arabic, and vitriol. "Paper was expensive, and so it was a serious offense for a child to spill ink on, or blot, his copybook."

Reading this, I wondered if Cook's devotion to detail, and his meticulousness as a mapmaker, had their origins here, as he sat terrified that he might spoil a sheet of paper or spill a drop of ink. The exhibit's concluding statement also gave insight into Cook's adult writing style. "Accuracy was highly valued, but not originality. There was no such thing as creative writing in the 18th century."

Cook attended this school for only three or four years; he was most likely taught by a local weaver who moonlighted as an instructor. During this period, the young boy also worked on the Scottowe farm, several miles outside the village. From here on, Cook would teach himself. But his brief time in this schoolroom was nonetheless a life-altering break. Without the basic literacy and numeracy he acquired at Ayton's small school he could never have become so expert at navigation, surveying, and astronomy.

In the schoolhouse, much more than at Marton, I felt able to conjure the young James: seated in the cold room on a hard bench, hunched over his quill, learning the workmanlike hand in which he would later pen more than a million words in his ships' logs and journals. But this pleasing apparition evaporated a moment later. On the way out, I noticed a small wall panel that said the school had been torn down in 1785, "due to the increase of poverty in the growing village." A poorhouse went up in its place. In other words, the Captain Cook Schoolroom Museum wasn't Cook's schoolhouse at all, despite the plaque we'd seen outside. It was a building erected six years after his death, and since refurbished to attract unsuspecting tourists like me.

Ayton, it turned out, had a history of hyping its Cook-related sites. Near the "schoolroom" stood a monument to "Cook's Cottage." This referred to the modest dwelling that Cook's aging parents built in 1755, on a parcel of "waste ground" in the village. In 1933, the cottage, by then derelict, was put up for auction with an advertisement that read: "Renowned as the home of Captain Cook's early days." The Australian state of Victoria bought the house at an inflated price and moved it to Melbourne, even transplanting the ivy that grew on its walls. And so it stands today, a popular tourist attraction and the oldest building in Australia, having been constructed fifteen years before Cook first sighted the Australian continent at what is now the east coast of Victoria.

There was one problem. The young Cook never lived in the cottage. By the time his parents built it, Cook was a Navy man and had been gone from Ayton for a decade; there's no evidence he ever spent a single night there. Also, drawings of the original cottage showed that it didn't much resemble the one taken to Melbourne; in the intervening two centuries, the building had undergone considerable change.

We walked across the road to the last of the Cook sites in Ayton: All Saints Church, which James attended as a child and where much of his family lay buried. This, at least, was the actual building Cook had known: a low, twelfth-century church with a heavy wooden door and a dark nave, illuminated—barely—by a Norman slit window. The church still had no heat or electric lights.

As we entered, an old man stepped from the shadows and introduced himself as Jack Greathead, a church guide. He showed us stones etched with eighth-century Celtic symbols, survivals from an Anglo-Saxon church that once stood on the same site. He also pointed at the dark wood pews, apologetically noting, "They're only from the eighteenth century."

"So Cook would have sat in them?" I asked. After our other stops, I was eager to inhabit some bit of authentic Cook space.

Jack shook his head. "Sorry, no." He explained that the Cook family would have sat in the back, in a portion of the church that had been torn down in 1880 to expand the graveyard outside. By then, Ayton had become a bustling village, and the church needed more room to bury all the dead. Jack led us to a space in the stonework by the door. "That's the charnel pit," he said. The ancient churchyard held so many bodies that gravediggers often struck earlier corpses. "So they'd throw the old bones in this hole," Jack said, retreating into the dark church.

Following Jack's directions, we wandered the crowded, lumpy graveyard until we found the Cook family plot: a single stone topped by a spooky, lightbulb-shaped angel's head, similar to those adorning old graves in New England. The inscription listed the five Cook children who had died young: Mary, Mary, Jane, William, and John. The recycling of Mary seemed especially poignant; Cook's mother had a sister named Mary, and it seems likely Grace meant to honor her.

Studying the dates on this cluttered stone, I calculated that James had been eight when the first of his siblings died. He lost two young sisters a few years later, and both his brothers when he was in his late teens and early twenties. Perhaps this helped explain the seeming coolness with which Cook later recorded the deaths of his shipmates. Well acquainted with death from an early age, he may have learned to armor his emotions. The headstone also spoke to Cook's hardy constitution. In the Darwinian world to which he was born, only the toughest made it to adulthood.

Two of his sisters also survived, although we know very little about them. Christiana Cook married a man named Cocker and vanished from the historical record. Margaret wed a fisherman, James Fleck, and moved to Redcar, nine miles from Ayton. One sad glimpse of the Flecks' connection to Cook survives. On England's northeast coast in the eighteenth century, smuggling brandy, silk, and other heavily taxed luxuries from the Continent was an extremely common occupation. James Fleck was charged with "running goods" in 1776, and wrote to his famous brother-in-law, claiming he was innocent and asking the captain for help.

But Cook was straitlaced. He wrote to an attorney about the matter, making it clear that he doubted Fleck's innocence and adding that he had neither the "time nor inclination" to intercede on his relative's behalf. No more is known of Fleck's fate, except that some of his and Margaret's descendants ended up in Australia. Cook left each of his sisters ten pounds sterling in his will.

Cook's mother and father left similarly faint traces on the historical record. Their names are etched on the gravestone in the All Saints churchyard, as "parents of the celebrated circumnavigator." But the church guide had told us this was a misleading nineteenth-century addition. Grace didn't lie beneath the stone; indeed, no one knew where in the churchyard she'd been buried. Her husband, who outlived her by fourteen years, moved to Redcar, where his daughter Margaret lived, and was buried near there. He was eighty-five at the time of his death: among eighteenth-century farm laborers, a Methuselah.

We know that Cook visited his aged father in 1771, between voyages, and that his will provided the old man an annuity of ten guineas. His father never received it; the elder James died just six weeks after his only surviving son, before news arrived in England that the captain had perished in "Owhyhee." This, at least, seemed a small blessing for a man who had endured so much hardship and family tragedy in the course of his long life.

I WANTED TO make one other stop near Ayton: the property outside the village where the Cooks lived and worked when James was a boy. It was still a working farm, a picturesque expanse of sloping pasture overlooked by Roseberry Topping. The land was private, so we leaned against a roadside fence, gazing at the sheep and cattle.

"Cook insight number three," Roger said, picking up where we'd left off on the pier in Whitby. "Cook always wrote about the livestock and seeds he left at every island. We think of him as a mariner, but he was a farm boy first, and he never lost that." I sensed something else. Growing up on a farm, working a plow and herding stock beneath Yorkshire's inclement skies, he would have developed an instinct for reading the weather, which served him well at sea.

A short way on, we saw a sign for a trail up Easby Moor, the highest point for miles around; James would probably have scaled it as a youth. Like farm work, climbing moors was excellent training for the future mapmaker. Almost everywhere Cook landed, he hurried up the nearest hill for a good look around.

Then again, Easby Moor didn't much resemble the hills that Cook scaled in Tahiti or New Zealand or Australia. Hiking up a steep path through a thinning cover of trees, we emerged on a bald summit swept by a howling wind off the North Sea, ten miles or so to the east. Easby Moor may well have been the spot from which Cook first looked out to sea—or at the "German Ocean," as the North Sea was then known. We couldn't see it now: the view was socked in by fog.

Instead, we studied a towering obelisk perched at the crest. It was the first monument in Britain erected in the navigator's honor, and easily the most colossal Cook memorial I'd yet seen. Curiously, it was also among the least heralded; I'd never read mention of it in any of my books on Cook. The monument's lengthy inscription perhaps explained why.

"Regardless of danger, he [Cook] opened an intercourse with the Friendly Isles and other parts of the Southern Hemisphere," it read in part. "While the spirit of enterprise, commerce and philanthropy shall animate the sons of Britain, while it shall be deemed the honour of a Christian nation to spread civilization and the blessing of Christian faith among pagan and savage tribes, so long will the name of Captain Cook stand out among the most celebrated and most admired benefactors of the human race." This Kiplingesque monument had been erected by one "Robert Campion Esquire" of Whitby, in 1827.

"I think that's the most unfortunate use of the word 'intercourse' I've ever seen," Roger said. "And I'm surprised all those 'pagan and savage tribes' haven't come over here and blown the thing up." He slouched off to pee in the heather, shouting over his shoulder, "Still, it's almost refreshing to see something so politically incorrect."

In the southern hemisphere, I'd learned to tiptoe around my admiration for Cook and had become used to hearing his name indelibly stained with the disease and dispossession that followed in his wake. In North Yorkshire, there was no such shame attached to his memory. Cook was a hero, plain and simple. Like Roger, I found this a bit liberating.

But I also felt wearied by the pendulum swing of historical memory. Cook, to me, wasn't the wicked imperialist that modern-day Maori and others imagined him to be. Nor was he the godlike figure that Robert Campion Esquire extolled, bestowing Christianity, commerce, and civilization on benighted savages. In remembering the man, the world had lost the balance and nuance I so admired in Cook's own writing about those he encountered.

But then, what *was* he? Everyone had an opinion—except Cook himself. His journals and charts allow us to follow every step and sail he took, down to the minutest degree of latitude. But Cook left us no map to his soul. Very rarely does he tell us *why* he did what he did, not just in the Pacific but throughout his life.

Descending Easby Moor, we found a plaque describing the surrounding landscape as "countryside which young James Cook knew and loved." If he "loved" it, why had he fled rural life as soon as he was able? After joining the Navy in 1755, Cook traveled home to Ayton only once that we know of. Nor did he ever express a sentimental attachment to his childhood terrain, at least not in his journals or surviving letters.

Even more enigmatic was this: Cook spent most of his career charting new territory and probably named more places than any person in history. Yet there's no evidence that he ever once called a river, shore, island, or promontory after any of the places he'd known during his childhood. And while he named countless landmarks after Admiralty bureaucrats, second-rate aristocrats, and sailors on his ships, he never gave this honor to any member of his own family.

As a chill twilight blanketed the moors, we left the Yorkshire countryside behind, as Cook had done, and followed his path to the sea.

JAMES COOK WAS about seventeen when he departed Great Ayton for Staithes, a small town on the North Sea coast north of Whitby, thirteen miles from his family's home. He'd secured work as a shop assistant to William Sanderson, a haberdasher and grocer. This seems, at first glance, an unlikely occupation for a farm boy and future navigator. But at the schoolroom museum, we'd learned that the teaching of arithmetic in Cook's day was "aimed particularly at preparing pupils for the shop-counter or merchant's warehouse." Also, Cook's later life revealed that he had a gift for mathematics. So it seems probable that his Ayton patron, Thomas Scottowe, recommended the quick-counting lad to William Sanderson, a friend and business associate in Staithes, just a day's walk away.

Staithes lay in a seaside crevasse so sheer that Roger and I couldn't see the small town until we'd plunged down a steep road from the cliff above. The road turned to cobble, slithering between close-packed houses and ending beside a seaside pub called the Cod and Lobster. The pub stood so close to the North Sea surf that a ship's bowsprit had once pierced its wall. Over beer and crisps, we scanned Beaglehole and other sources for the little that was known about Cook's time in Staithes.

During his eight months working at Sanderson's store, Cook slept under the counter, as was then the custom for shop assistants. Staithes was a small but busy seaport, and Sanderson's shop faced the water, just a few yards from the Cod and Lobster. According to local lore, the ships coming and going outside the shop's window entranced the young Cook, as did the tales told to him by visiting mariners. One day, a customer paid for an item with a shilling issued by the South Sea Company. Bewitched by the exotic coin, Cook plucked it from the shop till, putting another shilling in its place. One version of this tale (which made its way into every early biography of Cook) held that Sanderson accused his assistant of stealing the money, and as a result Cook ran off to sea.

"Calumny," Roger declared, when I read this aloud. "Locals just made up that story because Cook had the sense to leave. Can you imagine him spending his life as a grocer and haberdasher?"

Across from the pub we found a small home with a sign labeling it "Captain Cook's Cottage." This turned out to be as dubious as "Cook's Cottage" in Ayton. Long after Cook left Staithes, Sanderson's seafront shop succumbed to surf and storms. In the early nineteenth century, locals salvaged timbers from the wave-battered relic and erected a new store on the site of this cottage. Slight as this connection was, it remained the only physical remnant of Cook's time in Staithes.

It didn't take us long to tour the rest of town. Penned on three sides by high cliffs called nabs, Staithes was a picturesque tangle of alleys so narrow and precipitous that cottages piled almost on top of one another. Smoke coiled from every chimney. The ambience was cozy but claustrophobic, especially when set against the wide-open sea lapping at Staithes's feet. It was easy to imagine a restless and ambitious youth gazing out the window of Sanderson's shop and aching for escape.

Near the top of the High Street we noticed a gray stone building labeled "Primitive Methodist Chapel 1880," with a small sign beneath its stained-glass window: "Capt. Cook & Staithes Heritage Centre." Model boats floated in the window and wicker lobster pots perched by the door. It looked like another Cook tease.

The museum's first few rooms, stuffed with bric-a-brac, confirmed this impression. We studied a jumble of seashells, crab pots, old bonnets worn by local fisherwomen, and an intriguing notice for a 1797 fair in Staithes, which included a three-legged race ("maidens running in pairs" with their ankles tied together) and a man-and-wife race ("ye wife to be hugged either on the backe, in arms or by any other device. Husbands with light wives to be put back. No wheelbarrows allowed"). The notice suggested that life in eighteenth-century Yorkshire wasn't quite so pinched and prudish as I'd supposed.

"Is there anything in here to do with Cook?" Roger wondered aloud, as he studied a gag toy called "Big Mouth Billy Bass," which flapped its plastic tail and croaked the song "Take Me to the River." At the mention of Cook, a man suddenly materialized at Roger's side. "Oh, aye," he said. "You haven't even started yet."

Reg Firth was a large man with a gray mustache, gray hair tufted atop his head, prominent front teeth, and blue eyes that darted behind thick glasses. He looked like the March Hare. Reg led us from the warren of Staithes history into the nave of the former church, which now housed a two-story replica of Sanderson's shop: bay windows, a tiled roof, and candles, brooms, bolts of cloth, and other goods set out front. There was also a counter, fashioned from what had been the church pulpit, modeled on the one Cook slept under. The floor in front of the shop had been cobbled to resemble the street on which the store stood.

"The only thing wrong is the windows," Reg said. "They're four feet high and they should be five, but I was restricted for space." He wrung his hands, obviously vexed by this minute variance from the original. The window's wooden shutters also troubled him. "I believe these were salvaged from Sanderson's shop. But without carbon-dating, I can't be sure."

Reg bounded up a narrow flight of stairs to a vast room crammed from wall to wall, and floor to ceiling, with Cook memorabilia. This part of the onetime church still felt like a place of worship. The exhibits were arranged around the cycles of Cook's life, beginning with his birth in the mangerlike biggin in Marton and ending with his martyrdom at Hawaii. There were saintlike relics, such as a bottle of black sand from Point Venus, where Cook had trod, and a South Sea shilling "similar to the one Cook exchanged from the till of William Sanderson." The Word was carefully preserved on shelves filled with bound volumes, many of them ancient and rare. Framed quotes from Cook and his disciples adorned the walls. A few graven images lay mixed among this reverential display: a jigsaw puzzle of Cook's landing at Botany Bay, a toby jug of his head, a bottle of rum bearing his name.

After twenty minutes my head spun. There was no place for the eye to rest, and no way to uncover every treasure in less than a week. Reg hovered beside us, like a fussy shopkeeper, making sure each item was returned to its precise position the moment we moved to the next. Occasionally, he'd recommend a particularly valued object to our attention, such as blue bottle shards discovered by an English visitor to a beach in Cooktown. The Victoria and Albert Museum had confirmed that the glass was "free blown" and of eighteenth-century origin, possibly a gin bottle. The man who found the glass had given it to Reg because he liked the museum so much.

Other items reflected Reg's own scavenging, some of which broke new ground. Across one table spread William Sanderson's will, an extensive document. "Solicitors write out these wills, and every word has to be paid for," Reg said, "so of course it's very long." The will revealed that Sanderson, depicted in history books as a simple shop-keeper, had actually been a prominent merchant, banker, and landowner who left a considerable estate. "His wife and son ran it all into the ground," Reg noted, showing us the bankruptcy documents he'd also unearthed and put on display.

After years of foraging, Reg had amassed a collection so vast that he'd run out of space, cramming the overflow in drawers and beneath tables. "Makes for an exhibition, doesn't it?" he said, allowing himself an understated smile before bounding down the stairs to greet a new arrival.

During our hour-long tour, Reg had frequently called out to some-one we couldn't see, working downstairs. "Which drawer are the Tonga stamps in?" he'd yell, or "What year did Sanderson's son go bankrupt?" A meek female voice answered each time, invariably with a prompt and correct reply. This disembodied person seemed to play Cook's role, as dutiful shop assistant to the rather imperious Sanderson.

I went in search of this phantom and found Reg's wife, Ann, behind the counter of Sanderson's rebuilt store, which doubled as the museum gift shop. Dark-haired and slight, she was about as easy to draw out as a church mouse. But after twenty minutes of answering my queries with nods and "Oh, ayes," she mentioned something Reg hadn't. The couple had sold everything they owned to buy this derelict church fif-teen years ago, even living in a trailer park for seven years while they'd turned the chapel into a museum.

When I asked why, Ann shrugged and said, "It's what he wanted to do." She blushed and began fiddling with a display of Cook mugs. When Reg reappeared, I teased out a few more details. He said he'd worked previously as the captain of a fishing boat in Whitby, and served a term as Whitby's mayor. Then, at the age of forty-nine, he gave it all away to start this museum. "Cost me me boat, me house—everything—and years of hard work building this brick by board," he said. "Put me money where me mouth is, and me muscle too, didn't I?" He rubbed his fingers together as if counting coins. "If you haven't got the brass, you can't do nowt but what you do yourself."

For a man so careful with his brass, Reg struck me as having under-taken a midlife makeover more reckless than most. At two pounds sterling per visitor, the museum obviously wasn't a money-spinner. If anything, the couple seemed to have taken a virtual vow of poverty to sustain it. Reg offered me use of a creaking copy machine to reproduce documents in the museum, but he switched it off between copies, to save electricity. When Roger asked to use the toilet, Reg showed him to an outside building with a bucket nearby to collect rainwater for flushing.

When I asked why he'd given over his life to Cook, Reg looked a bit puzzled, as if he'd never really posed this question himself. "Maybe it began with the fishing," he said. "I spent years going out of the same harbor as him, traveling the same water, seeing the same sights." He'd always taken note of the Cook statue on a cliff above Whitby's harbor. "I'd go past it twice a day. It was like he was looking after me."

If so, Cook had cared for Reg well. In twelve years on the water, Reg had never once fallen in—a good thing, given that he couldn't swim. Nor had he ever broken down or called for help. "I try to do everything right, by meself, and if I can't, I don't do it." He looked around the museum. "If you get hold of something, you have to see it through to the end. Cook was like that, wasn't he?"

Reg led us to a glass case holding one of his most prized posses-sions: an eighteenth-century edition of Cook's third voyage, based on the captain's journal. Reg opened the volume to an introductory note, drawn from an entry Cook penned on July 7, 1776, as he prepared to set off for the Pacific one last time. Reg asked me to read Cook's pref-ace aloud.

" 'It is the production of a man, who has not had the advantage of much school education, but who has been constantly at sea from his youth; and though, with the assistance of a few good friends, he has passed through all the stations belonging to a seaman, from an appren-tice boy in the coal trade, to a Post Captain in the Royal Navy, he has had no opportunity of cultivating letters. After this account of myself, the Public must not expect from me the elegance of a fine writer, or the plausibility of a professed bookmaker; but will, I hope, consider me as a plain man, zealously exerting himself in the service of his Country, and determined to give the best account he is able of his proceedings.' "

I looked up. Reg's eyes brimmed. "That's all Cook," he said. "Joseph Banks would have said, 'I'm the greatest,' but not Cook. He's humble."

Roger was wet-eyed, too. "He could have put on airs, but he didn't," he said to Reg. "He was what he was, a simple Yorkshireman, to the end of his days."

Reg nodded. "Most places, they go for aristocracy, or people who seek it. When you go down to London, the museums are all Horatio Nelson. They've no time for Cook, who taught himself and didn't have money to buy into his job." Reg opened a drawer and produced a sheaf of insurance records for Cook's house in London. The building was only fifteen feet wide. The household goods Cook insured were just as modest, including plates, apparel, and a timber shed valued at ten pounds. "He wasn't looking for a grand home or a Lady Hamilton," Reg said. "He married a publican's daughter and lived simply. We have to stick up for him, don't we?"

By now, Reg and Roger looked as if they might start bawling. I felt awkward. Cook's humility and plainness were admirable qualities, but they didn't move me to tears. There was obviously a Yorkshire thing going on that I couldn't understand. Feeling left out, and a bit contrary, I raised the question that had come to me on Easby Moor. If Cook was such a homeboy, why hadn't he named any place after Marton or Ayton or Staithes—or spared a word in his voluminous journals for his beloved Yorkshire?

"He was working all his life. He died at his work, didn't he?" Reg said. "No time to write about himself or his boyhood, or even think about it. And he was too humble to name places after his own. Cook wasn't a vain man. Not like Banks, who took all the glory when he came home."

This seemed accurate. I'd been struck in Yorkshire by the fact that people didn't draw attention to themselves. Reg, in his gray pants and gray sweater and thick-soled gray shoes, was a case in point. Still, I was curious about why Cook seemed so intent on fleeing home: first the farm, then Staithes, and later the coal trade in Whitby. Reg had a theory about this, too.

"Farming's like religion, isn't it?" he said. "You roll it over, the same thing every year. Then he came here and looked at the North Sea, which was like a big road heading out, the M1 of his day. He was thinking, 'I don't want to be in a shop all me life.' So he goes to sea, but it's a coal ship. That's a monkey's job, you'd be black bright from working that coal every day. He wanted more."

It was an hour past closing time. We'd been in the museum all afternoon. At the door, I asked Reg one last question: Did he ever have the urge to pack up and travel as Cook had?

"No. Haven't got the brass. It cost Banks ten thousand pounds to go, didn't it?" He smiled. "But there's an offer on now to Hawaii that's cheap, even for a Yorkshireman. Might just go."

His offhand tone suggested this would never happen. Reg's attraction to Cook was entirely different from my own. While I was drawn to Cook's restless adventuring and plunge into the unknown, Reg worshipped the man's modesty, sense of duty, loyalty to home and country. Maybe it was good that we knew so little of Cook's inner life. As it was, each of us could fill him up with our own longings and imagination.

ON OUR FOURTH morning in Yorkshire, waking at a guest house we'd found near Staithes, Roger refused to get out of bed. Or rather, he got out of bed just long enough to devour a crippling repast of porridge, kippers, sausage, and eggs, then got back in. "Bed and breakfast, breakfast and bed," he said. "I feel a terrible ennui."

I flung open the curtains in a feeble attempt at reveille. The sky was gray and drizzly, as it had been every day. "Still leaden," Roger said. "Like my stomach. All the forces of the universe are focused on my gut." He burped. "I'm not homesick anymore. Can we pack up and go now? Head to the Costa del Sol for a week? Cook probably sailed near there."

I flipped open a pamphlet on the Cook birthday festival, and read the list of events still on offer. Happy hour at a brewery offering "Captain Cook Ale." Reenactors of eighteenth-century marine life, "drinking grog and cooking leftover rations." A shanty festival and other "fun for the kids."

Roger groaned. "I loathe the word 'fun.' It always means you're not going to have any. English code for 'utter misery.'" With that, he rolled over and soon began to snore.

I sprawled on my bed with a pile of books and read about the next stage of Cook's life. When he left Sanderson's shop in Staithes for the Whitby docks in 1746, he was about to turn eighteen, in those days a late age at which to begin life at sea. But Cook, once again, found a fine patron: John Walker, a Quaker shipowner and coal merchant who took James on as a three-year apprentice, perhaps because he knew Cook's earlier benefactors. Quakers, renowned for their thrift, integrity, and work ethic, prospered as shipowners the world over, as readers of *Moby-Dick* will recall.

Cook's stay in Whitby is much better documented than his earlier life, thanks in large part to a fortuitously timed act of Parliament. A new law, enacted just a year before Cook's arrival in Whitby, required that merchant seamen pay sixpence a month to support a fund for disabled sailors and the families of those who died at sea. To collect the levy, the government made copies of muster rolls from every merchant ship, including details of mariners' position and age, and the date and port of their entry and discharge.

From these records, it appears that Cook sailed for the first time as a "servant" aboard a coal ship called *Freelove*. The ship's name was richly ironic, given the terms of indenture common in that day. Apprentices agreed not to "haunt taverns or playhouses, play at dice, cards or bowls or other unlawful games, commit fornication or contract matrimony." In exchange, the master agreed to teach apprentices "the trade, mystery and occupation of the mariner," and to provide them with "Meat and Drink, washing and Lodging."

John Walker's ships traveled north from Whitby to load coal near Newcastle, then carried the cargo south to London. Cook also served on ships bringing timber from the Baltic and transporting troops to Ireland. But for nine years, as he worked his way up the ranks, Cook mostly performed the dirty, heavy business of toting coal, in waters and along coasts that are among the most storm-lashed and treacherous in Europe. Also, the mid-eighteenth century witnessed a climatic chill known as the Little Ice Age, when rivers and ports froze. It was easy to see why the coal trade was regarded in Britain as the "nursery of seamen," one that taught young men to handle tricky channels, shoals, currents, and tides—all skills that would serve Cook well in later years.

WHEN ROGER FINALLY stirred from his kipper-induced slumber, we returned to Whitby. Since our earlier visit, the wind had slowed to mere storm strength, allowing us to lift our heads and take in the town's theatrical profile. Whitby spread across steep hills on either side of the Esk. The buildings, roofed with rust-colored pantiles modeled on a Dutch design, cascaded in pastel waves down to the river. This made Whitby appear, at first glance, more continental than English. The spooky ruin of a seventh-century abbey perched on a crag looming over the town. Sacked by Vikings, rebuilt by one of William the Conqueror's knights, and dissolved by Henry VIII, the abbey and its graveyard also feature in Bram Stoker's *Dracula*.

Crossing the iron swing bridge that spans the Esk, we turned down Grape Lane, a cobbled thoroughfare so dark and narrow that it was originally known as "Grope." At the end of the lane stood a handsome redbrick building with a plaque by the door: "James Cook Lodged Here." This was the former home of Cook's employer, John Walker, and now a museum furnished as it had been in the eighteenth century.

The family rooms appeared modest and utilitarian, befitting a Quaker household, with bare walls and straight-backed cane chairs that looked about as comfortable as pews. Even the house's single looking glass wasn't there for vanity; mirrors reflected and thus amplified candlelight. The apprentices' quarters, in the attic, were about as airy as the mess deck of a coal ship. Sixteen young men crowded into a single, slope-roofed room, stringing hammocks between oak rafters made from ships' timbers.

In a corner of the attic, a wax manikin of the teenage Cook sat before a desk spread with trigonometric drawings. The Walkers' housekeeper, Mary Prowd, took a liking to the serious-minded James and made sure he had candles to study by at night, she later said, "whilst the other apprentices were engaged in idle talk or trifle amusements." When Cook returned to Whitby after his first Pacific voyage, the Walkers instructed Mary Prowd to treat the now famous man with due deference and reserve. But the housekeeper couldn't contain herself. At the sight of Cook, she embraced the former apprentice, exclaiming, with un-Quaker exuberance, "Oh honey James! How glad I is to see thee!" This anecdote was about as warm and fuzzy as Cook's story ever got.

Even without the wax effigy, it was easy to visualize the young apprentice pacing the attic's creaky floorboards, or gazing out a small back window at the river, so close that he could almost have stepped through the glass and straight onto one of Walker's ships. The house's austerity and gloom—some casements had been bricked in to avoid an eighteenth-century tax on windows—also threw into bold relief the museum's small display of exotica from Cook's voyages: a watercolor of Krakatoa, a drawing of bare-breasted Pacific islanders, a fly whisk from Tonga, tattooing needles from Tahiti. In this plain Quaker dwelling, they looked like artifacts from another planet.

We picked up a bunch of booklets about Whitby and Cook in the museum shop and headed for a nearby tearoom. By my second scone, the time-travel reverie I'd enjoyed in the Walkers' attic had been badly punctured. It turned out there wasn't hard evidence that Cook had ever lodged in the house. I consulted my bible—Beaglehole's biography—and found a footnote I'd previously missed. "Walker's house and its attic in Grape Lane are popularly regarded as the premises where Cook lived and slept," the historian wrote, "but the dates make this impossible." John Walker didn't occupy the house until 1752, after Cook's apprenticeship had finished. Before then, the Walkers lived in a house on the other side of the Esk that had since been torn down.

Our entire tour of "Cook Country" seemed doomed to this vexing pattern. In a landscape filled with centuries-old structures, some dating back a millennium, almost every building space associated with Cook had vanished: the biggin in Marton, the Ayton schoolhouse, the section of the church he'd sat in as a child, the Staithes store, and now the Walkers' one-time home in Whitby. "Funny, isn't it," Roger said, finishing off my scone, "that a man who traveled everywhere left so few footprints."

In a way, this seemed fitting. While every town and village associated with Cook wanted to claim him as a native son, Cook didn't truly belong to any of them. He was a wanderer for most of his life: a rebel against the rootedness and narrow horizons of his Yorkshire childhood. His real home, if he had one, was the sea.

However, one of the books we'd picked up at the Walker house hinted at a powerful local influence on Cook that I hadn't considered before. Titled, simply, *The Life of Captain Cook,* it was a slim volume written by a couple named Tom and Cordelia Stamp, who came at Cook from a very different perspective than other authors: as Whitby dwellers, as lifelong Quakers, and, in Cordelia's case, as a woman. I was especially struck by the book's list of "Quaker Advices" current in northern England during Cook's youth, which stated in part:

"Keep to that which is modest, decent, plain and useful. . . . Be prudent in all manner of behaviour, both in public and private; avoiding all intemperance in eating and drinking. . . . Walk wisely and circumspectly towards all men, in a peaceable spirit. . . . Let our moderation and prudence, as well as truth and justice, appear to all men, and in all things, in trading and commerce, in speech and communication."

To me, this read like a blueprint of Cook's adult character. The Stamps also pointed out that Cook lived with the Walkers at a very impressionable age, in his late teens and early twenties, and may have attended Quaker meeting with the family. On the walls of the Grape Lane house, we'd seen several letters Cook wrote to John Walker between Pacific voyages. While the letters were mostly reports on his Pacific travels, they also gave glimpses of the navigator's ambition and anxiety, and included rare mention in Cook's writing of "Providence." The fact that Cook wrote the letters at all, to a man whose employ he'd left twenty years before, suggested that the farm boy had formed a close bond with his Quaker mentor.

I found the Stamps listed in the local phone book. Cordelia answered my call. "Oh yes, please!" she replied, when I asked if we could stop by. "My husband's dead, but I'm still here. I've broken my leg and can't do anything. I'd love someone to talk to!" Whitby Quakers, it seemed, weren't quite so reserved as in Cook's day.

Cordelia's house, however, was appropriately plain: a modest brick cottage on the edge of Whitby. Cordelia also seemed without pretense, a woman of seventy-eight wearing a wool cap, loose blouse, long skirt, and one sensible shoe. A cast covered her other leg. She sat by an ancient electric heater, surrounded by the clutter of the small publishing company she ran from her house. The only decorations were a portrait of Cook and a photograph of a deceased dog named Buttercup. The pet's replacement, a Jack Russell terrier, tugged at Cordelia's shoelace as I asked her to expand on the book's thesis that Cook's character bore many "marks of the true Quaker."

"You see it first in his quietism," she said. "Quakers are quiet people, though you wouldn't know it listening to me. When you read the journals of Cook's men, they almost never quote him directly. He didn't waste words. When he talked, it was to get something done."

She reached for a pile of bubble wrap and gave it to the dog, which began ecstatically popping. "Then there's his modesty and plainness," Cordelia went on. "That's very Quaker. I don't wear a wedding ring, even though I was married forever. Quakers back then carried this to extremes. Men's jackets had no collars. Cook wasn't an extremist, but he was a no-frills fellow. Also, he had no room for religious ritual, at least not external ritual. He couldn't bear reverends on his ships and he almost never referred to the Deity in his writing. Belief is within oneself."

I'd been struck by this, too. Cook often used the word "superstition" when referring to Pacific beliefs, and implied that he felt the same way about Western religion. I'd put this down to Cook's Enlightenment faith in scientific inquiry. Closely related to this was a quality that, being a journalist, I much admired: Cook's clear-eyed objectivity and "just the facts, ma'am" style. To Cordelia, this also bespoke Quaker influence. "I went to a Quaker school in Great Ayton," she said. "Its motto was '*Magna est veritas*'—'The truth is great.' I'm a believer in that, and so was Cook."

I'd attended a Quaker school, too, for eight years, though I'd fidgeted during the required weekly meeting and the moments of silence before each class. I also disliked the fact that we couldn't skip school on military holidays, a recollection that raised another question about Cook. He wasn't, strictly speaking, a pacifist.

Cordelia disagreed. "He fired guns, but only as a last resort," she said. "And whenever he did, he expressed regret over it." She herself had served in the Signal Corps during World War II, scrubbing floors and operating telephones. "Quakers are peaceful, but they're not barmy. You do what you have to do."

Cordelia clumped out of the room to get more bubble wrap for her dog. While she was gone, I checked the list of "Quaker Advices" in her book, searching for holes in her argument. But rereading them, I felt the same eerie concordance with Cook's character that I'd noticed before. Quakers couldn't abide idleness, and nor could Cook, who always kept himself and his crew busy. Even the quality in Cook that least appealed to me, his customary humorlessness, was in the Advices; they warned against "foolish jesting" and "long and frequent conversation on temporal matters" because "there is leaven therein, which, being suffered to prevail, indisposes and benumbs the soul." Reading this, I realized how often, and usually in vain, I'd searched Cook's journals for some leaven therein.

Cordelia thumped back in, critiquing her thesis for me. "Of course, as a believer in truth, I have to acknowledge that the qualities I've described could reflect his father's Scottish background, too," she said. "Scots are dour, quiet, never daft. Or that's how they were in Cook's day. Now a lot of them are silly asses."

Her language reminded me of one Quaker dictate that didn't fit. What about the admonition to "swear not"? The journals of Cook's men include a number of references to his temper and profanity. A prissy Swede on the second voyage complained that Cook "stamped about the deck and grew hoarse with shouting" oaths, including repeated "Goddamns."

Cordelia laughed. "Oh, yes, Cook knew his language, I'm sure he cursed like a true Navy man. But when Quakers say they don't swear, what they really mean is that they won't take an oath. We'll affirm the truth but we won't swear to it."

Roger, by this point, was fed up with talk of religion, and he burst in with a question of his own: "If you'd lived in Cook's day, would you have found him attractive?"

"Oh, yes!" Cordelia cried. "I find the weather-beaten face in his portraits very handsome. And I adore tall men. No use for little chaps." This pleased Roger, who at six foot three regarded me, five inches shorter, as a virtual dwarf. "What about Mrs. Cook?" he asked. "Do you think she was crumpet?"

"Must have been, or she wouldn't have caught the attention of a man as observant as Cook," Cordelia said. "Of course, she may have chosen him. We often do. I think he was too busy to have much of an eye for the ladies. Still, I bet Elizabeth was a bonny lass."

Unfortunately, the only surviving image of Elizabeth Cook was a portrait painted of her as a very elderly woman. Her oversized bonnet and tight-lipped expression, which suggested she'd lost her teeth, made her looked pinched and severe. Cordelia had sold postcards of the painting at a gift shop she once ran in Whitby. "Gawpers would look at that picture and say, 'No wonder Cook went to sea. To get away from her!' " Cordelia shook her head. "Well, I used to be younger, too, but I'm not now."

Cordelia also took a sympathetic view of Elizabeth's character, a subject most male historians ignored or touched on very lightly. Beaglehole, for instance, wrote little about Elizabeth, except to lament the fact that she destroyed Cook's letters.

"I love her for that!" Cordelia exclaimed. "Long may she be revered for burning them all! When my husband died, I destroyed all our letters. I hate gawpers. She was his wife, it was her right. It was him and her. Good lass!"

However, this left us with virtually no record of their relationship. Elizabeth once revealed that she was always nervous on stormy nights, thinking of "Mr. Cook," as she invariably called him. We know nothing of Cook's longings. But Cordelia thought she sensed them in his journals. "You notice how tender Cook and his men are towards the animals on board, they're always going on about the goats and dogs and livestock," she said. "Part of that was practical, of course. But I think it was an expression of how much they missed their women, the presence of someone to care for."

This put her in mind of her own pet, whom she'd banished to the garage when the bubble wrap gave out. As we got up to go, I asked Cordelia to sign my copy of her book. "It's a good seller," she said. "Not because it's good, mind you, but because it's cheap. This is Yorkshire, remember. I'm the sole distributor and I keep the price at five pounds." With that she clumped off to free her dog.

Roger sighed. "Vibrant face, twinkling eyes, enormously good-humored, a real iconoclast. If she wasn't married to that dog, I could really go for her."

ALTHOUGH WE'D SKIPPED most of the week's Cook festivities, I was determined to catch the last: a "Captain Cook Commemorative Service" at St. Mary's Church, beside the ruined abbey in Whitby. It was at St. Mary's that coal ship apprentices were required to worship when ashore. Perhaps I'd have one last chance in Yorkshire to stand in some space that Cook had actually occupied.

Roger, church-averse as always, begged off and went to visit his mother instead. So on Sunday morning, I hiked up the 199 stone steps leading to the abbey. Bram Stoker, who visited Whitby in 1893 and used it as a model for the seaside town in *Dracula*, wrote of a black dog leaping from a wrecked ship and bounding up these steps to the churchyard, where it metamorphosed into a vampire. Stoker chose his spot well. The steep steps had wide landings designed for pallbearers to rest. In the clifftop cemetery, where Dracula took refuge in the tomb of a suicide, a sundial bore the eerie inscription "Our Days Pass Like a Shadow."

St. Mary's was low and Norman, like so many other churches in Cook Country. But the interior resembled no church I'd ever encountered, except in the pages of *Moby-Dick*. Like the whaling church that Ishmael visited in New Bedford, St. Mary's was an extension of the sea, fitted out by maritime carpenters with box pews hewn from ships' timbers, and recycled masts supporting the gallery. The three-decker pulpit, topped by a preaching box, towered above the pews like a crow's nest. Above it loomed a ceiling cut with transom windows similar to those in the great room of the *Endeavour*.

St. Mary's had no electric lighting, and no heat apart from a single coke stove. Each pew's distance from this fire reflected its occupants' place in Whitby's social hierarchy. When I asked a churchwarden where apprentices would have sat, he pointed me to a drafty alcove that was now unused and curtained off to save heat. "You might want to have a look at the seats," he said, pulling aside the curtain.

Crouched in the alcove's chill gloom, I studied the dark pews and found that almost every inch of the wood had been hacked and carved by generations of apprentices. The pews were a Rosetta stone of church boredom: initials and dates (the oldest being 1665), crude etchings of flags and ships, and other cuts too worn to decipher. I searched in vain for the letters "J.C." or a carving of the *Freelove*. Still, it wasn't hard to imagine the young Cook and his shipmates, numb with cold and tedium, discreetly wielding penknives as a preacher droned and the coke stove sputtered in the distance.

When the church bells began pealing, I took my seat in a pew marked "Strangers." Two nuns joined me in the box. Most of the other pews were filled with men in suits and women in huge hats, though one group in the upper gallery stood out: a small band of Dracula fans, "Goths," who favored black lace, frock coats, purple hair, and exposed, pierced navels.

Near them sat a local "fishermen's choir," which inaugurated the service with a song about herring.

> "Our market will not wait for God,
> And neither will it wait for men,
> It's get your fish upon the quay,
> Then turn and put to sea again."

A hymn followed as the minister strode down the aisle, followed by the Right Reverend Bishop of Whitby, who wore an enormous, teardrop-shaped miter and carried a crosier as tall as he was. I thought back to Cordelia's observation about Cook's dislike of religious pomp, and wondered what he would have made of this ceremony in his honor.

Ten minutes into the service, my nose and feet began to go numb with cold. The pew was so uncomfortably high and straight-backed that each time I tried to relax my posture I almost pitched onto the chill stone floor. Listening to hymns, psalms, lessons, and more herring fishermen's songs, I gazed dully at a clock and wished I'd brought a penknife to add some graffiti of my own.

The bishop stirred me from my torpor, climbing into the preaching box and reciting the beautiful lines of Psalm 107: "They that go down to the sea in ships, that do business in great waters," he called out in a booming voice. "These see the works of the Lord, and his wonders in the deep."

Then the bishop launched into a sermon about Cook that seemed to draw a long spiritual bow. Cook, he claimed, "set science and technology in the context of Christian faith." For the captain, the wonders of discovery and mathematics "spoke to the glory of God." Cook also had "a deeply held Christian understanding of life." The bishop concluded by bringing the message home to his listeners. "We of the church in our own age must similarly seek new ways of understanding. The same voyage of discovery is ours."

The choir sang another tune about fish, and then the congregants filed out of the church for a wreath-laying at the Cook statue topping Whitby's West Cliff. This was the figure that had so inspired the Staithes museum keeper, Reg Firth. The statue depicted Cook in his resolute navigator mode: legs spread wide, hands clutching the dividers used to measure distance on charts, the captain's commanding gaze aimed straight out to sea. The base bore two inscriptions: *"Circa Orbem"* ("Around the Globe") and *"Nil Intentatum Reliquit"* ("Nothing Left Unattempted"). It was the most striking monument to Cook I'd yet seen.

The day had turned frigid and threatening, and the wind whipped so hard across the exposed cliff that it carried away most of the prayers and tributes. "A son of this country and nation . . ." "His quality of courage, humanity, and diligence of service . . ." "As Nelson said, 'Only those associated with the sea can appreciate Cook. . . . '"

Whitby's mayor and other officials laid wreaths at Cook's feet and stood stiffly at attention. A vicar bowed his head and said, "Let us praise those who have charted new territory that others may safely follow, and may the memory of his life encourage us to greater things in ours." A cold, hard rain pelted down, but the ceremony continued with a prayer for the queen and a last song from the fishermen's choir, "Beacon Light."

I found myself unexpectedly moved, less by the memory of Cook than by the people gathered to honor him. The British were brilliant at this sort of ceremony: sincere, stoic, and understated—nothing like cynical Australians or syrupy Americans. Watching these few dozen faces lashed by freezing rain, their breath clouding as they uttered "God Save the Queen," I caught a glimpse of the grit and pride that had sustained Cook and his men, and that had once enabled this small, damp country to rule so much of the globe.

"Hold fast to that which is good," the bishop intoned in a final prayer. Then the crowd dispersed, popping umbrellas and retreating to their cars. I was about to do the same when the rain abruptly halted and a rainbow appeared, arching over Cook's statue and framing the navigator against the sea and sky. The moment was so unexpected and spectacular that I felt a sudden urge to pay my respects. But the only words that came into my head were "Happy birthday, Captain Koook. Happy two hundred and seventy-two."

Chapter 11

LONDON:
Shipping Out, Again

I have had a good dinner, for I have had a good *Cook*.
—JAMES BOSWELL, PUNNING AFTER A MEAL
WITH THE CAPTAIN IN 1776

"I regret to say," a voice intoned over the Tube's loudspeaker, "there is no service between South Kensington and Embankment, due to a person lying under the train."

Roger greeted this news by muttering, "Whenever I'm in London I feel like doing the same." He studied the sallow-faced commuters packed in the stalled train. "Everyone looks stupefied, as though they've swallowed a misery tablet." Newspapers shot up around us like shields, each one bearing a variation on the same headline: "Britain's Rail System Grinds to a Halt." "Taking the Train Today? Forget It." "Disaster Strikes Tube."

Great Britain, the nation that invented train travel and dispatched Cook around the globe three times, still couldn't manage to move people into and around its capital city. Our train ride from York had slowed to horse speed near London and taken twice as long as scheduled, owing (a disembodied voice told us) to "wet leaves on the track." Now, we inched and jolted beneath central London as the gratingly civil voice crackled over the loudspeaker again: "Sorry for the slow progress. Defective train at Aldgate."

The young Cook had been spared this. He traveled to London by sea, aboard Whitby colliers. Then, in the summer of 1755, he disembarked in East London and joined the Royal Navy. This marked yet another enigmatic departure in Cook's early career. His Whitby employer and friend, John Walker, had recently offered him command of a coal ship. At the age of only twenty-six, Cook appeared set for a relatively comfortable and secure career as a merchant captain. Instead, he enlisted in the Navy as an able seaman, just one notch up from the bottom of the maritime hierarchy. This job earned Cook a pittance and subjected him to the horrifying cruelties, privations, and dangers of life aboard the lower deck of eighteenth-century Navy ships. On his first vessel, the *Eagle,* scores of men perished from disease, and almost a quarter of the crew was killed or injured by a broadside from a French ship. British warships of the day set off with twice the number of sailors needed, in expectation of appalling casualties.

In 1755, when Cook enlisted, Britain was on the brink of war with France. He may have volunteered out of patriotism and a sense of duty—or to avoid being press-ganged, a fate that had befallen some of his Whitby shipmates. More likely, given what we know of Cook's tremendous confidence and ambition, he regarded the Navy as the route to far greater renown than he could ever achieve as a coal ship commander. In the event, Cook didn't remain a lowly seaman for long. Soon after he volunteered, his talents caught the eye of Hugh Palliser, a fellow Yorkshireman and fast-rising captain who would reach the pinnacle of the naval establishment, and look after Cook each step of the way.

Cook's skill at managing the men under him is well documented; much less heralded is his talent at managing those above him. From Thomas Scottowe, Ayton's lord of the manor, to Hugh Palliser, who became a Lord of the Admiralty, Cook showed a knack for attracting powerful patrons and maintaining their loyalty and support. These men were no doubt eager to take such a promising novice under their wing. But Cook, having grown up poor in a deferential and hierarchical society, also seems to have developed an instinct for flattering his superiors and enlisting them in the furtherance of his own aims.

This skill is evident in Cook's surviving letters, many of which are obsequious in tone. He also stroked his superiors with his choice of place-names. Cook honored Palliser with a bay, cape, and island group, and named one of his sons, Hugh, after his Admiralty benefactor. The captain also named so many Pacific sites for another exalted patron, the Earl of Sandwich, that the Admiralty later changed some of them.

"Sandwich Islands, Sandwich Sound, Sandwich Cape," Roger read out, as we killed time in the stalled Tube by tallying all the places named for the earl (who is best known for once having asked, while gambling, for a piece of meat between two pieces of bread—thereby bestowing his title on this combination, too). "Cook could at least have included some other foods. Scone Mountain. Pudding Island. Biscuit Hill." Roger shook his head. "He was the complete employee, the opposite of me."

Then again, Roger closely identified with Cook's decision to flee Yorkshire, which Roger had done at precisely the same age. The son of a World War II tank commander, Roger left school at seventeen, volunteered for the Leeds Rifles, his father's regiment, then went to work in construction. He'd done well at this and repeatedly been offered a top job by his employer. "When I was twenty-six, I had a glittering career ahead of me in the Yorkshire cement industry," he said. But Roger decided to take off and travel the world instead, and ended up in Australia. "Cement's like coal, a grubby unglamorous business. So I threw it all away for adventure. Why wouldn't Cook have done the same?"

In the end, as with so much of Cook's life, we could only speculate about his motives. But we could retrace his movements with some precision. Between 1755 and 1768, when Cook took command of the *Endeavour,* he rose steadily through the ranks, becoming a ship's master at twenty-eight. During this period, Britain was busily wresting Canada from France; Cook's principal duty was charting the St. Lawrence River and the coasts of Newfoundland and Nova Scotia. He quickly established himself as a brilliant surveyor and chart maker, jobs that combined his nautical, mathematical, and astronomical skills. "Very expert in his business," one of his superiors observed in a typical dispatch.

It was between voyages to Canada that Cook married Elizabeth Batts in 1762. Nothing is known of their courtship, except that it appears to have been brief: Cook returned to London from a voyage to Canada in mid-November 1762, married Elizabeth on December 21, and went back to sea the following April. This pattern continued for the next five years, with Cook spending only the winters in London between sails to and from Newfoundland (including his 1764 visit to a place called Unfortunate Cove, where, his ship's log reported, "a Large Powder Horn blown up & Burst in his hand which shatter'd it in a Terrible manner," leaving a scar that ran up to his wrist). In 1763, Cook bought a lease on a brick house in East London. There his children grew up, and there his wife would remain for twenty-five years.

London was as close to a home as the adult Cook ever had: his domestic base for the latter half of his life, and the place where he readied his ships and plotted his voyages with the Admiralty and Royal Society. It was also in London that the impact of his discoveries was most keenly felt: in science, commerce, and the arts. Cook's achievements contributed, in no small way, to London's becoming the headquarters of an empire that would ultimately span eleven thousand miles of the globe and rule over 400 million subjects.

You'd think, then, that Cook's memory and legacy would be stamped all over London, a city with more monuments and museums and historic plaques than almost any other. But the opposite appeared true. At Trafalgar Square, Roger and I joined hundreds of tourists craning their necks at Horatio Nelson, perched heroically atop his towering column. A hundred yards away, hidden behind Admiralty Arch, we found London's only monument to Cook: a modest 1914 statue of the captain in an oversized tricorn, gazing across a busy street at a memorial to marines who fought in China and South Africa in 1899–1900. The casual tourist passing this way could easily mistake Britain's greatest navigator for one among a legion of now obscure figures cluttering pedestals all across London.

The British Museum, at the time of our visit, had not a single Cook-related exhibit on display, and the Natural History Museum only one: a small sample of plant specimens that Banks and Solander collected in Australia. Even Greenwich's National Maritime Museum gave Cook short rations. While Nelson memorabilia occupied an entire wing, the Cook collection, which once merited a room of its own, had been scattered across theme exhibits such as Explorers, Trade and Empire, and Global Garden.

In a stairwell of the museum hung two of the three surviving paintings of Cook. The most famous, painted in 1776 by a renowned portrait artist, Nathaniel Dance, depicted Cook in imperial mode, wearing a gray wig and formal captain's uniform, his finger planted on a chart. The depiction of Cook's body, broad and imposing, didn't match the rawboned figure described by the captain's shipmates. Cook had sat only briefly for the portrait, forcing Dance to use a model to finish his work.

Much more compelling, to me at least, was the museum's lesser-known portrait by William Hodges, an artist on Cook's second voyage. Hodges had the advantage of spending three years at sea with the captain. His unheroic portrait of Cook—wigless and weather-beaten, with brown curls, deep-set eyes, prominent nose, jutting chin, and sloping shoulders—seemed as close to an image of the real man as we were likely to find. (The third surviving portrait, by John Webber, an artist on the third voyage, isn't so striking, though it has the historical virtue of showing Cook wearing a black glove, as he often did, to conceal the ugly wound on his right hand.)

We lingered in front of the Hodges portrait for some time, staring into Cook's rather weary and melancholic face. "The inner man," Roger declared. "It's all there. I see it for the first time."

"What?"

"Cook was an alcho, a total pisspot. Look at those eyes. Yellow and small, like peeholes in snow. He had a terrible hangover the day he sat for this painting, he can barely see out. And that big nose, shiny and crinkly, like crepe paper? A classic drinker's bugle."

"You're projecting yourself on Cook."

"No I'm not. Remember those three thousand gallons of Madeira he picked up on his first voyage? It was for Cook, not the crew. He wasn't a staggering, lurching drunk. But the grog explains some of his strange behavior, and why he fell apart in the end. He was down to one percent liver function, like me."

We continued to debate this the next day, during another torturous Underground trip to London's East End, where Cook spent most of his time in the city. Rather than try to navigate the tangled, Blitz-damaged streets (where even Cook might lose his way today), I'd arranged for a pilot: Clifford Thornton, president of the Captain Cook Society. Formed in 1975 by philatelists interested in Cook-related stamps, the society had since grown into a global network of Cook enthusiasts and historians who swapped opinions and arcane research queries about the captain. I'd joined the society and found its publications and online forum a tremendously useful resource.

But I knew nothing about Clifford Thornton, except that he'd once been a museum curator and now wrote an elegant "President's Message" in the society's quarterly newsletter, *Cook's Log*. From this, and from our e-mails (we'd never spoken), I'd conjured an elderly and eccentric Oxonian with long, swept-back gray hair, tweed jacket, public-school tie, and an unlit pipe hovering a few inches from his lips. So I was a little startled when we emerged from the Tube near the Tower of London to find a middle-aged man with close-cropped hair who wore corduroys, a windbreaker, and a student-style knapsack, and spoke with a northern England accent as strong as any I'd heard in Cook country.

Cliff, as he introduced himself, came from Stockton-on-Tees, an industrial town close to Middlesbrough, and now lived in suburban Essex, just outside London, where he worked supervising welfare services for the local council. "I'm a bit of a browser, nibbling here and there," Cliff said, checking his street map and striding briskly down Pepys Street and Seething Lane to our first stop: a church called St. Olave's, with a graveyard alongside that held the bodies of Samuel Pepys, 365 victims of the Great Plague, and a sixteenth-century woman identified as Mother Goose. "Cook's lieutenant, Pickersgill, probably worshipped here," Cliff said. "Just thought you might want to have a squint at it."

From there, he led us down a road called Crutched Friars and headed into Wapping, the Thames-side district that had once been the heart of maritime London. German bombs and urban renewal had transformed most of it since Cook's day. We passed new apartments and moorings for pleasure craft. Then the road turned from pavement to cobble, and condominiums gave way to old brick warehouses and pubs.

Cliff led us down moss-slicked steps that dropped to the river near Execution Dock, so named because pirates were once hanged there and left dangling until three tides washed over them. "I would put my money on it that Cook walked ashore right here from Whitby colliers," Cliff said, kneeling to pluck bits of old glass, crockery, and clay pipe from the dirty sand. He pointed at a riverside pub, one of thirty that had lined the Wapping waterfront in its eighteenth-century heyday. The owners of these pubs doubled as "undertakers," who undertook the business of unloading and selling coal. "It was thirsty work," Cliff explained. A coal heaver received a pint of beer during each hour he spent toting baskets of the grimy cargo up the steep stairs.

One of these riverside publican-undertakers had been John Batts, the father of Elizabeth Cook. Batts owned an alehouse called the Bell and leased Execution Dock. Cliff believed that Cook had become acquainted with the family while unloading coal here. He may also have lodged at the Bell, which stood just across the road from the dock.

The site of the Bell was now a parking lot. Cliff led us down the road to a church the Cooks attended, St. Paul's Shadwell, where their first child, James, was baptized nine months after their marriage. The church had been rebuilt in the nineteenth century and now bore almost no resemblance to the structure the Cooks had known. When I mentioned to Cliff that we'd been frustrated by the same pattern in Yorkshire, he nodded and said, "The best you can do is catch an echo of the man. You can almost never reach out and touch him."

The same was true of the houses that the Cooks inhabited, first in Shadwell—on a site that now lay in the middle of a road—and later in the nearby district of Mile End. Cliff led us from Wapping to Mile End through a maze of condominiums and housing estates that gave little hint of the area's maritime heritage, except for streets named Vinegar and Cinnamon, and buildings called after explorers: Franklin, Frobisher, Vancouver, Shackleton.

Mile End had changed even more since Cook's day. In 1763, when Cook purchased a sixty-one-year lease there, for a property bordered by a bakery, a wine vault, and stables, Mile End was an up-and-coming neighborhood at London's eastern edge, still fringed by fields and orchards. It didn't stay bucolic for long. By the time William Booth, the founder of the Salvation Army, began his work there in 1868, much of the neighborhood had become a crowded, impoverished slum known as Mile End Waste. Later came heavy bombing by the Germans in World War II. Once a magnet for Jews and other European refugees, Mile End now teemed with immigrants from Africa, the Middle East, and the Asian subcontinent.

Cliff led us past *halal* shops and ethnic restaurants to number 88 Mile End Road—or, rather, a plaque on the brick wall between 86 and 90 that read: "On this site stood a house occupied for some years by Captain James Cook R.N. F.R.S. 1728–1779 Circumnavigator and Explorer." Mrs. Cook stayed in the narrow brick terrace until 1788 before moving to Clapham, on the other side of the Thames. The building later became a kosher butcher's shop and survived the Blitz, only to be demolished in 1959 to expand a nearby brewery. The Australians were approached about buying the house, but feeling they'd been gulled once before, in the affair of "Cook's Cottage" in Great Ayton, they resisted. So the house was gone, and the garden behind it had become a parking lot.

We stood and stared at the wall, littered with windblown trash. Sitar music wafted from a textile workshop behind the house site. Muslim women in full-face veils hurried down the block while men in robes and skullcaps argued in Arabic before a coffee shop. "Cook didn't really need to sail around the globe, did he?" Cliff said. "If he'd stayed here long enough, the world would have come to him."

WE RETURNED TO Wapping for lunch at an ancient riverside pub called the Prospect of Whitby. Dark and low-beamed, with stone-flagged floors, the pub was named for a ship that had once moored behind it. As we sat outside, in the wan autumn sun, gazing at the Isle of Dogs, I asked Cliff the question that had nagged at me since our arrival in London: Why was Cook's memory so neglected in the city?

Cliff pondered this for a moment. "Britain loves its warriors," he said. "Cook wasn't blood and thunder like Nelson. He's a quieter, more peaceful figure, not your traditional hero." To some degree, he added, the American Revolution and Napoleonic Wars initially overshadowed Cook's voyages, so that the full impact of his discoveries didn't become apparent until the nineteenth century. Also, Cook's biographers never met the navigator; in popular imagination, he remained an opaque and stolid figure. This was in sharp contrast to the romantic Nelson, who carried on his adulterous affair with Lady Hamilton and perished triumphantly at Trafalgar with those immortal last words to his officer, "Kiss me, Hardy."

Cliff, however, felt that Cook was "starting to get his due." In his quiet way, Cliff had done a great deal to make this happen. He'd overseen the establishment of the Cook Birthplace Museum in Marton, written booklets and scholarly articles about the captain, and disseminated research around the globe through his presidency of the Captain Cook Society. I was surprised, then, to learn that Cliff hadn't really discovered Cook until midlife, even though the two men's birthplaces lay just miles apart.

"I'm a seaweed man by training," Cliff said. He'd begun his career as a marine biologist, dreamed of going into forensic science, then drifted into museum work instead, in part to support his growing family. This had led him to Cook. Though Cliff had since changed careers, he continued to immerse himself in the navigator as almost a second, unpaid occupation, and as an outlet for his detective instincts. "I love mysteries and investigation," he said.

Cliff opened his knapsack and spread bits and bobs of his latest research across the tavern table. This ranged from the fate of an obscure crewman on one of Cook's ships ("I've spent a lot of time at the India Office going through ships' rosters," Cliff said), to the design of the *Resolution*'s prow ("Been corresponding with a figurehead historian in New Zealand"), to the provenance of a painting of Whitby ("That story's still rumbling on, another bit of unfinished business"). For a skilled historical gumshoe like Cliff, Cook's story was the perfect fixation: global in reach, with a large cast of characters and a narrative so vast and intricate that you could spend years sleuthing each small part of the puzzle.

"This is my real obsession," he said, reaching into his knapsack again. "Finding Cook's bones." He brought out a spiral notebook filled with notes and copies of archival documents relating to the mysterious fate of the captain's remains. Cliff had unearthed an astonishing body of evidence, unknown to Beaglehole or other Cook scholars, suggesting that a piece of the captain had come back to England and may have survived to the present day. The labyrinthine paper trail led through Hawaii, London, and Sydney, though Cliff was still trying to fill several gaps in the historical record. "Don't know where this will end," he said. "In a way, I hope it doesn't."

Listening to Cliff, I quickly became infected by his passionate, quirky quest. "Why don't you come with us to Hawaii?" I said. "We'll go in February, on the anniversary of Cook's death."

Cliff, who had never left the U.K. except to attend a Cook conference in Canada in the 1970s, allowed himself a small smile. "I'll think on it," he said.

We parted beside the Tube stop at the Tower of London. When Roger and I reached the platform, a voice droned over the loudspeaker. "I regret to say," it began, before vanishing in feedback.

"All these Cook-mad Englishmen we've met are the same," Roger said, as we waited, and waited, for a train to appear. "They're isolatos. Trainspotters. A secret society, exchanging Cook trivia like a Masonic handshake." He peered down the empty track. "Actually, a trainspotter would come in handy right now."

Our flight to Sydney was scheduled to leave in a few hours. Roger reached in his pocket and fondled his plane ticket. "Blue sky, cold beer, happy people who don't lie under trains," he said. "I'm like Cook. Can't wait to get back to the Pacific."

TWENTY YEARS AFTER joining the Royal Navy in London, at the age of forty-six, Cook reached another crossroads in his career. In August 1775, within weeks of his return from the second Pacific voyage, he asked for and was granted a sinecure as captain of the Royal Hospital at Greenwich, a medical facility and home for aging sailors. The post offered a comfortable salary of £230 a year, plus living quarters, firewood, and a food stipend.

Elizabeth Cook may well have encouraged her husband to seek the hospital post. Since their wedding thirteen years before, the couple had spent less than four years together. When Cook returned from his second Pacific voyage, having been away six of the previous seven years, his two surviving sons, about to turn twelve and eleven, must have seemed virtual strangers to him.

But settling down for a life of professional and domestic quiet also felt strange to Cook. "My fate drives me from one extream to a nother," he fretted, soon after his return, in a letter to his Whitby friend, John Walker. "A few Months ago the whole Southern hemisphere was hardly big enough for me and now I am going to be confined within the limits of Greenwich Hospital, which are far too small for an active mind like mine. I must however confess it is a fine retreat and a pretty income, but whether I can bring my self to like ease and retirement, time will shew."

Time would show very quickly. A few months after the *Resolution* reached England, the Navy began preparing the ship for a return trip to the Pacific. The Earl of Sandwich and Sir Hugh Palliser, Cook's longtime Admiralty patrons, invited him to dinner and laid out their vision for the *Resolution*'s next voyage. Whom, they wondered, would the great captain recommend as its commander? Cook, according to his first biographer, Andrew Kippis, was so "fired" with excitement that he "declared that he himself would undertake the direction of the enterprise." One wonders if claret and port played some part in this declaration.

In any event, Cook's decision was undoubtedly what Sandwich and Palliser had hoped for all along. In February 1776, Cook sent another letter to John Walker. "It is certain that I have quited an easy retirement, for an Active, and perhaps Dangerous Voyage," he wrote. "My present disposition is more favourable to the latter than the former, and I imbark on as fair a prospect as I can wish. If I am fortunate enough to get safe home, theres no doubt but it will be greatly to my advantage."

COOK HAD ACCEPTED yet another mission impossible. His destination this time would be the top of the world, rather than its bottom, in quest of a channel instead of a continent. Cook was to search for the Northwest Passage, the much-dreamed-of shortcut between the Atlantic and Pacific that would enable British ships to reach the Orient without rounding the Capes. Surely, like a vast and temperate southern continent, a passage across the top of Canada *must* exist. Open ocean couldn't freeze, or so armchair geographers of the day believed. Parliament had even offered prize money of £20,000 to the crew of the ship that made the passage's eventual discovery. It awaited only an explorer of Cook's skill and fortitude to succeed where Baffin, Hudson, Frobisher, and so many others had turned back or frozen to death.

Cook's orders carried an added wrinkle. While other explorers had searched for the passage from the Atlantic side, Cook would approach from the far north Pacific. Only a few Europeans had ventured this way before, most notably Vitus Bering, who perished after his ship wrecked near the frigid sea named for him. And Bering, at least, had had the advantage of setting off from Russia's northeastern flank, in Kamchatka. Cook would have to sail halfway around the globe, entering the Pacific near New Zealand, then cross more than a hundred degrees of latitude to the largely uncharted waters of the north Pacific. For all he knew, there might be no land at all between Polynesia and the vaguely known territory that the Russians called Alaschka.

Cook had another, smaller mission to perform en route: taking home a Tahitian named Omai, whom Tobias Furneaux of the *Adventure* had carried to England on Cook's second voyage. By all accounts, Omai had been charmed by the British, and they by him. Joseph Banks squired him around London in a suit of Manchester velvet and white satin, and introduced him to King George, to whom the Tahitian blurted, "How do, King Tosh!" Omai attended the opera and sat for a portrait by Sir Joshua Reynolds. He skated on ice and swam in the freezing North Sea, novelties for a native of the tropics. According to the *London Chronicle,* Omai also became engaged "to a young Lady of about 22 years of age, who will go with him to his own country." The historical record makes no further mention of the engagement, or of the young lady.

Omai, like Banks before him, wasn't one to travel light. He took as baggage on the *Resolution* the many gifts he'd been given, including a suit of armor, a barrel organ, a jack-in-the-box, toy soldiers, and pewter dishes. Nor was this the only curious cargo that Cook carried as he set off from Plymouth on July 12, 1776, just under a year since his return from the second voyage. Cook's newfangled gear included a cork life preserver and "an Apparatus for recovering Drowned persons." Much more cumbersome was the menagerie he toted: a bull, two cows, and several calves, intended as gifts to the Tahitians from

King George, and a peacock and peahen, donated for the same purpose by the Earl of Bessborough. In Cape Town, Cook collected four
horses, sheep, and other stock, as added presents. "Nothing is wanting
but a few females of our own species to make the *Resolution* a com-
pleate ark," Cook wrote. The next year, when he'd unburdened his
ship at Tahiti, the captain confessed: "The trouble and vexation that
attended the bringing of these Animals thus far is hardly to be conceived."

Trouble and vexation, of all sorts, would plague the third voyage
from its start. The *Resolution*, battered by its Antarctic travels on the
second voyage, hadn't been properly refitted in dry dock—in part
because the fastidious Cook, believing he was headed for the Greenwich Hospital, didn't oversee the initial work. The ship began leaking
almost as soon as it left Plymouth, and rain poured straight in, soaking
the *Resolution*'s stores and sleeping quarters. Problems with the ship's
caulking, masts, and rigging would delay and divert Cook repeatedly
over the next several years.

The *Resolution*'s companion ship, the *Discovery*, was in better
shape, except for its captain, Charles Clerke, the good-humored,
wench-loving officer who had served Cook so well on his two previous
voyages. Shortly before setting off from London, Clerke landed in
prison, having agreed to answer for his brother's unpaid debts. Cook,
already behind schedule, sailed off without him. Clerke extracted himself three weeks later—"Huzzah my Boys heave away," he exulted in a
departing letter—and the *Discovery* caught up with the *Resolution* at
Cape Town. But the thirty-five-year-old Clerke had contracted tuberculosis in prison and would gradually weaken during the course of the
long voyage.

AS THE SHIPS sailed on from Cape Town to the Pacific, it also became
clear that Cook was ill—if not in body, then in spirit. He had turned
forty-eight in Cape Town, a ripe age for an eighteenth-century mariner.
William Watman, a gunner listed as forty-four years old at the start of
the voyage, was termed "an old man" by his shipmates when he died
three years later. Cook had been at sea for three decades and already

served a full and taxing naval career, as evidenced by the Admiralty's initial willingness to put him comfortably out to pasture at the Greenwich Hospital.

All eighteenth-century seafarers endured conditions that today seem insupportable. But even by the standards of that era, Cook labored under exceptional strain. He'd already sailed twice into the unknown, for three years at a stretch, traveling far beyond the range of reliable charts, mail contact, the prospect of passing ships, or the hope of any rescue if he got into trouble. Cook's status as commander, and his reticence, compounded this stress and isolation. By all accounts, he'd remained a solitary rock amid life-threatening crises: the Barrier Reef, Antarctic icebergs, attacks by islanders, and the diseases that carried off a third of the *Endeavour*'s crew. It seems fair to say that Cook didn't have a true day off during the six years he spent at sea commanding his first two Pacific expeditions.

Nor did he have much time off between voyages. Cook had already plotted a return journey to the Pacific by the time he finished his first, and he spent the intervening months preparing his ships, recruiting crewmen, and reporting on his travels aboard the *Endeavour*. The year's interval between his second and third voyages was even more hectic. Having initially planned to go to Greenwich, Cook had to play catch-up, rushing to prepare his ships and men for a departure originally scheduled for April, just eight months after his return.

Cook also had to fulfill the flattering but time-consuming obligations attending his growing celebrity. He set down the long account of his second voyage, sat for the portrait by Nathaniel Dance, and corresponded with admirers (including a French naval officer, to whom Cook wrote: "A man would never accomplish much in discovery who only stuck to his orders"). He also met other Fellows of the Royal Society at the Mitre tavern on Fleet Street, and dined with luminaries such as James Boswell, who wrote: "It was curious to see Cook, a grave steady man, and his wife, a decent plump Englishwoman, and think that he was preparing to sail round the world."

It seems doubtful that Cook found much time in this schedule to sleep in, enjoy his wife and children, or sit quietly by the fire at his home in Mile End. If he had, he might have reconsidered his impulsive decision to set off on a third Pacific voyage just months after returning from his second. Cook's letters to John Walker suggest another possibility; the captain may have been chronically ill-suited to a desk job and a staid domestic life.

COOK'S MOOD SHOWED clear signs of curdling in early 1777, when the *Resolution* and *Discovery* reached the Pacific. "We were persecuted with a Wind in our teeth," he wrote of his slow progress north, in what seems a revealing choice of words. Already behind schedule—the *Resolution* had left late, and the *Discovery* later still—Cook reluctantly abandoned his original plan to head north in time for the brief Arctic summer. Instead, he had to wait out the long northern winter by trolling between now familiar islands, and enduring all-too-familiar problems: theft, lecherous and drunken crewmen, warring chiefs, and the endless search for fresh provisions. He also had to deal with the nagging irritation of his poorly fitted ship. At one point, the normally respectful captain railed against the Navy Board in language so angry and accusatory that his superiors deleted it before publication of the voyage's official version.

On his two earlier journeys, Cook had generally confronted such challenges with equanimity, and shown a firm but fair hand in dealing with both crewmen and islanders. On his third voyage, he became, at times, an entirely different commander. Off the coast of New Zealand, someone on the *Resolution* started stealing food. Unable to find the culprit, Cook cut the crew's rations by a third. When his men complained, he accused them of "very mutinous proceedings." Such eruptions would become more frequent as the voyage proceeded north. Cook ultimately ordered lashings of forty-four men aboard the *Resolution,* more than twice the number he'd had flogged during each of his previous voyages.

As the third voyage proceeded to the island of Moorea, off Tahiti, natives stole a goat, and then another. In earlier such instances, Cook had taken a chief hostage, itself a harsh reprisal. This time, he ordered his men to burn houses and smash canoes. Even his admiring officers were stunned. Later, enraged at another Polynesian thief, Cook ordered his ship's barber to shave the man's head and cut off his ears. "I punished him with greater severity than I had ever done any one before," Cook acknowledged in his journal, though he expressed no regret. Instances of sudden fury toward natives would recur, ultimately at the cost of Cook's life.

At other times, the captain's instability manifested itself not with rage, but inaction. On his leisurely months-long revisit to Tonga, Cook heard frequent reports of a "very fruitful island" called "Fidgee," only a short sail away. He also learned of "the largest of all the islands" in the region, known as "Hammoah." Yet Cook failed to set off in search of either Fiji or Samoa—strangely passive behavior for a man whose hunger for new discoveries had once seemed limitless. Even more aberrant were Cook's occasional navigational lapses. In the Bering Sea, he became so confused by the location of one island that he repeatedly mistook it for a new site, and gave it three different names.

If the change in Cook's character seems clear, the causes for it are not. Cook gave no hint of distress in his journal, at least not directly. And his men tended to find excuses for their captain's erratic behavior, or wrote about it obliquely. One journal keeper, for instance, referred to Cook's escalating temper tantrums as "heivas," the foot-stomping Polynesian war dances.

Cook's deterioration may have reflected a physical breakdown. The first signs of declining health had surfaced during the second voyage, when Cook suffered from a rheumatic fever and later from the "Billious colick" that confined him to his bunk for a week. Stress seems to have contributed to his stomach trouble. In 1773, after almost wrecking against a reef off Tahiti—and bellowing at his men during the tense escape that followed—Cook went below in the company of Anders Sparrman, the Swedish naturalist. "Although he had from beginning to end of the incident appeared perfectly alert and able," Sparrman wrote, the captain was now "suffering so greatly from his stomach that he was in a great sweat and could scarcely stand." Sparrman dosed Cook with brandy, which seems to have given the captain at least temporary relief.

Sir James Watt, a surgeon-admiral in the British Navy who has made an exhaustive study of health aboard Cook's ships, believes that the captain's ailments represent "a classical picture of intestinal obstruction." Watt suspects the blockage was caused by a roundworm infection. This, in turn, caused a vitamin B deficiency, which produces fatigue, constipation, irritability, depression, and loss of interest and initiative—in other words, chronic, personality-changing symptoms that seem to match those exhibited by Cook.

Ulcers and a gallbladder infection are other possible culprits. On the third voyage, Cook also complained of sciatica, or what he called "a sort of Rheumatick pain in one side from hip to the foot" (at one point he described Tahitians giving him a bone-cracking massage that provided "immediate relief"). We also know that Cook was treated on the second voyage with opiates, the only effective painkiller in the medicine chests of ships' surgeons. Given the intensely addictive nature of opiates, and the stomach problems they often produce, it seems conceivable that Cook struggled with drug dependency as well.

Alternatively, or on top of these problems, Cook may have been simply exhausted, psychologically as well as physically. At times on the third voyage, he showed signs of disillusion with the whole business of exploration, and with the ills his own discoveries had brought to native peoples: disease, greed, thievery, prostitution. "Cook," the historian Bernard Smith speculates, "increasingly realised that wherever he went he was spreading the curses much more liberally than the benefits of European civilization."

Nor did Cook have anyone to lean on or confide in, even if he'd been so inclined. Charles Clerke was sick with consumption and captain of a separate ship. By Cook's side on the quarterdeck of the *Resolution* were the stolid American, John Gore, and the young William Bligh, who was already exhibiting the petulance that would land him, a decade later, on a longboat cast adrift from the *Bounty*.

There were several sensitive and literary men on the voyage who might have provided Cook with the sort of broadening company that Joseph Banks had offered on the *Endeavour*. Lieutenant James King, for instance, was a parson's son, educated at Oxford and in Paris, who corresponded with Edmund Burke. He and others on the third voyage wrote so prolifically that they collated a weekly paper at sea. (Sadly, it is lost to history.) But most of these men were much younger than Cook and far inferior in rank. They no doubt felt intimidated by their captain, a reserved man who was already a celebrity.

Finally, there was the frustration of the mission itself. As Cook headed north through cold and fog, with no sign of a route to the Atlantic, he came to suspect that the Northwest Passage was a chimera, like the fabled *terra australis*. Given all these pressures—his illness or fatigue, the exasperating condition of his ship, the hardship and frigid futility of the third voyage—it seems unsurprising that Cook showed signs of falling apart. The real mystery may be how he managed to hold on to his sanity and health as long as he did.

Chapter 12

ALASKA:
Outside Men

This region is the empire of the winds.
—IOANN VENIAMINOV, A NINETEENTH-CENTURY
RUSSIAN PRIEST IN THE ALEUTIAN ISLANDS

After my ride on the replica *Endeavour,* and several queasy sails with Roger in Tahiti and Australia, I'd hoped to avoid anymore travel by sea. But plotting Cook's path to the Arctic, I couldn't see a self-respecting way to avoid the *Tustumena,* an Alaskan ferry that closely followed the route Cook sailed in the summer of 1778. The state-run ferry traveled along Alaska's southwestern peninsula and into the Aleutian Islands, which form a twelve-hundred-mile tail arcing toward Kamchatka. The ship's last stop, a Bering Sea port called Dutch Harbor, lies beside Unalaska Island, the only place in the far north where Cook had prolonged contact with people rather than with walruses.

Unfortunately, to reach Dutch Harbor, the *Tustumena*—named, aptly, for a glacier—churned through some of the roughest seas on the planet. When I phoned the ferry office in Alaska for a schedule, I learned that the *Tustumena*'s most recent voyage, in June, had run into eighty-knot winds and twenty-five-foot waves, forcing the ship to stand off Dutch Harbor for half a day, tossing and pitching until the wind slowed enough for it to land without wrecking the dock.

"Sounds abysmal," Roger said, when I asked if we should book tickets for the ferry's July run. "You'll puke yourself to death. I wouldn't miss that for the world."

We decided to trim a few days off the weeklong ferry trip by flying from Anchorage to Kodiak Island, the *Tustumena*'s first stop. At a bed-and-breakfast, I told the owner we'd be checking out the next day to catch the ferry. She burst out laughing.

"Is it that bad?" I asked.

"Oh, no, I wouldn't worry," she said. "The captain's very seasoned." Meaning, I guess, we wouldn't drown. However, her beds were the last we'd see for the rest of the week. The few cabins aboard the ferry, which made the Aleutian run only once a month, from May through October, had been booked long ago. At a store in Kodiak, we bought thin foam mats. I'd also brought a sleeping bag, unlike Roger. "I'm Australian, I'm tough, I'm an idiot," he said, unfurling his meager pad on the ferry's cold steel deck, beside a massive smokestack. The hundred-odd passengers who had boarded before us had already staked out the indoor flop space.

As the ship pulled away from Kodiak, a horn bellowed and the smokestack roared to life. If the cold and swell and midnight summer light didn't keep us awake, the noise surely would. "At least we'll be the first ones into the life raft," Roger said, studying an alarming-looking vessel mounted near the rail. Labeled "Totally Enclosed Lifeboat," it was a submarinelike pod that deployed by shooting down a ramp and then making a twenty-foot freefall into the sea. Anything less robust wouldn't have stood a chance in Alaska's roiling, frigid waters.

We left the deck to explore the rest of the 296-foot-long *Tustumena*, a no-frills vessel built in 1964. The only entertainment on offer was a claustrophobic game room with three vertigo-inducing video machines—the last place I wanted to be in heavy seas. The ship's tiny bar was vacant, except for a man buying a packet of "Motion Ease." In the adjoining dining room, a lone couple tucked into gravy-choked Salisbury steak. This also seemed the wrong place to settle in for the rough ride ahead.

In theory, we could stand on the deck and gaze at the magnificent scenery—if the fog ever cleared. I'd packed field glasses, as well as half my library, including an article on motion sickness. Scanning it, I

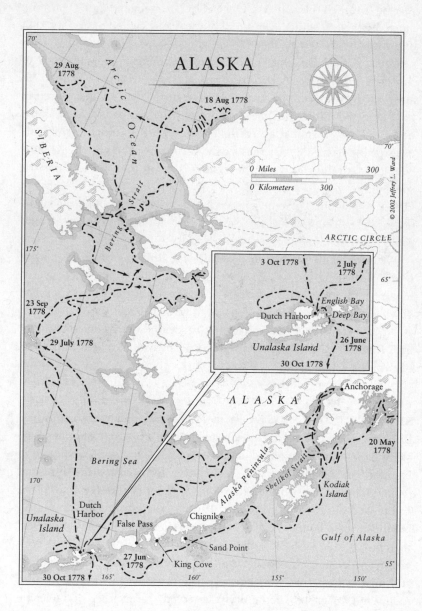

ALASKA

29 Aug
1778

18 Aug 1778

Arctic Ocean

SIBERIA

Bering Strait

0   Miles   300

0   Kilometers   300

© 2002 Jeffrey L. Ward

70°

ARCTIC CIRCLE

175°

23 Sep
1778

29 July 1778

65°

3 Oct 1778   2 July
                  1778

English Bay
Dutch Harbor   •Deep Bay

Unalaska Island   26 June
                        1778

30 Oct 1778

A L A S K A

•Anchorage

60°

Bering Sea

20 May
1778

170°

Alaska Peninsula

Shelikof Strait

*Kodiak
Island*

Dutch
Harbor

*Unalaska
Island*

False Pass

Chignik•

•Sand Point

Gulf of Alaska

55°

30 Oct 1778   165°

27 Jun
1778

King Cove

160°   155°   150°

learned that the two worst things to do in rough seas were reading and peering through binoculars. Our fellow passengers didn't promise much distraction, either. Almost all of them had sacked out by six P.M., exhausted by the trip so far.

Then, a few hours out of Kodiak, an announcement crackled over the ferry's PA system. A documentary on Arctic wildlife was about to air in the forward lounge. Eager for diversion, I quickly lost myself in footage of adorable sea otters, whose fur, the narrator said, was the densest of any mammal on earth. Then another announcement came over the loudspeaker. "There is a gale warning for tonight. Please stow your gear carefully and use the handrails at all times. There may be some motion."

Roger laughed. " 'Some motion.' In a gale! That's like when the doctor says, 'You may feel some discomfort' as he snaps on a glove and asks you to bend over for a prostate exam."

We tottered up to the deck. The ship was already swaying. I climbed into my sleeping bag while Roger slumped on his mat and covered himself with every scrap of clothing he could muster. Then I washed down several Dramamine with a can of tomato juice.

"You'll look like you're bleeding to death when you throw that up," Roger said, reaching for a rum bottle instead. "I may die out here, but at least I'll be numb."

AFTER SAILING ACROSS the Pacific, Cook encountered North America at present-day Oregon and coasted north to British Columbia, paralleling the route I'd traveled in the replica *Endeavour*. He anchored in Nootka Sound, west of today's Vancouver, to provision his ships and replace a rotted mast on the *Resolution*. Then, in the spring of 1778, he crawled north toward the 65th Parallel, the latitude at which he'd been instructed by the Admiralty to start searching for inlets and rivers that might lead to a "Northern Passage." Cook's ship leaked constantly; his charts were hopeless, and so was the weather: constant rain and mist interspersed with hail, sleet, and snow. "A thick fog and a foul Wind," Charles Clerke dryly observed, "are rather disagreeable intruders to people engaged in surveying and tracing a Coast."

Cook duly named whatever land he glimpsed through the fog,

though some of his choices seem to reflect his gloomy view of the coast. He named Cape Suckling for a captain whom Beaglehole describes as "weak" and "unimportant." Kaye Island honored a toady-ish rector who had curried favor with Cook's family; the island's name has since been changed to Kayak. Probing what seemed a wide, promising inlet, Cook dubbed it Sandwich Sound, after his Admiralty patron. But when he explored an arm of the passage and discovered that it led nowhere, Cook left a name that echoed his disappointment: Turnagain. A statue of the captain, gazing out at glacial silt, now stands near the site, at the edge of present-day Anchorage.

The scattered people that Cook encountered during this long, dismal coasting seemed like freaks to the English. Natives stuck bones draped with beads through large slits cut beneath their lower lips. "This Ornament is a very great Impediment to the Speech and makes them look as if they had a double row of teeth in the under Jaw," Cook wrote. One alarmed sailor, he added, "called out there was a man with two mouths."

Cook, however, admired the local attire: cloaks of beaver and otter fur. The inhabitants were unaware of their value in Europe. One chief accepted a single bead in exchange for ten skins that crewmen valued at several hundred pounds sterling, or roughly twenty times a seaman's annual wage. "There is no doubt but a very beneficial fur trade might be carried on with the Inhabitants of this coast," Cook concluded.

As usual, he was right. Within a decade of his visit, British fur traders—including several men who had sailed on the *Resolution* and *Discovery*—would swarm the coast of Canada and Alaska, with grave consequences for both the coast dwellers and their furry game. Cook also anticipated this impact. "Foreigners would increase their [natives'] wants by introducing new luxuries amongst them," he wrote, "in order to purchas which they would be the more assiduous in procuring skins."

As he pushed on, through "constant Misty weather with drizzly rain," Cook would discover that this inexorable transformation was already under way.

I WOKE SOMETIME in the night, when a man stepped on my head. The gale had spilled me across the deck and hard against the bathroom door. I caterpillar-crawled in my sleeping bag so the man could get past. The ship shuddered and bucked. Sea spray soaked my bag; wind buffeted my face. I felt as though I were trying to sleep through the rinse-and-spin cycle at a Laundromat.

After a few minutes I gave up and slumped against the ship's rail. Roger, sprawled nearby, looked like a Mathew Brady photograph of the Gettysburg dead: limbs twisted, clothes scattered, mouth curled in a stunned O. At least he could sleep. I rummaged in my rucksack for a flashlight and Cook's journal. "The gale increasing with a thick fog and rain," he wrote of the *Resolution*'s sail through these waters. "A prodigious swell rolling in upon the shore."

I poked my head over the rail. Thick fog and rain, no doubt about that. The swell *felt* prodigious, but I couldn't really tell. All I could see were whitecaps foaming atop black sea, like froth dollopped on espresso. The man who'd stepped on my head lurched out of the bathroom, gray-faced and trembling. There but for the grace of God . . . and the horse dose of Dramamine I'd swallowed before bed.

I turned to Charles Clerke's journal. As always, he played the everyman to Cook's Übermensch. "We have now a very staggering gale," he wrote, describing the same storm that Cook judged "increasing." As for Alaska, neither the sea nor the land impressed the *Discovery*'s captain. "This seems upon the whole," Clerke wrote, "a damn'd unhappy part of the World."

Dawn broke early and gray aboard the *Tustumena*. Tired but elated at having survived the gale, which died down at daybreak, I went to the bridge to see if I could chat with the captain. Several men occupied the large, glass-enclosed wheelhouse, checking banks of switches, computer terminals, and blipping screens. The helmsman offered to show me around, spouting acronyms for various guidance systems. A machine that looked like a heart monitor charted the depth and contour of the sea bottom. One fax spat out weather reports; another produced Coast Guard communiqués. "This gear will do everything except wash dishes," the helmsman said.

Tearing off a computer printout, he reported that the gale during the night had reached force seven on the twelve-notch Beaufort scale, with forty-five-knot gusts and a twelve-foot swell. "No big deal compared to what we often see out here," he said. When I asked why conditions were so extreme, he pulled out a chart and swept his finger across the Pacific. "It's wide-open sea all the way to Hawaii," he said. "The wind and ocean have a long time to build up before slamming into us."

The Gulf of Alaska was also a cauldron for ferocious storms, created when cold Arctic air met warm Pacific currents. At the moment, we were steaming through the Shelikof Strait, a notorious wind tunnel between Kodiak Island and the Alaskan mainland. Ahead lay the Bering Sea, renowned for its unrelenting fog and frigid wind. The helmsman showed me a circular window set into the bridge's front glass. It was designed to heat up and revolve, keeping a peephole clear when the rest of the windshield iced over.

A trim man with a graying beard joined us on the bridge. This was the captain, Bob Crowley, who had piloted the *Tustumena* for twenty-five years. In that time, he'd seen mountainous "rogue waves," ships in distress, and even circus animals on the ferry getting sick. "On bad trips," he said, "this looks like a hospital ship." The crew had to make announcements asking passengers to use toilets and vomit bags so as not to clog the sinks and water fountains. Occasionally, conditions got so bad that passengers bailed out, disembarking at remote stops along the way. Others drank too much and had to be handcuffed to the bar. Two suicidal men had even jumped overboard; one of them drowned.

I asked the captain if he ever thought about Cook, who had sailed these same waters in a wooden ship less than half the length of the *Tustumena*, without engines or weather reports or radio contact. He answered me by going to a computerized chart plotter and clicking a mouse. Our position, course, and speed flashed onto the color monitor. The computer also calculated the speed and direction of approaching vessels and the contour and distance of the shore. The captain shook his head. "What Cook did, it's hardly even comprehensible," he said. "This is a graveyard for ships. I wouldn't risk a day sail out here without all these instruments."

JUST BEFORE NOON, the ferry stopped at a small port called Chignik, a native word for "big wind." Ringed by towering, snowcapped peaks,

Chignik could be reached only by ship or small plane. We had an hour to wander onshore while the ferry unloaded cargo. Roger and I stepped off the gangway and into the middle of a Chignik summer's day: forty-five degrees, cold rain, and a howling wind. The old wooden pier led straight to a warehouse crowded with men hacking fish. This plant, and a nearby cannery, drew a few hundred seasonal workers to Chignik, which had a year-round population of only seventy.

A Mexican worker leaned against the wall of the fish plant, smoking a cigarette. "Here, we just cut, gut, and head," he said, adding that he earned $5.75 an hour, plus overtime, for working twelve-hour shifts, seven days a week. He shared a bed, sleeping while his bunkmate worked. The man pointed out the workers' quarters before returning to the line: barracklike buildings decorated with homemade signs saying "Hilton," "Hyatt," and "Waldorf."

We hiked through the rest of the village, across planks laid over mud. Most of the buildings were low and ramshackle; the only tall one, Chignik's church, had blown over in a storm a few years before. At the town's general store, I asked the shopkeeper what people in Chignik did for fun. "Fun?" he replied. "Wait for the ferry to come in."

We trudged back through the rain to the dock. Roger glanced up at the fog-shrouded mountains walling in Chignik. "The place is a gulag," he said. "Not one concession to sentiment or aesthetics." By comparison, the ferry now seemed luxurious, and we stretched out on our foam mats, munching peanuts from the general store. I went to the rail to snap a picture and returned to find Roger inside my sleeping bag. "I'm looking forward to becoming better acquainted with this," he said, zipping himself in. "I'll be like one of those Mexican workers, using the bed when you're not."

In the afternoon we passed a point Cook had named Foggy Cape. I couldn't see it through all the fog. Near here, the English had a strange encounter with natives in kayaks. "An Indian in one of them," Cook wrote, "took off his cap and bowed after the manner of Europeans." When sailors dropped the man a rope, he attached a small wooden box before paddling away. Inside the box was a paper covered in Russian script. None of the crewmen could read the writing, but they guessed it was a message from shipwrecked sailors.

In fact, as the English later learned, the note was a receipt for tribute, or tax, paid by the natives to Russian fur traders. Cook had reached the eastern edge of Russian influence in the region. After Vitus Bering died in 1741, having just sighted the Alaskan mainland, his sailors built a boat from their shipwrecked vessel and sailed home, carrying a rich load of seal, fox, and otter pelts. This sparked a frenzy among Russian fur traders, who spent the next three decades probing east along the Aleutians and onto the Alaskan peninsula.

The early traders were a brutal lot. They seized women and children as hostages until native men hunted furs for the Russians. This custom gradually evolved into a tribute system, paid in pelts. When natives resisted, by attacking small trading parties, the Russians retaliated by slaughtering them by the hundreds with musket and cannon. By 1778, when Cook arrived, the natives had become sub-Arctic serfs. The men who paddled out to the *Resolution* were probably fearful that the visitors were Russians, coming to extract more tax. Hence their "acquired politeness," as Cook called it, and their tendering of the receipt for tribute already paid.

This wasn't the first time Cook had encountered Pacific peoples who'd seen Europeans before. But in other places Cook had visited, that contact had been very limited; some of it had occurred more than a century before Cook's arrival. In Alaska, Cook, for the first time, met natives in the early throes of the upheaval wrought by sustained European contact. The picture he and his men came away with proved a melancholy preview of what lay in store for the societies Cook himself had opened to the West.

AT TEN O'CLOCK on our second night at sea, the *Tustumena* arrived at Sand Point, a larger and somewhat more salubrious outpost than Chignik. A Little League team awaited us on the dock. They would ride the ferry to the next stop for a game, then wait for the ship's return trip to travel home four days later. A crewman said that residents of these remote, scattered settlements also timed high school proms and other occasions for the ferry's monthly round-trip. The communities were too small to stage such events on their own.

We hiked a half mile to the center of Sand Point, which was dusty and silent, except for a shedlike tavern with a corrugated metal roof and a sign by the door: NO WEAPONS. Inside, a dozen men hunched around the bar, where they'd obviously been for some time. A woman with a black eye played pool with a man clad in the local uniform: duckbill cap, dirty quilted vest, flannel shirt, and blue jeans.

"Lemme buy you boys a beer!" a man slurred as soon as we reached the bar. The others quickly competed for our company. Strangers were obviously a welcome novelty in Sand Point. After several incoherent conversations, I was relieved to find a half-sober patron named Ken Cheek, a broad-shouldered, ponytailed man with broken teeth. He turned out to be the bar's bouncer. On most nights, Ken said, he had to muscle a troublemaker or two out the door. Repeat offenders risked banishment from the bar for a year—a dreadful fate in a settlement offering few other diversions. "There's a hamburger joint called Bozo's," he said, "and twelve miles of paved road to drive. That's about it."

Ken said the others at the bar were salmon fishermen, currently on strike because the price paid for their catch had fallen by half, to only forty-five cents a pound. (Fish farms in countries such as Chile and Norway had glutted the market.) Given the dangers of fishing in these waters, it wasn't worth risking a trip for a wage that barely covered expenses. "So they sit in here all day," Ken said. "If you stick around another hour, you're sure to see a brawl."

Instead, I disentangled Roger from the grip of a babbling man and headed back to the ferry. It was midnight, still light outside. "It's a permanent Dark Age back there," Roger said. "I've never met such basic *Homo sapiens.*"

We weren't in much better shape, curling on the cold deck for another night at sea. At least there was no gale this time, and I managed a few hours of fitful sleep before the ship stopped again, at six A.M., at a place called King Cove. I prodded Roger awake for a walk onshore, but he shook his head and climbed in my sleeping bag. Almost no one else bothered to disembark, and it was easy to see why. The wind blew so hard that I was almost crawling on all fours by the time I reached the end of the long pier.

Taking refuge in the first building I came to—the harbor office—I found four men sipping coffee and staring out the window. They had jet-black hair, small black eyes, and high cheekbones. "A bit fresh out today," I said, as a conversation starter.

One of the men looked at me strangely. "This is a nice day today," he said. "Last month we clocked the wind at a hundred and thirty-seven miles an hour." A radio crackled: the Coast Guard reporting that a fishing boat was in trouble. "Second this week," the man said. "They'll fish 'em out with a helicopter."

Rick Koso was a fisherman. In King Cove, as in Chignik and Sand Point, fish was the only game in town. "You can drive a few miles in one direction and four in the other," Rick said of the village, which was enclosed on all sides by mountains.

"What about hiking?"

"It's all pretty steep," Rick said. "Plus there's bears. One mauled a little kid a few years ago, right down the road. People haven't gone out much since then."

"Don't you get cabin fever?"

Rick smiled. "You mean the Aleut stare? You get that. Wind at a hundred clicks, driving rain, day after day. You get sort of wigged out." He assumed a blank, haunted expression. "That's the Aleut stare."

I was curious to learn more, but I had to crawl back down the pier in time for the ship's departure. A heavy fog settled in, and there was nothing to do but take turns in the sleeping bag and watch for occasional glimpses of the distant, treeless mountains. "This country is more broken or rugged than any part we had yet seen," Cook wrote of this landscape. "Every part had a very barren appearance." Roger studied the same scene and declared: "It's monstrously dull. We've been out here two days. Cook did this for months, with nothing to do but think up names." A desolate inlet emerged from the mist. "Buggery Bay," Roger christened it, "because there's bugger-all there."

After a momentary stop at another bleak outpost called Cold Bay, of which I learned nothing except that the settlement merited its name, we pulled in to the village of False Pass. This marked the true beginning of the Aleutian chain. Before leaving home, I'd consulted several atlases to plot the ferry's course. The Aleutians stretched so far west that most maps of America didn't even include them, unless with a small box in the corner of the page for Alaska.

False Pass appeared deserted. I toured the settlement's clump of low buildings and found little except a sign on the locked schoolhouse: "Please make sure the door latches. We don't want the wind to tear it off." The nearby library had a light on inside. I poked my head through the door and found an Aleut teenager studying a rack of months-old magazines. She looked at me through thick round glasses, a bit startled, as if a bear had wandered in.

"I'm from the ferry," I said.

"Oh." She fussed with her hair and introduced herself as Jana. She told me False Pass had eighty residents, including thirteen students. Jana, at seventeen, was the only one of high-school age.

"Do you get lonely?" I asked her.

"In summer, some fishermen come here who are about my age," she said. "But it'd be nice to have a girlfriend I could talk to about them. Someone I could ask, 'What do you think they're thinking?'" She blushed. "But I like it here. If you want to get away from other people, all you have to do is walk for five minutes."

This was certainly true. Still, I wondered if Jana longed for the world she read about in the library's magazines. "One thing, yes," she said. "I wish we had gardens here, like in other places. But it's hard to grow things. All we have are wildflowers." She plucked a gardening magazine from the rack to take home, then turned off the lights. I sprinted back to the ferry just in time for its departure, unsure whether to feel sorry for this solitary teenager at the end of the world, or to envy her remove from the pop culture and brand-name junk that mesmerized so much of adolescent America.

ON JUNE 26, 1778, sailing blindly through fog, Cook was "alarmed at hearing the Sound of breakers on our larboard bow." He quickly brought the ship into the wind and dropped anchor. When the gloom cleared, the English discovered that they'd narrowly avoided wrecking against rocks, and now lay beside a grassy island. "Very nice pilotage," Clerke wryly observed, "considering our perfect Ignorance of our situation." Cook, echoing the relief he'd felt at escaping the Great Barrier Reef eight years before, wrote in his journal: "The Island we were now at I called Providence from the providential escape we had in first making it."

Short of fresh water, Cook sailed along the coast until he found a harbor. Men paddled kayaks out to the ships, and one of them overturned. The English fished out the kayak's occupant and brought him aboard the *Resolution*. Cook took him to his own cabin for dry clothes. "He dressed himself with as much ease as I could have done," Cook wrote, adding that the man's own garb—a shirt made of whale's gut, and an undergarment of bird skins with the feathers worn against the body—had been patched with cloth of "European or such like manufacture."

Cook also learned that natives called the island "Oonalaschka," which he substituted on his chart for the earlier "Providence." But the season was advancing and Cook couldn't spare time to explore the island. Sighting a passage to the north, and favored by a southerly breeze, he sailed on, into the Bering Sea. For the rest of the brief summer, he fought steadily north, touching on the shores of western Alaska and northeastern Siberia. The English battled cold, "a nasty jumbling sea" (Clerke's words), and fog so dense that men aboard the two ships had to beat drums, fire guns, and ring bells to alert each other of their positions. At times, Cook had no guide other than "the roaring of the Sea Horses," or walruses. Their braying warned the fog-blind captain of the treacherous ice shelves on which the animals perched.

These "sea monsters," as one crewman called them, prompted a revealing dispute between Cook and his men. The captain dispatched boats to slaughter nine walruses, some of them almost ten feet long and half a ton in weight. Cook, characteristically, declared the walrus meat to be fine eating: "marine beef," he called it, with fat as "sweet as Marrow"—far preferable to the ships' dwindling rations of salt meat, which he promptly curtailed. Many of his men begged to differ.

"Captain Cook here speaks entirely from his own taste which was, surely, the coarsest that ever mortal was endued with," wrote midshipman James Trevenen. To Trevenen, walrus fat resembled "train-oil instead of marrow." As for the flesh, another crewman termed it "disgustfull" and "too rank both in smell and tast as to make use of except with plenty of pepper and salt and these two articles were vary scarce." The walrus meat caused some crewmen to vomit, leaving them with nothing to eat but their scant rations of bread.

"At last the discontents rose to such complaints & murmurings," Trevenen wrote, that Cook "restored the salt meat." The captain, in other words, had almost provoked mutiny with his dietary fanaticism: another distressing sign that Cook was losing touch with his men and perhaps his own faculties.

By this point, the men were also heartily sick of Arctic sailing. Cook had probed beyond 70 degrees north, well inside the Arctic Circle, and almost precisely the southern latitude he'd reached off Antarctica. Finally, encountering ice "which was as compact as a Wall and seemed to be ten or twelve feet high," Cook decided to turn back, having now traversed more than 140 of the earth's 180 degrees of latitude, as well as its entire longitude several times over.

As the ships retreated south in late August, heavy snow fell and the temperature rarely rose above freezing. "Ice was seen hanging at our hair, our noses, and even at the men's finger ends," Lieutenant John Rickman wrote. "Hot victuals froze while we were at table." Then the *Resolution* sprang a fresh leak. Cook had no choice but to return to the providential island of Oonalaschka where he'd stopped briefly before entering the Bering Sea.

WE SPENT OUR last night on the *Tustumena* in the bar. Since the trip's inaugural gale, the passage had been relatively calm, much to Roger's disappointment. "I was so looking forward to seeing you wan and feeble with seasickness. I'm going to be robbed of that experience." The other passengers also roused from their torpor, and several joined us at the bar: oil workers, fishermen, birdwatchers frustrated by the mist and rain. I felt thwarted, too. Except for the fog and my brief forays ashore, I'd experienced little of the landscape or native culture Cook had encountered.

Then, at eleven P.M., a vision appeared through the bar window: clear skies and a spectacular view of two peaks with the distinctive, cratered tops of volcanoes. A puff of steam drifted from one volcano, and its heat had melted the snow near its summit.

"Combustible mountains!" I shouted. This was Clerke's memorable phrase for volcanoes. Shuffling in my pack, I found English drawings that exactly matched our view, as did Cook's journal entry. "A narrow cloud, sometimes two or three one above the other, embraced the middle like a girdle," he wrote of the taller of the volcanoes, which rose more than nine thousand feet. "The Column of smoke rising perpindicular to a great height out of its summit and spreading before the wind into a tail of vast length, made a very picturesque appearance." This was about as ripe as Cook's prose ever got. After so much fog, he must have felt the same exaltation I did at actually glimpsing some scenery.

Before long, the fog returned, enveloping the *Tustumena* for the duration of its wet but placid passage through the Bering Sea. We arrived at Dutch Harbor at six in the morning. In the dawn gloom, the port appeared eerie and industrial: a flood of orange light, fuel tanks, cranes rising through the mist, and massive container ships. Dutch Harbor was a commercial fishing boomtown, with an annual catch greater than that of any port in America. Roughly half of all fish caught in U.S. waters now came from the Bering Sea and passed through this remote harbor.

From the dock, we made our way past fish-processing plants and turned down Salmon Way to the Grand Aleutian Hotel, a chalet-style monolith fronted by concrete pillboxes. During World War II, Dutch Harbor served as a major U.S. military installation and came under attack from Japanese aircraft. The hotel's walls and floors swayed as we tottered to our room and collapsed. Waking that afternoon, I walked up the road to a car rental office, where I procured a rattletrap that looked as though it had clocked three times the fifty thousand miles listed on the odometer. Wind, salt, sea air, gravel roads, and snow-melting chemicals weren't kind to Aleutian cars.

I roused Roger for a trip across the short bridge to Unalaska Island, Cook's "Oonalaschka." When the *Resolution* and *Discovery* returned to the island after their wretched Arctic sail, the English found even clearer evidence than before that other Europeans were nearby. A native came aboard bearing "a very singular present considering the place," Cook wrote, "a rye loaf or rather a pie made in the form of a loaf, for some salmon highly seasoned." Cook guessed that this dish was a "present from some Russians in the Neighbourhood." To find them, he dispatched John Ledyard, a young American marine whom the captain judged "an intelligent man."

The Connecticut-born Ledyard would later become one of the great solo adventurers of the eighteenth century, and his extraordinary trip across Unalaska may have inspired his later career. He set off with Aleut guides, unarmed except for bottles of wine and spirits as gifts for the notoriously bibulous Russians. On the first night, the party reached a village where Ledyard slept on fur skins, sharing quarters with several women who "were much more tolerable than I expected," he wrote. "One in particular seemed very busy to please me."

The next day, Ledyard boarded a skin kayak in which the only passenger space was the vessel's enclosed interior, between the two paddlers. After a long, cramped trip, during which he was unable to see out of the stuff-space, Ledyard was hauled from the kayak by two "fair and comely" Russians, the first European strangers he'd seen in two years. They fed Ledyard boiled whale and drank his rum "without any mixture or measure." That night, Ledyard watched as "the Russians assembled the Indians in a very silent manner, and said prayers after the manner of the Greek Church." The next morning, he joined the Russians in a steam bath, and promptly fainted. His hosts restored him with a swig of brandy and a breakfast of whale, walrus, and bear, which "produced a composition of smells very offensive at nine or ten in the morning."

Ledyard returned to the *Resolution* with three of the Russians. Although they lacked a translator, the English and Russians had a fine time comparing charts and astronomical instruments. Cook found the Russians "immoderately fond" of strong liquor, but he relished their company, as did his men, starved as they were for Western contact. "To see people in so strange a part of the World who had other ties than that of common humanity," Lieutenant James King wrote, "was such a novelty, & pleasure, & gave such a turn to our Ideas & feelings as may be very easily imagined."

Cook later entrusted the Russians with a chart he'd made of his northern voyage, during which he'd surveyed some three thousand miles of coastline, much of it never accurately mapped before. He also gave them a letter to the Admiralty, in which Cook wrote that he planned to resume his search for the Northwest Passage the following spring. "But I must confess I have little hopes of succeeding," he wrote, noting several "disappointing" circumstances, including the scarcity of safe harbors and his suspicion that "the Polar part is far from being an open Sea."

Cook's skepticism was well founded. A northwest passage *did* exist, but it wasn't navigable for eighteenth-century ships. Not until 1906 would Roald Amundsen complete a three-year voyage across the top of Canada, via Baffin Bay and the Beaufort Sea. No commercial vessel made it through until 1969. As for the "Polar part" Cook referred to, this route was first navigated in 1958—by a nuclear-powered submarine, traveling beneath the Arctic icecap.

In this sense, Cook's third voyage proved a replay of his second. The Northwest Passage was an ice-bound fantasy, of no commercial use to eighteenth-century Britain, just as the fabled southern continent turned out to be a frigid, uninhabitable wasteland. Cook's principal geographic achievement in the north would once again be negative discovery and the puncturing of myth—an appropriate legacy for so hardheaded a navigator.

THE PRESENT-DAY town of Unalaska, of which Dutch Harbor was an industrial extension, occupied the site of the Russian settlement that John Ledyard had visited by kayak. At first glance, Unalaska didn't look un-Alaskan at all. It was cold, damp, and gray, with the same frontier feel as the villages we'd visited on the ferry. The small downtown resembled the set of a John Wayne Western: wide main street, peeling wooden shop fronts, a few saloons, and unpaved side roads lined with makeshift houses. One incongruous building towered above the rest: an onion-domed Russian Orthodox church. Its graveyard was filled with triple-barred Orthodox crosses that were inscribed with surnames like Tutiakoff and Shishkin. A plaque on the redwood building, part of which dated to 1808, labeled it the oldest Russian-built church still standing in America.

Orthodox monks and priests first arrived at the Aleutian fur-trading camps fifteen years after Cook's visit. In contrast to Christianity's impact on Polynesia, Orthodoxy proved a welcome salve to the oppressed Aleuts. Churchmen condemned the harsh practices of the fur traders, who had, until then, operated under the creed, "God is in his Heaven and the czar is far away." A remarkable reverend, Ioann Veniaminov (later canonized as St. Innocent), created a Cyrillic-style Aleut alphabet, translated the liturgy, and opened a school. Once baptized, Aleuts exchanged native names that translated as "Made the Mammal Bleed" or "Covered with Grass While Sleeping" for Russian ones; the use of Russian names survived, with the Orthodox faith, to the present day.

We arrived at the church just as Saturday vespers was about to begin. The churchwarden, Moses Gordieff, showed us around the interior, which seemed at once ornate and austere: the floors were of plain wood, there were no pews, and the walls glittered with gold-leaf icons. Moses lit brass candelabras and led us to a few icons painted by Aleut artists in the early nineteenth century. In one, of the Apostle Mark, the artist had to imagine a cow, since he'd never seen one. The creature's head looked like a seal's. Another icon, of St. Andrew, substituted bare volcanoes for trees and mountains, making the background true to the stark Aleutian landscape.

Moses was soon joined by an elderly man and three middle-aged women who acted as lay readers; the church's itinerant priest was currently visiting another island. The women hunched over a prayer book while we stood to the side. Moses explained that congregants stood during services—hence the absence of pews—and men and women worshipped separately. The brief service consisted of dirgelike chants and a liturgy that incorporated English, Unangan (the island's Aleut dialect), and Slavonic, or church Russian.

On the ferry, I'd read an account by the nineteenth-century priest Veniaminov, about his years in Unalaska. "Aleuts are not very talkative," he wrote. "They can spend a whole day or days with you without speaking a word." The Aleut character evidently hadn't changed much. After the service, I tried to ask the few congregants about the church and the community. They answered me with polite nods, or a simple yes or no. "Please come again," Moses said, closing up the church. "When the weather is nice like this, we don't get many people. They prefer to be outside."

We stepped back into the cool, misty evening. Roger lit a cigarette. "God can see me in there," he said, "and doesn't like what He sees." Roger nodded suggestively at a tavern across the road. It was Saturday night, prime time at Unalaska's notorious bars. My *Rough Guide* to Alaska reported that the town's premier nightspot, the Elbow Room, had been named the second roughest bar in America, and was famed for "near-constant fights and people left bleeding out in the snow."

We found the Elbow Room, an A-frame antique of purple clapboard, on an unpaved lane by the water. The interior was utterly functional, like almost every other structure we'd seen in the Aleutians: low ceiling, cheap panel walls, dartboard, a few booths, and a dozen bar stools. The one aesthetic touch seemed a joke, given the context: a painting behind the bar of a classical nude, reclining on a day bed and illuminated by a museum-style down light. Just beneath this work stood bottles of every liquor known to mankind.

We perched at the bar beside several brawny men in peaked caps and stained overalls. They were talking about fish. One wore a sweatshirt cut off at the shoulders. Another was a human tattoo. I asked them a few questions about fishing, and offered to buy a round. The men shrugged and ordered refills of Coke.

"I drank so much booze here in the seventies and eighties that I'm still trying to clear out my bloodstream," explained a Caterpillar mechanic named Paul. In those days, Unalaska had been in the throes of a king crab boom, with boats harvesting tons of the pricey crustaceans. Deckhands could earn tens of thousand of dollars in a week, if they were willing to endure a grueling job with the highest death rate of any in America. Boats often iced over and sank; waves swept men overboard; 750-pound crab pots crushed limbs and skulls.

"You had guys coming in here with twenty thousand bucks in their pockets, feeling an inch from God," Paul said, "desperate to see how much of it they could blow on drink, drugs, and cards before going out to risk their lives again." The scarcity of women heightened the tension. Paul told us the standing joke in town: "There's a willing woman behind every tree in Unalaska." Earlier in the day, we'd passed three wind-bent spruces planted by the Russians—trees whose existence here was so remarkable that they'd been designated a national historic landmark. "You'd see knifings, guys shotgunned off bar stools, people stuffed in crab pots as bait," Paul went on. At one time, the Elbow Room's few windows were covered in plastic sheeting rather than glass, to diminish the damage when men flew through them.

Things had calmed down considerably in the past fifteen years. King crab had been so heavily fished that the crab season lasted only a few days now. Most boats fished instead for halibut and a codlike species called pollock: still dangerous work, but nothing like crabbing. Unalaska had also become a factory town, filled with fish-processing workers, most of them Asian and Latino. "They prefer Carl's," Paul said, referring to a pub down the road. "It gets busy there around midnight, then when Carl's closes at three, everyone comes over here. If you want to see some action, that's the time to come."

It was only ten o'clock. We decided to pace ourselves, and took a long, bracing walk through the cool air. At midnight, as we headed for Carl's, Roger looked longingly in the direction of our hotel. "I could be sleeping, which I haven't done in a week, instead of going to talk to another pack of wild men about fish."

"We'll ask them about Cook," I said.

"You'll be met with complete indifference. 'Cook? Did he fish?' "

Carl's was a cavernous joint crowded with men and a handful of women. Almost everyone wore jeans, heavy boots, and caps and jackets bearing the names of fish plants and crane operators. Roger went to order a beer and was instantly corralled by a drunken man who began shouting in his ear. The only word I caught was "halibut."

Leaning against the bar, I chatted with a black man named Luther. He worked the sanitation crew at a cannery, hosing fish guts twelve hours a day, seven days a week, for a $550 paycheck plus room and board at a drafty company bunkhouse. The way Luther described it, the "slime line" at fish plants drew workers from the dire side of the global economy: Vietnamese and Somali refugees, Mexican grape-pickers, busted gamblers, men on the run from the law and their families in the Lower Forty-eight.

Luther's background was different. He'd been born in New York and was six when his father announced that the family was moving to

Alaska. "I asked my mom, 'Are we going to live in an igloo and eat fish?' " He laughed. "I wasn't far off."

Luther had tried fishing, on offshore trawlers that were little more than seaborne sweatshops. "Slave ships, what we call them," he said. The constant, repetitive labor of cutting and gutting fish caused a painful affliction known as "claw." Men's hands cramped so tight they couldn't uncurl them. On his first day out, Luther noticed baseball bats in the bridge and remembered thinking, "That's cool. We'll have a ball game on some island." Then he learned that the bats were for beating ice off the windshield and deck. His first season out, fourteen boats sank, and the seas were so rough that they broke the windows on his boat. A few months before my own visit, a fishing boat left Dutch Harbor and sank with all fifteen hands aboard, the worst single accident on an American fishing vessel in fifty years.

When Luther headed for the bathroom, I freed Roger from a fish filleter at the bar who'd been lecturing him about pollock. As we stepped outside, Roger told me that most of the pollock became surimi, the processed meal used to make fake crab, fishcakes, and fast-food products. He'd also learned that a Samoan drinking at Carl's had recently beaten someone to death with a bar stool. "He was probably sick of hearing about fish," Roger said. "I've never so not enjoyed drinking. This town will get me off the piss, like that Coke-sipping mechanic we met."

It was two A.M. as we trudged through the cold to the Elbow Room. Inside, the atmosphere seemed surprisingly calm—perhaps owing to the presence of two muscular cops who wore body armor and carried Colt revolvers, as well as pepper spray, retractable batons, and enough spare ammunition to kill everyone in Unalaska. We settled at the bar beside a broad-shouldered Aleut with a white brush cut and a windbreaker labeled "Alaska Hydraulics." This turned out to be the Elbow Room's owner, Larry Shaishnikoff.

"Come to see a fight?" he asked, quickly sizing us up. "Not tonight. Not with the law in here."

Larry spoke with the clipped, slightly accented voice of the few other Aleuts we'd met. Sentence fragments slid out his thin mouth as if slipped through a mail slot. This seemed the Aleut way, now as in Cook's day: nothing wasted, not even breath. "We don't get mean fights," he said. "Guys take it outside. They come back in, clean up, start drinking again." Larry didn't mind the bar's notoriety. "Good for business," he said.

Larry had bought the bar for $800 in the 1960s, when crab fishermen began pouring into the town. He'd invested almost nothing in décor. "Seems to work," he said. "No one's here for the scenery." Even if they were, the dim lighting, the cumulus of cigarette smoke, and the damaged condition of most patrons would prevent them from seeing much.

Larry had a second job as a commercial fisherman. His father had been raised paddling skin kayaks and hurling spears at seals. "Dories and guns had changed all that by the time I came along," he said. But Larry still hunted walrus and sea lion, as native Alaskans were entitled to do. Given Cook's problems with "marine beef," I was curious to know how Larry felt about the animals' taste. "Cook was right—it's delicious," he said. "Dark and gamy, with lots of oil and fat."

Larry had been drinking double shots of whiskey for every one of our beers. Then he started buying us whiskeys, too. Things began to blur. I giddily bought a round for the dozen or so people seated at the bar. Then drinkers poured in from Carl's. I weaved to the bathroom and found myself standing at the urinal beside Luther, my companion from earlier in the night. I asked him if he'd ever tasted walrus. "Yeah," he said. "It tastes like Crisco, with mass."

At five A.M. the barmaid rang a bell, signaling last call. "Three for the road," Larry said, lining up shots of Baileys Irish Cream and insisting we join him. After the first shot, he slumped forward, eyes bulging, unable to breathe. Roger hugged him around the chest and slapped his back. Larry revived, and drank another shot. "My wife's dead, I am tired of living," he said. Downing the last shot, he said he'd be going out in two hours for a weeklong fishing trip with his son. "He gets nervous out there," Larry said. "It's best if I'm with him."

The barmaid turned on the lights. They barely penetrated the tobacco fog. We stumbled into the Alaskan dawn, red-eyed and coughing. Roger slumped on the curb. "That was a monster piss-up, a real bender. I'm so rat-assed I'm sober." We fumbled in our pockets and discovered that we'd spent all but a few of the $250 with which we'd begun the night. "If we'd spent that much on drink in Sydney, we'd be in the hospital by now," Roger said, as we staggered in the direction of the hotel.

COOK AND HIS men spent almost a month at Unalaska, repairing and provisioning their ships. With the hard work of probing the Arctic finished for the year, Cook eased up, allowing himself and his men some much needed shore leave. Roaming the hills, Cook catalogued a vast array of berries. "One third of the people by turns had leave to go and pick them," he wrote. Cook hoped that the fruit, coupled with the spruce beer he served his men, would combat "any seeds of the Scurvey." He also permitted the crew to drink with the Russians and trade with natives, whom the captain judged "the most peaceable inoffensive people I ever met with."

In particular, Cook admired the Aleuts' "engenuity" and "perseverance" in adapting to their hostile environment. Over knee-length skin jackets that Cook likened to a "Waggoners frock," the Aleuts wore hooded parkas made of gut, with drawstrings around their necks and wrists. This outfit, and the well-sealed kayaks, kept Aleuts dry during long days at sea, where they proved "very expert at striking fish" from their silent, maneuverable craft. Fishermen also wore visored caps to shield their eyes from rain and glare, and decorated their hats with sea lion whiskers and ivory figurines that were believed to endow hunters with supernatural powers.

Aleut women, Cook wrote, were skilled "Taylors, shoe makers and boat builders," and they wove rye grass baskets of stunning "neatness and perfection." He also took note of the curious way Aleuts warmed themselves with a blubber-oil lamp. "Placing it between their legs and under their garment," he wrote, they "sit over it for a few minutes." Cook was struck as well by the way natives had integrated Western conveniences into their daily routine, including Russian cloth and brass kettles.

But he also sensed that Russian influence wasn't altogether benign. Many young Aleut males had been "taken, perhaps purchased, from their Parents," and raised by the Russians. Aleuts also lacked defensive weapons—evidence, Cook suspected, of "the great subjection the Natives are under." He'd guessed correctly; Russians had disarmed the

Aleuts to guard against revolt. "They do not seem to be long lived," Cook added of the natives. He saw "very few" that he judged above fifty years old. This was probably because old people were particularly vulnerable to Western disease and other depredations arising from Russian contact.

Cook made note of another imported blight: Aleuts' insatiable hunger for tobacco. Russians meted out nicotine in quantities just large enough to keep natives addicted. "There are few if any that do not both smoke and chew Tobacco," Cook wrote of Aleuts, "a luxury that bids fair to keep them always poor." The sex-starved English also exploited this addiction. Charles Clerke put it plainly: "The compliment usually paid for a beauty's favours was a hand of Tobacco: for one of inferior Charms, a few leaves of this valuable Weed."

On Cook's first voyage, it was Joseph Banks who had provided a running commentary on native women. On the third voyage, this role was filled by David Samwell, a young Welsh poet and surgeon's mate who seems to have spent most of the journey admiring "fair Damsels" and "nymphs," and calculating how to bed them. He described one such encounter in Unalaska in vivid and rather disturbing detail. Led by an Aleut guide, he and four other crewmen hiked to a settlement beside a "deep Bay" near the English camp. At first, Samwell saw no signs of habitation, except for fish hanging out to dry, which "makes [the village] appear at a distance like a Glovers' Yard." On closer approach, he saw semi-subterranean shelters, covered in sod, with "a hole in the top of them, which we descended down a Ladder."

The interior of this longhouse stank of fish, Samwell wrote. Also, "a large Bowl of stale Urine" sat near the center. The inhabitants were filthy and louse-ridden. None of this deterred the single-minded Samwell, or his companions. "Having been used to many strange Scenes since we left England, we spent no time in staring about us with vacant astonishment," Samwell wrote, "but immediately made love to the handsomest woman in Company, who in order to make us welcome refused us no Favour she could grant tho' her Husband or Father stood by."

Samwell doesn't shed any further light on this "in Company" congress, which sounds to modern ears like a gang rape. But he later observed that Aleut women permitted the English "taking them promiscuously according to our fancies," so long as "We had but a leaf of Tobacco." On the Alaskan mainland, natives had a tradition of welcoming travelers with the offer of their women; it is possible that Aleuts hewed to the same custom. More likely, given their subjugation by the Russians, Aleuts reckoned it was prudent to grant Europeans whatever they requested. "We pigged very lovingly together," Samwell wrote of a later such foray, "the Husband lying close to his Wife & her Paramour & excercising such patience as would have done Honour to a City Husband while we engrafted Antlers on his Head."

Both Samwell and Cook noted that the Russians disapproved of the English behavior. They "seemed to lament our depravity in having Connection with those who they said were 'neet Christiane,' that is not Christians," Samwell wrote. He appended a dirty joke. "This Circumstance may restrain these godly People from meddling with any other Fur in these regions than that of the Sea Beaver." Russian abstinence, however, wasn't absolute. Before long, Samwell observed that many sailors had succumbed to "that fatal Distemper," presumably introduced by the fur traders.

In a rare digression from sex, Samwell also made passing mention that one of the *Discovery*'s anchors had been damaged. Cook put his armorers to work forging the iron into small tools to trade on the ships' return to the tropics, where Cook planned to wait out the winter. In particular, Polynesians valued iron adzes modeled on their own, called *to'i;* for these, they would trade many hogs. "Nothing," Samwell fatefully observed, "went so well as these Tois."

ON THE AFTERNOON following our all-night drinking bout, I left Roger asleep, slugged down a quart of coffee, and attempted a restorative walk through the wind-blown rain. I made it one block before seeking refuge inside a building marked "Museum of the Aleutians." This proved a sobering stop. The small, excellent museum traced Aleut culture from its beginnings in a migration from Siberia some ten thousand years ago, to its near extinction in the past two and a half centuries. Studying the exhibits, I was struck, like Cook, by the stunning "engenuity" and "perseverance" of the Aleuts in surviving one of the harshest environments on earth. Lacking trees, metal, and land animals apart from small hares and fox, Aleuts exploited every available resource to its ultimate extent. A single sea lion, for instance, yielded food, blubber oil, bone tools, fishhooks (from the teeth), and fish lines (from the sinews); the flippers became boot soles, and the intestines and esophageal membrane were woven into waterproof parkas or used to make skylights for subterranean houses. Even the troughs of urine in Aleut homes, which had so disgusted Samwell, served a purpose: softening animal skins and making dyes.

Yet Aleuts, who had endured for millennia in these harsh surroundings, barely survived one generation of Western contact. The Russian fur traders who arrived in the last half of the eighteenth century numbered only a few hundred. Yet during that time, the Aleut population of about fifteen thousand fell by more than 90 percent. Russians killed roughly five thousand Aleuts outright. They also dispersed the population, carrying off young males to hunt furs in the uninhabited Pribilof Islands, or as far south as Russian trading posts in California. Epidemics and famine took an even greater toll, caused in part by Russian hunting of sea lions. Food had always been scarce in the Aleutians, particularly in late winter as stores ran out: the native word for "March" translated as "When They Gnaw Straps."

The Aleutian Islands became American territory following William Seward's famous purchase of Alaska in 1867, and for seventy-five years the remote Aleuts survived in a state of benign neglect. Then came World War II, when the Japanese bombed Dutch Harbor and seized several islands farther out along the Aleutian chain, the first occupation of American soil by a foreign army since the War of 1812. The inhabitants of the occupied islands were taken to camps in Japan, where only twenty-five survived. The United States evacuated the rest of the Aleuts, ostensibly for their own protection, interning them at wretched camps in southeastern Alaska, where many of them also died. Because of wartime censorship, the Aleuts' plight remained unknown to the American public. Not until 1988 did the U.S. government formally apologize to the Aleuts and pay compensation of $12,000 to each of the camps' few hundred survivors.

I found the museum's director, Rick Knecht, in a back office, studying drawings of Steller's sea cow, an extinct species named for a naturalist who had traveled with Vitus Bering. Rick, a veteran archaeologist, looked as though he'd just come in from the field—or, rather, the tundra. He wore a lumberjack shirt, fleece vest, heavy boots, and tan pants made of double-layered canvas. Deep-set gray eyes and a bushy, graying beard lent his handsome face a biblical cast, appropriate to his period of study. Rick had recently excavated a site dating back nine thousand years, believed to be the oldest coastal settlement in America, predating even the civilizations of the Tigris and Euphrates.

Given this, I doubted he'd have much time for Cook, who had visited only a nanosecond ago in archaeological terms. But as Rick took a phone call, I noticed a sketch by one of Cook's artists hanging behind his desk, as well as a Union Jack set against a white field—a royal ensign of the sort Cook displayed on his ships. Volumes on Cook's voyages filled his bookshelf. When I asked Rick about this, he seemed a bit embarrassed.

"Cook's just a personal interest," he said, "something I do for fun." He pointed at a pile of research papers he'd published, with titles such as "Trace Metals in Ancient Hair from the Karluk Archaeological Site." Rick smiled. "Cook's about seven thousand years outside my principal area of expertise."

"So why are you interested in him?"

Rick glanced out his window at fog and rain and distant, snow-capped peaks. "This place is pretty extreme," he said, with considerable understatement. The previous winter, 189 inches of snow had fallen on Dutch Harbor. For much of the year, the sky was dark for all but a few hours, and the weather was too cold and windy for people to step outside. "By the end of winter," he quipped, "you pass people on the street with half-moon dents on their foreheads from leaning on shotgun barrels." Yet Rick, a Michigan native who had excavated his way ever farther from civilization during several decades as an archaeologist, felt most at home poking around the globe's fringes. He wondered sometimes whether Cook was the same.

"Cook keeps seeing the edge and can't resist leaping off it. Neither can I." He laughed. "So we end up in godforsaken places like this. Leaper colonies."

He shuffled papers and resumed his curatorial mien. "Of course,

Cook's voyages are also an invaluable resource," he said, leading me to the museum's latest acquisition: a sketch by the *Resolution*'s artist, John Webber, titled "Woman of Oonalashka." The drawing showed a pretty, round-faced young woman with cheek tattoos, a dangling nose ring, and a Mona Lisa smile. For Rick, the sketch offered a trove of detail about traditional clothing, hairstyle, and native adornment, including the bone labrets that Aleuts wore. (A labret is an ornament worn in a slit between the lower lip and the chin.) Webber's portraits of Aleuts offered the only visual evidence of what islanders looked like at the time of Western contact.

Webber had also drawn the subterranean settlement where David Samwell enjoyed the "favours" of an Aleut woman. Rick had used these sketches, and Cook's charts, to locate the remains of the village, as well as the nearby inlet, now known as English Bay, where the crewmen had set up camp during their stay on the island. The sites lay at the unoccupied eastern edge of Unalaska, reachable only by a strenuous day's hike, or by a long boat ride through the Bering Sea. "Some day I'd like to do a proper archaeological survey," Rick said. "It'd be cool to find a button with an anchor on it and be able to say, 'Cook was right here. He walked on this ground.' "

We talked about Cook for a while longer, and by the time we'd finished, Rick was on the phone, lining up a fishing boat to take us to English Bay later in the week.

BACK AT THE hotel, I prodded Roger awake. "Found a Cookaholic," I said triumphantly.

"You woke me up to tell me *that*? Town's full of pisspots, not counting me."

"*Cook*-aholic," I repeated. "An archaeologist. He's taking us on a boat to see where Cook landed."

"Did he talk about halibut?"

"Not a word."

"Pollock?"

"No. Just Steller's sea cows."

"Do we have to eat one?"

"They're extinct."

"Thank God for that." Roger sat up, holding his head. "A boat ride would be nice. Fresh air, howling wind, mountainous seas. It'll clean me right out."

We spent the two days before our trip exploring the environs of the town. Unalaska had only thirty-eight miles of road, much of it unpaved and bordered by the fantastic detritus of the fishing industry: sprawling salvage yards, five-story-high piles of crab pots, mountains of cable, nets, hawsers, floats. The landscape also bore scars from the Second World War: ruined bunkers, zigzag trench lines, rotted wooden barracks. At a school playground, children frolicked in a concrete pillbox. Cabanas and Quonset huts thrown up during the war had become permanent dwellings; even an old latrine block had been renovated and occupied. In the midst of this jerry-built, war-warped landscape rose brilliant public edifices, including a new school, gym, library, and city hall. Halibut and pollock might make for boring bar talk, but the tax that Unalaska levied on fishing boats had brought tens of millions of dollars pouring into local coffers.

We wandered down to the waterfront, a thin strand of dirty sand with a sweeping view of the majestic, and still unspoiled, mountains surrounding the harbor. Salmon jumped from the water and bald eagles swooped all around us. The birds' heavily feathered legs made them appear trousered, their sharp beaks and eyes as proud and piercing as those pictured on the dollar bill. For one of the few moments since our arrival in the Aleutians, I felt the wild, whalish grandeur that loomed just beyond every speck of humanity.

Feeling as expansive as the landscape, I went over to chat with an old Aleut fisherman who stood by the water's edge. I smiled and asked, "What are you casting for?"

"Fish."

"How do you cook it?"

"Don't. I dry it."

"How long for?"

"Till it's dry."

He reeled in a pink salmon, filleted it on the beach, and tossed the refuse toward the eagles, which swooped and caught the guts midair. "Salmon run from now to September," the man said, casting again. He tapped his chest, and said he'd recently had triple bypass surgery. "I got a lot of goddamn problems." His wife had died not long ago after drinking 190-proof alcohol. Three of his children had also perished. "Booze got one of them, too." Another had frozen to death; the third died young of diabetes. "But I'm still here," the man said, reeling in another fish. "Just hope I live till the salmon season's over."

We left him casting and wandered down the beach to a graveyard and a small park filled with memorials: to fishermen lost at sea, to drowned Coast Guard patrols, to wartime casualties. "This tree grows in memory of WWII servicemen and women who planted trees," one plaque said. Beside it stood a shrub, stunted and brown, about ten inches high.

At the museum, I'd learned that the Aleutian campaign was not only a tragedy for natives but also a military bloodbath. The 2,370 Japanese on the island of Attu fought almost to the last man; only eighteen surrendered. American troops fighting on Attu, many of them equipped with clothing intended for desert warfare, suffered a casualty rate second only to that on Iwo Jima in the Pacific theater. Fog, cold, and friendly fire killed and injured as many men as the Japanese did.

"This whole part of the world is one big cemetery," Roger said, studying crosses commemorating foreign seamen who drowned while passing through nearby waters. He spotted a fresh-dug grave that still lay empty. "Ready-made for me," Roger said, "after our next visit to the Elbow Room."

This reminded me of one other stop I wanted to make. Rick Knecht had recommended that I talk to an elderly Aleut named Ben Golodoff who lived two doors down from the Elbow Room. Rick said that Ben knew more than anyone in town about the old days in Unalaska. Roger chose not to go. "I've had enough sadness for one day," he said, heading off to chat with a solitary yachtie he'd spotted in the harbor.

I FOUND BEN Golodoff and his wife, Suzi, finishing a dinner of salmon pie, the same dish an Aleut had presented to Cook on his arrival at Unalaska. Suzi called the dish by its Russian name, *pirogi*, and gave me a slice of the doughy, onion-flavored pie, with pickles on the side. She said other Aleut dishes included *galupsy*, or stuffed cabbage leaves, and a jellied meat or fish called *studen*. Ben poured me a cup of black tea, or *chai,* as he called it. "In the old days we'd have used a samovar," he said.

Ben was a trim man of sixty-eight, with bushy white sideburns and small black eyes. He settled on a couch covered in seal furs, beneath an icon of the Virgin Mary. Like other Aleuts I'd met, he seemed reticent and watchful. Suzi, an émigrée from Washington State, gradually prompted her husband into answering my questions about his childhood in Unalaska.

"We were more Russian than American," he said. His parents spoke Russian and Unangan as their first languages. Ben went with his father to steam houses where the men beat each other with grass. Aleuts were also keen chess players. Ben said old people had told him that Aleuts cried back in 1867, when the Russian flag came down and the Stars and Stripes went up.

"The Russians were murderers in the early days," he said, "but Orthodoxy changed that, and the black robes still ruled town when I was a boy." Unlike the Protestant missionaries in Polynesia, Orthodox churchmen hadn't tried to stamp out all vestiges of native belief. Shamans still practiced in Ben's childhood, using medicinal plants. Aleuts also believed in folk creatures known as outside men: banished souls who roamed the fringes of villages and haunted the inhabitants. "If your mother wanted you to come in from playing," Ben recalled, "she'd say, 'The outside men will get you!'"

World War II changed everything. Ben was eight when he and other Aleuts were evacuated to an abandoned fish cannery in southeastern Alaska. It was there that he climbed his first tree, discovered apples and oranges, and listened at night to the howling of wolves in the deep woods. "I was a boy, it was a big adventure," he said, "but the old folks had a very hard time." Many elders died from diseases that ran through the unsanitary camps, and with them went much of the old culture. Ben's mother died at the end of the war; others remained in hospitals or sanatoriums, never to return home.

Ben and his father came back to Unalaska to find their house ransacked. Aleut fishing boats had also vanished. GIs had used the town's Orthodox church as a dance hall. Four of the island's eight villages had to be abandoned; the refugees moved to Unalaska or in search of wage labor to towns outside the Aleutians. There were so few natives left that they lost the tribal status they'd had before the war.

"People tried to resume the old ways," Ben said, "but they'd lost most of the skills and tools." The war also brought roads, electricity, and other amenities to what had been a traditional fishing village. "We became used to certain things, and dependent on cash to get them," Ben said. It was, in some respects, a twentieth-century replay of the transformation that occurred when Europeans first arrived with tobacco and other goods.

Ben and other Aleut children entered new government schools, where they were punished if they spoke Russian or Unangan. Aleut parents also urged their children to embrace American ways. Having been interned during the war because of their race, they saw assimilation as a form of protection. In the 1950s, at the height of the Cold War, Ben joined the Army and listed his religion as Russian Orthodox. A military recruiter told him, "You can't be that—you're not a Commie, are you?" So Ben put down "Catholic" instead. He "went south," to the Lower Forty-eight, and gradually, without really realizing it, became Americanized.

Ben later returned to Unalaska and went to work on a salmon boat, where he met Suzi. They'd made a good life for themselves and built a new house on the site of Ben's childhood home. But Ben sometimes wondered if more had been lost than gained. "I like to pick up the phone and turn up a thermostat as much as anyone," he said. "But we've lost our identity, our self-respect."

Ben saw evidence of this in the ills afflicting many of his Aleut neighbors: alcoholism, domestic violence, suicide, welfare dependency. It was the same set of pathologies I'd encountered in other indigenous communities. When I mentioned this to Ben, he sat silently for a few moments.

"I've never met an Aborigine or Maori, but I think I can see the connection," he said. "We're outside men, aren't we? Left out. Haunting the edges." He paused. "Here, we had the Russians, then the Americans, then the war. All that change, there's a sense of defeat, a guilty conscience. You can't help wondering, 'Why did we lose it all?' A lot of people just give up, they turn to booze or kill themselves or do nothing."

Things were slowly changing for the better, thanks to several factors: the government apology and reparations for wartime suffering, the restoration of islanders' tribal status, and the influx of fishing dollars. All this had helped Aleuts rebuild their lives and restore a sense of dignity. "We're starting to realize it wasn't our fault," Ben said. Like other indigenous peoples, Aleuts were also reclaiming their traditional ways. Local schools now taught native dance, language, and crafts, and young people attended a summer "culture camp" at which Ben and other elders taught. Aleut adornments, even the labret, were being revived—in part because body piercing and tattooing had become fashionable among young people across America.

One model for this revival of Aleut style was the 1778 Webber drawing I'd seen at the museum: the woman of Unalaska. Ben and Suzi had a print of it on their mantel, across from the Virgin Mary. An icon of a lost world. Ben studied the woman's face. "She looks happy, doesn't she?" he said.

ON THE DAY of our boat trip to English Bay, we found Rick Knecht at his museum office, pulling on knee-high rubber boots, triple-ply Gore-Tex pants, and a waterproof jacket. "It's wet and wild today," he said. "We could get clobbered out there." Then he gulped down what he called "the Coast Guard cocktail": high-octane Dramamine, mixed with uppers to counteract the drowsiness caused by seasickness pills. Luckily, I had some leftover pills from the ferry ride, and Rick offered us spare wet gear. "I feel like a human condom," Roger said, as we clumped to the dock in our foul-weather duds.

Rick's wife, Melia, stood waiting on the pier. A compact, athletic-looking beauty with short blond hair, Melia supervised longshoremen at a nearby dock. There were two other passengers: Mona and Richard, Arizonans who introduced themselves as "installation artists." They were completing a project about the wartime evacuation of Aleuts, and wanted to visit an abandoned village near English Bay. "Installation art is an environment you create," Mona explained. "We won't tell a literal or narrative story about the evacuation; it'll be more metaphorical."

"I'll record some sound, pick up the vibrations of the grass,"

Richard added. "Everything has its own pitch." He'd already recorded celery grass growing at another site. "The idea is to pick up whatever echo you can of the past." Listening to Mona and Richard, it was hard to keep a straight face—particularly with Roger silently mouthing "wankers"—until I realized we were seeking much the same thing.

The skipper, John Lucking, interrupted us to give a quick safety briefing about his fishing boat, *Hot Pursuit*. As we motored out of the harbor, he switched on a radio to catch the marine forecast: "Small craft advisory with periods of heavy rain, areas of fog, temperatures in the upper forties, winds fifteen to thirty miles per hour with occasional higher gusts."

John chuckled. " 'Winds fifteen to thirty with higher gusts'—that's a big window. They leave it wide open to interpretation." He said the weather changed so quickly in the Bering Sea that forecasts were always this broad, rather like astrological readings. "When passengers ask me how the weather will be, I always tell them 'bad.' By the end of the day, I'm sure to be right."

As the boat hit choppy swell outside the harbor, I fled the claustrophobic wheelhouse and joined Rick on the windy back deck. Distraction, I'd learned, was the best defense against seasickness. So I drilled Rick with questions about his journey to "the edge," as he'd put it when we'd spoken earlier.

"The story of my weirdo life?" He laughed. Rick said he'd become interested in archaeology while accompanying his father, a physician, on his rounds among Native American communities in northern Michigan. By the age of ten, Rick had filled the family basement with arrowheads, fossils, and other curiosities. His father was also a keen hunter and fisherman, and he took Rick on wilderness trips. "He always said that he spent his workday saving lives, so he wanted to spend his free time killing things."

Rick didn't share this bloodlust, but the wilderness skills he'd learned as a child had proved invaluable during his years as a "shovel bum" in Alaska. Among other misadventures, Rick had once been stranded when a bush pilot took off without him; he'd been shot at by a drunk loner in an isolated cabin; and he'd survived several near drownings in boats swamped by huge, frigid waves. "Nothing really *that* scary," Rick said. He paused, then added, "Well, there was one helicopter ride."

Seven years ago, Rick had flown with two women colleagues to survey a remote archaeological site. As they swooped low over the island, the helicopter's rotor slowed and then snapped. The women began hugging and praying as the pilot prepared to crash-land. "I wasn't that worried," Rick said. "I'd bounced off runways in bush planes and figured it would be like that."

Instead the helicopter hit hard and "pitch-poled," catapulting end over end. When Rick came to, he felt spray on his face: blood spurting from an artery in the pilot's gashed head. The two women seemed to have been crushed by the wreckage. Rick had a bone sticking out of his finger, a broken foot, cracked vertebrae, and ruptured intestines. The pilot somehow staunched his own wound and put out a fire before the fuel tank exploded. He and Rick extracted one of the women and the three lay on the ground, shocked and bleeding.

"That's when the grizzly burst out of the woods," Rick said. "It was spring, he was hungry, and we were covered in blood—his favorite sauce."

The pilot chased the bear off by firing a flare. Eventually, the helicopter's emergency beacon drew rescue helicopters. Miraculously, all four passengers survived. "It may sound twisted, but I wouldn't trade that crash for anything," Rick said. "It's great to be at the edge and make it back alive."

Melia joined us on the back deck. I asked her how she'd ended up with this lunatic for a husband. Melia laughed. Men outnumbered women in Unalaska by three to one, so finding a date wasn't a problem. "The odds are good," she said, "but the goods are odd."

So was her wedding to Rick. They'd married atop the wheelhouse of a fishing boat in a remote island cove. A geologist friend officiated (in Alaska, anyone can legally preside over a wedding), the skipper served as best man, and a male deckhand acted as maid of honor.

"Sounds romantic," I said.

"It was, in a way," Rick said, "except that we had to spend our wedding night in the cabin of this tiny boat with three other guys listening in."

Melia shrugged. "That wasn't the worst part," she said. "The boat ride to get there was really rough. We projectile-vomited the whole way."

As she spoke, our boat lurched and icy water washed over the deck. We'd entered Unalga Pass, between the Pacific Ocean and the Bering Sea, a strait known for its fierce current. I was just starting to feel queasy when we rounded a point and motored into a sheltered inlet. The hills surrounding it were so green that the color looked enhanced, as if in an animated film. Rick brought out copies of sketches by Cook's artists, sealed in plastic sheeting, and held one up against the landscape. "Look at the boulders, the waterfall, the shape of the hills," he said. "It's hardly changed at all since Cook was right here."

We anchored in seven fathoms of water, just as the English had, and rowed ashore—in a rubber dinghy rather than a wooden pinnace. While the other passengers poked around the rocky beach, I followed Rick through a field of purple lupins and tall rye grass. "This is it," he said, reaching a spongy plateau. Invisible to me at first, but obvious to the archaeologist, was a slight, perfectly square elevation, about twenty feet across. "That's not native," he said. "It's an obsessive, Western thing to put down a perfect square of sod, with neat, ninety-degree corners."

Consulting English charts and journals, he'd determined that the plateau corresponded to the site of an observatory Cook had erected. The sod was laid to create a perfectly level platform for surveying and astronomical instruments, and to protect the gear from the wet ground. Last time Rick visited here, he'd brought a handheld global positioning system. With a touch of a button he'd read off the exact longitude and latitude of this site. The English had struggled to do the same with clocks, telescopes, and a trough of mercury, called an artificial horizon, in which their observations were reflected. They'd calculated their position with remarkable accuracy. "Still, I wonder what Cook would have paid for a GPS," Rick said.

This time, Rick had brought a metal detector. "The odds aren't good that we'll find anything," he said, "but the goods would be fantastic." As he surveyed the sod, Rick's face lit up with the puckish zest of a boy digging for Ottawa arrowheads in northern Michigan. He swept the ground with the metal detector's bagel-like ring. At several points it beeped, shrill and insistent. Rick began working the fine dirt with his fingers.

"In subarctic tundra, stuff sinks about an inch a century," he said, "so if there's anything here it won't be very deep." I joined in, thrusting my fingers into the soil and uncovering a dark, nail-shaped scrap. "Sorry," Rick said, studying my find. "It's just fern root." We tried a half-dozen other spots: more beeps, more fern root.

Rick said false readings were common in Aleutian soil, which contained a lot of "bog iron." Even so, I felt possessed by the thrill of prospecting for Cook treasure and could have kept going for hours. "It's addictive, eh?" Rick said, tugging me back to the beach. He told me about a few finds he'd made at other coastal sites: silver pieces of eight, wooden masks, messages in bottles. "It can be eerie, like someone talking to you from the past."

This put him in mind of Cook again, and as we waited for the dinghy to collect us, Rick told me more about why the captain spoke to him. "I'm forty-seven, the same age as Cook when he set off on the third voyage," he said. "You have to wonder why he did it." Rick paused. "There's been some recent discussion in academic journals about a gene for a 'novelty-seeking personality.' Apparently, it has adaptive value. Prehistoric people who trekked out of Africa may have relied on intrepid, nervy individuals to lead the journey. I reckon Cook had that gene." Rick smiled. "Today, a guy like him would probably be diagnosed as having attention-deficit disorder and dosed with Ritalin."

Returning to the boat, we motored out of the cove and around a point to the sheltered inlet Samwell had called "deep Bay." Rick took out another of Webber's sketches, which showed the mounds of semi-subterranean homes, with ladders and Aleuts poking out the top. As at English Bay, the contour of the background exactly matched the shore we now gazed at. Then we landed and walked into the drawing, to the site of the dwellings. Nothing remained except shallow depressions overgrown with chest-high grass.

"They were like bunkers," Rick said. "The whole adaption was to the wind." He cleared away the grass and dug down a few inches to expose the hard-packed floor of one house. We also found scraps that Rick identified as charcoal, the edge of a stone tool, a small piece of whalebone, and the remains of a driftwood rafter. We scanned with the metal detector, but the chances of finding anything here were even more remote than at English Bay. Samwell and his companions had stayed only a few hours; at best, they might have left a nail or some other small item as recompense for sex. "Given what happened here," Rick said, "we'd probably have better luck finding a DNA sample in the soil."

With sunset approaching, we motored on to the site of Biorka, a village abandoned after World War II. All that remained were a few collapsed roofs. While the installation artists positioned microphones by the beach grass and driftwood, Rick pointed to a nearby island, where Russians had slaughtered Aleuts in reprisal for an attack on fur traders. Rick had surveyed the site and found dozens of skeletons, including one with a Russian knife still embedded in its rear.

"All these ghost villages make you feel sometimes like you're part of a toxic culture," Rick said. This was an uneasy sentiment I'd often shared while following Cook's travels and surveying the damage done in the captain's wake. When I said so to Rick, he added: "A lot of people want to blame Cook and others like him, because they were the first to get in and start nibbling. The sad truth is that we're the real locusts. Some of the worst destruction is taking place right now, by us, even though we know the consequences."

Aleuts had lived and fished in settlements like Deep Bay for thousands of years. Now, except for a few depressions in the earth, invisible to the untrained eye, nothing remained. Americans from the Lower Forty-eight had occupied Unalaska in large numbers for only the past sixty years. Yet the mark we'd already left on the landscape—gouged hills, pillboxes, rusted cars, rotting crab pots, oil-polluted soil—would probably linger for a millennium.

It was also very recent contact that had done the most damage to the abundant marine life that sustained the thrifty Aleuts for centuries. As we turned back to Dutch Harbor, a few otters frolicked in our wake, poking their whiskered noses just above the water. We also caught glimpses of porpoises and harbor seals, and passed a sea lion "haul-out," where a dozen of the blubbery giants sprawled like misshapen tires on the beach.

"Twenty years ago, you would have seen four times that number,"

Rick said. No one was sure what had caused this precipitous decline, but sea lions became caught in fishing nets and other debris, and competed for the same bottom fish that boats hauled out by the ton. With their numbers down by 80 percent since 1970, the sea lion had recently been put on the endangered species list. Several types of otter, seal, and whale had narrowly avoided extinction.

"The whole history of Western contact in Alaska is extractive," Rick said. First fur, then whales, then gold, then oil, and now mining of the sea for crab, halibut, and pollock. Once the water was fished out, there wouldn't be much left, except ice. "And global warming's taking care of that," Rick said. The polar icecap was retreating so rapidly that scientists predicted the Northwest Passage would soon be navigable for much of the summer.

This brought us around to Cook again, and to another of Rick's notions about the captain's character. Rick had read that accountants, and others whose work demanded extreme precision and control, often came from chaotic or troubled backgrounds, such as a home with an alcoholic parent. He imagined that Cook's boyhood might have led him along the same path. "Here's this child prodigy—almost a Mozart or a chess master—growing up in a crowded hovel filled with animals and death and maybe lots of drinking. He's got little in common with his peers. Math becomes his refuge."

Cook runs away to sea and turns his math skills to surveying and navigation. "Making charts, studying stars, plotting voyages—it's a way to control his environment," Rick hypothesized. This monomania proved both a strength and a weakness. It accounted for Cook's factual exactness and objectivity. But it also contributed to his impatience and periodic tantrums. "He's like Mr. Spock in *Star Trek*," Rick said. "He can't stand it when others are being imprecise or illogical." As a commander, accustomed to total control, he also resented any challenge to his authority. Hence the face-off with his crew over walrus in the Arctic, and other incidents that seemed to unhinge him.

Rick's theory was intriguing, if not wholly convincing. Cook clearly had an exceptional flair for mathematics, and he often behaved in ways that today would earn him the label "control freak." If Rick was right in imagining that Cook came from a troubled family, this might also explain his seeming lack of sentiment about the world he'd left behind. But while the captain may have been a loner, he obviously possessed a human touch; without it, he never could have bent both sailors and islanders to his will. He also took risks: calculated risks, but very dangerous ones nonetheless. In mathematical terms, the man was much bigger than the sum of his parts.

I shared this with Rick as we motored into Dutch Harbor at midnight. He smiled and said, "That's what's fun about Cook. You can read almost anything into him you want. It's like predicting the weather here. Take your pick—sun, rain, wind, storms—and some part of it is sure to fit."

AS OUR DEPARTURE from Unalaska approached, I realized that flying out of the Aleutians was as wretched as ferrying into them. The tiny, mountain-enclosed airport had one of the shortest runways in America, only 3,900 feet long. Departing planes carried half the normal payload and positioned passengers toward the back, so aircraft could make a rapid ascent and swerve to avoid slamming into the volcano near the end of the runway. The wreckage of a DC-3 that hadn't made it remained distressingly visible on the mountain's face.

The airport also lacked radar guidance. Fog, storms, and high winds were so frequent that roughly a third of scheduled flights were canceled due to weather: reputedly the highest rate at any airport in the world. Since Unalaskans relied on the daily flights to and from Anchorage for their mail, newspapers, and periodic escape, they made a sport of watching the sky and guessing whether "Alaskaflot" would risk landing. According to the local rule of thumb, if fog reached as low as a World War II bunker that stood midway down a mountain behind the airport, no plane would land. The bunker had remained shrouded for almost the entirety of our week's stay, and conditions didn't look much better on the day of our scheduled departure.

"Have a good trip, guys," said a woman at the drive-through espresso shack that we visited each morning. "And if you don't, I'll see you tomorrow."

Roger groaned. "It's like Devil's Island here. You never get off this place." We drove on to the airport. A sign near the entrance said: "Caution: Road Crosses Runway." We joined other passengers gazing into the fog for evidence of incoming aircraft. Rain sheeted onto the tarmac. "At least there's not much wind today," I said to the man standing next to us.

"Actually, that's a problem," he replied. "If there's no wind, the plane can't get enough lift to clear the mountains." The man worked as the city's engineer and evidently knew what he was talking about. I asked him about the DC-3 pancaked against the volcano, and another plane that had recently burned after its engines sucked up slush during takeoff. "They were both pilot error," he said, as though this would be somehow reassuring.

Half an hour after the plane's scheduled arrival, we heard a rumble overhead. Seconds later, a small jet materialized out of the fog and bounced down the runway. The other passengers applauded and headed for the gate. Roger popped a Valium. Rick Knecht had told us that takeoffs were often so hair-raising that even local fishermen, who braved death every day in the Bering Sea, became weeping wrecks. Rick referred to these flights as "pukers and screamers."

Roger gazed at the still, dismal sky. "Look, even that crow can't get any lift," he said, pointing. "I can't see the volcano, but I bet it's got my name scrawled across it." On board the plane, he gazed out the window at a slate-colored wash of rain and fog. The plane roared down the runway and jumped like a jackrabbit, wings barely off the tarmac before the jet banked sharply right, bumping along a carpet of cloud. After a few horrible minutes, the plane reached smooth subarctic air and rode it all the way to Anchorage.

I opened Cook's journal and read about his own departure from Unalaska on October 26, 1778, one day shy of his fiftieth birthday. "We put to sea," he calmly wrote, barely bothering to mention the rain, hail, and snow, which pelted his ships so ferociously that part of the rigging gave way, killing a seaman and injuring several others. "My intention," the captain added, was to proceed to the tropics "and spend a few of the Winter Months." Then he would return to the Arctic to continue searching for a northwest passage.

A week before, Cook had also completed his report to the Admiralty, which he hoped the Russians would deliver. Despite the captain's doubts about finding a passage to the Atlantic, he pledged every effort toward "the improvement of Geography and Navigation," and signed himself, "Your most obedient humble servant." The letter, dated October 20, 1778, made its way by Russian ship from Unalaska to Kamchatka, and by dogsled and horse-drawn sleigh across the steppes to the British mission in St. Petersburg, finally reaching London on March 6, 1780, more than a year after Cook's death. It was the last dispatch the captain's superiors would ever receive from his hand.

Chapter 13

HAWAII:
The Last Island

Chiefs are sharks that walk on the land.

—HAWAIIAN PROVERB

Ten months before leaving Unalaska, on his way north from Polynesia to America, Cook had stumbled on an island cluster unknown to the West. Sprinkled across the watery vastness of the central Pacific, thousands of miles from America or Asia, the isles lay farther from continental land than any archipelago on earth.

Cook and his men had just sailed six weeks and more than 2,700 miles from Bora-Bora without seeing a soul. Yet the islanders who came out in canoes to greet the English, Cook wrote, were "of the same Nation as the people of Otaheite and the other islands we had lately visited." His lieutenant, James King, thought the men in the canoes—tawny-skinned, tattooed, and muscular—most closely resembled Maori, who dwelled five thousand miles to the south.

Cook consulted his charts and calculated that he had now met islanders of similar ethnicity and language sprinkled across a third of the earth's latitude and longitude. "How shall we account for this Nation spreading it self so far over this Vast Ocean?" he wrote.

Historians and anthropologists are still trying to answer Cook's question. Most scholars believe that voyagers in sailing canoes set off from Tahiti between A.D. 100 and A.D. 300, navigating by the stars to what are now the Hawaiian Islands. A millennium or so later, more migrants arrived from the islands of Raiatea and Bora-Bora. Although Spanish ships passed near Hawaii in the sixteenth century, the islanders had remained sealed off from the outside world for centuries, and had never encountered Europeans until Cook and his men arrived one January day in 1778.

"I never saw Indians so much astonished at the entering [of] a ship before," Cook wrote, "their eyes were continually flying from object to object." Offered beads, the natives asked if they were edible. The Hawaiians also marveled at china cups, which seemed to them a wondrous form of wood. In exchange for a single sixpenny nail, they gave the English several pigs. But it was the vessel's commander that awed islanders most of all.

"The very instant I leaped ashore, they all fell flat on their faces, and remained in that humble posture till I made signs to them to rise," Cook wrote. As he walked inland, "attended by a tolerable train," a guide "proclaimed" his approach, causing natives to prostrate themselves until Cook passed. "In all their conduct, islanders seemed to regard us as superior beings," Lieutenant James King wrote; their regard for Cook, he added, "seemd to approach to Adoration."

The English spent only three days ashore, but they filled their journals with superlatives equal to any they'd composed about Tahiti. Island flowers "sent forth the most fragrant smell I had any where met with," Cook wrote. He judged island sweet potatoes the largest he'd ever seen, taro root "the best I ever tasted," and native canoes "shaped and fited with more judgement than any I had before seen." Best of all were the islanders themselves, "an open, candid, active people" who traded on the most favorable terms of any in the Pacific. "We again found our selves," Cook wrote, "in the land of plenty."

This bounty included island women. They were bare-breasted, wearing short cloth wraps, shell bracelets, and feathered "ruffs," the crewmen's phrase for leis. "As fine Girls as any we had seen in the south Sea Islands," enthused David Samwell, the lustful young Welshman. "They seem to have no more Sense of Modesty than the Otaheite women, who cannot be said to have any."

There was only one catch, so to speak. Cook forbade his men from having relations with women, lest they bring "the venereal" to these

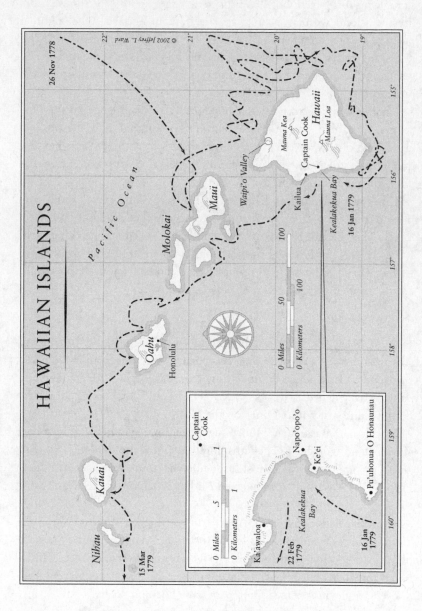

HAWAIIAN ISLANDS

© 2002 Jeffery L. Ward

26 Nov 1778

Pacific Ocean

Maui

Molokai

Waipi'o Valley

Mauna Kea

Hawaii

Captain Cook

Mauna Loa

Kailua

Kealakekua Bay

16 Jan 1779

Oahu

Honolulu

Kauai

Nihau

15 Mar 1779

0 Miles   50   100

0 Kilometers   100

Captain Cook

Napo'opo'o

Ke'ei

Pu'uhonua O Honaunau

0 Miles   .5   1

0 Kilometers   1

Ka'awaloa

Kealakekua Bay

22 Feb 1779

16 Jan 1779

untouched islands. He dispensed twenty-four lashes to an infected sailor who disobeyed, but this proved an inadequate deterrent. Sailors dressed island women as men to sneak them aboard. One night, a party of twenty crewmen had to stay ashore because the surf was too heavy for boats to pick them up. Island women, one crewman coyly wrote of that evening, "were determined to see wether our people were men or not."

Charles Clerke had no better luck enforcing abstinence on the *Discovery*. "Seamen are in these matters so infernal and dissolute a Crew," he observed, "that for the gratification of the present passion that affects them they would entail universal destruction upon the whole of the Human Species."

Cook was nonetheless delighted by his brief island stay—and by the three months' worth of provisions he'd acquired at minimal cost. As a mark of his esteem, he gave to the islands his favorite name: Sandwich. It was to this paradisiacal outpost that Cook steered once again after leaving Unalaska, anticipating a pleasant winter's sojourn that would afford his men all "the necessary refreshments."

THE ALOHA AIR jet from Honolulu to the Big Island of Hawaii swooped toward a runway that was hard to pick out from its volcanic surrounds. "It's one big Pompeii down there," Roger said, as the plane banked over a bed of black rock. "They could have skipped all the bitumen and just painted lines on the lava."

Roger had passed the short flight reading Samwell's rhapsodies about island women. " 'They absolutely will take no denial,' " he read aloud. " 'They would almost use violence to force you into their Embrace.' I love that! Maybe even I'll have a chance here. Can't wait to land."

I was eager to arrive, too. Apart from jet-lagged stopovers at Honolulu airport, en route to and from Australia, I'd never visited the state of Hawaii or the island that gave it its name. Like most Americans, I had a soft-focus image of the place: bronzed surfers, grass-skirted hula dancers, honeymooners sipping rum from coconut shells.

Not that our trip was shaping up as a romantic getaway. In Honolulu, we'd been joined by Cliff Thornton, the Captain Cook Society president, who had shown us around London's East End. Much to my surprise, Cliff had accepted our invitation to commemorate the February 14 anniversary of Cook's death. "I feel a loss that there is nowhere I can go and honor Cook," he said in a late-night phone call, telling me of his decision to undertake only his second trip abroad, and his first in more than twenty years.

I was glad to have Cliff along, though we made for an odd threesome. Among other things, I'd learned that he was a teetotaler and former Mormon who had done missionary work in England. He and Roger seemed to enjoy each other, swapping laddish tidbits about British TV serials, rugby and cricket, and Yorkshire jokes told in slang I couldn't comprehend. But as we crowded into a compact sedan at the airport, I couldn't help wondering how our crew would hold up over the week ahead.

We sped between fields of lava from the Kona airport to Kalaoa to Kailua to the King Kamehameha Hotel. (The Hawaiian language has only twelve letters, half of which seem to be "k.") When Mark Twain visited Kailua in 1866, he found "a little collection of native grass houses reposing under tall coconut trees—the sleepiest, quietest, Sundayest looking place you can imagine." One hundred and thirty-five years later, it was clogged with hotels, souvenir shops, superstores, and gridlocked traffic.

Our budget suite at the King Kamehameha offered a view of the hotel's heating and cooling system. Wandering downstairs for the evening luau, we joined a crowd of rotund Americans decked in leis, eagerly trying to learn the hula from a Hawaiian dancer. "Right foot out, hands on hips, slow and sensual," she shouted, rotating in her orange wrap. A hundred tourists mimicked her motions, rather less sensually. Then the crowd swarmed around an all-you-can-eat Polynesian buffet.

"How does a nation become so great when its population is such a dirge?" Roger asked, watching diners stack pyramids of food on their plates. "It must be a few individuals who do the great things. The rest are just consumers." He sipped his tropical punch and gasped. "It's nonalcoholic!"

During the feast, Cliff snapped pictures of an enormous woman in a *muʻumuʻu* crooning to the plink of ukuleles. But he, too, seemed dispirited by the luau's parody of traditional Hawaiian culture. "I wonder what Cook and his men would think if they landed today," he said. Roger shook his head. "Samwell would take one look at the crumpet and climb back in his bunk."

A few minutes later, Roger did just that. As he sprawled on his bed with an ashtray and a tumbler of rum balanced on his chest, idly perusing the adult offerings on the in-house movie channel, Cliff took the Gideon Bible from its bedside drawer and began searching for passages to read on the anniversary of Cook's death. That was still five days away. It was beginning to look like an interesting week.

AFTER A HARD month's sail from Unalaska, the *Resolution* and *Discovery* reached the Sandwich Islands again in late November 1778. On his earlier visit, Cook had touched at the archipelago's northern tip. This time, he arrived at the chain's southeastern end, off the island of Maui. His exhausted men, who had warmed themselves in the Arctic with memories of the archipelago and its fleshly delights, were desperate to go ashore. But Cook resolved to coast the islands without landing, so he could control trade, meting out his dwindling store of barter items and avoiding a quick depletion of the local food supply at any one place. He was also determined, as before, to keep the islanders free of the "Venereal distemper."

Sadly, the damage was already done. Many of those who paddled out to the ships had swollen penises and other signs of disease, evidently spread from the islands Cook had visited eleven months earlier. Still, Cook barred any contact. "Young Women came along side," lamented Samwell, "making many lascivious Motions & Gestures, but as we lay under the forementioned restrictions in respect to our intercourse with them we could not as yet conveniently admit them."

As if this were not torment enough, Cook also cut back on sailors' alcohol. He wanted to conserve what remained of the ships' spirits for his next Arctic probe. So he ordered a decoction brewed from island sugarcane, and declared it, characteristically, "a very palatable and wholsome beer." This provoked a reprise of Cook's dispute with his men over walrus meat in the Arctic.

"Not one of my Mutinous crew would even so much as taste [the beer]," Cook fumed in his journal. When he ended all brandy rations as punishment, his "turbulent crew" went so far as to write him a letter, complaining not only about the grog rations but also about their scant food allowance. Cook was oddly unaware that his men were still subsisting on the short rations he'd imposed in the north. He agreed to restore full fare, but held the line on alcohol. A midshipman wrote that the captain regarded the crew's letter "as a very mutinous Proceeding." The captain also told the crew that if they didn't like sugarcane beer, "they might content themselves with Water," and "that in the future they might not expect the least indulgence from him."

Cook, it seems clear, was losing command of his judgment, his temper, and his crew. His next journal entry, a rambling passage covering an entire week of sailing, provides further evidence of his disintegration. In heavy seas, part of the *Resolution*'s rigging gave out. This prompted the captain to blast the quality of his "cordage and canvas" and other "evils," and to blame the Navy Board—headed by his longtime patron, Sir Hugh Palliser—for providing him with inferior goods.

In writing this, Beaglehole observes, Cook surely "knew what he was talking about." But the captain's public and accusatory language—which Palliser later made sure was deleted from the voyage's published version—was so far from the deferential tone Cook usually adopted toward his superiors that it signals, once again, how much his mood had soured.

On the last day of November 1778, the ships reached the largest of the Sandwich Islands, called by the natives O'why'he. "To the great mortification of almost all in both ships," James King wrote, Cook again refused to land. Instead, he slowly circled the island for an agonizing six weeks, trading with natives in canoes and sailing through the heaviest seas he'd ever encountered in the Tropics. This discomfited not only the men—"We were jaded & very heartily tired," King wrote—but also the island women who had come aboard despite Cook's prohibition. "The motion of the ships by no means agreed with our poor friends," wrote the surgeon's mate, William Ellis. "In the midst of their amorous intercourse," the women "overflowed their unfortunate swains, with a stream not the most pleasing."

Rounding the island's southern tip, the ships coasted a lee shore unlike any the English had seen before. Ellis described it as covered in "large tracts of a dark and almost black matter, which we at first supposed was the soil which the natives had dug up and manured; but we afterward found it was the product of a volcano." Cook, short of water, finally decided to land. On January 16, 1779, he sent his master, William Bligh, to probe a wide bay. Bligh reported that it offered safe anchorage and fresh water. As the *Resolution* and *Discovery* sailed into the harbor, a fleet of a thousand canoes swarmed around the ships, filled with people singing and rejoicing.

"I have no where in this Sea seen such a number of people assembled in one place," Cook wrote. "Besides those in the Canoes all the Shore of the Bay was covered with people and hundreds were swimming around the Ships like shoals of fish." One crewman estimated the crowd at 15,000. So many climbed aboard the *Discovery* that the ship heeled.

The natives also treated Cook with even greater awe than those who had greeted him a year before. A *kahuna*, or priest, presented him with a pig, wrapped him in red cloth, and murmured an incantation. Then he escorted the captain and several of his men ashore. "As soon as we landed," Cook wrote, the priest "took me by the hand and conducted me to a large Morai," or open-air temple. "Four or five more of the Natives followed."

With these words, James Cook's pen falls silent, and remains so for the last month of his life. Why this faithful diarist suddenly stopped writing upon his dramatic arrival in Hawaii—or, if he didn't stop, what happened to his journal's last pages—is one of the many mysteries wreathing the captain's stay at Kealakekua Bay.

THE MAN AT the boat-charter company sounded puzzled by my request. "You don't want to fish," he said.

"That's right."

"Or scuba-dive."

"No, thanks."

"Snorkel? Watch whales?"

"That'd be nice, but really we just want to do the one thing and come back."

I sensed a shrug at the other end of the phone line. When we met Pat Cunningham at a boat ramp the next day, I understood why. His skiff, *Striker,* carried two 140-horsepower outboards, a sonar "fish finder," and an arsenal of lethal-looking truncheons and gaffes. Pat normally took out deep-sea anglers from Japan or California. Hiring *Striker* for a few hours of touring the coast was like taking an armored personnel carrier to the corner store for a quart of milk.

Still, his boat seemed the best option for the reconnaissance we had planned. Kealakekua Bay, twenty miles south of our hotel, was now a state marine sanctuary. We wanted to approach it for the first time by sea, as the English had done, and briefly scout Cook's death site without deflating the aura of our anniversary commemoration a few days later.

In the event, Pat Cunningham proved an excellent guide. Like many whites in Hawaii, he was a refugee from the mainland who had reinvented himself on the islands. Nothing about this deeply tanned, windcreased fisherman in board shorts and reflector sunglasses bespoke his actual background: farm boy from Zelienople, Pennsylvania. He also seemed completely at home describing the weird coastline we skimmed past, alternately lunar and lush, and utterly unlike anything in the continental United States.

"That's the cinder cone of an extinct volcano," Pat said, pointing at a rust-colored hillock. "And see that path winding down the mountain like an overgrown ski trail? That's an ancient *holua* slide." Centuries ago, Hawaiians created steep ramps made of smoothed lava stones, then covered them in slippery fronds and raced down the mile-long chutes on wooden sleds, sometimes launching into the sea.

If they tried the sport now, they'd land in a golf course. As we continued down the coast, we saw another links and gated golf community under construction, with sprinklers watering grass strips pasted onto the lava. Pat said that runoff from the piles of imported topsoil had already washed into waters that had once been classed "double-A pristine," among the clearest and cleanest in the world. There was also a risk that the pesticide-laden silt might wash into the ostensibly protected waters of Kealakekua Bay.

"I don't understand," Cliff politely interjected, adopting the tone of his day job as a bureaucrat in England, where history and open space are zealously protected. "Why haven't state planners put a stop to this?"

"Planners?" Pat guffawed. "This is America, bud. We don't plan." Under Hawaii's zoning laws, golf courses were regarded as "agricultural." The developers had also hired many locals to work on the project, defusing and dividing the opposition, which included not only environmentalists but also native Hawaiians who were upset that the golf course was disturbing ancient, unmarked graves.

Cliff was still silently fuming when we rounded a point and entered Kealakekua Bay. I'd purposefully avoided looking at photographs of the bay or reading tour books so that I could see the place, as much as possible, through the eyes of Cook and his men. Kealakekua's essential outline hadn't changed much since the eighteenth century. The mile-wide, half-moon bay was bordered by a soaring cliff and anchored at either end by a flat peninsula. But none of the English drawings or writings about the bay had prepared me for the 180-degree majesty of the scene.

In the distant background loomed the sloping volcanic bulk of Mauna Loa ("Long Mountain"). The cliff rising from the bay was a sheer thousand-foot wall of lava, half a mile across, plunging so sharply to the water that the shoreline was impassable. The cliff's face was multihued, separated into bands of black and bluish-gray and rust and chocolate, and pitted with lava tubes, miles-long cavities formed as the crust of the molten rock cooled. Miraculously, this lava precipice sprouted life: plugs of feathery beige grass that looked at a distance like shredded wheat spilled from the ledge above.

At the cliff's base, a strand line of bleached coral speckled the black lava boulders. And the water lapping against the shore was a color I'd never seen before, mingling patches of violet, ink, and royal blue, yet startlingly clear. Pat said visibility in the bay's water often reached more than a hundred feet. Spinner dolphins frolicked off the boat's bow, poking their bills above the surface before arcing out of the water, one right after another. It was easy to see why Hawaiians had named this place Kealakekua, meaning "Pathway of the Gods," and used the caves in its honeycombed cliffs as sepulchers for their highest chiefs.

I was jolted from my reverie by Cliff. He grabbed my arm and pointed at the bay's northern peninsula, on which stood a monument to Cook. "What's happening over there?" he shouted. I'd momentarily forgotten all about Cook's death site. From English paintings, I'd gotten the impression that it occupied center stage at Kealakekua, and that the obelisk marking the site would dominate the bay. In reality, the scale and grandeur of Kealakekua were so overwhelming that a casual visitor could miss the monument altogether, if not for its color: a sliver of white, silhouetted against the black-lava shoreline and brilliant green foliage covering the north end of the bay.

As we motored closer, I saw what Cliff was shouting about. A copper-colored youth, shirtless and shoeless, crouched at the obelisk's base, wielding what looked like a piece of charcoal and a can of spray paint. We could just make out the words GO HOME on the obelisk's pedestal.

"The bastard's besmirching the monument!" Cliff yelled. Rushing to the bow, he looked as though he might grab one of Pat's fishing truncheons and hurl himself ashore.

"Just hold on a minute," I said, grasping Cliff's arm. The journalist in me wanted to interview the graffiti artist before Cliff attempted some weird reversal of the violence that occurred on this site in 1779.

As we pulled up to the jetty by the monument, the message became clear. On one face of the obelisk, large block letters spelled WHITEY GO HOME. On another side was scrawled:

C R O O K

A

P

T

Rotten fruit had been thrown against the monument, its pulp splattered like birdshit against the white surface. The monument's inscription had also been crudely hacked away so that the word "discover" was now almost illegible, and the two o's in "COOK" formed eyes of a cartoonish face sketched around the captain's name.

As I stepped ashore, the youth looked up at me and frowned. He appeared to be about twenty, Gauguin-handsome, with long brown hair, brown eyes, and a white shell necklace strung across his sinewy brown chest. "Idiots," he said. "They must have come in the night." Then he returned to his painstaking labor, chipping at the WHITEY GO HOME with a piece of lava and spray-painting over it. "We don't want tourists to get the wrong impression about Hawaii," he said.

Cliff paced on the jetty: face tight, eyes slitted, his rage directed as much at me as at the young man. "It's all right," I called out. "Someone else did it. He's cleaning it up."

Cliff's face went slack and he came up to us, looking suddenly penitent. "I want to thank you," he said, reaching out his hand to the young man, whose name was Gary. Then he sloped off with Roger to walk along the beach.

Gary worked as a lifeguard on a catamaran that brought snorkelers to the bay. The vessel's captain had spotted the graffiti and dispatched Gary to clean it up. I asked him why Cook made someone angry enough to deface the monument.

Gary didn't answer. I sensed I'd been too abrupt. This was America, but I was also still in Polynesia, where people tended to be wary of blunt questions from white strangers. Gary chipped and sprayed for a minute, then lit a Kool and sat on the pedestal.

"A lot led up to that killing," he said. "We treated Cook like royalty, like a god, and he stabbed us in the back."

"What do you mean?"

"He vandalized our holy places and buried his own men there. That enraged people. So anger built up and Cook paid the price." Gary stubbed out his cigarette. "After Cook came the trashing of our culture. No more hula. No more Hawaiian language. My mother could hardly speak a word of it. What I know of the language I learned in school."

It was at school, too, that he'd learned most of what he knew about Cook: how the captain had played God and let his men infect all the women with syphilis. "This was probably the healthiest place on earth before his ships arrived," Gary said. "Cook said ten thousand or more people lived around this bay. And how many now? Maybe a few hundred, most of them *haole*." "*Haole*" was the Hawaiian word for Caucasian: it translated as "without breath," possibly a reference to Europeans' inability to speak the native tongue.

Gary's version of Cook's visit startled me. Not because it was negative; I'd come to expect that in the Pacific. Rather, I was struck by how closely he echoed the view of Cook that had been promulgated by New England churchmen more than 150 years ago. The first American missionaries who arrived in Hawaii in 1820 were only a generation removed from the Revolution, and the War of 1812 had ended just a few years earlier. The missionaries were Anglophobes, and they were determined that America rather than Britain establish dominion over the islands. So, along with fire-and-brimstone Christianity, they created a Satanic caricature of Cook, based in part on the writings of John Ledyard, the American marine on Cook's third voyage. A patriotic New Englander who had trained at Dartmouth to become a missionary, Ledyard returned to America after Cook's death and published an unflattering account of the captain's behavior in Hawaii.

The basics of the missionaries' denunciation ran as follows. Cook was a genocidal libertine who (according to one tale) slept with a princess and let his men make prostitutes of Hawaiian women, infecting them with the "loathesome disease." He spat on Hawaiian belief by desecrating their temples. Worst of all, he blasphemed the Almighty by allowing himself to be worshipped by idolators as a false god.

"Sin and death were the first commodities imported to the Sandwich Islands," wrote the Reverend Sheldon Dibble, who compiled much of the anti-Cook dogma in an 1838 island history. Cook, Dibble concluded, "was punished by God with death." Dibble's history became an enduring island textbook. Later writers cribbed from him and expanded on the list of Cook's sins, even blaming the captain for introducing the mosquito to Hawaii. Judging from my chat with Gary, this view hadn't changed much.

Still, Gary didn't approve of vandalizing Cook's monument. "I'm part *haole,* part Hawaiian, like most people here," he said. "I can't disown half of me. I just wish my Hawaiian half hadn't gotten fucked over so badly."

He hoisted a plastic garbage bag to clean up around the monument, leaving me to study the obelisk's scarred inscription: IN MEMORY OF

THE GREAT CIRCUMNAVIGATOR CXXXXXN JXXEX XXXK R.N. WHO DXXXXXXRED THESE ISLANDS ON THE 10TH OF JANUARY A.D. 1778 AND FELL NEAR THIS SPOT ON THE 14TH OF FEBRUARY A.D. 1779. The obelisk had been erected by Britons living in Hawaii in the 1870s, and was later ringed with eighteenth-century cannon, their muzzles raised and joined by a chain. Admirers aboard visiting ships had also added commemorative plaques and signposts along the jetty. Many of these had been toppled or pried out.

I found Cliff and Roger sitting on a rock a short way down the shore. Cliff gazed out to sea. Roger eyed a nearby beach where a woman was tying up a kayak. "Tall, leggy, stud in her navel, probably a tattoo under that string bikini," he said. "A naughty girl, just my type." Then two portly men appeared and helped her pull the kayak ashore. "Oafs!" Roger shouted. He stood up, irritated, and slipped on the sea-slick lava, barking his shin. "Cook wasn't killed at all," he groused. "He tripped on one of these rocks and hit his head. The Hawaiians were blameless, but they had to take the fall because Cook was clumsy."

I asked Cliff how he felt about finally seeing Cook's death site. Before he could answer, Roger blurted, "Cliff was weeping while you talked to that bloke."

"Was not."

"Were too. You had a tear in your eye. You took your glasses off to wipe it away."

"That was sweat." Cliff paused. "Okay, I was upset. First I was choked up with indignation at that lad. Then I felt guilty for having those bad thoughts about him. Then I saw all those plaques left by people who came here before me. I had a hard swallow and needed solitude."

There wasn't much chance of that now. Bright, jellybean-colored kayaks crowded the bay, and snorkelers flippered all around us—nothing like the graceful outriggers and swimmers who had swarmed the English ships "like shoals of fish." We returned to the jetty and climbed back on Pat's boat. As we motored out of the bay, humpback whales arced out of the sea, spouted, and then "fluked," their tails fluttering for a moment as they dove deep in the water. A flat patch of sea—a "footprint," Pat called it—remained visible for several moments after the whales went down. Roger and I scrambled to the bow for a better view and called back to Cliff to join us.

"I didn't come to see whales," he said, still gazing back at Kealakekua. "I can see them on the telly."

ON JANUARY 17, 1779, the day of Cook's last journal entry, Lieutenant James King described in detail the extraordinary scene that unfolded when the captain went ashore. On the beach stood men carrying wands tipped with dog hair, intoning the word *Erono,* or *Lono,* while islanders fell to their hands and knees, bowing their heads to the ground. Cook and a few of his men were escorted to a waterside temple, a raised stone platform with a wooden railing that supported twenty human skulls. A priest named Koah then led Cook through a series of rituals, during which the captain remained "quite passive, & sufferd Koah to do with him as he chose," King wrote.

Cook ascended a rickety scaffold, where the priest wrapped the captain in red cloth. The captain also followed Koah's lead by prostrating himself before carved images and kissing them. Then Koah held up one of Cook's arms while King supported the other, as more prayers were said and a crowd continued to chant "Lono." Processions of men presented the captain with sugarcane, coconuts, sweet potatoes, and other food; a putrid hog also figured prominently throughout, and was repeatedly handled by Koah.

The ceremony ended with another priest anointing Cook's face, head, hands, and arms with masticated coconut. During the feast that followed, the priests "insist'd upon Cramming us with hog," King wrote. For once, the omnivorous Cook lost his appetite. "The Captn recollecting what offices Koah had officiated when he handled the Putrid hog," King wrote, "could not get a morsel down, not even when the old fellow very Politely chew'd it for him."

The English had learned a rudimentary Polynesian vocabulary, and the Hawaiian language was similar enough to that of Tahiti for crewmen to communicate with their hosts. Even so, after watching the "long & rather tiresome ceremony" at the temple, King admitted that he "could only guess at its Object & Meaning, only that it was highly respectful on their parts."

Scholars have been debating the ceremony's significance ever since. Most believe that Hawaiians regarded Cook as a manifestation of Lono, a potent fertility god and also an ancient, divine king who had exiled himself after killing his wife in a jealous fit. Each year, during a season known as Makahiki, Hawaiians celebrated Lono's symbolic return to seed the ground with winter rain. As part of this fertility rite, priests circled the island carrying an icon of Lono: a tall crosspiece draped with bark cloth.

The Hawaiians' deification of Cook may therefore have resulted from an extraordinary coincidence between island belief and the timing and nature of the captain's arrival. The English ships, with their masts and spars and sailcloth, resembled the native image of Lono. The ships arrived off Hawaii during the Makahiki season and circled the island in a clockwise direction, mirroring the Lono procession. Finally, the ships dropped anchor in Kealakekua Bay, Lono's onetime home and site of a temple, or *heiau,* honoring him. It was there that Cook was greeted as the returned god; hence the moment when King and the priest held out the captain's arms, duplicating the Lono icon.

In the view of the American anthropologist Marshall Sahlins, the principal champion of the Cook-as-Lono school, Cook's reception, and all that followed, can be understood in ritualistic terms. It was a "cosmic drama," Sahlins writes, in which "Cook obliged the Hawaiians by playing the part of Lono to its fatal end."

This thesis has sparked one of the most famous and vitriolic debates in recent academic history, pitting Sahlins, a renowned scholar at the University of Chicago, against Gananath Obeyesekere, an esteemed anthropologist at Princeton. In a book-length broadside, the Sri Lanka–born Obeyesekere attacks Sahlins's thesis as imperialist nonsense. Hawaiians were far too rational to mistake a white, foreign-tongued sea captain for a Polynesian god, Obeyesekere argues. Rather, they regarded Cook as a figure akin to their own high chiefs, and treated him with the same respect—in part because they wanted to enlist the English in their internecine wars, as many Polynesians had tried to do before. It was Cook's own actions, rather than island cosmology, that led to his eventual death.

Both men's arguments are so intricate and compelling that it is difficult to judge who is right. But it seems clear that Hawaiians treated Cook with exceptional awe, and in what James King called a "very Abject & slavish manner." The question is why. Kealakekua Bay appears to have been split between two somewhat competitive communities. At one end, near the temple, lived members of the priestly class. At the other dwelled the island's king and his chiefs. The priests may have genuinely believed Cook was an incarnation of Lono—or judged it in their interest to declare that a god had arrived. The king and chiefs, who didn't always trust the priests, may have seen it in *their* interest to flatter and placate the potent English with gifts and honors.

Tellingly, the Hawaiians initially treated the *Discovery*'s captain, Charles Clerke, with almost as much ceremony as they accorded Cook. But the everyman Clerke wrote that he "disliked exceedingly putting so many people to such a confounded inconvenience," and asked the priests to stop all the "singing and fuss." Clerke also seemed oblivious to the sacredness of royal flesh, at one point clapping a chief on the shoulder until one of the man's retainers "gently took away my hand, and beg'd I wou'd not touch him."

Clerke survived this faux pas, but Hawaiian commoners could not. They were subject to the harsh Hawaiian system of taboo, or *kapu,* which dictated that touching a chief, or even walking on his shadow, was punishable by death. "Equality in condition," King observed, "was not the happiness of this Island." Commoners bore the added burden of supplying almost two hundred hungry sailors with vast quantities of hogs, fruit, and other provisions.

"We live now in the greatest Luxury," David Samwell wrote, on the ships' second day in the bay, "and as to the Choice & number of fine women there is hardly one among us that may not vie with the Grand Turk himself." The currency of sex, as at Tahiti, was the nail. "Our Men pull as many [nails] as they can," Samwell wrote, and Hawaiians yanked them out as well. "Was there not a strict Eye kept over them we should have the Ships pulled to pieces at this place."

More seems to have been at work than metal lust. Even by Polynesian standards, Hawaii was a highly eroticized culture. Sexual initiation occurred very young, and the hula was often designed to arouse the gods or to praise a chief's genitals. Samwell recorded the words of a song accompanying one dance. They translated as: "A penis, a penis to be enjoyed/Don't stand still, come gently/That way, all will be well here/Shoot off your arrow."

Marshall Sahlins calls Hawaiian culture "Aphrodisian," and cites as evidence a nineteenth-century missionary who complained that islanders practiced twenty forms of intercourse—and had as many words for coitus. "If any one term were selected to translate the Seventh Commandment," Sahlins writes, "it was bound to leave the impression that the other nineteen activities were still permitted."

The island's king at the time of Cook's visit was an emaciated, palsied man of about sixty who nonetheless kept innumerable wives and concubines, as well as young male retainers known as *aikane*. Their "business is to commit the sin of Onan upon the old King," Samwell wrote. "It is an office that is esteemed honourable among them & they have frequently asked us on seeing a handsome young fellow if he was not an Ikany to some of us." Samwell also surmised that Hawaiians freely practiced "That Unnatural Crime which ought never to be mentioned," namely sodomy. And even he was shocked by their carved figures. "The leud postures and actions in which these are represented," he wrote, "would offend the Ear of Modesty to recount."

The English had also arrived at the lustiest moment in the Hawaiian calendar. The Makahiki season celebrated the fertility of the land, and Lono's return in search of his bride. So there may have been a ritualistic aspect to islanders' frantic coupling with sailors, particularly if Hawaiians saw Cook and his ships as divine. The English noticed women stuffing the umbilical cords of newborns between the ships' boards, perhaps believing the vessels would carry their infants' spirits to the heavens.

Given all this—Hawaiians' lavish hospitality, the homage they paid Cook, and the sexual ardor displayed by native women—it isn't surprising that the English were quickly lulled into a false sense of security. "Their behavior," concluded Samwell, "is so obliging and friendly that no quarrels could possibly arise in our intercourse with them."

THE DAY AFTER our boat ride, we drove down the coastal road from the King Kamehameha to Kealakekua Bay, paralleling the route we'd taken by sea. I'd known before coming to Hawaii that it wasn't an unspoiled paradise, but the island's snarled traffic surprised me. So did the haze, which I at first mistook for smog. It was actually what locals called vog, a high-level drift of sulfur dioxide–bearing clouds from an active volcano at the island's south end. The island newspaper even carried a daily "vog index" on its weather page.

It took us an hour to crawl the twenty miles from Kailua to Keauhou to Kainaliu to a community just above Kealakekua Bay called Captain Cook. "I'm surprised they don't spell it Kaptain Kook," Roger said. The town lay atop the thousand-foot shelf overlooking Cook's death site, though its name was only indirectly tied to the captain. A century ago, a local coffee company called Captain Cook maintained a small post office. The company had since gone, but the post office stayed, even though Captain Cook wasn't an incorporated township.

Like the other coastal towns we'd passed through, Captain Cook seemed a curious hybrid of old businesses run by Japanese-Americans (who were once the majority population on the island) and more recent establishments of a distinctly New Age cast. Near a shiatsu massage clinic, I saw a business card in the window of a whole-foods bakery that read: "I am Dolphins. Dolphin swimmer. Cetacean ambassador. Gemini communicator. Cyberspacialist." Also striking were the wanted posters at the post office, which identified suspects as "Portuguese-Filipino-Hawaiian" or "Japanese-Korean" or some other mélange. Hawaii was the sort of place where you felt conspicuous being just the one thing, particularly if that happened to be a bland *haole*.

Estimates of the Hawaiian Islands' population at the time of Cook's arrival range from 250,000 to a million. By the mid-nineteenth century, disease had made that number dwindle to about seventy thousand. Immigration from China, Japan, and other countries, as well as intermarriage and outmigration by Hawaiians, diluted the native presence still further. Today, only nine thousand "pure" Hawaiians remain; they constitute less than one percent of the state's 1.2 million people. Another 200,000, or 18 percent, are classified as part Hawaiian.

Near Captain Cook, we turned off the main highway and onto a frangipani-fringed, breadfruit-splattered road that wound around the cliff above Kealakekua and down to the bay. We passed a macadamia nut mill and a fragrant coffee-roasting factory, then entered the k-free but still tongue-twisting village of Napo'opo'o. At its edge stood the temple, or *heiau,* where Cook had been escorted by the priests on his first day ashore. The temple still stood, but all we could see was the outer wall of its high stone platform. A rope blocked the steps leading up to it, with a handwritten sign saying "KAPU. Sacred site. No Trespassing." On the steps lay various offerings: stalks, fruit, rocks wrapped in fronds.

On the black sand beach in front of the *heiau,* several heavily pierced young *haoles* were building a shrine of their own out of pebbles and shells. A short way back from the water, near where priests had once bathed in a sacred pool (now a brackish swamp), we found dreamcatchers hanging from trees and a throne-shaped stone adorned with corals and crystals.

While Roger and Cliff lingered on the beach, I walked over to a parking lot that appeared to double as Napo'opo'o's social center. A half dozen people sat drinking beer around tables made from telephone cable spools, with tattered beach umbrellas perched on top. A man wiggled his thumb and pinkie at me—the Hawaiian wave, or *shaka,* similar to the one I'd seen in Tahiti and New Zealand—and then pointed to a folding chair beside him.

"Want a nut, brah?" he asked, cracking a macadamia. The man had long black hair; a red bandanna was tied around his head. He looked like a cross between an aging rock star and a Zero pilot. His name was Cornell Shimamoto. "Mostly Japanese and who knows what else," he said, when I asked about his background. The others were of indeterminate ethnicity, appearing to range from mostly Hawaiian to mostly New Age *haole.* After we'd sat silently for some time, I asked about the temple and the *kapu* sign.

"It used to be, like, a sacred site," one man said. "Then *haoles* started walking all over it and putting towels down to dry. They closed it."

"Who's 'they'?" I asked.

He shrugged. "You know, *they.*" He lit a joint and passed it around. I'd noticed a "Sovereign Kingdom of Hawaii" license plate tacked to a tree in the parking lot. I'd read that some Hawaiian radicals had declared a provisional government, seeking return of native land and sovereignty, and symbolically seceding from the United States. I asked if *that* had something to do with *they*.

"Oh yeah, we're the sovereign kingdom right here," the man with the joint said, giggling.

"I'm chancellor of the exchequer," Cornell added.

"I'm queen!" a woman in his lap said, before convulsing in stoned laughter. I tried another tack. It was Makahiki season, just as it had been when Cook arrived. Maybe that explained the offerings at the *heiau,* and the *kapu* sign. I asked Cornell whether Hawaiians still celebrated Makahiki.

"Sort of. You party down. Music, beer, dope, dancing." He passed me the joint. "Isn't that why you're here?"

Why *was* I here, smoking pot in a parking lot at eleven A.M.? "I'm looking into Captain Cook. Know much about him?"

"The one who invaded Hawaii?" the woman said. "He was a rich man, one of the Big Five." This referred to the five agribusiness companies that had effectively ruled Hawaii for much of the twentieth century.

"Not exactly," I said. "He was killed just over there across the bay. I'm trying to find out more about that."

The woman shrugged. "All the famous people get killed. JFK. Martin Luther King. Captain Cook."

I was starting to feel a little like Cook's lieutenant, James King, struggling vainly to divine the "object and meaning" of the ceremony he'd witnessed at the temple a hundred yards away. Then, as I got up to go, a legless old man in a motorized cart tugged at my arm. "Few people you need to see," he said. "Arthur Kukua, down the road in Ke'ei. He's got one of Cook's bombs. And Henry Leslie, lives up in Captain Cook. He works for the British, looking after that monument." Before I could ask the man a question, he motored off in his cart.

KE'EI LAY AT the end of a rough, unpaved road a few miles south of Napo'opo'o. We found Arthur Kukua at a picnic table beside his small bungalow. A wiry old man, he sat drinking beer with his daughter, Leinora, a pretty woman of about forty with a flower in her hair. Neither of them seemed the least surprised to find three *haoles* wandering up and asking about Cook's "bomb."

"It's inside, I'll get it," Arthur said, returning a moment later with a cannonball, about the size of a large coconut. Cliff studied it for a moment and raised his eyebrows. He said it looked identical to the sort of ammunition once carried by British ships. Arthur led us down to the shore and pointed at the shallow water. "Right there's where I found it," he said. "I was spearfishing one day and there it was on the sand. It is unusual for me to see a cannonball. I like old things, so I keep it ever since."

That was all Arthur knew about it. We sat on the lava shelf for a while. Coconuts swayed in the breeze, and water lapped gently against the shore. Beneath the trees lay outrigger canoes covered in fronds. Leinora said she had a farm up the hill, where she grew coffee and macadamias. Like a lot of Hawaiians, she'd tried working in Honolulu and on the mainland, but came home in the end. "I didn't like the life," she said, "it was only about work."

Some of the homes in Ke'ei still had no electricity or running water, she told us. Most appeared ramshackle, with the same indoor/outdoor living area as Arthur's: a table, a few chairs, some corrugated metal to keep off the rain. "In this climate you don't need much," Leinora said. Though it was winter in Hawaii, she wore flip-flops and board shorts, as did most of the people we'd met. There was a dreamy, laid-back air to Ke'ei that reminded me of Tahiti outside Papeete, and Tongatapu beyond Nuku'alofa. For all that had changed, Polynesia still offered glimpses of the pleasing simplicity that appealed to Cook and his men.

But Hawaii was starting to remind me of Tahiti and Tonga in another, less pleasing way. The island's traditional culture and belief system had been so ravaged by disease, colonialism, and missionaries that it was almost impossible to reconstruct. Arthur pointed out a carving in the lava shelf that appeared to be an ancient petroglyph. When I asked him what it signified, he shrugged. "I have no idea," he said. "Anyone can make up a story. People that does know aren't here anymore, are they?" He hoisted his cannonball and headed back to the house. "It's up to you, what you believe."

IN THE FIRST weeks after their arrival in Kealakekua Bay, the English enjoyed an idyll reminiscent of their first contact with Tahitians a decade before. While women were the main attraction, crewmen occasionally lifted their heads from their hammocks to admire other aspects of island society. They judged the chiefly cloaks—made from as many as half a million bird feathers apiece—the finest garments in the Pacific. They were also astonished by Hawaiians' skill and joy in swimming through heavy surf. "Young boys & Girls about 8 or ten years of age play amid such tempestuous Waves that the hardiest of our seamen would have trembled to face," Samwell wrote. James King considered islanders "to be almost amphibious."

Charles Clerke noted something else: a "convenience for conveying themselves upon the Water, which we had never met with before." He described it as a thin board, six or eight feet long and shaped like a paper cutter. "Upon this they get astride with their legs, then laying their breasts along it, they paddle with their Hands and steer with their Feet." Hawaiians rode these boards on top of high swells, calling their sport *he'e nalu,* or wave sliding.

The Hawaiians, for their part, marveled at the English and their strange and seemingly magical ways. Historians in the early nineteenth century gathered natives' memories of first contact with Europeans. Islanders recalled thinking that the English had loose, wrinkled skin (clothes), angular heads (tricorns), volcanoes in their mouths (burning tobacco), and "a treasure hole in their side" (pockets). Their ships seemed like temples, "having steps going up into the clear sky, to the altars on the outside."

Samwell wrote that Hawaiians were mesmerized by the ships' clocks. The English, consulting these instruments constantly as they studied the sky, seemed to regard timepieces as gods commanding the heavens. Hawaiians also gazed with wonder at English writing, which they took to be a form of decorating cloth, like their own tapa work. And they relished English "novelties." Native women wanted mirrors, and the men craved anything made of metal, a substance they'd occasionally encountered in pieces of floating wood, probably from Spanish ships.

A fortnight into this delightful visit, two events clouded the English stay, at least in hindsight. Cook needed firewood, a scarce commodity on the lava-covered hills ringing the bay. He asked James King—who acted the part Banks had on the first voyage, of intermediary with natives—to inquire whether the English could buy the fencing around the temple. King wrote that he "had some doubts about the decency of this proposal," but the wood was "readily given." Sailors also carried off carved idols, one of which King returned at the request of the priests.

That same day, William Watman, the "old" sailor of forty-seven who had come out of retirement at Greenwich Hospital to sail a second time with Cook, died of a stroke. "The Chiefs knowing of his death expressd a desire that he might be bury'd on shore," King wrote, "which he was accordingly upon the Morai" (the English persisted in using the Tahitian term for temple rather than the Hawaiian word, *heiau*). Hawaiians watched the Christian service, then added chants of their own, throwing a pig and coconuts into Watman's grave.

The next day, King wrote, the king and chiefs "became inquisitive as to the time of our departing & seemed well pleas'd that it was to be soon." The islanders then collected a veritable Mauna Loa of food and trinkets—the largest offering King had seen in the gift-mad Pacific—and entertained their guests one last time with wrestling and boxing matches. The English reciprocated by igniting fireworks. Early on the morning of February 4, 1779, accompanied as they'd been on their entrance to Kealakekua by hundreds of canoes, the *Resolution* and *Discovery* sailed out of the bay.

One of the saddest to leave was King, who had made such an impression on Hawaiians that natives assumed he was Cook's son, and asked the lieutenant to stay. But King, almost alone among the crew, sensed the danger inherent in Hawaiians' apparent worship of the English. "They regard us as a Set of beings infinitely their superior," he wrote. "Should this respect wear away from familiarity, or by length of intercourse, their behaviour may change."

AFTER FINDING COOK'S bomb, we continued down the coast to Pu'uhonua O Honaunau, a historic park that encompassed one of the most sacred sites in Hawaii. Its centerpiece, a massive stone enclosure known as the "place of refuge," had served as a safety valve for the harshness of the *kapu* system. A taboo-breaker who managed to flee here by land or sea could shelter within the refuge's seventeen-foot-thick walls and win absolution from the priests. The park also included a canoe landing, a chiefly residence, a fish pond (the Hawaiians had practiced aquaculture), and a reconstructed temple very similar to the one Cook visited at Kealakekua Bay, with a paling, fierce carved images, and a scaffold, or oracle tower, from which the priests petitioned their gods.

What struck me about the vast park, apart from the sophistication it revealed of precontact Hawaii, was its kinship with sacred sites I'd visited thousands of miles to the south, in Tahiti, Raiatea, Tonga, and even New Zealand. Polynesian society had not only been astonishingly far-reaching; its belief system—including the notions of *tapu* and *mana*, and the worship of *ti'i* representing ancestral gods—had proved incredibly durable, surviving in its essential form for many centuries, even in the outermost reaches of Hawaii, Easter Island, and New Zealand.

Yet, as in other parts of Polynesia, traditional culture began unraveling within a generation of Cook's visit. By the end of the eighteenth century, ships were pouring into Hawaii, bringing muskets, swivel guns, grog, and disease. In 1819, Hawaii's alcoholic young king, under heavy pressure to adopt Western ways, went out in a boat, drank for three days, then came ashore and broke the taboo on eating with women—effectively destroying in a bite the *kapu* system, and with it the temples, idols, and centuries-old structure of belief.

A year later, New England missionaries sailed into this spiritual vacuum and wasted little time teaching the "naked savages," as they called Hawaiians, the depravity of the hula and other traditions. By 1837, the decline of the native population and its culture was so pronounced that the Sandwich Island Institute (a precursor of the famous Bishop Museum) was formed to document what remained of Hawaiians' tools, music, and customs. "In but a few years it is to be feared that they will be spoken of as a people who were but are not," wrote the institute's vice president. "Shall we coolly see these things pass before us without one effort to preserve a memoria of what the people were?"

As part of this work, the Bishop Museum later restored the place of refuge I was now visiting. At the park office, I found a native Hawaiian ranger with the wonderful name of Blossom Sapp. She'd grown up by Kealakekua Bay and had worked at the park for thirty years. In that time, she'd seen a resurgent interest in traditional belief—though the people embracing it were mostly New Age *haoles*.

"There's a lot of crystal people who come here," Blossom said, "a lot of meditation, a lot of chanting, a lot of lost or sick people trying to heal. We get them all." Visitors often left offerings like those I'd seen on the steps of the temple at Kealakekua Bay: rocks wrapped in ti leaf (a symbolic way of giving back a bit of the land), oils, jewelry, even alcohol and Spam. "After a while we just collect and bury it," she said.

There was another twist. The New Age had rubbed off on native Hawaiians. "A lot of locals come here now saying they feel a different 'energy' or a healing 'spirit,'" Blossom said. "I didn't hear those words from Hawaiians twenty-five years ago. It's all sort of washed together, the old beliefs, the new ones, the whole 'aloha' notion of love and welcome." She didn't see any harm in this. New Age pablum might not be very true to ancient Hawaiian practices, but on balance it was preferable to *kapu* and human sacrifice.

Still, while traditional belief may have mellowed, political anger hadn't. Many native Hawaiians were jobless and landless, effectively second-class citizens in what had once been their own country. In the late 1980s, when the park had introduced a $2 entry fee, many Hawaiians refused to pay. "They don't want to pay to visit what they feel is their own land," Blossom said.

Resurgent nationalism had also deepened the long-standing vilification of Cook. One outspoken sovereignty activist, Haunani-Kay Trask, had publicly labeled Cook "a syphilitic, tubercular racist" and declared her pride in the fact that Hawaiians, unlike other Pacific peoples, had made sure the captain didn't leave their shores alive. "We can defend our honor by declaring that at least *we* killed Cook, and having done so we rid the world of another evil *haole*." Her sister and fellow activist, Mililani Trask, had picketed a mall that once hosted a Captain Cook festival, and demanded that a coloring book glorifying Cook be pulled from shops. She also stated of the Cook monument at Kealakekua: "We have an obligation to trash that place."

Blossom didn't subscribe to this view. "Sooner or later the islands would have been found," she said. "Cook didn't steal the land or squash the culture, but his arrival brought others who did. So a lot of people just see him as the first bad guy, a symbol of everything bad that followed."

Blossom had her own, tangible reminder of Cook's visit: a cannonball, just like Arthur Kukua's. She'd inherited it from her grandparents and displayed it on a shelf at home. I asked her why she kept it. Blossom shrugged. "Cook's part of our history, whether we like him or not."

AFTER LEAVING KEALAKEKUA Bay, the *Resolution* and *Discovery* sailed north for three days, toward the Alenuihaha Channel between Hawaii and Maui, one of the roughest passages in the Pacific. In a heavy gale, Cook's ship once again failed him: the base of the foremast had rotted so badly that it shifted off the plate holding it to the hull. The ship also leaked. Making the necessary repairs in heavy seas was too risky. Cook saw no other option but to return to the known safety of Kealakekua Bay.

"All hands much chagrin'd & damning the Foremast," King wrote, as the ships bore away. One can only imagine Cook's chagrin, given his shaky state of mind and earlier tirade at the Navy Board about the shoddy outfitting of his vessel.

When the English sailed back into Kealakekua Bay, only a few canoes came out to greet them. "This in some measure hurt our Vanity," King wrote, "as we expected them to flock about us, & to be rejoiced at our return." One reason for the muted response was that the king had put a taboo on the bay until he could come greet the English himself. But when he did arrive, he asked why the ships had returned. The king seemed not to believe—or seemed to be displeased by—the reason given.

Soon after, thieving by islanders became rampant. And when barter resumed, Hawaiians demanded that they be traded iron daggers modeled on their own wooden ones. Cook's armorers duly forged the weapons from two-foot-long spikes aboard the ships. Then, on February 13, just three days after the ships' return, the last traces of hospitality vanished. Islanders harassed a watering party, and when marines were dispatched, natives laughed and jeered at them.

A scuffle broke out, one sailor hit a chief with an oar, and the crowd pelted crewmen with stones and beat two of them severely. Also, someone stole a pair of armorer's tongs, perhaps to forge daggers on his own. When Cook, who was ashore at the time, learned of the theft, he joined in a confused chase after the man believed to have taken the tongs. But islanders purposefully misdirected Cook. The captain ended up wandering in circles for three miles.

Returning to the ship in a state of rage, he told King that the natives must not "imagine they have gaind an advantage over us." He had also issued orders for the marines to load deadly musket balls rather than birdshot, and to fire at the first sign of further "insolence." At dusk on February 13, a tense quiet descended on Kealakekua Bay.

AT DUSK ON our fourth day in Hawaii, I left Cliff and Roger at a coffee shop and went in search of Henry Leslie, the Cook monument caretaker I'd heard about at the parking lot in Napo'opo'o. He lived in a suburban-style subdivision in Captain Cook, on a road called Captain Cook. Two massive dogs lunged at my throat as I entered the yard. I stopped just beyond the reach of their chains and shouted over their baying to a child standing in the doorway. "I'm looking for Mr. Leslie."

"Which one?"

"The one who looks after the Cook monument."

"Which one?"

"Henry."

"Which one?"

At this point I felt like shaking the child, except that two man-eating dogs blocked my path. Then a woman appeared, and I explained myself all over again. She called inside and three men emerged. One introduced himself as Henry Leslie III, though he went by the name Sonny. Next to him was his son-in-law, also named Henry. Then came Sonny's son, Randy. All three looked after the monument from time to time. As if this weren't confusing enough, I had trouble making out their faces in the dwindling light. Nor could I tell their silhouettes apart: all three were big-gutted men in shorts, bare feet, and duckbill caps, holding beer cans.

"Come on in," said Henry or Henry or Randy. I glanced at the dogs. "Mind if we talk out here? It's a beautiful evening." They came out and leaned against pickup trucks parked in the drive. Sonny dipped from a can of Skoal and explained that he was the third Henry Leslie to look after the Cook site, which had a very peculiar legal status. In 1877, a Hawaiian princess and her husband deeded the property to the British consul in Hawaii, for the express purpose of erecting a monument to Cook. Sixteen years later, a cabal of American sugar planters and missionaries' sons overthrew the queen of what was then still the independent kingdom of Hawaii; soon after, the U.S. Congress voted to annex the islands. So the monument site, a little over fifty by a hundred feet, was a legal anomaly: a tiny piece of Britain lying within American territory.

At the time the monument was built, the Leslies were one of the few families still living and fishing at Ka'awaloa, the village at the north end of the bay where the king and chiefs had resided during Cook's visit. The British hired Sonny's grandfather as caretaker, for a modest stipend. The job had since been passed from son to son. "Funny to think, isn't it," Sonny said, pausing to send a gob of snuff juice at one of the dogs, "that my family's looking after a monument to a man our own ancestors probably helped knock off."

The caretaking job, which paid $70 a month, basically involved tending the grounds within the chain enclosure, the only bit that belonged to Britain, and replacing vandalized plaques or toppled signposts. When I told the Leslies about the graffiti I'd seen the other day, Sonny shrugged. "There's some crazy, lazy people who have nothing better to do than blame someone else for their problems."

The Leslies had no time for that. Sonny worked as a construction-crew foreman, Randy installed swimming pools, Henry ran a photographic studio. Sonny and Henry were also employed at the golf-course development I'd heard about during our boat trip. I asked if they had any qualms about the project's disruption of the environment, and of Hawaiian graves. "It's jobs, you can't stop progress," Henry said. "But my dogs don't agree."

"What do you mean?"

"They won't get out of the truck when I'm there," he said. "The dogs can sense spirits, and the spirits are very strong at that place."

Henry's job was to take photographs of archaeological sites in the development area. "They found some bones while building Fairway Six," he said. "There's a way to handle that. You remove the bones to another place, put herbs in the original grave, and consecrate the spot with a blessing. That wasn't done with these bones. So there's been some ups and downs ever since."

"Like what?"

"People getting sick. Hearing things. Machines not working. The spirits just want to go home but they can't."

I sensed my questions were making the Leslies uncomfortable. Sonny had excused himself and gone inside. Randy stared at his feet. Even the dogs had gone quiet. I changed the subject and told Henry about my plan to visit the Cook site on the anniversary of the captain's death. Henry nodded sympathetically. "If his spirit's haunting you," he said, "best to put him to rest."

Chapter 14

KEALAKEKUA BAY:
A Bad Day on Black Rock

I cannot forget Cook's death. It is a sublime death in all
respects, and it is also beautiful that the majesty of the
untamed world has claimed its rights on him.

—JOHANN WOLFGANG VON GOETHE, 1781

Sunday, the fourteenth of February, 1779, dawned fine, with land and
sea breezes—and the *Discovery*'s cutter stolen from its mooring. This,
the ship's largest boat, was crucial to the crew. Its theft was also a
mark of "insolence" that Cook could not stand, unstrung as he was by
the previous day's troubles, including his goose-chase after the burglar
of the armorer's tongs. Cook ordered a blockade of the bay, and the
ships began firing cannon at canoes trying to run it.

Around seven A.M., James King came aboard, having spent the
night onshore. He found Cook "loading his double Barreld piece."
King was Cook's trusted lieutenant, but when he spoke to Cook, the
captain cut him off. A moment later, Cook went ashore with ten
marines, and posted armed sailors aboard two of the *Resolution*'s
boats, the pinnace and launch, in the water near the lava shoreline.

Cook planned to do what he had done many times before in the
Pacific: seize a chief and hold him until stolen goods were returned.
This time, he went straight to the top, marching the marines into the
chiefly village of Ka'awaloa and ordering the marines' lieutenant,
Molesworth Phillips, into a hut where the king lay sleeping. The king
agreed to return to the ship with Cook. But as the party neared the

water, a crowd formed. The English had shot a chief dead at the other end of the bay, as he tried to run the blockade, and at some point news of this had reached Ka'awaloa.

One of the king's wives tried to stop her husband from going any farther. "With many tears and intreaties," Molesworth Phillips later reported, she "beg'd he would not go onboard." Two chiefs also held the king back and made him sit down. "The old Man now appear'd dejected and frighten'd," Phillips said of the king. The lieutenant also observed that an "immense mob" of several thousand people had gathered, surrounding Cook and the ten marines. "It was at this period we first began to suspect that they were not very well dispos'd towards us," Phillips said.

The lieutenant suggested to Cook that the marines form a defensive line by the water, and the captain agreed. The crowd let the marines pass, but they also started collecting spears and rocks. "An Artful Rascal of a Priest," Phillips said, began "singing & making a ceremonious offering of a Coco Nut to the Capt." The lieutenant suspected this was meant to distract the English from "the Manoeuvres of the surrounding multitude."

At this point, Cook abandoned his plan of taking the king hostage, telling Phillips, "We can never think of compelling him to go onboard without killing a number of these People." The stage seemed set for a tense but peaceful withdrawal. Cook "was just going to give orders to embark," Phillips said, when a man in the crowd "made a flourish" with an iron dagger and threatened to throw a stone at the captain. Cook fired the barrel of his gun loaded with buckshot.

This caused no injury: the man wore the thick woven mat used by Hawaiian warriors as protection in battle. But the gunfire, a novelty to Hawaiians, incited the crowd. Islanders began stoning the English and trying to stab them. Cook shot again, killing a man. Then he ordered the marines to fire and called out, "Take to the Boats."

The marines unleashed a volley into the crowd, but before the English could reload, the Hawaiians surged forward, dipping their battle mats in water, in the apparent belief that this would protect them from the flaming muskets. Sailors in the boats, a short way offshore, started firing into the crowd as well. "The business was now a most miserable scene of confusion," reported Phillips, who was stabbed and beaten with a stone. "All my People I observ'd were totally vanquish'd and endeavouring to save their lives by getting to the Boats."

Phillips had lost sight of Cook, but the men aboard the pinnace and launch saw the captain standing with his arm outstretched, apparently beckoning the boats to come closer to shore. The pinnace's men rowed in. But the launch's commander, Lieutenant John Williamson, either misunderstood Cook's gesture or ignored it, and ordered his men to row farther out.

Cook struggled to the shoreline: a ledge of lava, covered in shallow water. He was about ten yards from the safety of the pinnace, if only he could swim.

Strange as it seems today, swimming was a skill that most eighteenth-century mariners lacked. Some had a superstitious dread of the sea. Others may have been discouraged by their superiors from learning to swim, lest this enable them to desert. Cook would have had few if any opportunities to swim during his childhood on Yorkshire farms. He spent his first two decades at sea plying the frigid waters of the German Ocean and the North Atlantic. Nowhere in the many accounts of his voyages is there a single mention of the captain swimming. Samwell and two of Cook's officers stated plainly that he could not swim.

"Captain Cook was now the only Man on the Rock," Samwell wrote. The captain stepped into the shallow water, one hand shielding the back of his head from stones, the other clutching his musket. The Hawaiians appeared hesitant to pursue him. "An Indian came running behind him, stopping once or twice as he advanced, as if he was afraid," Samwell wrote, "then taking [Cook] unaware he sprung to him, knocked him on the back of his head with a large Club taken out of a fence."

Cook staggered, fell to one knee, tried to rise. Another man rushed up and stabbed the captain between his shoulder blades with an iron dagger. Cook toppled into knee-deep water and the crowd fell on him in a frenzied group assault. "They now kept him under water, one man sat on his Shoulders & beat his head with a stone while others beat him with Clubs & Stones," Samwell wrote. Then they hauled Cook's body onto the rocks and continued the stabbing and beating. "As soon as one had stuck him another would take the Instrument out of his Body and give him another Stab."

It was just after eight o'clock in the morning, an hour or so since Cook's departure from the *Resolution*, and only minutes since the skirmish had erupted. Cook and four marines lay dead: the others, all of whom were badly wounded, had struggled to the pinnace, one pulled aboard by his hair. Seventeen Hawaiians had also been killed, including four chiefs; many more were injured. It was, by far, the bloodiest encounter of Cook's long Pacific career. And it occurred so suddenly and unexpectedly as to seem unreal to Cook's men, many of whom had witnessed the fight from the boats, or through spyglasses from the ships anchored in the bay.

"A general silence ensued throughout the ship, for the Space of near half an hour," wrote George Gilbert, a sailor on the *Resolution*. "It appearing to us some what like a dream that we cou'd not reconcile our selves to for some time." This collective shock gave way to grief, "visible in every Countenance," Gilbert added. "All our hopes centered in him; our loss became irrepairable." Samwell wrote that the men returning in the boats "cryed out with Tears in their Eyes that they had lost their Father!"

It isn't clear whether they meant "Father" in the religious or familial sense. Perhaps both. Just a few weeks before, the ship's crew had seemed "mutinous" to Cook. Clearly, sailors often bristled under his stern command; James Trevenen, an admiring midshipman, frankly labeled him "the despot." Yet the captain's towering presence in sailors' lives was a source of security as well as terror. Cook might be a wrathful god at times, but he also seemed all-powerful in his skill at leading his "People" through a watery wilderness of gales, reefs, ice fields, and encounters with hostile natives. He must have seemed to his men a talisman, indestructible, a commander whose decade-long triumph over peril brought glory not only to himself but also to those he carried home safely.

Trevenen put it best. "I (as well as most others) had been so used to look up to him as our good genius, our safe conductor, & as a kind of superior being," he wrote of Cook's death, "that I could not suffer myself, I did not dare, to think he could fall by the hands of the Indians over whose minds & bodies also, he had been accustomed to rule with uncontrouled sway."

The death scene was all the more shocking for its many ironies.

Cook, who had often excoriated his men for violent intemperance toward natives, succumbed to precisely that, marching ashore with a menacing but inadequate force and opening fire at the most charged moment possible. A Quaker-influenced child of the Enlightenment, Cook died with a gun in his hand, having just killed a man. The dagger that felled him was forged from one of the iron spikes that Cook himself had ordered for his ships before leaving England, "to exchange for refreshments" and "to be distributed to [natives] in presents towards obtaining their friendship." The final irony was that Cook died, not in warlike New Zealand or Niue, but on an island where he'd been greeted as a god, and where he'd felt so secure that until the final day he had ordered his men to go ashore unarmed.

So what went wrong? The anthropologist Marshall Sahlins offers a ritualistic analysis. The ships' initial sail from Kealakekua Bay roughly accorded with the end of the Makahiki season, marking Lono's departure and the symbolic return of royal sovereignty. When Cook returned to the bay, he was now out of sync with the ritual cycle, and confounded Hawaiians' prior understanding of him. Also, the Makahiki traditionally closed with a mock battle in which the king reappropriated the land from Lono. Curiously, the day before Cook's death, an island warrior asked the captain if he was a *kanaka koa,* or fighting man. Cook displayed his badly scarred hand as evidence that he was.

It is also possible that islanders had come to doubt the divinity of Cook and his men: first with the death of the sailor Watman, then when the damaged *Resolution* limped back into the bay. Gods weren't supposed to suffer these sorts of setbacks. Nor did gods feel physical pain. In the early nineteenth century, Hawaiian historians collected stories about Cook's death. One recorded the surprise felt by a warrior named Kalanimano, allegedly the first to strike Cook. "Lono cried out because of the hurt. Then Kalanimano thought, 'This is a man, and not a god, and there is no wrong. So he killed Lono.'"

English journals suggest a much more prosaic explanation for the sudden change in islanders' demeanor: put simply, the sailors had worn out their welcome. It was no small matter to keep several hundred men supplied with food, water, and sex. James King, the most perceptive man aboard, wrote that sailors' ravenous appetites, their frantic barter for provisions, and the absence of women on the ships all suggested to Hawaiians that the English were in exile from their own starved land.

"Our quick return seemed to create a kind of Jealousy amongst them with respect to our intentions," added George Gilbert, "as fearing we should attempt to settle there, and deprive them of part if not whole of their Country." Some of this jealousy may have been sexual. King observed a chief beat his wife after she briefly took the arm of an English officer. Later Hawaiian stories also told of islanders becoming agitated by their women's affection for sailors.

Finally, in the view of several crewmen, there was simmering anger over the English having carried off and burned the fencing around the temple, as well as taking idols. According to the American marine John Ledyard, such "sacrilegious depredations," and other English actions that "oppressed" islanders, made Hawaiians heartily sick of their visitors and unhappy to see them return. "Our former friendship was at an end," Ledyard wrote, "and we had nothing to do but to hasten our departure to some different island where our vices were not known, and where our extrinsic virtues might gain us another short space of being wondered at."

This is an unusual and incisive remark—if trustworthy. Beaglehole, a very discerning judge of sources, regards Ledyard as an unreliable and extremely prejudiced observer. But the anthropologist Gananath Obeyesekere draws on Ledyard and other diarists to posit a darkly provocative thesis. Not only was Cook never Lono; he was Joseph Conrad's Kurtz, "the civilizer who loses his identity and goes native and becomes the very savage he despises." In Obeyesekere's view, Cook's actions in Hawaii betrayed a heart of darkness that was always present—most conspicuously on the third voyage, when Cook flogged natives, cut off their ears, and burned islanders' homes and canoes. Obeyesekere also alleges a cover-up by Cook's contemporaries and biographers to conceal damning evidence of the captain's true character.

One doesn't have to accept Obeyesekere's argument—and I don't; it seems far too selective, ignoring the many instances of Cook's humanity—to recognize the discomfiting questions it raises. Cook was a diligent diarist, and his clerks made copies of his journals while on board. By his third voyage, Cook was famous, and both he and his men knew that the captain's words were destined for wide publication. It therefore seems very strange that he left no record of his last month in Hawaii, or that, if he did, his journal entries vanished.

Beaglehole cites evidence that portions of Cook's writing from the third voyage mysteriously disappeared after reaching England. It seems possible, as Obeyesekere suspects, that these missing pages exposed thoughts and actions so disturbing that someone made sure they were "lost," just as Cook's tirade about his ship's condition was later deleted from the official account of the voyage.

Cook's crewmen also may have exercised self-censorship. It would have been especially impolitic to disparage the captain following his death. Instead, many sought a scapegoat in Lieutenant John Williamson, commander of the launch during the fray at Kealakekua Bay. A number of crewmen claimed that Cook could have been saved if the men in Williamson's launch had rowed in closer to shore and kept up a steady fire.

Several crewmen later challenged Williamson to duels. One sailor even claimed that after a lodge of Freemasons was formed on the homeward journey, Williamson bribed his fellow masons with brandy "to promise, as brothers, that they would say nothing of his cowardice when they came to England; so, by this trick, he saved his bacon." Curiously, Williamson went on to become a naval captain—only to be court-martialed after a Napoleonic battle for "disaffection, cowardice, disobedience to signals and not having done his duty in rendering all assistance possible."

Charles Clerke, who took command of the *Resolution* after Cook's death, conducted an on-the-spot inquiry, mainly by debriefing Molesworth Phillips, the marine lieutenant who had been by Cook's side. Clerke didn't assign any blame to Williamson. He also seemed at pains to exonerate Hawaiians. "The unhappy catastrophe which befell us I do think appears by no means the effect of premeditated intention," he wrote, "but of an unfortunate string of circumstances tending to the same unlucky point, one action irritating another till they terminated in the fatal manner."

Sadly, the "unhappy catastrophe" was far from over. The *Resolution*'s damaged foremast, and its astronomical gear, remained on shore. Also, the Hawaiians had carried off the mangled corpses of Cook and the four marines. Clerke couldn't sail from Kealakekua Bay without attempting to recover them. As for the stolen cutter that had led to the fracas, it was never recovered, having been torn apart for its treasured iron.

FEBRUARY 14, 2001. 0600. Breakfast room of the King Kamehameha Hotel. Empty except for Roger, Cliff, and me, plus a few elderly insomniacs spooning bran flakes. I pulled a crumpled checklist from my pocket.

"Bible?"

"Aye," Cliff replied.

"Beaglehole?"

"Got it," Roger murmured.

"Booze?"

"What's left of it."

"Let's go, then."

I sounded more in command than I felt. We'd gone to sleep only a few hours before, following a rum-soaked rant by Roger. At the last minute, he'd balked at our plan: a dawn hike to Cook's monument, where we'd commemorate the captain's death at the precise hour it occurred on the same day in 1779. Just before our planned anniversary, we'd learned that the hike followed a long trail so steep and arduous that running up it was part of a local ironman competition.

"I won't make it, I'll be an embarrassment," Roger said as we'd climbed into bed. "I'm already an embarrassment but I'll be more of one. I'm not an ironman, for chrissakes. I'm a few years from needing an iron lung."

"The ironmen *run* it," I reminded him. "We're just going to walk down. And we have all day to get back up."

"You two walk," Roger replied. "I'll ride down in the motorboat again. But I won't pick you up—just like Williamson in the launch. I'll shout 'Sorry, lads, can't make it in!' and motor off. We're interested in verisimilitude, aren't we? My last name's Williamson. It's important that I show tremendous cowardice. My namesake has to be dishon-ored in all his dishonor. I'll fuck it up completely, I promise."

Roger had finally talked himself to sleep, rum glass still in his hand, and was jolted awake by the hotel's robotic wake-up call. Now, an hour later, he sat in the car, red-eyed and mute. Cliff glanced at his watch and said chirpily, "At just about this moment two hundred and twenty-two years ago, Clerke was telling Cook that a Hawaiian had pinched the *Discovery*'s pinnace."

"Pinched whose penis?" Roger grumpily replied. "Anyway, it was a cutter." We drove in silence, passing an oddly named funeral home: Dodo Mortuary. "You can take me there after I collapse on the hike," Roger said.

The sun was just starting to edge above Mauna Loa as we parked in high grass beside the trailhead to Kealakekua Bay. Cliff shouldered a large duffel bag, the contents of which he hadn't disclosed. Roger toted the rum bottle. I hoisted a small knapsack. At first, the going was easy and pleasant, the path wide and carpeted with sodden grass. High reeds rose on either side, with pastures and lychee orchards just beyond. A cockerel crowed. Cliff paused to study purple flowers still wet with dew. We could have been out for a ramble in the English countryside.

Then, after about half a mile, the path became steep and strewn with boulders, and the air turned sultry. We had to pick our way slowly, goatlike. The view opened up, a bare and forbidding expanse of black, wavy lava. "A petrified sea," Mark Twain called it. After five days in this strange terrain, I'd begun to see that not all lava looked alike. Some of it formed ropey piles, like giant cow pies. Other bits were jagged, very rough on the feet. Much better were the smooth patches, black and almost billowy. I'd read that these variations had to do with the different temperatures at which lava cooled.

"On the whole a pleasant Spot," Samwell wrote of the surrounds of Kealakekau Bay, "tho' it must be owned that there is no part of it or near it where a Man can walk with any pleasure on account of the ragged Lava hurting the feet."

It took us an hour to reach the plain beside the bay, where the vil-lage of Ka'awaloa had once stood. Here, the trail led through a grove of gnarly kiawe trees, an imported mesquite; it had almost supplanted the palm trees that grew here at the time of Cook's visit. Lichen covered the lava, and coconut husks littered the path, giving off a dank, ripe odor. The woods ran right up to the shore and the small patch of ground enclosing the Cook monument.

Roger and I collapsed beside the obelisk while Cliff went into a frenzy of maintenance, doing more in half an hour than the site's caretakers had probably done in a year. He picked up trash: flip-flops, Coke cans, food wrappers. He pulled up long grass and patched the seawall with stones. Then he went to work resurrecting a toppled sign, pushing it upright and hefting lava boulders to wedge around its base. Red-faced and sweaty, he stood back to admire his work. "We put them up, they knock them down, we put them up again," he said.

Cliff hoisted his duffel bag and slipped behind the monument. He emerged in a clean white shirt and a Captain Cook Society tie, navy blue with Cook's face below the knot. "I brought this shirt and tie ten thousand miles for this occasion," he said, pressing out wrinkles with his palms. Cliff reached in his duffel again and brought out the Gideon Bible. "Shall we, gentlemen?"

Roger and I stood up and faced the obelisk. As Cliff held the Bible open, reading glasses perched on his nose, he looked rather like a country curate. He began with Exodus 32, in which God reprimands Moses for allowing his people to worship a golden calf. Then Cliff turned to Exodus 34. "You shall destroy their altars, break their sacred pillars, and cut down their wooden images," Cliff read, "for the Lord, whose name is Jealous, is a jealous god."

Cliff closed the Bible and gave a short sermon on the passage's resonance. It spoke to the danger of Cook allowing himself to be treated as a god, and the missionaries' belief that the captain had been struck down as a result. "It also speaks to the danger of *us* making Cook a god, of treating him with too much veneration," Cliff concluded.

He reached in his duffel again and brought out a volume of poetry, turning to "The Rime of the Ancient Mariner." William Wales, Cook's astronomer on the second voyage, later taught mathematics at a school attended by Samuel Taylor Coleridge. Wales's stories of the *Resolution*'s harsh journey through Antarctic ice and tropical doldrums, and the published accounts of Cook's voyage, strongly influenced the young Romantic poet. Cliff had highlighted several verses from the

"Rime" that seemed to echo Cook's travels, and handed the book to Roger to read aloud.

> *The fair breeze blew, the white foam flew,*
> *The furrow followed free;*
> *We were the first that ever burst*
> *Into that silent sea.*
> . . . .
> *Day after day, day after day,*
> *We stuck, nor breath nor motion:*
> *As idle as a painted ship,*
> *Upon a painted ocean.*

It was my turn to read. I'd brought excerpts from English diaries in which Cook's men tried to explain their captain's death. I read first from the journal of James King, perhaps Cook's greatest admirer. He saw the captain as a tragic hero, blinded by his many triumphs: "A long course of success, which C Cook had in his intercourse with Indians, had taken away, as was natural, part of that wise distrust he formerly had." Charles Clerke thought Cook put too much faith in musket fire's power to frighten natives. Events, he concluded, "would not have proceeded thus had not Capt Cook first unfortunately fir'd." Other diarists took note of the captain's renowned temper and intolerance of theft. "He was not accustomed to having his intentions frustrated by any person," wrote George Gilbert, "and had but little command over himself in his anger."

When I finished reading, Cliff shook his head. "Cook didn't know how to go backwards, did he? He'd always been in control and for once he wasn't in control of the situation, or of himself."

"He was blowing every fuse in his brain," Roger said. "It wasn't his greatest day. He doesn't come out of it covered in stardust."

Cliff stared at the lava shoreline. "A bad day on black rock," he concluded. "I'm fifty-two, a little older than Cook was. I have days like that, too."

He went to his duffel bag again and brought out a wreath. Procuring this had proved a challenge: most florists on the island were busy filling Valentine's Day orders. Cliff had finally found a man making leaf hatbands and asked him to enlarge one to wreath size. Cliff had also affixed a certificate to the wreath: "In affectionate memory of Captain James Cook R.N. Died at Kealakekua Bay 14 February 1779. From members of the Captain Cook Society." The certificate carried Cliff's contact details and the society's Web address.

"We can always use more members," he explained. Then he turned to Roger, fellow Englishman and a former soldier in Her Majesty's Army. The two of them marched several paces from the monument, turned, stood erect, then solemnly approached the obelisk, as if laying a wreath at a military cenotaph.

Roger raised the rum bottle. "To Cook!" he intoned, taking a deep pull and passing the bottle to Cliff, who stared at it uncertainly, having never tasted rum. "Think of it as communion wine," Roger said. Cliff tossed a bit down and gasped, "That's bloody awful!" Roger and I drained the rest. After our short night and long hike, the rum went straight to my head.

Only one ritual remained. Cook's men had honored the captain by firing the ships' cannons. It seemed only proper that we attempt something similar. Roger had bought the rum and Cliff the wreath. Since I was the American representative, it naturally fell to me to purchase firearms. I'd trolled dozens of shops on the island, hoping to find one of the toy guns of my youth: a tin pistol with bubbly pink caps that you loaded one by one. But the only gun I could find was a plastic snub-nosed revolver that seemed to have been modeled on a Saturday night special. The caps came in rings that you slotted into the revolver's retractable barrel. Apparently, no self-respecting youth in the twenty-first century would be caught dead reloading, as had happened to Cook's marines.

I raised the gun in the air and fired twenty-one shots in quick succession. The caps made a barely audible pop.

"That was pathetic," Roger said.

Cliff patted my shoulder. "It's the thought that counts."

He glanced at his watch. It was just after eight o'clock. I was reminded of William Bligh's account of the fight on the shore: "The whole affair from the Opening to the End did not last 10 minutes." I felt hollow and shocked, like the men aboard the *Resolution* and *Discovery*.

The morning kayak and tourist-boat traffic had arrived in the course of our ceremony. Swimmers poked up all around us in blue flippers, lime-green snorkels, and fogged masks. A few people floated inside inner tubes. Several came over to gawk at the odd spectacle we presented: a clean-shaven man in a white shirt and Captain Cook tie, holding a Bible; a tall, shambling figure in shorts and T-shirt, cradling an empty rum bottle; and a third man, looking dazed, clutching a plastic revolver.

"What's going on?" a man called out, looking curious and a bit concerned.

"Captain Cook died here exactly two hundred and twenty-two years ago," Cliff said.

"Oh."

Cliff, ever the missionary, walked to the end of the jetty and lectured the man about Cook's death and the significance of his voyages. The tourist flippered off, and a gaggle approached in kayaks. "Is this something to do with Valentine's Day?" a woman asked.

"No. Different anniversary," Cliff said. "Captain Cook's death."

"Can we still eat chocolates?" she asked, laughing as she paddled away.

Roger sprawled on the obelisk's pedestal and fell asleep beneath the still faintly visible WHITEY GO HOME graffiti, the empty rum bottle at his feet. After a while Cliff gave up proselytizing, and I wandered with him along the shore, searching for a small tablet placed to mark the exact spot where Cook had fallen. Sailors visiting the bay in the decades following Cook's death were invariably shown "the very rock on which the truly great man lost his life," as a Russian captain put it in 1804. Natives also pointed out a nearby coconut tree damaged during the skirmish. The site became an early tourist trap where natives peddled rocks, coconuts, daggers, and other "relics" that they claimed had figured in the great navigator's death, a number of which later ended up in museums around the world. The circus master P. T. Barnum even claimed to have the club that felled Cook in his collection of Native American curiosities.

Visitors to Kealakekua also carried off chunks of the lava shelf. By the 1830s, very little of it remained. Then, in 1928, on the sesquicentennial of Cook's "discovery" of Hawaii, the local historical society placed a tablet on what was left of the rock. The tablet was quickly stolen, and replaced by a new one. But as the lava shelf gradually subsided into the sea, this one had also disappeared, and yet another tablet was installed, on a rock shelf fifty feet back from the original. Cliff and I found it poking just above the shallow water. Part of the tablet was loose, as though someone had tried to dislodge it.

Still, standing on the puckered rock ledge beside the tablet, I felt I could conjure the scene on February 14, 1779. The footing was tricky: water sluiced over the rocks and formed gullies between them. It was easy to see why the boats couldn't come in close enough for Cook and his men to climb aboard. There was also ample ammunition lying around: handy chunks of lava, well formed for throwing.

I gazed out at the bay, the sheer volcanic cliff, the long sloping ridge of Mauna Loa: a beautiful and exotic panorama. "So this is it, Cook's final view of the world," I said. "He must have felt a long, long way from home." I was tired, and still tipsy from the rum; the image of Cook's last moment made my throat catch.

"I doubt he had time to think about it," Cliff said. "His last thought was probably 'Come on, lads, get the boats in and let's get out of here!' "

Most likely, Cliff was right. Cook was a man of action and died that way. Then again, combat wasn't his element. He'd rarely experienced it during his voyages, and had never seen crowded, chaotic fighting like that which unfolded here. "You can see how he was cornered," Cliff said. "He probably couldn't see the others well, and it was hard to keep his footing. It was every man for himself. He had nowhere to go but in the water."

Cliff looked at me and tilted his head in the direction of the bay. I nodded. We left our clothes on the rock and waded into the water. At the end of the rock shelf, the water became deep and clear, and parrotfish flitted all around. Cliff, whose pallid torso and legs looked as though they'd never been touched by sunlight, paddled uncertainly in the shallows, too close to the rocks. He emerged with ugly cuts all over his feet and shins.

"Left my blood on the rocks," he said. "A blood brother to Cook."

"You've already outlived the man," I pointed out.

Cliff smiled wanly. "I've just outswum him, too."

ONCE THE SHOCK of Cook's death began to abate, the desire for revenge set in among his men. Even Charles Clerke, who was so wasted by tuberculosis that he could barely leave his bed, wrote a day after the melee: "I had some notion of taking a stout party onshore, making what distruction among them I could, then burn the Town, Canoes &c."

As if the death of Cook and the marines weren't incitement enough, the Hawaiians gloated over their victory. The day after the fight, they began taunting the English, strutting on the beach in the uniforms of the dead marines and brandishing Cook's sword. Several men also bared their backsides and slapped them. Worse still, the Hawaiians gave no sign of returning the bodies. They told the English that Cook's corpse "was cut to pieces & carried a great way off," King wrote. "They talk'd with unconcernedness & seeming Satisfaction of having thus dealt with it."

Then, on February 16, under the cover of dark, a priest who had always been friendly to the English came out in a canoe, carrying a bundle containing Cook's thigh. The rest of the body, he said, had been burned "with some peculiar kind of ceremony," Clerke wrote, "and the bones distributed among the king and chiefs." James King believed the priest had brought Cook's flesh as a friendly offering, and had defied the chiefs in so doing. But others on the ship didn't react that way.

"Distraction & madness," one sailor wrote, "was in every mind, and revenge the result of all." The next day, a native paddled out, twirled Cook's hat, and flung stones at the ship while a crowd on shore laughed and jeered. "This was too gross an insult to bear," wrote Clerke, who responded by firing the ships' cannons into the crowd on the beach. He then sent an armed party ashore to collect water and issued the men ambiguous orders: Don't provoke a fight unless provoked to do so.

When islanders threw stones at the watering party, the English shot six of them dead. Later, when the stone-throwing resumed, sailors went berserk, setting fire to about 150 homes, including those of the priests. Then they shot at the fleeing inhabitants. "Others of the

Natives who stayed in thier houses were run thro' by Bayonets," wrote the *Discovery*'s surgeon, John Law. "When they [the sailors] had Murdered these Defenceless people they severed the heads and stuck them on the boats as Trophies." Crewmen put two of the decapitated heads atop poles and waved them at natives gathered on a nearby hill. They also seized and bound an elderly man, and taunted him with one of their ghastly trophies.

This barbarous spasm certainly qualifies as the Kurtz-like behavior condemned by the anthropologist Obeyesekere. But the episode can also be read as a testimonial to Cook's leadership, and as partial exculpation of the harsh discipline he doled out to his men. The sailors were a very rough lot, and so long as Cook was captain, their most violent and destructive impulses were kept in check: by unceasing labor, by the lash, and by Cook's generally restrained and humane example. Charles Clerke, a more populist commander than Cook, and desperately ill, couldn't keep a lid on his men's brutality. Nor did he condemn it, although James King did. "Our people in this days transaction did many reprehensible things," he wrote of the slaughter, which he blamed on the men's desire for vengeance. "A common sailor with such a disposition & suffered to have its full operation, would soon equal the Cruelty of the most savage indian."

AT MIDDAY, WE began the long hike back from Cook's monument, pausing a third of the way up to search for the last stop on our pilgrimage: the Puhina O Lono, or mortuary temple, where Cook's body was taken after his death. Hawaiians believed that *mana,* or godly power, resided in hair and human bones, particularly the jaw, because of its association with speech. So islanders dissected Cook's body on a large flat stone and roasted it to remove the organs and flesh. These parts were regarded as refuse and generally thrown in the sea. Hawaiian stories, collected decades later, told of two boys having eaten Cook's heart and innards, thinking they belonged to a dog. One Cook-hating Hawaiian historian, an early convert to Christianity, even claimed that Cook's entrails were used to rope off a cockfight arena, while his hands became flyswatters. "Such is the end of the transgressor," he wrote.

Scholars differ as to whether the ceremonial baking of Cook's body represented a symbolic sacrifice and offering of a potent enemy to their war god, or an instance of the reverential treatment that Hawaiians accorded their own high chiefs. What is clear is that Cook's bones became revered objects, rather like saints' relics. For years afterward, priests carried Cook's remains from temple to temple in the annual Lono procession. In the early nineteenth century, a visiting missionary learned that Cook's bones were kept in wickerwork and covered in red feathers, as were those of Hawaii's most revered kings. Like royal remains, Cook's were also hidden in various sacred places, such as the caves above Kealakekua Bay, the nearby temple to Lono, and other sites around the island associated with the god. Only a few priests would have known their precise location, and the secret probably died with them when the old religion was abandoned in the 1820s.

Questions also shroud the precise disposition of the remains that Hawaiians returned to the English, in several bundles: part of Cook's legs and arms; his hands and feet; and his skull, minus the jaw. King wrote only that these body parts "were put into a Coffin & thrown into the sea." Sailors tolled bells and crossed the ships' yards, setting them awry: a naval mourning custom, intended to give vessels a disheveled appearance. By committing Cook's remains to the deep, the English unwittingly completed Hawaiian burial rites; they tossed body parts lacking *mana* into the sea.

As Cliff had revealed to Roger and me during our visit to London, that wasn't quite the end of the story. In 1824, the Hawaiian king Kamehameha II, a convert to Christianity, decided to sail to England with his queen aboard a whaling ship commanded by Valentine Star-buck. Cliff had discovered nineteenth-century documents mentioning that the king carried with him an arrow made from Cook's shinbone, which Kamehameha hoped to present to the captain's widow, or to the nation. But both the king and queen contracted measles and died soon after their arrival in London. Cliff was still trying to track down the whereabouts of the arrow, which apparently remained in England and had been mentioned in a letter as late as 1878.

The bodies of Kamehameha and his wife were returned to Hawaii aboard a ship commanded by Anson Byron, cousin of the poet George. It was Anson Byron who first sought out the temple where Cook had been cut up and burned. He erected a ship's capstan bar with an inscribed copper plate, which read, in part: "This humble monument is erected by his fellow countrymen, A.D. 1825." Like other monuments to Cook at Kealakekua, it hadn't fared well. Forty-one years after Byron's visit, Mark Twain described the temple as "a large inclosure like an ample hogpen," with the inscription on the capstan no longer legible. Twain added, "This [the temple] is not properly a monument, since it was erected by the natives themselves, and less to do honor to the circumnavigator than for the sake of convenience in roasting him."

We'd seen the temple site marked on local maps, and spotted it fifty yards from the main trail on our return hike. "So that's where Cook was cooked," Roger declared, too tired to care. He continued up the steep path without us. Cliff and I scrambled over the rough lava for a closer look. The local historical society had restored the site in 1928, setting Byron's oak post in concrete, laying a new plaque under glass, and adding a gate. The plaque was now gone, the gate rusted and almost off its hinges. But the post survived, a flagstaff with no flag.

There wasn't much else to see, just a tumbling rock enclosure with a few shrubs struggling through the rubble. Cliff pulled weeds from between boulders in a vain effort to tidy the site, but gave up after a few minutes, his shirt soaked with sweat, his hands black with lava. Since arriving in Hawaii ten days before, he had spent hours at museums and libraries in Honolulu, and on the Big Island, vainly searching for more clues about the fate of Cook's remains. "I felt like I had a mission to lay him to rest," he said, slumping on a rock. "Now I don't know what else to do." He looked toward the cliffs above the bay, filled with caves that once served as sacred graves. "If he's up there somewhere, I'm content."

I sat down next to him and gazed out at the scene. Perched on a bluff, the temple site offered a commanding view of wide-open ocean and part of Kealakekua Bay, with a glimpse in the far distance of the sacred "place of refuge." There were no snorkelers or kayakers cluttering the vista: almost no sign of humanity as far as the eye could see. I looked at the wooden post and thought back to all the Cook monuments I'd visited: imperial statues, ugly cairns, grandiosely inscribed obelisks. Somehow, this humble pillar of ship's oak, sturdy and lone, seemed the most eloquent and appropriate memorial of all.

THE NEXT DAY, I woke up late to find Cliff composing an ode about Kealakekua Bay. "It's not Coleridge," he said, showing me the last stanza:

> Whilst high above the sea-birds call
> And o'er their leafy plain,
> The cliffs maintain their silence
> On what secrets lie within.

Cliff was scheduled to fly home the next day, a little ahead of us. Both he and Roger seemed content to lounge around the hotel. But there was one more person I wanted to see, a man I hoped could answer some of the questions about Cook's death that still nagged at me. Herb Kawainui Kane was a noted painter of Hawaiian historical scenes and a one-man engine of the islands' cultural renaissance. Among other things, he'd helped design and sail a lateen-rigged outrigger from Hawaii to Tahiti and back, to demonstrate how Polynesians had spread across the Pacific by celestial navigation. Best of all, he took a particular interest in Cook and lived in Captain Cook, on a bluff overlooking Kealakekua Bay.

"On a clear day, I can see the monument from here," Herb said, as we settled on his verandah. On a foggy, voggy day like this one, the view was still spectacular. Beneath us spread Herb's garden and orchards, a panorama of hibiscus, macadamia, avocado, coconut palm, and coffee. Brilliant saffron finches swooped from tree to tree. This was the edge of Kona's coffee country, a twenty-mile slope where morning sun, afternoon cloud, and almost daily rain created a microclimate ideal for producing mild, aromatic beans.

Herb didn't look quite like anyone I'd met in Hawaii. Seventy-two, tall, with a full head of dark hair, he wore pressed white trousers, a white sweater, and deck shoes—almost formal attire in a place where most people went around in shorts and sandals, and donned a loud aloha shirt if they felt like dressing up. Herb's features, Asian, yet large and rugged, were also unusual.

"I'm chop suey, like everyone else here," he said, when I asked about his lineage. His father, part Hawaiian and part Chinese, had left the island as a young man and worked his way around the mainland, ending up in Wisconsin, where he met Herb's Danish-American mother. This polyglot background, and Herb's own time on the mainland—he'd attended the Art Institute of Chicago and worked in the city for many years as a graphic artist—informed his paintings of Hawaiian historical scenes.

"It's a little like method acting," he said. "I want to get inside the heads of Hawaiians *and* Europeans at the time of first contact, try to think like they did." Herb found it relatively easy to do this with Cook and his men, thanks to their journals and artwork. Recapturing the mind-set of eighteenth-century Hawaiians was much harder, even though Herb had known many traditional folk during his childhood in a remote valley at the other end of the island.

"Every Polynesian village had what was called a *wahanui,* or big mouth," he said. "They were adept at divining what an interviewer wanted to hear and feeding it to them. A lot of anthropologists have fallen for that, believing everything they're told. And a lot of Hawaiians today want to sanctify anything that comes down through their own culture. But you can't take everything at face value."

English sources could be unreliable, too. Herb opened one of his many books on Cook to a famous watercolor by John Webber, the *Resolution*'s artist, showing Hawaiians paddling a sail-rigged canoe. What made the work so striking was the men's attire: weird, medieval-looking helmets crafted from gourd, with eye holes and nose holes, fern crests poking out of the top, and beardlike strips of tapa hanging from the chin. None of these masks had survived to the present day, nor was there any record of them apart from Webber's paintings and sketches.

Webber's oft-reproduced image had spawned a contemporary, popularized imitation: cheap little helmets of the same design, made of coconut or plastic rather than gourd. I'd seen them for sale at souvenir shops and hanging from rearview mirrors. Herb said that Hawaiians regarded them as a generic symbol of their culture, and as a lucky charm.

While Herb regarded Webber's work as an irreplaceable window into eighteenth-century Hawaii, he also brought an artist's critical eye to bear on the painter. Influenced by the Classical revival in Europe, Webber and other artists tended to endow Polynesians with idealized Greco-Roman proportions. "Too lean, too long in the leg," Herb said. Later engravings of the work magnified Webber's distortion, making the men much too big in relation to the canoe's hull and rigging.

Herb showed me his own rendition of the scene, one of a dozen paintings he'd done of Cook's visit to Hawaii. He'd corrected the scale and detail of the canoe, reduced the number of men in it, and added bold, high-contrast coloring that was truer to the way Kealakekua Bay looked on a summer's day. "I was curious," Herb said, "to re-create what it was Webber really saw."

Herb had gone to much more meticulous extremes while crafting his masterwork, *The Death of Cook, February 14, 1779*. Webber's famed rendition of the same scene included obvious inaccuracies, such as placing the skirmish at the base of Kealakekua's dramatic cliff rather than on the flat plain near Ka'awaloa. Webber also substituted a sandy beach for the black lava shelf on which the fighting occurred.

Webber's image became a model for many later works by artists who hadn't witnessed the scene, and both painters and writers gradually mythologized Cook's death into a heroic act of martyrdom. Several crewmen, for instance, later wrote that Cook had raised his arm at the end, not to call in the boats but to halt his men from firing on natives (no one had advanced this notion at the time of his death). One famous painting, *The Apotheosis of Captain Cook,* showed Cook being carried into the heavens above the bay by the figures of Fame and Britannia.

In his own work, Herb stripped all this away like so much bad varnish. He depicted Cook in the canvas pants he'd probably worn, rather than the formal britches and hose shown in most paintings. Herb painted Cook's dagger-wielding assailants in the brilliant red-and-yellow feathered dress of chiefly warriors. Herb had even contacted Hawaii's Hydrographic Office to plot moon phases on a computer, so he could estimate the tide at eight A.M. on February 14, 1779. From geologists he learned that the lava shoreline had subsided precisely twenty-eight inches since then. So Herb snorkeled out to study the contour of the submerged lava shelf. Finally, because English diarists described the day as having been sunny, Herb painted Kealakekua with the sharp early-morning shadows it would have had at the instant of Cook's death.

The result was a historical reconstruction that gave the scene a documentary quality, about as close to the original moment as it was possible to get. Losing myself in the painting's detail, I felt the same time-travel thrill I'd often experienced when gazing at Civil War photographs. Herb had drawn together the past and present, art and science, the English and native perspective. It was a painterly version of what I'd been struggling to do in my own search for Cook.

Herb brought the same balance and precision to his writings about the captain in books and scholarly journals. On the debate over whether Hawaiians saw Cook as Lono or merely as a potent chief, Herb thought the problem was largely semantic. "There's no word in Hawaiian for religion or for 'god' as we understand it today," he said. Missionaries, who tried to make sense of Hawaiian belief in Christian terms, mistakenly took the word *akua* to mean "god," when it actually conveyed a deeply non-Western concept more akin to "spirit." Herb believed that precontact Hawaiians had no sense of a separate, supernatural sphere. Rather, *akua* represented ancestral spirits within nature whose powers were greater, but not wholly different, from those of ordinary men.

In Herb's view, you didn't need a Ph.D. in anthropology to understand what happened when Cook became wrathful and threatening toward the king on February 14. "He started the day by firing cannons at canoes and sending out armed boats," Herb said. "That's going to get people nervous." Then, marching ashore with his marines and going up to the king's house, "Cook does the unmentionable social blunder of all ages—waking someone up. And he sends his underling, Phillips, in to do it. Very bad form." Later, as tensions rose by the water, Cook blundered again by opening fire. "What he doesn't seem to understand is that the people around the king are bodyguards, it's their role to put themselves between the ruler and any potential danger." The rest, as they say, is history.

This wasn't a particularly ennobling vision of Cook's death. But I found it satisfying, like Herb's paintings. Stick to the facts. Consider both sides. Don't embroider what's already a good story. An homage, really, to Cook's own way of seeing.

Herb brought out a bottle of wine and offered a final thought. In his efforts to get inside the heads of both sailors and Hawaiians in 1779, he'd begun to wonder if the two groups had had more in common with each other than they did with either Europeans or Polynesians today. "Your average sailor, your Jack Tar, was from a farming background, and from a very hierarchical society," Herb said. "He did what other people told him to do, he lived in fear of his superiors, probably resented them too. He wasn't a son of the Enlightenment, he was a superstitious, tradition-bound, often violent person."

Sailors' religious beliefs and material culture were obviously very different from those of Hawaiian commoners. But in broad human terms, their status and outlook had kinships. "Most of the big changes that define modern life, things like technology and democracy, have come since Cook's day," Herb said.

He therefore suspected that contact between the English and Hawaiians might have been richer and more nuanced than we tend to think. "The sex, for instance. I don't believe it was simply prostitution. In a way, the women were doing sexually what the priests were doing ceremonially with Cook: bringing strangers into their society. And hoping, no doubt, that once the English felt at home they'd feel obliged to reciprocate."

We watched the sun set over Kealakekua Bay. "To me, a lot of the story is about trying to break down walls, on both sides," Herb concluded. "It's a pity we don't remember it that way."

LATE THAT NIGHT I woke in our hotel room at the King Kamehameha, though it took me a few moments to figure out where I was. I'd spent half my working life on the road and often awakened in unfamiliar places, feeling so dislocated that I'd reach for Geraldine, or walk into a wall thinking it was the door to my bathroom at home. This was an aspect of travel I found both unsettling and exhilarating, as though I'd drifted away from any real mooring in time or place and become a true wandering Jew.

Lying awake, listening to Roger's rummy snores, I thought about

Herb's parting comments and the chord they'd struck in me. I'd been traveling the Pacific, on and off, for only eighteen months, during which I'd been tethered to home by telephone, e-mail, and hotel TV. I couldn't even begin to grasp what it had been like to stay continuously at sea for twice that long—and, in Cook's case, to make such a voyage three times—completely cut off from familiar surroundings, with the strong possibility that you'd never return home. Shipboard routine provided an anchor of sorts, with its bells and watches, dreary rations, and the claustrophobic companionship of other sailors. But there were no women on board, no old people, no children. For Cook and his men, the life they'd known in England must have come to seem very unreal.

I tried to imagine, then, how the men felt each time they came ashore in Hawaii or Tonga or Tahiti, however strange these societies may have first seemed to them. Fresh food, terra firma, and female flesh were, no doubt, the main attractions of land. But there must have been something else: a desperate need to connect, for lack of a better word. They must have felt it particularly after their long, brutal sail to the frigid, scantly settled Arctic. Pacific islands became a home away from home, however tentative. The friendships the English formed with islanders, their eagerness to learn the local language, their tattoos, and their fascination with native customs and rituals—all this spoke to a desire to feel at home and fit in.

Islanders, for the most part warm and hospitable and curious, reciprocated. Tahitians adopted individual crewmen as *tiao*, or friend, a complex relationship that included the exchanging of names (hence, chiefs became *Toote* while Cook assumed their names). The English didn't completely understand this custom or the reciprocal obligations it implied. But as Herb said, the two peoples may have felt a kinship, or forged one, in a way that was hard to appreciate now, influenced as we are by the horrors that resulted from first contact, and by the prevailing notion that all viewpoints are "culturally determined," creating an almost unbridgeable divide between Western and non-Western societies. "A sort of Intimacy & dependance on each other began to come on," the astronomer William Wales wrote of the *Resolution*'s brief stay during the second voyage at the New Hebrides, where the

English and islanders had initially exchanged only arrow shots and musket fire.

For all the violence and exploitation that occurred during Cook's voyages, what struck me in the end was that the English, and those they encountered, had managed to communicate and, in most cases, to get along. The two groups came from opposite ends of the globe, usually knew nothing of each other, and often had not so much as a single word in common. Yet they almost always made themselves understood: with a smile, an embrace or nose-press, the presentation of a plant as a sign of peace, the offer of a gift. Hostile or derisive gestures—not just the brandishing of weapons, but the baring of buttocks and other taunts—also seemed to have universal meaning.

Among the many examples of this Esperanto, one encounter on the third voyage illustrated it best. Seeking a safe harbor in Nootka Sound, on the coast of today's British Columbia, the English found themselves surrounded by natives in canoes who appeared more alien than any they'd ever confronted. "It will require the assistance of ones imagination to have an adequate Idea of the Wild, savage appearance & Action of these first Visitors," wrote James King, the most charitable observer aboard the *Resolution*. The natives' faces were "bedaub'd with red & black Paint & Grease, in no regular manner," King wrote; they had "small black Eyes void of fire" and an "expression of the countenance unmeaning"; and some wore "frightful" masks of distorted bird and animal faces. At the sight of the English, they worked themselves "into the highest frenzy," King added, shaking rattles and "uttering something between a howl & a song."

Cook calmly offered beads and medals to a man standing in one of the canoes. "He threw into the Ship in return some dried herrings," King wrote. Then "a man repeated a few words in tune, & regulated the meaning by beating against the Canoe sides, after which they all join'd in a song, that was by no means unpleasant to the Ear." Sensing that they'd gratified the English, the natives repeated the song.

"We judg'd they might like our musick, & we ordered the Fife & drum to play a tune," King wrote, as dusk fell on Nootka Sound. "They Observed the Profoundest silence, & we were sorry that the Dark hind'red our seeing the effect of this musick on their countenances. Not to be outdone in Politeness, they gave us another song, & we then entertain'd them with French horns, to which they were equally attentive."

The English ended up staying almost a month in Nootka Sound, with "no serious quarrels," King wrote. They engaged in a lively trade with coastal dwellers, dined on wild garlic and spruce beer, and compiled a lexicon of several hundred words and phrases, including "What is your name?," "friendship," and "Admiration or applause." King and other crewmen continued to enjoy natives' music and came to admire their exceptional skill at wood carving, as well as the boldness and fierce "independency of spirit" that had initially struck the English as bellicose.

To the young lieutenant, on his first Pacific voyage, all this was noteworthy. Cook, who had witnessed many such scenes during almost a decade of exploration, didn't bother to mention the first meeting at Nootka Sound in his journal. But his actions, and the words he wrote about many other such encounters, reveal the captain's extraordinary confidence not only in himself, but in the commonality of man.

If there was an overriding message in his journals, it was that people, the world over, were alike in their essential nature—even if they ate their enemies, made love in public, worshipped idols, or, like Aborigines, cared not at all for material goods. No matter how strange another society might at first appear, there were almost always grounds for mutual understanding and respect.

This was a radical notion in eighteenth-century Europe. And it seemed relevant to me more than two hundred years later, at a time when so much of the world appeared perilously divided along ethnic, religious, and ideological lines.

THE NEXT DAY, we drove to the airport to drop Cliff off for his flight back to London. I gave him an awkward hug while Roger joked that Cliff was now a world traveler, obliged to keep exploring. "Hell no," he said, hoisting his duffel bag. "I'm going back to my secure little hole in England. I may never go anywhere again."

Roger and I still had twenty-four hours on the island. It was our last day in Polynesia, the end of our long voyage in Cook's wake. Some part of me still felt restless for new territory. So I cajoled Roger into forsaking a lazy day on the beach and driving to the north end of the island, to a place called the Waipi'o Valley. Herb Kane had spent much of his childhood there, and his paintings of Waipi'o depicted it as a wild and magical place. Waipi'o also had a connection to Cook that I wanted to explore.

We drove away from the sunny Kona coast and into arid, empty ranchland. Then, as we climbed the slope of Mauna Kea—Snowy Mountain, James King called it—the landscape turned wet and cool. Hawaii was really two islands, the leeward side dry and lava-covered, the windward flank fertile and soaked, one of the wettest places in America.

The narrow road leading to Waipi'o ended at a precipice overlooking the mile-wide valley, which opened onto the sea. Only horseback riders, hikers, and four-wheel-drive vehicles were allowed on the rugged switchback winding down to the valley floor. The few walkers we saw straggling up were breathless and drenched in sweat. "Oh God, ironman stuff again," Roger said. "I'll take in the view from up here." He glanced over the edge and retreated to the car, easing back the seat and closing his eyes.

I headed down the switchback, grateful for the quiet and solitude. I'd spent just a week in the constant company of Roger and Cliff. Little wonder that Cook, sequestered for months aboard his cramped, overcrowded ships, often headed off for a solitary hike as soon as he reached land.

After a half-dozen turns, the view from the trail opened up. I could hear waves crashing on the beach. Birds swooped back and forth across the valley, wafting on air currents. From here, Waipi'o resembled a lush version of the Grand Canyon: an immense trench, more than a thousand feet deep, with a river snaking along the valley floor. It took me half an hour of scuffling in a backward-leaning trot to reach the bottom, which was marked with an alarming road sign.

WARNING! WARNING!
DO NOT STOP—STOPPING MAY BE HAZARDOUS.
ROAD FLOODS. SLIPPERY WHEN WET.
ENGAGE FOUR-WHEEL DRIVE. PROCEED AT YOUR OWN RISK.

Not surprisingly, there wasn't a vehicle in sight. Except for the caw-ing birds and crashing surf, the scene was silent. A steady rain pelted down. The valley before me looked jungly, the way I imagined the Mekong Delta or an Amazonian rain forest: swamped paddies, huge-fronded palms, trees dripping with rain and fruit, the whole scene so green it seemed to vibrate. More than at any moment in my Pacific travels, I suddenly felt very far away, alone in a landscape utterly for-eign to me. Funny that this should happen in my own country, an hour's drive from a cookie-cut sprawl of fast-food joints and tourist hotels.

I plunged on, my normally nature-impaired senses alert to every sound and smell. I tasted a berry, red and tart, and picked pink flowers and other plants I couldn't identify. Closing my eyes, I listened to the thrum of insects. Where a stream ran across the road, I took off my sandals and left them in some bushes, along with my soaked shirt and knapsack.

Herb Kane had told me that during his childhood, the six-mile-long valley supported hundreds of farmers, as well as a general store, churches, and a Chinese temple. The valley had also been rife with ille-gal stills, brewing the ti plant into a potent liquor called *okolehao,* which translated as "iron ass." Now, very few people remained, and the handful of farmsteads I passed appeared ramshackle.

After walking a mile or so, I spotted a man with his head under the hood of a pickup. He seemed a bit startled to see a barefoot, shirtless stranger wandering into his yard, soaked with rain and clutching a bunch of leaves and berries. I asked him how much farther it was to the base of a waterfall I'd seen cascading down the mountain on the distant side of the valley.

"You won't get there, not today," he said, wiping a wrench on his trousers. "Road's flooded." The man was heavily tattooed and looked, like so many other people on the island, to be a mix of Hawai-ian and Asian. He studied me for a moment and asked, "You a plant collector?"

"Oh. No. Just picking a few things. Wondered what they were."

I held my small bouquet out to him and asked what grew in the val-ley. "Taro mostly, and ferns, red ginger, monkey paw, mango, guava, orange, coconut, apple, banana, breadfruit, lotus, candlenut. Few other things." He paused. "You can throw a seed out the window of your truck and it takes root here. It's about the most fertile place on earth."

"Lono-land," I said. He looked at me strangely, as if I was on drugs. I'd seen a lot of hippies in Hawaii; many of them probably chose the valley for hallucinogenic hikes. "Lono, the god of fertility," I went on. "He rode down from the heavens on a rainbow to woo his bride by the waterfall here." This was one of the stories I'd read about Waipi'o.

"Oh yeah, I heard that one, lots of rainbows here," he said. "Then Captain Cook came and they thought he was Lono and killed him. They say he's buried up in the cliffs beside the waterfall."

I'd heard that one, too. In the many Hawaiian stories about Cook's bones, several mentioned that his remains had been secreted in a cave in Waipi'o, where island royalty had been buried for centuries. In pre-contact Hawaii, Waipi'o was the Valley of the Kings, a religious and political center, and home to a place of refuge like the one I'd visited near Kealakekua.

"What do you think, is he up there?" I asked.

The man shrugged. "Dunno, brah. You'd need a rainbow to check it out." He chuckled, shook his head, and stuck it back under the hood of his pickup.

I walked on until I reached water running waist-high across the road: as far as a man could go. The rain sluiced down, and the cliff tops were lost in mist. I could just make out a few caves in the rock face, far above. I waited awhile, hoping for a rainbow, then turned to begin the long trip home.

EPILOGUE:

A Period to His Labours

Ah! Those were the glorious days; but we are all going
now. —ALEXANDER HOME, MASTER'S MATE,
RECALLING COOK'S VOYAGES

In June 1779, four months after leaving Hawaii, the *Resolution* and *Discovery* reached the Kamchatkan harbor of St. Peter and St. Paul. Charles Clerke dispatched a letter to the Admiralty, informing his superiors of Cook's death. He also pledged to push on with the search for a northern passage: "Whatever can be done, shall be done."

The *Resolution* "leaked confoundedly," Clerke wrote, its trusty chronometer had stopped, and the captain's health was failing fast. But he pushed his ships to 70 degrees north, just a few miles short of the latitude Cook had reached the previous summer. Then the sea, once again, became "Choak'd with Ice."

Retreating south toward Kamchatka, Clerke grew too weak to write. He dictated a final letter to Joseph Banks. "My ever honoured friend. The disorder I was attacked with in the King's bench prison has proved consumptive," Clerke began. "It has now so far got the better of me that I am not able to turn myself in my bed, so that my stay in this world must be of very short duration. However, I hope my friends will have no occasion to blush in owning themselves such."

Clerke recommended several of his men for "a share in your friendship" and promised Banks the plants and artificial curiosities collected on the voyage. "Now, my dear and honoured friend, I must bid you a final adieu. May you enjoy many happy years in this world, & in the end attain that fame your indefatigable industry so richly deserves. These are most sincerely the warmest and sincerest wishes of your devoted, affectionate, departing servant."

Clerke departed four days later, at the age of thirty-eight, and was buried in Kamchatka beneath willows planted by his crew. Clerke, remembered by one sailor as a "wag and lusty extrovert," would have appreciated the leisure his men enjoyed in Kamchatka, courtesy of their Russian hosts: bear hunting, fiddle playing, and country dancing. Catherine the Great was a great admirer of Cook and his men, and a monument to Clerke still stands near his burial site in Petropavlovsk.

John Gore, the stolid American survivor of his fourth Pacific voyage, took command of the *Resolution* for the long homeward journey, unaware that his native land had declared its independence from Britain more than two years before. James King commanded the *Discovery*. In Macao, on the Chinese coast, sailors sold the pelts they'd collected in Canada and Alaska. News of the astronomical prices they received—as well as Cook's writing about the commercial potential of the Pacific Northwest—would ignite the fur trade and spark the trailblazing of American "mountain men."

The stop at Macao proved the crew's last bit of good fortune. Reaching the coast of Britain in the summer of 1780, after four years at sea, the ships couldn't land because of contrary winds, and lingered for an agonizing month off the Orkneys. Samuel Gibson, the marine who had deserted in Tahiti on the first voyage, only to sail with Cook twice more and survive the fight at Kealakekua Bay, made his way ashore and married. He died of disease just a few days before the ships finally reached the Thames on October 4, 1780.

Clerke's letter from Kamchatka had preceded the ships to England by nine months. When Elizabeth Cook received the news, she was embroidering a waistcoat of Tahitian cloth for her husband to wear at court. With no body or grave to mourn over, she took to wearing a ring containing Cook's hair. Widowed at thirty-eight, with three sons, she also felt the loss of the "easy retirement" at Greenwich Hospital once promised to her husband. In 1781, she wrote to Lord Sandwich, pleading for proceeds from the published history of Cook's third voyage. "Consider us for such compensation as you may deem us deserving of by his merit," Elizabeth wrote, in a fine, clear hand, "untill his unfortunate Death put a period to his Labours whereby we became great sufferers from his not returning safe home."

Elizabeth eventually received half the profits from the history, which sold out within three days of its publication. She also garnered a generous pension and other gratuities that afforded her a comfortable lifestyle, attended by a footman. Elizabeth may have drawn consolation, too, from the praise lavished on her husband's memory. Medals were struck, panegyrics written, a coat of arms posthumously conferred. The Theatre Royal in Covent Garden staged a show called *Omai: Or, a Trip Round the World,* which ended with a tapestry of Cook's apotheosis lowered onto the stage as a chorus of "Indians" sang: "Mourn, Owhyee's fatal shore/ For Cook, our great Orono, is no more."

Elizabeth also took comfort from her three surviving children, whom she described in a letter as "my greatest pleasure now remaining." Two had gone to sea very young and had risen much more quickly than their father had done a generation before. By listing Nathaniel and James on the *Endeavour*'s muster roll when they were only four and five, Cook had hastened their naval careers.

This proved, however, no blessing. Nathaniel Cook was a fifteen-year-old midshipman when his ship went down in a hurricane off Jamaica. His older brother, James, began his naval education at the age of eleven and made commander at thirty. On a winter's night in 1794, he boarded a longboat on the south coast of England to take command of his first ship—and was later found stripped of his clothes and possessions, with a wound to his head, dead on the shore of the Isle of Wight. The longboat's crew was never discovered.

A few months before James washed ashore, his brother Hugh, the last of the Cooks' six children—he was born just prior to his father's departure on the third voyage—went to study for the clergy at Cambridge. Described as a "fine tall youth," Hugh was the only Cook child of whom a portrait survives. He appears in the painting as a handsome scholar of seventeen, with his father's long straight nose but none of the captain's austerity. Soon after arriving at Cambridge, Hugh contracted scarlet fever; he died on his parents' wedding anniversary. James Cook's line had ended.

Elizabeth Cook retired to her bed for two years, and then lived for another thirty-nine, donning black on the anniversary of each of her children's deaths. She survived to the age of ninety-three and was buried beside two of her sons in Cambridge. Elizabeth left part of her considerable estate to "six poor widows" in the parish of Clapham, where she'd dwelled for the latter half of her life. The only monument to her memory is a small fountain in Australia.

The soft job that Elizabeth had wished for her husband, as captain at the Greenwich Hospital, went instead to John Gore. The next ranking survivor of the third voyage, James King, was also promoted to captain, and took several veterans of Cook's journeys along on his first command. They were at King's bedside in Nice when he died at the age of thirty-four from tuberculosis, as had so many of Cook's officers. The men may well have contracted the disease from one another in the close quarters of Cook's ships.

Many other young men who served under Cook went on to distinguished naval careers—posthumous testimony to the captain's skills as a mentor. More than twenty of them became commanders; Isaac Manley, just twelve when he joined the *Endeavour* as Cook's servant, and Isaac Smith, a sixteen-year-old midshipman on the same ship, both rose to the rank of admiral, outstripping Cook. George Vancouver, who sailed on the second and third voyages and was almost beaten to death at Kealakekua Bay, later commanded his own great voyage of exploration to the Pacific, during which he completed and corrected Cook's survey of the North American coast.

Others became freelance adventurers, most notably John Ledyard, the Connecticut-born marine. Dispatched to fight the Americans in the closing days of the Revolutionary War, he deserted, sold his story of the third voyage, and concocted his own grand scheme for exploring the north Pacific. With the encouragement of Thomas Jefferson, Ledyard set off on a solo walk across Russia, with the intention of sailing from Siberia to Alaska and then crossing the uncharted interior of the North American continent from west to east. Ledyard's circumambulation of the globe was aborted at Irkutsk, where he was arrested as a suspected spy and escorted back west to the Polish frontier.

Undaunted, Ledyard went to London and, with Joseph Banks's help, won sponsorship from the Association for Promoting the Discovery

EPILOGUE

of the Interior Parts of Africa, to lead an expedition in search of Timbuktu and the source of the Niger. Ledyard got as far as Cairo, where he died of food poisoning at the age of thirty-seven. Jefferson's dream of one day dispatching Ledyard from Kentucky to the west coast of America would have to wait for two men by the names of Lewis and Clark.

Others who served under Cook also went on to colorful, if not always illustrious, ends. Lieutenant James Burney abandoned his wife, eloped with his half sister, and wrote "An Essay by Way of Lecture, on the Game of Whist." The talented artist William Hodges gave up painting for banking, at which he quickly failed, and soon after died of a laudanum overdose. Then there was William Bligh, whose story needs no repeating, except to note that several veterans of Cook's voyages were set adrift with the captain following the mutiny on the *Bounty.* The irascible Bligh also nursed a lifelong grudge toward his shipmates on the *Resolution,* accusing them of failing to recognize his navigational achievements. "I must take another opportunity, to declare," he groused in a letter to Burney in 1791, "that the Sandwich Islands published with Cook's Voyages are entirely my survey—the Friendly Islands the same." Bligh would go on to survive two more mutinies and die old and bitter in 1817.

The hundreds of men who served on Cook's lower decks left much fainter tracks on the historical record. Some fought in the American Revolution and Napoleonic Wars, or ferried convicts to Botany Bay. One sailor wrote a song about his voyage with Cook. Others fell on hard times and wrote to Joseph Banks in hopes the wealthy botanist would remember them. "I am one of the Men that went round the world with you and Captain Cook," began a letter from a crippled seaman in 1808, a full forty years after the *Endeavour*'s voyage. Banks kept a careful record of such correspondence. "Gave him a guinea" was a typical reply.

Banks also became, in effect, the executor of Cook's legacy. As president of the Royal Society for forty-one years, he promoted the colonization of Australia and the many voyages—by Bligh, Vancouver, the London Missionary Society, and others—that expanded on Cook's discoveries and helped build the empire. Banks turned Kew Gardens into an experimental plot for plants from around the world. He also dispatched sheep and cattle to Australia and dispensed human skulls and other curiosities to collectors and anatomists across Europe. (Australian Aborigines are now seeking the return of shields and spears the English took from Botany Bay, as well as skeletons spirited away by later visitors.)

With time, the rakishly handsome young botanist of the *Endeavour* voyage became fat, jowly, and gout-ridden. Banks died in 1820 at the age of seventy-seven, with no known offspring, just eighteen days after resigning as president of the Royal Society. His great botany collection now resides in the herbarium of London's Natural History Museum, in polished wood cabinets from Banks's Soho house. But Banks never completed the multivolumed work he'd planned on the *Endeavour*'s botanical discoveries; not until the 1980s were the hundreds of copper plates made from Sydney Parkinson's drawings finally published.

Cook's ships met with similar neglect. The Navy sold the *Endeavour* in 1775, then leased it back to transport Hessian mercenaries to fight against the Americans. The *Resolution* was sold into the whaling trade. In a believe-it-or-not twist, marine archaeologists have recently discovered that the two ships came to rest in the same waters, at the bottom of Newport Harbor in Rhode Island. When a French fleet threatened the harbor in 1778, the English formed a blockade by sinking a convoy that included the *Endeavour* (which had been renamed the *Lord Sandwich*). Divers are still trying to determine which of the scuttled ships matches the size and build of Cook's vessel. The *Resolution,* meanwhile, ran aground at Newport in 1794, and now lies buried beneath landfill.

ONE PIECE OF the puzzle still lingered: the fate of Cook's remains. Cliff Thornton, back in England, regaled me with e-mails about his ongoing search for the arrow allegedly made from Cook's shinbone. He'd managed to track the relic from an exposition in London in 1886 to its transfer, soon after, to the government of New South Wales in Australia. From there the trail went cold.

I delved into the archives, following Cliff's leads, and found a card catalogue at the state library in Sydney devoted to "Realia," or relics. A librarian escorted me to a back room to inspect the Cook-related items, including a tiny lacquered box in the shape of a coffin, inscribed with the words "Lono and the Seaman's Idol." The coffin's lid slid open to reveal a watercolor of Cook's death, a lock of the captain's brown hair, and a carving that read: "Made of *Resolution* Oak for Mrs. Cook by Crew."

But I couldn't find the arrow, even though it was listed as belonging to the library's collection. Further digging led me to the nearby Australian Museum, where I met with the head anthropologist, a professorial English emigrant named Jim Specht. He seemed amused by my tale and insisted that there was no such artifact in the museum's possession. But he agreed to have a look in the museum's vast "Pacific storeroom."

I followed Jim through aisles lined with trays until he located a box marked "H68 Arrow." Taking it to a brightly lit table, Jim donned white gloves and opened the box. Inside lay an arrow of about two and a half feet in length, with a metal point, feathered fletching, and a shaft made from a bamboolike stem affixed to a pale, mottled substance, five inches long and roughly the diameter of a pencil. An old card inside the box said: "Arrow stated to be partly made from the small leg bone of Captain Cook."

Jim turned the artifact in his hands. "It's definitely bone, perhaps the tibia," he said. "But this arrow is not Hawaiian. There are no fletched arrows in the tropical Pacific." He showed me other arrows from the region, most of them dartlike and, indeed, unfletched. "It just doesn't ring true," he said. "The Hawaiians thought Cook was a demigod. Why would they turn his leg bone into an arrow? It seems disrespectful."

In the museum's library, we found two "authenticating documents," attesting to the arrow's provenance. One, from a prominent English surgeon in 1828, stated: "This Arrow was given by the King of the Sandwich Islands, when in England, to one of his Attendants, with the assurance that the bone attached to it was a part of the leg-bone of Captain Cook."

Jim also unearthed pictures of arrows from the west coast of Canada, which closely resembled the one in the box. "These jokers were all over the north Pacific," he said of Cook and his men. "Maybe they brought the arrow to Hawaii from someplace else." The seventy years during which the arrow apparently resided in England also raised questions. Museums were filled with Cook relics of dubious or unknown origin.

I might have left it at that, but not Cliff. He kept up a steady stream of correspondence with the museum, sharing each new shred of evidence. Among other things, he'd learned at the Bishop Museum in Honolulu that the bones of enemy chiefs were often fashioned into fishhooks and arrows; possessing *mana*, the bones were believed to give fishermen and hunters a better chance of success. Turning bones into tools could also be a way of spitting on one's enemies. It seemed plausible, given the ill repute into which Cook fell in Hawaii, that his shinbone had been made into an arrow as a mark of disrespect. As for the fletching, Cliff speculated that someone had added it in England, to make the arrow resemble prevailing images of "Indian" weapons.

Eventually, officials at the Australian Museum became as intrigued as Cliff, and they agreed to study and test the arrow. When I went back a second time, Jim Specht and his colleagues began a long and technical discussion of DNA testing, and how the bone would have to be matched with mitochondria from Cook's maternal line. Cliff had thought of this, too, and contacted Australian descendants of Cook's sister Margaret. They had agreed to give DNA samples.

Jim took me down to the museum's photo lab, where a technician X-rayed the bone. While we waited for the prints to emerge, Jim and another anthropologist speculated about the result.

"Marine mammal," Jim predicted.

"I'll say bird," his colleague replied.

"There's another question," Jim said, smiling. "If it is Captain Cook's bone, should we clone him?"

When the X ray was done, it showed nothing but a dense white mass, providing no clue as to its origin. Months later, the museum sent the arrow to a Sydney hospital for a bone scan. This, too, proved inconclusive. A forensic archaeologist studied the arrow and test results. "The bone density falls well within the human range," she told me. However, marine mammal couldn't be ruled out. If the bone was human, she added, it belonged to the tibia or femur of "a robust, active, large male." But only a DNA test could take the investigation further. The museum, concerned that extracting a DNA sample might damage the arrow, balked at conducting the test; months more have passed without a decision.

I felt frustrated by these tantalizing clues, and by the glacial pace of museum and laboratory work. But Cliff was philosophical. "This is one *leg*end that refuses to lie down quietly," he punned. "Long may the search go on." In a way, this seemed fitting. Cook spent a decade seeking a fabled continent and passage, and died without finding them. More than two centuries later, the truth about his remains still eluded discovery. He'd left one very personal riddle for the rest of us to solve.

ON MY LAST night in Sydney, I went for a parting "piss-up" with Roger on his yacht, *Aquadisiac*. The next day I'd be flying home with my family to the Blue Ridge foothills of Virginia, a landlocked domain that was about as far as you could go from the Pacific. "Swallowing the anchor" was what mariners called it when they finally gave up the sea. I'm a landsman, so this suited me. But Roger still felt restless. For all his moaning during our many trips together, he'd become as hooked on Cook as I had, and couldn't bear to settle down again in Sydney.

"I finally understand the man," he said, uncorking a third bottle of chardonnay. "Cook traveled because he liked to run away. It solves all life's problems."

Roger had hatched a scheme to continue traveling in Cook's wake. He'd sold his car—even sold the contents of his wine cellar—so he could muster the funds to buy a proper seagoing yacht. "I'm going to quit my job and just set off after Cook, for the sheer hell of it," he said. "I won't take a goat, but I'll sail as far as *I* can go, which might only be five miles."

As I write, nine months later, Roger is moving out of his apartment and onto the forty-one-foot yacht he recently bought for his oceangoing adventure. In the meantime, he'd also managed to ride a Russian ship to Antarctica, a destination I'd dodged. Reaching the continent, Roger set up camp with other passengers on an ice shelf, then wandered off to toast Cook with a bottle of rum. He passed out on the ice and might have frozen to death, like Banks's drunken servants in

Tierra del Fuego, were it not for a young doctor from Texas who dragged him into her tent. She'd since followed Roger home to Sydney.

"For once I didn't have you along as deadweight," he said, explaining his Antarctic success during a late-night phone call. "Then again, maybe she took me into her tent only because she wanted to keep warm."

IN VIRGINIA, I often put my five-year-old son, Nathaniel, to bed with tales of Captain Cook, while tracing his adventures across the inflatable globe hanging above Natty's bed. One night, after Natty fell asleep listening to the story of Cook's death and dismemberment—his favorite episode—I lay awake, drowsily recalling the distance traveled, then got up and placed a toy arrow alongside Natty's globe. If I poked it through the plastic, starting at our home, it would emerge in the blue latitudes off Australia, close to where Cook sailed on the *Endeavour*.

In the early nineteenth century, wealthy families in Europe and America adorned their homes with wallpaper depicting scenes from Cook's voyages, including Tahitian dancers, Tongan wrestlers, and Cook's final struggle on the beach in Hawaii. Dufour, the French company that manufactured these "scenic papers," advertised its product as not only decorative but didactic—useful in teaching children about geography, botany, and exotic peoples, as well as inspiring them to great things.

The notion seems quaint today. Natty enjoys my stories of Cook's adventures, though he prefers to hear about wizards and hobbits. He has spent a third of his life in Australia; his room in Virginia is filled with stuffed koalas and kangaroos, and books about Aborigines. The antipodes doesn't seem strange or unimaginable to him.

If a company like Dufour were to design wallpaper today, it would probably craft images of men on the moon, or weightless astronauts on space stations. This, too, was part of Cook's legacy. He was one of the world's great explorers, but also among its last. In his wake, other discoverers filled in the few remaining blanks on the map. Eventually, there wasn't anyplace left on earth where no man had gone before.

Tucking Natty in, I liked to think that he might become an explorer of a different sort. As Rick Knecht, the Alaskan archaeologist, had told me during our boat ride to Cook's landing site, there was evidence of a "novelty-seeking" gene in humans' makeup. Cook, because of the early deaths of his own children, wasn't able to pass this trait along. But maybe I could, if not genetically then with my stories about the navigator.

When adults ask Natty what he wants to be when he grows up, he always smiles mysteriously and says, "An adventurer." Making lists of supplies and companions for his future exploration fills much of his playtime. Natty's mission, like Cook's, isn't always clear: the destination is often secret or imaginary, and it tends to change from day to day. But I rejoice in the endeavor.

NOTES ON SOURCES

As I hope I've made clear throughout this book, any study of Cook depends to an extraordinary degree on the encyclopedic work of John Cawte Beaglehole. The New Zealand historian, who died in 1971, published the first accurate and comprehensive edition of Cook's journals, including scholarly introductions, long excerpts from crewmen's diaries, and scores of official documents. Before Beaglehole, entire continents of Cook material remained unexplored, embroidered, or inaccessible to the general public. His four-volume edition of the journals is a masterpiece of thorough and judicious scholarship.

For this reason, I've relied on Beaglehole's edition rather than on the many earlier versions of Cook's travels, such as John Hawkesworth's three-volume work in 1773, *An Account of Voyages undertaken . . . for making Discoveries in the Southern Hemisphere*, which adapted Cook's words and blended the captain's writing with that of Joseph Banks and earlier Pacific explorers. In almost all cases, I've also used Beaglehole as my guide in navigating the shoals of eighteenth-century names, titles, and spellings.

Also invaluable to me were Beaglehole's essays, his annotated edition of Banks's journal, and his last work, *The Life of Captain James Cook*. In Beaglehole, Cook found the biographer he deserved: a fair, factual, tenacious, and humane man of astonishing breadth. Beaglehole isn't infallible or completely without prejudice; he's occasionally too forgiving of Cook, and overly harsh in his assessments of the naturalists Banks and Johann Forster. But his biography of Cook, published posthumously in 1974, remains the gold standard for books about the captain.

In the thirty years since Beaglehole's death, new sources have come to light. Also, the past three decades have seen a flowering of scholarship by and about Pacific peoples. So while any study of Cook must begin with Beaglehole, it shouldn't end with him. Two recent works that I found indispensable were Ray Parkin's *H.M. Bark* Endeavour, a very accessible, beautifully illustrated look at Cook's first ship, crew, and voyage, and John Robson's *Captain Cook's World*, which provides clear maps and concise exposition of Cook's circuitous travels, in Britain and Canada as well as the Pacific.

In a more analytic vein, Bernard Smith combines brilliant art criticism with literary and historical insight, particularly regarding Cook's legacy. Smith's *European Vision and the South Pacific* and *Imagining the Pacific* also include some of the best reproductions of art from Cook's journeys. Another Australian scholar, Greg Dening, skillfully dissects eighteenth-century seafaring and the encounters between Europeans and Pacific Islanders. In *Mr. Bligh's Bad Language,* Dening makes frequent reference to Cook and ranges across disciplines to craft one of the most original books I read in the course of my research. Typical of Dening's contrarian approach is his examination of the number of lashes doled out by every British captain in the Pacific during the eighteenth century; this tally reveals that Bligh, despite his reputation, was a mild commander compared to Cook and others.

Gananath Obeyesekere, a Sri Lankan–born anthropologist at Princeton, offers a harsh, postcolonial critique of the navigator and of the mythmaking that occurred in his wake. Obeyesekere's *The Apotheosis of Captain Cook* is a polemic, often wrongheaded (in my view), but always provocative. As with Smith and Dening, I found that reading Obeyesekere sharpened my own thinking about Cook and provided an antidote to the hagiographic, Anglocentric tone of much that's been written about the captain. Other, excellent interpretations of Cook and his legacy can be found in several books of essays, most notably Robin Fisher and Hugh Johnston's *Captain James Cook and His Times*, Margaret Lincoln's *Science and Exploration in the Pacific*, and Walter Veit's two-volume *Captain James Cook: Image and Impact*.

Though no biography comes close to Beaglehole's in depth, several offer lively introductions to Cook for readers who don't want to brave the New Zealander's 750-page tome. Alistair MacLean, the author of best-sellers such as *The Guns of Navarone*, knows how to tell a good story, and he does so in *Captain Cook*. One of the most recent biographies, Richard Hough's *Captain James Cook*, is very traditional in its approach, but it also provides a readable summary. Lynne Withey takes a broader, more anthropological approach in *Voyages of Discovery*, integrating the perspective of Pacific peoples in a way that most others have not.

For readers interested in Joseph Banks, Harold Carter's *Sir Joseph Banks* is the most comprehensive biography. Patrick O'Brian, the famed sea novelist, brings his lively style and eye for color to his shorter, more readable biography, *Joseph Banks*. The botanist's *Endeavour* journal is available online at http://slnsw.gov.au/.

For primary sources, apart from Cook's and Banks's journals, I relied for the most part on the Mitchell and Dixson Libraries at the State Library of New South Wales in Sydney, which houses the best collection of Cook-related manuscripts in the world. Also very useful to me were the libraries and exhibits at Sydney's National Maritime Museum, the Bishop Museum in Honolulu, the National Geographic Society in Washington, D.C., the Natural History Museum in London, and other repositories in Tahiti, New Zealand, Alaska, and Niue. I'm indebted to the curators and librarians who assisted me in each of these places. I also drew a great deal of information from the Captain Cook Society, which publishes a quarterly "log" and provides the best clearing-house for contemporary research at www.CaptainCookSociety.com.

For readers interested in works about travel in the modern Pacific, there are countless paeans to swaying palms and twitching hips. A few works stand out from this tired genre. Paul Theroux's *The Happy Isles of Oceania* is an acerbic, amusing, and insightful travelogue that covers an astounding amount of the Pacific, including many of the places I visited. Theroux can be brutal, but he's never dull. And it's a mark of Cook's appeal that a writer as skeptical as Theroux observes: "It is impossible to travel in the Pacific, even for a short time, and not develop an admiration for this hero of navigation and discovery, who was—amazingly, for a great captain—a thoroughly good man."

Simon Winchester's *Pacific Rising* offers an informative overview of the ocean and its history. And while Jonathan Raban's *Passage to Juneau* isn't, strictly speaking, about the Pacific, it's the most probing book I read about travel in the vast territory Cook covered. Raban sails the northwest coast of America in the path of Cook's disciple, George Vancouver, and casts an original and illuminating eye on both shipboard life in the eighteenth century and the legacy of European encounters with natives. Like Theroux, Raban also appreciates Cook's accomplishments. "Cook's rise in the world was a fabulous occurrence—a phoenix, born in smoke and ashes," Raban writes. "Cook proved that there was room for wild untutored genius in the upper echelons of eighteenth-century England."

The *Lonely Planet* and *Rough Guide* for each of the countries I visited provided lively and generally accurate introductions to Pacific history and culture, as did the *South Pacific Handbook*. For a more academic treatment of the region, I often turned to *The Cambridge History of the Pacific Islanders*.

For readers interested in additional sources, here are a few comments on individual chapters. Details on the mentioned works are in the bibliography.

PROLOGUE: *The Distance Traveled*

In describing the aftermath of Cook's death, I've relied on the journals of his men, particularly Charles Clerke, James King, and David Samwell. For Hawaiians' treatment of the dead, I found the writings of Marshall Sahlins and Roger Rose particularly useful. My overview of Cook's career and legacy is informed by many sources, especially the writings of J. C. Beaglehole and Bernard Smith.

1 PACIFIC NORTHWEST: *One Week Before the Mast*

For details relating to Cook's ship, Ray Parkin's *H.M. Bark* Endeavour is essential, both for Parkin's detailed drawings and for the background he provides on eighteenth-century seafaring. Also useful are the publications of the H.M. Bark *Endeavour* Foundation and its historian, Antonia Macarthur; the foundation's Web site is www.barkendeavour.com.au. Sydney's National Maritime Museum, in conjunction with the National Library of Australia, has produced an excellent CD-ROM, *Endeavour*, which combines journal extracts with graphics of the ship and the lands it visited.

There are dozens of books on the exploration and mapping of the Pacific. Among the most useful to me were J. C. Beaglehole's *The Exploration of the Pacific* and Peter Whitfield's *New Found Lands*. I've dealt only briefly with the complex subject of cartography and navigation. For those interested in further reading, John Noble Wilford's *The Mapmakers* is the best place to start.

Joan Druett's *Rough Medicine* provides many grisly details about shipboard health and diet. The most exhaustive study of this subject in relation to Cook is an essay by Sir James Watt, a British naval surgeon, titled "Medical Aspects and Consequences of Cook's Voyages," published in Fisher and Johnston's *Captain James Cook and His Times*.

The aphorism quoted at the start of the chapter is from Marcus Rediker's *Between the Devil and the Deep Blue Sea*.

2 TAHITI: *Sic Transit Venus* and 3 TO BORA-BORA: *Sold a Pup*

I don't read French well enough to comment on the extensive writings about Tahiti and neighboring islands in that language. Translated works or ones written in English that I found useful include Teuira Henry's *Ancient Tahiti*, Etienne Taillémite's *Bougainville in Tahiti*, Jose Garanger's *Sacred Stones and Rites*, and John Dunmore's *French Explorers in the Pacific*. David Howarth's *Tahiti: A Paradise Lost* provides an excellent overview of European contact and its dire results. I also profited from my interviews with two academics at the Université de la Polynesie Française in Tahiti, Sandhya Patel and Serge Dunis, as well as with government adviser Alexandre Ata and journalist Al Prince.

4 NEW ZEALAND: *Warriors, Still*

For such a small country, New Zealand seems to produce a striking number of great historians. In addition to Beaglehole, there is James Belich, whose *Making Peoples* is a lucid, engaging, and balanced history of New Zealand to the late nineteenth century. Anne Salmond's *Two Worlds* is a gem of a different sort: a richly detailed, almost microscopic look at early contact between Maori and Pakeha, much of it focused on Cook's voyages.

For the recollections of Te Horeta, the Maori boy who witnessed Cook's arrival, I've drawn on several nineteenth-century versions of his story, particularly the one published in John White's *The Ancient History of the Maori*. I gathered added details from my interviews with Maori still living in Mercury Bay, and am indebted to Peter Johnson of the Ngaati Hei.

5 BOTANY BAY: *In the Pure State of Nature* and 6 THE GREAT BARRIER REEF: *Wrecked*

Robert Hughes's *The Fatal Shore* doesn't dwell for long on Cook's visit to Botany Bay, but it brilliantly and exhaustively details the *Endeavour*'s legacy: the creation of the world's largest prison and the devastation of Aboriginal society. He also paints a grim, vivid portrait of the working-class world from which convicts—and many of Cook's sailors—came. While some Australian scholars have challenged Hughes's analysis as overly dark, dramatic, and polemical, *The Fatal Shore* is indispensable for anyone interested in the early history of white Australia.

Also controversial, and invaluable, is the work of Henry Reynolds, who has written several books detailing the dispossession and devastation of Aborigines. Reynolds is a campaigner as well as a scholar, and some of his research has recently come under fire. But he attempts to document, in a way that few other Australians have been willing to do until recently, the horror and extent of white-on-black violence. Other works on Aborigines that I found useful include Lyndall Ryan's *The Aboriginal Tasmanians*, John Mulvaney and Johan Kamminga's *Prehistory of Australia*, and a book of essays printed by the University of Sydney's history department, *Maps, Dreams, History*.

Bill Bryson's *In a Sunburned Country* is a fun and informative overview of Australia and its history. Also lively are Tim Flannery's well-edited anthologies about Australia's settlement and exploration: *The Birth of Sydney* and *The Explorers*. For information on Botany Bay, Daphne Salt's *Kurnell* provides the best overview.

As I've mentioned already, Sydney is blessed with the Mitchell and Dixson Libraries. The Mitchell's exhibit in 2000 on maps of *terra australis*, and a lecture there by the library's curator of manuscripts, Paul Brunton, were also very useful to me. Brunton dismisses claims, based on the so-called Dieppe maps, that the Portuguese "discovered" Australia before the Dutch, so I haven't covered this issue in my book. But a new work, published in Britain too late for me to include it in my research, treats this subject at length: Victoria Collingridge's *Captain Cook: Obsession and Betrayal in the New World* (Ebury Press, 2002). Other works dealing with early voyages to, and maps of, Australia, include J. P. Sigmond and L. H. Zuiderbaan's *Dutch Discoveries of Australia*, and Robert Clancy's *The Mapping of Terra Australis*.

Finally, I am indebted to the very helpful librarians at my onetime employer, *The Sydney Morning Herald*, who helped me find news stories on Cook, Aboriginal affairs, and contemporary Australia.

8 SAVAGE ISLAND: *The Hunt for Red Banana* and 9 TONGA: *Where Time Begins, and Goes Back*

Not surprisingly, there isn't a great deal of literature on Niue. For overviews of the island's history and culture, I mostly relied on Percy Smith's *Niue: The Island and Its People* and Edwin Loeb's *History and Traditions of Niue*. Two excellent monographs at the Niue Archives detail Cook's visit: Thomas Felix Ryan's "Narratives of Encounter" and "Palagi Views of Niue."

Any historical study of Tonga should begin with the extraordinary story of William Mariner, a young clerk who survived the massacre of his shipmates in 1806, lived on the islands for four years, and later told his tale to Dr. John Martin, who published it as *Tonga Islands, William Mariner's Account*. The book provides rich detail of Tongan life and culture in the early-contact period. For twentieth-century Tongan history, the most useful book to me was Elizabeth Wood-Ellem's *Queen Salote of Tonga*. I also profited from dozens of issues of *Matangi Tonga*, an excellent newsmagazine published in Nuku'alofa.

10 NORTH YORKSHIRE: *A Plain, Zealous Man* and 11 LONDON: *Shipping Out, Again*

No part of Cook's life is more shrouded in mystery and myth than his early years in the north of England. In my efforts to distinguish fact from folklore, I'm indebted to *Captain Cook in Cleveland*, a booklet by Clifford Thornton, formerly head of the Captain Cook Birthplace Museum in Marton. In Great Ayton, I found two other useful booklets: Joyce Dixon's *History Under the Hammer*, about the history and sale of "Cook's Cottage," and Dan O'Sullivan's *The Education of Captain Cook*. In Staithes, as I've mentioned in the text, the Captain Cook and Staithes Heritage Center contains an astonishing trove of artifacts and documents relating to Cook's life. Also useful to me were the exhibits at the Captain Cook Memorial Museum and Whitby Museum.

In London, I turned to two experts at the Natural History Museum. Roy Vickery, a curator in the botany department, showed me around the herbarium and its collection of specimens gathered by Joseph Banks and Daniel Solander. Neil Chambers, research curator of the museum's Banks Archival Project, gave me access to some of the botanist's vast correspondence, which he has since edited and published (*The Letters of Sir Joseph Banks* [London: Imperial College Press, 2000]). The letters, many of them never transcribed before, make for astonishing reading, including one from a Lincolnshire magistrate who sent Banks a statement about local people vomiting live frogs. The best source for scarce information about Cook's time in East London is *Captain James Cook Endeavours*, by Julia Rae.

12 ALASKA: *Outside Men*

Steve Langdon's *The Native People of Alaska* is an excellent introduction to Aleuts and other indigenous residents of the state. Historians Stephen Haycox at the University of Alaska in Anchorage, and Lydia Black, professor emerita at the University of Alaska in Fairbanks, helped me with research relating to Russians in Alaska. The state is also blessed with first-rate museums, including the Anchorage Museum of History and Art, the Alutiiq Museum and Archaeological Repository in Kodiak, and Unalaska's Museum of the Aleutians. I can also recommend two beautifully illustrated publications by Alaska Geographic, *The Bering Sea* and *Russian America*. Two other works gave me a feel for contemporary Unalaska: Ray Hudson's affecting memoir, *Moments Rightly Placed*, and Jerah Chadwick's beautiful poetry in *Story Hunger*.

13 HAWAII: *The Last Island* and 14 KEALAKEKUA BAY: *A Bad Day on Black Rock*

It is impossible to research Cook in Hawaii without becoming mesmerized by the duel between the anthropologists Marshall Sahlins and Gananath Obeyesekere—and also, at times, bewildered by their contretemps. (Sahlins rebuts Obeyesekere at one point by writing: "The notion that a substantive statement can be ignored on the presumption that its author was directly or indirectly influenced by a priori missionary belief involves the fallacies of ignoratio elenchi and petitio principii.") I've given a very abbreviated version of their views in the text. But as the title of Sahlins's main work on the subject— *How "Natives" Think: About Captain Cook, for Example*—makes clear, this debate isn't simply about whether or not Hawaiians viewed Cook as a god. Sahlins and Obeyesekere are really arguing over the fundamental and bedeviling question of how best to understand cultures very remote from our own, whose beliefs have been heavily filtered by Western sailors, scholars, and missionaries.

For that reason, I found the Sahlins-Obeyesekere debate relevant to the whole enterprise of understanding Cook's contact with people across the Pacific. Anthropologist Clifford Geertz offers a probing, noncombatant's view of their face-off in his November 30, 1995, essay for *The New York Review of Books*, titled "Culture War."

While scholars argue over the meaning of Cook's death, untangling the many versions of what transpired at Kealakekua Bay on February 14, 1779, is like interviewing ten witnesses to a car wreck. Molesworth Phillips's report on the skirmish, given to Charles Clerke soon after it occurred, is probably the most reliable record we have. To a lesser degree, I've also drawn on the journals of other crewmen, particularly David Samwell, who gathered the testimonies of others and wrote a short book about Cook's death (to which, rather bizarrely, he appended an essay "respecting the introduction of the venereal disease into the Sandwich Islands").

There is ongoing debate about whether the Spanish visited Hawaii in the sixteenth century. Captain Rick Rogers deals with this at length in his well-illustrated *Shipwrecks of Hawaii*, and he was kind enough to share additional research with me in Honolulu. The Hawaiian proverb quoted as the epigraph of Chapter 13 is from Greg Dening's *Mr. Bligh's Bad Language*.

EPILOGUE: *A Period to His Labours*

My information about the fate of the *Endeavour* and *Resolution* comes from a visit to Newport, where I met with Dr. A. K. Abbass, the director of the Rhode Island Archaeology Project. I also consulted researchers involved with the hunt for the *Endeavour* at the National Maritime Museum in Sydney. Updates on the continuing search can be found online at www.rimap.org/.

For the story of Cook's bone, I turned to the Australian Museum and the State Library of New South Wales, the Bishop Museum in Honolulu, Clifford Thornton of the Captain Cook Society, and Estelle Lazer, a forensic archaeologist at Sydney University.

SELECTED BIBLIOGRAPHY

Adams, Mark and Nicholas Thomas. *Cook's Sites: Revisiting History.* Dunedin: University of Otago Press, 1999.

Alaska Geographic. *The Bering Sea.* Anchorage: Alaska Geographic, 1999.

Alaska Geographic. *Russian America.* Anchorage: Alaska Geographic, 1999.

Alexander, Michael. *Omai: Noble Savage.* London: Collins and Harville, 1977.

Beaglehole, J. C. "Cook the Writer." Lecture Delivered at the University of Sydney. Sydney: Sydney University Press, 1970.

———. *Endeavour Journal of Joseph Banks,* volumes 1 and 2. Sydney: Angus and Robertson, 1962.

———. *The Exploration of the Pacific.* London: A. & C. Black, 1934.

———. "The Death of Captain Cook." *Australian Journal of Science,* vol. 26, April 1964, pp. 297–304.

———. *The Journals of Captain James Cook on His Voyages of Discovery* (four volumes and a portfolio). Cambridge: Cambridge University Press, 1955–68.

———. *The Life of Captain James Cook.* Stanford: Stanford University Press, 1974.

———. "On the Character of Captain James Cook." London: Royal Geographical Society, 1957.

Beddie, M.K. *Bibliography of Captain James Cook*. Sydney: The Library of New South Wales, 1970.

Belich, James. *Making Peoples: A History of the New Zealanders from Polynesian Settlement to the End of the Nineteenth Century*. Auckland: Allen Lane, The Penguin Press, 1996.

Besant, Sir Walter. *Captain Cook*. London: Macmillan, 1894.

Brosse, Jacques. *Great Voyages of Exploration*. Sydney: Doubleday, 1983.

Bryson, Bill. *In a Sunburned Country*. New York: Broadway Books, 2000.

Byron, John. *Byron's Journal of His Circumnavigation, 1764–1766*. Edited by Robert Gallagher. Cambridge: Cambridge University Press, 1962.

Cameron, Ian. *Lost Paradise*. Topsfield, Mass.: Salem House Publishers, 1987.

Carter, Harold. *Sir Joseph Banks, 1743–1820*. London: British Museum, 1988.

Chadwick, Jerah. *Story Hunger*. Cliffs of Moher, Ireland: Salmon Publishing, 1999.

Clancy, Robert. *The Mapping of Terra Australis*. Sydney: Universal Press Pty. Ltd, 1995.

Collett, Harry. *Whitby*. Whitby: Dalesman Publishing, 2000.

Davidson, J.W., and Deryck Scarr, editors. *Pacific Island Portraits*. Canberra: Australian National University Press, 1976.

Davies, Norman. *The Isles: A History*. Macmillan, 1999.

Daws, Gavan. *Shoal of Time: A History of the Hawaiian Islands*. Honolulu: The University Press of Hawaii, 1989.

Day, A. Grove, editor. *Mark Twain's Letters from Hawaii*. New York: Appleton-Century, 1966.

Dening, Greg. *Islands and Beaches: Discourse on a Silent Land Marquesas, 1774–1880*. Chicago: Dorsey Press, 1980.

———. *Mr. Bligh's Bad Language: Passion, Power and Theater on the Bounty*. Cambridge: Cambridge University Press, 1992.

Denoon, Donald et al. *The Cambridge History of the Pacific Islanders*. Cambridge: Cambridge University Press, 1997.

Diamond, Jared. *Guns, Germs, and Steel*. New York: W. W. Norton and Co., 1997.

Dibble, Sheldon. *A History of the Sandwich Islands*. Honolulu: Thomas G. Thrum, 1909.

Dixon, Joyce. *History Under the Hammer*. Booklet published by the North York Moors National Park, 1996.

Druett, Joan. *Rough Medicine: Surgeons at Sea in the Age of Sail*. New York: Routledge, 2000.

Dugard, Martin. *Farther Than Any Man: The Rise and Fall of Captain James Cook*. New York: Pocket Books, 2001.

Dunmore, John. *French Explorers in the Pacific*. Oxford: Oxford University Press, 1965.

Elder, Bruce. *Blood on the Wattle: Massacres and Maltreatment of Australian Aborigines Since 1788.* Sydney: New Holland, 1988.

Ellis, W. *An Authentic Narrative of a Voyage Performed by Captain Cook and Captain Clerke.* London: G. Robinson, 1782.

Ellis, William. *Narrative of a Tour Through Hawaii . . . Manners, Customs, and Language of the Inhabitants of the Sandwich Islands.* London: H. Fisher, Son and P. Jackson, 1826.

———. *Polynesian Researches During a Residence of Nearly Eight Years in the Society and Sandwich Islands.* London: H. Fisher, Son and P. Jackson, 1829.

Estensen, Miriam. *Discovery.* Sydney: Allen & Unwin, 1998.

Evans, Julian. *Transit of Venus: Travels in the Pacific.* London: Secker & Warburg, 1985.

Eyraud, Arlette. *Tahiti Today and All Its Islands.* Paris: Les Editions du Jaguar, 1992.

Fisher, Robin and Hugh Johnston, editors. *Captain James Cook and His Times.* Canberra: Australian National University Press, 1979.

Flannery, Tim. *The Birth of Sydney.* Melbourne: The Text Publishing Co., 1999.

———. *The Explorers.* Melbourne: The Text Publishing Co., 1998.

Forbes, David. *Encounters with Paradise: Views of Hawaii and Its People, 1778–1941.* Honolulu: University of Hawaii Press, 1992.

Fornander, Abraham. *Ancient History of the Hawaiian People to the Times of King Kamehameha I.* Honolulu: Mutual Publishing, 1996.

Forster, Johann Reinhold. *Observations Made during a Voyage Round the World.* Honolulu: University of Hawaii Press, 1996.

Fox, Edward. *Obscure Kingdoms.* London: Penguin Books, 1995.

Garanger, Jose. *Sacred Stones and Rites.* Paris: Société des Oceanistes, 1979.

Gilbert, George. *Captain Cook's Final Voyage: The Journal of Midshipman George Gilbert.* Honolulu: University of Hawaii Press, 1982.

Gould, Rupert. "Bligh's Notes on Cook's Last Voyage" and "Some Unpublished Accounts of Cook's Death." *The Mariner's Mirror,* vol. XIV, no. 4, October 1928.

Gray, William. *Voyages to Paradise.* Washington, D.C.: The National Geographic Society, 1981.

Henry, Teuira. *Ancient Tahiti.* Honolulu: Bishop Museum, bulletin no. 48, 1928.

Hiney, Tom. *On the Missionary Trail.* New York: Atlantic Monthly Press, 2000.

Hough, Richard. *Captain James Cook.* New York: W. W. Norton and Co., 1995.

Howarth, David. *Tahiti: A Paradise Lost.* New York: Viking Press, 1985.

Hudson, Ray. *Moments Rightly Placed: An Aleutian Memoir.* Fairbanks: Epicenter Press, 1998.

Hughes, Robert. *The Fatal Shore: A History of the Transportation of Convicts to Australia, 1787–1868.* London: Collins Harvill, 1987.

Institute of the South Pacific. *Niue: A History of the Island.* Government of Niue, 1982.

James, Van. *Ancient Sites of Hawaii.* Honolulu: Mutual Publishing, 1996.

Joppien, Rudiger and Bernard Smith. *The Art of Captain Cook's Voyages: The Voyage of the* Resolution *and the* Discovery, *1776–1780.* New Haven: Yale University Press, 1988.

Kaeppler, Adrienne. *Artificial Curiosities: Being an Exposition of Native Manufactures Collected on the Three Pacific Voyages of Captain James Cook, R.N.* Honolulu: Bishop Museum Press, 1980.

Kane, Herb Kawainui. *Ancient Hawai'i.* Hawaii: Kawainui Press, 1997.

———. *Voyagers.* Bellevue, Wash.: WhaleSong, 1991.

King, Dean. *A Sea of Words: A Lexicon and Companion to the Complete Seafaring Tales of Patrick O'Brian.* New York: Henry Holt, 1995.

Kippis, Andrew. *The Life of Captain James Cook.* London: G. Nicol, 1788.

Langdon, Steve. *The Native People of Alaska.* Anchorage: Greatland Graphics, 1993.

Langford, Paul. *A Polite and Commercial People: England, 1727–1783.* Oxford: Oxford University Press, 1989.

Ledyard, John. *A Journal of Captain Cook's Last Voyage to the Pacific Ocean.* Chicago: Quadrangle Books, 1963.

Ledyard, Patricia. *The Tongan Past.* Nuku'alofa: Vava'u Press, 1982.

Leed, Eric. *The Mind of the Traveler: From Gilagamesh to Global Tourism.* New York: Basic Books, 1991.

Lincoln, Margaret, editor. *Science and Exploration in the Pacific: European Voyages to the Southern Oceans in the Eighteenth Century.* Suffolk: The Boydell Press, 1998.

Loeb, Edwin. *History and Traditions of Niue.* Honolulu: Bishop Museum, 1926.

Macarthur, Antonia. *His Majesty's Bark* Endeavour: *The Story of the Ship and Her People.* Sydney: Angus & Robertson, 1997.

Mackay, Joseph. *Historical Poverty Bay.* Gisborne: J. A. Mackay, 1949.

MacLean, Alistair. *Captain Cook.* London: William Collins and Sons, 1972.

Maddock, Shirley. *Far As a Man May Go.* Auckland: Collins, 1970.

Major, R.H. *Early Voyages to Terra Australis.* Adelaide: Australian Heritage Press, 1963.

Malo, David. *Hawaiian Antiquities.* Honolulu: Bishop Museum Press, 1951.

Mariner, William. *Tonga Islands, William Mariner's Account,* as told to Dr. John Martin. Tonga: Vava'u Press, 1991.

McDougall, Walter. *Let the Sea Make a Noise: Four Hundred Years of Cataclysm, Conquest, War and Folly in the North Pacific.* New York: Avon Books, 1993.

Mitchell, T.C. *Captain Cook and the South Pacific.* Canberra: Australian National University Press, 1979.

Selected Bibliography

Moorehead, Alan. *The Fatal Impact: An Account of the Invasion of the South Pacific, 1767–1840.* New York: Harper and Row, 1966.

Mulvaney, D. J. *Encounters in Place: Outsiders and Aboriginal Australians, 1606–1985.* University of Queensland Press, 1989.

Mulvaney, John and Johan Kamminga. *Prehistory of Australia.* Washington, D.C.: Smithsonian Institution Press, 1999.

O'Brian, Patrick. *Joseph Banks: A Life.* London: Collins Harvill, 1987.

Obeyesekere, Gananath. *The Apotheosis of Captain Cook: European Mythmaking in the Pacific.* Princeton: Princeton University Press, 1992.

Oliver, Douglas. *The Pacific Islands.* Honolulu: The University Press of Hawaii, 1975.

Parkin, Ray. *H.M. Bark* Endeavour. Melbourne: Melbourne University Press, 1997.

Parkinson, Sydney. *Journal of a Voyage to the South Seas in HMS* Endeavour. London: Caliban Books, 1984.

Philbrick, Nathaniel. *In the Heart of the Sea: The Tragedy of the Whaleship* Essex. New York: Viking Penguin, 2000.

Pike, Glenville. *Queen of the North.* Brisbane: Watson, Ferguson & Company, 1979.

Pohlner, Howard. *Gangurru.* Milton, Queensland: Hopevale Mission Board, 1986.

Polack, J. S. *New Zealand: Being a Narrative of Travels . . . Between the Years 1831 and 1837.* London: Richard Bentley, 1838.

Raban, Jonathan. *Passage to Juneau.* New York: Pantheon, 1999.

Raban, Jonathan, editor. *The Oxford Book of the Sea.* Oxford: Oxford University Press, 1992.

Rae, Julia. *Captain James Cook Endeavours.* London: Stepney Historical Trust, 1997.

Rediker, Marcus. *Between the Devil and the Deep Blue Sea: Merchant Seaman, Pirates, and the Anglo-American Maritime World, 1700–1750.* Cambridge: Cambridge University Press, 1987.

Rennie, Neil. *Far-Fetched Facts: The Literature of Travel and the Idea of the South Seas.* Oxford: Clarendon Press, 1995.

Reynolds, Henry. *Dispossession: Black Australians and White Invaders.* Sydney: Allen & Unwin, 1989.

———. *The Other Side of the Frontier: Aboriginal Resistance to the European Invasion of Australia.* Ringwood, Victoria: Penguin Books, 1982.

Rickman, John. *Journal of Captain Cook's Last Voyage to the Pacific Ocean on* Discovery. London: E. Newbery, 1781.

Rienits, Rex and Thea Rienits. *The Voyages of Captain Cook.* London: Hamlyn Publishing Group, 1968.

Robson, John. *Captain Cook's World: Maps of the Life and Voyages of James Cook R.N.* Sydney: Random House, 2000.

Rodger, N. A. M. *The Wooden World: An Anatomy of the Georgian Navy.* London: Collins, 1986.

Rogers, Captain Richard W. *Shipwrecks of Hawaii.* Honolulu: Pilialoha Publishing, 1999.

Rose, Roger. *Reconciling the Past: Two Basketry Ka'ai and the Legendary Liloa and Lonoikamakahiki.* Honolulu: Bishop Museum Press, 1992.

Ryan, Lyndall. *The Aboriginal Tasmanians.* Sydney: Allen and Unwin, 1996.

Ryan, Thomas. "Narratives of Encounter: The Anthropology of History on Niue." Ph.D. thesis, University of Auckland, 1994.

———. "Palagi Views of Niue." Auckland: Auckland University Bindery, 1984.

Sahlins, Marshall. *How "Natives" Think: About Captain Cook, for Example.* Chicago: University of Chicago Press, 1995.

———. *Islands of History.* Chicago: University of Chicago Press, 1985.

Salmond, Anne. *Two Worlds: First Meetings Between Maori and Europeans, 1642–1772.* Auckland: Viking Penguin, 1991.

Salt, Daphne. *Kurnell.* Sydney: Clarion House, 2000.

Samwell, David. *A Narrative of the death of Captain James Cook . . . and observations respecting the introduction of the venereal disease into the Sandwich Islands.* London: J. Robinson, 1786.

———. *Captain Cook and Hawaii.* London: Francis Edwards, 1957.

Scott, Dick. *Would a Good Man Die? Nuie Island, New Zealand and the Late Mr. Larsen.* Auckland: Hodder and Stoughton, 1993.

Sharp, Andrew. *The Voyages of Abel Janszoon Tasman.* Oxford: Clarendon Press, 1968.

Sigmond, J. P. and L. H. Zuiderbaan. *Dutch Discoveries of Australia.* Adelaide: Rigby Limited, 1979.

Smith, Bernard. *European Vision and the South Pacific, 1768–1850.* Oxford: Oxford University Press, 1969.

———. *Imagining the Pacific: In the Wake of Cook Voyages.* Melbourne: Melbourne University Press, 1992.

Smith, Edward. *The Life of Sir Joseph Banks.* London: John Lane, The Bodley Head, 1911.

Smith, Percy. *Niue: The Island and Its People.* Suva: The Polynesian Society, 1983.

Sobel, Dava. *Longitude: The True Story of the Lone Genius Who Solved the Greatest Scientific Problem of His Time.* New York: Walker and Company, 1995.

Stamp, Tom and Cordelia Stamp. *The Life of Captain Cook.* Whitby: Caedmon of Whitby Press, 1978.

Stanley, David. *South Pacific Handbook*, fifth edition. Chico, Calif.: Moon Publications, Inc., 1993.

Stokes, John. *Heiau of the Island of Hawaii: A Historic Survey of Native Hawaiian Temple Sites*. Honolulu: Bishop Museum Press, 1991.

———. "Origin of the Condemnation of Captain Cook in Hawaii," published in the Annual Report of the Hawaiian Historical Society, 1930.

Taillémite, Etienne. *Bougainville in Tahiti*. Paris: Société des Oceanistes, 1972.

Theroux, Paul. *The Happy Isles of Oceania: Paddling the Pacific*. New York: Putnam, 1992.

Thomas, Nicholas. *Entangled Objects*. Cambridge: Harvard University Press, 1991.

Thornton, Clifford. *Captain Cook in Cleveland: A Study of His Early Years*. Middlesbrough: Middlesbrough Borough Council, 1978.

Tooley, R. V. *The Mapping of Australia and Antarctica*. Holland Publishing, 1985.

Turanganui a Kiwa Landfall. Gisborne: Logan Print Ltd, 1994.

Veit, Walter, editor. *Captain James Cook: Image and Impact*, vols. 1 and 2. Melbourne: The Hawthorn Press, 1972.

Villiers, Alan. *Captain James Cook*. New York: Charles Scribner's Sons, 1967.

Westervelt, W. D. *Hawaiian Historical Legends*. New York: Fleming H. Revell Company, 1926.

White, John. *The Ancient History of the Maori*. Wellington: The Government Printer, 1887.

Whitfield, Peter. *New Found Lands: Maps in the History of Exploration*. New York: Routledge, 1998.

Wilford, John Noble. *The Mapmakers: The Story of the Great Pioneers in Cartography from Antiquity to the Space Age*. New York: Alfred A. Knopf, 1981.

Wilson, Derek. *The Circumnavigators*. New York: M. Evans and Co., 1989.

Winchester, Simon. *Pacific Rising: The Emergence of a New World*. New York: Simon and Schuster, 1991.

Withey, Lynne. *Voyages of Discovery: Captain Cook and the Exploration of the Pacific*. Berkeley: University of California Press, 1987.

Wood-Ellem, Elizabeth. *Queen Salote of Tonga: The Story of an Era, 1900–65*. Auckland: Auckland University Press, 1999.

Young, Rev. George. *The Life and Voyages of Captain James Cook*. London: Whittaker, Treacher, 1836.

Zimmermann, Heinrich. *Zimmerman's Account of the Third Voyage of Captain Cook*. Wellington: W.A.G. Skinner, 1926.

ACKNOWLEDGMENTS

My travels, like Cook's, introduced me to a world of wondrously hospitable strangers. Apart from Sydney, all the places I visited were new to me. I knew no one at any of my destinations before arriving. The following people were especially welcoming and helpful: James Pouant, a great teacher in Tahiti; Sheila Robinson and Anne Iranui McGuire, my warm and inspiring guides in New Zealand; Ian Stubbs, Reg Firth, and Doug Worton, fellow Cookaholics in North Yorkshire; Herb Kawainui Kane, the Renaissance man of Hawaii; and four sailors who kept me afloat and amused on the replica *Endeavour*: Todd Vidgen, Karen Angel, Mike Randolph, and Steve Featherstone.

I owe a special debt to Clifford Thornton, president of the Captain Cook Society. Cliff accompanied me in person during part of this journey, and in spirit for all of it; he is one of the world's true explorers, circumnavigating the globe every day from his computer in Essex. I'd also like to thank the other members of the society, who entertained and informed me with their online dispatches. I'm proud to belong to your fraternity and hope, like Charles Clerke, that my Cook-mates "will have no occasion to blush in owning themselves such."

I'd also like to express special gratitude to Rick and Melia Knecht of Unalaska, Alaska, the most intrepid couple I've ever met: great company, great readers, great adventurers. I'll never forget the Elbow Room, the Bering Sea, and Dutch Harbor's airport—and hope never to see them again. Please come visit me in Virginia.

Acknowledgments

While new and distant friends assisted me every step of the way, it was two New Yorkers who made this journey possible. Kristine Dahl urged me to undertake it, and helped launch my endeavor with the largesse of Joseph Banks. John Sterling navigated the book into print with Cook-like calm, vision, and courage. You two are my Lords of the Admiralty; I look forward to future voyages together. Thanks, too, to Jolanta Benal, for an eagle-eyed copy edit that saved me from countless errors and embarrassments.

I also owe an immeasurable debt, yet again, to family and friends who kept me on course with their editing and encouragement. Most of all my wife, Geraldine Brooks, who patiently endured my long absences, and my even more taxing presences, during which she lived through and edited every chapter, several times; my mother and line editor without peer, Elinor Horwitz; my big-picture brother, Josh Horwitz; and inspiring fellow writers Joel Achenbach, Brian Hall, Jack Hitt, Rich Ivry, Michael Lewis, Lisa Michaels, William Powers, Martha Sherrill, and Ken Wells. Love and thanks to you all.

Finally, and fulsomely, I want to thank my co-traveler, Roger Williamson, an intoxicating companion who helped me keep my sense of humor and nautical direction throughout. I'm sorry (though not very) that I skipped Antarctica; you did better without me. I'm honored to be your Beaglehole, and hope that these pages are the tribute you merit. Cheers, mate.

INDEX